HOUSE OF COMMONS SESSI

FOREIGN AFFAIRS COMMITTEE

Third Report

THE EXPANDING RÔLE OF THE UNITED NATIONS AND ITS IMPLICATIONS FOR UNITED KINGDOM POLICY

VOLUME II

Minutes of Evidence
and Appendices

Ordered by The House of Commons *to be printed*
23 June 1993

LONDON: HMSO

235–II

The Foreign Affairs Committee is appointed under SO No 130 to examine the expenditure administration and policy of the Foreign and Commonwealth Office and of associated public bodies.

The Committee consists of 11 members. It has a quorum of three. Unless the House otherwise orders, all Members nominated to the Committee continue to be members of it for the remainder of the Parliament.

The Committee has power:

(a) to send for persons, papers and records, to sit notwithstanding any adjournment of the House, to adjourn from place to place, and to report from time to time;

(b) to appoint specialist advisers either to supply information which is not readily available or to elucidate matters of complexity within the Committee's order of reference;

(c) to communicate to any other such committee its evidence and any other documents relating to matters of common interest; and

(d) to meet concurrently with any such other committee for the purpose of deliberating, taking evidence, or considering draft reports.

The Committee has power to appoint one sub-committee and to report from time to time the minutes of evidence taken before it. The sub-committee has power to send for persons, papers and records, to sit notwithstanding any adjournment of the House, and to adjourn from place to place. It has a quorum of three.

The membership of the Committee since its appointment on 13 July 1992 is as follows:

Rt Hon David Howell, *Guildford* (Chairman)

Mr Dennis Canavan, *Falkirk West*
Mr Mike Gapes, *Ilford South*
Mr David Harris, *St Ives*
Rt Hon Michael Jopling, *Westmorland and Lonsdale*
Mr Jim Lester, *Broxtowe*
Mr Ted Rowlands, *Merthyr Tydfil and Rhymney*
Rt Hon Peter Shore, *Bethnal Green and Stepney*
Rt Hon Sir John Stanley, *Tonbridge and Malling*
Mr David Sumberg, *Bury South*
Mr Robert Wareing, *Liverpool West Derby*

The cost of printing and publishing this Volume of Evidence is estimated by HMSO at £18,111.

TABLE OF CONTENTS

Page

LIST OF WITNESSES

LIST OF MEMORANDA INCLUDED IN THE MINUTES OF EVIDENCE

CORRECTION

Page 82.

Title of Table should read:

ANNEX E:
OUTSTANDING CONTRIBUTIONS TO THE UN REGULAR BUDGET
AND PEACEKEEPING OPERATIONS AS AT 31 OCTOBER 1992

LIST OF APPENDICES TO THE MINUTES OF EVIDENCE

HOUSE OF COMMONS SESSION 1992–93

FOREIGN AFFAIRS COMMITTEE

THE EXPANDING ROLE OF THE UNITED NATIONS AND ITS IMPLICATIONS FOR UK POLICY

MINUTES OF EVIDENCE

Tuesday 27 October 1992

FOREIGN AND COMMONWEALTH OFFICE

Sir David Hannay, KCMG and Ms Glynne Evans, CMG

Ordered by The House of Commons *to be printed*
27 October 1992

LONDON: HMSO

£7.50 net

235–i

MINUTES OF EVIDENCE

TAKEN BEFORE THE FOREIGN AFFAIRS COMMITTEE

TUESDAY 27 OCTOBER 1992

Members present:

Mr David Howell, in the Chair

Mr Dennis Canavan	Mr Ted Rowlands
Mr Mike Gapes	Sir John Stanley
Mr David Harris	Mr David Sumberg
Mr Michael Jopling	Mr Robert Wareing
Mr Jim Lester	

Memorandum submitted by the Foreign and Commonwealth Office

THE EXPANDING ROLE OF THE UNITED NATIONS AND THE IMPLICATIONS FOR UK POLICY

INTRODUCTION

1. After nearly 45 years hobbled by the Cold War the world now looks to the United Nations to do what the founding fathers set it up to do. The end of the Cold War gave the United Nations a new lease of life. The beginnings of this could be seen with the close consultations between the five permanent members of the Security Council (P5) over Iran/Iraq in 1987. Since then there has been ever closer co-operation amongst the P5 leading to a number of important UN endeavours, for example in Namibia and in Cambodia. It was the role of the UN in the Gulf Crisis, however, which propelled the organization back into the centre of world politics. There it has remained.

2. Following Iraq's invasion of Kuwait, the Security Council passed twelve Resolutions, which formed the legal basis for the reversal of Iraqi aggression by an international coalition operating under UN authority. Since April 1991, when Security Council Resolution 687 set specific terms for the formal cease fire in the Gulf War, the Security Council's agenda has continued to grow. It is now addressing a wider range of issues than ever before. Ninety Security Council Resolutions have been adopted since SCR 687, 18 of them mandatory under Chapter VII. The new-found spirit of co-operation within the Security Council is demonstrated by the fact that the veto has not been used since May 1990.

3. The UN's effectiveness has, however, brought new problems. Demands on the organisation have increased. Parties to regional conflicts everywhere tend to look to the UN for solutions. The pressure which this imposes is increased by the fact that many of these new or re-emerging conflicts are not inter-state conflicts in the traditional sense, but conflicts within the borders of existing states.

4. In his annual report this year the UN Secretary-General Mr Boutros Boutros-Ghali drew attention to the extraordinary expansion in the responsibilities of the United Nations. Taking 1987 and the end of the Cold War as a starting point, his report cites the expansion in the activities of the Security Council and in peacekeeping operations. In 1987 there were 49 Security Council meetings and 43 Consultations of the Whole; in the first 7 months of 1992 alone there were 81 meetings and 119 Consultations of the Whole. The Security Council passed 14 resolutions in 1987; 46 in the first 7 months of 1992. Since 1988 13 new peacekeeping operations have been organized, the same number as in the whole period between 1948 and 1987. Peacekeeping costs for 1992 are 4 times higher than the previous highest annual figure. At the beginning of 1992 the number of UN military personnel and civilian deployed on peacekeeping operations was roughly 11,500. Today the figure stands at 51,000 including new deployments in Somalia and Bosnia-Herzegovina. The UK is now a major contributor. When the UK contingent is deployed to Bosnia, we will have over 3,000 members of the armed forces under UN command, which will make us the third largest contributor after France and Canada.

5. Traditional peacekeeping is no longer limited to the purely military. Recent operations including a significant civilian component (for example for election monitoring in Angola or providing a neutral environment for free and fair elections in Cambodia) and an ever increasing role in cases of humanitarian need, as with the deployment of UN guards in Iraq. In response to the UN's expanding role in cases of humanitarian emergency, the Organisation has sharpened its own internal mechanisms. UNGA Resolution 46/182, stemming from an Anglo/German initiative, created the new post of Co-ordinator and Department for Humanitarian Affairs (DHA). DHA is now responsible for co-ordinating efforts in Somalia and in issuing appeals on behalf of all parties in complex emergencies involving several agencies, for example in Iraq. In the case of Bosnia-Herzegovina, the UN and UNHCR are mounting a combined operation with a UN force offering protective support for relief convoys and for the evacuation to safety of detainees from camps.

The cost of printing and publishing these Minutes of Evidence is estimated by HMSO at £4,119.

6. At the beginning of this year as Dr Boutros-Ghali took up office the UK, as President of the Security Council, took the initiative in convening the first ever meeting of the Security Council at Head of State/Government level. The Summit took place in New York on 31 January and was chaired by the Prime Minister. The meeting invited the UN Secretary-General to prepare a report on ways in which the UN could reinforce its capacity for preventive diplomacy, peacekeeping and peacemaking. On his own initiative, the Secretary-General added a fourth topic which he called post-conflict peace building.

7. The Secretary-General's report, under the title of "Agenda for Peace" was published on 17 June. It is a wide-ranging document which was welcomed by the Security Council in a declaration on 30 June. This stated that the Council "trusts that all organs and entities, in particular the General Assembly, will devote particular attention to the report and will study and evaluate the elements of the report that concern them". It has already become a focus of attention during the current session of the UNGA. In his speech to the General Assembly the Secretary of State for Foreign and Commonwealth Affairs welcomed the report on behalf of the EC and its Members. He said that the "Secretary-General's ideas are a very important collection of proposals which all UN bodies but notably the Security Council and the General Assembly should follow-up swiftly." A copy of this speech will be placed in the Library of the House of Commons.

PREVENTIVE DIPLOMACY

8. For people living in areas on the verge of conflict preventive diplomacy is far more effective than the most successful peacekeeping or peacemaking operation which inevitably must follow the outbreak of violence. The EC Monitoring Mission established by the CSCE in July 1991, originally established as a peacekeeping mission in the former Yugoslavia, and currently operating under the direction of the British Presidency, is developing its role in this area. It will soon begin monitoring events on the borders of the former Yugoslavia in Hungary, Bulgaria and Albania. This is in precisely this area of preventive diplomacy that regional organizations have a major contribution to make, working in collaboration with the UN to tackle potential threats to international peace and security. We shall continue to look carefully case by case at similar preventive deployments where the UK may be able, at the request of a government or of the parties concerned, to help with conciliation and/or humanitarian assistance.

PEACEMAKING

9. We want the UN to put an increased effort into peacemaking under Chapter VI of the UN Charter, and under Chapter VIII, acting together with regional organizations when appropriate. We have particularly welcomed the willingness of the UN to share the peacemaking burden in Yugoslavia. Following consultations between the British EC Presidency and the UN Secretary-General, an international Conference on former Yugoslavia, involving for the first time all key leaders, was held in London on 26 and 27 August. The objective was to develop a comprehensive framework for tackling all elements of the crisis. The Conference is the first joint EC/UN exercise and indeed the first formalized joint approach between the UN and a regional organization.

10. On other aspects raised in the Secretary General's report, the imposition of sanctions under Chapter VII often causes economic difficulties to third countries. Article 50 of the Charter does not provide a wholly effective remedy because the Security Council cannot provide financial or economic assistance. The remedy must ultimately lie in the hands of international financial institutions who are well placed to assess and to take into account the economic difficulties caused to third countries by the imposition of sanctions. We support in principle the Secretary-General's call for states to accept without reservation before the year 2000 the general jurisdiction of the International Court of Justice. We also welcome greater co-ordination between UN specialized agencies in dealing with circumstances contributing to a dispute or conflict.

11. Under the heading of peacemaking the Secretary-General's report contains a number of proposals that Member States should earmark forces for enforcement action and peacekeeping. These include the suggestion that Member States should make forces available to the UN Security Council on a permanent basis. The UK, in conjunction with other EC Member states, has responded to the Secretary-General's questionnaire on forces which could be made available for peacekeeping. We welcome the approach in President Bush's statement to the General Assembly on 21 September, in which he called on member states to maintain troops available for deployment on peacekeeping duties at short notice. He proposed that such units should train together and that there should be co-operation in planning, crisis management and intelligence for peacekeeping. He promised full US collaboration. France has also offered to earmark a further 1,000 men to be on call to the UN, in addition to the 6,000 already on UN service. The Secretary General's idea of "peace enforcement" units raises issues which will need to be discussed in some depth. In the British view, these are probably best addressed on a case by case basis. The objective must be to assess whether the circumstances are right for deployment of UN forces, or forces acting under UN authority.

PEACEKEEPING

12. The Secretary-General calls for an improvement in training of peacekeeping personnel. We have welcomed this, as we have the proposed expansion of the military advisers office in New York. The establishment of a pre-positioned stock of peacekeeping equipment would, however, be costly and uneconomical. In our view, it would be better for governments to agree to keep appropriate equipment on standby for use by the United Nations. The EC and its Member States have declared support for the proposed peacekeeping reserve fund, subject to satisfactory arrangements for financing.

POST-CONFLICT PEACE BUILDING

13. The Secretary-General also draws attention to the importance of efforts to identify and support structures which will consolidate peace and establish confidence after a conflict has been resolved. The UN is playing a crucial role in El Salvador, Cambodia and Angola in helping to rebuild national structures and new democratic institutions.

14. We agree with the Secretary-General that the removal of mines must be high on the list of priorities of any post-conflict peace-building agenda.

REFORM OF THE SECRETARIAT AND GENERAL ASSEMBLY

15. In February 1992 the Secretary-General instituted what the UN described as the "first phase" in the restructuring and streamlining of the Organization. Twelve offices and departments were abolished as separate entities. This produced a net reduction of 14 high level posts. These welcome moves also involved a shift of focus to the political and peacekeeping departments of the Secretariat. The United Kingdom has been active in encouraging a second phase of reform.

The United Kingdom has also supported moves to rationalize and streamline the work of the General Assembly in order to revitalize the organ.

IMPLICATIONS FOR UK POLICY

16. The UK has a central interest in a strong and effective United Nations. As the Foreign Secretary said in his address to the UN:

> "international order is threatened in the short-term by the unleashing of extreme nationalism and challenges to the rule of law. In the medium-term, the inescapable challenge is to reinforce the system of collective security based on the UN. Respect for good government and human rights must move to the centre of the stage".

The UK is an original signatory of the Charter. As a permanent member of the Security Council the UK has a special responsibility for upholding the principles of the Charter and for maintaining international peace and security. We wish to see a stronger UN as was demonstrated in our decision to convene the special Security Council summit of Heads of State/Government in January 1992.

17. Until recently the P5 countries did not normally participate in peacekeeping operations. We were an exception with troops in UNFICYP (UN Force in Cyprus) and UNTAG in Namibia. This convention was finally abandoned in 1991 when UNIKOM (UN Iraq/Kuwait Observer Mission) was established and for the first time, all the P5 deployed troops to a UN peacekeeping operation. At that time we, and each of our P5 colleagues, deployed 20 officers to act as observers. Since then we have deployed: 15 observers to MINURSO in the Western Sahara, 8 observers and a 260-strong Field Ambulance Unit to UNPROFOR I in Croatia and 38 observers, a mine clearance training team and a 70-strong naval component to UNTAC in Cambodia. With the imminent deployment of about 1,800 British soldiers to UNPROFOR II in Bosnia-Herzegovina our total troop contribution to the UN will exceed 3,000 and will make us the third largest troop contributor. Details of UN peacekeeping operations is at Annex A and UK participation at Annex B.

18. The total UN peacekeeping budget for this year is approximately $3 billion of which the UK share is 6 per cent. In addition to this, our direct contribution to UNPROFOR II will be approximately £100 million. The UK therefore has a keen interest in adequate and cost effective funding for peacekeeping operations. The key to adequate funding lies in the readiness of Member States to pay their assessed contributions in full and on time. We also support better arrangements in New York for the organization and funding of peacekeeping operations. We have appointed a military adviser to the UK Mission in New York. We welcome the establishment of a group of qualified persons to examine the longer term financial security of the United Nations. Subject to satisfaction on the details of financing, we also support the idea of a peacekeeping reserve fund.

CONCLUSION

19. In "Agenda for Peace" the Secretary General has come forward with the bold response we looked for in commissioning the report. At the same time, he has made clear that the UN is currently suffering from an "excess of credibility". Expectations that the Organization can respond to and resolve crises in every continent are high. As Dr Boutros-Ghali rightly notes, the UN is not however equipped financially or structurally to cope with all the problems it faces. We are committed to working with the Secretary-General to help him cope with his expanding agenda. This includes, not only threats to international peace and security, but such major issues as the environment, the protection and promotion of human rights, the effects of famine and mass migration and, not least, the problems of development. We shall work with him to find lasting solutions to his financial problems. As a Permanent member of the UN Security Council, Britain will continue to play a leading and constructive role.

ANNEX A

SUMMARY OF UNITED NATIONS PEACEKEEPING FORCES BY COUNTRIES MILITARY COMPOSITION AS AT 30 SEPTEMBER 1992

Contributors	*Missions* *UNTSO (Jerusalem)*	*UNMOGIP (India/Pakistan)*	*UNFICYP (Cyprus)*
Australia	13		
Austria	14		405
Belgium	2	2	
Canada	20		575
Chile	4	3	
China	5		
Denmark	11	7	352
Finland	22	5	7
France	24		
Ireland	20		8
Italy	8	8	
Netherlands	15		
New Zealand	4		
Norway	17	5	
Russia	34		
Sweden	35	8	9
Switzerland		5	
United Kingdom			789
United States	35		
Uruguay		1	

ANNEX A *(cont)*

Contributors	*Missions* *UNDOF* *(Israel/Syria)*	*UNIFIL* *(Lebanon)*	*UNAVEM* *(Angola)*
Algeria			16
Argentina			15
Austria	540		
Brazil			(f)1,415
Canada	218		15
Congo			14
Czechoslovakia			15
Egypt			12
Fiji		725	
Finland	414	544	
France		500	
Ghana		889	
Guinea Bissau			5
Hungary			15
India			15
Ireland		755	15
Italy		52	
Jordan			15
Malaysia			15
Morocco			15
Nepal		851	
Netherlands			15
New Zealand			12
Nigeria			15
Norway		876	15
Poland	156		
Senegal			15
Singapore			8
Spain			15
Sweden		587	15
Yugoslavia			12
Zimbabwe			15

ANNEX A *(cont)*

Contributors	*Missions* *UNIKOM* *(Iraq/Kuwait)*	*ONUSAL* *(El Salvador)*	*MINURSO* *(W.Sahara)*
Argentina		7	7
Australia			45
Austria		7	1
Bangladesh		7	1
Brazil		3	
Canada	(c)92 1	1	32
Chile	(d)50		
China		15	19
Denmark	(e)44	7	
Equador			3
Egypt			9
Fiji		9	
Finland		7	9
France		15	30
Ghana		8	1
Greece		7	1
Hungary		7	
India		8	
Indonesia		7	
Ireland		8	6
Italy		5	6
Luxembourg			40
Kenya	8		10
Malaysia	8		1
Nigeria	7		1
Norway	(f)23 8		
Pakistan	9		1
Peru			15
Poland	7		2
Romania	7		
Russia	15		
Senegal	7		
Singapore	7		
Spain	5		
Sweden	(g)30 8		
Thailand	7		
Turkey	7		
United Kingdom	15		15
United States	15		30
Uruguay	8		
Venezuela	7	3	15

ANNEX A *(cont)*

Contributors	*Missions UNTAC (Cambodia)*	*UNPROFOR I (Croatia)*	*UNPROFOR II (Bosnia-Hercegovina)*
Algeria	18		
Argentina	2	900	
Australia	30g 533j		
Austria	17		
Bangladesh	920		
Belgium	2	620	100
Bulgaria	819		
Cameroon	14		
Canada	96g 47	350c 900	1,200
Chile	42b 11		
China	448		
Czechoslovakia		500	
Denmark		900	110
Egypt		400	
Finland		300c	
France	200d 987	1,100g 1519	2,000
Germany	125f		
Ghana	900		
Guinea	1		
India	375f 997		
Indonesia	1,752		
Ireland	17		
Jordan		900	
Kenya		900	
Nepal	910	900	
Netherlands		884 360j	400
Nigeria	34d 48g	900	
Norway	40j 26	100e	
Pakistan	1,002		
Philippines	117g 1		
Poland		900	
Romania	84b 16		
Russia	30 14g 27	900	
Singapore	57		
Spain	2		400
Sweden		100	
Switzerland	25		
Tunisia	887		
Ukraine	710	400	
United Kingdom	70b 51	300f	1,800+
United States			50
Uruguay	875		
Venezuela	50		
Yugoslavia	42b 89		

a) Civilian medical & air personnel
b) Patrol Boat Crew
c) Engr. Unit
d) Air Unit
e) Post and Movecon Unit
f) Medical Unit
g) Logistic Unit
j) Comms. Unit

ANNEX B

BRITISH PARTICIPATION IN UN PEACEKEEPING OPERATIONS

Operation	*Total Size*	*British Contribution*	*Total Cost US $m*	*British Cost US $m*
UNIKOM	250	16 observers	67.2	4.0 plus MOD costs (full) £0.6m
MINURSO	230	15 observers	58	3.5 plus MOD costs (full) £0.54m
UNFICYP	2,176	800	VOL	£1.7m cont. plus MOD costs (full) £25m
UNTAC	16,000 troops plus 69,000 civ and local	38 observers 13 MCTU 70 naval unit	1,690	101.4 plus MOD costs first yr £0.17m last six months (full) £2.5m
UNPROFOR I	15,300	292 Field Amb. Unit 8 observers 5 HQ UNPROFOR	675	40.5 plus MOD costs first yr £1.8m subsequent yrs (full) £10.5m
UNPROFOR II	6–7,000	1,800 Infantry plus Logistic support		£100m approx.

Examination of witnesses

SIR DAVID HANNAY, KCMG, UK Permanent Representative to the United Nations, examined. MS GLYNNE EVANS, CMG, Head of UN Department, Foreign and Commonwealth Office, further examined.

Chairman

1. Sir David and Ms Evans, first of all, welcome to this Committee and our warm thanks to you both for being able to be here this morning, in particular Sir David; I am not sure whether you have flown all night just to be here or whether you happened to be here anyway. We are extremely pleased indeed to have the opportunity of meeting you here and indeed this Committee hopes shortly to have opportunities of meeting you, as it were, on your patch in New York when we visit the United Nations the week after next. The Committee is seeking to clarify and formulate some views for a report to the House starting very much from the sort of outline set out in Mr Boutros Ghali's report "Agenda for Peace", trying to see how British policy should respond to that and what our objectives are in relation to the United Nations. That is the background. May I therefore begin by addressing a question to you, Sir David, but Ms Evans also please feel very ready to chip in and vice versa if questions go the other way, we like to be quite informal about that aspect of things. It is a general question to start the proceedings. Is it sensible to view the United Nations as a cohesive body that can become very politically powerful now the Cold War has ended or is it, once again, going to turn out to be a house divided where, in this case, the divisions will be new ones between the rich North and poor South and other fault lines? Are we being optimistic in seeing a new and unified UN or is there a genuine hope there?

(Sir David Hannay) Well, Mr Chairman, thank you and Members of the Committee very much for inviting me today. No, I did not fly overnight last night I came on Sunday and look forward very much to seeing you in New York the week after next.As to your question, I think it is first of all, reasonable to register that the UN has put in a

[Chairman *Contd*]

much more effective performance since the end of the Cold War, is very much closer to what the founding fathers believed it should be doing, that is to say exercising the primary role for ensuring international peace and security than it has ever done before. There is no doubt that following the end of the Cold War, which has enabled the five Permanent Members and the other 10 non Permanent Members of the Security Council to work together on a whole range of issues, the UN has been put to the test in the last three years. I would argue myself that the UN has not been found particularly wanting. In that context it has been able to formulate policies which are the response to very serious problems which have arisen in different parts of the world and where the UN has had to deal with threats to international peace and security: reversing aggression in Iraq, trying to cope with disintegrating situations in Somalia and Yugoslavia. I would not however entirely depart from the note of caution in your question, namely that we cannot simply assume that this is going to go on like this, that you can extrapolate a trend line which says the UN is performing effectively and simply carry it on to the future like that. It will depend, of course, on the political will of the Member States to back the UN and that is a crucial part of it because no international organisation has a life of its own separate from the life of its Member States. The UN is no more immune from that requirement than anybody else. It will depend on that; and that is very much crystal ball gazing. What will the world look like in three years time? If we had tried to answer that three years ago we would have got it comprehensively wrong. There are downside risks as well as upside opportunities. It is in our interest as a medium sized country with a stake in collective security to see if we can do our best to make sure the upside advantages are taken and the downside risks are avoided. I would not argue they do not exist.

2. Would you, Ms Evans, as head of the UN Department at the Foreign and Commonwealth Office, like to add to that?

(Ms Evans) When the Secretary-General was here and spoke at Chatham House he spoke of an excessive credibility on the part of the UN. It is a body which the international community collectively and separately now turn to and look to to resolve their problems. There is demonstrably a degree of political will as Sir David has said. The UN is better placed to respond, in some cases better than others. At the moment we have a growing list of missions, good offices, in various part of the world, from Africa to the former Soviet Union. The UN is not going to be able to provide a response in each and every case but it is perhaps at least going to be able to chart, indicate at least, some possibilities. It is an evolving area and as Sir David has said we cannot predict.

3. What about the suggestion that really with America the only super-power left and Russia very weak, the UN is becoming too much of an American agenda, dictated by them?

(Sir David Hannay) I do not think that is a very realistic criticism myself. If you look at the Gulf Crisis, for example, it was not a purely American agenda. The need to reverse an absolutely open aggression such as took place by Iraq against Kuwait was a need that was very widely perceived in the Arab world and the rest of the world. Small countries around the world realise they are always at risk against their better armed neighbours. If there is not available, as there was during the Cold War, often a kind of proxy who came in and saved you because you were his friend, then the only force for collective security is the United Nations. I think there is some reality in the view that if there is an American super-power and there are no other super-powers (because of the collapse of the Soviet Union) then indeed America is going to be an important influence in the United Nations but this is merely reflecting reality. It is not the same thing as saying the UN is completely dominated by the United States. You only have to look at the voting record in the Security Council to see a very large number of resolutions adopted unanimously.

Mr Sumberg

4. In relation to taking action as opposed to voting with the United States, the operation in the Gulf would have been completely impossible so far as the UN is concerned. Therefore, it would seem to me that at the end of the day action, particularly in military terms, by the United Nations depends on the United States supporting that military action. If it failed to do so we would not have taken action in the Gulf. I cannot see another situation where we could take military action in an effective large way without United States' backing.

(Sir David Hannay) I would not disagree with your analysis. I think in the case of Iraq it was not credible to believe that the UN could have, on its own, mounted an operation like Desert Storm. You were dealing with the fourth largest armed forces in the world, admittedly perhaps not quite as strong as was originally thought but nevertheless a formidable array of weaponry and it required someone like the United States to be on the side of the coalition to be leading the coalition, for it to be credible and for the aggression to be effectively reversed. I think this case was probably a little bit atypical and I do not think we can argue by extrapolation from that to other cases that might come up, quite apart from the fact that a lot of problems might arise in places which do not have the same amount of force needed to be countered by the international community. We must never forget what the United States was doing was simply applying the resolutions of the Security Council. It was not acting on its own and that would probably be the case in other places. I do not disagree with you if it comes to enforcement, and I think most people would very much hope that would be the exception rather than the rule.

Mr Rowlands

5. Sir David, you said it was in the United Kingdom's interest to help to avoid the downside risks. Could you give us an example of the downside risks and how you avoid them?

(Sir David Hannay) There are a whole lot. One is what you might call overstretch, that is to say what Ms Evans has spoken about, the United Nations being asked to do more than it can do. That has two sides to it: one is maintaining the sense of proportion between what the UN takes on, not as it were dashing into every situation even ones which are very unpromising in legal or practical terms; the other is trying to expand resources available to it to achieve an elasticity of the resources available today in men, logistics and finance. We can play a bit of a role, although modest, in both sides of the equation. Then there are risks which you have to register as being unpredictable, that is to say some falling out among the five permanent members for example, as a result of events of a kind over which we have no control and that will, of course, hamper UN cooperation and action. It will not necessarily mean we will return to the old Cold War situation where there were two blocs, as it were, countering each other's positions in the United Nations but it could be a less cohesive situation than the one now. In those circumstances we would want to be working to try to reduce the frictions, if possible, and to ensure the UN remained an effective force. Those are just a few of the downside risks and there are probably many others I have not described.

6. Are there any present day activities, particularly in the heightened role of the UN, which fall into the first category you describe, that is basically ones we would not desire to get further involved in, or do you think every existing involvement is justified?

(Sir David Hannay) I would find it difficult to say that any of the existing involvements are not fully justified. There are some cases where many people have argued the United Nations should have got involved earlier—Somalia is an example of that—where there were conceptual problems as well as practical problems, the conceptual problems being there was not a clearcut threat to international peace and security, to which a response was required. It was more a massive humanitarian disaster gradually coming to be seen as a case for international intervention in a way it was not seen some years ago. I could not put my finger on one which I would say is not justified. But there are problems, for example in the former Soviet Union where there is a tendency to say: "Please get the UN in" which are very unpromising for UN action, where it is really a kind of civil war between two factions in a post-communist situation where you would want to be very cautious.

7. Georgia for example?

(Sir David Hannay) Georgia is one where a certain amount of caution is needed and Tadzhikistan is another one. We were bombarded by letters from the President of Tadzhikistan last week asking for UN intervention in Tadzhikistan in circumstances where it was very unclear what the UN would be coming in to do, or whether it would be appropriate so to do it, or politic to do so. You would need to make much more use, as the Secretary-General is doing, of fact-finding missions and good offices and so on to probe the situation and to see if it is an appropriate case for intervention by the international community.

Chairman: We are drifting on to a subject we want to come on to in greater detail in a moment, that is the criteria for intervention in these kinds of conflicts. Could we concentrate on the broader issue for the moment.

Mr Wareing

8. I want to take up the point the Chairman raised initially about the dominance of the United States as the one super power within the United Nations. Can you conceive of any situation arising where it would be possible to launch the sort of action that was taken over Kuwait in an area of the world where the United States was at odds with the United Nations? For example, if a situation was to arise within, we would say, Latin America and the United Nations resolved to take a line of action, is it conceivable that that action could be taken involving military activity without the United States' involvement or at least coalescence?

(Sir David Hannay) I think the answer must be no, because the United States remains a permanent member of the Security Council, it remains a power which has a right to veto Security Council action. Such action in any part of the world could only be a UN action if it was authorised, or undertaken, by the United Nations. If you will forgive me for saying so, I do not recognise this analysis as applying to any situation likely to happen; but to follow you down that purely theoretical path, I would assume the United States would not allow the United Nations' Security Council to decide in that sense.

Sir John Stanley

9. You referred to Somalia and we are very much aware, of course, of the criticism that has been raised as to the alleged dilatoriness of the UN's involvement. You suggested there was some uncertainty as to whether there was locus here for the United Nations, might I put it to you there was the clearest possible justification for the United Nations' intervention on humanitarian grounds and this was pressed for very strongly by the development agencies in this country and elsewhere, conspicuously by the Save the Children Fund. How would you justify the fact that the United Nations' serious involvement took so long to arrive in Somalia?

(Sir David Hannay) I will try to answer you in two parts. Firstly, I will start by saying I think the criticisms of the whole international system in

[Sir John Stanley *Contd*]

respect of Somalia are to some extent founded. We have to recognise this and we have to learn from certain mistakes that were made over Somalia. For many months, even years, it was assumed the problem in Somalia required effective humanitarian relief purveyed by agencies like the World Food Programme, the World Health Organisation and so on. This was tried and the Red Cross and non-governmental organisations were working there. This was tried for many, many months with decreasingly successful results as the internal security situation broke down and it became basically impossible to distribute relief, for the people providing relief to get it to anybody other than the gunmen and so on. It took a long time before people perceived there was a problem that required a Security Council operation of military protective action. It was quite unprecedented really, and it was a big conceptual jump to get over because it was difficult to argue with much conviction there was a threat to international peace and security in Somalia, which is the primary reason for peacekeeping and for deploying military forces. Gradually it became clear that was necessary and that is what is now being done. If I could say this about the two parts of the equation: the humanitarian organisations for a very long time were fundamentally opposed to any form of military intervention, as were a lot of the people on the ground, and the change in opinion in the non-governmental organisations and humanitarian organisations towards favouring a UN military involvement is a pretty recent development. You do not have to go back many months to find people saying: "Please keep your troops away, they will merely make things worse for us". That opinion has shifted and there is emerging a consensus which is even communicating itself to most of the factions in Somalia, that these peacekeeping protectors who are coming in, 3,500 or so, will perform an absolutely essential task which will enable the humanitarian workers to get on with their tasks. It is quite recently that shift of opinion has taken place. You will find many quotes from humanitarian organisations saying: "Please keep them out, they will make things worse".

10. Could I put it to you that what in fact did change fundamentally the climate was the American political decision to become involved militarily in terms of deploying military aircraft with military security in a major airlift operation to Somalia and was that not a factor that basically did produce a fundamental change in the scale of effort that the world was prepared to make in Somalia itself?

(Sir David Hannay) No, I am sorry, I do not think so. The Security Council authorisation of the deployment of protective forces came before that American change in position, in fact. I do not think it is correct to describe the American operation as a military operation. They have themselves described it very firmly as a humanitarian one. They are not involved in the provision of protective forces on the ground in Somalia. They are using their air force, air lift capability, to bring in supplies. That is a good thing and something which everyone involved in the operation is enormously grateful for. But I do not think they were the catalyst in quite the sense you describe it.

Chairman: Our questions are broadening into the "new" types of conflict the UN is involved in. Mr Lester?

Mr Lester

11. Is this not the nub of the argument, Sir David, in fact the whole type of conflict one envisages in the future is much more likely to follow the pattern of Somalia and Yugoslavia? We can talk of other parts of the world where intervention in one form or another is increasingly necessary and it is the basis upon which one can make that intervention. I know the UN and I would like you to tell us whether the way you think the UN was originally organised can cope with this question of sovereignty where people claim you cannot interfere in the sovereign affairs of the country where quite clearly there is anarchy and there are no sovereign affairs. Does this attitude change to adjust to what is sovereign? Mozambique, where there has been a civil war for the last 17 years causing enormous problems for all the surrounding areas, without the sovereignty of Mozambique you cannot intervene but you can pick up the tab for the millions of refugees in Zimbabwe or Malawi. It is a new concept of what the UN can do in terms of describing sovereignty and how the non aligned movement sees the sovereignty. I know they are very jealous of the fact it should remain perhaps in the old fashioned sense and where does enforcement come into it? We are moving slowly towards enforcing when one puts humanitarian aid in Yugoslavia, Bosnia and Somalia.

(Sir David Hannay) I think you have asked some very important questions but ones which are extraordinarily difficult to answer in a hard edged way. I will try to say a few things. I think the United Nations, and here that I mean the Security Council, also to some extent the General Assembly, has gradually been moving in its approach to these issues and has been evolving. There has been a big shift in the last two or three years from what was previously considered conventional wisdom. Article 2.7 of the Charter which says you cannot intervene in internal affairs meant there were no-go areas. That has rather changed now and to a lot of people's surprise, including some of the people who have supported the action in Somalia. For example, the United Nations is doing things that would have been absolutely off limits some years ago. The same is true of some aspects of what is going on in Yugoslavia too. All that has happened without any change in the Charter. It has happened by a kind of organic process, an evolution of opinion and nobody was more surprised than some of the Members of the Security Council when it was the African Members, i.e. non aligned Members, of the Security Council who came and said: "We believe we must put UN troops into Somalia to protect

[**Mr Lester** *Contd*]

the aid effort." That was an extraordinary shift but it was a shift which came, you might argue, from the right direction because it was not forced on anyone. It came as a result of an evolution of opinion. I would not like to say how far that will carry us. I do not think it will probably carry us to enforcement in such circumstances which is a very big jump, to going in by force to enforce things. That is a very big jump. I would regard that as a rubicon which has not yet been crossed. It would be very difficult to cross. I would also myself argue against any too conceptual an approach to defining how things have changed in these doctrines. The minute you start to write this down on a piece of paper it would disappear because there would be fundamental objections to re-writing Article 2.7 of the Charter. You can imagine the sort of reaction of some countries who would consider that to be a licence to anyone to interfere anywhere. I would argue very strongly for a kind of pragmatic, organic approach such as is going on now, whereby the UN is proving itself more adaptable than some of us would have given it credit for many years ago.

12. Is there anything that can be developed in terms of intervention? As Sir John has suggested many of us close to Somalia recognised the situation, watched it evolving with horror. The fact, for instance, in Southern Sudan as soon as somebody is shot, which is desperately wrong, then the UN withdraw from Southern Sudan and leave a desperately difficult situation. Is there any way in which the credibility of the UN, indeed the terms of contract of the UN's operation, could not necessarily mean when anybody is shot they have to leave the theatre?

(Sir David Hannay) I would not like to get too far into individual cases like the Sudan because it is a very sensitive one and I do not think it would help anyone for me to express too strong views about what the UN should do in that situation. I would hope the experience of Somalia and the way in which the UN's approach of dealing with a humanitarian disaster of this sort has evolved would mean if a similar one occurred—heaven forbid—somewhere else in the world there would not be the same time lag because there would not be the same hang ups. People would say: "We tried a protective humanitarian effort in Somalia and it worked". That is a very big assumption right now. We still have to show it works. But if it works, then of course it will be a precedent and it will be something people will turn to more quickly in the future if a similar situation arises. That must be the hope, there will not be a time lag in coming to their assistance. The other thing I would argue is that you cannot establish blueprints of a situation. Almost every situation in every country is different and they require a bit different treatment by the UN, by its humanitarian agencies, by the Security Council. It is very difficult to argue from blueprints. There will never be an exact carbon copy of Somalia.

Mr Lester: Do you think the organisation now can cope with this new form? The fact is we have the traditional set up with all the different agencies competing for funds, competing for authority. Is the organisation as you see it now in a form to deal with that?

Chairman: Can I intervene there because we would like to come on to the structure of the organisation in detail in a moment. If we can stick to the tasks at the moment and come back to that.

Mr Harris

13. I gather really what you are saying is there is a very real danger because of the success and because of the demands and pressures and precedents and the organic growth, the United Nations is in danger of becoming completely overstretched?

(Sir David Hannay) Well, I do not myself feel that that is an imminent danger although I think it could arise. But I would argue that the United Nations has shown great adaptability in the last two or three years, has shown considerable elasticity. It has, for instance, gone, as you know from the document circulated to you, from deploying 11,000 peacekeepers at the beginning of this year to 51,000 now. It is spending four times as much on peacekeeping this year than it has ever spent in previous years and yet, if that is not too flippant a way of putting it, it is about the same distance from bankruptcy this year as it was this time last year but at a much higher level of expenditure. That seems to show there is real support for the United Nations because real money is being stumped up by these members in unparalleled amounts. Is that infinite? Well, obviously it is not infinite but I do think the organisation, both in practical terms and in conceptual terms, is showing the ability to adapt as it goes along and to me one of the most important things about an international organisation is that it can adapt to circumstances. It seems to be doing that quite well but it produces creaks and groans and strains in so doing of which we are all very conscious and which cannot be wished away.

14. Has any thought been given at all to winding up some of the longstanding peacekeeping operations or winding them down? It seems to me one cannot go on adding remorselessly to the tasks being put on the United Nations.

(Sir David Hannay) You have touched on probably one of the most difficult aspects of UN peacekeeping which is how to get out. We are getting more and more experienced in ways of how to get in and the UN is becoming more and more adaptable about the things it gets into and the things it does when it gets in, for example organising elections, protecting human rights as well as deploying peacekeepers, training civil police. The gamut of the United Nations' activities in a peacekeeping situation in somewhere like El Salvador or Cambodia has greatly expanded. One thing nobody has yet cracked is how do you get out. It is not true that the United Nations has never got out of a peacekeeping situation satisfactorily, harmoniously and effectively. It has, and Namibia is one

[**Mr Harris** *Contd*]

example. The United Nations saw the country through to independence, oversaw the elections and then it left. There are no UN peacekeepers in Namibia now and Namibia is living in peace under a democratic government as a member state. That is the paradigm. But there are other cases where it has not worked like that, for instance in Cyprus. Cyprus is a bad case which has dragged on and on and the UN involvement has continued. I think most people think it has saved Cyprus and the two communities there from worse but it has not brought about a solution. We have to face the fact there are one or two places where it will be difficult to wind down, for example in Angola we are faced with a difficult situation where one of the parties is contesting the outcome of the election that the UN went to organise and which the UN representative has considered to be, broadly speaking, fair and free. In one analysis you would say just pull them out and tell them they cannot have this. But that is a very difficult decision to take. There will be many voices saying you cannot walk away from a situation where thousands of people have been killed in civil strife. With international involvement, when things have gone a little bit wrong or get a little bit difficult you cannot just walk away. I do not think the walk away solution is terribly appealing. We have to recognise, and all of us in New York recognise, there is a real problem as to how to get the UN out. The UN presence sometimes seems to become very comfortable.

Mr Canavan

15. Sir David, you refer to an evolution of opinion as to whether the United Nations should intervene in the internal affairs of nation states but you appear to be opposed to actually writing anything down about this. Will not this evolution of opinion almost certainly in the passage of time lead to demands for an amendment to the Charter, particularly Article 2.7, because people will start quoting precedents and say: "If you did it in country X why did you not do it in country Y" and there will be accusations of double standards and so on. Will it not be better to think ahead in terms of at least writing down the basic principles on which intervention in internal affairs by the United Nations could be justified?

(Sir David Hannay) I think there is a perfectly reasonable case to be advanced in the sense you advance it. But I do not myself find it compelling in the circumstances we live in, and not just because I come from a country that has not got a written constitution and tends to believe in an evolutive approach. Frankly it is not realistic to suppose 179 members, or whatever the number is, of the UN whose agreement would be needed for a charter change are going to agree about the redefinition of, say, Article 2.7. The United Nations would, frankly, tear itself to pieces if it tried to redefine this concept. I think there is a lot of empirical evidence that the membership in the institutions in which they are represented, the Assembly, the Council and so on, are prepared to recognise the need in practical terms to do things differently from the way we did them some years back and to regard some taboos as no longer being what they were. As a practitioner you tend to argue that we will get further and be more effective by using that kind of approach than by defining a right of intervention. There are voices raised that say there should be in the United Nations' Charter the right of humanitarian intervention. That is the view propounded by Monsieur Kirchner, the French Minister for Humanitarian Affairs, but most of us feel that if this debate was started it would make it more difficult to do the things we are doing now.

Mr Rowlands

16. You said earlier on, understandably, cautions have been felt over intervention in internal conflicts in, say, the former Soviet Republics, if they get hotter and hotter how is the UN going to say no when you have a perfectly similar situation that has evolved in Yugoslavia where the UN has got more and more deeply involved? How can we make a distinction between the break up of the Soviet Republic on Muslim, Christian, Orthodox grounds, the sort of situation we have got deeply involved in in the case of Yugoslavia?

(Sir David Hannay) I think it will be rather difficult to do. But I do not myself believe that having a great debate about the right of intervention would actually help to make those decisions.

17. I understand that.

(Sir David Hannay) You cannot, in the end, dodge having to take these issues as they come. But I think the Secretary-General could develop, and is developing, more instruments for dealing with them. His ideas of fact-finding missions are important. His ideas of using his own good offices are also important. Then there are others, other forms of preventative diplomacy, putting in civilian monitors or observers, as has been tried by the EC in South Africa and in Yugoslavia. These are various concepts and ideas being developed now which may make the criterion we have to apply when dealing with new situations easier to apply.

Chairman

18. In order to give Sir David's voice a rest, I do not know whether Ms Evans would like to add anything to that? Mr Gapes, you now ask your question but, Ms Evans, do feel free to come in.

(Ms Evans) If I could just make one point. There is in a sense a tension between the two lines of questioning, one when the UN goes in and the second how to get the UN out after it has gone in. One of the practices the UN has followed in what I will call broadly peacekeeping operations is certain general criteria which are the consent of all parties, not only the Government but any parties within the state in ex-Yugoslavia, for example, for preference, there is a more or less durable ceasefire and an ongoing political process that is the key that will help end the process of participation. I think these are factors that would also guide people

[**Chairman** *Contd*]

when you go beyond, perhaps, the fact-finding missions of the kind the Secretary-General is proposing in the former Soviet Union, in Georgia, Latvia, and whether that is taken forward and whether the UN can contribute in any sense beyond identifying political solutions. Is there a need to go in? Do circumstances exist, is it possible to see an end to such a process? When you are talking about humanitarian intervention it is also important to remember one further aspect is the consent of the two contributors. There needs to be a balance between the acute suffering the international community wants to respond to and which it can do something about, as in the case of Somalia, and the willingness of the people to deploy troops into a very difficult situation. These points perhaps reinforce the case for looking at problems on a case by case basis. That is why it is difficult to think of a universal role or, indeed, a further article. All these things can be done within the existing highly flexible Charter.

Chairman: Mr Gapes on this and then structure.

Mr Gapes

19. Is not the big problem that the UN is not a democratic organisation and in practice the big and powerful countries can lean on the smaller and weaker countries and get them to comply with certain things and therefore I can quite easily understand why people do not want things written down with principles because then you can use pragmatic approaches depending upon the particular circumstances at the particular time. Is there not a great danger in that though that many third world countries will see it as a conspiracy by the United Nations and its closest allies to get what they want? You have already said, Sir David, the United States would not allow circumstances to arise where its policy was not being pursued or decisions were taken contrary to its interests. Is there not a danger that for perfectly understandable reasons approaches are taken on a pragmatic basis but that then leads to enormous resentment in large numbers of the third world countries?

(Sir David Hannay) I do not think that arises over this question about whether you define a right of intervention because it is the third world countries who do not want the right of intervention to be defined in a more flexible and interventionist way. I am sorry, I do not think it arises in the way you put it. The question about democracy in the United Nations is, I think, very difficult to define. Some aspects of the Charter of the United Nations are not about democracy in the broad sense of the word. The idea of having a Security Council of 10 or 15 or more Members, which takes decisions about international peace and security is not obviously a democratic concept. But it was a concept which emerged after the Second World War in the light of the failure of the League of Nations. It was felt there needed to be a restricted member body which could be principally responsible for international peace and security and the fact that that body had a lot less members than the overall membership of the UN was present from the very beginning.

Chairman: This leads on very nicely to the whole issue of the structure of the United Nations in the face of all these new tasks. Mr Jopling?

Mr Jopling

20. I wonder if you could talk to us about the efficiency of the organisation, as you see it. We have read of the Secretary-General's first phase reforms in reducing I think it was 12 offices and departments and the reduction of 14 high level jobs. What has been the effect of that? What are we pressing for in phase two of his reforms? I wonder if you could talk to us about how better the UN could improve its co-ordination with its different, or between its different, agencies? Finally, how well you think the UN co-ordinates its activities with non-governmental organisations around the world?

(Sir David Hannay) Yes, I will try. They are three pretty broad questions. On the Secretary-General's reforms, he did, as you say, reduce sharply the number of Under Secretary-General posts which had, in the view of most of Members of the United Nations, grown like Topsy over the years without any clear definition of their functions. Some of them were definitely not worthy of having Under Secretary-General posts and there was a lot of doubling up, overlapping and so on. What the Secretary-General did at the beginning of the year was I think admirable and necessary. What we are asking that he do, and what he is beginning to do now, is to follow that down through the machine to the lower levels, where there are also overlaps, and offices which were unnecessary. He is beginning to do that, to get a more coherent structure in the UN Secretariat. Your second question was about the agencies and that is a much more difficult one. The problem is many of these UN agencies have a constitution and a structure entirely of their own and they are not the servants of the Secretary-General. He cannot order them around. The United Nations' High Commission for Refugees, he cannot order Mrs Ogata around. That may be a good thing or a bad thing but it is a fact. So the problem of the agencies has to be done by persuasion as much as by decision by the Secretary-General. He is talking and putting a lot of effort into trying to make an organisation called the Administrative Co-ordinating Committee, which brings together all of the agencies with himself chairing it, to make that a more effective and policy orientated body. It is definitely an up-hill task but it is one in which he deserves our support. The third question are the relations with NGOs which is, I think, a very crucial one as NGOs become more and more active in fields like humanitarian relief, the environment and so on. We ourselves have been very active in the field of the environment in pioneering a new and more intensive relationship between NGOs and inter-governmental UN institutions. We are going to try to continue that in the discussions which are starting in New York now for setting up a thing

[**Mr Jopling** *Contd*]

called the Sustainable Development Commission decided by the Rio Summit this year to carry forward the body of decisions on the environmental programme made by Rio. We want to see the non-governmental organisation more directly involved in dialogue than they have been in the past. In the humanitarian field it is a much more practical working relationship problem, not just a policy problem but on the ground working together. I sometimes feel frankly there is a little bit too much finger pointing on both sides, particularly when things go wrong. It is absolutely clear things have gone wrong in a place like Somalia. The United Nations in the form of its co-ordinators on the spot have got to have better working relationships with the non-governmental organisations. I know the new Under Secretary-General for Humanitarian Affairs, Mr Eliasson of Sweden, has that high up on his agenda. He is beginning to organise monthly meetings both through his officials in Geneva and his own offices in New York with non-governmental organisations. He is trying to pull all this together better. It is a complex field but one which needs improvement.

21. Would you mind enlarging on what you think the Secretary-General ought to do in phase two? We are told in the Foreign Office paper the United Kingdom has been active in encouraging the second phase of reformation. Will you tell us please what you are encouraging them to do?

(Sir David Hannay) Well, I will be cautious about it because one of the things we are encouraging him to do is to be an effective manager. The Secretary-General is the top manager of the United Nations. You should not spend too much time micro-managing other people's management. We wish to give him general encouragement to follow his rationalisation down below the level of Under Secretary-General to Assistant Secretary-General, directors and so on. We are not going along with a blueprint and saying: "This is how the Secretariat should be organised" or "Why not do this to this Department". That would be inimical to his being the top manager of the United Nations. In the end he has to manage it for himself. We may think our ideas are very rational and good but there are 178 other people with ideas as well. The last thing you want is everybody pitching in with their own blueprints. We are encouraging him to carry out managerial reforms in the Secretariat of a rational kind but we are not trying to micro-manage.

Mr Lester

22. In terms of one instance, what you said about rationalisation, is there a reverse process? Does anybody look at the considerable expansion of work of the Human Rights Commission in Geneva and the many more cases of human rights worldwide which are still trying to be dealt with on the same budget with the same people? Surely we could rationalise where there is overlap but is there any mechanism where there has been a considerable increase in the workload and an increase in the support of the work the Human Rights Commission does but they have not got the people to do the work properly?

(Sir David Hannay) The European Community did make representations to the Secretary-General recently to ask him to try to find more staff for the Human Rights Commission, particularly for its work on Yugoslavia but in other areas too. He has found some more staff within his existing manpower capacity. That is the precise answer to that question. More generally speaking, yes indeed, part of the rationalisation we are seeking to encourage him to do is to adjust priorities in the way in which a government would do and to switch people from one area of lower priority to another of higher priority. Obviously human rights is one area you have identified, peacekeeping is another, the Department of Humanitarian Affairs is another. The problem is that international organisations are less adaptable than national governments to changing priorities. It is very difficult indeed to prise people away from one department and get them sent to another department, far more difficult than in national administrations where the political imperatives of elections and new governments or whatever it may be tend to be followed through to the civil service level. One should not under-estimate the difficulty of doing this but, equally, we are very much pressing the Secretary-General to reflect his priorities and the priorities of 1992 in the structure of the Secretariat.

Mr Jopling

23. Let us go back to the organisation and structure so far as the Security Council is concerned. There have been various suggestions made as to how it should be changed and we have had Anthony Parsons' paper where he suggested membership of the Security Council should be increased to 20, the Permanent Members to 10. When the Foreign Secretary was in front of us he said: "The Government was not persuaded on the case for seeking to reform the Security Council". Can I ask you, Sir David, what is the background to that approach? Is it that we object to any changes on the merits of the case or is it that to make changes would be rather like a Government Minister bringing a Miscellaneous Provisions Bill into this House? You have to change the Charter and if you are in the process of changing the Charter people can bring 101 other changes into that process. We think it is better to leave it alone rather than to let anyone else tinker with the Charter in the broadest sense. Why is it we are saying there should be no changes to the Security Council?

(Sir David Hannay) I do not think we are saying that in a dogmatic spirit. We are saying the case has not been made to our satisfaction that the work of the Security Council will be better served by a Council of different membership than at present. The idea you mentioned, Tony Parsons' suggestion, it is not terribly easy to see the membership agreeing to have five new Permanent Members and thus change the balance between the Permanent and non-Permanent Members. At the moment there are five Permanent and 10 non-

[**Mr Jopling** *Contd*]

Permanent Members in the Council. He has suggested there should be 10 Permanent and 10 non-Permanent Members. That changes the balance of non-Permanent Members who rotate. The membership outside would not find that a very attractive proposition. Our own feeling is the Security Council has only in the last two or three years begun to realise the potential. It has begun to perform the functions laid down in the Charter of having the primary responsibility for international peace and security. For the first time it has begun to do this with reasonable effectiveness, not 100% success but with reasonable effectiveness. It has done so, broadly speaking, with a very consensual approach. There have been a large number of decisions taken by the Security Council in the last two or three years with unanimity, or 13/14 votes. That does not look like an organisation that is very divided. Confronted with that we are not persuaded of the case for change. But that does not mean to say we are not part of the debate about whether or not it is desirable to change the make up of the Security Council. Everyone in the United Nations is part of that debate. It is a debate running in the corridors very actively now.

24. You say the case is not made for change in the Security Council. I accept the Parsons' criticisms are very much wider but will you explain to us what we say as Parliamentarians travelling around the world, meeting our German and Japanese friends, how do we explain to them the case is not made for having Japan and Germany as Permanent Members of the Security Council at this time, bearing in mind their contribution to the United Nations, I read in the Parsons' paper, is twice that of Britain and France?

(Sir David Hannay) I would hope you would not consider me cowardly if I ducked that question. I honestly cannot go beyond what the Foreign Secretary said on the subject. The question is not posed in those terms because there is no possibility of the totality of the membership agreeing to include Japan and Germany in the Security Council as Permanent Members; but no-one else. It is posed in much wider terms. It is not a narrow question in the way that has been posed. I hope you will forgive me because I do not think I want to get further on that ground.

Chairman

25. We are not trying to divide you from the Foreign Secretary and you are too old to get divided from him in this Committee, but Mr Jopling's point is a more central one. Clearly this world is not the same as in 1945, there are completely new forces at work, the debate there is ought we not to be taking a more leading part in the reshaping of the United Nations otherwise if we stand back saying the case is not made others may gain the upper hand in the debate about the reformation. That is the worry I think.

(Sir David Hannay) The United Nations' Security Council is not as it was designed in 1945. The Council set up in 1945 had five Permanent Members and only five non-Permanent Members. At a later stage the decision was taken to add five more to that, so the 15 Member Council has been going for about 15/20 years. I do not think anybody is suggesting the situation is frozen permanently but frankly I am not at this early stage after the Security Council has begun to operate as it was designed to operate, particularly convinced by the arguments for wholesale reform.

Sir John Stanley

26. Sir David, the right of veto by Permanent Members of the Security Council has not been used since May 1990 but would you agree in the event of a further material reformation of the membership of the Security Council that right of veto belonging to Permanent Members is likely to have to go?

(Sir David Hannay) Well, I think that is one of the reasons why the case for reform is not as appealing as it might be. I think we could have an enormous argument about the right of veto in circumstances where it has ceased to be a central issue in the United Nations. It has ceased to be so because it was last used in 1990 which more or less coincided with the end of the Cold War. What I would call everyday vetoes have gone out of fashion and the veto has become what it was originally designed by the founding fathers to be, a recourse of absolutely last resort by Permanent Members if they felt vital national interests were at stake. It is now so regarded tacitly by everybody at the UN. Therefore to poke up a debate on this now when it is not being used as much as it was in the days of the Cold War in tit for tat operations would, I think, be rather self-destructive. It is not at the heart of how the UN functions now in the post-Cold War era.

Mr Wareing

27. I understand your reticence, as it were, on questions about Germany and Japan being admitted to the United Nations but in the Security Council's desire to ensure there is a peaceful world I think few of us would argue the European Community has in fact increased the possibility of hostilities between Germany and France for example. With that in view have any discussions taken place with the United Nations, or in your own conversations with other people, on the possibility of regional representation taking place with individual Member States? I am thinking in terms of the European Community being a Permanent Member of the Security Council. Should we perhaps not be thinking along those lines, moving in that direction in order to consolidate regional supranational organisations which are definitely promoting peace?

(Sir David Hannay) I think to start with the European part of your question, the Maastricht Treaty which deals in part of it with progress towards a Common Foreign and Security Policy rather explicitly makes it clear that it is not envisaging a European seat in the near future because it

[**Mr Wareing** *Contd*]

makes provision for the two existing permanent members and any other European Community countries that are non-permanent members of the Security Council to consult with and work very closely with the other members so that they defend European Community decisions and policies in the Security Council. I think this implies that nobody in the European Community was thinking of the point of a single European seat on the Security Council being reached in the very near future because the Treaty itself does not envisage it being reached. Insofar as the great debates that have raged in Europe in recent months have shown that progress in the years ahead is likely to be less dramatic and rapid than had been thought possible perhaps one or two years ago, that really merely reinforces the point. As to regional representation in general, in a sense that already exists. The non-permanent members, the ten non-permanent members, are distributed regionally. There are three Africans, there are two Latin-Americans. This is how the elections are worked. So if four Africans tried to get on to the Security Council, they would not get on. It is agreed that there should be three Africans and there are ways in which the regional groupings distribute the seats. In a way that brings in different parts of their regions. The idea that regions should be represented by a permanent member is, I think, quite contentious because some of the largest countries in the world that might aspire to permanent membership are not always accepted by all members of their region as countries they would wish to have representing them. So I think to take it beyond the point it has got already whereby there is indeed a regional balance in the Security Council would be quite contentious.

Mr Sumberg

28. Sir David, I get the impression from all that you have said that the Government takes a very pragmatic, non-doctrinaire approach, "Don't stir up the hornets' nest for fear of what we are going to find", in the sense that, "Don't lay down the principles of intervention because we would never get an agreement. Don't actually look at the institutions and try and reform them because we never could and that would create even greater problems". Is there not a danger that we are going to be in a reactive position rather than a proactive position and the problems will throw themselves up and we are totally unprepared for dealing with them and, therefore, we are trying to fall back on a basis of trying to cope with each situation case by case? Is there not an intrinsic danger of that both in the institutions themselves and indeed in the way the UN operates as a whole?

(Sir David Hannay) I am sorry if I have given that impression because I would not want to give you the impression that we are entirely reactive and not proactive. We have in fact been at the forefront. In the evolution of the Security Council and the UN's practice and its involvement in a whole number of problems that have come before it and I think we have played a very leading role. The number of resolutions that we have sponsored in the Security Council is very high indeed and they have led to things like the ending of the Iraqi aggression in Kuwait and so on. Where I answered very cautiously, I think, is to questions about changing the constitution, as it were, changing the institutional framework. But we are in favour of the Secretary-General rationalising and making his Secretariat more up to date and more capable of dealing with the problems of today, so it cannot, I think, be said that we are totally reactive. But we are rather dubious about the wisdom of starting a fundamental constitutional discussion about the Charter over the question of the right of intervention or about the reform of the Security Council.

Mr Canavan

29. I have a question about the General Assembly. Sir David, do you see a future developing role for the General Assembly? Do you, in your own words, see another evolution of opinion that more power ought to be vested in the General Assembly rather than the Security Council and would that necessarily require an amendment to the Charter?

(Sir David Hannay) I would argue that it is very important that we do not see the relationship between the General Assembly and the Security Council as a zero-sum gain. If the UN is as a whole getting more influential and more respected than it was before, and I believe it is, then there is a lot for both institutions to do. But they operate in quite different ways and it is important that they do not get involved in a turf battle. For example, it seems to me that the Security Council in recent years has not usurped any of the privileges of the General Assembly; it has merely done its job as laid down in the Charter. But it has done it rather more effectively than it did it in the past. Now, there is a case for saying that the General Assembly has to develop and redefine its own role more than it has done up to now and we, Britain, and we, as a member of the European Community, have been very much forward in this. For example, the two main issues that were debated and settled in the General Assembly in 1991 were the setting up of an arms register of transfers of conventional weapons and the establishment of a completely reformed Department of Humanitarian Affairs, an Under Secretary-General, Mr Eliasson, at its head and with a revolving fund at its disposal. Those were both ideas put forward by Britain and endorsed by the European Community and they were the meat and drink of last year's General Assembly. This year we are looking at the follow-up to Rio which is of general interest to everyone and which is going to be a main theme of this year's General Assembly. We are also working very hard in the General Assembly, on some parts of the Secretary-General's "Agenda for Peace", for example, his idea that there should be a modest start-up fund for peace-keeping operations so that there should be some funds available right at the beginning of a peace-keeping operation. This the European Community and Britain support. What we have got to do is to give the General Assembly

[**Mr Canavan** *Contd*]

a more effective role, but not to look on it as one that has to be achieved at the expense of the Security Council.

Sir John Stanley

30. Sir David, you referred earlier to the fact that we are increasingly getting involved in international situations where there is an armed conflict dimension either actual or potential and of course around the world both national governments and international defence organisations have always found it much better in planning for such eventualities to have some form of permanent military staff that can engage in contingency planning. The United Nations had a Military Staff Committee initially, but I understand it has been wholly moribund since 1945. The Russian Government and the French Government, we understand, are in favour of its revival to take into account the new circumstances in which the UN finds itself and I should be grateful if you could tell us the British Government's view of that particular proposal.

(Sir David Hannay) I would like to, if I might, distinguish between two quite different things. One is the Military Staff Committee which was established under the Charter and which, as you correctly say, has never transacted any effective business and remains a kind of empty shell. It is a committee set up of the five permanent members, meant to be, I think, at chief of defence staff level. The second element is the military advisers' staff in the UN Secretariat which was set up some years ago to provide the Secretary-General with military advice in peace-keeping operations and which is very much a living part of the peace-keeping operations area of the Secretariat. Now, to take the second first, we would like to see that military advisers' office strengthened. We believe that it is now too small for the tasks that are required of it with this very large expansion in peace-keeping operations. We would like to see the Secretary-General being helped by attachments, secondments and so on to boost this military advisers' staff and, thus, to help the peace-keeping effort to have better and more up-to-date military input. The Military Staff Committee, the other facet, I think we are unconvinced that needs the Sleeping Beauty treatment. The problem about it is that because it is composed of the military chiefs of the five permanent members, to revive it would be intensely divisive. It would arouse all the susceptibilities that are aroused by the collective activities of the five permanent members already, but worse because it would be in the military field. So I think we are really unconvinced of the desirability of reviving that committee. But these are two quite different aspects and on the strengthening of the Secretary-General's military advisers staff we are strongly favourable.

31. You indicated, however, that the British government's view is that the present extent of that military advice is inadequate. Could you tell the Committee what is impeding this very necessary strengthening of those military advisers to the Secretary General?

(Sir David Hannay) Well, it is being strengthened. He is getting some additional staff. For example, earlier this year we worked with the UN establish a de-mining adviser, a permanent official who could advise all peace-keeping operations on the problems of mine-lifting. This has become a dramatic problem as we discovered in one after another of UN areas of activity in Cambodia, in Afghanistan and elsewhere. There was a critical problem of de-mining. There is now a former British military officer who we identified and who is now part of the military adviser's staff for that. The Secretary-General is also shortly getting a police adviser which has become necessary as the United Nations is becoming involved in civil police work and training in a number of peace-keeping operations. So the staff is evolving but it probably needs to go quicker as like everything else it is being dealt with in a great rush at the moment because of the number of operations that are coming on to the table which require day-to-day dealings and this tends to impede changing the structure. But the Security Council has given encouragement to the Secretary-General to strengthen his military staff and I am sure he will respond to that.

Chairman: We touched earlier on the changing nature of peace-keeping and peace-enforcing and peace-building and so on but this really takes us to the heart of the "Agenda for Peace" document and I think Mr Gapes would like to pursue some of its contents in more detail.

Mr Gapes

32. The memorandum we received from the Foreign and Commonwealth Office refers in paragraph 11 to the Secretary-General's proposals for peace enforcement units. It seems to me that it is very cautious. It says that these should probably be addressed on a case-by-case basis. Could you explain why the Government is so cautious towards this concept given the great needs that there are for speedy action internationally and the number of potential actions and number of eventualities that we have already touched on?

(Sir David Hannay) I think the answer is in the word enforcement. This really is carrying the UN into a new area and it is one where not only the British but many of the membership are very cautious. This is where the UN does not simply go in to monitor or police a cease-fire agreed between the parties and with the consent of them but goes in to enforce something, ie it takes sides. Now I do not think that anyone after the Gulf crisis can argue that this is inconceivable in the sense that the UN did take sides, quite rightly, then when it authorised the use of force after many months of trying to achieve the reversal of the aggression by non-forceful means. But to go on from that to saying that it is the UN in blue helmets that should go in and do the enforcing is quite a big jump. I think a lot of people feel that time and careful study is needed before making that jump. The Secretary-

[**Mr Gapes** *Contd*]

General himself has now said in a number of discussions that he regards this issue of UN direct involvement in enforcement as a lower priority issue than the ones of preventative diplomacy, of strengthening the peace-keeping role of the UN and of strengthening the peace-building role of the UN. He realises this is something that will have to be debated rather carefully and discussed and cannot be dealt with in a great hurry.

33. Would you not agree that it would be preferable to have a structured United Nations involvement with international legitimacy than the ad hoc arrangement which might then be susceptible to criticism that it was just being driven by the United States, Britain and France and some other countries with others reluctantly going along with it?

(Sir David Hannay) I am sorry I would not like to give a clear-cut answer to that question of choices. I think there are real problems. I do not accept that the action in the Gulf was other than an action with total international legal legitimacy. It was authorised by the Security Council and I do not believe that it was unsatisfactory in the sense that we discussed earlier that the degree of force that was necessarily proportionate to deal with the aggression was a very large amount of force, an amount of force that frankly it is not credible to believe the United Nations itself will be able to muster in the short-term.

34. Can I pursue that please. I am not arguing with you about the legitimacy of the United Nations decisions in the Gulf. I am thinking in terms of the new world that we are moving into and I am concerned that we might find north-south conflicts, conflicts about energy supply and conflicts about access to resources where unless there is a proper structuring within the UN framework these kinds of tensions which are there could come to the forefront and it might be regarded that conflicts in particular regions are being taken seriously because of certain countries but in the other regions they are not being taken so seriously because there is not seen to be a vital strategic interest in that.

(Sir David Hannay) Well, I would answer you by saying that there is no evidence in the daily practice of the UN now that indicates that imbalance. For example, the UN is very actively involved in Somalia and Angola and almost certainly within Mozambique now that the peace agreements in Rome turn to the UN to apply them. I do not honestly think that in any of those countries now that the Cold War is over is there any great strategic interest but there is a massive humanitarian interest and a massive interest of the international community to help end civil war and bring about elections and some kind of pluralist society and so on. I do not think the UN is being found wanting that way and I do not think it is applying a criterion of "Is there some natural resource in Somalia or Mozambique that we are all trying to get at?" So I am sorry, I am just trying to plead "not guilty" on behalf of the UN.

35. I am not arguing that the UN is doing that. I am saying there may be occasions where certain members of the United Nations take an action internationally and maybe with the legitimacy of the United Nations, but it would be better if it was done by the United Nations itself in its own name and then there would be fewer political problems with some countries internationally.

(Sir David Hannay) Can I just respond by saying that the point of view you are expressing is put forward quite often in New York. It is a lively debate that is going on now in this but has not reached a conclusion yet and I am sorry to say that I cannot come down on one side or the other at this stage.

Mr Rowlands

36. Can I offer a slightly different scenario. It is one that we have seen on our television sets quite vividly in the last few months and that is of UN military personnel cowering watching their headquarters and their barracks being blown to smithereens in Sarajevo and in a state of helplessness. Now is there somewhere in the existing rules and the forward peace-enforcement principles which would still nevertheless remove the image of UN military cowering and appearing helpless. In view of the fact we are going to have UK troops in blue helmets in similar circumstances, is there some way between the two propositions that we should explore?

(Sir David Hannay) I do not want to get involved in the "rules on engagement" issue which is a purely military issue and which I think has been dealt with in another Committee by a Minister when he gave evidence. But one of the reasons why we and the French are providing much more robust equipment for the troops we are deploying in Bosnia and Herzegovina is to avoid some of the helplessness that occurred in Sarajevo. The protection of humanitarian convoys, an operation which is beginning to be deployed now, and ought to be in operation within two or three weeks is equipped to a higher standard and much less lightly equipped than some previous UN operations have been. But I do not think it does a service to anyone to suggest that we are probing our way to a more aggressive UN role. I think frankly that puts people very greatly at risk when you say that.

37. There seems to be quite a lot of risk now.

(Sir David Hannay) Yes. There is indeed risk. If you look at it, UN peace-keepers have lost many lives not just in Yugoslavia but over the years in South Lebanon and elsewhere. It is no point anyone suggesting that the UN peace-keeping operations, even of the classical sort, have been risk-free. They have never been risk-free.

(Ms Evans) I would just like to say, Mr Chairman, that I have been to Sarajevo twice and in fairness to the UN troops there, I think the pre-

[Mr Rowlands *Contd*]

sentation on television does not give the full picture. There are a lot of——

38. These images are wrong that we have got, are they?

(Ms Evans) No, I am just saying it is not the full picture. The situation is dangerous and it is volatile, but besides people cowering there are a lot of very brave men doing a job in difficult circumstances.

Mr Jopling

39. I wonder whether Sir David has read the paper Sir Anthony Parsons sent to us.

(Sir David Hannay) I am sorry, I have not.

40. All I say is that on page 20 he does have a paragraph which begins with the words, "The Yugoslav operation has been a classic case of how not to do it" and it ends in the last sentence, "All this has created an impression of dither and muddled thinking in an admittedly extremely complex situation". Can I ask you, therefore, throughout the whole of this crisis in former Yugoslavia, do you believe that a lot of lessons have been learnt which if we are to have either a continuation of the Yugoslav drama or otherwise, that the reaction by the United Nations is less likely to make people like Tony Parsons talk about "dither and muddled thinking"?

(Sir David Hannay) Well, if you ask me the question, "Have lessons been learnt?", yes, lessons have been learnt. To give you one example of a lesson that was learnt, we have all learnt that the original division between the peace-making activities of the European Community and the peace-keeping activities of the UN was a not very helpful distinction and that it was more important to fuse our efforts, as we have done since the London Conference in August. That has led to a completely different structure in which there is a joint EC/UN peace-making effort with Lord Owen and Mr Cyrus Vance and a great structure of task forces with distinguished international UN faces like Mr Ahtisaari working on the constitution for Bosnia and Herzegovina and that is producing a very purposeful and more effective approach. Whether it is going to do the trick is of course another matter, but it does represent, I think, lessons learned. In the same way on the peace-keeping front, the EC monitors and the UN troops are working now in a much more coherent and concerted way. For instance, in implementing the deal which Mr Vance and Lord Owen managed to get for the withdrawal of the Yugoslav army from the Prevlaka peninsula, this was worked up by the EC monitors and the UN working together. The EC monitors and the UN are now policing that demilitarised area together and we are producing a much more concerted effort, so that is another way in which I would say that lessons have been learnt. I think if I might say so about Yugoslavia, the key is in the dying fall of Sir Anthony Parsons' sentence about the "admittedly extremely complex nature of the situation". That is nothing short of the real truth. The situation has elements of aggression, that is, the activities of the authorities in Belgrade in interfering and in pursuing what are in shorthand called "Greater Serbia ambitions", but it also has elements of civil war in the sense that there are three communities in Bosnia who are within the confines of Bosnia and Herzegovina fighting tooth and nail and often in a very inhuman way. It is this sort of mixture of elements which makes it a much less black and white, much less clear-cut case than the aggression, for example, of Iraq against Kuwait.

Mr Gapes

41. My question actually relates to Yugoslavia. The "Agenda for Peace" document talks about the post-conflict peace-building. It may be a little bit optimistic or premature to talk about that, but do you see any possibility that in Croatia or elsewhere in the Balkans or potentially elsewhere in the region that concept is going to have any real benefit or any real virtue or is it just unrealistic and is it just words on a piece of paper that in no way can be applied on the ground?

(Sir David Hannay) I think it is somewhere between the two. I think that there will be an urgent need in a Yugoslavia post-conflict, former Yugoslavia, that is to say, a country divided into a number of emerging independent countries, to rebuild. The destruction is terrible—and the international rehabilitation effort, as in Cambodia, will have to be very substantial and the UN may well have a role to play in that. There will also be elements of economic co-operation. These countries who will be independent have of course lived as a single economic unit and their most important single economic relationship, each of them, is with the European Community, so there will be a great deal to be said for trying, as Lord Owen's and Mr Vance's conference is, to focus also in the longer term on economic co-operation amongst themselves and between the individual former Yugoslav countries and the European Community. So I do not think that peace-building is at all off the agenda; quite the contrary, I think it will be very necessary because there will still be great frictions and great bitterness between these protagonists in what has been an appalling conflict even if we succeed in bringing peace and getting them to live side by side with each other. The way to avoid a recrudescence of these problems will be in these areas of economic rehabilitation, co-operation with the rest of Europe and so on.

42. What specific role do you think this country could play?

(Sir David Hannay) This country?

43. Yes.

(Sir David Hannay) Well, one part of it will be as a member of the European Community because I think the relationship between the European Community and the individual countries of former Yugoslavia will be absolutely crucial. If you look at the level of their economic activity which is

[**Mr Gapes** *Contd*]

affected by their relationship with the European Community, it is very high, so I think that we as part of the European Community will have a major role to play in that relationship. But then we will also have a role to play in the more short-term rehabilitation, helping refugees to go back to their homes, helping to deal with the short-term problems of destruction and warfare, as part of the international community and through institutions as differing as non-governmental institutions, the Red Cross, the High Commission for Refugees, to which we are contributing very heavily, and so on.

Mr Wareing

44. On the question of Britain's role in the process of peace-building, I just wonder what facilities, what assistance is given to Lord Owen and Cyrus Vance by the Foreign Office. What staffing arrangements are there for the two negotiators, for Lord Owen and Cyrus Vance, and do we give any assistance? Are there regular briefings given by the Foreign Office to David Owen and at what level of clearance?

(Ms Evans) Mr Chairman, Lord Owen and Mr Vance have a staff that is contributed by the UN and by the EC Member States. Among them is Mr Peter Hall who was formerly British Ambassador to ex-Yugoslavia. I cannot give you a detailed breakdown. If you would like to have the precise data, we can certainly write to you. Lord Owen has an interactive relationship with the European Community and Mr Vance one with the UN Security Council. Lord Owen will give and receive briefings with the Member States, particularly with us as Presidency, and of course we would give him whatever help he would ask for, so there is a very regular, continuing process of contact. In fact this morning there is a meeting of the Steering Committee of the London Conference taking place in Geneva where I think they will be airing various ideas for peace-building, particularly in Bosnia, for the future.

45. I was wondering how many people are actually assisting him in Geneva. What is the level of staffing?

(Ms Evans) It is not more than about—I cannot give you the precise breakdown—half a dozen what you might call "teeth staff". In addition there are support staff.

(Sir David Hannay) Perhaps if I can just add that the structure of the conference in Geneva consists of, I think, six task forces, three of which are being chaired on the European Community side. There is a German Ambassador, who is chairing the Committee on minorities and a former Commission official is chairing the task force on economic cooperation and the task force the succession to the former Yugoslavia was headed by the late Henry Darwin, the legal adviser to the Foreign Office who, as you know, sadly died recently. The UN is providing leadership in the task force on Bosnia Herzegovina, that is Mr Ahtisaari who was the UN special representative in Namibia, a man of very great experience, who is now the Secretary-General of the Finnish Ministry who has taken leave of absence. Mrs Ogata is in charge of the humanitarian task force which is a way of avoiding overlap or conflict over the humanitarian work that has already been done; and there is an Argentinian UN official who is in charge of the confidence-building measures task force. So these are six task forces on top of which sits a steering group which is chaired by Messrs Owen and Vance and as you have heard the Owen staff contains a considerable FCO element. The Vance side is staffed by UN secretariat officials who have been seconded from secretariat duties in New York to help Mr Vance, people like Mr Boothby who was a British official in the disarmament part of the Secretariat who is now working on a three or six month attachment to Mr Vance.

Sir John Stanley

46. This question really relates, Mr Chairman, to the situation in Yugoslavia which Sir David did touch on and the cooperation really between the UN and EC. Do you see a conflict between these two in this sense, that the two organisations may not be entirely sure who is doing what and so forth?

(Sir David Hannay) No, I do not see any conflict at all. They are working together remarkably well. Lord Owen and Mr Vance have known each other extremely well for many years. They were both Foreign Ministers at the same time, when Cyrus Vance was Secretary of State in President Carter's administration and Lord Owen was our own Foreign Secretary. And they work together, as far as I can see, very closely and very effectively. Again further down the line in the humanitarian field and in, for example, the work that has been done by the EC Monitors who are taking quite a bit of the load off the UN in areas where military observers are not strictly necessary and our civilian observers are able to do the task, that cooperation is really working excellently and the British Presidency, the head of our EC Monitors, Ramsay Melhuish works very very closely with General Nambiar and General Morillon.

47. You see it as a genuine partnership which can work? Do you see that being extended to other areas of the world in the sense the UN may well wish to devolve its activities to other organisations not specifically the EC?

(Sir David Hannay) This is an area of great interest in the Secretary-General's "Agenda for Peace" document. It is one to which he attaches a lot of importance. I think one has to recognise that it will be more realistic to use it in some parts of the world than in others. For example, in Asia there is no real regional support organisation with any security responsibility so it is not very easy to look to that. In Africa the OAU has not had a very successful track record in the past although it may have a more successful one in the future. I think Europe is the area to which the Secretary-General looks with greatest interest because it is not only the European Community which is work-

[Sir John Stanley *Contd*]

ing very well with the UN in Yugoslavia but there is the Conference for Security and Cooperation in Europe which took a big step forward this summer in the Helsinki Conference when it adopted a document which gave it some potential especially in the peace-keeping field. Also the Charter that was agreed by an earlier CSCE summit, the Paris Charter, has elements in it which are more far-reaching than the Charter of the United Nations because it goes into the whole field of ethnic minorities, human rights and so on. So I think that there is a great deal of interest in what the CSCE could do and this, of course, is given added point by its involvement in the former Soviet Union. Just to give you some examples of how the CSCE can potentially be useful take the Nagorno Karabakh problem. One of the problems there is that the Azerbaijan government will not accept that there is a threat to international peace and security in which the UN should become involved because that means admitting that it is an international problem and not a problem within Azerbaijan, Nagorno Karabakh as you know, being an enclave which is inhabited by Armenians but is internationally recognised as being part of Azerbaijan. But both the Armenians and the Azerbaijanis do recognise that the CSCE and the Paris Charter are relevant and they are prepared to see some CSCE involvement. There is a similar situation in Kosovo where the government, the Belgrade authorities, will not accept that there is an international responsibility there because they say it is part of Serbia but they do accept there is a CSCE responsibility. So it may be that as time goes on and as the CSCE becomes better equipped—at the moment it is still very much in its infancy in the peace-keeping area—it may very well come to be an adjunct of the United Nations in that sense and if it does the Secretary-General has made it clear, and I think all the Members of the Security Council have made it clear, that would be very welcome.

48. To pick up your one word "adjunct". Who is going to be calling the shots in the sense that when the CSCE or the EC is acting, who is directing the operation? Is the authority and decision-making in New York or is it based elsewhere? That is the key, is it not?

(Sir David Hannay) I think it would depend very much on what the nature of the involvement was. But I think on all sides there is a willingness to learn as we go along and not be too rigid about who is calling the shots, as you say. We are on a fairly steep learning curve in this area and I think it is not wise to be too dogmatic about it.

Mr Jopling

49. Do you think the Organisation of American States could be considered in Latin America?

(Sir David Hannay) Yes, I think the Organisation for American States definitely has to be considered as one of the regional organisations that has a real potential there. It has been grappling with the issue of Haiti, alas so far with not very evident success but it has been grappling with it and I think it could well have an expanding role in that area, particularly if it maintains the sort of homogeneity it has been able to achieve since all the governments there represented are elected governments.

Mr Wareing

50. Taking on the question of Yugoslavia and the point Mr Rowlands made before about the United Nations representatives there cowering against the gunfire that was going on, is it really realistic to assume that United Nations' involvement can be completely restricted to aiding the humanitarian convoys getting through? Is there not something to be said in view of the umpteen ceasefires there have been and all of these have been broken and the amount of deception that has been going on from all sides, Croatians and Muslims as well as Serbs within Bosnia, is there not a case for insisting that there should be some UNPROFOR presence within each military unit be it Bosnian, Croatian or Serbian in Bosnia to ensure that the ceasefire is enforced and that, in fact, we know when it is not who is responsible?

(Sir David Hannay) Well, the short answer is that there is no ceasefire in force at the moment. There have been a number of attempts to broker a ceasefire, each one of which has failed and the Vance/Owen duo have been very careful not to put as their primary objective negotiating yet another in the endless series of broken ceasefires. They are trying to bring about something rather wider which is a cessation of hostilities throughout Bosnia Herzegovina, a de-militarisation of Sarajevo and, of course, if they did so and got the agreement of all the parties and the effective implementation of the parties to that, then I am sure there would be implications for the mandate of UNPROFOR which would have to be brought back to the Security Council in that context. But I do not want to venture onto that ground now. The present mandate is perfectly clear. It is to protect humanitarian convoys and this is, of course, a high priority with winter coming on and a small adjunct to it is to offer protection to detainees released from these terrible camps if anyone like the ICRC ask for such protection. Those are the two mandates that have been given to the extended UNPROFOR operation in Bosnia.

Mr Wareing: I wonder what your observations would be about the arguments some people use. I appreciate that, for example, the United Nations forces in Krajina and eastern Slavonia are in fact protecting, and correctly protecting, the Serb minority which is in those enclaves, but some people have argued that the presence of UNPROFOR in those areas is merely consolidating the annexation of parts of Croatia by Serbia. I do not feel that myself, but this is an argument which is used. Is there not a danger here of putting the United Nations in this sort of action?

Mr Jopling

51. Like Cyprus.

(Sir David Hannay) Well, I think almost all the choices are hard ones to make, but I think you do have to remember that the situation in Slavonia and in the Krajina, not so much in the Krajina where there was not a great deal of fighting, but in Slavonia was a cessation of a really horrible form of fighting, the bombardments of Vukovar and Osijek which a mere year ago were troubling us every bit as much as the situation in Sarajevo is now. So if you ask, "Is the stationing of UNPROFOR in these enclaves better than that?", I have an unhesitating answer "Yes". Is it a solution? No, it is not a solution; it is a holding situation and the only satisfactory solution is to move on to constitutional arrangements which recognise that frontiers cannot be changed by force, but also recognise that ethnic minorities must be given rather extensive rights with regard to their language, their schools and so on and their local administration.

Mr Wareing

52. If I may just ask one other question on Yugoslavia and the imposition of sanctions against Serbia, is there not a case for some flexibility here? I am thinking in terms of the media, sanctions against the media, because the western media, the international media can play a very leading part in helping to get opposition opinions within Serbia to the Serbian people who live in the villages. In Belgrade it is much easier because of the access to the newsprint, but if you are living in a village in southern Serbia, it is very difficult to get news other than through Belgrade television which puts or tends to put one side of the view within Serbia.

(Sir David Hannay) I think quite honestly it is difficult to fine-tune sanctions. Once you start fine-tuning them you come into a morass of difficulty. I do not wish to dispute your view that public opinion in Serbia and Montenegro is not well served in sources of information, although they are of course capable of receiving broadcasts like those of the BBC which will give them an objective view of what the outside world thinks of what is going on, but I am sorry, I do not honestly think that it is easy to fine-tune sanctions and say, "Let us let this product go through because it is going to help turn opinion in one way, but don't let us let that one in". I think that is a tricky road to go down.

Mr Lester

53. We know from all the questions how important the UN is, but many of us have been conscious of the problem of financing it which you referred to earlier, being as near to bankruptcy as you were before, and that you are spending four times as much money. What do you think about the suggestions of finding additional money from levying arms sales, international air travel, the ability to borrow from the World Bank and indeed the basis of current contributions, which I know is a source of concern in the United States?

(Sir David Hannay) Well, I think we will have to wait and see how the high-level committee the Secretary-General has set up, which is presided over, I think, by Professor Ogata of the Japanese Central Bank and Mr Volker and with help from people like Sir David Scholey gets on. It is going to look into a number of these ideas the Secretary-General has floated, but I would tend to take the view myself that the problem is not so much the system of financing, which is a system basically founded on a GNP- influenced key, as the record of countries in paying up. It is the arrears that are the real problem. We now have added to the American problem, although, to be fair, one must recognise that the Bush Administration has made major efforts in the last two years to get back on the right road of paying its assessments, a Russian problem which is not due to lack of political will, but it is due to a lack of money and that is quite serious. When I said that the UN was no nearer bankruptcy this year than it was last year, it was perhaps a little flippant to express it that way, but the conclusion I wanted to draw was that because the UN was actually financing peace-keeping at a much higher rate this year than it was last year, the system was not quite as broken as we think it is. It is as broke, but not as broken as we think it is. It is coping better than you might suppose because it has actually financed these huge operations in Cambodia and in Yugoslavia and I suppose if we had sat here this time last year and said, "Could the UN finance that?" we would have all sucked our teeth a bit, but it has managed to do it. So I do not think there is something fundamentally wrong with a GNP-based system which is the one the UN has got and it does have the effect in fact that those who can afford to pay better for international peace and security pay more than those who can afford to pay less. It is a fairly equitable system, although there are inequities in it which are familiar to anyone who knows about international keys. For example, some countries like the Gulf countries and Saudi Arabia pay remarkably little, as we would see it. But these are rather small inequities compared to the general equity which I think is there. I think you can spend an awful long time destroying a system and then have to put together something which is almost like it all over again.

54. Has it been successful the idea of providing additional funds in advance of situations going on, UNHCR and another one you have mentioned, because one of the concerns many of us have had is the idea of having to go round with a begging bowl when a thing has actually happened in order to get the money in order to do it which seems a very odd way of proceeding?

(Sir David Hannay) Well, the UN has been doing quite well in a number of areas this year. For example, the appeal that went out for rehabilitation for Cambodia was over-subscribed at the Japanese-sponsored rehabilitation conference that took place in Tokyo. It was over-subscribed and it was very well worked up in advance. Mrs Ogata

[**Mr Lester** *Contd*]

has proved a formidably effective fund-raiser who has managed to persuade the main donors to fund her activities because they believe they are worthwhile. So I do not think one should say that the present system is not working. Mr Eliasson's revolving humanitarian fund, he has been drawing on it, for example, to strengthen the staff of the humanitarian co-ordinator in Mogadishu. That was exactly the sort of thing that this fund was set up to enable him to do, a kind of expenditure that could not have been found anywhere else very quickly in the UN system and so he has drawn 2 or 3 million from his revolving fund for that and that is, therefore, beginning to prove its worth.

Mr Jopling

55. We see in the Foreign Office paper that the Government supports the idea of the peace-keeping reserve fund, paragraph 18. How practical a possibility do you think that is at the moment?

(Sir David Hannay) I think it is perhaps not quite correctly called a "reserve fund"; it is a start-up fund.

56. I am quoting what is in the paper.

(Sir David Hannay) I am sorry because in shorthand we call it in New York a start-up fund. The Secretariat come to the Security Council and say for example, "We would like, to have a UN operation in Mozambique and it will cost approximately $130 million". The Security Council agrees to the operation. The money then has to be voted and assessed through a rather complex process which means going through a number of budgetary committees and is probably voted by the General Assembly only about four or five or six weeks later and then levied on the Member States on their percentages. So there is a bit of a time lag before any money starts to come in and that is often the moment at which the UN Secretariat need to be actually spending money on the transport of troops to the place which has been authorised, on getting equipment and so on. So this start-up fund is designed to give them a kind of drawing capacity in the early stages which will be repaid when the assessment comes through and therefore would keep it topped up. The Secretary-General talked about a really very modest start-up fund of 50 million dollars which is in today's peace-keeping terms pretty small but which we think would be genuinely useful. We are hoping we will get a decision to set up a start-up fund by about Christmas and that is what we are working to. I do not want to guarantee that because there are complexities about where the money should be drawn from but that is the hope and I think it is a genuinely useful idea. It is just to fill in that short period at the beginning.

Mr Canavan

57. To what extent should the work of other UN agencies such as UNHCR and UNDP be seen as part of the UN's conflict prevention activities and also while you are at it could you give us a brief up-date on the possibility of the UK re-joining UNESCO?

(Sir David Hannay) On that last one, I am sorry I cannot. It is not something that is handled through my office and I cannot give you any idea on UNESCO. On the question of UNHCR, it is of course very close to many conflict situations. It gets deeply involved often from a slightly earlier stage than the Security Council does. There is quite a big overlap and that has been clear in Somalia and clear also in Yugoslavia and it has been clear in Cambodia where the work together has been very good. In Cambodia, for example, the return of refugees from camps in Thailand has gone remarkably smoothly and it has been dovetailed in and helped by the deployment of troops in Cambodia which has enabled the refugees to go back in reasonable security and to start taking up their lives again. The UNDP is a little bit further removed from the action but of course the developmental dimensions of peace-building is that after you have got some kind of settlement, getting a country back on its feet is something which UNDP has a great deal to contribute to.

58. Could you give us a brief report on progress on the post Rio proposed conference of technology transfer from developed to under-developed countries?

(Sir David Hannay) That is the one that the British government is sponsoring next year, is it not?

Chairman

59. Yes, it is.

(Sir David Hannay) It is one of the initiatives announced in Rio by the Prime Minister. I am sorry I cannot off cuff give you an answer; it is being organised in London. The UN follow-up to Rio is being actively debated in New York. There is going to be a General Assembly debate on it on Monday when Mr Howard, the Secretary of State for the Environment, is going to deliver a speech on behalf of the European Community. We are working very hard to set up this Sustainable Development Commission which was decided in Rio which is to be the follow-up body to Rio to make sure the commitments of Rio are implemented and to progress-chase, to work out what more commitments might be needed in the years ahead. This decision should be taken by Christmas and the SDC should meet for the first time in the early months of next year.

Mr Lester

60. In terms of UNDP in Burma and the politics how do we get the liaison that prevents UNDP spending development money in Burma when the rest of the UN are trying very hard, because of its human rights record, to prevent any support for SLORC which it regards as an illegitimate regime?

(Sir David Hannay) I am slightly unsighted to tell you the truth on the UNDP programme of activity in Burma. I am sorry but I think it is very

[**Mr Lester** *Contd*]

much grass-roots stuff on education and so on. I do not think it is a very high level. I am feeling a bit hesitant.

(Ms Evans) I think the last UN Council did look at the issue and I think it reached a satisfactory conclusion. I am not sure. It is certainly a point that Members are very conscious of.

Mr Rowlands

61. We had a debate in September in the House on Iraq, Somalia and Bosnia, three completely disparate situations but they do have two themes in common: one was the role of the UN and the second one was the enormous number of arms that allowed the warfare and the carnage to take place. Way back in October 1991 the permanent five members of the Security Council supported the idea of an arms transfer register and I would like to know how much progress we are making on what I think could be one of the practical issues and solutions where we could reduce the areas of conflict by reducing the number of arms available?

(Sir David Hannay) The progress on the register is good. The decision to set it up was taken last December. It was a British initiative, as you know, together with the other European partners and the Japanese and that decision was taken at a speed which most people regarded as extraordinary by UN standards. There has now been a meeting of the panel of experts which has defined the reporting requirements for that and that has been a unanimous conclusion which will be endorsed in this General Assembly and the register goes into effect from the 1 January 1993, the reporting requirement, that is. So we will begin to see whether it is effective. It is a transparency measure and not a control measure. We must not try to sell it as a control measure when it is only a transparency measure although transparency hopefully will lead on to something which is nearer to control. We will begin to see how that works next year. If I can just say this on the three countries. In a way it illustrates how difficult it is to generalise because in the Yugoslav case, it is indeed awash with arms but practically all of them have been made in Yugoslavia because the Yugoslavs were one of the big arms' producers. It has made its living for many years by shipping arms overseas and when it came to organising a civil war of its own it had an awful lot of this stuff and indeed factories are still producing it.

62. In Somalia —

(Sir David Hannay) In Somalia it comes from outside and that is an outside problem.

63. Is there any role for the Military Staff Committee in establishing a system of armaments regulation under articles 26 and 47(1) of the UN charter?

(Sir David Hannay) I think at the moment we are at the stage more of informal consultation between the five permanent members not through the Military Staff Committee but through their political/military directors in their foreign offices. Unfortunately the Chinese have for the moment announced they are not coming to further meetings as a result of their irritation at the American decision to sell aircraft to Taiwan but we hope that that decision can be reversed. It has not been presented as set in concrete and we hope that it will be possible to take these consultations further and to start to think of ways in which we can not out bid each other in supplying arms, particularly to very sensitive areas of the world. But it is in its early stages on an informal basis rather than in the Military Staff Committee which sets up very strong contrary vibrations in other Members of the United Nations.

64. But you paint a hopeful picture?

(Sir David Hannay) I hope I have not painted too hopeful a picture because it is a fairly intractable problem but we have been pushing and will continue to push to give meaning to these five power consultations.

Sir John Stanley

65. Sir David, can I just come back once again to Somalia. You said in the earlier part of your evidence that the UN had made mistakes in relation to Somalia. Could you tell the Committee what specific mistakes you had in mind and what are the specific lessons you believe have been learned?

(Sir David Hannay) I am afraid I do not want to enter into it. I think there has been, if I may say so, too much finger pointing about Somalia. The lessons are now being learnt, I hope. We have got to all now put in a major concerted effort. But I honestly do not think it would be helpful to point fingers. I am sorry. There were mistakes of coordination that were made. I think there were weaknesses of coordination and also the results I think show that anybody who says we put in a wonderful performance, "we" the UN or anyone else, then we have to look at the situation before our eyes. We have to understand that. I am sorry I do not want to enter into specifics.

Mr Jopling

66. Sir David, you have just told us and you told us earlier on this morning that you did not see a role for an expanded Military Staff Committee. We have actually had a paper from Brian Urquhart of the Ford Foundation in which he does argue for an extended role for the Military Staff Committee. Can I ask you are there very many people around the UN who take the contrary view to you and can see an extended role for that Committee?

(Sir David Hannay) I think there are a certain number and I greatly respect Sir Brian whose experience of the UN and its peace-keeping is a very great deal more than mine. I know that has been his view for many years and he continues to argue it. There are others who share it and it is a subject much discussed at seminars and meetings of that sort. I am afraid I remain not entirely convinced. I

[**Mr Jopling** *Contd*]

am worried about the divisiveness inherent in it, that it is the military staffs of the five permanent members which I think would increase the tensions within the system if we tried to move on this. What we definitely need to do is increase the degree of military advice that gets to the Secretary-General. I think it is better to think of building up the military advisers office in the peace-keeping office and by developing a dialogue, at the military level, between the main peace-keeping contributors and the UN Secretariat. That is something we are moving on. We have had a number of senior serving officers in the UK to New York now for meetings both about specifics like the Bosnia operation and to discuss general issues of the "Agenda for Peace". This dialogue is being built up in our case and it is being built up in the case of the French and of the Americans and I think that kind of informal network of dialogue may be better than a structure called the Military Staff Committee.

Sir John Stanley

67. Sir David, one of the specific lessons learned from Yugoslavia which you did refer to was the desirability of fusing the efforts of the EC and the UN. In South Africa recently I found some considerable lack of clarity as to the respective roles being played in that country as between the EC and the UN. Would you agree that that too may be an area where it would be better for the EC and the UN to fuse their efforts earlier on rather than later?

(Sir David Hannay) No, I would argue that the fusion took place from the very beginning in South Africa. It was in fact the Secretary-General when he came here at the beginning of July before there were any observers in South Africa or indeed before the issue of sending observers to South Africa had become a concrete one, but when it was about to become so because of the Boipatong massacre and the desire of both the ANC and the South African Government to see some kind of external involvement, he proposed to the Prime Minister and to the Foreign Secretary that we should fuse our efforts, the EC, the UN and the Commonwealth because they also were considering it. That is what we have done. I do not wish to dispute your discovering that there may be some uncertainty about exactly how to do that, but I know from the telegrams I see that there is a very active consultation going on between the UN observers who are headed by a lady from Jamaica and the EC observer team which we are helping to set up. It is still early days. The first people are just arriving there and I think the details of how they are inserted into the National Peace Secretariat structure to help implement the national peace agreement are being worked out. Some of them are allocated to Judge Goldstone, to help him in his work. All that takes a little working out, but there is frankly no lack of co-ordinated effort. We are all working together on this and it was an idea the Secretary-General put to us as Presidency of the EC right at the beginning and we followed it through from the beginning.

Chairman: Sir David, your answers this morning, and Ms Evans, have been enormously thorough and full and I hope our questions have been thorough—they have certainly been full, and perhaps a little too full—but either way we are immensely grateful to you and to Ms Evans for giving us a very wide range of information and insights on this enormous subject. There are many other areas that we would like to pursue, and I have found it hard to stop the questioning, but I think I must now and I would like to thank you and Ms Evans very much indeed for coming before us.

Printed in the United Kingdom for HMSO.
Dd.5060492, 12/92, C6, 3398/3B, 5673, 224484.

ISBN 0-10-279093-0

HOUSE OF COMMONS SESSION 1992–93

FOREIGN AFFAIRS COMMITTEE

THE EXPANDING ROLE OF THE UNITED NATIONS AND ITS IMPLICATIONS FOR UK POLICY

MINUTES OF EVIDENCE

Wednesday 25 November 1992

OXFAM

Mr Tony Vaux

CARE

Mr Julian Hopkins

SAVE THE CHILDREN

Mr Michael Aaronson and Mr Mark Bowden

Ordered by The House of Commons *to be printed*
25 November 1992

LONDON: HMSO

£8.95 net

235–ii

WEDNESDAY 25 NOVEMBER 1992

Members present:

Mr David Howell, in the Chair

Mr Dennis Canavan	Sir John Stanley
Mr Mike Gapes	Mr David Sumberg
Mr David Harris	Mr Robert N Wareing
Mr Peter Shore	

Memorandum submitted by Julian Hopkins, National Director, CARE Britain, on behalf of CARE, the international relief and development agency

INTRODUCTION

CARE works with the world's poor in Africa, Asia and Latin America. It is the largest non-political, non-sectarian organisation working in the developing world. In 1991–92 its combined relief and development project funding was £300 million.

CARE helps poor people to improve their circumstances and quality of life. Through a worldwide network CARE manages over 300 self-help projects in 50 developing countries, focusing on emergency relief and rehabilitation, primary health care, agriculture and environmental conservation. CARE is widely regarded as being pre-eminent in emergency relief, logistics and rehabilitation work.

CARE's work is managed and supported by CARE International, which is a family of 11 members, in Australia, Austria, Britain, Canada, Denmark, France, Germany, Italy, Japan, Norway and the USA.

9.500 national and 500 international staff are employed by CARE worldwide. Each of the 50 CARE developing country offices has established monitoring and reporting systems to ensure that funds are spent in the most cost-effective way. Each country office has also established close working relationships with agencies of the United Nations, where appropriate.

CARE Britain was established in 1985 and funds CARE projects with the support of the British Government's Overseas Development Administration, the European Community, corporations, trusts and individual donors.

The evidence in this document has been compiled from a number of recent submissions requested from CARE's Country Directors, who are the senior staff responsible for CARE's operations in the field.

GENERAL

There have been an unprecedented number of humanitarian disasters and emergencies in recent years. Most of them have been "man made", in developing countries where civil strife is out of control, and where security is consequently severely lacking.

These situations very often result in serious instability, vast movement of populations, famine, disease and human suffering on a scale very rarely witnessed in the developed world.

Because these emergencies are not overcome in a matter of weeks, and can develop into long-term problems, they tend to overlap.

The international community therefore finds itself dealing with a number of "crises" concurrently. This is a fairly recent phenomenon. It has serious consequences in terms of speed of response to a new emergency, and can be a drain on human and financial resources which can hinder effective action.

NGOS/SOMALIA

In responding to emergencies, NGOs such as CARE have obtained a sustained degree of support from governments and the private sector, and have been able to channel aid to where it has been most needed in an effective way. Over the last three years, for instance, CARE has trebled the income it has raised for emergency programming, rehabilitation and food aid in those countries where critical conditions have existed, such as in Somalia, Ethiopia, Sudan, Mozambique, Iraq and Cambodia.

The cost of printing and publishing these Minutes of Evidence is estimated by HMSO at £5,196.

These initiatives have been welcomed, but there has been growing concern that the relief organisations have been resourceful and flexible to a degree not always matched by the UN agencies.

In Somalia, for instance, CARE began its activities in the early eighties. Its major function initially was providing food to 800,000 refugees from the Ogaden. CARE established a programme under the name "Emergency Logistics Unit" which continued until 1990 when the security situation worsened considerably.

CARE maintained a reduced presence during subsequent conflicts, providing emergency assistance to the population of greater Mogadishu. Following the fall of Barre, CARE formed a cordial relationship with the United Somali Congress (USC), and maintained its relief programme throughout 1991/92, except for a suspension of activities between January and April 1991, and does so to this day, but only under the most difficult conditions imaginable.

In Somalia, as the world at large has seen for at least 4 months, relief operations carried out by CARE and other NGOs have been severely hampered by banditry and insecurity. CARE has been able to maintain its operations, in the rural areas of southern Somalia as well as in Mogadishu, only by hiring security guards ("Technicals") to protect food convoys, staff and supplies. Even with such "security", there have been many casualties and incidents which have hindered the relief operation. After ICRC, CARE now has the largest NGO programme in Somalia.

It is accepted that the security situation in Somalia is more extreme than in most other countries where CARE works. There is no government structure, no legislature, and no recognised police or security force. There are estimated to be approximately 1 million males in Southern Somalia who carry weapons and ammunition at all times. There are many observers who would not be surprised if full-scale fighting between the various warlords and their clans breaks out once again.

Such is the situation facing the United Nations, in a country where the NGOs have taken the initiative in the interests of the suffering people, but now find themselves without sufficient security in order to achieve the humanitarian results required.

The United Nations has so far failed to respond.

THE UN/SOMALIA

Governments and NGOs have agreed that the size and adequacy of forces sent to Mogadishu have been insufficient. A force of 3.500 would be barely adequate (500 have been stationed so far). Additional troops are essential. Authority should be given for the UN Commander in Mogadishu to exercise his own military discretion in location. These and other critical requirements were being advocated in August this year, and yet no effective action has been taken.

It is believed that local security structures need to be established with the warlords. If the UN did once have a mandate to recruit, train and equip local Somali forces, the opportunity for this may have been lost. Nevertheless, this should become a priority for the UN. CARE has had to take upon itself the task of paying local Somalis to provide protection, as explained above, **but this is properly a UN role which the UN now needs to formalise, belatedly**.

The UN leadership should grant the UN Envoy to Somalia full authority to make on-the-ground decisions, without reference to New York.

The first priority of the peace-keeping forces should be to provide security for the delivery of relief supplies by Somali, international NGOs and other organisations, to those who are at the greatest risk. This is a UN role which has not been started, and it is a serious and justifiable complaint that nothing has been achieved.

It is acknowledged that the difficulties in negotiating with the Somali warlords have contributed to the lack of effective action by the UN, but it is generally believed that the other basic cause has been the over-centralised and bureaucratic workings of the UN in New York.

A welcome step forward was the announcement of the UN 100 day plan for Somalia, and the appointment of Dr. Philip Johnston, Chief Executive of CARE USA, as Co-ordinator of the plan.

However, there remains a critical need for UN observers in Somalia to monitor developments and provide early warning of military movements which could lead to factional conflicts and thus to potential threats to NGO operations.

It is believed that the UN has adequate mechanisms to deal only with structured conflicts. The situation in Somalia, and many others elsewhere, represent a different type of "unstructured" conflict, with very large numbers of displaced people. The UN response in Somalia has thus been woefully inadequate.

THE UN AGENCIES

CARE experiences varying degrees of efficiency in dealing with UN agencies around the world.

UNITED NATIONS HIGH COMMISSION FOR REFUGEES (UNHCR)

The mandate with which UN agencies work is often the problem. With UNHCR, for instance, the mandate is often in need of renegotiation, with reference to UNHCR's relationships both with countries which generate and those which harbour refugees. UNHCR needs to be given more powers, and needs to be pro-active in advance of likely refugee movements. Its mandate should extend to the internally displaced. Decision making should be decentralised to regional or local staff.

UNHCR has produced simple guidelines for small-scale programmes. These are termed "Quick Impact Projects". The rationale for the scheme is for NGOs to implement immediate assistance for returnee refugees in their resettlement areas, financed from a special UNHCR fund. The guidelines for the scheme have been changed no less than three times in as many months, however, and confusion remains as to the procedures to be followed in obtaining access to these funds. In Cambodia, this has been the cause of serious difficulties which are still not resolved.

In general respects, CARE's experience is that UNHCR's planning and response times have often been poor, due to the quality of expatriate staff assigned to programmes. A commendable flexibility is gradually being introduced, which bodes well for the future.

WORLD FOOD PROGRAMME (WFP)

WFP performance has often been impressive and valuable. WFP activities in transporting food in Ethiopia were creditable, although "Food for Work" programmes have been subject to corruption and inefficiency.

There is often a low level of field autonomy, with management imposed from Headquarters. CARE's experience in Mozambique was that this hampered operations to a serious extent.

However, with the appointment of the new Director, WFP is improving.

UNITED NATIONS DEVELOPMENT PROGRAMME (UNDP)

UNDP's role in emergencies is critical, and sometimes the lack of UNDP's line authority over other UN agencies creates operational difficulties and causes delay in response time. This matter is in need of urgent attention.

UNDP will often assume responsibility for a programme in taking over from UNHCR, when the latter withdraws, as in Cambodia. UNDP has developed its own implementing agency. Some confusion remains as to the precise role of UNDP, particularly for approval of funds for NGOs' operations, or in developing their own projects.

EMERGING CONCLUSIONS/THE WAY FORWARD

That the UN is a large and unwieldy bureaucracy is a widely accepted truth. It is a grave issue, moreover, and the situation need not exist. An apparent lack of urgency is often explained by delays in the use of elaborate procedures. The kind of flexibility being encouraged within UNHCR in Iraq, for example, in enabling rapid responses to be made in changing situations, is welcome. It is believed that this has been made possible by rotating staff between Geneva and the field; Headquarters staff are consequently familiar with the situation on the ground. CARE believes that this example should be followed in UN agencies generally.

CARE believes there is too much evidence of a lack of clear authority on the ground. There should be a UN Co-ordinator in every country, to lead the various UN teams. At the present time, there is a tendency for UN agencies to compete with each other, rather than working with each other, and with NGOs, in co-operation.

It is suggested that the UN Secretary-General should be asked to consider the feasibility of a plan to meet with the Heads of all the UN agencies which get involved in emergency responses, to agree and promulgate clearer lines of operational procedure to country representatives.

In addition, CARE urges that the UN is more assertive in its peace-keeping role, and in facilitating humanitarian relief. Does the UN have a mandate and the support of Members to deal with situations more assertively? Are there mechanisms in place within UN structures to apply appropriate and effective pressure on opposing sides involved in conflicts, to allow the UN to implement its overall mandate? Are there adequate mechanisms in place for independent monitoring and evaluation of peace-keeping and humanitarian relief activity? These are some of the questions CARE believes should be addressed.

Memorandum submitted by OXFAM

THE UNITED NATIONS RESPONSE TO HUMANITARIAN CRISES: THE UNPRECEDENTED CHALLENGE

Introduction

Like the United Nations, Oxfam is working in humanitarian crises in a rapidly-changing world which seems increasingly disaster-prone. Our relief work is matched by support for long-term development. Yet over half of our expenditure in the South of US$80 million in 1991–92 has been for communities suffering from conflict. In Africa, this figure rises to over 70 per cent. Disasters, increasingly the products of deliberate policy, are blocking the prospects for development.

With the UN, we hope, we are working towards a more effective, more integrated response to humanitarian crises. This paper is not therefore a list of final answers, but some questions and suggestions arising from our experience of current disasters. It covers three main issues:

— The Deficit of Determination

— Putting the Poor First

— The Need for Co-ordination

Background

Within the United Nations, the last twelve months have witnessed significant changes in its role in humanitarian emergencies. The Department for Humanitarian Affairs was established following the General Assembly's resolution in December 1991. The new Secretary-General, Dr Boutros-Ghali, took up his post in January 1992, and in March implemented the first round of restructuring of the UN system, rationalising the number of Under Secretaries-General. In July, Dr Boutros-Ghali published his "Agenda for Peace", looking forward to a heightened UN role in preventive diplomacy, peacemaking and peace-keeping.

Much of this has arisen from the opportunity provided by the end of the Cold War. For forty-five years, the United Nations' mission was largely blocked. That obstacle has now been removed; there has not been a veto in the Security Council since May 1990.

At the same time, the threat to millions of the world's citizens, and challenge to the UN, is greater than ever. In the last ten years, more than 1.5 million children have died in wars. More than 4 million have been disabled by land-mines, bombs, firearms and torture.

Conflict and consequent humanitarian crises have increased as the stability of superpower rivalry has been removed. The promise in 1990 of a new world is turning into the reality of a decade of disasters.

The demands upon the United Nations have therefore risen. There are now twelve peace-keeping operations around the world, costing US$2.6 billion in 1992, compared to twenty-six from 1948 to this year, totalling US$8.3 billion.

Despite this increased level of activity, and the beginning of reforms, there has been widespread criticism of the UN's performance in response to recent humanitarian emergencies. There has been disappointment that the DHA, in its first year, has not been able to effectively co-ordinate the actions of different UN agencies.

The Deficit of Determination

The ability of the United Nations to achieve its humanitarian objectives is still restricted by inadequate funding from member governments. The Secretary-General has warned of placing too *much* credibility upon the UN: of creating an imbalance between the demands placed upon it and the resources given to it.

UN relief operations are consistently underfunded. In October, for example, the DHA and SADC (Southern African Development Community) reported that there was still a shortfall of US$287 million for the DESA (Drought Emergency in Southern Africa) appeal.

Many NGOs also experience this imbalance between needs and resources, as more and more is expected of them by the UN, donor governments and public. NGOs and the UN therefore share enormous expectations upon them in responding to the humanitarian crises of the new world 'order'. Both need to be properly resourced.

In Angola, the limited resources committed to the United Nations to monitor and verify the transition from conflict to peace and democracy was one factor which contributed to the renewed fighting once the election result was disputed. While the Secretary-General's diplomatic intervention will be vital in getting Angola back on course to a second round of Presidential elections, it will also be vital for the UN to be adequately resourced if it is to demobilise the separate armies, and monitor and verify this further election.

Donor governments must fund the United Nations to fufil the tasks which they have mandated it to undertake. This will be essential to its credibility—and also to prevent short term under-funding leading to longer-term problems and demands upon their resources.

The United Nations is also at times inhibited from effective action by a failure of political will in the Security Council. When the Security Council shows its determination, as in Iraq in 1991, the UN can intervene dramatically. When it does not, millions of people can be left unprotected against the actions of their own governments or other political forces.

In 1992, Oxfam has witnessed the dichotomy between the vast needs and the response which the UN is able to deliver in several countries. In Sudan, millions of people are still suffering from the civil war which has been continuing, unresolved, since 1983. The UN's Operation Lifeline Sudan has failed to access and bring relief to all those in need. The United Nations is neither able to offer protection for the increasingly difficult work of international NGOs, nor monitor human rights violations against citizens of Sudan. The United Nations should urgently turn its full attention to the growing crisis in south Sudan.

For Somalia, the Secretary-General has been able to activate a greater response by challenging the international community to respond in the same way as for the former Yugoslavia. Yet the increased determination has not been sufficient to overcome the obstacles to deploying UNOSOM troops to protect the delivery of relief.

Despite the commitments from the Security Council to place 3,500 United Nations guards at various strategic points for the entrance and distribution of humanitarian relief, this has not happened. Only 500 have arrived in Somalia, and have not been seen on duty in their first five weeks in the country.

The inadequacy of this response has meant humanitarian agencies are without the security cover which the UN declared that it would provide. As a result, it has been impossible to carry out urgently needed relief work in Bardera because no agency's security can be assured. This raises the question of the extent to which a UN military presence to protect relief should await the consent of local warring parties.

There is still not the will to put the interests of poor people first. The greater degree of action in Iraq and the former Yugoslavia, where Western interests, as well as peace, were threatened, suggests that the United Nations remains more accountable to its most powerful members than to its poorest citizens.

PUTTING THE POOR FIRST

The UN has often allowed the interests of the nation state or of other political forces to prevent access to those in need and the effective delivery of relief. In Ethiopia, the United Nations observed the Mengistu government's sovereignty over the areas controlled by the Eritrean and Tigrayan opposition forces, and was therefore unable to assist the populations suffering from famine. This role was left to NGOs operating at some risk, and with limited resources, across the border from Sudan.

The question of whether the sovereignty of the nation state should be allowed to prevent access to those suffering is part of the wider issue of how much the United Nations should be restrained by the requirement to act only with the consent of the various parties in a country. Our experience in Somalia shows that this can leave NGOs without the necessary security umbrella to deliver relief. Yet the experience of Iraq and the former Yugoslavia shows that the UN does, at times, have the will and ability to protect relief against the wishes of local warring sides.

Can this protection be implemented consistently and transparently? Should the UN's response to humanitarian needs be based upon life-threatening suffering as *the* over-riding principle? If this is agreed, should this be put into effect through formal UN agreements, setting down criteria for action, or determined by the circumstances of each case?

To be effective, a non-partisan humanitarian approach requires the monitoring of humanitarian needs and human rights to trigger United Nations action. Oxfam has witnessed the lack of this monitoring in south Sudan, where critical needs are not being addressed.

Without humanitarian monitoring and triggers, the only real initiative for UN action will remain with the host government or the more powerful UN members.

Can the UN's monitoring and consequent interventions not be distanced from such a close relationship from the host government? Should the Department for Humanitarian Affairs be able to operate outside normal diplomatic procedures, with free access to non-government parties and areas, under the principle that humanitarian concerns override all others?

THE NEED FOR CO-ORDINATION

The need for NGOs in areas of conflict to work under a UN security umbrella has been addressed above, as an example of better collaboration between the UN and NGOs.

Yet within the UN system, the lack of co-ordination has limited the effect of the UN's response. For example, when UNHCR withdrew from northern Iraq this spring, it transferred its supplies to its own operation in the former Yugoslavia, leaving UNICEF, taking over responsibility in Iraq, without them.

This year's start to the restructuring of the UN has promised changes. The numbers of Under Secretaries-General reporting to Dr Boutros-Ghali has been rationalised, and the Department for Humanitarian Affairs has been established. In advocating such a new body, Oxfam had hoped that it would be able to co-ordinate the work of UN agencies involved in humanitarian affairs, particularly UNICEF, UNHCR and WFP.

Unfortunately, other UN agencies have not co-operated eagerly with the DHA, and governmental and NGO criticism of the lack of UN co-ordination has reached a new intensity over Somalia. It is not Oxfam's purpose to attack the United Nations, however, but to suggest a direction which may lead to better co-ordination.

The Department for Humanitarian Affairs should have stronger powers over the function of other UN agencies in humanitarian crises, to direct their responses in co-ordinated, effective strategies. The DHA can also help facilitate the co-ordination of NGOs to ensure the maximum use of limited resources.

This paper has not sought to be exhaustive, and has not included issues of great concern which we are investigating, notably the elimination of land-mines, the restriction of the sale of conventional arms, and the accountability of UN agencies.

SUMMARY

Oxfam believes that people are more important than governments, UN agencies—and NGOs. We present a view that the interests of any of these bodies must be subsidiary to non-partisan, effective humanitarian action.

The United Nations is the only international body that can overcome many of these problems: to press for access and to protect those agencies, including NGOs, which are at present not able to deliver relief in all circumstances which demand it.

The UN also is uniquely placed to assess and monitor humanitarian needs and human rights, in a non-partisan manner, and initiate responses.

None of this is possible without the political will and financial resources of member governments, nor of better co-ordination within the UN system itself. The deficit of determination must be overcome, and it must be done with an urgency which reflects the scale and escalation of the disasters confronting us all.

Memorandum submitted by Save the Children

INTRODUCTION

The recent startling transformations in the international political order have had swift and unpredictable results. The disintegration of communism as a unifying economic and political principle in the former Soviet Union and countries of Eastern Europe has had global repercussions. Positive results of the easing of superpower tensions include the moves towards peace in such areas as Angola, Ethiopia, Afghanistan and Cambodia, and a new ability within the United Nations to obtain agreement on security and humanitarian initiatives. Negative results include the fragmentation of states as demands for self-determination and autonomy resurface and the continuing human effects of the Cold War. This new world order based on US hegemony does not yet guarantee that humanitarian action will be driven by an even-handed response to need rather than political attitudes towards governments, strategic priorities, intercultural factors or media attention.

However, the roots of conflict and disaster did not all lie within Cold War rivalries. Economic disparities, demographic imbalances, religious fundamentalism, political extremism and national boundaries encompassing diverse populations which lack means of participating in their respective political processes all contribute to continued civil conflict and unrest, exacerbated by environmental degradation, climatic change and human displacement. It should also be noted that the proliferation of sophisticated weaponry has changed the nature of war, especially intrastate conflicts.

Save the Children (SCF) has been involved in humanitarian response since its foundation in 1919 but has become increasingly disturbed over the last two to three years by the inability of the international community to establish mechanisms which ensure that the complex emergencies resulting from these factors receive appropriate attention. During 1991 SCF was among those calling for major reforms to the international system and contributed its own ideas to the debate. Momentum for reform built up, culminating in the UN General Assembly Resolution of December 1991 on the "Strengthening of the Co-ordination of Humanitarian Emergency Assistance".

Save the Children welcomed the resolution, the appointment of the Under Secretary-General for Humanitarian Affairs, and the establishment of the Department of Humanitarian Affairs—UNDRO (DHA). However, although the Guiding Principles of the Resolution are exemplary, as its anniversary approaches the strengths, weaknesses and limitations of this institutional response are becoming apparent.

In the following sections Save The Children presents evidence based on its experience in Somalia which illustrate some aspects of humanitarian response which are still deficient. Save the Children is aware that the DHA did not become fully established until March/April 1992: nevertheless the account is still relevant as it helps to illustrate the constraints on the DHA and which issues still need to be addressed if effective response mechanisms are to be developed.

Please refer to Annex 1 for a chronology of events in Somalia and Annex 2 for a background to Save the Children's work in Somalia and Somaliland.

SOMALIA

From the time of Mohamed Siad Barre's coming to power in 1969 until he was ousted at the end of January 1991 the basis of Somali politics was a system of client and patron built upon traditional clan relationships. When the linchpin of that system was removed a vacuum was left at the centre which the southern warlords have been trying to fill, while the north broke away claiming independence as Somaliland. At the time of Siad Barre's fall there was extensive need for reconstruction: there was total economic breakdown at all levels including the collapse of local food markets. The banking system was also destroyed, resulting in cessation of the once substantial remittances from abroad.

1. SPEED OF UN RESPONSE

1.1 Response from the Fall of Siad Barre until October 1992

Although it must be acknowledged that there are increasing demands being made on the UN, the lack of urgency in responding to the Somalia situation is difficult to understand in view of

(a) warnings from other agencies, and

(b) the UN's own early warning systems.

SCF had maintained its office and administration in Mogadishu during the civil war and was able to resume operations within two months of the fall of Siad Barre, beginning with the rehabilitation of

Mother and Child Health (MCH) Centres. The ICRC and other non-governmental organisations (NGOs), which included Medecins Sans Frontieres and SOS, also demonstrated that it was possible to respond to humanitarian needs. All these agencies drew attention to the deteriorating humanitarian situation. SCF first called for the UN to re-establish operations in Somalia on 22 February 1991.

Although the situation deteriorated significantly in September 1991 the response of SCF and ICRC at this point was to **expand** their programmes to attempt to meet the growing needs.

In November 1991 Andrew Natsios of the United States Office for Disaster Assistance (OFDA) called for UN involvement. This was reinforced by US Congressional hearings.

There were two Security Council Resolutions on Somalia, in January and July 1992. The driving force behind both was Cape Verde. The first requested "the Secretary-General immediately to undertake the necessary actions to increase humanitarian assistance of the United Nations and its specialized agencies to the affected population in all parts of Somalia in liaison with the other international humanitarian organizations and to this end appoint a co-ordinator to oversee the effective delivery of this assistance". Despite this and the March ceasefire there were still long delays, despite the growing pressure and presence of agencies like UNICEF who were aware of the acute needs.

There were a number of technical missions which visited Mogadishu briefly and in mid-1992 a 90 Day Action Plan was produced but was not acted upon.

It was not until 10–11 September that "as part of an overall effort to determine ways to accelerate relief efforts in Somalia" (Introduction, 100 Day Action Programme, October 1992) that the UN Under-Secretary-General for Humanitarian Affairs, Mr Jan Eliasson led a high-level Inter-Agency Mission, including Mr James Grant to Mogadishu. This visit was more than one month after the public outcry and media coverage over the suffering in Somalia reached a peak

In mid-October 1992 a 100-Day Action Programme for Accelerated Humanitarian Assistance was presented at a pledging conference in Geneva.

On 27 October Ambassador Sahnoun, the UN Secretary General's special representative in Somalia, resigned after being cautioned by Boutros Boutros Ghali about the level of his public criticism of the UN response.

1.2 Security Issues

It appears that issues of security rather than sovereignty prevented the UN from acting more decisively. Guidelines on security seem to have curtailed even humanitarian intervention. Undoubtedly security was an important issue and ICRC, UNICEF and NGO personnel, both national and expatriate died. However, other agencies have mandates and internal arrangements which do not restrict the activities of their personnel to such an extent. In view of other inconsistencies concerning the deployment of UN personnel in situations where personal security is a problem, the present guidelines could be modified to allow for more flexibility in acute emergencies.

SCF made attempts to assist UNICEF overcome the the UN security restrictions during 1991. UNICEF brought staff back in to Somalia for a brief period in August 1991 but had to pull out in September. SCF employed two expatriate UNICEF staff as consultants with SCF contracts for three months, one in Mogadishu and one in Somaliland.

1.3 Sovereignty Issues

There is currently widespread debate concerning the balance between sovereignty and human rights. *Agenda for Peace* contributes little to this debate, restating the tension that lies at the heart of the UN Charter between the sovereignty of the state and individual human rights. It is increasingly accepted, however, that Article 2.1 of the UN charter no longer constitutes an absolute barrier against outside interference. Resolution 688, which insisted "that Iraq allow immediate access by international humanitarian organizations to all those in need of assistance in all parts of Iraq", may prove to be one-off rather than a precedent but it reflects and contributes to an evolving awareness of the importance of safeguarding human life. It also demonstrated the fact that governments are coming under increasing scrutiny as the positive obligations of sovereign governments to their own people are being emphasised.

The question of external agencies overriding sovereignty did not arise in the same way in Somalia. The issue that arises is how to provide an effective response to needs in the absence of a clearly defined sovereign government. Although there was uncertainty following the fall of Siad Barre as to what constituted the sovereign or legitimate government UN agencies could have re-established themselves in the period between February and August 1991 when UNICEF and WFP attempted to re-establish their programmes, by which time law and order had deteriorated. UNDP and WHO stated that it was not possible unless there was a properly constituted government.

By December 1991 the UN was in dialogue with clan leaders and the wording of the January Security Council Resolution "at the request of Somalia" indicates that sovereignty was not then an issue in the sense that those who wished to deliver humanitarian assistance would have to override it. From that period the issue was how to obtain a ceasefire between the factions to allow aid to be imported and distributed by accredited personnel.

1.3 Staffing Issues

There has clearly been a problem recruiting suitable personnel for posts in Somalia. Although moves are being made with the establishment of the DHA the UN does not appear to be equipped for fast mobilisation with experienced personnel whom it can call upon.

2. Conserving Government Structures.

After the fall of Siad Barre some government infrastructure remained intact, ministries still functioned, and there were Somali professional and technical personnel in post in some cases working without pay, who needed support. The principle that outside aid should be tailored to local circumstances was still applicable. SCF and the ICRC continued to work with national staff and communities.

In February 1991 SCF's objective was to rehabilitate basic health services by reactivating the health centres which had not been damaged by fighting and resume Mother and Child Health (MCH) services at Benadir Hospital in Mogadishu. Throughout 1991 and 1992 SCF pursued this objective, basing their feeding programmes at the Health Centres and over that period extending both the MCH and the feeding programmes.

In its slowness to engage at that early period the UN missed the opportunity of conserving and strengthening government structures and supporting the many committed and competent Somalis who demonstrated their willingness to keep systems operating.

As the situation deteriorated the humanitarian imperative became predominant but from the end of the civil war there was also the imperative to halt the damage being done to the development process. It was vital to re-establish trade and resuscitate the local economy. It would have been easier to attempt this in early 1991 than very late 1992.

Undoubtedly representatives of UN agencies found it extremely difficult to deal with Siad Barre's regime towards the end of its period of rule and the distaste felt for the lack of co-operation, corruption and nepotism by many of those attempting to administer assistance programmes was shared and understood by NGO representatives. The decision not to engage with those who had ousted Siad Barre is not so easy to understand, however. UNDP despite having $50 million remaining in its budget said there were no government structures to work with and its budget could only be used for development purpose. It appeared to be the policy of UNICEF and other agencies not to work through government structures. What aid they did manage to bring in was channelled through NGOs.

NGOs questioned and challenged this decision. Ambassador Sahnoun was also to question it in a public statement eighteen months later.

Throughout the post civil war period a similar situation pertained in the north-west (Somaliland). There is no major hunger or starvation as yet in Somaliland but as the government is unrecognised external assistance is extremely limited. The Ministries of Health and Education are attempting to function and teachers have continued to work without pay.

3. Effectiveness of Response

3.1 The Importance of an Overall Strategy

Effective aid requires a comprehensive view of overall needs and the likely impact of interventions. In the case of Somalia an overarching strategy based on an informed analysis of the political and economic realities was lacking from before the fall of Siad Barre. This lack of analysis led to a failure of both the humanitarian and political initiatives.

3.2 Political and Humanitarian Linkages

In Somalia, as in most of the recent and current complex emergencies where civil conflict is inextricably linked with the need for humanitarian assistance the delivery of that assistance in accordance with principles of non-partisanship and independence is difficult. Those in need of humanitarian assistance are hostage to political developments and those in the business of delivering the assistance must find ways of relieving the suffering without compromising their principles.

The resolutions of the Security Council on both Somalia and Yugoslavia reflect the interrelationship between humanitarian assistance, the political situation and peacekeeping. *Agenda for Peace* also stresses the linkages between political and humanitarian action but gives little guidance on how these are to be strengthened in practice. The Somali experience demonstrates the problems which can arise when there is a division of responsibility between Departments of Political Affairs and Humanitarian Affairs. Important questions of policy remained unaddressed because of lack of clarity about who was responsible for the overall situational analysis. At one level it led to individual incidents such as those that marred James Jonah's visit in January 1992, but more importantly it meant that no strategic decisions concerning a relief effort could be made. Somalia presented problems that required a combined approach and creative thinking. The continued failure to provide an adequate analysis is likely to limit the effectiveness of increased humanitarian efforts.

The circumstances demanded a large scale relief programme within which SCF and other smaller NGOs could perform their "normal" functions, as part of a co-ordinated international effort. The UN agencies both before and after the establishment of the DHA hold the key to such co-ordinated efforts. NGOs in Somalia have developed ways of relating to those wielding local power but ideally the UN should provide a political umbrella under which NGOs can work. Whereas it is acknowledged that the security of the port, the airport and the roads running from them into the vulnerable areas was vital to a major relief effort, efforts to address both the humanitarian and political problems could have been made concurrently.

Those agencies who remained in Mogadishu learnt through experience to work through local power structures and became creative in the way they delivered food. They realised that it would not be possible to set up the perfect logistical food distribution system. If vulnerable groups were to be fed clan fighters had to be fed in order to prevent them looting food. Agencies on the ground took a pragmatic approach which enabled them to make some progress in the delivery of humanitarian assistance even though the security problem was not solved.

3.3 The Importance of Information and Analysis

To most observers the situation in Somalia appears anarchic. This may be true in the sense that there is no organised central power but it is not true in the way the word is currently being employed to describe wholly random violence. The violence exists for several reasons including the protection of legitimate activities for example trade, protecting visiting delegations; for the protection of social order within defined areas, as well as the pursuit of central power. Of particular note are trade and looting. The former because relief is seen as directly interfering with trade and the latter because many of those employed in looting are primarily doing this for want of an alternative source of income.

Despite the continuing violence there is some social cohesion and organisation; locally, at district level, for example the district committees and in the formation of "Ministries". At least in the example of Mogadishu and health there is a limited amount of working across the lines.

The following factors have to be taken into consideration when relief programmes are planned;

— the bypassing of emerging structures, legitimate, effective or not, by aid providers causes offence to Somalis.

— if relief is seen to give advantage to one group over another, it will lead to violence.

— if relief is seen purely as feeding the starving i.e. food for distribution, and not in terms of cash, organisation, or employment creation, it will be at best obstructed or met with violence, at worst it becomes a factor which adds to violence, not least violence directed against the relief system.

— high value food stuffs such as rice will exacerbate looting. They should be put through markets and lower value grains be used for food aid.

These issues should be borne in mind as the UN Action Plan becomes operational. It should be implemented bearing in mind that a detailed consideration of the issues indicated above is the only possible way to proceed. This will involve careful negotiation and the use of Somali structures.

In order to function effectively in all parts of Somalia including Somaliland SCF has found it necessary not only to establish and maintain links with Somali institutions and communities but also to conduct studies and operational research programmes into the functioning of underlying political, economic and social structures. For example, a study of the ethnic and political movements was commissioned which enabled SCF to understand the complex clan relationships which currently dominate life in

Somalia. Nutrition surveys of Somaliland's major towns and of rural Somaliland were conducted after the destabilising events of November–December 1990. The rural survey not only gauged the extent of acute malnutrition but also obtained a broader picture of the food economy. Using experienced expatriate and national staff information on environmental conditions, rainfall, livestock holdings and condition, harvests where there was cultivation and food markets was obtained. The survey (and a similar one in the adjacent region of the Ogaden in Ethiopia) produced numerical information on the current population and the proportion of "returnees" in rural communities. These surveys, intended for the aid community in general, offered unique baseline information and provided an important overview of the regional economy. Information on the "terms of trade" of grain for livestock, the need for veterinary drugs as a vital contribution to reviving the local economy, and the need for a campaign of water point rehabilitation contributed to a regional overview from which strategies could be developed, not only to target relief, but to lead to longer term revitalisation of the economy of the region.

The two UN "Action Plans" are little more than lists of projects with price tags which were presented to donors as "consolidated appeals". In the case of the 100-Day Action Programme it did appear that Ambassador Sahnoun and representatives of the DHA wished to work with NGOs and incorporate them in an overall strategy. To date this is not happening. In Somalia the UN has no information officer. It has one radio communications frequency for use by all its agencies which is constantly in use. There is no UN security channel.

In July/August 1992 UNDP funded a report which provided an overview of development needs.

There have been instances where it appears that those at the lower levels who do gain understanding of issues on the ground are overruled by those at higher levels at a remove from local understanding.

The NGO Consortium in Mogadishu has issued a statement in which it makes clear that the enforced resignation of Ambassador Sahnoun has jeopardised the relief effort. To have an effective command structure there has to be a person in the field who can make judgements relatively unconstrained by those above him in New York. Ambassador Sahnoun had gained an understanding of the local situation. His experience of working with the local clan leaders determined the way he introduced UN guards.

3.4 Relationships with NGOs

In a situation where information was difficult to obtain, particularly on the feasibility of mounting relief operations the visiting UN teams did not take advantage of the knowledge and expertise of the operational NGOs. This was also important in terms of identifying Somali structures and people with whom co-operation could still be effective.

Mr Hashim (UNDP) visited Mogadishu for one day in April 1991 and for one in May. A WHO representative visited Mogadishu for two hours in May. Neither made contact with operational NGOs.

In December 1991 David Bassiouni non-resident representative for UNICEF returned to Mogadishu but did not communicate with NGOs for 10 days.

In November 1992 NGOs are still doing 80–90 per cent of all relief and rehabilitation work. The UN as a whole has to recognise the nature of NGOs and develop ways of working with them. NGOs have now established their own Consortium with an independent budget, premises and information officer to coordinate NGO activities.

4. UN Co-ordination

4.1 Strategic Framework

The important issue of co-ordination is subordinate to the issue of the overall strategic framework. The role of co-ordinator or co-ordinating or lead agency is vital to the success of an effective emergency operation but there has to be a strategic framework in place before a systematised operation can begin.

4.2 Confusion Over Who Plays Co-ordinating Role

The institutional framework pre-dating the establishment of the Department of Humanitarian Affairs (DHA) appeared to impede UN engagement and co-ordination in Somalia from the fall of Siad Barre. Both before and after the DHA came into being there was a series of appointments of special representatives and co-ordinators. For agencies on the ground there was confusion about who was in charge.

At the time of, and immediately after the fall of Siad Barre (January 1991) there was no formal UN involvement in Somalia, other than UNICEF material support for NGOs, including SCF. UNDP was the lead agency but the UN resident representative, Mr Hashim, formerly based in Mogadishu, was based in Nairobi. UNDP took a more cautious and conservative approach than UNICEF or later WFP.

In August 1991 UNICEF and WFP sent former Somali programme staff back to Mogadishu, but evacuated staff in September.

On 2 February David Bassiouni was made UN Emergency Co-ordinator for Somalia. In May Ambassador Sahnoun was appointed UN Secretary General Special Representative.

All those who were associated with Ambassador Sahnoun in Somalia welcomed his attempts to overcome problems in Mogadishu and his attempts to speed up the relief operation. He tried to establish operations within a framework.

4.3 The Involvement of the DHA

The establishment of the DHA created a new opportunity for the UN to come to grips with the situation in Somalia. However Mr Jan Eliasson was immediately despatched on a round of visits to international trouble spots when it could be argued that a better investment would have been made in concentrating on the detailed planning of his office. In the event, key decisions about practical arrangements were taken too hastily and were based on the views of people and institutions that were part of the system which it had been decided to reform. The decision to split the political and operational activities between New York and Geneva was particularly damaging to the effectiveness of the new institution, undermining good administration and dividing scarce logistical resources, but most of all helping to perpetuate an artificial barrier between functions that are—as we have argued above—inseparable when suffering is caused by political factors. We understand that this decision was taken at the urging of donor governments and of UN agencies headquartered in Geneva. We remain unconvinced that their arguments outweighed the case for unified control. It has, however, also not helped that subsequently the two-way liaison visits of top management between New York and Geneva have fallen far short of the regular monthly exchanges originally promised.

5. LEARNING FROM THE SOMALI EXPERIENCE

(1) It is as yet unclear what will prompt UN co-ordinated humanitarian intervention when there is no request by a sovereign government. There appears to be no capacity to launch a co-ordinated response when there is a request.

(2) Present security guidelines constrain the response.

(3) Lack of a strategic framework dilutes the effectiveness of the response.

(4) The role and authority of the DHA is as yet unclear. The traditional lack of co-ordination between agencies at country and regional level continues, and gaps still exist. At the Under-Secretary level there is confusion over the division of responsibility between Political and Humanitarian Affairs. Whilst it may be clear in principle that the UN Secretary-General's Special Representative has an overview of political and humanitarian affairs at the country level, in practice this makes the role of the DHA co-ordinator even more unclear.

(5) In situations such as Somalia where UN agencies lack information on which to base a response independent experts and operational NGOs should be consulted.

ANNEX 1

CHRONOLOGY OF EVENTS IN SOMALIA
1991–1992

1991

January

Siad Barre ousted. USC interim government created on 29 January under the presidency of Ali Mahdi Mohammed.

18,000 mts of UNHCR food looted in Berbera, NW Somalia.

1 February

SCF's report on the situation in Somalia recommends that a feeding programme should start.

4 February

SCF's relief programme begins in Somalia. UNICEF provide support for NGOs, and SCF in particular, in the form of vaccines, medical equipment, etc. No other UN involvement. UNDP is the lead agency for Somalia with Mr Hashim, ex UNDP resident representative in Mogadishu, now based in Nairobi. The UN stance is that the insecurity does not allow for UN operations.

15 February

SCF sets up five feeding centres in Mogadishu.

22 February

SCF writes a letter to the Independent calling for the UN to re-establish operations in Somalia.

February/March

Opportunities for re-engagement exist. Some structures remain; ministries functioning and there is only sporadic violence. The UN sends in a reconnaissance team.

April

Hashim visits Mogadishu for one day. He does not have any contact with NGOs on the ground. UNICEF, under the umbrella of SCF, posts Cliff Webster to Mogadishu as a way round the UN security guidelines.

SCF expands its feeding programme to ten centres.

May

Hashim visits Mogadishu again for one day but does not contact NGOs. WHO representative Dr Bargogar visits Mogadishu for two hours.

Malnutrition levels worsen and SCF expands its feeding programme to 12 centres.

August

The UN returns. UNICEF and WFP send staff to Mogadishu on a two week rotation using former Somalia programme staff now based in Nairobi.

September

The UN evacuates from Mogadishu. SCF partially evacuates for seven days. Fighting between Aideed and Ali Mahdi signifies the end of nascent structures and Mogadishu becomes factionalised on a clan basis. Other parts of southern Somalia are controlled by different clans.

7,000 mts of food arrives in Mogadishu but is blocked in the port.

SCF expands its programme to sixteen feeding centres to try to meet the food needs of the population.

November

No food stocks in Mogadishu. Evidence of great social distress with a resultant increase in looting. Outbreaks of fighting occur mid month.

Andrew Natsios of OFDA calls for UN involvement. US congressional hearings call for UN involvement.

An ICRC worker is killed in Mogadishu: a UNICEF doctor is killed in Bossasso.

24 December

UNICEF returns to Mogadishu but does not communicate with the NGOs for ten days.

David Bassiouni arrives to prepare for Jonah's visit.

1992

16 January

Jonah's mission to Somalia. Jonah stipulates that aid will be conditional on a ceasefire. There is no action. The visit is compromised and the mission did not meet all concerned parties or consult with clan elders.

January

ICRC bring food into Merca.

2 February

UN nominate Bassiouni as representative for Somalia.

February

UNICEF plan a feeding and health programme.

7,000 mts of wheat flour and dried skimmed milk is looted.

March

Mogadishu ceasefire comes into effect negotiated by Jonah.

SCF carries out an assessment of conditions in Belet Weyn.

April

UNICEF become operational with a feeding programme and distribution of tents.

May

Ambassador Sahnoun is nominated as UN Secretary General Special Representative.

SCF open feeding and health centre in Belet Weyn.

May-June

The first UN shipment of food (2,000 mts of wheat) arrives since the ceasefire.

July

A team of 50 UN observers arrive in Mogadishu.

August

The UN Security Council accepts Sahnoun's report recommending that Somalia (including the north west) be divided into four zones for the distribution of food aid.

28 August

The USA airlift starts.

10–12 August

Inter-agency mission, including Jan Eliasson and James Grant visit "to determine ways to accelerate relief effort".

12–13 October

Presentation of 100 Day Action Plan to donors in Geneva.

27 October

Sahnoun resigns.

ANNEX 2

SAVE THE CHILDREN FUND (UK) IN SOMALIA

Background

Save the Children has been involved in relief and development programmes in Somalia since 1952 when it established a home for abandoned children in the town of Hargeisa, and later feeding centres in the 1964 famine. In 1980 refugee health and feeding programmes were established for Ethiopian refugees in the north-west, at which time a long standing relationship with the Somali Refugee Health Unit (RHU) also began. As emergency needs diminished assistance was extended to work in the Somali community, particularly Mother and Child Health (MCH) services in the north-west region as a whole.

In 1985 SCF decided to expand its work in Somalia. The country, affected by drought, civil unrest and a large refugee problem, has one of the highest child and maternal mortality rates in the world. Government health services were in a serious state of decline and ill equipped to provide basic health care for mothers and children. SCF commenced a programme of technical assistance to the national immunisation programme, and at the same time responded to a new influx of refugees in the north-west. In April 1988 it further expanded its operation with the aim of assisting the Somali Ministry of Health (MoH) improve basic MCH services in Mogadishu. SCF was involved in improving the skills of the MCH staff, upgrading the existing clinic buildings and in the development of management systems.

The period 1988 to 1991 saw a deterioration in the political situation with clan conflicts seriously disrupting life throughout the country as the efforts to replace Siad Barre degenerated into a series of conflicts in which clan leaders and ex-generals battled for supremacy. In the process the capital was destroyed and the north of the country declared itself independent. There was serious economic decline, acute food shortages and soaring inflation. The human rights record of the Siad Barre government and the failure of economic reforms lost the regime the support of major donors. With the exception of the Japanese all donors reviewed and decreased their assistance.

The security situation in most parts of the country declined sharply. SCF withdrew some expatriate staff temporarily in mid-1989. Those in key posts in the MoH remained in order to be able to respond to an emergency situation if it arose and the team was re-established in November 1989. Some expatriate staff withdrew to Nairobi in early December 1990 when the civil war reached its peak.

1991

In January 1991 Mohammed Siad Barre was finally ousted by the United Somali Congress (USC). After Barre fled Ali Mahdi, of the Hawiye clan was appointed interim President by one faction of the USC, the Manifesto Group. His appointment antagonised General Aideed who had led the USC forces against Barre and the unresolved disputes between these two men dominated the following months, erupting into full scale fighting in June, September and November. By December 1991 up to 5,000 were thought to have been killed and 15,000–18,000 injured. Hospitals were overloaded with casualties. The only NGOs remaining in Mogadishu were the ICRC, MSF and the International Medical corps (IMC). CARE remained until the November fighting.

In the final days before Siad Barre's downfall the destruction of Mogadishu, murder of members of the Hawiye clan by the President's troops and comprehensive looting became more intense. There was destruction of power lines and communications. There was no electricity except privately generated power. The government of the United Somali Congress had no foreign exchange and was without reserves of local currency.

During the most intense period of fighting Dr Hussain Mursal and other Somali staff maintained an SCF presence despite the shelling of the office in which an administrator lost his life, and the looting of vehicles. A working structure still existed. Dr Mursal's contacts and information network were to continue to prove invaluable throughout the following months of shifting clan alliances and fighting.

It was decided in February 1991 to attempt to rehabilitate basic health services by reactivating the health centres which had not been damaged by fighting and resume MCH services at Benadir Hospital. This was agreed with the new Minister of Health, Dr Nuur but he left during the later part of the year and the only health initiatives came from NGOs. SCF funded incentive payments for a small emergency committee of health staff and together with this group worked to operate the MCHs with MoH staff. This committee was the only instance of paid government employees in Somalia.

It was also agreed to provide "wet" supplementary feeding to children under 80 per cent WFL at these centres. During the first three months of the project 5 MCH centres and 2 therapeutic centres were established in the city and a further two feeding centres and one therapeutic centre were established in the "Fairground" area where an estimated 8,000 displaced people and former refugees had gathered. During this period the programme was managed by Dr Hussein Mursal, using national staff recruited from the amongst pre-war MCH and Refugee Health Unit staff.

In July 1991 SCF's emergency programme entered a new phase with the arrival of seven expatriate medical staff to strengthen the technical management, supervisory and training support capacity of the programme. With the recruitment of a Field Director Dr Mursal was enabled to spend more time on the technical management of the project as Medical Co-ordinator.

1992

SCF has seen the major objective of 1992 as continuing the main components of the 1991 programme;

— Continuing the development of the MCH programme and opening new MCH/feeding centres

— Continuing ration distribution to those families with children under 80 per cent weight for height where possible

— Continuing to develop the immunisation programme within the existing MCHs

— Development of the antenatal facilities within the MCHs

— Developing the MCH centres into a general health centres.

However, because of the violence of the last months of 1991 the numbers of displaced around Mogadishu had grown and it was decided to open MCHs in camps for the displaced, provide clean water, latrines and shelter and open and supervise feeding programmes in camps where there was a high level of malnutrition.

In June SCF expanded its emergency programme to include Belet Weyne district, and the towns of Jelalaaxi and Bulo Burti. In villages south of Mogadishu SCF has provided maize and vegetable seeds to 5,000 farming families. Seeds were distributed in time for the rainy seasons, April/June and September/October.

SOMALILAND

Somaliland is under the control of the Somali National Movement (SNM) which has declared independence but has not been afforded international recognition. There has been a high degree of insecurity but it is currently more stable. Save the Children is working with both the Ministries of Health and Education, in so far as these both exist, in an attempt to rehabilitate these services. SCF is currently planning to make local food purchases in order to stimulate local economy and pay teachers.

Examination of witnesses

MR TONY VAUX, Emergencies Co-ordinator, OXFAM, MR JULIAN HOPKINS, National Director, CARE, MR MICHAEL AARONSON, Director, Overseas Department, and MR MARK BOWDEN, Director, Africa, Save the Children, examined.

Chairman

68. Gentlemen, could I begin by welcoming you this morning: Mr Hopkins, National Director of Care—you must say if I have your titles wrong—and Mr Vaux, Emergencies Co-ordinator of OXFAM, is that correct?

(Mr Hopkins) Yes, indeed.

69. We were hoping, and still are hoping, we are going to be joined by Mr Mark Bowden of Save the Children and Mr Aaronson, also of Save the Children, but they appear to have been delayed along the way and have not appeared, so perhaps they will join us later. Anyway, that will give more air space for the two witnesses we do have. We are extremely grateful that you are with us and we are looking forward to hearing your expert views, based on deep practical experience, about the UN involvement in humanitarian and major emergency issues. Could I say if I ask a question of one of you, if the other wishes to answer as well, please do so. We have now been joined by Mr Aaronson and Mr Bowden, who are Directors of Save the Children, respectively in the Overseas Department and the Africa Department, is that correct? Am I describing you correctly?

(Mr Bowden) Yes.

70. I would like to begin with a general question and perhaps I could put it to Mr Hopkins of CARE. From your perspective, what are the major problems that have emerged in the recent United Nations responses to humanitarian and security related emergencies? We do seem to have more humanitarian challenges and more disasters and emergencies piling on to the plate of the international community and the UN than ever before, and in the midst of this the non-governmental organisations play an ever more vital role and the world seems to rely upon your work filling in the niches, making the thing operate, giving teeth to various internationally sponsored activities increasingly. Therefore, I suspect you have some views on how all these are working together, given the new proposals for a new and enlarged role for the UN, certainly new responsibilities. So with those observations, Mr Hopkins, would you like to share some thoughts with us?

(Mr Hopkins) Thank you, Mr Chairman. I would answer, first of all, by saying that, as far as CARE is concerned, we would say that the situation in Somalia is as severe as any elsewhere in relation to how the UN is responding and, indeed, how the NGOs themselves are responding. I would then cite the former Yugoslavia as another area where the UN presence is critical and I could

[**Chairman** *Contd*]

probably, if time permits, point to the situation in Angola, where there are growing problems and the resurgence of old problems. I am not quite sure how you would like to proceed on this but certainly as far as CARE is concerned we have quite a lot to say about Somalia at least. Would you permit me to move on?

71. Yes. I think what we would like you to do—not that we do not want to hear as much of your views as possible—is, first of all, to tell us how CARE relates or does not relate to the UN agencies and their involvement and then after that, but still at the beginning, we would like to ask about your relations with the United Kingdom agencies, donor agencies and the Overseas Development Administration, and how, as a major NGO, you are getting on with them. But could you focus what you have to say, without feeling too constrained, on where the United Nations personnel and your own work cross paths in Somalia or wherever?

(Mr Hopkins) Yes. I ought to preface my remarks by saying that, first of all, CARE works in 50 developing countries. We work in relief, rehabilitation, logistics and long-term development, and in very many of those countries we have close working relationships with the various UN agencies represented. As a general rule, those relationships are productive and subject to monitoring and discussion and they work reasonably satisfactorily. However, one has to say that in recent years, and particularly over the last few months, there seems to have been a very large number of emergencies occurring, which have not been disasters which have perhaps been dealt with in a matter of weeks; they have been emergencies which have had profound and long-lasting implications for the people of the country in question and in terms of the humanitarian response needed by the international community. It is that prolonged engagement and involvement which is causing problems, in our experience, in those countries where there are not what one might call structured conflicts, where there are unstructured conflicts, where there is anarchy, where there is no government or where there is difficulty because one has to deal with several leaders. It is in those countries that problems are occurring, between the NGOs and the UN agencies, where the system is perhaps breaking down or does not work at all. CARE is, if I may say so, well-known for dealing with and responding to emergencies and providing logistical support, and in doing so it comes up against these problems quite frequently, in particular in Somalia in recent weeks. CARE has a large network overseas; it employs some 10,000 staff, of whom about 9,500 are national staff employed within those countries, and, contrary to some reports which have been appearing lately in the press about NGO operations overseas, one should stress it is a professional organisation with management structures in each of those countries where it works and it is through those structures that it aims to deal with the various UN agencies that are represented there. It is, I am afraid, the case that we are finding that where there are these problems of conflict such as in Somalia, where different clans are fighting each other and where there is no government, no legislature, it is in those situations where no leadership is apparently forthcoming from the UN and no co-ordination has been apparent for some time. There the NGOs have difficulties and perhaps are filling a role that is properly the role of the UN. For example, in Somalia, as you may well know, some of the NGOs that are working there have no alternative but to hire protection to protect food convoys to provide the relief that is required. The UN's assistance and support for those operations has been minimal. The attempts by the UN to find political settlement have not worked and from a practical day to day point of view the situation has been a disaster. The NGOs—and I speak for CARE but I think, I hope, I speak for a dozen or more that are working in Somalia now—have done their level best to deliver assistance to starving people but it has got to the stage where the humanitarian effort is severely at risk unless the UN presence is co-ordinated and the role of the UN is clarified. There is some belated strategy which has the approval of New York which is now being implemented satisfactorily by the representatives in the country, in this case in Somalia. I should explain that the Chief Executive of the CARE organisation in the States was recently appointed on a secondment basis as co-ordinator of the UN One Hundred Day Plan in Somalia. He has been doing this job for about three weeks. From his initial findings and his involvement with Ambassador Kittani, who succeeded Sahnoun, he is making some very strong recommendations which he was discussing in New York with Mr Eliasson two days ago. If I may, I would just like to mention, to illustrate the gravity of the problem, the sort of points that were being made by the co-ordinator, Dr Johnston. He was saying that the Security Council should act now to change the rules of engagement for the 3,500 troops it has already approved for Somalia. It should empower their commanding General to deploy them to any location in Somalia where relief operations require protection. He is saying once the General in charge of UN troops is empowered to move the troops where they are needed most, the majority should be deployed to Mogadishu and assigned to secure the port and airport and provide protection for convoys of food which, at the moment, as I have said, is not being provided. He is saying cartels of Somali traders are currently hoarding Somali currency and thereby artificially controlling the dollar-shilling exchange rate. The UN and the World Bank should be asked to form a bank for Somalia in order to limit the influence of these cartels. The Security Council should pass whatever resolutions are necessary to succeed in these matters. However, one has to go further and say that because of the difficulties of co-ordination and clearer lines of command and perhaps the lack of authority given to the field representatives—and Somalia is not an exception in this case—all kinds of problems have occurred and the UN response to the crisis in Somalia, as far as CARE is concerned, has been sadly lacking. As a

[**Chairman** *Contd*]

result of which, in spite of the enormous amount of effort NGOs have made, we are still seeing people dying, we are still seeing extraordinary amounts of suffering and it has got to the stage where really something has to be done in order to save many, many tens of thousands who otherwise would die.

72. Thank you for that very sombre assessment which I think confirms all our views there are many problems and indeed Somalia is tragically a graveyard of many hopes at the moment about a better world order. I am going to ask Mr Aaronson if he would like to comment on the general question about relations with the UN because I know, Mr Aaronson, you have to leave for Geneva shortly and you are in charge of the Overseas Department.

(Mr Aaronson) Thank you very much. Could I first of all apologise for arriving late, my colleague and I narrowly avoided giving evidence to the wrong Committee! I am glad we made it in the end. I am sorry I have to go to Geneva, as you have said. In response to your general question, I think the thing that strikes us most from the non governmental organisation perspective is the lack of clarity within the UN about how the different actors in humanitarian assistance should relate to each other. There is an obvious complementarity between non governmental organisations, bilateral donors, UN agencies, inter-governmental organisations, and we do not seem to be exploiting that. It seems to us, on the NGO side, that the burden of responsibility which has now been laid upon the UN actually sits very heavily, I would say too heavily, on their shoulders. Perhaps what needs to be done is to ease that burden by making it clear to them and everybody else that they do not have to do everything. I think Somalia is a very good case where, as I agree with Julian Hopkins, they have not performed well. One of the problems is expectations have perhaps been unrealistic. I think some of the things people have looked to them to do actually are better done by others. From our point of view, just to illustrate that clearly, it is absolutely vital that there is an overall political and security framework within which we can do our job and that is obviously what is going wrong in Somalia at the moment. If that framework is not there no-one can operate effectively. We would see the work to produce that framework as being the responsibility of the UN. When it actually comes down to providing material assistance I think they are not necessarily as well placed to do it as some of the other agencies. There seem to be expectations of what they will deliver which put them in a difficult position and do not produce a good result. It seems to me there is a lot of work to be done in trying to achieve greater clarity about how the UN agencies and UN system generally relates to the work that others are doing and, of course, vice versa. I would make that point first. I think the particular problem facing the UN agencies is lack of capacity to undertake the sort of analysis of humanitarian needs and to produce a workable strategic plan to respond to those needs. The famous One Hundred Day Plan in Somalia is not a plan at all because there is no real analysis of needs. It is more a pious wish list of things they would like the donors to come up with. We feel very frustrated because we feel we have the capacity to help with that analysis. We are on the ground, we are involved in a way UN agencies are not and we argue very hard that we and others should be involved at the earliest possible stage in developing the analysis of what the needs are and suggesting what the response should be. On the whole that does not happen, on the whole these famous consolidated appeals are put together by people deciding from Geneva or New York, with minimal consultation of people on the ground. I think that is a major weakness in the system. My second point is I do not think the UN takes advantage of the opportunities that are available to it, as it were, to use us and draw upon the experience and contacts we have. My third point is to do with the lack of clarity and co-ordination within the UN system itself. A lot has been said about this, certainly Save the Children Fund was very supportive of the establishment of the Department of Humanitarian Affairs last year and we continue to be supportive of the concept of there being one point within the system which is given the responsibility for co-ordination. But what we have seen over the last year is a hopeless task being placed on Mr Eliasson and his colleagues because he has not had the consensus really within the UN system and from the UN agencies as to what his role is. I do not think he has the authority from the UN; he certainly has not had the resources. He has had to scrabble around for office space, for fax machines, for suitably qualified staff, and I think that the task he has been given has actually been completely impossible. I do not think anybody could have done what has been asked of him. So we would certainly still advocate strongly for a centrally co-ordinated body within the UN system to be given the authority and the resources. There does need to be a debate about what exactly is meant by co-ordination. It is a very frightening concept to many of the UN agencies. They need to be reassured that it does not mean they are going to be controlled by somebody else. On the contrary, it means their task is going to be made easier because somebody is making sure the bits of the jigsaw fit together. So lack of co-ordination is still a major issue but what it all adds up to is a lack of authority in the field and certainly in Somalia and many other places the credibility of the UN has totally evaporated and that is tragic because it renders them powerless to carry out the task which is theirs. If we talk about the legitimacy of a humanitarian operation, with particular reference to sovereignty and the UN Charter and the balance between humanitarianism and sovereignty, for example, I think the particular point I would make is that legitimacy is as much about delivery, it is as much about performance as it is about mandates and constitutions. There is a great deal of legitimate

[**Chairman** *Contd*]

discussion about mandates and whether the UN Charter allows the sort of humanitarian intervention that one would want to see. But I should point out that to a certain extent discussion about mandates is a smokescreen because I think that if the UN could be assisted to deliver more it would have the legitimacy which it lacks at the moment and would be able to operate even within its existing mandate.

Chairman: As you have to go, we are going to pursue this with you for a moment because obviously Mr Bowden and his colleagues would like to say something, and I have not yet asked Mr Vaux to speak.

Mr Harris

73. As Mr Aaronson has touched quite considerably on this vexed question of co-ordination, or lack of co-ordination rather, I wonder if I could ask you and perhaps Mr Hopkins who you think should have the co-ordinating role, who should be responsible for co-ordination? Should it be the Secretary General, should it be the Department of Humanitarian Affairs or whoever, or do you not much care who does it so long as somebody gets a grip of the situation?

(Mr Aaronson) I would be very tempted to agree with you that it must be for the UN and for the Secretary General to decide how they want to organise this. I think we are entitled to insist that there is effective co-ordination and perhaps that is also an area where we would expect the member governments of the United Nations, the member states, also to insist that they use their weight and their authority, because again I think it is too easy, as it were, just to blame the UN. We have to remember what the United Nations is and certainly governments get the UN they deserve and it is up to people in the Security Council and elsewhere to insist that effective co-ordination takes place.

74. I do not know if Mr Hopkins would like to clear that point.

(Mr Hopkins) I would support what my colleague said. I think the marginal preference, as a personal view, as it were, might be for the Department of Humanitarian Affairs to take a co-ordinating role. I think we have all seen, particularly in more recent times, that the UN is becoming in many situations the protagonist rather than just the broker and I think that all this calls for a degree of co-ordination which has been severely lacking is needed. It seems from an outsider's point of view to be logical for the Humanitarian Affairs Department to undertake that role, but I think the important thing I would add is that it should not be too high in the hierarchy, that the management structure should reflect the need for co-ordination at the operational level.

Chairman: I want to bring Mr Vaux in on this if we are going to have a general discussion on co-ordination now rather than later.

Sir John Stanley

75. Mr Aaronson, in your paper you make the point that a period of some 20 months elapsed between February 1991 when the SCF called for the UN to re-involve itself in Somalia and the autumn of 1992 before that involvement got under way in a material way. Do you consider that the critical impediment to UN involvement was the UN's reluctance to get involved in a situation where there was not a security environment that was acceptable; in other words, there was a civil war going on? Do you regard that as being the overwhelming factor or do you regard the overwhelming factor as being a sheer lack of political will, either by the UN or, perhaps just as important, by the member states within the UN to address what was going on in Somalia, which was vividly evident around the world, thanks to the mass media? Was it a lack of political will by the governments really to drive the UN to get involved? Was that the important factor or was it the security situation in Somalia?

(Mr Aaronson) I think that is a very difficult question to answer. Certainly the security situation was used as the reason for not getting involved. I suspect that it was a lack of political will, both within the United Nations and, as you suggest, on the part of the governments, who could and should have been insisting that more was done. I think a third factor is what I was talking about earlier, which is the lack of capacity. I think because the problem looked so difficult to the UN it was yet another reason not to get involved. I think if they had taken better advantage of the people who could have helped them and worked with them, they would not have got themselves into such a mess. I have to say that part of that lack of capacity does come down to lack of capacity of people who are actually dealing with the situation. I think if the full story is told it will be seen that some people took the easy way out when actually there were alternatives open to them and they did not pursue them. But obviously the security environment has been horrendous and it would be churlish to underplay that. We have all found it very difficult and anybody who has worked in Somalia—and let us not forget some UN agencies have been there for most of the time and some UN people have been as brave as anybody else—anybody who has worked there at all I think deserves recognition. So the security has been horrendous but I think actually you are right that the fundamental problem is a lack of political will and a lack of ability to address the problem.

76. To what would you attribute that lack of political will? It is an appalling indictment of governments around the world that here was one of the most ghastly famines with the most visible evidence of appalling suffering on a vast scale taking place and yet over a year elapsed before governments around the world were really prepared to address it and say, "We cannot just go on passing down the other side of the road," which is effectively what has happened for a year at least?

(Mr Aaronson) I think one of the problems is that the international community has a crisis man-

[**Sir John Stanley** *Contd*]

agement approach to the problems of Africa and tends to wait until things get bad before it steps in, whereas it should be focusing much more on the preventive side. It should be thinking much more in terms of solid and sustained rehabilitation so that crises do not recur. Unfortunately, what we seem to have is a tendency to hope the problem will go away until such time as, as you say, it does appear on the television screens and a political imperative to do something is thereby created. I think Africa just needs to rate rather more highly in the priorities of the international community and particularly of the, what one might call, donor community than it does at present.

Chairman

77. We are broadening this opening question rather on to co-ordination deliberately because we want to catch Mr Aaronson. Before I move on, Mr Bowden do you want to add anything else on the questions we have been doing so far or will you reserve yourself until later?

(Mr Bowden) I have one simple point on co-ordination and it complements what Michael was saying about Somalia and why the UN were not engaged. There is a constitutional incapacity within the United Nations to make the strategical analysis. You cannot have the co-ordination unless there is a shared analysis of the problem. At no stage has there been an analysis of the problem in Somalia, there was nothing for people to go on. That is the fundamental issue.

78. What is the alternative? Are you saying nation states or super powers like America or the former super power Russia could have done a better job bilaterally or we have to invent something else?

(Mr Bowden) I think there is a real problem within the United Nations as to whether they can be allowed to express an opinion on political matters, many of the states within the United Nations find it very difficult if the United Nations itself expresses a viewpoint about the legitimacy of government or the direction things are going. In the case of Somalia it was very peculiar because in the end there was no government and the United Nations found itself with perhaps a role but not the capacity within the organisation to try and analyse the problem. They should have built that up, perhaps in the Department of Humanitarian Affairs, because I think as we were saying earlier, and in our evidence too, all the plans we have seen are, in a sense, a wish list of project proposals rather than analysis so they need that capacity to be effective. The United Nations needs to find a mechanism for developing analysis and they need to be allowed to do that or providing a forum in which the major actors can provide that analysis along with member states.

79. It is time we heard from Mr Vaux. Oxfam is involved, we would like to hear your views.

(Mr Vaux) If I can just go back to the wider context. We will go on to make profound criticisms and strong criticisms of the UN but I think all this must be seen in the context of the end of the Cold War and the lack of interest, certainly by super powers and governments around the world, in the sorts of issues we are talking about and the tendency to push humanitarian consequences on to the UN and on to NGOs which I think fundamentally is an impossible position to be in. The UN is not set up to deal with problems of, particularly, African States which are, many of them, in very serious problems after the end of the Cold War. During the Cold War they were propped up by one power and given assistance that has been removed. This coincides with a period of agricultural stagnation. It is not just the United Nations is facing a crisis, it is Africa is facing a crisis. The two are running together and so it is not surprising the UN has failed. This is also in the context of a feeling of tension between northern governments and southern governments which is based on a feeling that the north is prepared to make a lot of noise and say: "Next such and such should happen, humanitarian problems should be removed and so on" but not actually finding the money to do it. This tension comes across many issues such as the Rio Summit, the sort of clashes that occurred there with the feeling the north is talking more about ideas and wish lists rather than actually being prepared to sacrifice money in order to make these things happen. The role that we see, as a humanitarian organisation, for the UN, particularly in these conflict situations, is primarily this one of co-ordination. We do expect the UN to fulfil that role and I fully agree with Mike, I think we have the right to expect that and that has been very disappointing in recent years. We also expect it to be an intermediary between us as humanitarian organisations and governments, particularly the government of the country we are working with, and as a means to influence world opinion and to bring about action especially when there are underlying political or military problems. The problems then, the criticisms of the UN revolve around the issue of national sovereignty. First of all, this seems to be a crisis, one where the UN seems to be unable to decide clearly on its mandate to intervene in the case of massive humanitarian crises such as in Sudan at the moment as well as Somalia. We feel that while the UN itself has dithered over these issues also there has been a lack of clear direction and clear involvement from the Security Council to give some backing to the UN in backing a more pro-active position on these kinds of issues. The second point of failure within the UN is to do with the quality of staff in the UN and again I think this refers to what Mike was saying about one of the reasons for the failure in Somalia does seem to have been staff who were unsuitable for the professional job of relief management. I think one of the causes of this is the appointment of staff not according to their ability and qualifications but according to the internal diplomacy of the UN and particularly having to fulfil, in most circumstances, quotas for different

[**Chairman** *Contd*]

nationalities rather than getting the right person for the job. We have heavily criticised the UN, with Save the Children, over their Ethiopian operations in 1988/1989 when they seemed to have staff who were simply not competent for the job of relief management. The third area of criticism is the lack of openness, self-analysis and accountability within the UN. Again, if I can refer to that Ethiopian operation, it was a very serious failure when 300,000 refugees went into Ethiopia suddenly in 1988/1989, the UNHCR in particular failed very very badly. There has been no serious analysis of why that failed, no public hearing, such as the one we are in today, to find out what went wrong and to put it right. There has been no objective evaluation and there never is in UN operations. There is no real calling to account. There are internal evaluations, many of which are kept private but there is no mechanism by which the public, including us as interested parties, humanitarian organisations, can call the UN to account not because we want to push the blame on to people but because we want improvements for the next time round. If there is no learning process what guarantee can we have, after this fiasco of Somalia, anything will be better next time?

80. That is extremely interesting.

(Mr Vaux) I just have a couple of other quick points I would like to make. I think the structural issue has already been mentioned. The structure of the UN is far too complex. The structure of the UN on humanitarian affairs is very unclear and in particular its relationship to organisations like WFP and UNHCR which have been doing a good job. The management line is not clear. Finally, their relationship with NGOs, such as ourselves, is not good. There is a tendency in the UN to come in as an organisation which takes hold of everything, which organises everything. For instance, this One Hundred Day Programme in Somalia which was referred to is simply a list of what NGOs were doing anyway and has been rescheduled as if it was a UN plan. I think the NGOs who were part of that process were not satisfactorily consulted in the way that document was brought about. The document came out from New York and the role of NGOs in humanitarian relief has not been properly encouraged and accepted. They treat NGOs at a distance and their natural axis is to be much closer to the donor nations or the governments of the country concerned rather than a close relationship with those concerned. There is an attitudinal relationship we would like to see.

Chairman: I want to come on to the question of intervention in sovereign states, but before that did you want to ask about UN complexities?

Sir John Stanley

81. This Committee, of course, is the Departmental Committee for the Foreign Office and ODA so I would like to ask you in relation to Somalia, in particular, your assessment of HMG's performance through FCO and ODA in trying to make a worthwhile British contribution to that crisis?

(Mr Aaronson) I would like to lead off on that. I think from the Save the Children point of view the ODA response has throughout been timely and generous and we have not, as I recall—Mark Bowden may wish to add to this—had any problems in securing support from ODA when we have asked for it. I think what we have found obviously frustrating is the sort of things we have been talking about, the failure of the system as a whole to deliver on Somalia, and we would certainly look to HMG as representing an important donor nation with a seat on the Security Council to be as active as possible in the Security Council and elsewhere, in the General Assembly and, indeed, within the EEC, because I think one thing that has not happened in Somalia is a concerted European Community approach to the problem and I think that could conceivably also have helped.

Chairman: Mr Aaronson, again I am looking at the clock and we are slightly bending our order of questions. You mentioned, as did Mr Bowden, the vital issue of analysis before one has any effective pattern and can deal with these situations. This, of course, takes us into the world of preventive diplomacy and Mr Wareing wanted to ask some questions on that.

Mr Wareing

82. Obviously this is very important and I think Mr Aaronson and the other witnesses have already emphasised the fact that NGOs are, as it were, kept at a distance by the United Nations and I think this is borne out by the fact that "Agenda for Peace" by Mr Boutros-Ghali does not make any reference at all to the role of NGOs. Do you feel that, in terms of fact-finding and early warning, NGOs could have a very important role in preventive diplomacy? Could you say how you think the United Nations could better use the information and expertise that you have? What would be the processes involved? Somalia, of course, is probably a good example. You were there before the United Nations.

(Mr Aaronson) We have the privilege of working very closely with people on the ground in the countries in which we are working and there are a number of benefits and, therefore, we do have a unique perspective and are perhaps able to provide early warning of various things happening. I think the way for the system to take advantage of that—and it comes back to a point we touched on earlier—is that the UN is a very centralised bureaucracy and it has people in the field who are given very little scope and very little authority. I think what needs to happen is that people at local level need to be given the mandate, the responsibility, to work with those of us on the ground and carry out this analysis and produce these recommendations, for them then to be fed up through the system to where decisions can be taken, whereas what tends to happen at the moment is, as I said before, that people tend to come out on assessment missions from New York or Geneva or

[**Mr Wareing** *Contd*]

wherever and they have not possibly got the time to take advantage of the experience on the ground and they go back to the centre with an imperfect job done imperfectly. So I think the UN system has to become less centralised, less bureaucratic and has systematically to take in the views of people in the field at an early stage in the process of analysis and recommendation.

83. What actual liaison takes place already between the NGOs and the United Nations agencies? Could I just say an idea that springs into my mind, that when you talk about decentralising the United Nations, do you think there is perhaps a case, bearing in mind what Mr Hopkins said about a case for co-ordination at the operational level, for having some sort of permanent representation, a consulate, say, of the United Nations, in the potential trouble areas? I noted before you mentioned that it was a problem even getting an office to instal a fax machine, which seems to me preposterous for a world organisation.

(Mr Aaronson) On the first question about contacts between the UN and NGOs, I am sure my colleagues will agree that there is a huge range of contacts. I hope we have not given the impression that they do not talk to us at all and we do not talk to them. We do, all the time. I think it is more a question of how those contacts are perceived and how they perceive the status, if you like, of the dialogue they have with us. One of the things which is very frustrating for NGOs is that the UN always want to put us in a big box labelled "NGO", with one front door and one person to talk to. For example, in Geneva I am going to a meeting of something which calls itself the Steering Committee on Humanitarian Response. This is a group of NGOs that have organised themselves because they have common interests and can benefit from sharing their experiences, but as far as the UN is concerned, it is a golden opportunity to say, "We do not have to talk to anybody else now because we have this wonderful committee and they can deliver the NGOs for us." This is something we have to resist and we have to get used to this. It is horses for courses. If we are talking about Somalia and a plan of action for Somalia, they must talk to those NGOs who are serious players in the context of Somalia and the only way they can do that is by talking to them on the ground. It is not a case of talking to people in New York, Geneva or anywhere else; it is a case of liaising properly with people on the ground. That is my answer on contact. On the question of permanent representation, one of the problems is that there is no single, as it were, UN ambassador in a country and that is one of the hitches in the system. It is one of the things that leads to poor coordination and leadership and I do feel that the UN needs to give much more thought to how it is going to give the power on a permanent basis to somebody who can actually make sure that all the different bits of the UN apparatus are represented in a country and work effectively together. This is obviously part of the rationale for the DHA but that only comes into it during a time of crisis and it seems to me it is every bit as important for that to happen on a continuing basis at least to try to avert crises. If there were better co-ordination in terms of insecurity, there would be fewer crises.

Chairman: Mr Aaronson, I think we must let you go to your committee in Geneva otherwise you will be late for that. Thank you very much. We can come back to these issues later because other witnesses may have comments on them. We would like to pursue this question of intervention in clan wars, tribal wars and wars where there is no government.

Mr Canavan

84. I would like to take a brief supplementary on the point raised by Sir John Stanley about the British Government's response to the situation in Somalia, because there have been allegations made against the British Government that the response is inadequate and when these points are put to government representatives the reply you get often is along the lines: "We have been very generous. The money is there. The problem is not the lack of money. The problem is the difficulty in getting the food to the people who are desperately in need." What I wanted to ask the witnesses was, are they, in fact, satisfied with the British Government's response (a) in financial terms and (b) in whatever case we are using within the United Nations to try and get better co-ordination and to try and make the delivery of food more efficient?

(Mr Hopkins) I would respond by saying in relation to your question (a) in terms of the quantitative response, I think it has been perfectly adequate and, indeed, let me say generous. I would agree that the problem in terms of the way that the relief effort has been mounted has not been lack of resources. There has not been, as far as we are concerned in CARE, any problem at all in getting a satisfactory response from the ODA for funding. It is more difficult, frankly, for us to comment on your second question which is to do with, perhaps I might say, the pressure that the Government might put on the UN in order to get a better coordinated response from the UN, because one does not know frankly the details of the discussions that are taking place formally or informally. All one can say is that the evidence suggests representatives have been meeting in a timely way and it is no reflection on the Government that they have not been successful. However, speaking for my own organisation, we do exchange information with the ODA constantly and I know that the ODA, the Minister, does make use of that information so I would, in general terms, respond by saying that we would not wish to be critical in any way at all.

Chairman: Thank you.

Mr Canavan

85. On the question of humanitarian intervention, Mr Vaux raised a question of national sovereignty and the UN mandate. The submission from Save the Children states that one lesson of

[**Mr Canavan** *Contd*]
the Somalia experience is it is unclear what will prompt UN co-ordinated humanitarian intervention when there is no request by a sovereign government. In what circumstances do you think humanitarian concerns justify United Nations' intervention in sovereign states, particularly in cases where there is no invitation to come in on the part of the sovereign government?

(Mr Bowden) I can start on that. I think, in fact, the United Nations has now given itself the mandate to do that if they are requested, not by the political leadership but by the people of the country, to intervene. I think the case of Somalia was there were various requests being made by significant groups of the population who wanted UN involvement precisely because there was no government and they wanted support in maintaining institutions and trying to provide some framework for society. I think there is a legitimate case, not just on grounds of the need for urgent humanitarian relief but also where there is a collapse of government and the people of the area are looking for some framework within which to operate, for the UN to come in. Can I also add partly to the previous question as well: I think there has been a lack of political will, in general terms, when the Siad Barre Regime collapsed, for anybody to get engaged. It does relate back to the fact the UN is the one we deserve. If there had not been pressure in the first place, and if it was not just in response to a request from people for more help, from members of the United Nations, from neighbouring governments and others to say: "Look there is a problem, you ought to go in" they may have been pushed a bit earlier. There was not any impetus from the outset in the first six or nine months.

(Mr Vaux) We realise this issue of intervention despite national sovereignty or against the wishes of the sovereign government is a very very tricky issue indeed but we do feel it is one that should be openly and formally talked about and discussed rather than just being left on a case by case basis. With the UN and American intervention on behalf of the Kurds in Iraq there were special circumstances, but in the case of Sudan where such an issue may possibly arise or Somalia, it will be left to political and diplomatic discussions behind the scene. I think this is not really acceptable or in the interests of humanitarian relief that it will ultimately just be done on political grounds so we would also propose that the British Government should take an active part in codifying the sort of circumstances in which intervention might take place and the sort of negotiations that would take place. Clearly nobody is going to go for humanitarian interventions in every situation and, broadly speaking, what we would propose is where there is a massive humanitarian crisis or violation of human rights that the world should be able to intervene but the mechanism by which that should be done is extremely unclear. It is an area where the British Government can be more active and where we, as humanitarian organisations, certainly with Somalia and Sudan, need a much clearer position.

(Mr Hopkins) The mandate needs to be looked at itself. The relevant Article which, I believe, prohibits technical intervention without the permission of the host government, clearly has to be looked at. Then the procedure also needs to be looked at and I agree with my colleagues on that. It is interesting that in the case of Northern Iraq it was action by the Allied Forces that helped to co-ordinate the relief effort that resulted in safe havens which resulted subsequently in intervention by the UN. It seemed to me to be totally chronologically illogical and resulted in a lack of co-ordination. You cannot anticipate every single detail of every operation. It does seem to us with the developments there are, particularly in Africa, that the UN has to prepare for situations where it will not be possible to get some sort of intervention agreed with the host government. There may not be a host government and clearly the guidelines, the rules of the game, have to be looked at and Her Majesty's Government could no doubt play a role there.

86. You seem to be referring there to the possibility of having another look at the UN Charter.

(Mr Hopkins) Yes.

87. And presumably even amending the UN Charter.

(Mr Hopkins) Yes.

88. But in practical terms are there criteria whereby an accurate assessment can be made as to whether the level of suffering in a particular situation is so severe, particularly if that is being caused by a manmade disaster, as it were, civil war or whatever, are there practical criteria which can be applied whereby you could say: "This justifies humanitarian intervention in this sovereign state despite the fact the sovereign government does not want us or explicitly forbids it."?

(Mr Hopkins) I think it goes back to the point Mark Bowden made earlier, it hinges on the assessment. In that respect our plea is quite clearly that the NGOs should be involved in such assessments and in planning stages and if they were then the criteria would be less difficult to deal with. It would be based on on the ground experience and know-how and a proper assessment of what the implications of various actions might be.

Mr Sumberg

89. You talked about the codifying of the terms and conditions of intervention, that the UN should look at those. If I recall rightly, the advice this Committee received from a number of diplomatic sources—evidence it has been given—is that would be extremely dangerous in the sense the UN would get bogged down in a very theoretical discussion on these interventions. We are all learning new ground rules and the important thing is obviously—and I am sure you would agree—to get the aid and assistance to where it is most needed. I wonder if you would like to address that aspect of it? You talk about problems in the UN, problems with thought lines, lines of communications, surely

[**Mr Sumberg** *Contd*]

in calling for codifying, those are going to be revealed and the attention is not going to be on doing the most effective job but frankly in arguing what circumstances require intervention?

(Mr Vaux) It is a difficult question and I do not think we would want to be in the position of saying what the code should be. On the other hand, it is a real crisis situation where just saying, "Should it be left to the UN ambassadors to consider in New York?" has not worked in the past and there is no reason to believe it is going to work any better in the future. The UN does not seem to be able to deal with the current situation in Sudan or Somalia in terms of agreeing what level of intervention is possible. Somalia is relatively easy; Sudan is much more difficult, but I think while we would not want to push everything forward into an endless and unproductive debate, especially at a time when, as I said, the relationships between the north and the south are not necessarily very good and there is a lot of fear about this issue, some progress can be made beyond saying, "Let us fix this issue on each case behind the scenes," because it will be left far too much to particular NGOs and it will be kept to external things like the Kurds in Iraq, where we will actually see things happening.

Chairman: One of the arguments in New York that this Committee heard is that authority requires force and peace will require peace enforcement and the Americans would suggest they would like to see the marines involved but it is not quite clear how that would help.

Mr Gapes

90. I have looked very closely at the document from CARE. Mr Hopkins, you say on page 4 that: "A force of 3,500 would be barely adequate (500 have been stationed so far)," and you say: "Additional troops are essential," and you make the very interesting point about whether the UN should actually recruit local Somalis to play a military role within the UN forces. I wonder, firstly, what the attitude of the other agencies is to that suggestion, and secondly, is there not a danger that all this mounting pressure for large, potentially heavily armed UN forces, either introduced from outside or recruited locally, could very clearly compromise the role of UN personnel in a particular situation and may cause great difficulty for NGO staff as well and adversely affect the possibilities of getting through the aid which is required? And is there not a particular danger—and I would be interested in the comments of all three of you on this—that if you start recruiting local personnel in a military role you may be playing a role in supporting one faction or one tribal group against another, or be perceived to be doing that, even if it was not your intention?

(Mr Bowden) I appreciate the question very much because it is something we are unclear about, what the role of the peacekeeping forces is in Somalia and what it should be. I think the military situation, certainly in Central and Southern Somalia, is such that you could say 15,000 troops would not be enough if what you are trying to do is get food securely delivered without loss to beneficiaries wherever you need it. So you have to look at a different role for the UN forces and that has not been determined. What has also not been determined about Somalia is where the deployment should be. Part of the problem we have is that there are very different problems in different parts of Somalia. In the north-west of Somalia there is more legitimacy of clan militias and these militias are asking for both a degree of militarisation and training to make them a somewhat better force. That would be a useful role for the UN to restore order to clan militias on an organised basis with the assistance of the local police force. I am not sure whether that role is possible in the south, therefore you have to go for a more strategic analysis and say, "What is it we need to secure? Do we want a policy of safe havens in Southern Somalia? Is that going to create large-scale concentration camps within those areas that are safe, where there is a total dependence on outside food and assistance, and that requires a different deployment of troops and forces, or do we require more of an observer force which would safeguard key areas such as port and airport and provide security to relief personnel, but we cannot guarantee food delivery to the end beneficiaries." So the whole issue relates to the form of relief role the UN has and how it is going to deploy its forces.

91. I would be interested in the comments of the other witnesses.

(Mr Vaux) You pose some difficult moral questions there because OXFAM, like other agencies working in Somalia, hires gunmen to protect our work there, and I suppose in that sense we could not argue against the UN doing the same, but there is a very serious problem, as Mark said, which is the danger of simply strengthening the gunmen, their military force, whereas what we want to do is strengthen the elders and the clan leadership, who are not at the moment the same by any means as the gunmen. They seem to be quite detached. So we would be working against ourselves if there were a massive UN use of gunmen because all the money would go to those gunmen. They would charge enormous amounts of money, which would boost their military base. I think the problem for me in saying all this is that it is very difficult to propose an alternative to the greater use of military intervention in Somalia the way things are going, but nobody knows, of course, what would actually happen until it is tried.

Chairman

92. Can you see a sort of UN government emerging in the area, like the old UN trusteeships, although we are not allowed to use that word any more?

(Mr Vaux) I think that is one of the things people are very much afraid of. What we would like to see is the emergence of the more traditional leadership and that external forces should back them

[**Chairman** *Contd*]

rather than doing a take-over situation by the UN, which would simply hold the lid on at best and then a conflict would emerge in a year or two when either the money runs out or people's attention goes elsewhere. So that is not really a solution.

(Mr Hopkins) I agree with Mr Vaux. I think the key has to be the UN working very closely with the clan leaders rather than some sort of superimposed structure which is not going to work politically. In the meantime, it is an interesting statistic—it is an estimate but probably not too far out—that even with 3,500 UN forces in Somalia they would be outnumbered 300 to one by armed men already in Somalia. In that context it is not an unreasonable thing to say 3,500 is probably inadequate. Yes, CARE takes no satisfaction in paying for security protection but it feels that it is justified in the context of the humanitarian relief programme that it and the other NGOs are involved in, but it is wrong in principle that an NGO should have to do this and there is no reason, if the NGO can actually do it from a practical point of view, why the UN could not do it, provided it was part of an overall strategy which involved some sort of introduction of a proper police force. There is no police force in Somalia; it is disbanded. Some of the security personnel who have been employed by the NGOs are, in fact, ex-police force officers, but it should be a high priority to plan the re-establishment of the police force, which might mean that the onus on the UN to build up protection forces within each clan area for the delivery of food might be less. Quite clearly, as long as NGOs are going on delivering relief supplies and needing protection, they will do what they have to do to safeguard the safety of their own staff, but I think one would like to see that scaled down in due course, provided there is something introduced under the auspices of the UN to replace it. I see nothing wrong, given the severity of the situation in Somalia, with the UN being seen to be instigating such arrangements without necessarily being responsible for the regime. This has to be done in conjunction with the clan leaders. Frankly, the only way, for the time being at least, that NGOs are going to be able to retain some security cover is by, as we do now, recruiting security personnel from the clans where they operate, where they are predominant. You cannot—and forgive me if it is saying the obvious—operate without protection from representatives of the clans in areas where other clans are in control. So that is why, as you probably gather, the NGOs have to switch crews from area to area in order to ensure some sort of continuity of protection. I see why this is regarded as being a fairly controversial state of affairs but it is a very extreme situation and I, for one, cannot think of another one quite like it.

Sir John Stanley

93. Again to help our understanding of the Somalian situation, could you tell us whether it is your judgment that Ambassador Sahnoun's resignation was precipitated because of a major difference in policy between him and whatever instructions he was getting from New York or did it come about simply because of his personal sense of frustration seeing the scale of the need that was there and his inability to get the UN system to deliver the goods? Was there a policy issue and if so can you shed any light as to what it was?

(Mr Hopkins) There appears to be a policy issue now if what he is quoted as saying is correctly attributable to him, in that he is now publicly saying things which are clearly at odds, from a policy point of view, from the line the UN has taken up to now. It would be wrong to suggest that has always been the problem. You would have to ask him in order to get a proper view on that. What is clear is that he was extremely frustrated at not being able to make progress because he did feel he was not being given the authority from New York, that he had to keep referring back to New York in order to make decisions. The communications between New York and Ambassador Sahnoun were clearly inadequate because there was evidence from time to time he did not know what was being said about the situation in Somalia by the UN in New York and perhaps, for all I know, they did not know what he was doing or saying at the same time. His frustration was borne of a commitment, which I think everyone who knows him applauded, which was to make a very substantial personal contribution. Quite clearly his removal from the scene is a very very sad loss. I think the answer to the question in all honesty has to be if he has always held the views that are attributed to him now then quite clearly there must have been a policy problem as well as practical difficulties in relation to communication and a lack of authority devolved from New York to the field.

Chairman: In a minute we want to come back to the agonies of running relief operations on the ground but Mr Gapes has another question.

Mr Gapes

94. I have one more question: if the UN is to get more involved militarily in conflicts like Somalia or elsewhere, is there not a danger that this could undermine its political mediation role between groups, clans, factions, whatever? From your experience on the ground would you like to comment on that question?

(Mr Vaux) Yes, I think the problem can be seen the other way round that in the past it has been a weakness of the UN that it has been too much aligned to the sovereign government. If we take the famine in Ethiopia in 1984/1985, the UN organised substantial assistance through the Ethiopian Government and did a good job generally and had a very good co-ordinator but it did nothing in Tigre and Eritrea, which were the worst areas of the famine, because they were under rebel control. The UN had no co-operation or communication with those rebel groups, as a result there was a massive humanitarian tragedy. I think we have to be prepared for situations like that on a

[**Mr Gapes** *Contd*]

much bigger scale now with the breakdown of nation states widely occurring in Africa and Eastern Europe and the Soviet Union, the definition of a sovereign state being much more difficult. There is a need for NGO assistance to reach the people in need regardless of the political situation. These are issues which again the British Government could usefully take up and try to find a solution to. I think the plea from humanitarian organisations like us is a solution must be found because otherwise we are left simply trying to deal with rebel groups with no security protection. With cross border operations into places which are theoretically illegal there is no protection from British diplomatic sources. For instance, our work in Northern Somalia, for several years we have not had any assistance from the British Government in terms of diplomatic cover because they have no clear position on the SNM in Northern Somalia. So everything we did there was entirely at our own risk even though it was funded by the ODA.

Mr Sumberg

95. Mr Aaronson talked about the great dangers which all of you and UN staff face in these situations. I wonder if you would like to give us your thoughts on the UN roles which apply here, whether you think they should be changed in relation to UN staff to remain in areas which are currently deemed to be dangerous and also so far as the specialised agencies are concerned could they really come out when there is a danger? What rules should apply? Should the UN be looking at this?

(Mr Vaux) Again this is a very very difficult question. I think one of the ways forward on this is to reduce the involvement of UN staff as such. Permanent UN staff could perhaps become the core of an operation and the actual staff working in countries like Somalia, doing the practical work, could be taken on for those special operations and taken on at their own risk. Obviously they would have to be compensated accordingly. I think the problem occurs when you want to transfer people from a safe place position in somewhere like the Seychelles to Mogadishu, they do not want to go. Then you get a farcical situation as happened in Somalia, where the UN offices were supposed to be in Mogadishu but for various reasons most of the staff were sited in Nairobi. They were earning enormous sums *per diem* but added nothing to the Somalian situation. This, according to the Africa Watch Report, has been one of the reasons why there has been a problem with a lack of UN presence in Mogadishu over the years.

(Mr Hopkins) It is a very tricky question. All I can say is how CARE operates. CARE understands it is asking its personnel working in Somalia at the present time to take certain unavoidable risks so there has to be contingency planning for dealing with certain situations. In Somalia, where the position is so volatile, you can get changes in different areas from day to day. You might have to evacuate one particular town one day and be able to go back in the next day. The plea I would make is that one person, and it has to be the person responsible for co-ordinating the operations on the ground, has to be given the authority to be able to press the evacuation button. CARE works in the following way, that in each of the 50 countries where it is operational it has a director who is responsible for all the personnel in that country and the country director is empowered to evacuate the staff if he or she feels the circumstances are such either from the country itself or from different areas within the country. That is an onerous responsibility to have but we feel it is the only way to do it because it is impossible to detect day to day affairs of that nature from New York, Geneva, London or anywhere else many thousands of miles away from where the situation is occurring.

(Mr Bowden) If I could go back to the original part of the question about the UN rules on security and whether it has hindered operations, in the chronology we prepared of events I think it is very clear from that that the UN security guidelines were being used certainly to stop UN personnel working in the country and, indeed, the UNDP resident representative stopped other staff from going in there, even when agencies such as UNICEF wanted to work there, so the rules are sadly lacking. But the other important issue to bear in mind is the security situation, and I think our concern at the time was that we were working there quite heavily. In fact, I was in Mogadishu in the first six months after Siad Barre fell and in Northern Somalia on and off and security was quite good in those days, certainly far better than it is now. So because the security was deemed by one particular person to be inadequate for UNICEF, they avoided early engagement in Somalia when security was far better than it is now. So it is as much a matter of assessment of a situation that is commonly shared and understood as well as the rules.

Chairman: We have already discussed quite a bit the question of running relief operations effectively and the co-ordination of UN agencies and there was a question about the resignation of Ambassador Sahnoun, but we would like to ask more detailed questions on the issue of delegation of authority.

Sir John Stanley

96. Could I, first of all, ask one point of clarification on the paper which I was not certain about. In the Save the Children paper there is a reference to the fact that the UNDP was refusing to release any resources for emergency work. I do not know whether that was general or in Somalia, but the CARE paper refers to the UNDP role in emergency work. Could you help reconcile those together, please?

(Mr Bowden) I think at the time that the Siad Barre government collapsed there was a vacuum and the UNDP were the lead agency, as always, and still had a country representative for Somalia, who had moved by that time to Nairobi. In his role as the head of the UN in Somalia he refused to release any moneys at that early stage. That

[**Sir John Stanley** *Contd*]
should not be confused with the fact that under the new Department of Humanitarian Affairs set-up they have involved UNDP and the UNDP representative is usually the lead person in emergencies. I think we are confusing the particular events in Somalia right after the collapse of Siad Barre and the general role that UNDP has within the emergency framework.

97. The central question I would like to ask is on the effectiveness of the UN operation as you see it as NGOs. The thrust of your papers is that there should be far greater delegation of real authority down into the UN staff in the country and particularly to the senior UN person in an individual country. Do you believe that within the UN as it is at present structured that is a realistic objective to try to go for or do you think that the diffusion of a multiplicity of separate organisations back in New York is always going to conspire fundamentally against having a strong single country UN director who is in a real position to co-ordinate UN operations?

(Mr Bowden) I think that at the moment is the case in Somalia but what I would like to clarify is the role of New York as opposed to the separate UN organisations. What we now see in Somalia is a structure which is the worst of both worlds, where we have a UN New York structure which is a Secretary General structure. In fact, there is a joke in Mogadishu about the UN warlords as opposed to the Somali warlords, because you will find each bit of the UN was represented under Ambassador Sahnoun, so that Marrack Goulding's section was represented and James Jonah's section was represented and they were in a sense all fighting for authority over, shall we say, the other UN agencies such as the World Food Programme, UNICEF and UNHCR, who have a separate line of command going back to Rome, Geneva or wherever, and it was that mismatch, I think, that has led to a very confusing situation within the whole structure. So in a sense there are two problems of co-ordination in that there is the UN Secretary General's office in New York and the various Under Secretary General's roles and the other UN agencies, and really the only way we see there being a solution is for the Department of Humanitarian Affairs or one central group agreeing to a centrally agreed plan to analyse the problem and then deploy the resources appropriate to meet it.

(Mr Vaux) Could I endorse very strongly what Mark has said. Firstly, yes, totally, these strong co-ordinators in country have worked very well when there have been such people. Unfortunately, some of them have been inappropriate people. So the quality of the person is also important, but then the issue of clear delegation of authority does seem to run right through the UN and is at the root of this difficulty you are referring to of mixed messages coming from New York, Rome and Geneva, because the messages are coming from all three. It is an intolerable position for any in-country representative of the UN and it is not surprising that Ambassador Sahnoun eventually resigned. I think the issue is clear delegation by the Secretary General to make sure that with a situation like Somalia people know who is in charge, so that, for instance, with Somalia he can say that Eliasson is in charge or Jonah is in charge but not that both are in charge or several other Under Secretaries General are in charge, which is the present state of affairs, unfortunately. The signs are that the Secretary General is not moving to clarify the relationships between those Under Secretaries General, and this is an area where we would think again the British Government could be active to insist that there is a clearer demarcation, that we learn something from Somalia and so, looking at this fiasco in retrospect, we should say which Under Secretary General should have total authority in this situation.

Chairman

98. Mr Vaux, in your OXFAM paper you draw attention to the problem of placing too much credibility upon the UN and creating an imbalance between demands placed upon it and resources available. We have heard Mr Hopkins' very clear statement on the Somalia scene that the resources approval from the United Kingdom was not a problem, but generally I think you are making a very much wider point that, as we sensed in this Committee in New York, huge new demands are pouring in on the UN and its agencies at every turn in the post-Cold War world and there are just not the personnel, the military or the cash to begin to address these. How do you see this imbalance being resolved?

(Mr Vaux) I think solutions to the problems we have been talking about are likely to cost a lot of money in pushing forward to a solution to the problem we are talking about, such as being in a position to intervene in an effective way in the future. That is going to cost money. I think we are also looking back then to the crises that have hit various UN organisations. I particularly remember the crisis that hit the UNHCR in 1989/90 when they almost had to stop feeding the refugees. So the British Government has allocated a significant and appreciable proportion of aid to UNHCR and other multilateral organisations. We are not particularly criticising Britain but Britain in its role as part of the world community should be active in ensuring that adequate resources are available and this may mean that, although within the aid budget as a whole, Britain's contribution to multilateral agencies is adequate, the totality of the aid budget, including multilateral agencies, may need to be increased if we are to deal satisfactorily with these massive humanitarian problems.

(Mr Hopkins) Yes, I agree with that. I would like to add that the impression one gets is that the bureaucracy itself is incredibly expensive, that coupled with the kind of initiative which Tony has advocated, there obviously needs to be a very thorough study of the methodology and cost-effective-

[**Chairman** *Contd*]

ness of the UN and its agencies. Any multinational company facing its shareholders with this kind of performance would have a public relations problem, and a real problem, I would have thought of gigantic proportions and probably would have called in management consultants many years ago. It is strange to us that these problems which have been apparent for some time do not appear to have been addressed and it appears that with some reorganisation and rationalisation greater use of existing resources could be made. NGOs themselves over the last few years, clearly most recently in the recessionary times, have had to review the way they operate to become more cost effective, why not the UN?

99. Mr Bowden do you want to add anything?

(Mr Bowden) We gave evidence to the Foreign Affairs Committee on the Horn of Africa where we were making the same points not least the fact time and again the issue is far more the effective deployment of resources the UN has rather than the fact there are not sufficient resources. Nobody would expect the United Nations or indeed the international community to solve all of Somalia's problems. They are looking for an effective intervention.

100. The impression we get as a Committee again and again is while multilateral aid may in theory be a good thing and beneficial to the British economy as a matter of fact when it comes to organisation and efficiency the multilateral organisations, indeed the EC as an organisation for aid giving, compare very unfavourably indeed with our own local administration here in London. It goes against the grain of dedicated officials to see aid put in their hands. That is a conundrum we have to somehow address. We have to focus on it. Could I come to the final question that is responsible for the theme which has been going through all our questions this morning. What can we do about making the UN and its agencies better co-ordinated between the two, better co-ordinated within the UN, within the various deputy under secretary-generals and so on and their departments? Is the Agenda for Peace idea the right way forward remembering that really says: "Let us make the Security Council more powerful". I am not sure whether we want to reform it but let us give it an enhanced role. How do you in the front line, as it were, the cutting edge in the NGOs view that kind of prospect and how do you think the NGOs are going to be given a better opportunity to feed their views into the UN organisation in a reformed state? Which of you would like to unburden yourself first?

(Mr Bowden) I will start unburdening myself. I think some of the points we have been making throughout are important. The first one to me, which I think Tony Vaux made earlier, which I find most important is the issue of accountability. There is a genuine lack of accountability within the United Nations' systems at all levels. I think Michael Aaronson was trying to make the same point in saying we get the United Nations we deserve. We have to participate fully in making them accountable. There have to be the structures, the UN has to be accountable not only to member states but actually to the people they are assisting. One of the great concerns I think in Somalia is aid is being, in a sense, done to the Somalians rather than with their active co-operation or involvement and that is perilous in terms of any long term solutions. The United Nations should also be accountable, as I hope all voluntary agencies are, to the benefits of assistance, that is sadly lacking. I think an improved accountability within the UN is a very key measure because from that we will get more effectiveness and with more effectiveness I think the UN will have more legitimacy. If you are seen to be running good and effective operations you create legitimacy, you do not get it just by your mandate. I see accountability as the critical area. The other thing which I think is important is the proper devolving of authority within the countries in a clearly understood way. This goes not just for the representative in the country but at lower levels as well. The whole structure is incredibly centralised, everything goes back to New York, Rome or Geneva from even Hargeisa in North West Somalia, everything has to go right the way back through the system and back down. That has to change, people have to be given more responsibility and in a sense they have to be trusted. The UN has to trust its own staff. If we bring in those two changes we will see a much enhanced system. While I share your view that the EC is perhaps less effective than ODA, it has started to move to devolve its own authority in the way other governments have and other institutions have. They have, for example, improved the lead time on food by allowing far more devolved authority so it does have benefits in large organisations to do that. There are benefits to be gained and I think the United Nations has to be shown that.

(Mr Vaux) I wholeheartedly agree with what Mark has said. There has to be accountability and reviewing of successes and failures and learning from them is very important and devolving. We can see there are certain parts of the UN where there is, for various reasons, devolved authority for the work such as early warning systems in the FAO or the emergency units in the WFP. There are these facilities and they are run by extremely able people. They do achieve something. This needs to go right the way through the system; at the moment it does not and everything is referred back and there is never any action and the planning which is done is just done on paper. Going back to the work of the Security Council, this is where I think the British Government should take very active steps and say the present situation of the world mechanisms for dealing with humanitarian crises is inadequate. It cannot just be left to the consideration of each case as it happens but there must be a real look at the right of the world, of the world's people to intervene when thousands or hundreds of thousands of people are dying somewhere and the government concerned is not in a position or does not wish to help. That is not acceptable. People in this country when they see that on the television say: "That is

[**Chairman** *Contd*]

just not acceptable." Something has to be done at the UN Security Council to make sure it does not happen again.

(Mr Hopkins) On that point I would agree and say there has to be an acceptance that the role of the United Nations inevitably is going to go beyond just peacekeeping, in being a referee, in protecting humanitarian aid at least, and that involves new challenges. There is clearly a role to play, as my colleague has said, for the British Government taking a lead there in advocating how that change might be achieved. The other point I would just like to finish on, as my colleagues have said during the morning, is that one of the problems is undoubtedly the calibre of staff deployed, particularly overseas, by UN agencies. We advocated in CARE's written evidence, limited use of rotating staff between headquarters and the field in order to equip staff who are then deployed to the field with an overall picture and indeed to have people in headquarters who have that benefit of field experience. We, the NGOs, find that ability to exchange personnel is extremely beneficial in terms of operational efficiency and co-ordination and one would like to see that as a human resource policy followed more vigorously by the UN agencies rather than putting people in slots for reasons which have nothing to do with their expertise or the needs of the jobs in question. So expertise on the ground, which his what is needed, and indeed further awareness at headquarters' level of the further problems on the ground, can only be helped by such a policy of rotation.

Mr Wareing

101. On this question of utilising the expertise of NGOs, is there anything to be said in any reform of the United Nations' organisation for, as it were, institutionalising the connections between the NGOs and the United Nations? I am thinking in terms of some sort of advisory council that might be there at the disposal, at all times, of the United Nations without necessarily adding to the cost burden of the UN? You are there already on site, as it were, you can communicate, allow the information to go to New York through some sort of advisory council. I do not know whether that would cut across the traditional role of non-governmental organisations but what is your view on that?

(Mr Vaux) There are meetings called every now and again, liaison meetings between the UN and NGOs, and our experience is that they are very unsatisfactory kinds of meetings because there is no clear agenda; there is nothing specific on the table; it is just talk about the general relationship. Far more effective are meetings when there is a crisis, when there is a real issue to be discussed, such as what to do in Somalia, then to have a meeting when it is clear to everybody round the table that there is an issue to be discussed and a possibility of using the meeting in order to make a conclusion. Too many of the UN/NGO meetings are purely for form's sake and sharing of information, not really involvement and decision-making. The other aspect of UN/NGO co-ordination is that some of the UN organisations have made moves to try and make contracts with NGOs to take on certain sectors of their activity. This is an interesting development. We have not actually gone down this track ourselves in OXFAM, because we are afraid that we would simply become a part of the UN, that what we do would be, as it were, diluted by this connection. We feel they could do their job working closely with us, but we should keep our independence and integrity so that we are able to do the things we can do well as best we can rather than fit into their system. This has been going on in the past but certainly some organisations have made closer links in that way.

Mr Gapes

102. I would like to ask about the UNHCR. Some of the things that have been said today are quite strong criticisms, and in some of the papers. Would you say that situation has improved since Mrs Ogata was appointed? Specifically, I heard a reference to the UNHCR operation in the Shia areas of Iraq and I would like your comments on that?

(Mr Bowden) It is a very difficult one. I think Mrs Ogata has made a difference to the UNHCR in overall policy levels but I think that there is still a major problem within UNHCR in terms of being able to improve its technical expertise and effectiveness. Certainly its operations in the Horn of Africa show no signs of improvement. Refugees in Kenya are facing the same problems as refugees in Ethiopia or Somalia have faced over the last ten years in terms of delivery of services to them and basic protection rights. So from the ground it does not look a great deal different.

(Mr Vaux) Can I say on this issue of improvement, the way you phrased it is interesting. You ask, has Mrs Ogata improved the UNHCR. In a way it should not be the leader of the organisation, his or her characteristics, as to whether an organisation is good or bad and UN agencies are viewed in this way because they are so top-heavy and depend on the leadership. A good leader in any UN organisation is almost invisible, is one who has devolved authority and is not visible in that way. In fact, Mrs Ogata is behind some of them and probably the improvements are attributable to that.

Chairman: The time has gone on and you have been extremely illuminating in what you have had to say this morning, very clear, and we are extremely grateful. You have been, while critical of some areas, on the whole constructive and, in your personal view, rooted in realism in what you are doing, which is all the more remarkable when you are facing such appalling challenges. I do, on behalf of the Committee, thank all three of you and Mr Aaronson for your time and effort and, of course, for the continuing work you do in your immensely valuable organisations. Thank you very much indeed.

Printed in the United Kingdom for HMSO.
Dd.5060558, 1/93, C5, 3398/3B, 5673, 225992.

ISBN 0-10-283493-8

9 780102 834932

HOUSE OF COMMONS SESSION 1992–93

FOREIGN AFFAIRS COMMITTEE

THE EXPANDING ROLE OF THE UNITED NATIONS AND ITS IMPLICATIONS FOR UK POLICY

MINUTES OF EVIDENCE

Wednesday 2 December 1992

FOREIGN AND COMMONWEALTH OFFICE

Rt Hon Douglas Hogg, MP, Mr T Aust, Mr W Patey, Mr S Bridges, Ms T Holland and Ms J Douglas

---

Ordered by The House of Commons *to be printed*
2 December 1992

LONDON: HMSO
£11.00 net

235–iii

WEDNESDAY 2 DECEMBER 1992

Members present:

Mr David Howell, in the Chair

Mr Dennis Canavan
Mr Mike Gapes
Mr David Harris
Mr Peter Shore
Sir John Stanley
Mr David Sumberg
Mr Robert N Wareing

Memorandum submitted by the Foreign and Commonwealth Office

INTRODUCTION

The Foreign Affairs Committee has requested further evidence from the Foreign and Commonwealth Office on the expanding role of the United Nations in the form of answers to a list of questions.

FINANCE

1. Could the FCO provide the Committee with a memorandum on the funding of the UN? This would include a detailed breakdown of all assessed and voluntary contributions to the UN, to peacekeeping operations and to UN agencies, together with details of the contributions by other countries to the UN (including information about arrears) and to peacekeeping operations.

Answer

A separate memorandum has been prepared.[1]

2. Will HMG be agreeing to the UN Secretary-General's recommendations for financing future peacekeeping operations set out in para 73 of "Agenda for Peace"? If not, what alternative proposals will HMG be making?

Answer

The key to financing peace-keeping operations is for States to pay their assessments in full and on time. In addition, the UK, together with the other Members of the EC, fully supports the Secretary-General's idea of establishing a Peacekeeping Reserve fund. The cost of UN peacekeeping has increased to more than $3 billion in 1992 and there is now undoubtably a case for increasing the reserves available to cover expenditure in the period between launching new operations and the collection of assessed contributions.

3. On what grounds did HMG agree to pay the costs of the British military contribution to UNPROFOR II? Does HMG expect this arrangement to continue beyond the end of the initial 12 month period of deployment?

Answer

The Secretary-General announced in Plenary of the London Conference on former Yugoslavia on 27 August that:

"It is my intention to submit to the Security Council . . . a report recommending that UNPROFOR's mandate and strength be enlarged to enable it to provide (this) support to UNHCR-organised convoys delivering food and essential supplies in all parts of Bosnia Hercegovina. Discussions continue with a number of Member States who have expressed a readiness to contribute military personnel . . . for this expansion of UNPROFOR's operations. I am asking Member States to provide such contributions at no cost to the United Nations".

We responded to the Secretary-General's call to Member States to provide troops to UNPROFOR in Bosnia without seeking UN reimbursement (which normally totals some US $1,000 per man per month and therefore represents only a small percentage of the costs incurred).

We have always made clear to both the United Nations and our fellow troop contributors that our military contribution to this operation will be reviewed after one year. This remains our position. It is impossible to predict what financing arrangements may apply to the operation after this time.

[1]See supplementary memorandum, p.62.

The cost of printing and publishing these Minutes of Evidence is estimated by HMSO at £6,912.

PEACEKEEPING AND PEACEMAKING

4. What factors did HMG take into account in replying to the Secretary-General's questionnaire to member states concerning their possible earmarked contributions to UN peacekeeping operations? Did HMG consult with other members of the Permanent Five or the European Community before submitting their response?

Answer

The Secretary-General's questionnaire was circulated in 1990; there are no plans for an update. The UN now prefer to conduct bilaterals with Member States on their possible contributions.

When we submitted our response to the Secretary-General's questionnaire on Requirements for UN Peacekeeping Operations it was covered by the statement that:

"Given existing national commitments it is not possible for the United Kingdom to state, even in principle, that we would be able to make available specified manpower for UN Peacekeeping operations. We would however consider any request from the UN for such assistance..."

We remain in close touch with our P5 colleagues on all aspects of UN Peacekeeping which are dealt with in the Security Council. The EC has made a series of common statements in the Special Committee on Peacekeeping and set out their ideas most recently in the Foreign Secretary's speech at UNGA commenting on Agenda for Peace.

5. The British Permanent Representative to the UN, Sir David Hannay, told the Committee that the Secretary General realises that the issue of peace enforcement is "something that will have to be debated rather carefully and discussed and cannot be dealt with in a great hurry". Does this attitude encourage the Government in its cautious approach to these issues? Is HMG's attitude to peace-enforcement units (Agenda for Peace, paragraph 44) shared by other Security Council members?

Answer

So far as we can judge there is little or no support among other Security Council members or more widely among the UN membership for the idea of peace enforcement units. The view that the issue is one which will require a great deal of thought before it can be pursued further is widely held.

6. Will HMG continue to support the continued presence of UN peacekeeping operation in Cambodia if the Khmer Rouge move from non-participation in the forthcoming elections to a campaign of violence and intimidation?

Answer

The UN Transitional Authority in Cambodia (UNTAC) is mandated to stay in Cambodia until a new government is formed, that is, three months after elections, which are due to take place in April/May 1993. UNTAC's present role is based on the assumption that all parties co-operate in implementing the Paris agreements. It is too early to say what adjustments might be made should the Khmer Rouge continue to refuse to co-operate.

PREVENTIVE DIPLOMACY

7. What measures can be taken to strengthen preventive diplomacy? What role does HMG see the regional organisations playing in preventive diplomacy?

Answer

Individual states, General Assembly and the Secretary-General could all make greater use of existing rights under the Charter to draw to the attention of the Security Council any potential conflict. In particular, the Secretary-General might make greater use of his powers under Article 99 of the Charter to draw to the attention of the Security Council situations which might pose a threat to international peace and security. The Secretary-General could also make more use of fact-finding missions and of his good offices to defuse points of tension, and where appropriate to make direct contact between the parties. This is already happening, for example in Moldova, Nagorny-Karabakh and Georgia. The UNSG has now proposed to the Council a deployment of UN observers in Macedonia; this would be the first time there has been such a pre-emptive deployment.

There are discussions in New York about the preventive deployment of monitors/observers at the request of the government or all parties, to help with humanitarian assistance or help defuse tension. This should also be considered on a case-by-case basis. The despatch of monitors to South Africa by the

United Nations, EC and the Commonwealth, is one precedent, the European Community Monitoring Mission in the former Yugoslavia another.

The spread of democratic values itself is also a form of preventive action to cultivate an atmosphere in which conflicts are solved by dialogue rather than force. Promotion of good government and the use of election monitors are useful tools of preventive diplomacy.

Greater co-ordination between United Nations and regional organisations is a crucial part of more effective diplomacy, whether it be in sharing information on likely trouble spots or the provision of monitors. Regional organisations could themselves do more to take preventive action to stop disputes deteriorating.

8. What methods does HMG consider can be employed to assess whether and when internal conflicts are likely to require international dimensions?

Answer

The Secretary-General is already making greater use of fact-finding missions to ensure that action taken by the Security Council or by the Secretary-General under Article 99 of the Charter is based on the fullest possible understanding of a situation. Member States could also provide the Secretary-General with information on issues of concern. There is also room for a strengthening of the departments of the Secretariat responsible for information gathering and analysis.

HUMANITARIAN ISSUES

9. Does HMG agree that the UN should be ready in principle to involve itself in humanitarian relief inside countries where internal conflict is threatened or maybe taking place?

Answer

The principle of provision of relief by the UN in areas of internal conflict is well established. The UN is increasingly acting upon that principle. We support both the principle of such intervention in cases of extreme humanitarian need, and the relief operations of this type in which the UN is involved. In former Yugoslavia the UNHCR has been delivering relief to areas affected by internal conflict in Bosnia-Herzegovina since the middle of this year—first by airlift to Sarajevo and more recently in a large scale road convoy operation. Such relief operations can (for example: in former Yugoslavia, Somalia) be supported by units of UN troops mandated to provide protection. Elsewhere (for example: Afghanistan) the UN humanitarian agencies are operating in conflict areas *without* military protection. We have demonstrated our support for such UN operations by financial assistance and, in the case of military protected operations by our provision of British troops for protection duties, (for example: Iraq, former Yugoslavia).

10. What factors will influence HMG in deciding whether or not to support the UN's actual involvement in specific cases?

Answer

Each humanitarian emergency arises from different causes and has different characteristics. Our policy is to consider each emergency on a case-by-case basis. This clearly involves evaluating carefully the circumstances of the emergency and possible action, both nationally and within the UN. In the case of complex emergencies, particularly those in areas of internal conflict, any decision endorsing UN action will almost invariably involve consideration within the UN Security Council. If we believe nationally that the circumstances of a specific emergency warrant UN involvement we will support such action in the Security Council and work to ensure the UN response is the right one. But we took the lead in encouraging the UN to develop the concept of *protective support* for humanitarian assistance operations in Bosnia.

11. What criteria does the government employ in assessing whether the level of suffering caused by a man-made disaster is such as to justify intervention in a sovereign state?

Answer

We do not have a formal set of criteria to apply in assessing whether or not the level of suffering in a particular emergency justifies intervention for humanitarian purposes. We examine each emergency carefully on a case-by-case basis. It would be wrong to try to set parameters for human suffering. The application of a set of criteria would inhibit the decision making process and limit the flexibility of our response. We firmly believe that the nature of the response should be matched to the scale of the problem. It was on this basis that we deployed troops to Northern Iraq last year and again during the current crisis in former Yugoslavia.

12. Does HMG regard it as essential that it should only intervene in another country when invited to do so by the government of that country? Was this principle breached in the case of the Iraq Kurds? Might the case of Kosovo pose the question in an acute form?

Answer

We believe that international intervention *without* the invitation of the government of the country concerned can be justified in cases of extreme humanitarian need. This is why we were prepared to commit British forces to Operation Haven, mounted by the Coalition in response to the refugee crisis involving the Iraqi Kurds. The deployment of these forces was entirely consistent with the objectives of SCR 688. In the case of Kosovo it is not possible at this stage to predict how events will unfold and whether any humanitarian operation under UN auspices will be necessary. As in all volatile humanitarian situations we shall watch developments closely and make decisions commensurate with the need.

HUMAN RIGHTS

13(a). What specific action has HMG taken in recent years in support of the UN's work in the field of human rights?

The UK is actively involved in all United Nations human rights bodies, particularly the *Third Committee of the UN General Assembly* and the *UN Commission on Human Rights (CHR)* to which we were re-elected in 1991 after a one year absence. In this year's Commission, we tabled or co-sponsored a total of thirty-two resolutions on human rights issues, most in conjunction with EC partners. We also play an active role in the Third Committee of the UNGA where, last year, we tabled or co-sponsored a total of seventeen human rights resolutions. The UK is also represented on the *Sub-Commission on the Prevention of Discrimination and the Protection of Minorities* and on two of the Treaty Monitoring Bodies, the expert supervisory bodies established pursuant to human rights treaties adopted within the UN system.

The UK makes annual alternating financial contributions to the UN *Advisory Services Voluntary Fund* and the *Voluntary Fund for Victims of Torture*. A new *Human Rights Policy Unit* was established in June 1992 to co-ordinate human rights policy within the Foreign and Commonwealth Office. This will ensure that the UK continues to play a prominent role in supporting the UN's work in the field of human rights.

13(b). Would HMG wish to see the UN playing a more prominent role in this area, and if so what steps will HMG be taking to try to bring this about?

Answer

Yes. HMG attaches considerable importance to the role of the UN in the field of human rights, in particular to improve the implementation of existing human rights instruments and in assisting countries in fulfilling their international human rights obligations. We shall play an active role in the *World Conference on Human Rights* to be held in Vienna in June next year. The Conference will address the problems of the implementation of existing human rights instruments, and explore ways of improving them.

We have and will continue to press, in appropriate UN fora, for measures to enable the UN human rights machinery to react swiftly to human rights crises. We are also pressing for increased resources from within existing UN budgetary constraints to be allocated to the human rights programme which is currently operating under severe strain. In particular we recognise the need for extra resources for the UN Centre for Human Rights to allow it to function effectively.

14. What criteria does HMG take into account when deciding whether to support intervention to safeguard human rights?

Answer

The appointment of a *Special Rapporteur* to investigate alleged human rights abuses in a particular country (eg Iraq), or a particular theme (for example, torture), is the *optimum action* within the UN human rights machinery. Before formulating a position on any resolution calling for the appointment of a Special Rapporteur HMG will take into account the *human rights record* of the country concerned, any *evidence of consistent and severe abuses* of human rights and the reaction of the government concerned to previous criticism of their human rights policy by the UN, individual governments and Non Governmental Organisations. Other considerations, including the state of the bilateral relationship, will also be a factor.

During the past three years the UK and other EC member states, have co-sponsored several resolutions on both country situations and thematic issues. These include, Iraq, Iran, Cuba, Burma, Former Yugoslavia, China/Tibet, East Timor, Romania, Afghanistan, Haiti, Israeli settlements in the occupied Arab territories, Disappearances, Summary & Arbitrary Executions, Ethnic Cleansing, Economic, Social and Cultural Rights, International Covenants, Convention on the Rights of the Child, Religious Intolerance.

15. What contributions has HMG made to the monitoring of elections by the UN?

Answer

In addition to the assessed financial contribution to large scale operations (which include election monitoring) for example, UNAVEM in Angola or UNTAG in Namibia, the UK has also donated £200,000 to the UN's new voluntary fund for electoral verification, money which will be used for the forthcoming UN electoral verification mission to the Eritrean Referendum. This is the biggest donation so far. UK observers also formed part of UNAVEM and UNTAG. We will consider sympathetically any requests for election observers to the UN operations in the Western Sahara (MINURSO) and Cambodia (UNTAC).

SECONDMENT OF UK SERVICE PERSONNEL

16. What service personnel have so far been seconded by HMG to which departments in the UN Secretariat and are any further secondments planned?

Answer

We have seconded two officers for successive six month periods to the Logistics Section and one for a nine month period to the Finance and Budgets Section, both departments of the Field Operations Division in the UN Secretariat. We have also sent a number of officers on short term secondments to the Secretariat to assist in the planning of major new operations (for example, UNPROFOR in former-Yugoslavia and UNTAC in Cambodia).

Serving officers have also been seconded to the United Nations High Commission for Refugees to work in the Air Operations Cell and to head the Convoy Planning Cell, both in Geneva, and to the Office of the Special Envoy in Zagreb.

In addition to these secondments, which will continue for as long as the costs can be met, Brigadier Paddy Blagden, a retired Royal Engineer, has become the UN's first full time adviser on mine clearance, working within the Department of Peacekeeping Affairs.

The UN Secretariat increasingly sees the need to reinforce the Military Adviser's Office during the critical planning and deployment phases of new operations by requesting short and medium term secondments from Member States. We stand ready to respond positively to such requests as often as we are able.

17. Has the UN secretariat requested service personnel with any specific expertise and if so, what?

Answer

The UN Secretariat have asked Member States to second military officers with specialist expertise in the following disciplines: building and works, transport, communications, supply, logistic operations, administration, budget and property. The UK currently provides a Royal Navy Lieutenant Commander (Supply) as Chief of the Logistics Unit and a Major (Accountant) from the Adjutant General's Corps as a Budgetary Planner in the Finance and Budget Section. Both officers fill specialist appointments, which the UN has requested the UK to fill. We intend to replace both at the end of their respective current 6 and 9 month secondments respectively.

NUCLEAR AND OTHER ARMAMENTS

18. The Committee was informed by the Russian Permanent Representative to the UN that, in addition to Russia, three other CIS states, Kazakhstan, Ukraine and Belarus, may have retained nuclear weapons under their control in their respective territories. Does HMG agree with this assessment and, if so, what steps is it taking to try to prevent this further proliferation of nuclear weapons?

Answer

Since the break-up of the Soviet Union, nuclear weapons have remained in four countries: Russia, Ukraine, Belarus and Kazakhstan. Arrangements for the control of these weapons were agreed between members of the Commonwealth of Independent States (CIS) in Minsk in December 1991. Former Soviet nuclear weapons are now under the unified command of the CIS strategic forces. Decisions affecting their use are a matter for the Russian authorities, in agreement with the leaders of Ukraine, Belarus and Kazakhstan, and after consultation with other CIS members.

Ukraine, Kazakhstan and Belarus have made clear commitments to the removal of all remaining nuclear weapons from their territories, and to accession to the Non-Proliferation Treaty as non-nuclear weapon states. In our contacts with all three countries we have welcomed these commitments and have emphasised that their full implementation will be essential to continuing the development of good relations with these countries.

19. In what forum are the western powers attempting to control and help destroy the nuclear and conventional weapons of the former Soviet Union, and by what means can his problem best be settled in HMG's view?

Answer

As regards nuclear weapons, we consider that the solution to this problem lies in the safe and rapid implementation of nuclear arms control agreements in the former Soviet Union. We and our NATO allies are working closely together to provide technical and material assistance with the elimination of nuclear weapons due for destruction. These efforts are co-ordinated in NATO's Ad Hoc Group on Nuclear Weapons in the Former Soviet Union, which met most recently on 16 November.

On conventional weapons, states in the area of the former Soviet Union west of the Urals are parties to Conventional Armed Forces in Europe Treaty (CFE), which was provisionally applied from July 1992 and entered fully into force in November. The Treaty lays down precise methods and timescales for the reduction of Treaty-limited equipment to residual levels which come into effect 40 months after entry into force.

20. What lessons for the future of arms control and monitoring can be learned from the experience of the UN Special Commission in disarming Iraq?

Answer

There are essentially two principal lessons for other multilateral verification regimes. First, there are many practical lessons on the conduct of inspections, such as organisation, team composition, logistical support and establishing teams in a short period which would be applicable in any future repeat of the UNSCOM experience. This body of experience will be invaluable. The pitfalls and mistakes that were made can be avoided. The second, and the most important lesson is that the unprecedented inspection powers were only possible because of Iraq's defeat in the Gulf War. Iraq was seen as an aggressor power which posed a serious threat to regional security. This ensured that there was no difficulty in securing passage of SCR 687. Whilst many states, especially in the Third World, may have been a little wary about the powers being conferred on the Commission, Iraq's behaviour overcame any doubts. There were initially two members of the Security Council who were ready to side with Iraq—Yemen and Cuba—but they were in the minority.

Nevertheless Third World states are cautious about accepting that the intrusive powers available to UNSCOM should be repeated in any multilateral treaty. Thus any repetition of the UNSCOM/IAEA process will have to be either case-specific, or linked to an identifiable process. It would also need to be supported by the authority of a mandatory Security Council Resolution.

21. In the light of the International Atomic Energy Agency's experience in Iraq, how does HMG consider that IAEA safeguards procedures could be strengthened?

The revelations about Iraq's extensive covert nuclear weapons programme highlighted the need to strengthen verification procedures which are vital to confidence in the NPT. The United Kingdom, together with European partners, has proposed a series of measures to strengthen IAEA safeguards. Two of these, support for "special inspections" and early provision of design information on nuclear installations have been approved by the Agency's Board of Governors. Special inspections allow the Agency, in states with comprehensive safeguards agreements, to inspect sites other than those formally declared as containing nuclear material. Of course conducting such inspections is a sensitive matter. The Board's reaffirmation that the Agency does have the right to conduct them is a step which will help make it more difficult for a state party to the NPT to follow Iraq's example.

The UK, once again with European partners, is pursuing other voluntary improvements designed to provide the IAEA with greater information on transfers of nuclear materials, nuclear equipment and specialised non-nuclear materials.

THE UN ACTING AS GOVERNMENT

22. While in New York, the Committee gained the impression that the UN could more and more find itself acting as the effective government of fragmenting countries, such as Somalia. How does HMG view this substantial expansion of the UN's role?

Answer

Somalia is an almost unique case of a country without any form of effective government. The only similar situation is Cambodia, where UNTAC is taking over much of the administration of the country during the implementation of the Paris agreements. At the moment, these are unusual cases. We cannot unfortunately rule out similar situations arising in future. The UN may well have a role to play in helping restore or establish public administration and democratic institutions. But there are also constraints on the UN taking on this more interventionist role both in terms of the potential financial burden, and the provisions of the Charter as well as the attitude of other member states.

Supplementary Memorandum submitted by the Foreign & Commonwealth Office

UN FINANCE

INTRODUCTION

The UN and the organisations of the UN system are financed through a mixture of assessed and voluntary contributions. Assessed contributions represent a compulsory and legally binding obligation on Member States for the UN Regular Budget and for Peacekeeping activities. There are assessed contributions also to the Specialised Agencies. As a general rule operational activities by the UN in areas such as humanitarian and development assistance rely on voluntary contributions, while administrative costs are met through assessment. In 1990 the last year for which figures are available, total assessed contributions to the UN system as a whole were $2.6 Billion, while voluntary contributions $3.45 Billion. This memorandum concentrates on assessed contributions to the UN regular Budget and Peacekeeping Operations, although Annex A includes the voluntary contributions made by the UK in 1991 and Annex B indicates the major contributors/debtors to a number of the Specialised Agencies.

UN REGULAR BUDGET

The UN regular budget is set on a biennial basis and is financed by contributions from the Member States according to a sliding scale of assessments calculated on an individual country's capacity to pay (Annex C). It is current practice to measure capacity to pay in terms of the average national income of Member States over a ten year base period (1981–1990). The UN Statistical Office circulates an annual questionnaire to Member States for completion and return. About 90 per cent of Member States complete the questionnaires regularly. The Statistical Office collects published figures from the International Financial Institutes such as the IMF and IBRD for calculating the average national income of those states that do not complete the return.

The Scale is computed by the Committee on Contributions (CCONTS) using as a base point the national income statistics, but including such factors as low per capita income, debt burden, reliance on single crops and/or foreign exchange etc. In addition CCONTS apply a scheme of limits to ensure that member states' assessments do not fluctuate excessively due to changes in their respective capacities to pay. This preliminary working scale, after applying the ceiling and floor rates of 25 per cent and 0.01 per cent respectively is then "mitigated", that is, adjusted on the basis of mutual agreements between individual countries to take account of any perceived anomalies, to provide the final "capacity to pay" scale of assessments.

In addition to the regular budget scale there is also the ad hoc special scale for Peacekeeping where Developing Countries pay one-fifth or one-tenth of their regular rate while the Five Permanent Members bear a compensating surcharge (Annex D). The UK thus pays 6.102 per cent for peacekeeping as opposed to 5.02 per cent on the regular budget scale; France pays 7.293 per cent as opposed to 6 per cent and the USA 30.387 per cent as against 25 per cent.

UK POLICY ON THE FINANCING OF THE UN

During the 1970's the UN budget underwent a period of compound real growth which resulted in pressure from the major contributors to reform the budget process. Agreement was reached in 1986 to work for consensus on the content and level of the Regular Budget. This has made it easier to uphold the policy of Zero-Real Growth, backed by the other major contributors, (ZRG) under which new activities, mandated by the General Assembly, have to be financed either from a small contingency fund, by redeployment of existing resources or by deferment to another biennium.

ZRG has been the corner-stone of the UK's policy toward the financing of the United Nations and its Specialised Agencies for some ten years. It has proved to be the best tool available to the major contributors in controlling expenditure. Its consistent application across the system has served to put an end to the high rates of real growth, and has we believe, helped force greater transparency in the budgets of the organisations, induced improved efficiency and has given some impetus towards developing more rational priorities among programmes.

UN budget estimates are closely scrutinised by the Advisory Committee on Administrative and Budgetary Questions (ACABQ) which reports to the Member States in the General Assembly. The ACABQ has 16 members who serve in an individual capacity. Apart from the years 1980–83 and 1986–90, there has always been a British member. The UN accounts are audited by a Board consisting of the Auditors-General of three Member States. The Western member of the Board is currently Sir J Bourn in his capacity as Comptroller and Auditor General.

PAYMENT OF CONTRIBUTIONS

The UK endeavours to pay its assessed contributions promptly to both the Regular Budget and to the Peacekeeping accounts and we encourage other UN Members to do the same. Our contribution to the Regular Budget is made in two tranches. The first instalment is made in January the start of the UN Financial Year, the second in the first week in April, the start of our financial year. The UK is in addition, almost fully up to date on its contributions to the cost of UN Peacekeeping operations. In the financial year (1 April–31 March) 1991/92, UK contributed over £250 Million to the United Nations. (Full details at Annex A)

THE CURRENT CRISIS

The Secretary-General stated in his recent report on the work of the United Nations that "The financial resources of the Organisation are under acute strain". While adequate funding is agreed for both the UN Regular and Peacekeeping budgets, in practice some of the major contributors do not pay in full and on time in keeping with their obligations and have accumulated substantial arrears. The cash flow problems arising from late or non payment of assessed contributions affect the efficient planning and funding of UN operations, whether at UN Headquarters or UN Peacekeeping Operations in the field. At the end of October 1992, the unpaid contributions to the UN regular budget totalled $576 Million (details at Annex C). If the arrears to peacekeeping operations are added the total debt to the Organization is approximately $1.25 Billion. Put another way, at 31 October 1992 the arrears to the regular budget amounted to 55.5 per cent of the net annual expenditure, with 93 Member States in arrears. The major debtors are listed in Annex E. US arrears are a particular problem because their share represents 25 per cent of the UN Regular Budget, and over 30 per cent to Peacekeeping.

The US Administration under President Bush made very real efforts to pay off their accumulated arrears. The US recently paid $229 Million to the Regular Budget and approx $100 Million to various Peacekeeping accounts. They could pay a further $56.4 Million to the Regular Budget by the end of December. In addition Congress has appropriated $376 Million for Peacekeeping payments for US Financial Year 1993. Additional funds for regular budget and peacekeeping arrears will also be made available during the course of next Financial Year.

The Russian Federation also propose paying $130 Million of their arrears, primarily to the regular budget, before the end of their current Financial Year (31 March 1993), and a further $30 Million to their arrears for UNESCO and The International Atomic Energy Authority.

POSSIBLE SOLUTIONS

A number of proposals have been made to improve the situation, from the offer of incentives to member states that pay on time to interest charges for those that pay late. Under one particular scheme, the UN Secretariat would include in the UN Regular Budget a sum representing the additional costs to the Organisation resulting from late payments. Those Member States that paid on time would receive a discount from their assessment based on these additional costs; those paying late would however be liable for payment of the relevant proportion of the additional costs.

Although this scheme has merit and is similar to the successful schemes already employed in a number of the UN Specialized Agencies, suitable caveats would need to be included to safeguard the interest of states such as UK, Japan etc that pay promptly but in line with their own domestic appropriation provisions and budgetary cycles.

There have also been a number of emergency and alternative financing suggestions put forward by the Secretary-General and others, such as commercial borrowing, borrowing from the International Financial Institutions, levies on arms sales and air travel, worldwide lotteries etc. We do not favour these ideas as they are all open to the objection that they would increase the burden on the tax-payers and Governments of Member States that pay on time and in full without offering any guarantee that the performance of others will improve.

The Secretary-General, following presentation of his report "Agenda for Peace" and in conjunction with the Ford Foundation, has recently established an International Advisory Group to assess current arrangements for financing United Nations operations and to recommend improvements to them. The Group is co-chaired by Mr Paul Volcker, Chairman of James D Wolfenson Inc and former chairman of the US Federal Reserve and Shijuro Ogata, retired Deputy Governor of the Japan Development Bank and husband of Mrs Sadako Ogata UN High Commissioner for Refugees. The UK representative is Sir D Scholey, Chairman of Warburg Group. We await completion of the Group's report and any recommendations the Secretary-General may make.

Our position is clear that the major requirement is for Member States to pay promptly and in full as this alone will allow the UN to successfully carry out its mandated functions.

ANNEX A

Assessed Contributions	*Financial year 91/92*	*Calendar year 1991 (£)*
United Nations Regular Budget	26,549,477	25,598,167
World Health Organisation (WHO)	8,358,000	8,358,000
Food and Agriculture Organisation (FAO)	9,510,909	9,510,909
International Labour Organisation (ILO)	5,613,019	5,613,019
International Atomic Energy Agency (IAEA)	4,930,000	4,930,000
International Telecommunications Union (ITU)	–	1,789,000
International Civil Aviation Organisation (ICAO)	*2,129,520	*1,155,285
International Fund for Agricultural Development (IFAD)	2,300,000	2,400,000
International Red Cross (IRC)	8,060,000	10,360,000
League of Red Cross Sources (LRCS) now (IFRCS)	275,000	308,000
World Meteorological Organisation (WMO)	1,107,744	1,107,744
World Intellectual Property Organisation (WIPO)	–	480,000
Universal Postal Union (UPU)	623,476	1,277,060
United Nations Industrial Development Organisation (UNIDO)	2,709,000	–
International Maritime Organisation (IMO)	457,355	457,355
Permanent Court of Arbitration (PCA)	7,699	7,699
Committee for the Elimination of Racial Discrimination (CERD)	3,500	3,000
UN Committee Against Torture (UNCAT/UNCOT)	73,400	12,000
United Nations Observer Mission in El Salvador (ONUSAL)	456,293	456,293
United Nations Observers in Central America (ONUCA) (now terminated)	478,279	829,402
United Nations interim Force in Lebanon (UNIFIL)	5,259,314	–
United Nations Disengagement Observer Force (UNDOF)	1,384,371	–
United Nations Force in Cyprus (UNFICYP)	28,300,000	–
United Nations Iraq/Kuwait Observer Mission (UNIKOM)	*2,000,000	*2,000,000
United Nations Protection Force (Yugoslavia) (UNPROFOR)	Op started Feb 92	
United Nations Transitional Authority Cambodia (UNTAC)	7,164,103	
United Nations Advance Mission in Cambodia (UNAMIC)	1,166,839	
United Nations Angola Verification Mission (UNAVEM II)	1,600,000	1,600,000
United Nations Mission for the Referendum in Western Sahara (MINURSO)	8,265,226	–
TOTAL (A)		

*Exchange rate £1–$1.75

Voluntary Contributions	*Financial year 91/92*	*Calendar year 1991 (£)*
United Nations Force in Cyprus (UNFICYP)	28,243,272	
United Nations Development Programme (UNDP)	28,500,000	28,500,000
United Nations High Commission for Refugees (UNHCR)	30,513,000	29,276,000
United Nations Children's Fund (UNICEF)	12,857,000	13,718,000
United Nations Relief and Works Agency (UNRWA)	6,000,000	6,000,000
United Nations Border Relief Organisation (UNBRO)	470,000	484,000
International Fund for Agricultural Development (IFAD)	500,000	–
International Telecommunication Union (ITU) Conference Expenses (every 4 yrs)	–	–
WHO Human Reproduction Programme		2,550,000
WHO Onchocerciasis Research		900,000
WHO International Agency for Research in Cancer (DES)	535,000	
WHO and UNDP Tropical Diseases Programme		900,000
WHO International Programme on Chemical Safety	312,000	312,000
WHO-PAHO Caribbean Epidemiology Centre		226,000
WHO Cold Chain Support Immunisation Programme		70,000
WHO Action Programme on Essential Drugs and Vaccines		400,000
WHO Programme for Prevention and Control of AIDS		4,650,000
WHO Diarrhoeal Diseases Control		450,000
WHO Substance Abuse		200,000
WHO Acute Respiratory Infection Centre		200,000
General Agreement on Tariffs and Trade (GATT)	1,941,254	1,941,254
Food & Agriculture Organisation (FAO)	40,000	584,677
World Food Programme	17,770,002	15,505,594
IAEA Technical Assistance	1,196,000	1,196,000
United Nations Environment Programme (UNEP)	4,000,000	4,000,000
United Nations Fund for the Victims of Torture—funding alternatives with United Nations Voluntary Fund for Advisory Services	25,000 Not in	25,000 1991/92
United Nations International Drug Control Programme (UNDCP)	1,942,000	604,000
UNFDAC (Dir Project Pakistan)	Original payment	
United Nations Industrial Development Fund	635,471	
United Nations Educational and Training Programme for South Africa (UNETPSA)	75,000	75,000
United Nations Development Fund for Women (UNIFEM)	100,000	100,000
United Nations Association	24,000	24,000

Voluntary Contributions (continued)	*Financial year 91/92*	*Calendar year 1991 (£)*
WMO Voluntary Co-operation Fund	20,000	20,000
Polish Refugees in Lebanon	–	–
United Nations Centre for Human Settlements (UNCHS)		200,000
United Nations Fund for Population Activities (UNFPA)		7,500,000
ICCROM		

ANNEX B

FOOD AND AGRICULTURE ORGANISATION (FAO) 1992—US Dollars

Top 15 Contributors	*Assessed Contribution*	*Top 15 Debtors*	*Amount Owed at 13/11/92*
USA	99,976,515	USA	96,065,363
Japan	42,005,028	Brazil	14,984,222
Germany	34,529,020	Iran	4,510,240
France	23,061,584	Yugoslavia	4,541,812
UK	17,929,748	Turkey	3,501,428
Italy	14,730,270	Mexico	3,484,580
Canada	11,404,080	Libya	2,783,834
Argentina	8,389,973	Czechoslovakia	2,439,206
Spain	7,190,906	Venezuela	2,090,147
Australia	5,797,074	Kuwait	2,051,452
Brazil	5,353,582	Romania	1,426,457
Sweden	4,466,598	Nigeria	1,397,654
Belgium	4,308,208	India	1,362,154
Switzerland	3,991,428	Iraq	1,223,012
Iran	2,534,240	Poland	1,087,450

WORLD HEALTH ORGANISATION (WHO) 1992—US Dollars

Top 15 Contributors	*Assessed Contribution*	*Top 15 Debtors*	*Amount Owed*
USA	94,153,345	Russia	35,861,110
Japan	40,704,595	USA	17,316,949
Russian Fed	35,861,110	Brazil	5,295,015
Germany	31,976,815	Ukraine	4,586,535
France	22,004,970	Belgium	4,232,040
UK	16,497,530	Iran	2,502,165
Italy	13,895,515	Argentina	2,423,775
Canada	10,415,640	Poland	2,050,660
Spain	6,838,750	Italy	1,872,411
Netherlands	5,682,955	Mexico	1,712,820
Australia	5,442,005	Yugoslavia	1,654,540
Brazil	5,295,015	Belarus	1,011,230
Ukraine	4,586,535	Libya	1,006,800
Belgium	4,232,040	Venezuela	831,795
Sweden	4,066,550	Nigeria	722,625

INTERNATIONAL LABOUR ORGANISATION (ILO) 1991—Swiss Francs

Top 15 Contributors	*Assessed Contribution*	*Top 15 Debtors*	*Amount Owed*
USA	72,283,748	USA	40,103,419
Japan	32,672,253	Russian Fed	28,682,190
Russian Fed	28,682,190	Brazil	4,163,542
Germany	26,860,638	Iran	1,966,116
France	17,955,282	Argentina	1,879,377
UK	13,965,219	Ukraine	1,792,636
Italy	11,449,744	Yugoslavia	1,330,020
Canada	8,876,443	Libya	809,578
Spain	5,609,217	Israel	567,340
Netherlands	4,741,812	UAE	549,357
Australia	4,510,504	Nigeria	502,075
Brazil	4,163,542	Belarus	477,073
Ukraine	3,585,272	Iraq	346,962
Sweden	3,469,618	Cuba	260,222
Belgium	3,353,964	Philippines	260,222

UNITED NATIONS EDUCATIONAL, SCIENTIFIC AND CULTURAL ORGANISATION (UNESCO) 1992—US Dollars

Top 15 Contributors	*Assessed Contribution*	*Top 15 Debtors*	*Amount Owed*
Japan	38,103,984	Russian Fed	28,802,037
Russian Fed	28,802,037	Brazil	4,851,845
Germany	27,318,671	Ukraine	3,615,706
France	18,356,663	Belgium	2,483,246
Italy	13,133,976	Iran	2,348,664
Canada	9,518,269	Argentina	1,730,594
Spain	6,057,080	Venezuela	1,441,546
Brazil	4,851,845	Poland	1,421,559
Australia	4,604,617	Yugoslavia	1,297,946
Netherlands	4,573,713	Belarus	958,008
Switzerland	3,553,899	Turkey	821,937
Ukraine	3,615,706	Kuwait	766,045
Sweden	3,399,381	Libya	741,682
Belgium	3,244,864	Mexico	724,688
Saudi Arabia	2,935,830	UAE	648,973

INTERNATIONAL ATOMIC ENERGY AUTHORITY (IAEA) 1992—US Dollars

Top 15 Contributors	*Assessed Contribution*	*Top 15 Debtors*	*Amount Owed 18/9/92*
USA	55,616,982	USA	55,616,982
Russian Fed	22,002,076	Russian Fed	22,002,076
Japan	21,970,327	Ukraine	2,758,602
Germany	19,192,203	Brazil	2,045,348
France	12,470,061	Argentina	949,368
UK	9,336,644	Saudi Arabia	898,494
Italy	7,816,908	Italy	886,356
Canada	6,118,814	Venezuela	797,486
Spain	3,745,760	Belarus	734,145
Netherlands	3,282,970	Yugoslavia	647,532
Australia	3,099,109	Kuwait	645,160
Ukraine	2,758,602	Libya	601,568
Sweden	2,474,074	Poland	483,295
Belgium	2,336,999	Turkey	462,494
Switzerland	2,205,981	Israel	454,054

WORLD METEROLOGICAL ORGANISATION (WMO) 1990/91—Swiss Francs

Top 15 Contributors	*Assessed Contributions 1990/91 (%)*	*Top 15 Debtors*	*Amount Owed 31/12/91*
USA	24.65	Russian Fed	4,984,681 *
Russian Fed	10.23	USA	2,863,901 *
Germany	8.76	Brazil	1,262,884
Japan	8.53	Argentina	1,113,766
France	5.91	Ukraine	662,675 *
UK	4.97	Iran	363,383
Canada	2.94	Bolivia	328,024
Spain	1.79	Israel	320,943
Australia	1.65	Zaire	293,511
Netherlands	1.57	Yugoslavia	229,013 *
China	1.55	Kuwait	224,001
Brazil	1.37	Dominican Rep	198,187
Ukraine	1.36	Peru	185,998
Sweden	1.29	Turkey	185,159 *
Belgium	1.22	Mauritania	159,257

*this represents contribution due for 1991 alone; all other debtor nations owe for periods up to and including 1991

ANNEX C

STATUS OF CONTRIBUTIONS TO THE UNITED NATIONS REGULAR BUDGET FOR 1992
as at 31 October 1992
(United States dollars)

Member State	1992 scale of assess-ments (%)	Contributions payable as at 1 January 1992			Collection in 1992 ($)	Contributions outstanding		
		Prior years ($)	Current year ($)	Total ($)		Prior years ($)	Current year ($)	Total outstanding ($)
Afghanistan	0.01	92,442	98,482	190,924	93,125	0	97,799	97,799
Albania	0.01	0	98,482	98,482	98,482	0	0	0
Algeria	0.16	0	1,575,701	1,575,701	690,000	0	885,701	885,701
Angola	0.01	79,087	98,482	177,569	0	79,087	98,482	177,569
Antigua and Barbuda	0.01	171,218	98,482	269,700	80,000	91,218	98,482	189,700
Argentina	0.57	14,019,884	5,613,438	19,633,322	19,633,322*a*	0	0	0
Australia	1.51	0	14,870,668	14,870,668	14,870,668*a*	0	0	0
Austria	0.75	0	7,386,104	7,386,104	7,386,104	0	0	0
Bahamas	0.02	72,012	196,962	268,974	94,980	0	173,994	173,994
Bahrain	0.03	0	295,443	295,443	295,443	0	0	0
Bangladesh	0.01	0	98,482	98,482	98,482	0	0	0
Barbados	0.01	0	98,482	98,482	98,482	0	0	0
Belarus	0.31	1,520,157	3,052,922	4,573,079	20,000*b*	1,500,157	3,052,922	4,553,079
Belgium	1.06	0	10,439,026	10,439,026	10,439,026*a*	0	0	0
Belize	0.01	0	98,482	98,482	98,482	0	0	0
Benin	0.01	245,003	98,482	343,485	222,120	22,883	98,482	121,365
Bhutan	0.01	0	98,482	98,482	98,482	0	0	0
Bolivia	0.01	0	98,482	98,482	98,482	0	0	0
Botswana	0.01	0	98,482	98,482	98,482	0	0	0
Brazil	1.59	17,823,960	15,658,539	33,482,499	0	17,823,960	15,658,539	33,482,499
Brunei Darussalam	0.03	0	295,443	295,443	295,443*a*	0	0	0
Bulgaria	0.13	500,000	1,280,257	1,780,257	1,780,257*a*	0	0	0
Burkina Faso	0.01	190,468	98,482	288,950	6,700	183,768	98,482	282,250
Burundi	0.01	118,249	98,482	216,731	99,960	18,289	98,482	116,771
Cambodia	0.01	216,732	98,482	315,214	0	216,732	98,482	315,214
Cameroon	0.01	0	98,482	98,482	0	0	98,482	98,482
Canada	3.11	0	30,662,414	30,662,414	30,662,414	0	0	0
Capa Verde	0.01	92,131	98,482	190,613	111,233	0	79,380	79,380
Central African Republic	0.01	220,907	98,482	319,389	0	220,907	98,482	319,389
Chad	0.01	245,084	98,482	343,566	94,210	150,874	98,482	249,356

Table — *(continued)*

Member State	*1992 scale of assess-ments (%)*	*Contributions payable as at 1 January 1992*			*Collection in 1992 ($)*	*Contributions outstanding*		
		Prior years ($)	*Current year ($)*	*Total ($)*		*Prior years ($)*	*Current year ($)*	*Total outstanding ($)*
Chile	0.08	737,046	787,850	1,524,896	824,896	0	700,000	700,000
China	0.77	0	7,583,066	7,583,066	7,583,066*a*	0	0	0
Colombia	0.13	0	1,280,257	1,200,257	1,280,257*a*	0	0	0
Comoros	0.01	112,549	98,482	211,031	0	112,549	98,482	211,031
Congo	0.01	130,883	98,482	229,365	100,000	30,883	98,482	129,365
Costa Rica	0.01	147,005	98,482	245,487	10,000*b*	137,005	98,482	235,487
Côte d'Ivoire	0.02	0	196,962	196,962	0	0	196,962	196,962
Cuba	0.09	1,086,212	886,332	1,972,544	893,400	192,812	886,332	1,079,144
Cyprus	0.02	0	196,962	196,962	196,962	0	0	0
Czechoslovakia	0.55	0	5,416,476	5,416,476	5,416,476*a*	0	0	0
Democratic People's Republic of Korea	0.05	0	492,407	492,407	492,407	0	0	0
Denmark	0.65	0	6,401,290	6,401,290	6,401,290	0	0	0
Djibouti	0.01	116,441	98,482	214,923	50,000	66,441	98,482	164,923
Dominica	0.01	0	98,482	98,482	48,909	0	49,573	49,573
Dominican Republic	0.02	713,316	196,962	910,278	10,000*b*	703,316	196,962	900,278
Ecuador	0.03	90,131	295,443	385,574	149,457	0	236,117	236,117
Egypt	0.07	36,686	689,369	726,055	726,055	0	0	0
El Salvador	0.01	206,818	98,482	305,300	169,926	36,892	98,482	135,374
Equatorial Guinea	0.01	360,891	98,482	459,373	250,000	110,891	98,482	209,373
Estonia *c*	–	–	–	–	–	–	–	–
Ethiopia	0.01	0	98,482	98,402	98,482	0	0	0
Fiji	0.01	0	98,482	98,482	98,482	0	0	0
Finland	0.57	0	5,613,438	5,613,438	5,613,438	0	0	0
France	6.00	0	59,088,830	59,088,830	59,088,830*a*	0	0	0
Gabon	0.02	0	196,962	196,962	196,962*a*	0	0	0
Gambia	0.01	239,125	98,482	337,607	105,882	133,243	98,482	231,725
Germany	8.93	0	87,943,875	87,943,875	87,943,875*a*	0	0	0
Ghana	0.01	0	98,482	98,482	98,482	0	0	0
Greece	0.35	0	3,446,848	3,446,848	3,446,848*a*	0	0	0
Grenada	0.01	171,218	98,482	269,700	78,000	93,218	98,482	191,700
Guatemala	0.02	503,964	196,962	700,926	164,400	339,564	196,962	536,526
Guinea	0.01	13,044	98,482	111,526	79,087	0	32,439	32,439

Table — *(continued)*

Member State	*1992 scale of assess-ments (%)*	*Contributions payable as at 1 January 1992*			*Collection in 1992 ($)*	*Contributions outstanding*		
		Prior years ($)	*Current year ($)*	*Total ($)*		*Prior years ($)*	*Current year ($)*	*Total outstanding ($)*
Guinea Bissau	0.01	171,218	98,482	269,700	0	171,218	98,482	269,700
Guyana	0.01	222,953	98,482	321,435	272,438	0	48,997	48,997
Haiti	0.01	245,926	98,482	344,408	75,500	170,426	98,482	268,908
Honduras	0.01	167,076	98,482	265,558	167,143	0	98,415	98,415
Hungary	0.18	1,115,853	1,772,664	2,888,517	1,772,664*a*	0	1,115,853	1,115,853
Iceland	0.03	0	295,443	295,443	295,443	0	0	0
India	0.36	28,528	3,545,329	3,573,857	1,753,279a	0	1,820,578	1,820,578
Indonesia	0.16	0	1,575,701	1,575,701	1,575,701	0	0	0
Iran (Islamic Republic of)	0.77	6,708,766	7,583,066	14,291,832	6,708,766	0	7,583,066	7,583,066
Iraq	0.13	234,601	1,280,257	1,514,858	1,514,858	0	0	0
Ireland	0.18	0	1,772,664	1,772,664	1,772,664	0	0	0
Israel	0.23	3,827,944	2,265,071	6,093,015	1,636,405	2,191,539	2,265,071	4,456,610
Italy	4.29	0	42,248,513	42,248,513	42,248,513	0	0	0
Jamaica	0.01	92,131	98,482	190,613	46,066	46,065	98,482	144,547
Japan	12.45	0	122,609,322	122,609,322	122,609,322	0	0	0
Jordan	0.01	0	98,482	98,482	98,482	0	0	0
Kenya	0.01	190,626	98,482	289,108	57,360	133,266	98,482	231,748
Kuwait	0.25	0	2,462,034	2,462,034	2,462,034*a*	0	0	0
Lao People's Democratic Republic	0.01	0	98,482	98,482	98,482	0	0	0
Latvia *c*	–	–	–	–	–	–	–	–
Lebanon	0.01	92,131	98,482	190,613	0	92,131	98,482	190,613
Lesotho	0.01	0	98,482	98,482	98,482	0	0	0
Liberia	0.01	203,212	98,482	301,694	62,400	140,812	98,482	239,294
Libyan Arab Jamahiriya	0.24	1,379,673	2,363,553	3,743,226	860,000*a*	519,673	2,363,553	2,883,226
Liechtenstein	0.01	0	98,482	98,482	98,482	0	0	0
Lithuania *c*	–	–	–	–	–	–	–	–
Luxembourg	0.06	0	590,888	590,888	590,888	0	0	0
Madagascar	0.01	46,565	98,482	145,047	74,536	0	70,511	70,511
Malawi	0.01	0	98,482	98,482	10,000	0	88,482	86,482
Malaysia	0.12	0	1,181,776	1,181,776	1,181,776	0	0	0
Maldives	0.01	92,131	98,482	190,613	92,131	0	98,482	98,482
Mali	0.01	245,668	98,482	344,150	70,448	175,220	98,482	273,702

Table — *(continued)*

Member State	*1992 scale of assess-ments (%)*	*Contributions payable as at 1 January 1992*			*Collection in 1992 ($)*	*Contributions outstanding*		
		Prior years ($)	*Current year ($)*	*Total ($)*		*Prior years ($)*	*Current year ($)*	*Total outstanding ($)*
Malta	0.01	0	98,482	98,482	98,482	0	0	0
Marshall Islands	0.01	0	98,482	98,482	98,482	0	0	0
Mauritania	0.01	167,003	98,482	265,485	66,876	100,127	98,482	198,609
Mauritius	0.01	7,131	98,482	105,613	105,613	0	0	0
Mexico	0.88	0	8,666,361	8,666,361	8,102,727*a*	0	563,634	563,634
Micronesia (Federated States of)	0.01	0	98,482	98,482	98,482	0	0	0
Mongolia	0.01	92,133	98,482	190,615	92,133	0	98,482	98,482
Morocco	0.03	0	295,443	295,443	283,142*a*	0	12,301	12,301
Mozambique	0.01	76,742	98,482	175,224	98,482	0	76,742	76,742
Myanmar	0.01	0	98,402	98,482	98,482	0	0	0
Namibia	0.01	0	98,482	98,482	98,482	0	0	0
Nepal	0.01	0	98,482	98,482	98,482	0	0	0
Netherlands	1.50	0	14,772,207	14,772,207	14,772,207*a*	0	0	0
New Zealand	0.24	0	2,363,553	2,363,553	2,363,553	0	0	0
Nicaragua	0.01	248,802	98,482	347,284	98,732	150,070	98,482	248,552
Niger	0.01	245,961	98,482	344,443	94,340	151,621	98,482	250,103
Nigeria	0.20	1,965,272	1,969,627	3,934,899	1,141,265	824,007	1,969,627	2,793,634
Norway	0.55	0	5,416,476	5,416,476	5,416,476	0	0	0
Oman	0.03	0	295,443	295,443	295,443	0	0	0
Pakistan	0.06	0	590,888	590,888	590,888	0	0	0
Panama	0.02	466,400	196,962	663,362	158,173	308,227	196,962	505,189
Papua New Guinea	0.01	0	98,482	98,482	90,482	0	0	0
Paraguay	0.02	306,535	196,962	503,497	316,535*a*	0	186,962	186,962
Peru	0.06	790,549	590,888	1,381,437	247,749	542,800	590,888	1,133,688
Philippines	0.07	707,642	689,369	1,397,011	1,002,209*a*	0	394,802	394,802
Poland	0.47	0	4,628,625	4,628,625	4,628,625*a*	0	0	0
Portugal	0.20	0	1,969,627	1,969,627	1,969,627	0	0	0
Qatar	0.05	663,370	492,407	1,155,777	433,044	230,326	492,407	722,733
Republic of Korea	0.69	0	6,795,215	6,795,215	3,795,215	0	3,000,000	3,000,000
Romania	0.17	1,750,484	1,674,183	3,424,667	1,750,484*a*	0	1,674,183	1,674,183
Russian Federation	9.41	46,019,313	92,670,982	138,690,295	18,580,000*a*	27,439,313	92,670,982	120,110,295
Rwanda	0.01	92,131	98,482	190,613	39,429	52,702	98,482	151,184
Saint Kitts and Nevis	0.01	128,339	98,482	226,821	50,000	78,339	98,482	176,821

Table — *(continued)*

Member State	1992 scale of assess-ments (%)	Contributions payable as at 1 January 1992			Collection in 1992 ($)	Contributions outstanding		
		Prior years ($)	Current year ($)	Total ($)		Prior years ($)	Current year ($)	Total outstanding ($)
Saint Lucia	0.01	0	98,482	98,482	98,482	0	0	0
Saint Vincent and the Grenadines	0.01	64,893	98,482	163,375	108,621	0	54,754	54,754
Samoa	0.01	0	98,482	98,482	98,482	0	0	0
Sao Tome and Principe	0.01	256,667	98,482	355,149	98,482	158,185	98,482	256,667
Saudi Arabia	0.96	0	9,454,212	9,454,212	9,454,212*a*	0	0	0
Senegal	0.01	170,009	98,482	268,491	0	170,009	98,482	268,491
Seychelles	0.01	92,131	98,482	190,613	92,131	0	98,482	98,482
Sierra Leone	0.01	227,521	98,482	326,003	83,100	144,421	98,482	242,903
Singapore	0.12	0	1,181,776	1,181,776	1,181,776	0	0	0
Solomon Islands	0.01	82,502	98,482	180,984	0	82,502	98,482	180,984
Somalia	0.01	176,999	98,482	275,481	0	176,999	98,482	275,481
South Africa	0.41	45,007,168	4,037,736	49,044,904	0	45,007,168	4,037,736	49,044,904
Spain	1.98	0	19,499,313	19,499,313	19,499,313	0	0	0
Sri Lanka	0.01	0	98,482	98,482	98,482	0	0	0
Sudan	0.01	72,626	98,482	171,108	100,103	0	71,005	71,005
Suriname	0.01	92,131	98,482	190,613	0	92,131	98,482	190,613
Swaziland	0.01	0	98,482	98,482	81,659	0	16,823	16,823
Sweden	1.11	0	10,931,433	10,931,433	10,931,433*a*	0	0	0
Syrian Arab Republic	0.04	0	393,925	393,925	393,925	0	0	0
Thailand	0.11	0	1,083,295	1,083,295	1,083,295	0	0	0
Togo	0.01	84,233	98,482	182,715	84,234	0	98,481	98,481
Trinidad and Tobago	0.05	117,144	492,407	609,551	373,538	0	236,013	236,013
Tunisia	0.03	90,631	295,443	386,074	315,527	0	70,547	70,547
Turkey	0.27	2,896,285	2,669,546	5,565,831	1,823,201*a*	1,073,084	2,669,546	3,742,630
Uganda	0.01	75,404	98,482	173,886	0	75,404	98,482	173,886
Ukraine	1.18	5,758,172	11,620,802	17,378,974	70,000*b*	5,668,172	11,620,802	17,308,974
United Arab Emirates	0.21	0	2,068,108	2,068,108	2,068,108	0	0	0
United Kingdom of Great Britain and Northern Ireland	5.02	0	49,437,654	49,437,654	49,437,654	0	0	0
United Republic of Tanzania	0.01	92,131	98,482	190,613	92,131	0	98,482	98,482
United States of America	25.00	266,407,875	298.619,001	565,026,876	269,568,891	0	295,457,985	295,457,985
Uruguay	0.04	368,523	393,925	762,448	368,523	0	393,925	393,925

Table — *(continued)*

Member State	*1992 scale of assess-ments (%)*	*Contributions payable as at 1 January 1992*			*Collection in 1992 ($)*	*Contributions outstanding*		
		Prior years ($)	*Current year ($)*	*Total ($)*		*Prior years ($)*	*Current year ($)*	*Total outstanding ($)*
Vanuatu	0.01	0	98,482	98,482	0	0	98,482	98,482
Venezuela	0.49	0	4,825,587	4,825,587	4,825,587*a*	0	0	0
Viet Nam	0.01	0	98,482	98,482	0	0	98,482	98,482
Yemen	0.01	163,413	98,482	261,895	82,131	81,282	98,482	179,764
Yugoslavia	0.42	7,850,297	4,136,218	11,986,515	3,802,283*a*	4,048,014	4,136,218	8,184,232
Zaire	0.01	0	98,482	98,482	101	0	98,381	98,381
Zambia	0.01	171,718	98,482	270,200	28,669	143,049	98,482	241,531
Zimbabwe	0.01	0	98,482	98,482	10,000*b*	0	88,482	88,482
Total	100.02	439,383,945	1,037,471,596	1,476,855,541	901,020,946*d*	112,722,991	463,111,604	575,834,595

a Includes credit transferred from the Working Capital Fund.

b Credit transferred from the Working Capital Fund.

c As stated in General Assembly resolution 46/221 A, the assessment rates of Estonia, Latvia and Lithuania were determined by the Committee on Contributions during its fifty-second session. The assessment rates, which will be considered by the General Assembly at its forty-seventh session, are to be deducted from the assessment rate for the Russian Federation of 9.41 per cent.

d Includes $14,666,976, $30,627.709, $209.366 and $288,374 received from Australia, Canada, Colombia and Mexico, respectively, in 1991 towards the 1992 assessment and $98,746 that had been held in the suspense account in favour of six Member States.

ANNEX D

APPORTIONMENT OF THE COSTS OF ASSESSED PEACE-KEEPING OPERATIONS IN 1992

	Percentage share resulting from application of scheme for apportionment of costs of assessed peace-keeping operations			
	(1) Regular budget scale 1992–1994 %	*(2) Relative to group total a %*	*(3) Relative to grand total a %*	*(4) Per capita national income average 1980–1989 (United States dollars)*
A. *Member States referred to in paragraph 3 (a) of General Assembly resolution 43/232*				
China	0.77	1.667	0.936	333
France	6.00	12.987	7.293	10,894
Russian Federation	9.41	20.368	11.437	3,771
United Kingdom of Great Britain and Northern Ireland	5.02	10.866	6.102	8,954
United States of America	25.00	54.113	30.387	14,247
Subtotal	45.20	100.001	56.155	– b
B. *Member States referred to in paragraph 3 (b) of General Assembly resolution 43/232 and paragraph (a) of resolution 44/192 B*				
Australia	1.51	3.645	1.510	9,744
Austria	0.75	1.810	0.750	10,003
Belarus	0.31	0.748	0.310	3,825
Belgium	1.06	2.559	1.060	9,901
Canada	3.11	7.507	3.109	12,456
Czechoslovakia	0.55	1.328	0.550	2,478
Denmark	0.65	1.569	0.650	12,762
Finland	0.57	1.376	0.570	11,689
Germany	8.93	21.554	8.928	11,059
Iceland	0.03	0.072	0.030	13,484
Ireland	0.18	0.434	0.180	5,246
Italy	4.29	10.355	4.289	8,522
Japan	12.45	30.051	12.447	12,212
Liechtenstein	0.01	0.024	0.010	18,362
Luxembourg	0.06	0.145	0.060	15,810
Netherlands	1.50	3.621	1.500	10,364
New Zealand	0.24	0.579	0.240	7,519
Norway	0.55	1.328	0.550	13,410
South Africa	0.41	0.990	0.410	1,962
Spain	1.98	4.779	1.979	5,196
Sweden	1.11	2.679	1.110	13,456
Ukraine	1.18	2.848	1.180	2,963
Subtotal	41.43	100.001	41.422	– b

Table — *(continued)*

	Percentage share resulting from application of scheme for apportionment of costs of assessed peace-keening operations			
	(1) Regular budget scale 1992–1994 %	*(2) Relative to group total a %*	*(3) Relative to grand total a %*	*(4) Per capita national income average 1980–1989 (United States dollars)*
C. *Member States referred to in paragraph 3 (c) of General Assembly resolution 43/232, paragraph (b) of resolution 44/192 B and paragraphs 6–12 of resolution 46/198 A*				
Albania	0.01	0.084	0.002	887
Algeria	0.16	1.350	0.032	2,134
Argentina	0.57	4.810	0.114	2,519
Bahamas	0.02	0.169	0.004	7,552
Bahrain	0.03	0.253	0.006	6,180
Barbados	0.01	0.084	0.002	4,366
Bolivia	0.01	0.084	0.002	856
Brazil	1.59	13.418	0.317	2,030
Brunei Darussalam	0.03	0.253	0.006	13,146
Bulgaria	0.13	1.097	0.026	1,985
Cambodia *c*	0.01	0.084	0.002	80
Cameroon	0.01	0.084	0.002	884
Chile	0.08	0.675	0.016	1,525
Colombia	0.13	1.097	0.026	1,104
Congo	0.01	0.084	0.002	811
Costa Rica	0.01	0.084	0.002	1,348
Côte d'Ivoire	0.02	0.169	0.004	746
Cuba	0.09	0.759	0.018	1,991
Cyprus	0.02	0.169	0.004	3,914
Democratic People's Republic of Korea	0.05	0.422	0.010	798
Dominican Republic	0.02	0.169	0.004	952
Ecuador	0.03	0.253	0.006	1,084
Egypt	0.07	0.591	0.014	1,047
El Salvador	0.01	0.084	0.002	902
Estonia *d*	–	–	–	3,812
Fiji	0.01	0.084	0.002	1,546
Gabon	0.02	0.169	0.004	2,610
Ghana	0.01	0.084	0.002	432
Greece	0.35	2.954	0.070	3,778
Guatemala	0.02	0.169	0.004	1,083
Guyana	0.01	0.084	0.002	461
Honduras	0.01	0.084	0.002	742
Hungary	0.18	1.519	0.036	1,976
India	0.36	3.038	0.072	253
Indonesia	0.16	1.350	0.032	474
Iran (Islamic Republic of)	0.77	6.498	0.154	2,546
Iraq	0.13	1.097	0.026	2,138
Israel	0.23	1.941	0.046	6,079
Jamaica	0.01	0.084	0.002	1,068
Jordan	0.01	0.084	0.002	1,319
Kenya	0.01	0.084	0.002	320
Kuwait	0.25	2.110	0.050	15,504
Latvia *d*	–	–	–	4,153
Lebanon	0.01	0.084	0.002	581
Liberia *c*	0.01	0.084	0.002	392

Table — *(continued)*

	Percentage share resulting from application of scheme for apportionment of costs of assessed peace-keening operations			
	(1) Regular budget scale 1992–1994 %	*(2) Relative to group total a %*	*(3) Relative to grand total a %*	*(4) Per capita national income average 1980–1989 (United States dollars)*
Libyan Arab Jamahiriya	0.24	2.025	0.048	6,559
Lithuania *d*	–	–	–	3,471
Madagascar *c*	0.01	0.084	0.002	236
Malaysia	0.12	1.013	0.024	1,749
Malta	0.01	0.084	0.002	4,077
Marshall Islands	0.01	0.084	0.002	1,230
Mauritius	0.01	0.084	0.002	1,271
Mexico	0.88	7.426	0.176	1,921
Micronesia, Federated States of	0.01	0.084	0.002	1,828
Mongolia	0.01	0.084	0.002	797
Morocco	0.03	0.253	0.006	743
Nicaragua	0.01	0.084	0.002	898
Nigeria	0.20	1.688	0.040	733
Oman	0.03	0.253	0.006	4,799
Pakistan	0.06	0.506	0.012	327
Panama	0.02	0.169	0.004	1,900
Paraguay	0.02	0.169	0.004	1,295
Peru	0.06	0.506	0.012	1,001
Philippines	0.07	0.591	0.014	591
Poland	0.47	3.966	0.094	1,716
Portugal	0.20	1.688	0.040	2,608
Qatar	0.05	0.422	0.010	17,495
Republic of Korea	0.69	5.823	0.138	2,376
Romania	0.17	1.435	0.034	1,458
Saudi Arabia	0.96	8.101	0.192	8,528
Singapore	0.12	1.013	0.024	6,299
Sri Lanka	0.01	0.084	0.002	327
Swaziland	0.01	0.084	0.002	880
Syrian Arab Republic	0.04	0.338	0.008	1,865
Thailand	0.11	0.928	0.022	782
Trinidad and Tobago	0.05	0.422	0.010	4,654
Tunisia	0.03	0.253	0.006	1,108
Turkey	0.27	2.278	0.054	1,144
United Arab Emirates	0.21	1.772	0.042	17,470
Uruguay	0.04	0.338	0.008	2,388
Venezuela	0.49	4.135	0.098	3,082
Viet Nam	0.01	0.084	0.002	121
Yugoslavia	0.42	3.544	0.084	2,465
Zaire *c*	0.01	0.084	0.002	125
Zambia *c*	0.01	0.084	0.002	355
Subtotal	11.85	9.990	2.369	– *b*

Table — *(continued)*

	Percentage share resulting from application of scheme for apportionment of costs of assessed peace-keening operations			
	(1) *Regular budget scale 1992–1994* %	*(2)* *Relative to group total a* %	*(3)* *Relative to grand total a* %	*(4)* *Per capita national income average 1980–1989 (United States dollars)*
D. *Member States referred to in paragraph 3 (d) of General Assembly resolution 43/232, paragraph (c) of resolution 44/192 B and paragraph 9 of resolution 45/269*				
Afghanistan *c*	0.01	1.852	0.001	190
Angola	0.01	1.852	0.001	525
Antigua and Barbuda	0.01	1.852	0.001	2,123
Bangladesh *c*	0.01	1.852	0.001	152
Belize	0.01	1.852	0.001	1,128
Benin *c*	0.01	1.852	0.001	295
Bhutan *c*	0.01	1.852	0.001	118
Botswana *c, e*	0.01	1.852	0.001	943
Burkina Faso *c*	0.01	1.852	0.001	162
Burundi *b, c*	0.01	1.852	0.001	225
Cape Verde *c*	0.01	1.852	0.001	560
Central African Republic *c*	0.01	1.852	0.001	310
Chad *c*	0.01	1.852	0.001	152
Comoros *c*	0.01	1.852	0.001	318
Djibouti *c*	0.01	1.852	0.001	1,083
Dominica	0.01	1.852	0.001	1,209
Equatorial Guinea *c*	0.01	1.852	0.001	289
Ethiopia *c*	0.01	1.852	0.001	110
Gambla	0.01	1.852	0.001	272
Grenada	0.01	1.852	0.001	1,285
Guinea *c*	0.01	1.852	0.001	378
Guinea-Bissau *c*	0.01	1.852	0.001	257
Haitic	0.01	1.852	0.001	304
Lao People's Democratic Republic *c*	0.01	1.852	0.001	153
Lesotho *c*	0.01	1.852	0.001	431
Malawi *c*	0.01	1.852	0.001	162
Maldives *c*	0.01	1.852	0.001	352
Mali *c*	0.01	1.852	0.001	203
Mauritania *c*	0.01	1.852	0.001	428
Mozambique *c*	0.01	1.852	0.001	168
Myanmar *c*	0.01	1.852	0.001	186
Namibia	0.01	1.852	0.001	975
Nepal *c*	0.01	1.852	0.001	151
Niger *c*	0.01	1.852	0.001	265
Papua New Guinea	0.01	1.852	0.001	720
Rwanda *c*	0.01	1.852	0.001	271
Saint Kitts and Nevis	0.01	1.852	0.001	1,472
Saint Lucia	0.01	1.852	0.001	1,101
Saint Vincent and the Grenadines	0.01	1.852	0.001	940
Samoa *c*	0.01	1.852	0.001	557
Sao Tome and Principe *c*	0.01	1.852	0.001	390
Senegal	0.01	1.852	0.001	476

Table — *(continued)*

	Percentage share resulting from application of scheme for apportionment of costs of assessed peace-keening operations			
	(1) Regular budget scale 1992–1994 %	*(2) Relative to group total a %*	*(3) Relative to grand total a %*	*(4) Per capita national income average 1980–1989 (United States dollars)*
Seychelles	0.01	1.852	0.001	2,651
Sierra Leone *c*	0.01	1.852	0.001	339
Solomon Islands *c*	0.01	1.852	0.001	530
Somalia *c*	0.01	1.852	0.001	337
Sudan *c*	0.01	1.852	0.001	343
Suriname	0.01	1.852	0.001	2,544
Togo *c*	0.01	1.852	0.001	288
Uganda *c*	0.01	1.852	0.001	225
United Republic of Tanzania *c*	0.01	1.852	0.001	227
Vanuatu *c*	0.01	1.852	0.001	774
Yemen *c*	0.01	1.852	0.001	657
Zimbabwe	0.01	1.852	0.001	628
Subtotal	0.54	100.008	0.054	– *b*
New Member States not yet assigned to a group				
Armenia	–	–	–	3,052
Azerbaijan	–	–	–	2,696
Bosnia and Herzegovina	–	–	–	1,694
Croatia	–	–	–	3,153
Georgia	–	–	–	3,156
Kazakhstan	–	–	–	2,268
Kyrgystan	–	–	–	1,894
Republic of Moldova	–	–	–	2,959
San Marino	–	–	–	8,013
Slovenia	–	–	–	4,955
Tajikistan	–	–	–	1,599
Turkmenistan	–	–	–	2,063
Uzbekistan	–	–	–	1,817
Subtotal	–	–	—	– *b*
Grand total	100.02*f*		100.00	

ANNEX F

CONTRIBUTIONS TO THE UN REGULAR BUDGET AND PEACEKEEPING OPERATIONS AS AT 31 OCTOBER 1992

M S	*Regular Budget (US$ 000s)*	*M S*	*Peacekeeping (US$ 000s)*	*M S*	*Total (US$ 000s)*
USA	295,458	Russia Fed.	290,458	USA	462,391
Russia Fed.	120,110	USA	166,933	Russia Fed.	410,568
S.Africa	49,045	Japan	54,989	S.Africa	71,446
Brazil	33,482	Italy	31,071	Japan	54,989
Ukraine	17,309	Ukraine	29,323	Ukraine	46,632
Yugoslav	8,184	S.Africa	22,401	Brazil	39,067
Iran	7,583	Germany	21,986	Italy	31,071
Belarus	4,553	Spain	14,693	Germany	21,986
Israel	4,457	Poland	10,975	Spain	14,693
Turkey	3,743	Czechosl	9,307	Iran	13,173
Rep of		Belarus	8,254	Belarus	12,807
Korea	3,000	France	8.050	Poland	10,975
Nigeria	2,794	Iran	5,590	Yugoslav	9,898
India	1,821	Brazil	5,585	Czechosl	9,307
Romania	1,674	China	3,598	France	8,050
Peru	1,134				

Supplemtary Memorandum submitted by the Foreign and Commonwealth Office

SOMALIA: UN INVOLVEMENT

1. In January 1991 former President Siad Barre fled Mogadishu for his clan homelands in the south-west of Somalia. The factions who had opposed him fell to fighting amongst themselves. One group formed what it called an interim government, but none of the others recognised it, and it commanded no support outside of one part of Mogadishu. Reconciliation attempts in 1991 came to nothing, and in November fighting in Mogadishu began between factions led by self-styled interim President Ali Mahdi, on one side, and General Aideed (chairman of the United Somali Congress—USC) on the other.

2. The scale of fighting in Mogadishu from November was such that aid distribution became almost impossible. In January 1992 the UN attempted without success to negotiate corridors for the safe distribution of humanitarian aid. On 23 January the Security Council adopted SCR 733 demanding a cease-fire and requesting the Secretary-General to increase humanitarian assistance and seek political reconciliation.

3. A cease-fire in Mogadishu was negotiated in New York in mid-February and signed in Mogadishu on 2 March. On 24 April, SCR 751 was adopted, endorsing the Secretary-General's proposal to deploy 50 cease-fire monitors in Mogadishu and endorsing, in principle, the deployment of a security force in Mogadishu to safeguard humanitarian aid, subject to detailed negotiation with the factions.

4. Aideed held out against these proposals for some months in protracted talks with the Secretary-General's Representative for Somalia. (At that time Mohamed Sahnoun, now Ismat Kittani, following Sahnoun's resignation late in October). But by August Aideed had agreed, both to the 50 UN observers (who took up position in July) and to the armed guards. Pakistan agreed to provide 500 soldiers for deployment in Mogadishu, and the US Air Force carried them to Somalia in September.

5. Recognising the poor prospects for national reconciliation, in July 1992 the Secretary-General proposed a strategy of basing UN operations in Somalia on four regional zones, in addition to Mogadishu. This was endorsed by SCR 767 of 27 July. The Resolution also noted that, in the absence of co-operation by the various Somali factions, "other measures" to deliver humanitarian assistance were not ruled out.

6. The UN proposals also provide for the promotion of national reconciliation. The UN plans to work at local and regional level, both with the military factions and also civil leaders, in the hope of developing a framework for national reconciliation.

7. Following a report by a further UN technical team, on 25 August the Secretary-General proposed that up to 3,000 more UN armed guards should be deployed additional to the 500 in Mogadishu, to safe-

guard humanitarian deliveries in the four regions proposed for UN operations. This was endorsed by SCR 775 of 28 August. Canada, Nigeria, Egypt and Belgium have offered to provide troops. Canada is due to deploy 750 troops at Bosasso in the north-east during November 1992. Deployment at Berbera (north-west) is likely to follow, but no dates have been set. Local agreement has not yet been achieved for the other proposed locations—Kismayo (south) and Mandera (south-west, inside Kenya).

8. The south-west is the area most severely afflicted with starvation. The region is occupied by agriculturalists (most Somalis are nomadic herdsmen), and has been regularly fought across since Barre's downfall. Most recently, late in October, Aideed's forces, who had occupied the town of Bardera, were driven out by a faction led by General Morgan. Described by the press as pro-Barre (Morgan is Barre's son-in-law), Morgan's troops are probably not working for Barre's restoration, but are more accurately described as anti-Aideed. They are drawn from different clan factions, including Barre's, opposed to Aideed's Hawiye clan. (Though Aideed is in alliance with elements of one of these same factions opposing him. The clan/factional rivalries do not divide neatly.)

9. The cost of the UN operation as a whole is estimated at $129 million for six months. In mid-September the UN announced a 100-day action plan to accelerate relief efforts, including the delivery with the ICRC of 52,000 tonnes of food a month to all parts of Somalia. The plan was formally presented at a Somali donors conference in Geneva in October. The Geneva conference also discussed ways in which co-ordination amongst donors and the UN could be improved. A further such conference is tentatively planned for November in Addis Ababa, to which the Somali factions would be invited in order to seek their cooperation with UN efforts.

10. The UN Secretary General has recommended that UNOSOM be funded on the UN regular budget scale of assessment. If this is accepted, the UK share would be some $6.5m. for the first 6 months and $0.63m. per month thereafter

---

Examination of witnesses

Rt Hon Douglas Hogg, a Member of the House, Minister of State, Foreign and Commonwealth Office; Mr Anthony Aust, Legal Counsellor, Mr William Patey, Assistant Head, United Nations Department, Mr Steve Bridges, United Nations Department (UN finances), Ms Tricia Holland, United Nations Department (peacekeeping), and Ms Janet Douglas, United Nations Department (humanitarian affairs), Foreign and Commonwealth Office, examined.

Chairman

103. Minister, could I begin by welcoming you and your colleagues here this morning and thanking you not only for being here but for changing the time of your attendance at very short notice. We appreciate acutely in this Committee pressures on both your diary and those of your officials and so we are all the more appreciative that you were able to come this morning rather than this afternoon when the House will have its mind on other matters. The spread and size of your team really reflects the ever-widening number of activities which the Government finds itself involved in in relation to the United Nations which in turn is a reflection of the ever-widening number of roles the United Nations has been called upon to perform over and above its intention to reform itself. It is, indeed, those activities which have attracted the attention of this Committee and form the subject of our inquiry. What we want to seek your advice and that of your advisers on is a whole range of matters which this Committee has begun to inquire into following our visit a few weeks ago to the United Nations in New York. Could I begin, following that, by noting and pointing out to you that the wide range of peacekeeping operations the United Nations is now involved in has, I believe, more than doubled since 1988, and asking you how you feel about the rigour with which these activities have been thought out and the objectives identified? I think particularly about Angola and even more about Somalia, Cambodia and Bosnia, in all of which the United Nations is now deeply and increasingly involved. Are the objectives in your view sufficiently clear or is that an impossible demand?

(Mr Hogg) I think the answer is they are not always sufficiently clear. Moreover, the circumstances change so you have to develop the policy. Take, for example, Cambodia and ask yourselves what does happen if the Khmer Rouge does not participate in the election and then you see violence following the election or at the time of the election. The mandate runs out three months or thereabouts after the election. We are going clearly to have to address that question of the mandate if and when the Khmer Rouge do not participate or do cause violence and in that kind of way you have inevitably to change the mandate. You can see a similar situation developing in Bosnia. We started off with UNPROFOR I; that moved on so you got UNPROFOR II. We have so far resisted suggestions that we should use force of an aggressive kind, we are now contemplating what will happen in the event of there being further infringements of the no-fly zone regime. Therefore, policy does develop and I think it is impossible to set in concrete your objectives at the moment when you

[**Chairman** *Contd*]

embark on an expedition of any of the kinds I have referred to. It is a hazardous, uncertain undertaking.

104. Given that military men understandably like to start out with very clear objectives, rules of engagement and all the rest, can you give us any idea of whether when you come to change the mandate there are any ways of describing the different levels of mandate, starting from completely non-violent, non-engagement on any account, keeping the existing peace and moving gradually up through protecting your own people to active engagement with the enemy? Is it possible to talk in those terms?

(Mr Hogg) I do not think, Chairman, there are pre-set levels of gradation. I think what is in fact happening is that problems become apparent or previously had not been addressed and one then has to seek to deal with the problems as they emerge within what you can secure by way of an agreement in the Security Council. It is a pretty evolutionary process and one cannot conceal that fact. For example, in Somalia we are now seeing a boatload of Marines going off there and their role is clearly going to be much more adventurous than we previously contemplated.

105. Could you just share with us further thought on that very issue you have raised? What would be the effect of the deployment of a really very large number of American troops, which I think is now being mooted, in Somalia? What would their mandate be? A force come to establish a protectorate, rather in the language of colonial imperial days or how would they do it?

(Mr Hogg) I have been reading the transcripts and I know Mr Canavan rather objects to the language of imperial days, so I shall avoid using that kind of language. But clearly in countries such as Somalia where everything has broken down, and in particular it is not possible because of the lack of order to deliver relief supplies, you are going to have to ask yourself to what extent it is right by force to make the delivery of supplies possible. This matter has to be assessed finally by the Security Council, but it does seem to me—though one cannot bind the Security Council—that we are moving to a situation which will authorise armed troops to escort the delivery of supplies, and I should be very surprised indeed if that did not extend to a degree of action to enable that to take place. I do not know what the rules of engagement will be or what the ultimate decision will be. That seems to me the direction in which we are going.

106. Is this going to be a direction in which we are going to see the evolution of what United Nations blessed troops do by custom or are we going to be taking an area of legal reform and require actual changes in the powers accorded to the United Nations under its Charter and its Articles?

(Mr Hogg) I suspect the former. I would ask Tony Aust, the lawyer, to add to that but I suspect what we are going to see is an extension of the willingness of the Security Council to act in a whole range of areas which have previously been regarded as closed and an acceptance of our ability to deploy forces in areas which would previously have been regarded as internal. To some degree, events have brought this upon us—partly because the P5 line works a great deal more harmoniously than they did in the past for obvious reasons, and partly too because the dissolution of the Soviet Union has, in fact created tensions between now sovereign states when they were previously tensions between internal parts of the one Soviet state, and that has given rise to a competence and jurisdiction which previously did not exist, at least not obviously so.

(Mr Aust) I think the powers under the Charter are perfectly adequate. Although the United Nations is prohibited from intervening in the internal affairs of Member States, Article 2.7 of the Charter speaks of matters which are "essentially" internal affairs, and humanitarian matters are, of course, now matters of international concern. The prohibition of interference by the United Nations in internal affairs has also an important exemption: if you take action under Chapter VII, the prohibition does not apply. But to take action under Chapter VII, as is presently being considered by the Council, does require a determination that the situation or the dispute, is a threat to international peace and security. In the case of Somalia the Council has already reached that determination some months ago when it imposed an arms embargo because the lack of stability in the country was, of course, a threat to its neighbours, as was the refugee situation. So provided you can make a determination of a threat to peace and security, Security Council powers to deal with that situation are extremely wide, as we have seen with their actions over Iraq and over Libya and now over Yugoslavia.

Mr Rowlands

107. Following that, really all those actions we are talking about, particularly the Bosnian one—the Yugoslavian one, are under Chapter VII determinations?

(Mr Aust) Yes.

108. Because we have been grappling with the thought of what other criteria, if there were no changes in the United Nations Charter, you could devise or use, as it were, to govern the degree of United Nations intervention, short of trying to revise the Charter. One thing which crossed my mind (and we raised it before) is that where, in fact, the conduct of affairs within the territory caused a large-scale refugee problem to neighbouring territories, that would seem to be a reasonable criterion or justification for some form of intervention in territory which had previously been seen as the sovereign territory of a state.

(Mr Hogg) I think that we would reply to that by saying that it would be a factor which would justify making a Chapter VII determination.

[**Mr Rowlands** *Contd*]

109. Would you go through the Chapter VII route on each and every occasion where you wanted to put UN military personnel on the ground?

(Mr Hogg) I am not sure I would be quite so dogmatic about that because we did not use the Chapter VII route, I think, in North Iraq.

(Mr Aust) Resolution 688, which applies not only to northern Iraq but to the whole of Iraq, was not made under Chapter VII. Resolution 688 recognised that there was a severe human rights and humanitarian situation in Iraq and, in particular, northern Iraq; but the intervention in northern Iraq "Provide Comfort" was in fact, not specifically mandated by the United Nations, but the states taking action in northern Iraq did so in exercise of the customary international law principle of humanitarian intervention.

Chairman

110. In the very helpful answers your Department has provided, Minister—and I thank you for the work your officers have done on a whole range of questions the Committee have put to you after our visit to New York—we asked about intervention and humanitarian cases and what the criterion was and how you decide when any of these issues has reached the point where we should participate. Could you codify that a little more clearly for us?

(Mr Hogg) The honest answer to that is, most certainly not. Codification is one of the things which is quite impossible. It is a question of recognition and will, I think, depend upon the degree of suffering that we assess to be actually occurring, and the risk of it spilling over frontiers and thus causing serious problems to the tranquillity of adjoining states and, quite frankly, how bloody the business is. I cannot codify that in a legal language.

111. I think in a way that does answer the thought behind my question, particularly the point about spilling over into other areas. Maybe we will come back to that later. Could I just finally ask in this section: we have talked about the criteria and the difficulty of establishing for going into areas, but what about the conditions for pulling out; because if one goes in with open-ended goals or, indeed, ill, undefined goals, it does imply long-term involvement, and long-term involvement suggests that at some stage one has to think about how to get out as well as in?

(Mr Hogg) I think that it is probably impossible to answer that question in general; one could only seek to offer an answer with regard to particular circumstances or deployments. For example, in former Yugoslavia I can answer the question with regard to our own troop deployment, although I can only give a general reply. We are there for specific purposes, humanitarian in kind, the escort of convoys and the assistance of refugees. If we find that the risks we are being asked to carry are too high in relation to those objectives we will pull them out; or, in the first instance, we will pull them back to defensive positions and then, if our judgment continues that it remains too dangerous, we will pull them out. As to the term of the commitment, I can only answer again with specific replies. In Bosnia our initial deployment is for 12 months. We will look again at that deployment at the end of that 12 month period, or towards the end of it, and try and judge what the position there is, whether the objectives are still sustainable, and what the level of risk is. That is, in fact, the kind of approach that will be adopted no doubt at a larger level with regard to most of the problems where the United Nations is deployed.

Mr Shore

112. If we justify our original intervention in Bosnia on the grounds that what is going on in there and the rest of what was once Yugoslavia poses a threat to international peace and security, it really would be very difficult, would it not, to withdraw our presence simply because there had been no improvement in the threat to international peace and security, but because we had not yet deployed sufficient resources to carry out the mission? Would there not be, as it were, a continuing pressure for that once we had committed ourselves?

(Mr Hogg) I understand that point, Mr Shore, and of course it is a very fair one to make. I think it is important to remind yourself, and indeed the Committee, that within any Resolution there are many elements and, therefore, in a sense one is only addressing one part of the element. For example, the stop and search powers in the Adriatic and the sanctions regimes and the deployment of the SAMs are likely to go on in most circumstances. I was focusing on the deployment of ground troops, and I can only say to you that we put them in for a limited purpose, recognising that what could be secured by their presence is limited in character, and we are not prepared to run unnecessary or undue risk. I cannot quantify what I mean by that. It is, in a sense, a subjective judgement that you make in the circumstances that develop. We are not focusing on making peace by force, that was never our purpose.

Mr Harris

113. I wonder if I could follow that, Chairman. Is there not something of a conflict, or at least a dilemma, in what the Minister has just said and what he said earlier. He said earlier that we are in a evolutionary process as far as Bosnia is concerned and other places, but I think if one looks at Bosnia we are probably in an escalating situation, and I think the Minister touched on that. Is not the difficulty that, although troops have gone in with limited missions and the Minister says if there is any danger or that falls apart we pull them out, is not the reality that they are likely to be sucked further and further in? I notice in today's paper,

[**Mr Harris** *Contd*]

and I think the Minister touched on it in his earlier remarks, that in today's *Times* there is a suggestion that the Foreign Office has become quite hawkish, perhaps more hawkish than the Ministry of Defence, as far as Bosnia is concerned. If I may quote from the *Times*: "Senior officials in the Foreign Office are leaning towards the possibility of military action against the Serbs, including attacks on Serbian-held airfields to enforce the no-fly zone over Bosnia, and possible deployment of ground troops in Kosovo to prevent a general uprising there". The Minister himself did, I think, touch on the possibility of enforcing the no-fly zone. Perhaps he would like to enlarge a little on that. Is there some substance in *The Times* article, or is it just speculation?

(Mr Hogg) There is always a danger of being drawn in. I accept that the process of evolving policy sometimes does oblige you to go deeper than you originally intended, that is true (and I think the case of Somalia is rather a good example of that) although you always at each step have to ask yourself: is the deployment, or whatever you are deploying, and the risk thereby engaged, commensurate with the objectives you are seeking to achieve; and what is the next step beyond if you take the first step forward? So far as the no-fly zone is concerned, we do actually have a Resolution in place, and we have tried to ensure that it is implemented by the presence of monitors in various airfields, most airfields from which they are flying. There have been a large number of infringements, but no infringement of a combat kind, of which we are aware, since October 12th. Lots of aircraft have been flying, mainly to transport people, often VIPs, a certain amount of Medevac and a certain amount of training operation, but we are not aware of any combat operations. May I say, by "combat", I mean missions where lethal force has been in any way deployed. The question that we have to ask ourselves is whether we want to put in place a pre-emptive Resolution, in effect, saying we will enforce if there is any further breach, or whether we wish to await a breach and then put a Resolution of enforcement in place. That is a discussion which is now going on, not just within Government but within the membership of the Security Council and elsewhere. We have not come to a concluded view on that matter, but it is being urgently addressed.

Chairman

114. Our assumption at that point would be that this is going beyond humanitarian objectives and we are concerning ourselves with preventing further expansion threatening international peace and security?

(Mr Hogg) It flowed from a resolution that has already been passed because the resolution (I forget the number of it) already provides for no flying and, therefore, the question is whether you stand by and watch that broken or whether you put in place an enforcement provision for that which has already been passed. It is very difficult to see how you could stand idly by.

Mr Wareing

115. Are there not, Mr Hogg, some dangers—it always seems to me there are dangers—in the warning that has been given, indeed, by your colleague the Minister of State for Defence some time ago and which you have reiterated now, that, if in fact it gets rather too hot for our forces in Bosnia in regard to casualties, we will withdraw our forces? The danger I am referring to is the danger of limiting the usefulness of British troops within a United Nations force by saying to a potential enemy, "If you rough us up too much, then of course we will end the entire operation". Is it not best to keep your opponent guessing as to what you might do because to go along the path which I think we have gone along would suggest to some extreme nationalists (and there are all sorts of extreme factions there in Bosnia) that, if they cause enough United Kingdom casualties, then Britain will stop its role in the humanitarian operation in Bosnia? How do you feel about that?

(Mr Hogg) I am not in any way being critical of you and the view you represent—I hope you understand that—but you have not differed with the substantive policy, you are, in fact, at least not criticising the policy of withdrawing if we suffer unreasonable casualties. So can I proceed on the basis that at least we agree on the broad nature of the policy, at least we are not differing on that. You are asking me questions. Either I lie to you or I tell you the truth and the truth on the withdrawal is as I have stated it. The only way I can avoid not stating that is either to refuse to answer your question or to lie. We are a transparent system of government. If you ask me questions about what we will do in situation A or situation B, either I answer or I do not. You want me to answer. So it is not a criticism of you; but it is a structure of our government that I have to respond to questions you ask. The same question arose, for example, early on as to whether we would use force in aggressive circumstances. Now, there is the case of Mr Cormack whose constituency is in Staffordshire, and Mr Cormack has criticised us for saying early on in the conflict that we would not use force of an aggressive kind: I understand his point, it is a real one, but at the same time people like him or yourself will ask of Ministers "Do you intend to use force of an aggressive kind?" How do we handle that? We either answer truthfully or we do not answer at all.

116. There is the question of preventative diplomacy, is there not, involved in all of this. What about avoiding a conflagration by, as you say, keeping your opponent guessing because the Bosnian Serbs should be rather doubtful as to what will happen if there are British casualties?

(Mr Hogg) I understand that, but would you tell me what you want me to do when you ask me a specific question which has the effect of exposing

[**Mr Wareing** *Contd*]
our hand? The truth is, either you must not ask the question in the first place—and I do not blame you, I think you should ask the question—or you must not criticise me when I give an honest answer.

117. I criticise you for what has been said in the past.

(Mr Hogg) We have a problem here, do we not, because if I were simply to fudge it, you would criticise me for fudging it; if I were to lie to you, I should be brought before the Bar of the House; if I answer truthfully, you criticise me for removing uncertainty. I am in a jam.

Mr Wareing: Mr Hogg, you know all too well I would never stop criticising you.

Chairman: I think Talleyrand said "never too much zeal", perhaps we should rephrase that—"never too much clarification". Whilst we seek to understand these issues, we realise the very severe limits which diplomatic conduct of foreign affairs places upon the degree to which these things can be made explicit.

Mr Rowlands

118. We are all men of the world and understand the old-fashioned dilemma you describe. But in Cambodia, for example, is one of the most dramatic pieces of political engineering ever tried by an international organisation where a great deal has been put in place, we ourselves have made commitments, and the Japanese have committed enormous sums of money and for the first time got involved in this sort of activity. You then arrive at a situation where one party, the Khmer Rouge, decides to try to pull the plug on the whole and we hear from the papers that possibly three of our own soldiers have been caught in this kidnapping exercise that has been reported in the news. We have to assume, if we are willing to withdraw, whether from Bosnia or elsewhere, everybody else will have a right to withdraw and the whole scheme could get aborted (a) in Cambodia and (b) in Bosnia. Let us take Cambodia first: have we reached the stage where aborting this amazing piece of international political engineering, that is, getting an election going, is now a real danger, or do you still think we should hang in there and try to get a solution?

(Mr Hogg) The latter. I think we should hang in there and seek to get a solution. I do not think we are near to the point at which the Cambodia operation should be aborted. That applies also to Bosnia and in the whole of what was Yugoslavia. May I ask Mr Patey to come in?

(Mr Patey) In the Security Council a resolution was passed on Cambodia which very much says that the international community is hanging in there. They are calling on the Khmer Rouge to honour its commitment under the Paris Agreement and giving them the opportunity to do so, at the same time offering up the threat of further action should they not. So certainly the United Nations and the Member States of the United Nations have not given up on Cambodia. The commitment is for UNTAC to remain for three months beyond the elections which are due to be held in April / May. It would certainly be premature to talk about the United Nations pulling out.

119. I wondered if you could tell us about this news story about the soldiers and whether that is the case. At least in Cambodia there is a well-defined endgame. It is about elections and is a very well organised plan. In the case of Bosnia, where it is a humanitarian exercise, the endgame presumably is the equivalent of Cambodia, for Vance and Owen to establish a rather complicated new constitution for Bosnia. How far do we go on the ground to pursue that endgame or objective, which could mean a much greater deal of involvement of the United Nations and everybody else on the ground who have hitherto been engaged as opposed to just the humanitarian line.

(Mr Hogg) You have not asserted our sole role in what was Yugoslavia, Bosnia in particular, is humanitarian. It is obviously very important but it is not the sole role. You know in August we had the London Conference which brought together the United Nations and the European Community in what I think is a unique co-operation to provide the prospect of and mechanisms for a political settlement. So they are proceeding in tandem and we have got the two joint Chairmen heavily engaged, a working party now in Geneva, and we do have a number of principles formulated at London, but also subsequently worked out by the joint Chairmen, to guide the process of a settlement. One has to recognise though—and I am now talking about Bosnia as opposed to Serbia-Croatia—that one's ability, in fact, to bring about a settlement is extraordinarily limited. What one can try to do is to identify those solutions that will be unacceptable, not accepted by the world international community, and try to identify those principles which seem to us the most appropriate ones for the purposes of a constitutional settlement. At the same time you can set up fora, mechanisms which enable people to grope their way to a settlement reflecting these principles as and when they are willing to do so. You can also work on things such as ceasefires and trying to expand the area of tranquillity—there is not much of that in Bosnia—using in part your humanitarian forces for that purpose; but in the end we have to recognise that we cannot make peace in Bosnia and it is not an objective of policy to make peace through the deployment of force.

Mr Gapes

120. I have a couple of questions that follow on about Bosnia. You said earlier that you could not have peacekeeping by military means, or words to that effect. At what point in this Bosnian situation does the United Nations decide, or does the British Government urge the United Nations to decide, that we move from peacekeeping to something stronger? Linked to what, if we start getting to a

[**Mr Gapes** *Contd*]

situation where there are attacks on Bosnian/Serbian airfields or military facilities, are we not then making the humanitarian British forces sitting ducks for annihilation in retaliation without having any military protection, or adequate military protection, for them? My third question linked to that: could you now think that the recognition of Bosnia was actually premature, given what you have just said about the impossible situation we are faced with?

(Mr Hogg) I do not think that the recognition of Bosnia is premature, in the sense that a referendum was held within Bosnia which was a sufficient basis for recognition, and Bosnia complied with all the requirements that were established by Mr Badinter and within the EC. I think that it was a state that we had to recognise, applying ordinary criteria, in the same way that we recognised both Slovenia and Croatia.

121. But not Macedonia?

(Mr Hogg) Not Macedonia. I will answer Macedonia if you want me to, but can I do that separately. You then outlined what I do regard as a dilemma that we face. You are quite right in saying that if force is used against Serbian positions, by any force which is authorised by the United Nations, that will put at risk all the UN authorised deployments and activities within what was Yugoslavia. That has been an absolutely fundamental point which we have held to throughout this crisis. It is one of the reasons (though not the only reason) why we have turned our face against the use of aggressive force. It is not just the UK forces who are spread all over Bosnia, it is UNPROFOR II, it is the EC monitoring mission, the lorry drivers, and it is a very large number of people who are extremely vulnerable. If we use any kind of aggressive force they are at risk. We know that to be the case. Therefore, if we decide that we have to enforce, and then do enforce by lethal force, a no-fly enforcement regime we may well find ourselves incapable of operating on the humanitarian supply links for an extended period of time. Therefore, those of the world who say, "use force", have to trade against, one, the prospects of success flowing from the use of force, as against the fact that people will most certainly die, or are likely to die, because we are unable to deliver supplies. This is a tension. I think the truth of this is that we are likely, although not certain, to put in place an enforcement regime, and we will enforce but we do so with our eyes open.

122. If you are doing that is there not an argument that you would have to remove your humanitarian forces because they have not got the military capability or military support, and you have to actually withdraw humanitarian forces before you go in with military enforcement?

(Mr Hogg) Yes, absolutely.

123. What will that then mean for the refugees and the people who are starving at this moment who need the work of those humanitarian convoys to get through this winter?

(Mr Hogg) We have a dreadful dilemma, and you are right to identify it, and I do not shrink from it. If we decide to use force and use lethal force, and it may be possible to use graduated response (but that is a separate point) if we start shooting down aircraft what you say is correct. For a period of time, I cannot tell you how long, it is likely that we will not be able to deliver humanitarian supplies. We will find that UNPROFOR I forces, for example, in Krajina or UNPAs may well be at very serious risk and will have to pull back to defensive positions. That is a dilemma we have to face. It does not flow from that that you do not use force to enforce a no-fly regime, because it is in place and it is intolerable to have it flouted, but we have got to be aware of the consequences and I am not trying to conceal them from you.

Chairman

124. What would be the answer to the question about British interests if this is "upgraded" (if that is the right word) to peace enforcement? We were told by your distinguished office, or the previous Committee was told, that Yugoslavia was a *sui generis* affair and that, horrific as it all was, it all took place in the former Yugoslavian regime and was not a threat to international security. If we were to move to peace enforcement would people not say in this country, "What is the objective now, beyond the humanitarian one? Where is the international security threat to this island? Why are we raising the whole temperature in this area?"

(Mr Hogg) Chairman, again you identify, I think, a very real area of concern. Might I say, I would not like to use your phrase "peace enforcement", because I am drawing a distinction in my own mind between enforcing the no-fly zone, which seems to me something that can be relatively easily done by air power, which is available, and using your ground troops for a peacemaking function. We are not looking at that latter possibility at the moment, but we are looking at enforcement of the no-fly zone, so I would make that distinction. If you say to me, do I think (and I mean to say me) that we are pushing to the frontiers of what the British public believe to be our national interest, I think we probably are.

Mr Wareing

125. I think I must say, as Mr Hogg knows, I was very supportive of the Government's even-handed position over Yugoslavia, but that ceased in January 1992.

(Mr Hogg) Yugoslavia ceased?

126. Yes, the former Yugoslavia. In reply to Mr Gapes you quoted the Badinter report on Bosnia-Herzegovina. I think you will find, and your officials may correct me if I am wrong, that report did not particularly recommend Bosnia-

[**Mr Wareing** *Contd*]
Herzegovina and did not recommend recognition of Croatia and they felt that human rights had not been upheld, which is one of the reasons why we now have to have UNPROFOR troops in Krajina to protect the large sections of minority Serbs within the boundaries of Croatia. What I am very interested in is the role of preventative diplomacy. I wonder what role the United Kingdom is playing in improving the early warning systems of the United Nations. We have the possibility of something happening in Kosovo. It is very difficult because it comes within Serbia itself. We have the problems which are likely to arise in both Cambodia and Angola if the Khmer Rouge in Cambodia and UNITA in Angola did not accept the election results held under the United Nations auspices. How are we attuned to the United Nations earlier warning systems in areas of possible conflict?

(Mr Hogg) Firstly, I obviously do not want to split hairs with you, Mr Wareing, but on the question of Croatia my recollection is that Badinter originally reported (and I forget the exact date, but it may be around December 1991, and I am now speaking off the cuff) that Croatia's constitution was lacking in a number of material respects and that it was wrong to recognise until those defects had been put right. I think that then what happened was that the Croatian Government addressed those defects and the constitution was in fact changed, and that is why the recognition then took place. I am bound to say that I do not have a note in front of me.

Chairman

127. This Committee did visit Mr Badinter and went over his Croatian and Bosnian recommendations in detail, and they did not really sustain the case for recognition.

(Mr Hogg) I do not want to fall out with you on this point because I think it is some time ago and I have not focused on the detail step by step for some little while. I will ask Mr Patey to answer on the early warning point, but there are a number of things that we are doing within Yugoslavia which are designed partly to diffuse tension and partly to keep us more fully informed of what is happening. For example, in Kosovo there is now a team of four CSCE people who are there to report on the affairs there, most particularly on infringements of human rights but more generally, and I could see it might be helpful to reinforce them either by extending their numbers or alternatively—and this is slightly different—bolting on another team to them. That would have to be by consent of Serbia because, as I am sure you appreciate, Kosovo is part of Serbia. So far as Macedonia is concerned there are a variety of teams now in place there or shortly to go there doing much the same. They have been sent to look at the question of oil supply. There are what are called the SAMs, the Sanctions Assistance Missions, to advise on enforcement and a United Nations team is going too—it may have gone already—to determine whether or not it would be right to put any permanent presence there. So those types of things we are in the business of doing by way of a pre-empting early warning system. It may be that Mr Patey would like to speak a little more generally; I have been rather specific.

(Mr Patey) On the subject of preventive diplomacy and fact-finding missions, that is a key element in the Secretary-General's report "Agenda for Peace". We particularly welcomed that section of his report. The Secretary of State said that effort spent in preventive diplomacy is lot cheaper than what might follow. So we are paying particular attention to that. We have supported the Secretary-General in his attempts to strengthen areas of the Secretariat, the political areas where there is a need to gather information about potential areas of conflict, to act as an early warning system for the Secretary-General to enable him to exercise the powers which he already has under Chapter 99, to bring concerns about threats to international peace and security to the attention of the Security Council. So it is a question of enabling the Secretary-General to utilise the provisions within the Charter he already has. He has increased the number of fact-finding missions. The Secretary-General has sent the missions to Moldavo, Nagorno Karabakh and to Georgia. The UN has been active in sending missions and monitors to South Africa and the Minister has mentioned the activities in the former Yugoslavia. We support the Secretary-General in this. We have also offered to provide information and assessments from our own resources. There is a slight sensitivity in that there is a convention that the Secretary-General must request information and must not have information foisted on him. I think this may be a throw-back to earlier times when there was a worry that governments would seek influence through the provision of information; but we are willing to respond to requests for information. There is also a process going on essentially to strengthen those areas of the UN Secretariat who are tasked with providing early warning. Of course, it is open to any Member State, including the United Kingdom, to draw any matter to the attention of the Secretary-General or the Security Council and this happens in response to situations as they develop.

Chairman: Before we go on a complete world tour of every trouble-spot, I would like to move on to the central United Nations structure and its problems. Mr Rowlands.

Mr Rowlands

128. I assume we have reached preventive diplomacy. I think your description is very interesting and very important, Mr Patey, but it is going to be put to the test, I am afraid, one suspects, in rather more extreme circumstances. We have seen how impervious the Serbians are and have been to all forms of pressures and representations; ethnic cleansing has gone on in Bosnia. Now there is the dilemma, which has been vividly described by the

[**Mr Rowlands** *Contd*]

Minister, of how to limit that and put further pressure on the Serbians to obey the no-fly rules etc. Let us take Kosovo. Do you think the preventive diplomacy actions you described are going in any way to prevent the Serbians starting to behave towards the 80 per cent majority of Albanian Muslim people of Kosovo in anything but a rough way? Do you think the measures you have described are going to mean much to a gun-law Serbian leadership.

(Mr Hogg) I will answer specifically, then Mr Patey may wish to add. One cannot conceal that Kosovo could be the worst yet that is going to happen.

129. It has got the potential.

(Mr Hogg) Yes, it has got the potential. It is 90 per cent little Albania. The Serbs have very substantial forces already there, there is enormous tension and, so far as one can judge, a total denial of human rights so far as the Albanian population is concerned. It would only take a fairly casual incident to cause massive fighting throughout that region and we cannot necessarily stop that. What we can do is to re-emphasise our own views and our policy which is that Kosovo should be given autonomy similar to that which it had which was removed by Milosovic. One can make it plain to the Serbs that, if they use force, we are entering into a new ballgame. Most certainly their prospects of getting back into the international community and seeing sanctions in any way alleviated will be totally removed, and I can think of a number of situations that might well develop of which the least would be yet further tightening up of sanctions, but there are others.

130. To be honest, I just do not see——

(Mr Hogg) You are saying it does not add up. I agree with you in one sense. I am not in the position to say that if they use force against the Kosovans what will happen is that the international community will come down on them like a ton of bricks, whatever one quite means by that. I am not in a position to say that. All I can say is that they have exposed themselves to the whole range of extremely unpleasant possibilities.

Mr Gapes

131. Can I take you back to Macedonia? You did say you would come back to it. Is it not a little bit perverse that the Badinter Report recommended Macedonia as a pluralistic democratic system and Macedonia has not been recognised whereas in Croatia there are concerns about human rights but Croatia was recognised. Could you explain what the position of the Government is at this moment on this question?

(Mr Hogg) We are seeking to effect the compromise which would be acceptable to everybody on the question of the name. You are right in saying Macedonia satisfies all the ordinary criteria for recognition, yes. The problem is that the Greeks believe that the use of the word "Macedonia" in the name of that republic is intolerable so far as they are concerned and, therefore, they are seeking to persuade the Macedonians not to use the word "Macedonia" in the title applied to their country. The Secretary of State has appointed, as you probably know, a representative, Mr Robin O'Neil, who has been shuttling to and fro between Skopje and Athens trying to identify elements on which everybody can agree with a view to getting a settlement or compromise on this matter. It is that which we are seeking to deliver.

132. But the German Government was pushing for Croatia's recognition against the other eleven members of the Community, as far as many of us thought; yet Croatia was recognised. It seems that 11 governments in the Community are in favour of Macedonia's recognition and the Greeks are able to hold it up. Could you explain how this could be?

(Mr Hogg) We are trying to get a compromise on this. I hope a compromise may prove possible.

133. There was no compromise on Croatia.

(Mr Hogg) If compromise is not possible we have to determine what we do, and I would rather not say what one might do at this stage because we are still in the process of seeking a compromise. I think you also have to take into account—and this is, I think, an important point—that it is very desirable from the point of view of Macedonia that you should get Greek agreement to whatever happens because they have common frontiers and Greece could very well block those frontiers if things happened which they did not approve of, and therefore, if we can secure an agreement, let us try to do that. If not, we will face that when we come to it.

Chairman: If I could bring matters back to base, so to speak, I would like to get on to how we pay for all this growing area of activity which may well spread to the regions we have just been discussing. Mr Harris.

Mr Harris

134. Can I ask the Minister whether it is a distinction of Her Majesty's Government that a Peace Endowment Fund could meet the cost of any peacekeeping forces and replace the current system of assessed contributions?

(Mr Hogg) The short answer is, no. We would, however, favour another proposal, which is the peacekeeping fund which is designed to meet the start-up costs of a peacekeeping operation. There are proposals in place for that. The Japanese have come forward with specific proposals on how that should be funded, namely, by using arrears which should be carried forward into that fund, and by using unencumbered and unspent monies from previous peacekeeping operations which are still sloshing around and could be put into a contingency fund. We would favour a contingency fund—it is called the Peacekeeping Reserve Fund—which favours the start-up costs. The EC

[**Mr Harris** *Contd*]

has now actually got its own act together on the question of funding, and I know that Mr Bridges understands the technicalities better than I do, because it is a slight variation on the Japanese funding.

(Mr Bridges) The Japanese proposal as such at present recommends that there will be two windows of financing for the fund. 60m, as the Minister has said, will come from the unencumbered balances of two peacekeeping operations, and 90m will come from arrears to the regular budget and to other peacekeeping operations once they become available.

Chairman

135 That is dollars, is it not?

(Mr Bridges) Yes. There is no specification in the Japanese proposal of when and how the arrears from the regular budget and from peacekeeping operations will go into the reserve fund rather than to the regular budget or for the purpose for which they were originally intended. The EC proposal looks to nail that down. There are $60m sloshing around which could perfectly be used for the Secretary-General's start-up fund. In addition and once all arrears to the regular budget and its other working capital funds etc. have been topped up all subsequent arrears could also go into the reserve fund; thereby appeasing a lot of Member States who are concerned about the use of arrears, primarily for purposes for which they were not originally intended.

(Mr Hogg) Subject to that, we are basically content with the existing arrangement which is that peacekeeping operations are funded in an ad hoc way and under a special assessment which requires us to pay 6.102 of the cost.

Mr Harris

136. What criteria does the Government use in determining whether costs of individual peacekeeping operations are reasonable or not?

(Mr Hogg) I do not think I know the answer to that.

(Mr Patey) There is an advisory committee on budgetary questions in New York, and I think you met our representative when you were there, Mr Richard Kinchen. We have been represented on that committee for all but six years, since it was formed. It is a committee of 16 which scrutinises the various budgets, and is the UN's financial watchdog. There is an opportunity through that to establish that monies allocated are properly spent. They have an opportunity to ask the secretariat to provide explanations of reasonable costs, really like a select committee on finance, that is their role. Where the United Kingdom provides troops there is an additional scrutiny, in that the Treasury is responsible for scrutinising the Ministry of Defence estimates for the UK element in a peacekeeping operation. That is governed by normal government accounting rules. Then there is a UN mechanism for establishing that costs are fair and reasonable.

Chairman

137. Unlike UNPROFOR where we are paying, but in other areas where there are British personnel, is the thousand dollars per month per man rate low or above our actual costs?

(Mr Patey) Substantially below.

(Mr Hogg) The UNPROFOR II costs are estimated to be of the order of 120m per year.

Chairman: We have not discussed the intervention issue and I think it is relevant.

Mr Gapes

138. On this question of intervention, one of the consequences of the Gulf War was the decision that there would be a compensation fund from the United Nations. Is there any progress on that side? Is there any suggestion that further action should be taken to force the Iraqis to sell oil which would then be used both for compensation to people who were working in the region and also hostages from this country?

(Mr Hogg) I think you are referring to the 706/712 mechanism, the object of which was to enable a quantity of the Iraqi oil to be sold, and a proportion of the money from that sale to be placed into a special account to go for a number of purposes, most importantly (although not exclusively) the purchase of food and humanitarian supplies for Iraqis; but also my recollection is compensation of the kind you have just referred to. The position is that the Iraqis have not accepted 706/712 mechanisms, that is correct.

139. Is there any suggestion of any pressure or other action that will force them to carry out the decision of the United Nations with regard to this matter?

(Mr Hogg) There are the general pressures which flow from the sanctions regime, and we constantly make the point that if it is true that there is considerable privation within Iraq that is the fault of the Iraqi government, because the sanctions regimes themselves do not prevent the import into Iraq of either food or medicine or humanitarian supplies; and those who say that the Iraqis cannot afford them cannot sustain that argument because the Iraqis have available to them the 706/712 mechanisms.

Chairman

140. Could I just ask one further question on intervention and Iraq. The safe havens are still in place, are they?

(Mr Hogg) The North Iraq safe haven. One must perhaps be a little careful, Chairman, not to put them in the plural.

141. Are British personnel involved in the UN forces?

[**Chairman** *Contd*]

(Mr Hogg) There are British aircraft flying out of Turkey over North Iraq and, indeed, there are British aircraft involved in the no-fly zone in South Iraq.

Mr Canavan

142. Mr Aust referred earlier to a right under international law of humanitarian intervention as distinct from Chapter 7 of the United Nations Charter. I wonder if you could elaborate on that. Is there a generally agreed definition of this right under international law?

(Mr Aust) There is no agreement in the sense of rules which have been laid down by any international body, but the practice of states does show over a long period that it is generally accepted that in extreme circumstances a state can intervene in another state for humanitarian reasons. I think before doing so though a state would have to ask itself several questions. First of all, whether there was a compelling and an urgent situation of extreme humanitarian distress which demanded immediate relief. It would have to ask itself whether the other state was itself able or willing to meet that distress and deal with it. Also whether there was any other practical alternative to intervening in order to relieve the stress, and also whether the action could be limited in time and scope. These are the sort of questions which you would have to ask yourself before taking what is a very serious step and needs, therefore, to be fully justified.

143. Are there any other precedents, apart from resolution 688?

(Mr Aust) As I said, Resolution 688 did not actually authorise it but it did recognise there was a very serious situation in Iraq, particularly in North Iraq. Most of the precedents before that relate perhaps more to intervention in order to protect one's own nationals who are being mistreated or neglected by the territorial state. But international law in this field develops to meet new situations and that is what we are seeing now in the case of Iraq.

Mr Rowlands

144. Would that allow Albanians to intervene in Kosovo?

(Mr Aust) One has to be very careful in relying upon this principle because there is always the possibility of it being misused and, therefore, one has to ask oneself the questions I posed and I would not like to comment on an individual situation. It all depends upon the circumstances at the time.

Mr Gapes

145. Can I just come back on the answer given about this compensation for people who were damaged or hostages? From what you have said there seems no prospect then that the Iraqis are going to sell the oil and pay the money into the Fund. Does that therefore mean the people who were hostage or other people who lost their livelihoods have no prospect of any financial support for the foreseeable future?

(Mr Hogg) I think I would answer the question in terms of compensation from the Fund because, of course, there are social security provisions which are available in appropriate cases. So in response to the question on the Compensation Fund my understanding is that the money that was to be made available for compensation was, in fact, to come from the sale of oil under the mechanism established by those two resolutions and at the moment there is no money in the Fund.

(Mr Aust) There has been a very recent development: because Iraq has refused to export oil, a resolution was adopted recently by the Security Council requiring Member States to sequestrate the proceeds of previous Iraqi oil sales and to pay these proceeds, except in so far as they are subject to third party rights, into an escrow account opened by the United Nations. That account will then be used for, amongst other things, payments into the Compensation Fund which was established by Resolution 687. At the moment the Americans have paid in, I think, $20 million recently and voluntary payments have been made by Saudi Arabia and another state, so the Fund will now be available partly for compensation.

Mr Shore

146. I have one question on Somalia. The most spectacular intervention is now about to be made apparently by the United States in which 30,000 Marines are going to be deployed effectively to back up peacekeeping—I am sorry, humanitarian relief—if needs be by force. This is a very major precedent. What I would like to know is what authorisation specifically has been given for this and whether it comes under what might be thought to be a reasonable extension of the belief that the situation in Somalia is a threat to international peace and security because of its effect on refugees and so on in surrounding countries.

(Mr Hogg) I think the decision as to the exact nature of the deployment has not yet been taken. 30,000 is one option but the boatload of Marines is another option. They are different numbers. I think the boatload of Marines is 2,000 odd. The matter has to be addressed again by the Security Council in order to give the authority to the deployment in numbers. But I think that the first resolution from which all of this stems was a Chapter 7 resolution, was it not, which was based on the risk to adjoining states and the breakdown of peace in that region.

Chairman

147. Do you sense, Minister, a change of American policy going on, even as indeed one would expect, during this transition period? It sounds to me as though the Americans have changed their views on Somalia and Bosnia.

[Chairman *Contd*]

(Mr Hogg) I think it is very difficult to be clear about this. I think the answer is yes. However, throughout the discussions on Yugoslavia the Americans have made it very plain that they were not—anyway at that time—willing to put ground forces into what was Yugoslavia. That lack of willingness does not necessarily apply to the enforcement of the no-fly regime. It is clear from what they are prepared to do in Somalia that they are now reconsidering their general attitude on the deployment of ground troops in a peacekeeping role and, of course, what they are apparently prepared to do in Somalia is, I think, an important shift in their policy. So I think you are right to perceive a change.

Chairman: That is very interesting. It is something we obviously would like to pursue at another time and takes us on to our next issue. We sensed when we were at the United Nations the beginning of what might be called the regionalisation of United Nations activities and the hope that regional organisations would increasingly do the work of the United Nations. I think Mr Canavan has some questions on this.

Mr Canavan

148. What is the Government's view of the ECOMOG operation in Liberia? Has the situation in Liberia reached a point where the United Nations should take over the peacekeeping operation?

(Mr Hogg) I will ask Mr Patey to respond.

(Mr Patey) There was a recent United Nations Security Council resolution which endorsed the ECOMOG peacekeeping activities in Liberia and at the same time imposed an arms embargo. The West African states involved had come to the Security Council and asked for the Security Council's involvement and assistance and the response was the imposition of an arms embargo to stop arms reaching the various warring factions. Arms for ECOMOG's own use were exempted. The resolution also authorised the Secretary-General to send a special representative to Liberia to look at the situation in more detail and there is the possibility of a development of the United Nations role, but in terms of an answer to the general question ECOMOG is there, the United Nations supports the regional organisations in their efforts to solve any particular problem at a regional level. Chapter 8 of the Charter provides specifically for a role for regional organisations. But that does not preclude the United Nations as a whole providing appropriate support and that is what has happened in Liberia.

149. I have a couple of questions about NATO. Has the conception of the EC-UN operation in Bosnia been influenced by the use of NATO troops and a NATO command structure?

(Mr Hogg) NATO assets have certainly been made available to the operations in Bosnia and in Yugoslavia generally. NATO ships are engaged in enforcement in the Adriatic with stop and search powers recently conferred upon them, and NATO AWACS are playing a part in intelligence gathering and observation, and there are other NATO command and control units which have been deployed. You will also know—this is not quite an answer to your question—that NATO has resolved that it is willing to participate in the peacekeeping operations under the authority of the CSCE and, of course, the question of NATO assets being deployed under the authority of the United Nations peacekeeping operation is currently under consideration.

150. What do you think of the Canadian suggestion of using the European NATO bases in support of United Nations operations?

(Mr Hogg) I have not focused specifically on that question myself, but I certainly do think that regional defence organisations, of which NATO is the most prominent, obviously have an important role to play in peacekeeping because they have the assets and the control and command facilities. Therefore I do welcome very much the Resolution to use NATO forces under the authority of the CSCE; and I think one might well see very encouraging developments elsewhere with regard to the United Nations and NATO.

151. On the EC Sanctions Assistance Missions——

(Mr Hogg) The SAMs?

152. Yes, the SAMs appearing in countries bordering the Danube, how effective are they? Could you tell us whether this operation provides a good model for regional organisations assisting the work of the United Nations?

(Mr Hogg) Mr Canavan, my own belief is that they could do better. I am glad that we have got the SAMs in place. There probably could be more of them. What they are doing is assisting local customs officers and other officers both with advice and their physical presence, but I do think we need to build on them. Their role has been much reinforced by the Resolution (787), about a fortnight ago, which prevents the transhipment of goods across Serbia, down Macedonia, down the Danube and so forth, because that is going to enable them much more rigorously to control the flow of banned goods. In recent weeks whilst the overall sanctions have been pretty effective so far as Serbia is concerned, one cannot say that for the supply of oil and petroleum products, and they have been leaking into Serbia at quite an unacceptable rate. We have really got to get to grips with this. The 787 Resolution on transhipment provides the legal basis for that, but the SAMs have, I think, got to be further reinforced and we have got to find ways of making the whole system less porous. I hope I may have the opportunity of visiting the SAMs in the not too distant future to try and form some personal view.

Chairman

153. Conventional wisdom has been that sanctions do not work, or they may weaken a country but they do not change its resolve, which I think was the guidance we were given at the United Nations. Do you think as a result of these sanctions efforts—the sanctions efforts in the Gulf, the discussion of sanctions possibly against Libya—that a body of technique is building up in the UN on the advice of Member States about making sanctions and trade blockades more effective?

(Mr Hogg) The short answer is, yes, Chairman. I do not entirely agree about their lack of effectiveness. I have got some figures here on Serbia. Unemployment up 60 per cent; most of industry in short hours; inflation up 50 per cent. a month; industrial output down 75 per cent. since December 1989; and trade down 50–75 per cent. The effect on the domestic economy of Serbia has been very great. I accept, because it is Mr Canavan's implied point, that there has been a recent increase in the flow of oil and petroleum products to Serbia. For example, we see pump prices and queues at petrol stations much diminished. We have got to get a grip on that; but we have acquired a certain body of expertise but it can always be refined. For example, the stop and search powers which we are using in the Adriatic is drawn very largely on our experiences in the Gulf. We are going to learn a lot from the process in Serbia about how you actually make what are essentially fairly porous frontiers less porous. SAMs is a model, and we are going to have to build on the SAMs to coordinate their activities and get greater co-operation. We have a longish way still to go but we are making process.

Mr Wareing

154. In September I did see how effective sanctions were with the very, very long queues of traffic at petrol stations in Serbia between the Hungarian border and Belgrade. It is not just on the Danube where the need is. I saw for myself petrol being transported across the Hungarian, Yugoslav and Serbian frontiers. There is nothing to stop that and, of course, there are no sanctions on traffic moving between, say, Budapest and Belgrade, or Bucharest and Belgrade, Sofia and Belgrade even though there may be a United Nations embargo on oil. I do not know whether any dealings have been held between the Foreign Office and the Hungarian or Bulgarian governments in order to prevent that leakage?

(Mr Hogg) You are quite right. I would just put one proviso in what you are saying, Mr Wareing, if I may. We believe that Milosovic has in fact been releasing quantities of oil from military supplies so as to make the position less oppressive prior to December 20th elections. That said, I am not trying to conceal from you that there is a flow of oil into Serbia from the adjoining states. We are trying to get to grips with this. The Foreign Secretary did in fact last week summon the Ambassador from Bulgaria, Rumania and Hungary to discuss precisely this issue, and those Ambassadors communicated to the Foreign Secretary their resolve to comply with 787; but this is a constant process, and we make démarche representations whenever we have evidence of non-compliance. I accept that we have got to try and make enforcements across the Danube, along the Danube and across the ground frontiers more effective than they now are. I accept that and we will try and do that.

Chairman

155. A question, Minister, about the mobilising of the UN forces for all these tasks we have been discussing, and many more. I understand that now there are about 50,000 military personnel around the world operating under the UN auspices in one form or another, and presumably many other support staff. Do you enthuse to the idea that each responsible nation or willing nation should earmark and train part of its national forces to be able to participate in these endless requirements?

(Mr Hogg) There are two questions there, Chairman, if I may say so. On the matter of training, what I do think is true is that, looking forward, we are going to see peacekeeping under the authority of the United Nations, or maybe CSCE although that is a slightly different system, being very much more a part of the career of the typical British soldier than has ever been the case before. I think at the moment we have got in the order of 3,000, maybe a bit more, UK forces employed in peacekeeping. We have got 2,400 in UNPROFOR II; we have got the field ambulance in UNPROFOR I; we have the Cyprus force of 800; and we have one or two other deployments; we have a deployment in Cambodia and I have missed one or two others, the Sinai force. It is going to be very much a continuing role and it is going to increase and we have to train for that. Although we have a great deal of expertise there are others with even greater expertise, maybe the Nordic nations, maybe Canada, and I hope we will be training specifically along with them on this function. I personally suspect that what we will try and do in terms of deployment is usually to offer our logistic supports. The field ambulance in UNPROFOR I is a rather good example of that, together with the Engineers in Bosnia, together with the Signals Unit in Namibia. Those were rather specific things that we offered. I think that we probably would find it difficult to deploy infantry in substantial numbers, and maybe the present deployment is about as much as we could readily contemplate. On the question of earmarking forces specifically, although you have not asked a question prepositioning equipment, I think the answer is, no, on both counts. We are able, I think, to respond to the requirements on a case by case basis and that is what we should do. We are not in favour, and I am sure this is right, of prepositioning equipment in various parts of the world because the unpredictable always happens and you will probably

[**Chairman** *Contd*]
find that the equipment becomes largely irrelevant for that which you have to do.

156. That does actually put us in a minority, does it not? I understand that Mr Boutros-Ghali sent round a famous questionnaire saying, "What would you earmark for us in the future?" and we provided a nil return, as did, I believe, our American allies but several other countries said, "Yes, we will stand by at all times to provide X logistical support, Y armoured battalions and Z armoured personnel?

(Mr Hogg) The proof of the pudding is in the eating thereof. We have actually been very good in that regard. I have mentioned what we have done in Yugoslavia; there is also what we have done in Cyprus; and, Mr Shore was drawing attention to the fact of what the Americans appear to be contemplating now in Somalia. Whilst we are not in favour of earmarking troops, we are making contributions when requirements arise, and that will continue.

Chairman: Thank you. Could we now look finally in the last few minutes—I know we are all under time pressure; you certainly are, Minister—at the reform of the United Nations and your policies towards that. Mr Shore.

Mr Shore

157. I have no doubt that our own people in New York are not enthusiastic about reform of the Security Council and have perfectly good reasons for that attitude; that attitude, I believe, is also shared by many others there. But there is growing pressure against our position and I would like to have your view as to how long we can sustain our present attitude towards the Security Council and its membership.

(Mr Hogg) I suspect on this matter you and I think very much alike. There are no advantages that we can see in changing the composition of the Security Council. Indeed, there are no national advantages in doing that, for obvious reasons. Actually I do not think there are any pragmatic advantages in doing that, because in the last two or three years for a variety of reasons you know as well as I do the Security Council has actually been working rather well, especially, of course, with the constructive role of Russia in its capacity as a permanent member. There are pressures building up, you are right—pressures from the European Community in general and Germany in particular, Japan likewise—but there are other countries who would like to be permanent members. Nigeria is another. I hope we can maintain the present position because it is working. There is not any natural correlation between economic weight and permanent membership of the Security Council, but I also accept that we the United Kingdom as a permanent member and France as a permanent member have to be very sensitive to the views—I hope I am not now departing from the consensus view established—of our European colleagues and have to take them into our confidence, represent their views, discuss very much what the line should be, etc.

158. Of course, as you say, to be sensitive is one thing, but as I understand it, arising out of the European Community, there is even a wish that the Community itself should be represented.

(Mr Hogg) That is correct—a wish: one we do not share.

159. But the whole basis of that, of course, would be to accept that the European Community or the European Union had become a state.

(Mr Hogg) We are going to broaden the debate, Mr Shore, if we are not careful. I think we can stand on common ground. I thought we had stood on common ground, which was that the present structure of the Security Council is as you and I would wish to have it, and that is my position.

Mr Gapes

160. From what you have just said, can I take it that the position of the Government is absolutely against the Japanese membership of the Security Council?

(Mr Hogg) As I have said, the shape and structure of the Security Council as it is now is how we would like it to be in the future, but clearly we have to keep an eye on other people's views. But we do not want change—how else can I express it?

161. You do not want Japan?

(Mr Hogg) We do not want change.

Chairman

162. Although, of course, the Japanese argument is that paying the piper involves having at least some say in some of the notes in the tune.

(Mr Hogg) I well understand that, Chairman, but if you are asking if I support change, the answer is, no, I do not.

163. Let me go into a little more detail about the United Nations Secretariat which are attempting to streamline themselves and also a related question connected with the Japan issue about the sort of sharing of information so that people who are not in the permanent five but nevertheless pay large sums of money do not find that they, first of all, learn they have to pay the money and afterwards learn what they have got to pay it for?

(Mr Hogg) I think there ought to be much more flexibility here. I will ask my colleague to come in.

(Mr Patey) Japan is a current member of the Security Council, of course. There are two separate questions, the streamlining of the Secretariat and the one about the Security Council which I think the Minister has answered. Our position has been very much supporting the Secretary-General in his attempts to streamline the Secretariat. The first phase of his reforms involved reducing the numbers of under-secretaries general and making the

[**Chairman** *Contd*]

system of accountability within the United Nations clearer, avoiding overlap and strengthening those areas of the United Nations Secretariat which are under the most pressure. I think these are easily identifiable as the peacekeeping operations under Mr Goulding and also the Political Section under Mr Petrovsky. Those are areas where additional staff and additional resources have been made available, fortunately without requiring additional funds, by streamlining and redeployment. The next phase, I think is one that, while supporting the Secretary-General, we need to leave to him. I think Sir David Hannay when he was here said that we should not try to micro-manage the Secretariat. That is a view we take, that the Secretary-General has drawn the broad lines of how he would like to see the Secretariat develop and we support those broad lines—but it is really for him actually to decide in detail what he should do.

164. What about the specialised agencies? Should they be given a going over in the same spirit of structural reform?

(Mr Patey) The specialised agencies have their own constitutions and their own boards. They are brought together by the Secretary-General in a co-ordinating committee on which he sits with the heads of the agencies, so it is possible to inject ideas for reform. Member states of course, have a role and responsibility to encourage reform within individual agencies. I do not think there is a global approach you can adopt to the agencies. I think they have to be agency-specific and we are doing that.

Chairman: We are really out of time because of the other demands on your time, Minister, and we are extremely grateful to you. There are many other issues we have not even touched on, like Cyprus, San Salvador, Nicaragua and dozens of other places where the United Nations is deeply involved. That merely reinforces the point that to carry these responsibilities you have to be a global expert in detail on a vast range of issues. We do appreciate your willingness this morning to answer questions on some of them and also your willingness to attend.

Printed in the United Kingdom for HMSO.
Dd.5060562, 1/93, C5, 3398/3B, 5673, 226063.

ISBN 0-10-280793-0

9 780102 807936

HOUSE OF COMMONS SESSION 1992–93

FOREIGN AFFAIRS
COMMITTEE

THE EXPANDING ROLE OF THE UNITED NATIONS AND ITS IMPLICATIONS FOR UK POLICY

MINUTES OF EVIDENCE

Thursday 10 December 1992

Rt Hon Lord Owen

Ordered by The House of Commons *to be printed*
10 December 1992

LONDON: HMSO
£5.95 net

235–iv

THURSDAY 10 DECEMBER 1992

Members present:

Mr David Howell, in the Chair

Mr Mike Gapes	Mr Peter Shore
Mr David Harris	Sir John Stanley
Mr Michael Jopling	Mr David Sumberg
Mr Ted Rowlands	Mr Ted Rowlands

Examination of witnesses

RT HON LORD OWEN, A Member of the House of Lords, attending by leave of that House, Co-Chairman, Steering Committee of the International Conference on the former Yugoslavia, examined.

Chairman

165. Lord Owen, we are acutely aware of the hectic schedule under which you have to operate in your role as Co-Chairman of the Steering Committee of the International Conference on the former Yugoslavia. That makes us doubly appreciative of the fact that you have been able to give us time today to share your thoughts with us on the grim situation in the former Yugoslavia. We would like to start with some more general questions on the strategic situation as you see it and then go on to a number of specific issues, if we may. First of all, I should say would you like to make an opening comment or would you prefer we should go straight into the questions? Can we then have your overview of the current security situation in the former Yugoslavia and also what chances have your's and Mr Vance's constitutional plan, which I know you hope is the basis for, and is the basis for, the talks you are presiding over in Geneva. Can we start with that?

(Lord Owen) Well, thank you, Mr Chairman. It is very nice to be back in the House of Commons. The security situation on the ground is, to say the least, not good. On the other hand, I think we have to take account of what is the reality of what is often how it is reported. For example, there was yesterday evening a great alarm, and the day before a great alarm, about the fact Sarajevo was going to be cut off and a lot of stories were run on the basis that Sarajevo was cut off. What actually happened was there was fighting across the road and this gave the appearance of it being cut off and, quite wisely, the United Nations did not run any vehicles down that road for the period while the fighting continued but by seven o'clock that evening a recce patrol went through without any difficulty. I only say that because it is extremely difficult to get accurate reporting from the field and often what appears to be a traumatic event may not necessarily always be the case. For example, many people thought Travnik was going to be taken some weeks back, fortunately at the moment the situation as far as Travnik looks reasonably stable. I am well aware of the fact that the situation may change within three days. The overall picture is one of advance by the Bosnian Serb forces into areas which under no stretch of the imagination could they claim even by their own standards was territory in the past which has been populated by a majority of Serbs. They have encroached on areas traditionally Croatian and traditionally Muslim. Travnik is a very good example of a town which has never had anything other than a small Serb population and cannot under any circumstances be considered to be a town which could be tolerated to be occupied on a permanent basis by Bosnian Serb forces, or would be part of any province which was likely to be controlled democratically by Bosnian Serbs. Therefore, it seems to me it is an example of where the line of defence has already gone far too far and has got to be stopped. What can stop it is a separate question which we will probably come to at other stages. As far as the ceasefire that took place, the first time a ceasefire has been claimed while the UN EC Conference, which started on 3rd September, has operated, it arose in November as a result of discussions in the Mixed Military Working Group, it has not held and in that sense has not been a success as a total ceasefire, but as a reduction in overall hostilities it has had some considerable successes. The ferocity of the fire and of the battle in certain areas has not lapsed at all. That is particularly the case in the northern corridor right up to the top of Bosnia-Herzegovina where the Bosnian Serbs are intent on keeping open, as they see it, the supply line through to Serbia, the Croatians who are strong in the Bosanski Novi area, although they had to withdraw from that area, and the Muslims who are stronger below that corridor are operating a pincer-like operation. There have been fears over other areas of fighting in the west and the Herzegovina side with the Croatians. The military commanders, General Nambiar and General Morillon, in Bosnia-Herzegovina feel since the ceasefire they have been able to pinpoint areas of major military activity on the front line and they were able to get UN observers into many of the other areas and in those areas where there had been a history of fighting the ceasefire has relatively held. What we are seeing is that each side is pushing out the boundaries of the present front

The cost of printing and publishing these Minutes of Evidence is estimated by HMSO at £2,919.

[**Chairman** *Contd*]

line with political objectives in mind. That is how we see it. Jajce, which fell to the Bosnian Serbs, was again an area it was hard to see any reason why they would go there for political reasons and we feel that they went there because it has the two hydro-electric plants which supply Banja Luka and there had been interference in the electricity supply line. The situation remains extremely difficult and most recently we have had fighting starting again in Sarajevo at an intense rate. It is difficult to know who has started the firing, in most cases it is the Bosnian Serbs but there are many well documented cases where the Bosnia-Herzegovinian side have started the firing and we have also seen firing from their forces not only that is at the other side but into Sarajevo which complicates the whole question tremendously as to who is generating the firing. Certainly the majority around Sarajevo is being generated, we feel, by the Bosnian Serbs.

166. Is it possible to elaborate a bit on your statement that the various parties are pursuing political motives for carrying on fighting? It is a mystery to many people as to why endless killing goes on and why the ceasefire broke down. What are the driving impulses? What is the political agenda of each of the three groups? If I may put a question in your mouth, are the Muslims fighting in the hope of bringing the world more involved? Are the Serbian Muslims fighting to order to get a good position on the negotiating table? Are the Croatians fighting to build a greater Croatia? What are the driving forces of this endless madness?

(Lord Owen) It is very difficult to be certain. I have no doubt that the Bosnian Serb General Mladic is intent on having a very substantial part of Bosnia-Herzegovina under the control of his army. In that sense he is an expansionist which is part of a wider dream of a greater Serbia. There has certainly been a quite active involvement of the Bosnian Serb army with the policy of ethnic cleansing in the areas which they have controlled. I think it is very clear they have an agenda. The extent to which General Mladic is responding and under the control of the political forces, Dr Karadzic and others, is not absolutely clear, to be honest. It seems the military are calling more of the shots than they were say two or three months ago. Like everything in this whole area it varies greatly. There are clearly generals who participate in the Mixed Military Working Group on behalf of the Bosnian Serbs who appear to be genuinely helpful and searching for the cessation of hostilities. As far as Bosnian Croatian forces, they have in parts a joint military command with the Bosnia-Herzegovina Government forces. There was a breakdown in relationships between the two and that led to the fighting between their two forces and this was particularly damaging and destructive. That appears to be considerably better at the moment. The Bosnia-Herzegovina Government are, I think one has to understand, pushed back into ever smaller territory and therefore I think are sometimes striking out, perhaps their commanders at times also take military stances which may not necessarily have the endorsement of the Bosnia-Herzegovina Government. That was obviously the case when they ambushed the French humanitarian convoy and two French soldiers were shot and we have still not seen anybody brought to justice. Two French soldiers were killed and others were wounded and we have not seen anybody brought to justice for that. Motives are confused, there is little doubt the Bosnia-Herzegovinians do want to internationalise the conflict and bring others in. There is a problem over the Bosnia-Herzegovina Government. As you know the Presidency is due to end on the 20th of this month and there have been discussions between the Bosnia Croatian leaders under Mr Boban, and President Izetbegovic on the allocation of portfolios within the Boznia-Herzegovina Government. This does not appear to have been as yet fully agreed but there appears to be an arrangement whereby President Izetbegovic would be allowed to continue as President beyond the 20th and for the continuation of the war in exchange for the Bosnian Croatians and people who are the choice of Mr Boban and, therefore, representative of the present power structure in Bosnia Croatia having governmental positions. Their exact positions is being negotiated it appears to be over whether they wish to have the Prime Ministership, which appears to be pretty certain, and whether they wish to have a Defence Minister or a Foreign Minister. These negotiations are important in as much as they wish to be able to lay claim to speak for more than the Bosnian Muslims—I have not used the expression Muslim forces, I have called them Bosnia-Herzegovina Government forces. I think this is for them to decide if they wish to claim to represent more than the Muslim forces. Many people in Bosnia-Herzegovina hope there will be an agreement between the Croatians and Muslims at least but it does not appear to have been ratified yet.

Mr Shore

167. A supplementary to your discussion of probable aid to the protagonists: are the Serbians anywhere near fulfilling their expansionist goals? Is the fall of Sarajevo itself an objective for which they are striving?

(Lord Owen) It is very hard to be sure what anybody's objective is. So far as I can make a judgment, I think they do not wish to seize Sarajevo and had they wished to do so I think they could have taken Sarajevo over the last six months. I think they wish to bring political pressure to bear on the Bosnia-Herzegovina Government to some extent to protect parts of Sarajevo where there has traditionally been a Serb stronghold and to throttle but never asphyxiate. It is a pretty callous policy, it means you hold up aid convoys and then let some aid convoys through. You hold up air relief convoys but then let some through. I do not think at any stage have they decided to take Sarajevo and indeed I think it would be extremely foolish from their point of view to do so. As to their overall territory I think

[**Mr Shore** *Contd*]

they have already taken far too much, that is not to justify their war at all but this in on even their criteria of what they are meant to be dealing with. On the other hand one has to have one caveat, it is not a simple equation to take the population prior to the war of the Serbs, 34/35 per cent, and claim that would be the percentage of the territory they would be likely to have. The Serbs have always had, in Bosnia-Herzegovina, more territory because they are a rural population and the Muslims, who are not the overall majority but the largest single of the population groupings, have been concentrated very heavily in centres of urban population. I do not wish to think of Bosnia-Herzegovina in entirely ethnic map terms but it is certainly true to say more territory and more acreage is likely to be occupied in any sort of political democratic system that might emerge by Bosnian Serbs than by Bosnian Muslims.

Mr Wareing

168. Lord Owen, I do believe you have taken on one of the most difficult jobs that could have been asked of any man by the United Nations. I just wonder whether you would like to tell us how your mind has changed, if at all, I suspect it has, since you took up the position from what you are quoted as having said in a letter to the Prime Minister last July that military intervention is the only option for stopping what is happening in Bosnia? What are your feelings about that having been on the spot, so to speak?

(Lord Owen) Thank you for what you have said. I think it is a pretty difficult job. It was very obviously so when I took it up. It is greatly helped by working with Cyrus Vance. I think it is an interesting combination, the United Nations and the European Community. I think, looking at some of the articles and speeches I made at the time, I do not want to defend every paragraph or line in them but the thrust of them I stand by entirely. I think in any diplomacy you need pressure to bring parties to the negotiating table and I think those pressures are political, I think they are economic and I think they are military. I qualified very extensively what I wrote in the days when I was a free man and described the military pressures I thought were the ones to be considered. I did not consider it sensible to produce a military force which would interpose itself between the fighting forces, that remains my view. I think that would be a foolish thing to do. I think it was necessary to have a British contribution to the United Nations, that is what I wrote about at that stage, and which had not been done in Bosnia-Herzegovina and I pay tribute to the Prime Minister's decision to contribute British forces to the humanitarian efforts and support of convoys. I suspect this is something you will come on to but it is often remarked to me by Mrs Ogata, UNHCR, that the British contribution on the ground at Bosnia-Herzegovina at the moment is a very effective one and they are getting convoys through by a combination of firmness and conciliation and switching it on and off very well. The question one then comes to is the use of air power which is what I did advocate at that stage in the summer. It is well known I believed it was, and still believe it is, very unfair to the Bosnia-Herzegovina forces, Government forces, to be operating under an arms embargo, which I support as necessary, but it is unfair to operate under such an embargo when the Bosnian Serbs had control of the air and were combat flying fixed wing aircraft and were also flying helicopters. It was for that reason I was very glad to be able to negotiate, I think it was October 12th, with Dr Karadzic a no-fly agreement. I have to say I would not have been able to negotiate that agreement with Dr Karadzic if President Bush had said only a few days earlier that he was ready to enforce a no-fly ban. It was the knowledge that Dr Karadzic had that if we did not negotiate a deal there would be one which was imposed which made him negotiate. I do not wish to go into the details of the negotiation but I was able to say without any threat or bluster: "If you do not agree to this your combat aircraft will be taken out of the Banja Luka airfield". Since then we have had no combat aircraft flown, we think, certainly in combat missions of fixed wing. We are not so certain about helicopters but we have no proven case. We have a lot of UN observers around the country. We think although they are violating the no-fly ban they are not informing UNPROFOR of flights as they are bound to, by prior notification, or not allowing UN observers on to the air strip to inspect the aircraft, either fixed wing or helicopters, on leaving the airfield and on return. Sometimes it is a combination of these infringements or only one but they are infringing it now in substantial numbers. It is my view that is a serious breach of the UN Security Council resolution framed in Chapter VI language and that the Security Council will have to ensure this is fulfilled. It is true to say yesterday that Cyrus Vance and I went through with Dr Karadzic these infringements. We gave him chapter and verse of recent infringements in the last few weeks. We explained to him why we were able to corroborate this from a combination of UN observers and AWAC patrols NATO are operating and other information. We warned him if this went on we would not see any option for the Security Council other than for the Security Council to deal with this under Chapter VII. In my view if these violations continue this will happen. I do not decide when it will happen, or how it happens, that is for Governments and for the Security Council. I believe it is necessary that that threat exists and that a degree of air power is something which I do believe the West should hold quite legitimately over the Bosnian Serbs or anybody else who infringes. Some of the infringements of the no-fly ban have taken place by the Croatians going into Bosnia-Herzegovina as well.

169. I agree with you but can I ask your opinion on a point you made before. You said the military were calling more of the shots, I assume by that you mean more of the shots than Karadzic?

[Mr Wareing *Contd*]

Can you express a view as to who really controls the Bosnian Serbs, is it the military warlords, is it Karadzic or Mladic of Serbia? Views are expressed on this widely. You have seen people on the ground so to speak, can you express a view on this?

(Lord Owen) General Mladic is a very able gentleman, I do not think it ever does your case good to denigrate a personality or somebody with whom you may be disagreeing with their military policies. He came out first in his military class. He is, in his statement most recently in Pale to the Assembly, a believer and he gave the appearance of believing might is right, you create the facts on the ground through territorial aggression and you hold them and the world just has to live with that reality which is, of course, in direct contradiction with the London Conference principles, one of which is you do not take territory by military might. General Mladic used to be responsible for the fighting Serbian forces in The Knin which was one of the most difficult and bitter areas of Croatian territory. He was transferred from The Knin to Bosnia-Herzegovina by President Milosovic, at that time in charge of Serbian forces. That can be a pretty clear indication of where General Mladic sees some authority, I do not say total authority but I think President Milosovic still has an influence with General Mladic. I think there is an influence from Belgrade on General Mladic. He used to be in the JNA, the Yugoslav Army. I think he has some residual respect but nothing else for his senior military officers in the JNA but there are not many senior to him and I think he is pretty conscious of his position. Dr Karadzic, if you talk to him, does say he controls the military and he drew our attention only yesterday to the fact they have just got a new defence council which does not have General Mladic on it, he is not even a member of it. It nevertheless remains the view of those who have met General Mladic and seen the conduct of affairs that he is conducting the military operation to a very large extent under his own authority. I certainly feel the military flouted the agreement which I have agreed with Dr Karadizc over no-fly. The argument was put to me "How can you possibly have a no-fly ban and not allow training flights?" That is not, on the face of it, an unreasonable argument so that was dealt with because Prime Minister Panic offered these aircraft to be flown out to Yugoslavia on the basis they could have training flights to their heart's content over Yugoslavian territory. That was the agreement, combat aircraft would fly with their maintenance and pilots and they would continue to have the right to fly. That agreement was overturned, I believe, by the Commander of the Air Force in Banja Luka airport, who I have met, and General Mladic. They were not prepared to see their aircraft go outside the country. Of course it was agreed there would be no flights of combat wing full stop. They waited a few weeks and then they proceeded to fly what they call "training flights". They are now flying training flights and it is hard to make a distinction between training flights and reconnaissance flights.

Mr Rowlands

170. You describe the extent of the Serbian territorial control and also the military involvement in the whole conflict. I read with very great interest the constitutional proposals and the two seem to be the two ends of a very long spectrum. Could you tell us how you think step by step, or stage by stage, we can reconcile the present situation to the ideal objective?

(Lord Owen) I think it is very difficult to get into serious discussions of the sort of compromises that are necessary to get the constitutional proposals accepted while there is a battle raging. That is why we have always attached, if you like, importance to the two, the dual track approach, of the Mixed Military Working Group meeting in Sarajevo under General Morillon or under the Chairmanship of his Second in Command being on offer, they have had over 10 meetings, and the Constitutional Working Group which operates under Martti Ahtisaari who was in charge of Namibia at the time it was brought to independence. Yesterday and the day before we had discussions over the maps we sent to the parties, the map of Bosnia-Herzegovina split into Obstines which is the local government area and asked them to come up with maps and they have done so. I do not think it would help, they are actually meant to be private anyhow, to reveal the full extent of them but obviously the Bosnian Serbs have the map which is very familiar to you which is the existing front line. The Bosnia-Herzegovina Government came up with more than the provinces we had suggested, which was seven to ten, and the Croatian Government came up with a representation of where they thought there was more than 60 per cent Croatians on the ground. If you look at those maps even though on the face of it they look very far apart, it is not inconceivable that you could bring together a map between seven to ten provinces which would reflect quite a lot of the aspirations of the different parties because there are traditionally parts of Bosnia-Herzegovina where nobody can really contend one or other of them is very dominant but there are also some very, very difficult areas for mapping. Allied to that there is this concept which the Bosnian Serbs have that they are already an independent republic. It is not the first time people have declared an independent republic as part of their ambitions and they have had to be turned back. It is incompatible with the concept of Bosnia-Herzegovina as a country recognised by the United Nations that it can have within it three states who have independent foreign relations with other countries and conduct themselves, to all intents and purposes, as independent states. The Bosnia Serb position on that is not acceptable. I personally think that too will shift in negotiations and we have already come up with I think the most decentralised form of Government it is possible to have. The reason for that is where you have distrust, suspicion and—I hate to use the word but I think one has to—hatred, you cannot expect the functions of central government to be anything other than the mini-

[Mr Rowlands *Contd*]

mum, or those that no rational person can deny have to be conducted by a single state. The mechanism for dealing with that distrust is rotation of the key roles which, of course, has been a tradition in Bosnia-Herzegovina with respect for the Croatian, and the Bosnian Serb, and also the Muslim leaders. So I do not rule out a constitutional agreement broadly within the lines of our draft proposals. There obviously has to be give and take on both sides, it is only a draft. If the will exists—and I think the will will exist—if we can also reach a cessation of hostilities with which I link the demilitarisation of Sarajevo, I think it is hard to see a cessation of hostilities being viable without the demilitarisation of Sarajevo.

171. How can you create the will because it does seem to imply it is going to require the present Serb forces virtually giving up a large amount of what they have spent a considerable time fighting to get control over? There does not seem to be military capacity to push them back significantly enough to create a better negotiating position for the Bosnia-Herzegovina Government. What is the mechanism that is going to change the balance of power on the ground?

(Lord Owen) You put your finger on the problem we face which is what pressures have we got to achieve this? I am in the business of welcoming every pressure that comes, even from quarters not altogether helpful in other areas. The first pressure is that sanctions are operating against Serbia and Montenegro in Belgrade. This is considered to be an injustice in Serbia and considered to be an injustice in Montenegro. They will say they have not helped militarily the Bosnia-Herzegovena military since May of this year. There is quite a lot of evidence that this is, I will not say totally, but partially true. They gave them a pretty substantial military force when they left and when the JNA pulled out, they left vastly more than would be the normal allocation. The Bosnian Serbs, however, think this is an injustice which is on them. Sanctions are a blunt instrument, but is one of our ways of holding Belgrade to account for past errors if not present errors. That is a pressure on Bosnian Serbs. Sadly the oil embargo is no longer a pressure. It was a very considerable pressure even as much as six weeks ago when people were queuing for the best part of a day in Belgrade to fill their private car. That will come back in my view now we have stopped tankers coming through Bar, we are also tightening up in the Danube and have stopped transshipments. The economic sanctions have had a significant effect. It is a considerable pressure. It is felt therefore in as much as the Serb economy is pulled down also in Bosnia Serbia and Dr Karadzic admitted that yesterday. The other pressure which I consider to be an important pressure and the biggest area of miscalculation which the Bosnian Serbs made, maybe all Serbs made, comes from the Muslim leaders—I say leaders, I do think it is very necessary to remember there are millions of Serbs who thoroughly disapprove of what has been done by their leaders in their name and who would love this war to end, hopefully their voice will come out on the 20th December vote although there are problems there—the mistake they made was to under-estimate the capacity of the Muslims to fight. There was also the contempt of the rural farming community for the city slicker, they did not think moderate Muslims—they certainly were moderate—would fight back. They have fought back and they have fought back, given the fact they are largely a volunteer force, remarkably well. They have been sustained by the Islamic countries with substantial sums of money which has enabled them to buy quite a considerable amount of weaponry, not the heavy weaponry where they are undoubtedly at a disadvantage: tanks, artillery pieces. There is a growing recognition certainly very commonly found in Croatia and more commonly found by Serbs that there will be no peace unless there is an honourable settlement for Muslims. The fighting will go on and Bosnia-Herzegovina faces the real pressures of becoming a Lebanon. That is the real pressure. The Yugoslav Army want respectability, they want to be taken back and they want the old links they used to have with Russia, Byelorussia, the Ukraine, and other part of the CSCE, their politicians and leaders would like to be able to travel. They would like to feel their standard of living is improving and they want recognition. They want to be recognised and have their membership sustainable in the United Nations and other bodies. That is undoubtedly a factor. The Croats are another factor. The Croats by a combination with the Muslims threaten the Serbs. When that works effectively they become a much more effective fighting force and the Serbs do not get it their own way. This is a factor, the Croatian strength. All of these issues and the weariness of war and the widows' voice coming through are factors and pressures to bring about a negotiated settlement. There is also now the emergence, since President Bush's statement about enforcement of the no-fly ban, of a much stronger pressure beginning to be felt that the patience of the world is not unlimited and some further strengthening of military action might have to be considered. Certainly they have not got a total freedom to fly because of the no-fly ban.

Mr Harris

172. My question is relating to pressures and Lord Owen, thank you very much, has gone into great detail on that. Can I press him a little bit further on the military pressure or possible military pressure, the enforcement of the no-fly ban, very important. One recognises that but the real difficulty is the continuing fighting on the ground and not the no-fly ban, it is the continuation of ethnic cleansing. All the pressures Lord Owen has talked about, does he think they will be sufficient to bring the diabolical and devastating events in former Yugoslavia to an end or do we have to move further on the military front as Mr Ashdown was suggesting in the House this afternoon?

[**Mr Harris** *Contd*]

(Lord Owen) I think we do not have to enforce a no-fly ban, I think it can be done by negotiation. I still believe it is possible. One of the reasons why, apart from not wanting ever to use force unless you have to, I am more reluctant to move to enforcement which I assume would be from the air is it would have an effect on UNPROFOR forces and UNHCR forces. A lot depends on the level of enforcement necessary. The moment whether the United States or the Western coalition take up arms in the sense of taking out an aircraft or helicopter or an airfield, they immediately put at risk UNPROFOR forces and UNHCR forces. We must all be aware of that. Therefore enforcement at this particular stage in winter as opposed to in the summer poses a threat to the humanitarian aid effort. I know there is sometimes a tendency, even of Bosnia-Herzegovina Government forces, to discourage this humanitarian aid. All I can say is without that humanitarian aid effort we would have seen a very large number of people lose their lives and as winter closes in many will lose their lives anyhow and without the humanitarian effort many, many more numbered in tens of thousands. So we have to be careful that enforcement action is weighed very carefully on the scales. The disruption of the humanitarian effort, that disruption would come from our having to protect UNPROFOR forces, not just in Bosnia-Herzegovina but also in Croatia. There is a tendency to forget the other problems. We have this third of Croatia which is either in UNPAS or in "pink areas" or not fully in the control and under the operation of the Croatian Government. Now everybody will have their own view on this balance. It is a very difficult balance to strike. My own judgment is this: if despite the constant warnings and if despite the fact that we have shown all possible care in making it clear to General Mladic what is involved in continuing to flout the no-fly ban, if they go on doing it, despite say verbal warnings, a Chapter VII determination, and they then continue to go on with it we will be forced to enforce. This is my own personal view. This is for Governments to decide. The reason I would say is this: this type of person, General Mladic and President Milosovic, will always take a yard if you give them an inch and on this sort of thing history proves time and time again you have to have a clear line. You do not threaten what you are not prepared to commit to. Therefore, I am very keen nobody lightly enters into enforcement of the no-fly ban without realising its implications. Its implications are you might have to take quite severe action in terms of use of air power in Bosnia-Herzegovina. Were the Yugoslav Army or the Yugoslav Air Force to intervene you might have to escalate right up through there. We need to know what route lies ahead, where we are going, and having thought it through, if Governments decide to do it then I can personally see a rational case for doing it even if it means disrupting the humanitarian winter programme. It is not a course to embark on lightly. I think people need to think through the implications very carefully indeed. In case Mr Wareing says is that different from what I said in the summer, I do not think it is. In winter it is a fact we are fighting a war on two fronts, we are fighting a war between the Bosnian Serbs and the Bosnian Croatians and the Bosnia-Herzegovina Government but also a war against winter. That could take more casualties than any of the armed fighting.

Chairman

173. I want to come on to this specific question of the mechanics and dynamics of military involvement in a moment because it is the heart of the ugly choice we may soon be faced with. We must think through very carefully indeed the fear of one thing leading to another as it tends to do in these situations. Can we, keeping the general level still, look at how your analysis of motives on the ground or pressures on the ground does or does not raise hopes for the peace process. You mentioned your constitution you and Mr Vance have put forward, it is a little bit early to look at that. Except for a few maps being produced are these people in the mood to talk peace, particularly if there is an increased line up between the Muslims and Croatians?

(Lord Owen) I believe they are. I need, to some extent, to explain what this Conference is about, it is virtually in continuous session in Geneva. Many of these people are there on a permanent basis, they are talking about these questions in restaurants, in hotel foyers as well as in conference rooms. They have been conducting this at many different levels. In UNHCR, Mrs Ogata deals with the Humanitarian Working Group, they are discussing all the time how to get convoys through in her forum and in another forum chaired by Ambassador Berasategui. These are all confidence building measures.

174. Is that the Polish——

(Lord Owen) No, that is outside our conference. That is the CSCE. These are our confidence building measures. They are discussing if there is, as there has been only a few days ago, firing at the UNPROFOR plane which actually took out the patrol of General Morillon's plane which could have been very damaging, the Italian plane was shot down and four Italian people lost their lives, this is all being discussed in this Group and constitutes confidence building measures. They do not get all of the headlines but there is a lot of constant dialogue going on. There is discussion at the Succession Working Group which is looking at the sharing out of the embassies and the various, if you like, heritage of the former Yugoslavia. As I say, you are getting all the time a dialogue with these people. I do sense from nearly all this activity that started on 3rd September we are getting a climate where people are beginning to understand the framework and the structure of the problem and a possible negotiation. A problem is, as has already been commented round this table, that the Bosnian Serbs hold far more territory than is acceptable, therefore they have to be rolled back on territory.

[Chairman *Contd*]
They have to accept a constitution which would allow people to go back into homes they have been forced out of as part of ethnic cleansing. On the face of it Bosnian Serbs appear to accept some of these humanitarian provisions and have accepted an ombudsman for dealing with these questions. Whether that will really come through in the final negotiations to some extent remains to be seen. On the Mixed Military Working Group there are signs the Bosnian Serbs do not wish to extend the present front line but would be content to sit on that front line while negotiations went ahead. Where they are showing as yet a lack of realism is over Sarajevo and we have pressed and pressed and pressed that it is vital Sarajevo is demilitarised in a way that learns from the lessons of Beirut, not having green lines. We want an open city if it is at all possible which will obviously have to have a very heavy UN presence in order to protect Serbs from Muslims and Muslims from Serbs. I would argue all of those factors are coming to make it possible to have a negotiation, particularly when the election in Belgrade is over. It is very difficult now to get decisions from Belgrade. Yet I do not think you can get an overall settlement in Bosnia-Herzegovina without tackling some of the problems between Croatia, Serbia and Montenegro.

Chairman: That is a mostly encouraging assessment.

Mr Sumberg

175. One of the great dangers it seems to me of this is the widening of the conflict and that other parties could be persuaded to come in. We all saw you speak at the Conference of Islamic States, I wonder if you could tell us a little bit as to how seriously you take their ultimatum to the UN concerning the arming of Bosnian Muslims? What do you think they are likely to do if the situation continues as it has?

(Lord Owen) It was a thoughtful and courteous Conference but I do not think that should allow you or me to under-estimate the strength of feeling that exists amongst the Islamic community and their foreign ministers. I think there is, certainly I detect, a feeling amongst many Islamics who have been often very Westernised that for the first time they have questioned whether or not the action of the countries in which they may even be living, but certainly with whom they have had very friendly relations, are prejudiced against them. I believe we have to address that anxiety very seriously indeed. That was at one time a feeling amongst Jews, they were being discriminated against because they were Jews. There is a strong feeling about this amongst Muslims and it comes out in the arguments about the embargo. It is more than a feeling, it goes deeper than that, over ethnic cleansing. It is the appalling sights they see, the minaret or the mosque being poleaxed down; I know that Croatian Catholic churches have been affected and there have been raids against Bosnian Serb Orthodox churches. There are no innocents in this whole area. I am sure you are well aware of this, there are no innocents. There is however not an equivalence of guilt. Certain sections of people have been responsible for grievious humanitarian abuses and ethnic cleansing as practised is one of the most loathsome things we have seen on the Continent of Europe since 1939 to 1945. I therefore take Muslim anxieties very seriously. On the actual Resolution, the encouraging thing was how Prince Saud of Saudi Arabia, who chaired the Conference, brought all the criticism and Action Programme within the context of international action and in particular of the United Nations. It is not an ultimatum, it is a decision that if by 15th January—I think it is 15th January—various things are not done then there should be a debate in the Security Council, of course they can go to the Security Council and have a debate at any time. I think it is a warning rather than an ultimatum. Certainly Cyrus Vance and I left taking account of their views very seriously. But, on the other hand, I think we need to avoid a certain amount of exaggeration. Let us be realists, arms have got through to the Muslims in fairly substantial quantities. If you have money, and substantial amounts of money, in our modern world arms dealers ensure light arms get through. As I said earlier, the Muslim problem is they do not have enough tanks or artillery pieces, they are getting more and more missiles, anti-tank missiles, but probably not in sufficient numbers. Therefore this arms embargo had to be dealt with in Jeddah and we dealt with it openly. I warned them when Croatia was fighting against the Serbs there were many people who thought the predominant Catholic Croatians were being unfairly treated, discriminated against, and the embargo should be lifted, but we did not lift it. The reason we did not lift it has been because the traditional arms suppliers to the Serbs, if they see it lifted from one side, will be tempted to supply arms. It is a great tribute to President Yeltsin and his foreign minister that despite the fact they had strong links with the Yugoslav Army, there have been no arms supplies to the Yugoslav Army since the embargo started 14 months ago. Those who lightly say we should lift the arms embargo must realise the consequence, you have to lift it effectively for Croatia too because that is the only way arms come through. If you lift it you are not dealing just with Bosnia-Herzegovina, you are dealing with Croatia. I have not been able to get any assurance from anybody closely involved in this that this will not trigger a relaxation, perhaps initially clandestine and then overt, of arms supplies from the former Soviet Republics where we know there is sophisticated weaponry of this generation, the 1990s generation of weapons. If you look at Nagorno Karabach both sides have been supplied with multiple rocket launchers, fired with terrible devastation. We have not yet seen that type of military armament in Bosnia-Herzegovina. It is more the weaponry of the 1970s and early 1980s, not the 1990s. It is not yet sophisticated weaponry. Our fear, is you might temporarily address the imbalance—there is a real imbalance on the Muslim side, but it will not be long before that is dealt

[**Mr Sumberg** *Contd*]

with by other arms purchases. You then raise the whole level of military escalation. I think it is better to deal with that imbalance by things like no-fly bans, levelling the playing field in terms of that factor trying—as we did—to do something about the heavy weaponry and facing the fact Muslim Islamic countries will supply arms and see it is got through. Any Serbian who thinks the Muslims will not be well equipped over the winter months had better have another think. They will be better equipped, they will continue to fight. If you want peace there has to be a settlement which is honourable for the Muslims. They have not lost this war, there has been much too much glib reporting about the fact they have lost this war. There is still a substantial amount of territory which they have.

176. There is an imbalance of heavy weaponry?

(Lord Owen) Yes.

177. Would you therefore try and reduce that imbalance if not by letting arms go in at least using air power to deal with that imbalance, using the air power to deal with that as well as enforcement of the no-fly zone?

(Lord Owen) I think if you do that you come back to all the problems I have said about enforcement, about the effect on UNPROFOR, UNHCR and winter and take yourself into a bigger step than enforcement of the no-fly ban. My own view is at this juncture the only military option we should be considering is the enforcement of the no-fly ban. I do not rule out that option as I would never rule out any force option. I think there has been much too much ruling out of force options and not enough understanding that the language you might appropriately use in the American Senate or the American Congress these days with CNN is beamed straight into the decision makers and military headquarters in Bosnia-Herzegovina and everywhere else. In dealing with a war it is perfectly legitimate and right for democratic politicians always to retain the option of military force and not rule it out. Equally I personally do think where you have people already fighting on the ground you do not need to intervene with ground forces. I think there has been too much argument that because you use air power, therefore the next escalation is you have to put ground forces on the ground, I do not see the logic of that. This is not a reason for us to get involved in the ground war fight. I think that the question of whether or not to use air power to redress the balance of forces might arise if the Serbs were to pursue things like Travnik and Sarajevo. It might arise if we felt there was a grotesque interference with UNHCR convoys so the humanitarian effort was failing because of military interference. It might come if, despite the serious surge in negotiations you got no co-operation from Belgrade after the elections and there was no give in their negotiating position and the picture Mr Rowlands put forward, recurred where you could not roll them back, came up. All this is a matter for Government. I am in a strange position, I am not in Government, I can only advise. I tend to make my advice private, I do not make policy, all I can do is to respond to what Governments are ready to do. I took this job knowing full well they were not ready to go beyond the present parameters. I am perfectly happy to live within those present parameters. It was the London Conference decision that there should be no military flights over Bosnia-Herzegovina.

Sir John Stanley

178. Lord Owen, can I take what you said about the arms embargo slightly further? I am sure you would agree one of the most powerful military pressure points on both sides, bringing them towards negotiation, would be the diminishing supplies of weapons, most particularly in this case of military consumables: ammunition, anti-tank missiles and so on. Are you effectively saying you think both sides, in possibly slightly different ways, will be able to sustain fighting from within their existing stocks and from stocks they have managed to acquire from abroad or do you have any optimism that over the next few months both sides may come under real pressure in terms of available supplies of ammunition?

(Lord Owen) I do not think the Bosnian Serbs will come under pressure. I have already said I think the Bosnian Muslims will be supplied with enough money to be able to purchase from the arms trade illegally. I think Bosnian Serbs will not have the money but I think they already have the ammunition. Not only have we seen the fragmentation of Yugoslavia, we have seen the break up of the Yugoslav Army. I have not really focused on how much of a garrison that whole country, Yugoslavia, was. It was very substantially armed, it had its own munitions factories with considerable export capacity, it is still producing munitions, some in Bosnia-Herzegovina. They also still have very extensive supplies, some of which are still underground. I do not think, therefore, we can rely on the running down of munitions. I do believe the oil embargo was extremely important, that is the other thing armies have to run on. They have to have food and they can get that from the fields, but they have to have fuel. We have been ill-served by this. I noticed the other day some rather strong comments from the WEU Secretary-General. I think it is a little rich when you consider they were not stopping and searching in the Adriatic. I know that was the decision of the Governments, but we have had five oil tankers going into Bar and Montenegro at a time when we had the oil embargo. That substantially weakened one of the very important sanctions we had. Hopefully that will stop. There is now stop and search by both NATO and WEU Naval forces. We are still concerned that barges are coming down the Danube, quite large ones, with oil supplies. Trans-shipment stopped on 8th of this month, only two days ago. We have to face the fact that the stopping of trans-shipments through Serbia and Montenegro is having difficult effects on the economies of Bulgaria, Rumania and Macedonia.

[**Sir John Stanley** *Contd*]
We will have to try and help those countries, for the oil embargo is a way of stopping the military machine.

Mr Gapes

179. You referred to Bosnian Serbian forces and said that they are happy to sit on the present front line. You have just said you are not happy to have vast military forces and ground forces introduced. Is there not a contradiction in what you are saying? If you are trying to reverse ethnic cleansing does that not require you to be able to force the Serbs back or are you just simply talking about bombing these people until they retreat of their own free will? If that is the case is it not reality that the assumptions in your proposals, your constitution, and all those elaborate processes, have actually failed and that negotiations are not going to be necessary?

(Lord Owen) I do not think so. It seems to me that what you have said underlines the importance of the constitutional proposals, that you give them a structure of government and provinces, in some of which they would be in the majority and some of which would be contested politically because they were balanced. Then you give them the feel they will have within some of those provinces where they are a natural majority, which is also economically viable, for that is another important characteristic of a province, very considerable autonomy. Then the fear of being dominated by one of the other national groupings will be, to a very great extent, alleviated. That is the hope. I do not think it is a forlorn hope when you talk to people now sitting on this territory, they know they will have to come back from some of this territory. It was said to us on the Bosnian Serb map: "This is not a humble proposition", "You can say that again", we said. They know they will have to come back, the question is how far back and where. These are highly political matters rooted, unfortunately, in history. The Bosnian Serbs justify their claim, not just on the census details, which incidentally in their map they have got a very tenuous hold on, but the fact there was genocide of the Serbian people between 1939–1945 and they go back to the Austrian Hapsburg empire. We may all say that is absurd but that is what we are dealing with. I do believe you can roll it back, whether you can do it far enough I do not know. As far as rolling back ethnic cleansing, this is predominantly going to be a matter which will have to be done through legal measures. We have already got the agreement of all the principal parties that the documents forced out of people when they were forced out of their home and land and they have signed away their house and rights to land, these are null and void. The new constitution will declare them to be null and void. That is a different thing from getting Muslims back into the Prijedor region where there has been ethnic cleansing as a result of artillery fire and tanks rolling in and people being told: "This is a Muslim house" and a tank opens up on that house and destroys it. If you fly over from the sky it is an extraordinary sight. You see a row of houses and suddenly there is a hole and you cannot think what it was, then you realise that was a house. You see a patchwork quilt around isolated houses. It is quite discreet, what happens to a house, a Croatian; a Muslim house, sometimes a Serb house.

Chairman: Can we move on from what has been a fascinating tour of the issues in more detail to the military intervention and the whole question of deployment of force. You touched on it earlier but it is a central issue whether we are being gradually sucked in as though caught by our tie into the washing machine rollers in a greater degree of military involvement, or are there stopping points?

Mr Jopling

180. You said you tended to give your advice to the Government in private, and I am sure we would agree with you. Mr Hogg came to this Committee not long ago and told us that it is not clearly an objective of the Government at this time to seek to put ground forces into the area in a peace making role, and I gather from what you have said that would imply they were following your advice. You did go on to say you thought the only option, I think you said, was to seek to enforce the no-fly zone and you said, again I wrote down the words, "quite severe measures might need to be taken to do that" and I think you said even if it might upset some of the humanitarian activities which are going on. It is that point I really want to ask you about. First of all, I wonder if you could tell us how your mind is working as to how the no-fly zone might be enforced and what the implications for that might be for the humanitarian activities which are going on and in particular, of course, I am thinking of the position of the Cheshire Regiment which is engaged in that peace keeping and that humanitarian activity. I wonder if you could just help us explaining what you mean by "enforcement" of the no-fly zone and what you think the effect of that will be on relief workers and others?

(Lord Owen) I believe if you show enough determination you are going to enforce you will not need to enforce. I do not want to enforce. Having faced a persistent pattern of violations if you do not show a determination over the matter then those violations will become serious, they will start to use combat aircraft again which will be obviously a flagrant abuse. I do not seek to enforce, I seek there should be no military aircraft flying within the parameters. If we enforce I think we have to look at its implications and realise you change the nature of the military role which you currently have. You currently have a military role which I would argue is peace making but it is peace making within a limited remit to ensure humanitarian aid convoys get through. This is accompanied by a UN presence which I think gives reassurance to the population, many of them displaced people who have already come through a frightening experience of having their homes gutted or bombed or literally forced out. I think that UNPROFOR is a measure of reassurance. I think

[**Mr Jopling** *Contd*]

also when you meet sporadic fire and a limited military destruction often by local commanders not acting under the authority of higher command, a readiness to exchange fire and to push the convoy through is a perfectly legitimate use within the mandate and it again is peace making. What you have not got the authority to do is to fight the convoy through but then you have to remember what the convoy consists of, the convoy consists of civilians driving the lorries, it consists of UNHCR personnel accompanying the lorries. Some of the lorries are driven by soldiers but not many and you know you are subjecting a whole range of people to a very vulnerable situation along those sort of mountain roads. It may sound great to fight a convoy through and you might in some circumstances succeed in forcing a convoy through once but the chances are you will not succeed for a second or third time. I do not think there is another alternative to the humanitarian effort of cajoling, persuading, pressurising, occasionally responding to military fire and returning fire. I know it is a frustrating role and people argue it is a role soldiers should not do. I do not agree: to be asked to get a humanitarian convoy through is a legitimate task for our military in the world which we live in, whether in Somalia or Bosnia-Herzegovina. If you want to change that role to a more aggressive role, I do not think you can do very much more within the present mandate. For example, we are asked now to provide protection zones or safe areas, this has become a very fashionable proposition. The main proponent is the Austrian Government and the other day Mr Mock, the Foreign Minister, gave an interview, it was helpful, it clarified the issue. He was talking about putting a protection zone around five quite large cities like Travnik. Once you put perimeter security you have to defend that perimeter and if that perimeter becomes a front line you are then going to have to defend it against Bosnian Serbs. That is a complete change to the existing mandate and a step I would not wish to take without having carefully calculated its consequences. At the moment none of the governments contributing sizeably to the humanitarian convoy protection are prepared to entertain that role. The other danger is if you then pull the perimeter security back from the front line you then have the danger of a vacuum in which the Bosnian Serbs can think: "We can push the front line forward because they have a protection zone 10, 15 or 20 miles back". These protective zones—advocated for the best of motives—have a serious danger of encouraging ethnic cleansing. Most people who advocate them would be appalled if they thought that was what they were doing. UNHCR is not happy with the concept of perimeter security for some of those reasons. "Safe havens" is an attractive word. What has happened to try and deal with this is the French UN forces, in Bihac and the British and maybe the Spaniards have started to, if you like, have a zone of confidence around which where people who are worried tend to go and either are put in temporary accommodation or moved closer to military barracks. They are not providing military security but some form of security. You can have humanitarian aid and NGO voluntary activity and that may be a way in which we can give some help on this. My own feeling is I do not wish to concede the case to the Serbs that they have any justification in gaining another kilometre and their front line is now far far enough in. The safe zone is the existing area on this side of the front line. It would certainly mean a change in the mandate if you want to put in perimeter security, that is the next step up which some people advocate for the best of reasons. I do not exclude it: if Travnik were to fall and we saw the Serbian Army making relentless steps forward, we might have to consider it. We would have to consider other major aspects before we went to perimeter security. You would have to consider whether we have to effectively impose instead a ceasefire.

Mr Shore

181. Would not the sheer pressure of refugees and people driven from their homes, if there were to be a significant further advance by Serb forces, actually almost force you into a position where you would have to declare some parts of Bosnia to be safe havens, otherwise I do not know how many more people will be homeless?

(Lord Owen) I think Mr Shore has put his finger on what would be a horrendous prospect. It is widely thought if Travnik were to be attacked you might have 50,000 people on the road, a worse disaster than with Jajce. This is a continually changing scene, you have to be ready. I do not say I would not do that. I must say I think there are other options you would have to consider. It could be we would be facing genocide, people have used the word genocide very easily, it is a very grave term to use. I think if the Serbs were pushing that deep into territory which is normally occupied by Croatians, we would face bigger questions, put it that way. I would not at the moment do anything to encourage any Bosnian Serbs to think they have any right whatever to take Travnik. I think it is a good case on which to take our stance, it is not a Serb town under any circumstances. I think it is a good yardstick. If that fell I think many of the options people currently are talking about would have to be reviewed again. You could still come up against the argument we have had before about the effects of winter but by then you may not be in winter and you may be able to cast that particular apprehension off your shoulders and we would be more ready to take military action. I do not want to sound as if the negotiated settlement is off the agenda, I think it is on the agenda. I do not say it is going to be easy.

Chairman

182. Do you think the news, the fact of American willingness to use forces, to use large numbers of troops, let us be precise, very large numbers of troops in Somalia, no nonsense about a thousand here and there but 28,000 troops, two

[Chairman *Contd*]

divisions, has had any impact on the thinking among the Bosnian components?

(Lord Owen) I think it has. I think it has had some impact in Bosnia-Herzegovina but I think it has had quite a serious impact in thinking about Kosovo which is the other area which causes me, and I am sure all of you, very great concern because Kosovo could flare up without anyone in Belgrade having decided to implement the policy of ethnic cleansing or clamp down, you could argue there is enough clamp down in Kosovo or Pristina already. I think it has been indicated by the Americans they are prepared to intervene in the internal affairs of the country. It is a major and significant change. Preventive planning has been done with the full support of the NATO Secretary-General and in association with the Secretary-General of the UN.

Chairman: I think we would like to come to preventive diplomacy, if that is the right word for the other danger areas, in a moment if we have time. Could we just ask a question about the UN's own organisation and the present level of involvement. Mr Harris.

Mr Harris

183. Lord Owen, I wonder if you feel the military functions of the UN can and should be strengthened or improved in any way, often on the ground?

(Lord Owen) You have to recognise the UN is deeply stretched with Cambodia, Somalia, Angola, Mozambique and 16,000 troops in Croatia and 7,000 in Bosnia-Herzegovina quite apart from the traditional commitments like Cyprus. This does put a very considerable load on New York, particularly on the Under-Secretary concerned, Mig Goulding, and the Secretary-General himself. I think you do notice now when you are dealing with wars involving sophisticated weapons and modern industrialised countries, which I think the former Yugoslavia has to be considered at least in part as an industrialised country, you do have different considerations. It is one thing to run a United Nations' peace keeping force where you can rely on only small arms being used, it is another where you are running a peace keeping force into a situation where people have sophisticated aircraft. The Bosnian Serb forces have Frog missiles and they have other missiles as well, they have SAM missiles protecting some of their sensitive areas. You are planning in a sophisticated way when you come to talk about enforcement in the situation of Bosnia-Herzegovina, you are immediately talking about enforcement outside the UN, sorry, not relying only on UN forces. They would have to be forces earmarked for the UN and Secretary-General but from major nations of which obviously the United States is the most relevant one. You saw this in the Iraq/Kuwait war. What sort of mechanism do you need for the planning exercise? I think the UN Secretary-General has two options in these situations, either call on regional agencies, which he is entitled to do under the UN Charter, and in effect our Conference is this. I tend to think it will be more likely in the future for the UN to invoke a regional agency, in this case the European Community. It calls on European Community countries, to make a much larger contribution in terms of UN peace keeping forces, the UN Secretary-General did this, and we have responded. He asked us to fund it outside the normal UN financial rules to be responsible for our national contribution, again we have responded to this, even paying for the vast majority of the headquarters' costs. When that happens then inevitably slowly the relationship changes, instead of the old way where the UN tended not to have troops from the region and where you also had total UN control in New York, now you are bound to have the region having a larger say in the structure. I have watched this develop since September in a very interesting way. At times I think we Europeans have demanded too much and have actually damaged ourselves by not having enough "UN-ary" at a time when the UN wanted to set this up with the involvement of NATO and using some of its headquarters arrangements in a double-hatted arrangement. These issues have been resolved satisfactorily and we now have a sophisticated headquarters which have been helpful. NATO has helped provide AWAC patrols for no-fly enforcement, and NATO and the WEU do routine patrols for enforcement in the Adriatic and now they are stopping and searching. That is making a valuable contribution. When people disparage Europe and do not think Europe is doing enough we have to quietly say we are taking casualties, we are providing the vast bulk of the financial support for UNHCR and providing the bulk of upfront forces in terms of UNPROFOR in Bosnia and Hezogovina. In Croatia UNPROFOR has Russian crews and it was an interesting experience to go between the Belgians patrolling in the morning and the Russians patrolling in the afternoon, all under blue berets. We are now in an interesting world and in that world when dealing with sophisticated forces I think a Military Staff Committee does have a role and I would like to see the Military Staff Committee ratified. I do not believe it means the Chiefs of Staff normally attending, because the UN Charter is quite clear, when it says or their representatives. But I think the five permanent powers could give the Secretary-General on a permanent basis access to the sophistication of their intelligence, their satellite intelligence, their communications, their knowledge of modern warfare, their planning capacity so as to deal with things like the enforcement of a no-fly zone. We can either do this through a regional agency, like NATO or a Military Staff Committee, indigenous to New York, or as I personally prefer a bit of both. I cannot see how the UN will operate without this capacity, to use a technical term very fashionable at the moment, of blistering on and having a facility or capacity like AWACs or planning capacity from other agencies, sometimes regional and sometimes, in the case of the five permanent members, of the Military Staff Committee. You cannot run a UN operation of the sort we

[**Mr Harris** *Contd*]
currently have without extra planning facilities in some way being made available to the Secretary-General.

Mr Gapes

184. You have talked about the use of regional organisations. One of the problems in the former Yugoslavia is that the Secretary-General felt at the beginning he could not, or would not, fund an operation there so it was left for particular countries to participate. Does that not have dangers. As well as being necessary in these circumstances? Does it not have dangers linked to that? You have talked about the relationship between the UN and EC with regard to the International Peace Conference, I took it from what you said earlier about WEU and oil embargoes that you were quite critical of some European countries and the way in which this process was going on; could you enlarge on that, please?

(Lord Owen) I have no doubt we should have stopped and searched as soon as we thought it necessary to deploy naval forces in the Adriatic.

185. WEU collectively?

(Lord Owen) You cannot blame the UN, it reflects the Member States. You cannot blame WEU, it reflects the Member States. The organisations have to make the decisions. A problem, there were many different problems, for NATO is that Yugoslavia is out of area and there are constitutional problems in some countries; there is also the debate between using WEU and NATO. Historically, I do not like going too far back over what was wrong, we are now involving the United States in a way that was not hitherto done and we are involving the European Community and the UN. At the start of all this the United States did not want to be involved in Yugoslavia and the Europeans did not want them to be involved if truth be told. The European Community were very happy this should be a European event even to the extent of us developing our own peace keeping operation and we were not too keen to involve the UN. Peace keeping is a highly skilled operation and the UN has learned painfully its constraints and disciplines and I think we have now got the right combination US-EC-UN. The US is not ignoring a major global geopolitical problem with serious ramifications into the former Soviet Union. The issue of racism is one of paramount importance for the whole world. Europe is still fully committed, very much so. There are dangers for the UN in the region being involved because the region is committed. On the other hand, the region because of its commitments is readier to put forces in, readier to take risks and readier to pay money. I do not want to desert the idea of a global UN taking its contributions on a fixed system and taking commitments from a lot of varying countries, I think there are some situations where the Secretary-General in Yugoslavia has turned down troops from some contributory nations in the region which he thought historically were too inflammatory or for some other reason. This regional help is for the Secretary-General to determine. A soldier cannot have two bosses. The end result is the Secretary-General is responsible, he is in many ways the Commander-in-Chief although Cyrus Vance of course as his own representative has very real weight. I have all the telegrams I need from the Foreign Office; when I see them I share them when I think appropriate with Cyrus Vance, and he has all UN cables and I see them routinely as well. Our Conference is a pooled effort. The overall line of responsibility is from General Nambiar with overall responsibility for UNPROFOR to Mig Goulding, Under Secretary to the Secretary-General. Both co-chairman have direct access to General Nambiar and we can have direct access to Under Secretary Goulding and we can have direct access to the Secretary-General but the line of authority has not changed. We are not in the command loop in Geneva but we know everything that is going on, we think.

Chairman: Sir John Stanley would you like to ask a question.

Sir John Stanley

186. You have made reference to a number of significant assets that have been contributed by NATO, the AWACs, command and control naval forces in the Mediterranean. In addition there is an intangible benefit of having land forces operate alongside each other which have done so in many cases in NATO exercises. I would be grateful for your assessment of the worth of NATO troops. Do you regard it as being very useful or would you say it has been absolutely and is likely to be absolutely indispensable to the likely posture for the EC and UN peace keeping forces?

(Lord Owen) Well, I think it has been very helpful because if our headquarters' staff have been working for months and years together in an integrated unit, it is very much easier to fly them out to Sarajevo and carry on when you have a degree of commonality. That does not mean to say I think it should be a NATO headquarters, I think it has to be a UN headquarters and has to have UN staff at a variety of political levels and it needs UN civilian and political advice in particular. At one stage I think we were not getting sufficient UN political advice because of funding disagreements, that has been resolved and I think it is alright now. I think you would have to involve NATO to have an oil embargo, we need a naval presence, and WEU has also contributed. It is boring work, this business of just monitoring evasions, but essential. We could not have a no-fly ban without the AWACs system. These extra facilities, the theology about whether it should be NATO operating out of area or WEU, I think is for another day.

Chairman: Another Committee! Could we turn to what might have been done—without raking over too many old crises—to stop the atrocities we are now involved in and what we might do to stop the horrors spreading. You have mentioned Kosovo and Macedonia, those are very much in our minds.

Mr Wareing

187. Yes, Lord Owen, I wonder whether I can put my question by posing a scenario? Following a visit last year, and speaking to Presidents Tudjman and Milosovic, I came very strongly to the view—and I have a feeling you may share this view, I would like to hear it from you—a very large mistake was made by the European Community which contributed to the present situation by the premature recognition of Slovenia and Croatia, for instance, and Bosnia-Herzegovena on the other hand. Slovenia was not so much of a problem but in Croatia you had large enclaves of the Serbian population and a lot of the Serbian minority in Croatia has also been ignored by the European Community countries. The dash to recognise Croatia was in fact a very very erroneous move particularly in view of the fact the Badinter Report recommended only Slovenia and Macedonia. I know my colleague, Mr Rowlands, will be asking you questions about Macedonia and indeed if there is to be a solution at all in the former Yugoslavia it is the rights of those Serbs as well as the rights of the Muslim Croatians and it is the rights of those Serbs in Krajina where the UNPROFOR forces are being threatened by President Tudjman that they have to leave by March 31st and that could throw up the whole problem. How do you see that observation on my part? How do you see how we can learn from our past mistakes?

(Lord Owen) I was not there but it is a public fact—because neither have hidden it—both Lord Carrington and Cyrus Vance believed, as you do, that there was a premature recognition of Croatia and also they should not have moved on to the referendum and then the recognition of the Bosnia-Herzegovina. The original idea we would try to resolve all the negotiations over the constituent parts of Yugoslavia together and we would only recognise at the end was the right one. Personally, I think there is a much more fundamental question, which the European Community really has to ask itself: is the fundamental test of a European foreign policy that you all recognise on Day One simultaneously? I personally feel, having had to make a decision on recognition on a number of occasions, I remember Iran in particular, they are very very difficult decisions and they do reflect national history, national commitments, past and present and I think it is very difficult to judge correctly. It is perfectly understandable why the German Foreign Minister felt very strongly about the recognition of Croatia. There were a substantial number of Croatian emigres in the Republic of Germany. I am not saying he bent to pressure but there was an awareness of things as seen from the Croatian side. They strongly wanted it, understandably so, and in the old days that would have been recognised by Germany, there would not have been a pressure for all Community countries to follow suit. If you take another example outside the history of Yugoslavia, we will remember the recognition of Estonia, Latvia and Lithuania where for a variety of good reasons—I did not share them—there was a feeling it would offend President Gorbachev to recognise the Baltic States. Germany, France and Britain felt they had a wider agenda, more important agenda, for which it was not felt worth disrupting relations with the USSR. Denmark, a member of the Community, recognised at the same time as other Scandinavian countries—I was in the Baltic States at the time—it had a very considerable impact. It was, I think, the right decision to do. Irrespective of that it was a reflection of Denmark's own history, their own knowledge, their own intimacy in relations. I think we need to review this question of recognition, having to be unanimous for all the Twelve. There are lots of other actually rather more important issues which are a better yardstick of Community political co-operation, as it used to be called, Community foreign policy is developing through agreement amongst Member States. I think recognition is a very sensitive issue, to insist on unanimity.

188. On the question of what happens in, for example, the former Croatia now with the UNPROFOR forces established in Krajina and they are being forced to withdraw by President Tudjman by next March, is there a possibility of Krajina remaining inside Croatia with United Nations protection and yet having some local autonomy?

(Lord Owen) If you do not mind I really would prefer not to answer that question. Firstly, I think it is difficult to answer it at this stage and also this is a matter which will be negotiated over. I have indicated I do not think you will get an overall settlement of Bosnia-Herzegovina without tackling some of the problems of the United Nations' Protected Areas in Croatia. I think this has to be done with some understanding of Belgrade and Zagreb. I think this area will be addressed. We are, after all, a Conference not on Bosnia-Herzegovina, we are a Conference on the former Yugoslavia. I devote a very large amount of my time to Kosovo, Macedonia and Croatia as well as Bosnia-Herzegovina. In the particular scenario you paint I hope we will avoid some of the pitfalls you highlight in the negotiations over the next few months.

Mr Rowlands

189. If we think about it we know somehow the international community did not get the message across about ethnic cleansing and was not able to do enough to get rid of the thing on the ground. Given that experience what sort of message and what sort of stance are we going to have to take to make sure we do not have the barbaric behaviour of the kind we have seen in Kosovo where we are talking about a population of 90 per cent of different backgrounds from the Serbian masters?

(Lord Owen) I have actually answered the question. I think the appointment of Mr Mazowiecki and his terms of reference to make a new Report on Human Rights Abuses was important. I think the decision to appoint a Commission of Experts under Professor Carl Schengen was very important. They start their work now, they are assem-

[**Mr Rowlands** *Contd*]

bling the evidence. There is one extra element that has to be dealt with. There is no use assembling the evidence unless there is a structure for an ad hoc court and there is growing pressure to move towards the creation of an ad hoc court, a criminal court, which you could do under a Security Council Resolution. The other option through a General Assembly Resolution of creating an International Criminal Court would be non-discriminatory but it would take such a length of time that it would not catch the present problems, you have to do it through a Treaty and ratification. You are dealing with a long timescale. That loop has to be closed so that people can be tried for committing war crimes or other abuses of the human rights law. As to Kosovo, I think I said the danger of Kosovo is actually one only needs civilian unrest so dry is the tinder round there and the militia clamp down, panic spreads, people start to flee and by mistake everybody believes ethnic cleansing has started. The answer to Kosovo, of course, is to have a UN force in Kosovo now and to do what we have done in Macedonia which is to have a deployment. As you know under the Resolution the Secretary-General has had the report and has agreed a battalion of 700 people should go to Macedonia at the earliest stage. It will be debated in the Security Council. It is an open secret that it is extremely likely to be approved tomorrow. Ideally we would like to do the same with Kosovo but Kosovo is part of Serbia and that is important to state. We are not part of a succession movement. We are part of restoring to Kosovo autonomy which was taken away from them as recently as 1989.

190. This is the problem. Do you think the Serbs on the ground will listen to all this?

(Lord Owen) They were not accepting this. I think maybe it will change after the election but it is said the present government will not accept it and any government which had President Milosovic would not accept it. We, therefore, cannot get a UN force in without shooting our way in, which is out of the question. We have got CSCE monitors, we would like to get more. We have got UN monitors, we would like to have more. I think we have to try and show and demonstrate to the Serbians, particularly whatever government takes over after the election, that it is in their interests to involve the UN. In the major towns the militia is so distrusted there is no chance of them dealing with any civilian unrest. The UN would deal with it better in a way that would not lead to these repercussions. I do not rule out the hope of getting a UN presence in Pristina and some of the other major towns but at the moment we have met a completely blank wall.

191. You are using the language of persuasion, I understand that, but should there not come a moment as a result of what has happened in Bosnia when the language of ultimatum will come into place sooner or later?

(Lord Owen) I think that would only come in in the form of the second passage. I agree with preventative diplomacy but preventative diplomacy is by negotiation as envisaged by the Secretary General. You cannot fight a UN force within the framework of preventative diplomacy. I think it is perfectly open to the United Nations to say at any given point you have to accept a UN force and if you do not then we will take action so as to ensure you do accept it. Again, I think there are military options there which do not necessitate military force. If you are going to put forces in then you will have to put a substantial force; the JNA, the Yugoslav Army, is in Kosovo in substantial numbers. I think again you come back to the question of air power and it is possible to envisage an air power ultimatum under certain circumstances in which events begin to unravel. I am afraid in that whole region events could unravel very fast. I do think one has to have contingency planning ready and people know how they are going to act well in advance. I have reason to think that sort of contingency planning is being done now.

192. Macedonia is a more hopeful scene, how would you rate Macedonia?

(Lord Owen) I have to be careful how I talk about Macedonia because it is obviously a very sensitive issue. You are asking your questions fully aware of how sensitive it is. It is profoundly to be hoped Macedonia and Greece, who are neighbours and have a great deal of common interest, can resolve their difficulties peacefully and there can be the fullest political and economic co-operation between the two. That at the moment sounds a slightly pious platitude when faced with the severe dispute about what name the new country should be called. This will be discussed in some way at the Edinburgh Summit. The problem is the economy of Macedonia is already very weak. With our ban on transshipments of oil across Serbia and a ban on oil coming from Greece this means the only option open to Macedonia is to get oil through over the mountainous routes from Rumania and Bulgaria. That is very difficult to do. I do not think they can get sufficient oil. We are dealing with an economic problem in Macedonia and the strategic problem of Macedonia which is the biggest question.

Chairman: I think we have talked about sanctions earlier in some detail but there are one or two more questions from Mr Jopling on that before we close.

Mr Jopling

193. You rang a bell with me when you expressed your frustration at the pathetic way in which the international community has sought to enforce the sanctions which have been imposed. As one who has also been frustrated over many years by this inability, as one who years ago voted with the Labour Government in favour of oil sanctions against Rhodesia, I think you will understand what I mean. Will you tell us to what extent you think a lot of the bloodshed and agony over the

[**Mr Jopling** *Contd*]
last few months could have been avoided if those sanctions had been properly enforced? Also whether you would comment on the sanctions assistance missions which are currently in place and comment on how effective they are and what you would like to see in there to enable the international community much better to impose sanctions?

(Lord Owen) I think you are a little savage; "pathetic" is a pretty hard word to use.

194. Five oil tankers under the noses of this monitoring force, I describe as pathetic.

(Lord Owen) It is your word. I am tempted to follow suit. On the question of oil tankers, the idea oil would not come into Bar in Montenegro, was not handled as a serious question. The oil coming through by road is a more difficult one. The problem was to get oil through to Bosnia-Herzegovina which is an independent country recognised by the UN. There was a scheme of end user certificates and you had to prove at the border the oil was going to Bosnia-Herzegovina. There was naivety in believing by crossing Serbia it was not going to offload en route or find its way to the Bosnian Serbs. It was very noticeable a great number of those lorries were going to towns on the border in the control of the Bosnian Serbs. There was no doubt there was a black market and racket, we should have been aware of it earlier. The Sanctions Assistance Mission was one of the factors alerting us to the fact it was being broken. There was a great reluctance by the riparian states on the Danube to stop and search. They claimed it was not allowed for under their Treaty obligations. Now the Resolution has been passed there has been a toughening up, although there are still countries which are allowing barges with oil through. There have been countries which have, however, changed their end user certificates to Bar which will have an effect. As to the lives lost by it, I do think the main effect has been we have not got the pressure on Belgrade now in the month of December we would have expected to have which would have had, I think, an important effect on the elections and attitudes in Belgrade. It has had the counter-effect, that by needing to toughen up the sanctions it has been misconstrued by some supporters of Prime Minister Panic and President Cosic that we have deliberately spurned them and their efforts to be reasonable. We had no option but to do it but that is now how it is seen if you are in Belgrade. I think they have seen this somehow as a slap against them when Cosic and Panic were genuinely trying to get into a more constructive dialogue. They would claim it has instead helped Milosovic. We wanted a more constructive dialogue with Prime Minister Panic and President Cosic, who whilst a nationalist, wanting a Greater Serbia, wants it through different objectives. The effect of tightening sanctions has been to make some of these people rather discouraged, feeling the West think anti-Serbian. That is not the case, certainly not the case of our negotiating team. We recognise there has to be a settlement the Serbs can live with. Serbs were ready to live in Bosnia-Herzegovina or Croatia when it was part of Yugoslavia but the ground rules changed when they started to become independent countries. On this question of sanctions, all we can do is to apply them as firmly and clearly as we can and hope the pressures on Belgrade to act constructively will again win through. I think we have lost two months on the oil embargo but we have not lost on economic sanctions. But have got to be more conscious of the effect this sanctions policy is having on Macedonia and Bulgaria and Rumania, of who have weak economies. They are paying a substantial price for this. If we do not help them then we cannot expect them to implement sanctions properly.

Mr Wareing

195. Can I say that, in fact, in September sanctions appeared to be working very, very strongly in Belgrade. At that time people in the street were expressing the view that they would hope that the United Nations would lift their sanctions in response to Mr Panic's overtures. We are coming up now to the December 20th elections which you have already mentioned as being very, very important. Do you think, in fact, we can offer, as it were, an olive branch in some shape or form to the people to encourage support for Mr Panic? If, in fact, Mr Cosic and Mr Panic are able to deliver something they should be rewarded. What is your view of that?

(Lord Owen) You are an experienced politician, you well know how it is received if any American, French or German politician seeks to interfere in our elections. We have to be very careful in trying to influence the elections in Belgrade. I think all we can say with truthfulness and honesty is we have had more co-operation from President Cosic and Prime Minister Panic than we have had from the previous administration of President Milosovic. The elections are flawed anyhow. There are no Albanians standing in Kosovo and given the troubles they have had with basic freedom it is understandable. It is very hard to encourage them to do so. These elections will be monitored by outside observers if for no other reason than to try and ensure the television is rather more fair minded than it currently is. That does not avoid the fact the run up to the election on television has been biased and many other factors. The real problem is one significant power in Serbia is not going to participate in the elections. Montenegro has shown evidence of having a fairer democratic system for elections and agreed by opposite parties. In Serbia democracy leaves a lot to be found wanting. We will have observers and they will tell us what is happening during the election period. I am wary of trying to design a package which interferes with their elections.

Chairman

196. Lord Owen, when this Committee looked at the crumbling Yugoslavia in the last Parliament, we were advised by the Foreign and Common-

[**Chairman** *Contd*]

wealth Office in their view it was *sui generis*, in other words it was a terrible situation but a contained one, it would not spread. Do you believe that?

(Lord Owen) No, I never have done.

197. Therefore the final question: what do you fear most are the likely engines of spreading the infection? Where are the real danger points that might turn this not only into a Balkan punch-up but into a major war?

(Lord Owen) This is not a civil war pure and simple, though it has some element of civil war. It is not a war of aggression across frontiers although it has some element of that. It is a highly complicated situation which I think can very easily flow over into Eastern Europe and the Former Soviet Republics. I think the fact the Russian diplomacy has been so committed and so skilful under the Foreign Minister reflects their anxieties about the Caucasus which in many ways could be called Yugoslavia of the Former Soviet Union. There are ethnic disputes and territorial disputes of a very similar nature. I think it goes deeper than that and I have watched the various sophisticated commentators in this country and other countries, mainly in this country, arguing this is none of our business. I suppose this was the language of the 1930s. I do not think there are straight historical analogies with the 1930s, there are analogies with the past, the 1914–1918 break-up because of the Soviet Union and all that has happened there. I think ethnic cleansing is so odious and pervasive, it has racist elements that if we do not check it, it will go everywhere in Europe, not just Eastern Europe. This is a severe problem. I think racism is there below the surface, in all our societies. There are a lot of people who think you can solve these problems by herding people into separate areas and geographically sort people out which makes life more comfortable and easier. They delude themselves that you can send them home with financial incentives or move populations. Once you accept that philosophy it is not long before you harass them and browbeat them and kill them to deal with that. I do not think there is a deeper question than ethnic cleansing. Some people say to me it is a *Realpolitik* to give up Yugoslavia. Unfortunately it is a country which many people thought would be the first communist country to come into the European Community. It is a country many of our citizens have spent many happy hours in on holidays and they like and know the people, whether Serb, Croat or Muslim. The idea we can ignore it seems not *Realpolitik* but infantile and wrong. I think *Realpolitik*, by which I mean the determined pursuit of interest, which in my view is a praiseworthy objective of foreign policy, has to realise that this racism and ethnic cleansing has to be defeated at the earliest possible opportunity otherwise we know from history it will spread. Therefore, I do not think there is any enlightened do-gooding about being involved in trying to reach a resolution of the dispute in Yugoslavia. We have a deep interest in resolving it. I do finally just say this: that the mechanism of the International Conference on former Yugoslavia that was established through the London Conference is still alive and kicking. It is very easy to disparage it. I undertook this job in the full knowledge that I was going off to Geneva for at least six months. There has never been any illusion in my mind it was anything less than that and after four months I have not given up the negotiating process and am willing to stay there a year or a year and a half if need be to deal with it. Negotiations are often painful, long and receive many setbacks and often at the point of maximum dispair you often get the breakthrough. There are no simple military cleancut solutions to this but the steady application of pressure is essential and pressure is economic, political, moral and it is also, in my view, being ready to speak quietly, to hold a big stick and if threatened or challenged then you have to be ready to use the stick. Although I have been, I hope, honest about the gloomy and pessimistic side, I would not like to leave your Committee, Chairman, feeling the peace process is spent and there is no prospect of a negotiated settlement. I believe the prospect is there and with determination the more they realise we are not going to give up on this and we are going to reverse ethnic cleansing and have a constitution that reverses ethnic cleansing or they will be the pariahs of Europe, they will not be allowed into any of the European assistance programmes or European health programmes, I am confident we will reach a solution.

Chairman: That is a realistic but not totally pessimistic note on which to finish this very long session. We are deeply grateful to you for answering all our comments and questions and, of course, we wish you very well in the enormously difficult tasks that lie immediately ahead. Thank you very much indeed.

Printed in the United Kingdom for HMSO.
Dd.5060653, 1/93, C5, 3398/3A, 5673, 229416.

HMSO publications are available from:

HMSO Publications Centre
(Mail, fax and telephone orders only)
PO Box 276, London, SW8 5DT
Telephone orders 071-873 9090
General enquiries 071-873 0011
(queuing system in operation for both numbers)
Fax orders 071-873 8200

HMSO Bookshops
49 High Holborn, London, WC1V 6HB
071-873 0011 Fax 071-873 8200 (counter service only)
258 Broad Street, Birmingham, B1 2HE
021-643 3740 Fax 021-643 6510
Southey House, 33 Wine Street, Bristol, BS1 2BQ
0272 264306 Fax 0272 294515
9-21 Princess Street, Manchester, M60 8AS
061-834 7201 Fax 061-833 0634
16 Arthur Street, Belfast, BT1 4GD
0232 238451 Fax 0232 235401
71 Lothian Road, Edinburgh, EH3 9AZ
031-228 4181 Fax 031-229 2734

HMSO's Accredited Agents
(see Yellow Pages)

and through good booksellers

ISBN 0-10-283993-X

HOUSE OF COMMONS SESSION 1992–93

FOREIGN AFFAIRS COMMITTEE

THE EXPANDING ROLE OF THE UNITED NATIONS AND ITS IMPLICATIONS FOR UK POLICY

MINUTES OF EVIDENCE

Wednesday 27 January 1993

BRITISH RED CROSS

Mr M Whitlam and Mr G Dennis

Ordered by The House of Commons *to be printed*
27 January 1993

LONDON: HMSO
£6.80 net

235–v

WEDNESDAY 27 JANUARY 1993

Members present:

Mr David Howell, in the Chair

Mr Mike Gapes
Mr David Harris
Mr Jim Lester
Mr Ted Rowlands
Sir John Stanley
Mr Robert Wareing

Memorandum submitted by the British Red Cross

EXECUTIVE SUMMARY

This submission sets out only the views of the British Red Cross. However, the opinions of other components of the International Red Cross and Red Crescent Movement have also been canvassed.

The Movement has a unique neutral and impartial role which is recognised by governments. As such it co-operates with the United Nations within the limits of the mandates—complementary but distinct—of the two institutions. Co-operation would be improved in the field if the calibre of UN officials were higher and the chains of command clearer. It might be wise to move the UN Department of Humanitarian Affairs to Geneva.

Medium-term changes in the relief environment have arisen from the information revolution, and from massive deprivation of civilian populations in conflicts. The former threatens a distortion of priorities; the latter has led to a huge increase in displaced persons. It is all the more important for the Movement to retain its impartial judgement.

More recently, the end of Communism in this continent has given the West increased confidence to mount humanitarian actions. But it has also created new needs in Eastern Europe and the former Soviet Union, and the weapons distributed by the former adversaries are still around. The post Cold War UN in its greater freedom of action reveals more of its weaknesses.

Two major concerns to the Red Cross are the increased complexity and intensity of food security disasters and the lack of resources to meet them. The increased burden cannot be carried by humanitarian agencies alone. The UN has a role to play; so have governments.

The British Red Cross believes the UN could put more effort into peace-keeping. More generally, there is scope for improved co-operation between the humanitarian players. This requires flexible mechanisms for consultation and the establishment of principles and criteria for action. The Red Cross welcomes the setting up of the UN Department of Humanitarian Affairs. It is less effective than it could be due to its low status within the UN and to its small budget. The situation in Somalia should be examined for the lessons it teaches about management of the interface between military and humanitarian actions.

The UN should contribute to ensuring compliance with humanitarian law; to building indigenous disaster preparedness capabilities; to the dissemination of information on emergencies; to the execution of humanitarian actions in accordance with the principles of humanity, impartiality and neutrality.

THE PERFORMANCE OF THE UNITED NATIONS IN THE FIELD OF HUMANITARIAN ASSISTANCE

1. Introduction: Framework of the International Red Cross and Red Crescent Movement

The British Red Cross is part of the International Red Cross and Red Crescent Movement. The components of this Movement consist of the 153 recognised National Red Cross and National Red Crescent Societies; the International Committee of the Red Cross (commonly known as the ICRC), and the International Federation of Red Cross and Red Crescent Societies (called the Federation). These components share a common mission and Fundamental Principles, and they co-operate with each other. However, each component also has a high degree of independence, and a distinct role.

The 153 National Red Cross and National Red Crescent Societies are autonomous organisations, co-operating with their respective public authorities to meet the humanitarian needs of their own countries, in peace and in war. They also support each other's work, particularly in times of emergency.

As an illustration, the work of the British Red Cross, which was established in 1870, today lies in five main areas: an Emergency Programme for disaster assistance within the UK; a Community Programme,

The cost of printing and publishing these Minutes of Evidence is estimated by HMSO at £3,495.

including the provision of first aid cover at public events, Day Centres and services for disabled people; Training, such as in first aid, nursing and welfare; a Youth Programme, and an International Programme, embracing a tracing and family message service, the provision of personnel, food, medicines and relief goods for international disasters as well as the management of development projects overseas.

The existence of a National Red Cross or National Red Crescent in nearly every country means that unlike any other agencies, the Movement does not need to rely on expatriates or on transplanted alien structures but is able to use expatriate staff to manage specialist services and support those of the local community.

The ICRC is the oldest of the three components, being founded in Geneva in 1863. Its role as a neutral and impartial humanitarian intermediary is established in the four Geneva Conventions for the Protection of War Victims of 12 August 1949 and in their two Additional Protocols of 1977, and it has a customary right of initiative to offer its services to Governments and to other parties concerned, in situations not covered by those treaties. The ICRC sends delegates to visit prisoners of war, to inspect internment camps, to help trace and reunite families, and to organise relief in areas of armed conflict. It is also involved in the development and dissemination of knowledge of international humanitarian law. The British Red Cross supports the work of the ICRC by funding some of its work, by supplying people for its operations, and by taking management responsibility for parts of its programme.

The International Federation of Red Cross and Red Crescent Societies comprises all the recognised National Societies. It was established in 1919 after the First World War as the League of Red Cross Societies. The Federation encourages the creation and development of National Societies and co-ordinates relief activities in cases of natural disaster and the aftermath of armed conflict, for example in its work with refugees.

The Movement has three statutory bodies which are vital to the unity of the components. The most important of these is the International Conference of the Red Cross and Red Crescent, which is the Movement's supreme deliberative body and consists of delegations from the States parties to the Geneva Conventions (which now number 174 and thus comprise the vast majority of the international community) as well as representatives of the National Societies, the ICRC and the Federation. The International Conference examines humanitarian matters of common interest, including respect for and development of international humanitarian law. It was the International Conference which adopted the Fundamental Principles of our Movement, and the Principles and Rules for the Movement's disaster relief operations, copies of which are annexed to our submission.[1]

From the preceding remarks, the Members of the Committee will understand that there is a special relationship between the Red Cross and Red Crescent Movement and Governments, going back nearly 130 years.

In making its submission, the British Red Cross can only speak for itself. However, in formulating its remarks, our National Society has sought to draw upon the experience of the entire Movement.

2. The Movement's relationship with the UN

The Select Committee will understand that the Red Cross and Red Crescent Movement predates the United Nations machinery for mitigating human suffering, and that our neutral and impartial role is expressly recognised in treaties and other international instruments. Indeed, the Statutes of the Movement, which were approved by the International Conference of the Red Cross (which, as already noted, includes State representatives) in 1986, lays down three requirements for Red Cross or Red Crescent co-operation with other organisations. These are, first, that the components of the Movement must maintain their independence and identity; secondly, that the co-operating organisations are pursuing a purpose similar to that of the Movement (that is, they share similar goals), and third, that the organisations must be prepared to respect the adherence by the components to the Movement's Fundamental Principles, which include humanity, neutrality, impartiality and independence.

The Movement's Statutes also cover the relations between States parties to the Geneva Conventions and the components of the Red Cross and Red Crescent. The relevant provision refers to mutual support for humanitarian activities, and to the States' respect for the adherence by all the components to the Fundamental Principles. Given that the United Nations is a body of States, and that most UN members are also parties to the Geneva Conventions, this provision is also of some relevance.

[1] not printed

The United Nations has in fact recognised the independent character of the Red Cross and Red Crescent from its inception. The relationship of our Movement to the UN system is special, and sometimes needs to be at arms' length.

The ICRC has a unique relationship with the UN in that since 1990, it has had observer status at the UN General Assembly. This was granted in consideration of the ICRC's special role and mandates conferred upon it by the Geneva Conventions of 12 August 1949 (Resolution 45/6 dated 16 October 1990). Although a number of non-governmental organisations (NGOs) have consultative status with the Economic and Social Council (ECOSOC) of the United Nations, they do not have observer status at the General Assembly which is reserved primarily for the UN specialised agencies, regional international organisations, non-member States and a few national liberation movements. Unlike other NGOs, the ICRC's mandate under the Geneva Conventions and Additional Protocol I 1977 has vested it with a "functional international personality".

Thus, the ICRC co-operates with the UN at two levels: formal contacts at the General Assembly, and operational work in the field.

The Federation has consultative status with ECOSOC, and has a presence in the ICRC office in New York. Representatives of National Societies on occasion are called upon to represent the Federation at UN meetings. Like the ICRC, the Federation has permanent and case-by-case relations with subsidiary organs and specialised agencies of the UN, such as UNHCR, UNICEF, WHO, the World Food Programme (WFP), and UNDRO. However, the formal status of the Federation at the UN is equivalent to that of other international NGOs.

Contact between the UN and National Societies is both through the offices of associated institutions in Geneva and more directly through field operations.

Regardless of whether the body is the ICRC, the Federation or a National Society, co-operation operationally between the UN and the Red Cross/Red Crescent is undertaken within the limits of each other's respective mandates, which are complementary but distinct.

At headquarters level, there is regular contact between the UN and the Red Cross in Geneva, which on the whole is positive. Although the ICRC and the Federation are represented in New York, the British Red Cross would prefer to see the UN Under-Secretary General for Humanitarian Affairs set up his office in Geneva because this is where the co-ordination of disaster relief work and co-ordination of population movements (refugees) is better achieved. This apart, problems are more likely to arise in the field where the calibre of UN officials is more variable, and where chains of command are not always clear. This difficulty could usefully be addressed.

3. The Present Global Environment

As already noted, the International Red Cross and Red Crescent Movement operates in nearly every country. Consequently, we have a perhaps unique global perspective on matters of humanitarian concern as well as a unique operational capability which could be better used by the UN machine.

Other submissions to your Committee have described recent developments in the international order, which are also set out well in the Report of the UN Secretary General entitled "An Agenda for Peace" (1992). Building on what others have already stated, suffice it to say that the emergence of new States following the break-up of Yugoslavia and the former Soviet Union has set new challenges for our Movement and its relationship to the UN, for example, in our support of a new National Red Cross Society which may be the operating arm for one of the UN bodies in the delivery of aid. Our comments, therefore, will be limited first to a general overview of the current political and economic environment as it affects the UN and delivery of humanitarian assistance, and then we will wish to highlight two specific concerns.

(a) General overview

There are two significant medium-term changes in the disaster relief environment over the past two decades, which are distinct from but still relevant to, the short-term changes of the past couple of years, which will be discussed later.

The first of these significant medium-term changes is the key role of the media on the humanitarian stage. The global information explosion means that the victims of armed conflicts, from starving babies to shelled hospitals, are shown daily on television screens. As a result, there is increased pressure on donor governments, such as the UK; aid agencies, including the Red Cross, and the UN system to take action and to be seen so to do.

The media can also direct attention towards certain conflicts or disasters which lend themselves better to media coverage to the detriment of others. Although there is no hard evidence, we believe that such media attention affects the judgement of these responsible for funding international aid. This makes it all the more vital for the Red Cross and Red Crescent to preserve its objectivity. That is, our Movement must make its own assessment of the needs and try to respond to them according to our own criteria. These assessments put the victims first and not the political imperative, although the same may not be true of the UN. The ICRC in particular can only co-operate with the UN or others in such a way that it can preserve its independence, given its specific role as a neutral intermediary providing protection and assistance to specified categories of conflict victims. The Red Cross and Red Crescent Movement must be seen and must be accepted as being genuinely independent, avoiding manipulation by the media or by political interests.

Secondly, although after the Second World War no conflict leading to massive deprivation of civilian populations occurred for almost 20 years, beginning with Biafra and the Nigerian Civil War, such widespread dispossession of innocent civilians has now become the norm for disaster relief. Recently this has led to UNHCR being required to take on more tasks to meet the increased demand. This in turn affects the ability of the UN Department of Humanitarian Affairs to co-ordinate different parts of the UN disaster relief machine.

Referring now to the recent short-term changes in the disaster relief environment, the collapse of Communism in the former Soviet Union and in Eastern Europe has had four main effects on humanitarian assistance.

First, the Western powers, with little fear of conflict with former Communist powers, have been able to take humanitarian initiatives in response to geo-political imperatives (as in Iraq); to domestic or international pressure (Somalia); and to gain influence (the role of the United States Navy following the cyclones in Bangladesh). However, the West cannot necessarily take such initiatives so decisively where humanitarian considerations are weighed against other factors, as we have seen in Bosnia.

Second, the emergence of ethnic conflict, so far only at the very beginning, in Eastern Europe and the former Soviet Union places new demands on disaster relief capacity, hitherto needed primarily in the Third World. An issue which thus requires an even greater co-ordination of effort in order to make most effective use of limited resources.

Third, although the end of the Cold War has potentially freed the UN system to fulfil its original role as a forum for Governments to resolve conflicts, it has also revealed weaknesses in that system which remained hidden owing to the paralysis of the past 40 years. For example, the absence of a UN standing force means that there is no permanent machinery for the international community to express its will when such force is required.

Fourthly, and last, huge quantities of arms once supplied to client states by NATO or the Soviet Union are now left in the hands of all sorts of unstable regimes and would-be regimes. These are being used against aid agencies and perhaps suggest a greater role for multi-national forces such as UNPROFOR.

(b) Specific concerns

We have particular concern with two alarming developments in this present period of profound change which affect all humanitarian agencies. These concerns might be termed "complex emergencies" and "the humanitarian gap" respectively.

(i) *Complex emergencies*

By 'complex emergencies', we wish to highlight that the major food security disasters of today are no longer simple cases of cause and effect. Whether we are talking about Somalia, former Yugoslavia, Cambodia, Afghanistan, the Sudan or the former Soviet Union, contemporary disasters involve economic dislocation, drought or floods, the collapse of political structures, violence—ranging from all-out international war, through civil war to banditry—famine, and mass population displacements. In such circumstances, destroying or controlling food production and distribution has become part of the arsenal of the aggressor. Whether we like it or not, the provision of humanitarian aid is often seen by one faction or another as a political act. Despite the strictures of international humanitarian law, the blocking of humanitarian assistance is becoming part of the accepted arsenal of the politician and military commander.

This suggests a development of a new relationship between governments/UN/NGOS in delivery of aid. All partners now need systems agreed to cope with such situations. The relationship between the delivery of aid and the military is changing and needs to be recognised.

(ii) *Humanitarian gap*

The humanitarian gap or deficit is increasing. Food security disasters are not only becoming more complex: they are also becoming more frequent and more catastrophic in their impact. We believe that the prime reason for this is that the gap between the needs of the world's most vulnerable people, and the resources available to the humanitarian agencies to meet those needs, is ever widening. In 1980, some 100 million people were affected by major disasters; by the end of the decade this figure had risen to 230 million. Over the same period, as an illustration, the average annual response of the International Federation of Red Cross and Red Crescent Societies to disasters (representing just one component of our Movement) went up from 150 million Swiss Francs to 260 million, a growth of approximately 70 per cent. Clearly, the need for humanitarian intervention is growing exponentially and our ability to meet those needs is not keeping pace. For the first time ever, the UN and the Red Cross alike are having to set priorities and make choices. This requires a more cost-effective response and criteria to help with making these choices.

The Red Cross and Red Crescent Movement is not alone in facing this response crisis. Major NGOs face similar problems, as do the humanitarian agencies of the United Nations.

What are the causes of this humanitarian gap? Some are referred to every day, such as the debt burden, trading relations, environmental factors, an absence of so-called "good government" and the effect of structural adjustment packages on the most vulnerable. However, we would like to highlight one additional cause of the humanitarian gap, which is not normally included in commentators' lists: a declining willingness among States to accept responsibility for the disadvantaged members of their societies.

The relationship between the poor and vulnerable of the world on the one hand, and on the other hand, nation states and non-state humanitarian bodies has changed significantly. Increasingly States are reducing their responsibility for the welfare load. Many no longer feel an obligation to provide directly themselves a safety net for the poor. This is as true in the Northern hemisphere as in the South. The British Red Cross welcomes the fact that the United Kingdom's budget for overseas aid in 1993 was not cut and very much hopes that the revenue for such expenditure will remain secure in future.

The net result of this changing relationship is that more people are vulnerable to disaster and the aid agencies are being looked to to pick up the pieces. Even if the humanitarian organisations were able to solve all crises, which they are not, these bodies are not being supplied with the necessary resources to bridge the humanitarian gap. We are also concerned that the UN aid agencies with their bureaucracy—as well as the European Community—may be looking to the wrong solutions to meet this gap. Instead of trying to fit new aid delivery structures into their heavily bureaucratic machine, thus becoming even more operational, they should look to strengthening their links with agencies like the Red Cross so as to use their resources of cash, food etc. more effectively.

(iii) *The way forward*

The British Red Cross argues that faced with this situation, humanitarian agencies, particularly international agencies, must look for a new perspective on their work.

First, we have to move to increase the impact of our humanitarian actions both on the ground and in the corridors of power. The agencies must become more effective in their delivery of humanitarian assistance and more assertive of the rights of individuals and communities to both give and receive such assistance. Given that there is a bigger job for us to do, and we want to do it, humanitarian agencies must become more professional. As will be suggested later, the UN, in particular the Department of Humanitarian Affairs, could have a role in promoting this professionalism.

Secondly, the UN and other humanitarian agencies should no longer accept the status quo as given. Nation states and the international bodies they control must accept that it is an inherent responsibility of sovereignty to provide for the needs of the most vulnerable and to work to reduce that vulnerability. Within the limits of their own statutes, humanitarian agencies have a duty to advocate and lobby to ensure that these responsibilities are acted upon.

In summary, effective and professional humanitarian aid, and lobbying to reduce the root causes of food insecurity, must be the dual strategies for dealing with complex emergencies and for closing the humanitarian gap.

If this two-pronged attack on vulnerability is not taken, a point will soon be reached at which humanitarian agencies can no longer provide an effective, impartial and universal service to humanity. Such a situation would not be acceptable to the Red Cross and Red Crescent Movement and should not be acceptable to any humanitarian body.

4. The UN in recent conflict situations: The role of the General Assembly and the Security Council

The United Nations may be at its most useful when it provides a forum for the resolution of conflict, since conflict may itself be the source of the humanitarian emergency. The UN's activity in this area has been seen in Nicaragua, El Salvador, Cambodia, Sri Lanka, Afghanistan and former Yugoslavia. An armed conflict may also cause natural disasters, as in Mozambique, or exacerbate natural disasters, as evidenced in Somalia, Sudan and Ethiopia. It is the role neither of NGOs nor of the Red Cross and Red Crescent Movement to bring conflict to an end but only to alleviate its effects, and in the case of the ICRC, as mentioned before, it is the ICRC's specific role to act as an impartial and neutral intermediary between the parties to a conflict. The failures of the UN in conflict resolution, such as in former Yugoslavia and Somalia, speak for themselves. But patient diplomacy has over time had some effect, for example, in Angola, Cambodia and Central America, and may yet do so in Mozambique and elsewhere; the British Red Cross would like to see more effort put into this peacemaking role by the UN, as proposed in the UN Secretary General's Report on An Agenda for Peace.

However, the British Red Cross is not in favour of the proposition, which has recently become popular, that it is proper to use force to aid victims of conflict, as a kind of acceptable alternative to addressing the root causes of that conflict. In the light of the obstacles and refusals encountered by humanitarian action in numerous conflict situations, certain governments, that of France in particular, have advocated the institution of a right to intervene. But is this not yet another instance in which the exercise of such a right would depend primarily and directly upon the balance of power and thus be limited in scope? The military intervention conducted on humanitarian grounds in Iraq after the Gulf War in 1991, pursuant to Security Council Resolution 688, may have given rise to the illusion that resort to force might be an appropriate course of action for addressing other humanitarian crises. However, many observers feel that it would be premature to consider that operation, which was conducted in an exceptional political and military context, as having created a precedent. Moreover, not only is the so-called "droit d'ingérence" doubtful law, but it can also have undesired side-effects: No one wishes to have the United States, for example, intervene in Northern Ireland!

Still, this does not mean that use of force to assist victims is wrong *a priori.* In the case of Security Council action against an aggressor under Chapter VII of the UN Charter, aid for victims may be an essential corollary, as it was seen to be for the Kurds and Shias in Iraq. More recently, the Security Council authorised force to protect the delivery of aid in Bosnia-Herzegovina and in Somalia. However, the Red Cross and Red Crescent Movement may then have to stand back in order to preserve a proper neutrality between the contending forces in the interests of all victims, military and civilian, including those of future conflicts.

In the case of conflict where there is no effective authority—Somalia may be a case in point, and where UN diplomacy has failed, the choice may be between the use of measured force or death for millions. Clearly the Red Cross cannot argue for the latter and so in such circumstances the choice is clear. The British Red Cross recognised this to be the case several months before the UN took action in Somalia.

5. The UN's co-ordinating role for humanitarian actions

Your Committee has already heard some reflections on the need to improve the co-ordinating role of the UN. We would also like to address this issue, which we too regard as central. We will first make several general comments; then refer to the UN specialised agencies, and conclude this section with some specific remarks on the present situation in Somalia.

(a) General aspects

Increased co-operation between the many humanitarian players presently active on the scene of emergencies is an obvious need. Such co-operation would help to prevent duplication of effort and to augment individual effectiveness. Two distinct aspects of this effort towards greater co-ordination merit close consideration.

First, it is important to establish flexible mechanisms for consultation which will not slow down the decision-making process and will not render co-operation more complicated. Each conflict is played out in specific circumstances, and therefore, we cannot draw up hard and fast rules to apply in all cases. A consequence of this situation is to give decision-making authority to those on the ground.

Secondly, there is a need to establish principles and criteria for action which make co-operation feasible and eliminate any risk that humanitarian work will become politicised. In this respect, it might also be useful to define a common framework of ethical and operational principles to be shared by the many

NGOs whose activities are not based on treaties or mandates recognised by the international community. Such a framework or code of conduct would be a part of the drive for professionalism mentioned earlier as a way of closing the humanitarian gap and could be led by the UN.

Thus, all the players in the game need to place more emphasis on co-operation and consultation. This includes NGOs, the Red Cross and Red Crescent Movement, the UN system and other Governmental instrumentalities, such as the European Community. This is so not least for the reason that large scale interventions of which governmental agencies are capable often have to be carried through by the voluntary bodies which alone have the necessary machinery on the ground. As an illustration, in former Yugoslavia, the Red Cross is distributing the food brought in by UN agencies.

But the UN system should not believe that—speaking only for ourselves—we in the Red Cross and Red Crescent Movement are prepared to let co-operation and consultation be interpreted as co-ordination of us by them. As explained earlier, there are reasons both of principle and of practice which require our Movement to retain its separate identity and independence. More can be achieved for the victims by maintaining the complementary but distinct roles of the UN and of the Red Cross and Red Crescent

Finally, on the subject of general co-ordination, in all humanitarian emergencies, the collection and dissemination of accurate information is a pre-requisite of effective humanitarian assistance. The UN system has a mixed record of success and failure in this regard: we would urge that this essential function is strengthened at each and every opportunity.

(b) The UN specialised agencies

Conversely, the actions of the UN specialised agencies need co-ordinating one with another. The Department of Humanitarian Affairs (DHA) was set up to deal with this. It was born out of the failure of the UN system to address effectively the political and military complex of contemporary humanitarian emergencies, as seen from the plight of the Kurds following the Gulf War. The British Red Cross certainly welcomes this effort to remedy the weaknesses in the UN system but to date, the DHA has been ineffective.

Some of the reasons for the present failings of the DHA may be as follows. First, the budget for the Department is derisory. Second, the present status of the Under-Secretary General for Humanitarian Affairs may be insufficient. That is, it is well-known that the Heads of the UN agencies are powerful figures in their own right. Given that they have not been under the control of successive UN Secretary Generals, it is unlikely that they would answer to a newly-created subordinate official. As previously mentioned, if the Under-Secretary General for Humanitarian Affairs is to become effective, he should probably be based in Geneva where the aid community can give him best support, rather than in New York, and be given sufficient authority and budget.

The UN agencies function best where the task is reasonably clear, and there is a lead agency. The specialised agencies seem to function worst where there is a multiplicity of tasks, priorities are unclear and where, since no agency is in the lead, agency rivalries have free rein. A large part of the tragedy of Somalia was due to ineffectual co-ordination within the UN system and even to institutional rivalry. The same has occurred in the Sudan, Afghanistan, former Yugoslavia, Angola, Mozambique and Iraq.

It appears that the allocation to the UN system of Overseas Development Administration Disaster Unit funds has grown over the past two-and-a-half years. In our view, the British Government gets better value for money from the Red Cross, which has less bureaucracy, lower salaries, fewer overheads and more unpaid workers. The British Red Cross is of course very pleased with the assistance given by the ODA but given some of the constraints and the changing circumstances, perhaps more questions need to be asked of the UN about value for money, salary levels and overhead charges.

In addition, there is a case for saying that the Department of Humanitarian Affairs will never function better than it has done so far unless it controls more of the funds that governments provide. Perhaps the Under-Secretary General for Humanitarian Affairs should have some say in how extra funds voted for specific disaster situations are allocated between the UN agencies?

(c) Points arising from Somalia

The international military intercession in Somalia raises critical issues of humanitarian politics surrounding the use of military forces alongside humanitarian operations. We feel that the UN Department of Humanitarian Affairs has the mandate to seize the initiative and to provide the leadership and the forum to stimulate action on these matters, concentrating the debate on the original reason for the military intercession, namely the humanitarian concern. The British Red Cross believes that there are four main issues which need to be addressed. They are as follows:

(i) The interface between the international military forces and the humanitarian operations cries out for more effective management and co-ordination. Is the military intercession being carried out in a way which helps or hinders the humanitarian mission? Were reasonable structures set up to co-ordinate between the military and the aid agencies before the military intervention and/or during the action?

(ii) The movement of armed people out of Somalia across the Kenyan and Ethiopian borders ahead of the military forces has led the governments of those countries to ask the UN to play a role in policing the borders to stop such activity. This has profound implications for the rights of refugees in the area.

(iii) Given that the warring groups are likely to resume fighting when the immediate relief effort is completed, there is a requirement to look beyond the short-term needs. With all the focus on immediate relief in the newly secured areas, is a correct balance being struck between relief and rehabilitation and between one geographical area and another? Equally, are the technical rehabilitation staff accompanying the intercession force, working with or parallel to the humanitarian agency's rehabilitation programmes?

(iv) Real rehabilitation needs a political solution, disarmament, and economic rebuilding. All three have to happen together. Who is taking the lead in considering what happens after the relief operation? Can DHA act as the catalyst to bring together the UN agencies, the Bretton-Woods institutions, NGOs and the Somali parties?

Many organisations have a role to play in Somalia but given the absence of a national government, only one has the specific mandate to provide the co-ordination and leadership necessary to ensure that action stays focused on the real needs of the Somali people. That organisation is the UN Department of Humanitarian Affairs.

The recent intervention by the Americans is an indication of the failure of the UN peace-keeping force in this situation. We would assume that when and if US forces pull out, the UN will have made arrangements to deal with the resulting situation.

6. The UN compared with other Inter-governmental organisations

It can be both interesting and instructive to compare the humanitarian actions of the UN system with those of other inter-governmental organisations.

For example, the experience of European Community involvement in the early stages of conflict in Yugoslavia was not a happy one. EC monitors were drawn into actions which reportedly, were not in accordance with international humanitarian law. For example, during the Croatian conflict, EC monitors, in their negotiations, were equating persons protected under the Geneva Conventions 1949 with members of fighting forces. Powerful groupings such as the EC need to take care not to act in ways that confuse, rather than ease, the resolution of conflict and the relief of victims—perhaps by cutting across UN actions. In fact, there appears to be an urgent need for the UN and the EC to clear their lines. Rivalries between the two have been damaging in former Yugoslavia, and with the EC Humanitarian Office (ECHO) and the UN Department of Humanitarian Affairs each newly established and seeking a role, this competition and confusion can only be detrimental to the future of victims.

The British Red Cross welcomes the opening of a dialogue between NATO and humanitarian agencies, as took place at the Workshop on the use of military and civil defence assets in disaster relief, held in Brussels in December 1992. At the same time, "out of theatre" activities by NATO for humanitarian purposes are likely to cause problems unless they are restricted to actions under UN authority or to the provision of transport and other logistic support to humanitarian agencies—particularly the latter.

7. UN role in ensuring respect for humanitarian law

An important change since the end of the Cold War is the recognition by the international community of the importance of compliance with the rules of international law and respect for fundamental human rights as preconditions to the maintenance of international peace and security. This recognition should lead to increased respect for international humanitarian law, the main contemporary instruments of which are the Geneva Conventions 1949 and their two Additional Protocols of 1977.

Despite the fact that respect for international law and human rights is at the core of the new world order, in a number of current conflicts in different parts of the world, violations of humanitarian law are persistent. If we really want international relations to be based on respect for the rule of law, the international community must work for greater compliance with the existing provisions of humanitarian law. We must let belligerents know that they will have to answer for their acts to the international community. Article 1 common to the four Geneva Conventions, and to the first Additional Protocol, clearly defines the responsibility of States in this regard: the High Contracting Parties undertake to respect and to ensure respect for the Conventions—and, as appropriate, the Protocol—in all circumstances. Thus when one State or other party violates its undertakings under the Conventions or Protocol, all other State parties—which include the vast majority of countries (174 at the last count), must feel responsible. This Common Article 1 provides States with a suitable framework, free of all partisan or political considerations, for effective monitoring of the implementation of humanitarian law and for supporting the efforts and representations made by both the ICRC under its treaty-based mandate and other impartial and independent humanitarian organisations.

The UN can be an appropriate forum or mechanism for the exercise of this responsibility of States to ensure respect for humanitarian law. This role is expressly recognised in Article 89 of Additional Protocol I which stipulates that in the event of serious violations of the Conventions or of the Protocol, the High Contracting Parties undertake to act, jointly or individually, in co-operation with the United Nations and in conformity with the UN Charter.

With this in mind, the ICRC welcomed the adoption by the Security Council of Resolution 780, which established a commission to investigate grave breaches of the Geneva Conventions in former Yugoslavia. However, will this resolution remain an *ad hoc* measure, applicable to one conflict only and limited to a mere enquiry? Are States willing to go further and accept the jurisdiction of an international criminal court? We are inclined to doubt it, judging by the number of governments which have still not recognised the competence of the International Fact-Finding Commission established under Article 90 of Protocol I and the number which quite simply have not yet ratified the Additional Protocols, including, alas, the United Kingdom.

The point we wish to make here is that more could be done by the UN to promote compliance with international humanitarian law.

8. Concluding observations

We should like to conclude by making a few observations and by raising a number of questions pertinent to current humanitarian needs and the UN.

Our first comment is that the most important actors in alleviating a humanitarian emergency, especially in the early stages, are the affected State and the indigenous organisations, usually including the National Red Cross or National Red Crescent Society. The tendency towards developing multinational actions may ultimately have an adverse effect on the operational capabilities of the affected State and local institutions unless great care is taken. Thus, in addition to reviewing and expanding its own role, the UN must ensure that sufficient attention and resources are given to establishing effective national disaster preparedness systems as a means of reducing the need for multinational interventions.

In making this Submission to the Select Committee, we like many are left with a number of unanswered questions about the future. Without the framework of the Cold War for making decisions on priorities, what principles of humanitarian action will be applied? Will the end of the Cold War provide an opportunity to reaffirm existing humanitarian standards? In the absence of geographical motivations, will governments provide sufficient resources or show the political will to meet the needs of victims of conflict? Considering the heightened role of the United Nations, and particularly of the Security Council, should humanitarian action focus on assistance, and protection for victims or give priority to a combined political and humanitarian effort designed to tackle the root causes of conflict? To what extent should the United Nations, governments and independent humanitarian organisations co-operate in undertaking humanitarian operations? Might not a humanitarian operation dictated by Security Council resolutions be potentially governed by considerations of political strategy rather than by the urgency and magnitude of the victims' needs?

Many other questions exist; definitive answers may not yet be possible. The British Red Cross wishes to end its submission with one final remark. All humanitarian actions, including those involving the use of force, must be carried out in conformity with the principles inherent in any humanitarian activity, namely the principles of humanity, neutrality and impartiality. As I hope we have shown, we believe that the UN, despite its present shortcomings—many not of its own making, has an essential role in achieving this objective.

Examination of Witnesses

MR MIKE WHITLAM, Director General, and MR GEOFFREY DENNIS, Director of International Operations, the British Red Cross, examined.

Chairman

198. Could we begin this morning by welcoming you, Mr Whitlam and Mr Dennis. You are respectively the Director General for the British Red Cross and the Director of International Operations of the British Red Cross. We are extremely grateful to you for finding the time in your heavy schedule to share your thoughts with us on the views of the British Red Cross and, indeed, the work in respect of the British Red Cross in a whole range of difficult operations around the world which are now raising such huge humanitarian challenges. I think we would like to begin—because this is part of an overall inquiry into the very fast changing role of the UN and Britain's attitude to that changing role—with a very general question: The end of the Cold War has brought new struggles, new ethnic disputes (some of unparalleled horror), and new challenges in terms of protecting and saving human lives and trying to check the tide of human misery. How has the end of the superpower bloc world affected, in your view, the principles by which humanitarian action is applied?

(Mr Whitlam) Thank you, Chairman. In advance of that, perhaps I could just explain to the Committee in a few words how the Red Cross operates across the world so that you can understand where we are coming from.

199. I think that would be very helpful.

(Mr Whitlam) We are obviously here representing the British Red Cross, which is an independent national society, one of 153 national societies around the world. We determine the areas in which we wish to work, the programmes that we want to respond to and so on. We set our own priorities. We are part of the Red Cross Movement and liaise very closely with other national societies. If there is a major problem to address and we cannot address it on our own, we can work in very close partnership with other national societies from anywhere, and co-ordinate those activities through the Federation of Red Cross and Red Crescent Societies—which is based in Geneva. They would act as the co-ordinators in very general terms for programmes relating to natural disasters, population movements and refugees. There would be a close working link with the United Nations on programmes of that kind. Where we are dealing with work that is related to an armed conflict, we would almost certainly work through the ICRC, the International Committee of the Red Cross, also based in Geneva. That is the third part of the Red Cross Movement; it is the part that is Swiss based and neutral because it is Swiss. It is able to monitor the armed conflict and the use or abuse of the Geneva Conventions. We support them with people, goods and cash, and in certain cases take responsibility for parts of the programme. There are three components to the Movement. We try to co-ordinate to ensure that there is the most effective use of the resources from wherever, no matter in which part of the world we are working.

(Mr Dennis) If I could just add briefly to that. With the ICRC in conflict situations we would expect, as the British Red Cross, to act under their umbrella. We would not expect to come out with our own ideas necessarily, but we may come out with slightly different priorities underneath the umbrella of ICRC. With the Federation in disaster areas and in longer term development in some of the countries, ie, rehabilitation-type projects, we would expect to talk to them and, maybe, come up with our own ideas and discuss those with them. There is therefore a slightly different attitude towards the two bodies in Geneva.

(Mr Whitlam) If I may try and answer your incredibly difficult question, although it is very general. I think underlying the evidence that we have given to you in our paper, obviously is this whole question of the changing world in which we are living, and that has an impact not just on the United Nations and the way it has to work, but in the way that all aid agencies are having to operate. We, in our evidence, give a number of examples of how the changing environment affects the delivery of aid and the delivery of services across the world. For example, we mentioned the need for better co-operation and co-ordination and that, of course, is incredibly difficult in a world that is changing as rapidly as it is; but given the changes, of course, it makes that need for co-operation and co-ordination even more important. It also means that the relationships that the United Nations have with agencies like ours, like the British Red Cross, have to be much, much clearer perhaps than they have been in the past. They cannot remain as they have been over recent years. There is enormous pressure coming from all parts of the world on all the agencies concerned, on the UN, on ourselves and so on, and that means regarding resources, for the first time certainly in my involvement with the aid world (and that is a number of years) we are all having to make choices and decisions about where we can put the aid. That, I think, has implications for the UN, in the sense that it cannot do everything that is being demanded of it, any more than we can. Therefore, if there is a closer working relationship with agencies like the Red Cross Movement then we can decide together who can do what best; we have to decide what our role is, and how best to exercise that role. If I could again draw an example out of the paper we gave you, there have been, with the development of the Department of Humanitarian Aid, suggestions of new ways in which the UN might co-ordinate its operations. One of our concerns when that agency was established was that they would attempt, through that Department, to replicate or duplicate much of what other organisations were currently

[**Chairman** *Contd*]

doing. Our advice from day one has always been that, whilst we see the need for an agency like the DHA (and I can explain more about how we think that could work better), its role has to be primarily that of co-ordinating and ensuring that resources are made available from wherever. We do not need to re-invent the wheel and create a network of operating agencies like the Red Cross. The Red Cross exists in 153 countries, and wherever there is a disaster, whether it is a natural disaster or an armed conflict, often the people on the ground are the people who have to make the immediate decisions and decide how best to distribute aid, or whatever it is. In Croatia, for example, where the UNHCR have had a mandate to ensure that the refugees are cared for and that aid is distributed (and when I was in Croatia last year they had the mandate to distribute family parcels and things like that), the operating part of that programme is actually the local Croatian Red Cross Society. It was not even the Federation or ICRC; they were volunteers and the paid staff of the Croatian Red Cross. In terms of the refugees or the detainees who have been taken by ICRC out of some of the camps and moved to Karlovac, this has all been done under the umbrella of the Red Cross. It has been the Federation of the Red Cross that managed the camp in Karlovac and the Croatian and Bosnian and other national Societies who have actually undertaken the work. So the point I am making is that with the pressures on the aid world at the moment and the changing circumstances being as they are, we all have to understand much more clearly what our respective roles are and what we can offer and how best those can be co-ordinated.

200. Can I ask a question of my own now about how it actually works. Let us say a conflict, a man-made disaster, breaks out, people start killing each other in a particular area and the local Red Cross in that nation state (if that is what it is) or area, then say, "We must do something." Do they then contact the ICRC in Geneva and say, "This is getting very big. Could we have resources"? Just describe to me how it actually works.

(Mr Dennis) Basically, what would happen if a conflict arose in a new area is that we, the British Red Cross, and the ICRC in Geneva would be in contact immediately to try and find out through our own sources what was going on, because there are situations where some of our counterpart bodies, the Red Cross and the Red Crescent, are not able to deal with the situation on their own. So we also keep in contact ourselves, but the standard textbook way would be for the local organisation to contact the ICRC in Geneva and say, "We have a desperate problem here. Can you help us. This is roughly what we need." Often the ICRC brings in its own resources in order to check what is actually needed, but if the local society is strong enough and if they have identified the needs correctly, the ICRC will simply launch an appeal to the donor Societies, as they are called, which are the larger, wealthier parts of the Red Cross Movement such as ourselves, to say, "We need some help. Can you help us with this? There is a general appeal. We need"—it may be goods, blankets, people or whatever.

201. Would the French Red Cross and the German, Spanish and Italian branches of the Red Cross also be making contact to know how they could help?

(Mr Dennis) Absolutely.

202. So they would all be homing in?

(Mr Dennis) Yes, they would, but this would be co-ordinated. The thing I want to emphasise is this. Supposing it happened in Bangladesh, we would not just rely on the Bangladesh Red Crescent contacting Geneva and getting right all the information; we would have to make our own enquiries as well.

203. Just a small point: the Red Crescent is just another name for the same part of the operation? You are all part of the same operation?

(Mr Dennis) Yes, the Red Crescent is used in many Muslim countries.

Mr Rowlands

204. One question based on your experience and observation: can the local national Red Cross movements stay out of the politics? For example, do not the Croatian and Serbian Red Cross movements take sides in a sense?

(Mr Dennis) Let me start on that and Mr Whitlam can probably add something to it. By the mandate we have as the Red Cross and Red Crescent Movements, they must stay out of that. Obviously in some countries there are difficulties, in which case there may be opportunities where the ICRC or Geneva can have a look at the mandate they have, but they have to be totally independent.

205. They do it independently?

(Mr Dennis) Yes.

(Mr Whitlam) Perhaps I could add a further point and again we draw this out in our evidence. The whole question of political pressures versus humanitarian pressures is an issue we are all wrestling with, not just with the Croatian Red Cross or whoever but here in Britain as well. The demands that are being made on national Societies to respond are often either politically motivated, politically led, or they are led by the media. One of the advantages that we have as the Red Cross Movement is that we can step back from both the political pressure and the pressure of the media, because a particular event is photogenic or televisual, or whatever the expression is. We have to help no matter what the political arguments are on both sides and no matter whether it is televisual or not. So we can take decisions that are based on real need, on the needs of the victims, rather than on what we think are other pressures that are currently being placed on governments and on the UN. So I think there is a real determination for

[**Mr Rowlands** *Contd*]
the Red Cross Movement to remain outside the political pressure.

(Mr Dennis) Can I add one point that relates more to your question, and that is to underline the strength of the ICRC in Geneva. It has a mandate and a right to go in regardless of the local Society, so it has that added strength.

Mr Wareing

206. I was particularly interested in the answer which was given by Mr Whitlam because I remember at the outset he did say that the British Red Cross sets its own priorities, and I was rather relieved to find that the Red Cross organisation internationally and the British Red Cross are not simply steered by what is seen and shown in the media. I was going to ask the question, before he made that statement, that I think I am right in saying the International Red Cross and British Red Cross are not, in fact, dependent upon an initiative being pushed at them by the United Nations or any other governmental agency. I know that Karlovac has been mentioned and the plight of the Muslim refugees and prisoners-of-war has been very much highlighted in the British media. I have been given quite a lot of evidence to show that, indeed, the Serbians have also suffered considerably in the problems in Bosnia. For example, I have in my possession now a copy of the Italian magazine *Epica* of 16 December showing a prisoner-of-war camp (if you can call it that) inside Sarajevo where prisoners are held in dreadful conditions. Do you look at that sort of thing yourself?

(Mr Dennis) Yes.

207. Do you use your own initiative and say, "To hell with the media," so to speak, "we look at everything that we are involved in"?

(Mr Dennis) That is an extremely important point. We feel at times that the UN are pushed by the media. If you take the example of Somalia, the Red Cross were actually in Somalia at strength fifteen months or so ago, before there was anything on the news about what was going on there. In fact, we were one of the agencies who were raising some of the problems there and trying to highlight some of them. It is very dangerous that some of these situations are media run. If I can give you an example, three days ago I returned from Nepal where there are something like 70,000 Bhutanese refugees pouring across the border at the rate of 200 a day into the eastern part of Nepal, which is one of the poorest countries in that part of the world and cannot afford to look after these people. It worries me considerably at times that the media do not pick up some of these other issues. The other one I can add to that is some of the countries which have had serious problems and, I am afraid, are not, to the media, as interesting as they used to be. Sudan would be an example of this, where we would like again to see a stronger UN presence.

(Mr Whitlam) I would not want to leave the Committee with the impression that we are in a sense anti the media because obviously there is a lot of benefit to be gained from involving the media in some of the areas where we are working. Mr Dennis mentioned Somalia. It was about 15 months ago that the Red Cross were quite heavily involved in Mogadishu and certain parts of Somalia. When, last summer, I went out with a number of people to see the work of the Red Cross in order to determine what our involvement in the programme might be. We had a great deal of difficulty in persuading the media to come with us, but we do try, if there are areas that have been forgotten or that people feel are not areas they are particularly interested in, to persuade the media to come with us and on that occasion in the end we did manage to get ITN to come with us and that started the process of telling the British public that there was a problem there and that we and others needed support to help us actually to achieve something.

Mr Lester

208. On the question of the International Red Cross, which many of us have seen in many parts of the world and have tremendous respect for, you mentioned, Mr Dennis, that they had a right to go in. Could you clarify that rather more, because some of the problems that have occurred are when they might have had the right to go, they go in and then, as in the case of Ethiopia when the International Red Cross decided it could operate better on the government's side than on the rebels' side, fell foul of the government or fell foul of the rebels and they made it very uncomfortable for them in Tigre or Eritrea. This right to go in, just how powerful is it and what authority is there if the government turns round and says, "You might have come in but, thank you very much, we want you to go out"?

(Mr Dennis) It is a very difficult situation. We have the right by the Geneva Conventions to go into such a country. All the ICRC can do is to offer their services to such a country, and if they are blocked (as they have been in several instances in the world) then they have a problem getting in there.

(Mr Whitlam) I think this goes back to a question the Chairman asked originally about the changing situation. We now have new countries being established, not daily but certainly fairly often, and these new bodies have to be signatories to the Geneva Conventions and mean what they say when they sign the Conventions. I was in Iraq in 1991 when Iraq had actually signed up to the Geneva Conventions and were not, at that time, honouring the spirit, the technical meaning of the Conventions. By whatever diplomatic means we can, we have to try to gain entry where we think it is important. Of course, being apolitical means that in many cases we are unable to persuade governments, and that is where working with the UN is important. Clearly the UN has capabilities that the Red Cross Movement does not have.

209. Do you find that countries can be selective in terms of the use of the International Red Cross?

[**Mr Lester** *Contd*]

For instance, you mentioned Bangladesh where they welcome all the assistance possible when they have a disaster but where they may not let you go and see the Rohina refugees from Burma who are in desperate circumstances. Can you have a selective mandate, if one can put it that way, or can a government have a selective mandate?

(Mr Dennis) The government can; we have not. Again, it hangs on the words that Mike has just given: we have to rely on setting up such a relationship in the country and having the Red Cross or the Red Crescent Movement in a position where we can go in and address all the issues in a country. It is a very important point and I can add two things: it is not only in a conflict situation that we have such a problem. To quote one example in Pakistan recently with the flood situation, we could not get in when we wanted to. We actually had everything here on the ground ready to take action but the government were saying they thought they could assess the situation themselves. The other point I would like to add is that sometimes conditions for entry are put on us which we cannot accept, i.e. "You look after one part of the community and not another", or whatever, and we then say, "No", or try and find another way around.

Chairman

210. We will come to the UN and its agencies and how they work in a moment. Just finishing up this general section, given that there has been this recent expanded UN response to humanitarian and security related emergencies, what are the main headaches and problems created for the Red Cross?

(Mr Whitlam) I think one of the issues we have had to address very recently is the question we just referred to of access to an area within a country. If we take Somalia as an example, the International Red Cross was given access to Somalia and we were working there and were able to get aid into Somalia, but within Somalia we had the problem of delivering the aid to the people who needed it. This was a very good example, I think, of where the Red Cross, certainly for the first time in recent history, had to begin to address the question of armed protection for our convoys. I think there was certainly some debate, if not criticism, of the speed with which the UN became involved in the Somalia problem over the last 18 months, because it meant that agencies like our own and Save the Children, had to begin to use locally employed security teams, and I know you have had that explained to you. I think there was a feeling around that perhaps, had we had a closer involvement in the early days of that particular problem with the United Nations, we may have had "blue beret" protection from day one, and that would have made it easier. The whole question of how having military protection might affect our neutrality and impartiality is one that we are currently, within the Movement, having to wrestle with. Indeed, we have had meetings here in London and in Geneva in the last two or three weeks on this very subject. It is a very live issue and one that we are having to address. We have had delegates in the field who have been shot and killed in the last year or two in a way that perhaps has not been the case in recent years, and that is quite a worry and a problem.

(Mr Dennis) The Red Cross Movement have had two people killed this year so far.

Mr Lester

211. One in Somalia?

(Mr Dennis) Yes.

Sir John Stanley

212. Mr Whitlam, just continuing further on Somalia. You say in your very illuminating and very helpful paper that a large part of the tragedy of Somalia was due to ineffectual co-ordination within the UN system, and even to institutional rivalry. I wonder if you could elaborate a little bit further on that and indicate in which elements in the UN system you felt that the co-ordination was ineffectual, and where you felt that it was institutional rivalry within the UN?

(Mr Whitlam) I am happy to answer the question, but approach it from a slightly different and perhaps a slightly more positive way. There were certainly problems and difficulties of co-ordinating on the ground the distribution of the relief goods and making sure that when a Red Cross ship actually arrived in Mogadishu Port it was unloaded and distributed quickly. There is no national government, as you know, in fact I think the only national organisation in Somalia is the Somalia Red Crescent who have done a fantastic job over the last couple of years or so and, indeed, been the mainstay of all agencies, and NGOs, working in that area. It became quickly evident that there was a need for the NGOs to co-ordinate their work in Somalia, and that happened. There were regular meetings and decisions taken about how best each of us could work. The contribution, I think, from the UN was felt to be somewhat limited. They were playing their peacemaking role, and I know Ambassador Sahnoun in his negotiations with the "warlords" was doing a very good job in ensuring that people were coming together and trying to reach decisions about allowing the aid in. In that sense I think the UN was carrying out its role quite properly and helpfully. Rather than look back, if we look forward we now have the Department of Humanitarian Affairs and it seems to us that, here is the agency which perhaps could have taken a rather stronger role in Somalia, rather more quickly, in ensuring that whatever was available from within the UN system and then from within the NGOs, was better co-ordinated. We would want to see even now, if there is no national government established quickly in Somalia that is able to take forward the future role of Somalia, some response from the DHA to get a grip on all the various opportunities that might be available from the UN. In our evidence you will recall we talked about the complexity of disasters;

[**Sir John Stanley** *Contd*]

they are no longer very simple operations; there are issues about food; there are issues about health; there are issues about military protection, the economy of the country and so on, and somebody from the UN has to put it together. We believe the DHA, with a stronger mandate and perhaps rather more resources, can probably help achieve that.

(Mr Dennis) Could I continue on Somalia for a second. There are three things I would like to say. First of all, as far as co-ordination of the food and food distribution is concerned, there are many different methods of getting the food to the right people in Somalia and one of the processes we have used quite successfully, (because the Red Cross has certainly had a lot less food purloined than a number of other agencies), is a kitchen method, rather than handing out food to heads of clans and so on. We cook the food in kitchens and hand it out to people and in theory, although not 100 per cent in practice, the food is not seen by anybody until it is actually cooked and in a bowl and the family walk in. That sort of method is something we are discussing ourselves with other NGOs but we felt that a body like the UN could have been co-ordinating the distribution of food and actually discussing this. The second point, which all the agencies out there, discussed and co-ordinated, was who was doing what: who was looking after supplementary feeding, who was looking after medical outposts, who was looking after other supplies and so on. That only worked, I would suggest, because we were talking to other agencies in the field and I think there could have been a co-ordinating role. The third point I would like to raise is that one thing I felt in Somalia—I have had three or four trips there—is that there was nobody who could give you any information as to what was happening, unlike the former Yugoslavia, where the UN particularly and other agencies would be able to say, "There are troop movements in this and that direction." Of course, I understand that Somalia is much more difficult because we are talking about gang warfare to a great extent, but certainly there was a role, even if it was only partly carried out, for somebody to have some idea as to what was happening in the country, where were the gangs at the moment, which parts were likely to be attacked when the last relief flight departed at 3.30 in the afternoon, because then we were totally left alone.

(Mr Whitlam) We focused on Somalia but there are many other examples. Iraq after the Gulf War was also a very good example, where no-one on the ground actually took control of what was available to be used. We are not looking to work under the umbrella of the United Nations. Each of us, as non-governmental organisations, wants to maintain our independence and the Red Cross in particular because of our special mandate, but certainly in Southern Turkey and Northern Iraq shortly after the war when, slightly ahead of Operation——

213. Restore Hope?

(Mr Whitlam) ——whatever it was when the military were brought in. At that point the military did not know what they were coming in to do and some of the senior generals at that time were saying to us when we were there, "Look, we are here and we do not know what our function is," and wandering around Ankara and wandering about Dyarbakir were lots of people not sure how best to use the aid and the skills that they had, and it seemed to us there should have been somebody on the ground.

Chairman: I want to focus increasingly the discussion now on the UN and its operations and how they might be remedied.

Mr Gapes

214. Could I ask one quick question which follows on from what was said before. Where you have national organisations like the Somali Red Crescent clearly that is very helpful to your work. What happens in a country where you do not have that? Given that you are an organisation of international Red Cross and Red Crescent Societies, what happens in countries like Japan, India, China, Israel? How do those types of Societies relate to the International Red Cross and Red Crescent?

(Mr Whitlam) As I said at the beginning, there are 153 national Societies. I would be very hard-pressed to find a country that did not have a Red Cross or Red Crescent Society. I am sure somebody could tell me one. But there is a national Society nearly everywhere. One of our seven principles involves the notion of working alongside our other Red Cross and Red Crescent Societies and we would always co-operate locally. We put a lot of time, energy and money into supporting national Societies in times when there is not a conflict and in times when they do not have disasters, in order that they can build up their disaster preparedness programmes and their management systems are such that we can trust that the people who are working in those Societies are trained and ready to respond as soon as they are called upon to do so. So this is where we differ from many other NGOs in that we have people on the ground permanently who are being worked with and alongside all the time, so that we can respond almost to any disaster within hours, if not minutes.

(Mr Dennis) Could I add that I have just come back from Nepal and in that country we are actively looking at getting our own people to help with the management of the Nepal Red Cross Society, this also applies to a lot of other countries. Obviously if we enter a country and work in a country where we do not feel the local body is strong enough, we have to support them and quite often the support will tend to be at senior management level.

215. You talked about the relationship to the UN. What is now going to be the long-term relationship, in your view, given that the UN is taking a far greater role with regard to conflicts in particular countries and there is a debate about moving

[**Mr Gapes** *Contd*]

from humanitarian relief into some kind of peace-making or potential peace enforcement? Is that going to have an implication and what do you think that will mean for your own operations as an NGO?

(Mr Whitlam) I have a lot of sympathy with and would support the notion of the United Nations in its peacekeeping and peace-maintaining role. I think that is a very right and proper function for the United Nations to undertake. I mentioned earlier our support also for the Department of Humanitarian Affairs, which is the UN's attempt at trying to make sure that the various parts of the UN work together at times of real need. I think our concern is that the structure which is in a sense being imposed from the top on the UN will try, because of pressure from governments and the media, to get more and more involved in the operational part of the delivery of relief aid and so on, thus taking resources away from some of the other, we think rather more appropriate tasks that the UN would have. This is why we think that, whilst the UN, rightly and properly, should maintain its peacekeeping/peace-maintaining role—and maybe the way the world is going at the moment they have to talk with us about protecting the delivery of aid in a variety of different ways when we put it into various countries—the role that we can carry out because of the structure of the Red Cross Movement, because we have literally thousands of people on the ground in every country, means that we can be operationally very cost-effective and efficient, and it does not make sense to impose an expensive, over-bureaucratic structure in place of that system. We give in our written evidence an example of why we think that could work. We do not have the bureaucratic structure that the UN has to have by virtue of the way in which it is constituted. We do not pay the salaries, I have to say, which the UN pay, and we can be quick and cost-effective. So I think the implication for the Red Cross and other NGOs is that there has to be established in the future a slightly different working relationship between the UN and other operating bodies.

216. Your memorandum refers to the relationship between the delivery of aid and the military and the way that is changing. As the UN moves towards an agenda for peace-type proposals, peacemaking and peace enforcement, and the role of the military in trying to "solve conflicts" becomes more important, is there not a danger that NGOs like yourselves will get somehow, whether you want to or not, linked into this process, that you will require military convoys, military support? You have referred to Somalia but if you were in Bosnia today you would inevitably be dependent upon some kind of knowledge or contact with the "blue helmets" who are going through certain roads which are mined, etc. Are you worried? Are you concerned that your independence will be compromised and that you will be in a sense drawn willy-nilly into what could become very nasty military conflicts?

(Mr Dennis) I think we clearly have to be very careful that we are not drawn into it and do preserve our own identity and independence. But if you have a look at the situation in, say, Cambodia, there are certain aspects of what is happening there that work very well, in that there is a role for the UN; (eg in bringing back refugees into the country and resettling them), and within that we have identified, as have other agencies, certain aspects of that movement in which we can substantially help, and that is what we are doing. But the answer is that we do need this peacekeeping role for the UN in certain countries. We often have to stand back, see what is happening, have discussions with the UN and with other agencies, and then work out what is best for us to do for humanitarian needs or issues in that country.

(Mr Whitlam) You are right to point out that there could be a danger, there is no question about that; our actions can be misinterpreted. If we take two examples of where we have worked alongside the military in a very positive way: in Bangladesh where the Americans came in with their helicopters (in a way that we as the Red Cross Movement and, I suspect, the UN and other agencies could not have done) that was a very helpful thing to do. To put that sort of operation into an armed conflict area might have been quite difficult, because the complexity of negotiating American helicopters or whatever into Iraq at the time of the Gulf War would have been somewhat different. We do have to negotiate a relationship with governments in a way that enables us to make use of those sorts of services that the military have, but in a very positive and sensible way. We saw in the last few days the British helicopters being used to deliver ICRC delegates into the encampment of the 400 Israeli deportees. That again was co-operation in a way that was focusing on the needs of the people there and not the political imperatives. We are going to have to work this out. This is where those of us involved in this business have to sit down and actually plan for this new environment, and it is not happening as well as it might. Although we have regular contact in Geneva with the UN, and the NGOs here in Britain had a meeting with Mr Eliasson just a few weeks ago, it was the first time, it was an hour, it needs to be more regular and it needs to be more frequent in order to make sure we understand each other.

Mr Lester

217. Surely one of the problems in this co-ordination is the different rules of risk for members of the organisations, short of "blue berets". I wondered if you would like to comment. You have lost two people, but as I understood it with some of the UN agencies as soon as somebody feels there is likely to be threat they withdraw completely from the country?

(Mr Whitlam) Yes, and we would not.

218. I just wonder whether the co-ordination of the rules of risk need to be put together if you want to co-ordinate with the UN. It is no good

[**Mr Lester** *Contd*]

one agency saying, "We'll stay", and another one saying, "Thank you very much, it's too dangerous, we'll go", when you actually want to co-ordinate in that country.

(Mr Dennis) I think the answer to all of this is that each situation has to be looked at as it comes up. Clearly what is happening in the former Yugoslavia and Somalia, where military assistance is needed to provide some of the aid, is not ideal and not what we want. We have to stand back and say, "How can we best help in this situation?" We will stick to our principles, and we need to keep ourselves independent from whoever, including the UN; but there are situations where we literally have to sit down and say, "That's what we're going to do in this country". In answer to your question about who should pull out, Mike is right, because we often have an existing organisation on the ground, we tend to be the last people to pull out, if anybody does. It can only be done on a case-by-case basis, actually examining the situation when we are there.

(Mr Whitlam) I think there is perhaps a point which is worth stressing and that is the emblem we have, which is, in a sense, our protection. When any of us ever go into a country (and I am about to go into Baghdad again) the only protection we have is that red cross. We spend in the Movement a lot of time and a lot of energy protecting the emblem and the use of the emblem. We work here in Britain with the Ministry of Defence in ensuring that that emblem is not abused, and the Movement worldwide does the same. Very often we are dependent on the respect that the Red Cross emblem has worldwide in protecting us which is why we can stay often longer than other agencies.

219. I recognise that, but the point is about co-ordination and working together and having a unified operation—you have really got to have unified rules of engagement, to put it into military terms. It is very difficult to go into a situation if every agency has got a different rule of engagement which leaves you, as was the case in Somalia (you and Save the Children), virtually on your own, with the UN responsible for co-ordinating but actually feeling that they could not put any of their personnel on the ground.

(Mr Whitlam) Geoff mentioned the point about each situation being different, and I think that is right. I think if we try to co-ordinate and establish rules of engagement, or extracting our people in a way that everybody had to work to, that would be a long-winded process and might or might not be helpful; but I think in our paper we talk about the need for giving delegated authority and decision-making responsibility as far down the line as we can. If you take a country like Somalia, if there were a UN person in Somalia who had the right to make decisions alongside the folk they were working with, you could make a joint decision about whether it was or was not appropriate for all or parts of the operation to be pulled out. If the decisions are made in New York it is often very difficult to actually get any kind of co-ordinated approach to any disaster. Perhaps rather than going for some overall worldwide general agreement, it is a management problem of making sure that you have the people on the ground who can work together and jointly take decisions.

(Mr Dennis) You are absolutely right, obviously the best thing to do is to co-ordinate the situation. Although there are differences in each situation, if we had some guidelines, and perhaps it is for the UN to provide these, that would be much better.

220. If one took the case of Southern Sudan where one UN official was shot and I think the UN agencies have pulled out of Southern Sudan, does that mean there is no protection whatever in Southern Sudan, or are you there or is anybody there in a situation like there is in Juba?

(Mr Dennis) Because of the knowledge of the Red Cross and the Red Crescent Movement and the emblem we are quite often in a country where nobody else is. Again, it goes back to your point, the whole thing should, if possible, be co-ordinated and people should know what everybody else is doing.

Mr Gapes

221. Picking up the point, if you are the only people in a particular country, because the UN agencies have pulled out, does that mean that UN specialised agencies are not really the best organisations for delivering aid and that far more emphasis should be given to the NGOs?

(Mr Whitlam) Let me try and answer that but, first, could I refer you to page 9 of our memorandum which picks up the point I think Mr Lester was trying to refer to. Although we are not talking about rules of engagement, there we are talking about principles of delivery of aid and so on. We would argue very strongly of course that organisations like the British Red Cross and the Red Cross Movement are cost effective, efficient and very experienced in the delivery of aid. We make that point in a number of places in our memorandum. I think there are examples of where the UN system has been such, that the delivery of aid, because of political imperatives, has been slow or difficult. We would clearly feel that if we were to become, as NGOs, rather more the operational arms, with our staff who are very skilled in this area, then that would improve the situation. The scale of many of the operations around the world are such that you could not depend solely on NGOs, and it would be crazy to think we could. The UN has to be a significant part of the total aid operation, as do governments. We have seen recently governments wanting to become involved directly and take the credit for being involved directly in the delivery of aid. We have certainly seen this in relation to the European Community, with the setting up of ECHO, and the need for their high profile intervention which has sometimes caused some difficulties (but as we are not talking about the EC today I will not develop that). There is a need for all of us to be involved. The scale of operations are such

[**Mr Gapes** *Contd*]

that we could not do it on our own. We just have to make sure that we each understand what each of us has to offer and how best to use those skills. It is not always the operational part of the delivery of aid that the UN can do best.

(Mr Dennis) The peacekeeping role is nothing to do with us at all. That is clearly something outside our remit. There will be examples, and are examples are the moment, where the Red Cross and the Red Crescent Movement is in a country, or part of a country, and nobody else is. We would always hope that would be short-term, but then this is one of the advantages of the principles of the whole Movement of the Red Cross and the way it is perceived in some countries. It is hopefully seen as non-political—it certainly *is* non-political.

(Mr Whitlam) That special relationship often gets us into countries where the UN cannot get in, and that is an important point.

(Mr Dennis) I think in answer to your question, if the whole situation is co-ordinated, and you are talking about a short-term situation hopefully, then I do not see there is necessarily a problem.

222. With co-ordination inevitably the UN is going to play a big role?

(Mr Dennis) Absolutely.

223. Is there not then a question about at what level or what point that UN co-ordination means that you are somehow implicated with the Security Council resolutions or actions of UN decisions or UN agencies which may be contrary to your own wishes in certain situations?

(Mr Dennis) Again we have to be very careful. We have in such countries, as in any country, a particular mandate. My mandate is to get food to starving people, etc. and we concentrate on that. We report back to various people and, of course, let the UN know what we are doing and they can then co-ordinate the whole situation, but we have to pull ourselves away from the UN.

(Mr Whitlam) It would be wrong to say there are not resolutions that are helpful in the delivery of aid. There are UN resolutions which make it much easier for us to get aid into certain countries.

224. You have already referred to it in passing but your memorandum on page 10 talks about the ineffectiveness of the Department of Humanitarian Affairs and you make a suggestion about moving it from New York to Geneva. Do you think that would really make much difference? Are there not other proposals that maybe would make more difference, have more impact, for example, its work with regard to the UN agencies? You have also referred in your memorandum, as far as I can see, to the rivalries, that each person has his own empire and nobody wants to give up his empire to the UN, and you refer to the low level of the Under Secretary for Humanitarian Affairs within the hierarchy of the UN. Could you enlarge on that?

(Mr Whitlam) I think the point we are trying to make is that, given the role that the Department of Humanitarian Affairs is expected to make, we think it can best be made if it is in amongst the key agencies that are working in that field. As far as that is concerned, those agencies are in Geneva and they can be best co-ordinated there. It is one of a number of suggestions we have made to improve the level of capability of the DHA. We obviously realise there has to be a link back to New York and the Security Council and the rest of the UN network, and there would clearly need to be some regular contact, but the emphasis we think is in the wrong place. It is mostly based in New York with some involvement in Geneva, and taking UNDRO under their umbrella, as they have done from 1 January this year, makes some sense. It is going some way in the direction we would want but if they were permanently based in Geneva they would be able regularly to talk with, meet with, work out at times outside of crises, some of the difficulties we have been referring to. But that is not the only recommendation we have made. We are saying that there are problems within the UN system. With an agency like the DHA, which only has a small budget, a small number of people, I have to say perhaps an ambassador rather than a manager managing the service—I am not being personally critical here; I am just saying the job description for the person running the DHA has not been thought out as well as it might have been. But if you put all those things together, what you are looking for is a very different kind of operation. We talk in the memorandum about the number of internally displaced people in the world and the number of refugees. That has meant that the UNHCR has grown like a cuckoo in the nest in the sense that it has become an enormous agency in UN terms, but to bring somebody in without the authority and the budget actually to make sure the UNHCR part of the operation is co-ordinated with the other parts of the agency seems to us to be unhelpful. So whilst we are supporting the notion of the DHA—we think it is needed and would like to see it grow—those sorts of changes have to be wrestled with and have something done about them, and we make half a dozen suggestions as to how DHA could be helped to become more effective.

Mr Rowlands

225. Could I ask one question with respect to an earlier reply. You say you have to be diligently defending your emblem. Are there imposter groups going around parading as Red Cross organisations?

(Mr Dennis) Yes.

226. Doing what?

(Mr Dennis) Mainly because they see it as a form of protection. There are a lot of examples. I saw the other day a fleet of trucks going round Southern England. I stopped them and asked what they were doing. They were on their way to Bosnia with Red Cross emblems on them, which is against

[**Mr Rowlands** *Contd*]

the law; but they do it because they see that they will get some benefit. The rather strange part about that situation is that once they get to Zagreb or Split they realise that they cannot cross borders to go into Serbian-held territory or into Muslim-held territory and they tend therefore to come to the Red Cross anyway and say, "We have such-and-such on the back of our truck for you. Is it any use?"

(Mr Whitlam) Usually it is not.

Mr Lester

227. It also gives a reason for warring parties to shoot down planes with a Red Cross on them because they say they are taking weapons in?

(Mr Dennis) Absolutely. A lot of these people are doing very good things, I agree, but if you think of the situation where one of these trucks may have a driver who is only interested in one part of the problem and sits around and talks about that afterwards, yes, that is a very great danger to us.

228. In terms of the co-ordination of the role of the DHA, would you go so far as to recommend that the budget—because at the end of the day it is the money and how money is allocated that gives the power to anybody—should be under their control before it is dispersed to whichever subsidiary, in the sense that you meant in your document, and the UN agency should then carry out the funding rather than the budget-holders being the independent UN body, because to try and co-ordinate people who already have a right to spend the money in the way they want is extremely difficult?

(Mr Whitlam) I think it is difficult for us to comment on how best to manage the budget of the UN. We had some examples in 1991 where we were working with Kurdish refugees by funding parts of the UN and when we tried to get feedback from the UN as to how several million pounds of our money had been spent, it was difficult to get them to explain the way they do allocate funds. So it would be difficult to comment on that but what we do say in the memorandum is two things: first, that we think the budget for the DHA needs to be increased substantially. I think the Under Secretary General has a small amount of money at his discretion to allocate quickly at times of urgent and sudden disasters, but it is a very small amount of money in comparison with the budgets of UNHCR, UNDRO and others, for example. So I think there is a need to increase the departmental budget. We also recommend that it would be helpful to have, in a given disaster, the control of the budget for a given programme under DHA control rather than under the independent control of the different parts of the UN. We think that would then ensure that there was better co-ordination. It is about giving authority. You used the term "power"; maybe it is power, maybe it is authority. It is about making sure the resources are used to best effect. So we make those two recommendations or suggestions.

Mr Rowlands

229. You say on page 8 that you believe that the right of humanitarian intervention, *droit d'ingerence*, is doubtful law. Could you tell us why you think that?

(Mr Whitlam) I think we have seen examples or discussions about the right of intervention following on after the Iraq War and I think people are making generalised suggestions out of what was, I think, a very special circumstance. Our concerns are really about the integrity of a given country and its right, first of all, to look after itself and not have people coming in determining the way in which any organisation or any country should look after the victims of any of its own given disasters. Mr Dennis mentioned earlier the problems there were in Pakistan after the floods and the Pakistani government decided that it did not need external help. We only think that it does because either we have people on the ground or we see the television film footage because the camera crews managed to get in, but I think we have to leave it to the individual people on the ground to decide what assistance they need. We tongue-in-cheek talk about whether we would actually like to see the Americans coming in to sort out Northern Ireland but that might be the kind of long-term implication if we were all to accept the right of intervention in that way. It really does create all sorts of problems. We would find it very difficult to work under those circumstances because of our need to remain neutral and impartial.

230. Are you doubting that there should be any circumstances in which it would be right for the United Nations to intervene using force for humanitarian purposes?

(Mr Whitlam) We do not think there are, but the Security Council——

231. You do not think there are any such circumstances?

(Mr Whitlam) I think we would doubt that it would be normally helpful, yes. Iraq was a very special case, and I am not saying there are not exceptions. Iraq was handled in a particular way because that was how the Security Council felt and they had information that NGOs did not have. It would be quite wrong for us to take a view on those sorts of issues. The way it looks at the moment is that people are taking decisions about the right of intervention based on that one special situation in Iraq, where you have a government which, although it has signed up to the Geneva Conventions, has clearly breached the Geneva Conventions in recent times.

232. What about Somalia, for example, you do not think that United States' troops should go in and get the food aid moving around the country when virtually there is no government in place and no state of law?

(Mr Whitlam) The fact that the United States had to go in as it did was an indication of the failure of the United Nations to deal with the matter

[**Mr Rowlands** *Contd*]

sooner, and go in as the UN. We would perhaps have preferred to have seen some Somalian/UN initiative sooner and rather stronger, that would perhaps have put more than 500 "blue berets" in there than was the case when they came in. The 500 were fairly immobile and stuck around the airport and were not able to do a great deal. Maybe 3,500 or 4,000 people might have been able to assist those people working in Somalia sooner had they been there. It is a problem.

(Mr Dennis) It highlights the problem that we have. We have to stand aside from such situations. We cannot be seen, and should not be seen, to advise on such things. To a certain extent, sometimes frustratingly, we have to work around the system that is there. Clearly there are many countries where we have some ideas. If I could go back to Pakistan, I do not know fully the reasons why the government of Pakistan were not letting aid bodies go into the country at a time when we considered, and our people on the ground considered, we needed to help. That was the important thing, it was not just listening to the television and media here, we had a lot of people on the ground seeing the situation and advising us on the telephone that we needed to take action. There may well have been other reasons why the government in that country was not allowing us in; for example, perhaps they saw if they could control that situation themselves they would get voted in at the next election. I am not suggesting that was the situation there, but these sort of things happen.

233. Let us take Somalia and Iraq, you are saying in both cases a fundamental principle was breached, the integrity of a state's right to decide how it should arrange its affairs and even destroy a proportion of its own population, and that the Red Cross in that situation would not support or cannot be a partner to a UN intervention to safeguard people's rights, their lives and their welfare?

(Mr Whitlam) One of the problems which I recall I had in 1991 during the Gulf War and shortly afterwards was trying to explain to people why the British Red Cross was sending aid to Iraq without any conditions as to who in Iraq should use it. We had to remain impartial. There were people who were affected by the Gulf War. We had British troops in Iraq and a lot of people found it strange that we were there trying to feed people in Iraq. We are a humanitarian organisation and that is what motivates and drives the decisions we take to remain impartial and neutral. If the United Nations Security Council choose to pass a resolution which says there is going to be an intervention by a group of states in another country, that is a decision for the governments to take and we would then react to that accordingly, as we did in Iraq and we have done in Somalia.

234. It would not impede the efforts that you could make? If the international community, through the proper resolution and through the proper UN machinery, decides to make an intervention of a kind, even a military kind, for humanitarian reasons that legitimises your effort?

(Mr Whitlam) Yes, that is what the ICRC exist to do.

(Mr Dennis) I cannot emphasise enough, we cannot be seen to be in a position, and never are in a position, where we are suggesting that such and such a thing should happen.

Mr Wareing

235. Is not the difficulty though that you are dealing with different circumstances as between a country like Iraq where there are clearly defined divisions between the two sides? You had the unified command of the United Nations clear cut in the south of the country and in the north and in Baghdad you had the Iraqi military which was clear cut. Whereas in Somalia and Yugoslavia you have had a whole host (particularly in Somalia) of warlords in different areas, and whereas it is possible in the Iraqi situation, or more possible, to call upon military protection, be it Iraqi military protection in and around Baghdad or UN military protection, say, around the south of the country near Kuwait, it is a bit more difficult if there is not a unified command of, say, the Serbs in Bosnia and the Moslems in Bosnia. Therefore, would you agree with me that the United Nations perhaps in the latter circumstance, in the Somalia and Yugoslav circumstance, is better employed to try to diplomatically get some sort of unification and agreement between the various factions within, say, a particular area of Serbs or Muslims or whatever?

(Mr Whitlam) We referred earlier to the peacemaking and peacekeeping role of the UN, and I do not think the two are mutually exclusive. The role of the diplomatic negotiations to try and ensure that peace is either agreed and/or maintained is clearly a correct role for the United Nations, and it is not a role for NGOs like the Red Cross; in fact it is very clearly their function. Equally, we have argued from the Red Cross Movement that, for example, in Bosnia it may well have been appropriate, and may still be appropriate, for there to be some kind of temporary protective zones created by UN military personnel in order to get Red Cross and other aid into that part of the country. That has been resisted by the British Government and by a number of other people on the basis that it would take far too many people to repeat or replicate what happened in Iraq. That is not what we were suggesting. What we were suggesting in that circumstance was that we were being frustrated in our efforts to get aid into certain towns in Bosnia; people were starving and dying and suffering from cold and all the rest, and we had to find a temporary solution to get aid into that small area and move out. One solution was to use the UN forces as a way of putting a ring around the town, getting aid in and then everybody moves off, and at least there is some food on the ground. They are not mutually exclusive. You use the resources you have got to the best effect. The British Red Cross and the Red Cross Movement could not operate

[**Mr Wareing** *Contd*]
that sort of operation; it has to be a UN-type operation.

236. You disagree with the French proposition that there should be military intervention? I think it is the French Red Cross you have referred to in page 8 of your submission.

(Mr Whitlam) It is the French Government. We would disagree.

Mr Lester

237. I can understand your reluctance not to lead on this, but surely you would accept that one of the lessons we should have learnt, particularly after, is that the general public find it very hard to accept the idea of a sovereign nation who fight a civil war over tens of years, who find that we in the West and others will pick up the humanitarian tab for the destruction of their country and the starving people, while they use their money to buy more weapons and guns; and where the impact is not sovereign in the sense of totality of the effect within that country's borders, but it spreads out into all the surrounding countries causing enormous problems of refugees and enormous suffering. In those cases would you really suggest that we continue to behave the way we have in the past, or that we should learn a lesson, that we ought to be able to use the United Nation's system, first of all, diplomatically and any other way to say that this is not tolerable, and we will not permit 25-year wars which cause such massive disruption to so many people's lives, and so much effort from the NGOs and the humanitarian community in actually stemming the humanitarian consequences of what they are doing?

(Mr Dennis) I can only agree with you. In that situation, of course, we would like, say, in Somalia, somebody to have sorted out the situation so that we can actually concentrate on what we are supposed to be doing (a) because the flow of goods and funds to us, of course, is limited, and (b) because I have my own staff in such a country. So of course I would welcome anything that will stop, even in the short term, some of the problems so that we can actually get on with what we are trying to do.

Mr Gapes

238. Can I press you on the point about Iraq. What would you say to the argument that by giving aid to the area controlled by the Saddam regime without any conditions, you are, in fact, propping up his regime, and that instead of doing that, the NGOs and the international agencies and the UN and its agencies should be working to help those areas that are not under the control of that regime, either via Iran or via Turkey, as I think the Iraqi Democratic Opposition and the Kurds themselves are calling for? They say, "Aid does not get through to us. It just goes to Saddam's army and supports it." What would you say to that argument?

(Mr Whitlam) We had those arguments throughout the whole of 1991 and had to defend our position. We are not selective in whom we help. We would help any group in need and if you start from that premise, you cannot then say, "We will only put assistance into"—sticking with Iraq—"the north or into the south and leave Baghdad out." When we were putting aid into Iraq as the British Red Cross last year through the Federation, which had a base in Baghdad, and through the ICRC; the ICRC and the Federation had to negotiate access to Iraq with the Iraqi government of the day and in order to be able to operate there, there had to be signed agreements to operate in that way. In putting aid into Baghdad we identified those areas of need in Iraq that we could help, and food aid and medicines went to Baghdad and food aid and medicines went up to the north and to the south.

239. Not through Baghdad, though?

(Mr Whitlam) Yes, some did.

240. So to get to the Kurds it had to go through Baghdad?

(Mr Whitlam) The Red Cross aid went through Baghdad.

241. What happened when it got to Baghdad?

(Mr Whitlam) It was taken by the Federation through the Iraqi Red Crescent to 18 distribution centres managed by the Iraqi Red Crescent.

242. For the Kurdish population in the north?

(Mr Whitlam) And for some people in the south. The ICRC had a team in Basra working on medicines and water sanitation projects, but our access was always from Jordan to Baghdad.

243. Are you confident that everything that goes in gets to the people it is intended to reach?

(Mr Whitlam) We were pushed very hard on this, you may recall, as a result of our major campaign in 1991 for Kurdish refugees and other parts of Iraq and we sent a team out, I remember, over the Christmas of 1991 to follow through some of the aid we got through. They were counting bags of sugar and pounds of flour and found that none of our aid had gone missing; they were able to account for all the aid that had left Britain.

(Mr Dennis) That is done in every country we operate in. We very closely monitor everything we do, as in Somalia.

244. Did you in addition send aid through Turkey to the north?

(Mr Whitlam) I think we did. I remember shortly after being up in the mountains and we got access through from Turkey and certainly we were providing aid to the refugees who had gone up into the mountains and down into Turkey. So we were providing aid in that region certainly.

245. At this moment?

[**Mr Gapes** *Contd*]

(Mr Whitlam) We the British Red Cross are putting no aid into Iraq at this very moment.

246. But you are going to Baghdad?

(Mr Whitlam) I am going to talk to the Iraqi Red Crescent in a couple of weeks' time.

Chairman: Can we in the remaining minutes look at the refugee aspect again. I know we mentioned it earlier but there are one or two more questions.

Mr Harris

247. Could I apologise to our witnesses. I have the usual problem of being on two committees. We did touch on refugees earlier but what has been your experience of working with the United Nations High Commission for Refugees?

(Mr Whitlam) In the main it has been a very positive relationship. We link in, as I think we said in the paper, at various levels; in Geneva they talk to the International Red Cross bodies. On the ground, which is where we tend to see the operation from the British Red Cross point of view, we have British Red Cross delegates managing refugee camps and operations within UNHCR operations and it works very well in the main. One of the problems we have found in some areas, for example, is that I was in a camp in Kenya in Mombasa where there were UNHCR operations working alongside the Red Cross for Somali refugees, and the difficulty we had there was that we were providing aid to the Somali refugees in Kenya and the Kenyans, the local population in the area, were getting no aid even though they needed it. This was one of the problems with the UNHCR brief. The UNHCR have a brief to work with the refugees in the area and to run the camps and were not able actually to provide assistance in that area locally, and what we saw when we were there was Kenyans being employed by Somali refugees in the camp in order to get some kind of assistance. So this comes back to the co-ordination point. If the UNHCR were working in a rather more co-ordinated fashion than in the past it should not be in such tight boxes.

(Mr Dennis) Basically we work with the UNHCR very closely in every country where we are operating. Of course that also includes the United Kingdom because we operate a tracing service and other activities for refugees in the United Kingdom. If I give you an example of the Bosnian refugees who have come to this country so far, I went to Zagreb and discussed with UNHCR what is, in reality, a screening process set up for refugees coming back to this country. So we work together with UNHCR, liaise with them and then look after the refugees when they come here.

248. On that last point, there was controversy in the House of Commons about a particular party of refugees who were not given visas when they arrived, but the Government laid emphasis on the importance of refugees, when they come to this country from Bosnia, going through the official channels through the UNHCR. Is that a position you support yourselves?

(Mr Dennis) Yes, because our theory—and certainly the British Government feels the same—is that if you possibly can, you should leave refugees in their own area. There are a variety of reasons for that. One, which is not so minor, is that some people have been going to the former Yugoslavia taking adults or children who have been handed to them, and we then have the task, which sometimes is impossible or quite often very difficult, of trying to get those people back to their own families again eventually. So, yes, we certainly believe in the idea of having a screening process so that certain people should come out of a country when there is a particular reason, and the first plane load was largely because of medical reasons; the second plane load for more mental than physical reasons. Those people desperately needed some help and needed to come out of the country. We are talking about relatively small numbers. So I would wholeheartedly agree that there has to be a screening process and that the UNHCR should be given the mandate. The fact that there was another body who, if you like, went round the back door and suddenly arrived with certain refugees at the border, no, that cannot happen, otherwise why not take everybody?

249. I am surprised at the number of countries in which the British Red Cross is involved. Have you a figure for how many there are?

(Mr Dennis) How many countries we are actively involved in at the moment?

250. Yes, the British Red Cross?

(Mr Dennis) Something like 90 countries and in about 40 we have a substantial element of work. We have approximately 60 delegates overseas at the moment in something like 20 countries and in another 20 countries we are providing significant support, either with goods we procure or finance.

Chairman: A final question, because time has rushed by, on co-operation with regional organisations. Mr Wareing?

Mr Wareing

251. I notice that in your memorandum you refer to the damaging rivalries in the former Yugoslavia between the United Nations and the European Community humanitarian organisations. I wonder whether you would like to reflect on that and tell us just precisely what that means, what are those problems and how you are working along with these various organisations?

(Mr Whitlam) I think we have a very close working relationship with the European Community. They fund a significant part of our programmes. The European Red Cross Societies have an office in Brussels and we meet with them regularly to make sure there is regular liaison. I think, again, it comes back to the point we have mentioned on a number of occasions this morning, that of co-ordination. I was in the former

[**Mr Wareing** *Contd*]

Yugoslavia some time towards the latter part of last year and we were seeing and hearing stories about the lack of co-ordination on the ground. The UNHCR officials on the ground and the local Red Cross and Red Crescent Societies were actually quite angry about the European Community's attempts at putting aid into that part of the world. Aid was being procured and delivered, high profile stuff, lots of yellow stars and blue banners, but there was no delivery mechanism actually on the ground, and that was being left to local Red Cross and Red Crescent Societies (the Croatian Red Cross or whoever) often without any discussion or consultation. It was actually being landed on their doorstep in a way that was quite unhelpful. It would have been better to have had the discussions beforehand and agreed who was actually going to deliver through what mechanism. That was just the one example that we had. We are aware that there have been other similar examples.

Chairman: Mr Whitlam and Mr Dennis, you have given us an enormous amount of food for thought and some glimpse, and I suspect it is a limited one, of the enormous infrastructure of hope and care which is the Red Cross and Red Crescent across the entire globe in this very violent world. I think you have been very helpful to us in your very detailed replies to our questions. If we have missed things out we will learn more both from your memorandum and from further enquiries but, in the meantime, thank you both very much for being with us today.

ISBN 0-10-289693-3

Printed in the United Kingdom for HMSO.
Dd.0508705, 3/93, C6, 3398/3B, 5673, 233116

HOUSE OF COMMONS SESSION 1992–93

FOREIGN AFFAIRS COMMITTEE

THE EXPANDING ROLE OF THE UNITED NATIONS AND ITS IMPLICATIONS FOR UK POLICY

MINUTES OF EVIDENCE

Thursday 28 January 1993

FOREIGN AND COMMONWEALTH OFFICE

Rt Hon Douglas Hurd, MP, Mr Len Appleyard, CMG, and Miss Glynne Evans, CMG

Ordered by The House of Commons *to be printed*
28 January 1993

LONDON: HMSO
£5.10 net

235–vi

THURSDAY 28 JANUARY 1993

Members present:

Mr David Howell, in the Chair

Mr Dennis Canavan
Mr Mike Gapes
Mr David Harris
Mr Jim Lester
Mr Robert N Wareing
Mr Ted Rowlands
Mr Peter Shore
Sir John Stanley
Mr David Sumberg

Examination of witnesses

RT HON DOUGLAS HURD, CBE, a Member of the House, Secretary of State for Foreign and Commonwealth Affairs, MR LEN APPLEYARD, CMG, Political Director, Foreign and Commonwealth Office and MISS GLYNNE EVANS, CMG, Head of United Nations Department, Foreign and Commonwealth Office, further examined.

Chairman

252. Secretary of State, good morning and thank you very much for agreeing to be with us at very short notice and finding time in your incredibly busy schedule to share some thoughts with us on both immediate foreign policy issues and the broader context into which they fit, which in our case is our inquiry into the changing role of the United Nations and the changing policy of this nation in the light of that changing role. We would like to start by asking you some questions about the problems in the former Yugoslavia and then turn after that to Iraq and the UN. You have stimulated our proceedings this morning, Foreign Secretary, by making a very interesting speech yesterday at Chatham House which we have read with the greatest interest. It has a very gloomy title, "The New Disorder" and in it you rightly say that we cannot be everywhere and try to seek to define our objectives. While it is true we cannot be everywhere, is it enough just to analyze the new disorder which is so apparent? Could you not share with us some view of the objectives of this country in foreign policy terms, the picture of what kind of world we would like to see, given the one we do see at present is a terrible mess?

(Mr Hurd) I think the speech yesterday was designed to take a step back from immediate concerns and the immediate issues which face us and have a look at the world as a whole and, more particularly, British foreign policy in the world as a whole because I think the problems of the world have changed their nature quite clearly in the last two or three years and the nature of your inquiry now illustrates that point. I wanted to set the scene, do the analysis and also explain how in my view this country can play its part directly, but more often in the direct organisations which I analyzed in some detail and to which we belong and which are all adapting themselves slowly to these new circumstances. The difficulty is that the circumstances hit the organisations before the adaptation is complete. But I do believe, as I said in my speech, that we are going to continue to live in a world basically of nation states, a very large number of nation states, that in a proportion of those there are going to be conflicts, disorders, which compel our attention in a way which they did not before. I am summarising very briefly what I tried to say yesterday. There are those in this country who say, "Nothing to do with us. Keep out." and there are those who say, really whatever the tragedy, however distant, however difficult, "It is our job to deal with this, to stop these atrocities, this conflict." What I tried to do was to show how I have thought realistically we could play a worthy part in trying to deal with this new world disorder, with this disorderly world, without diplomacy, with our armed forces, with our other assets, in the context of the organisations to which we belong. That was really the attempt, but I am conscious it is a contribution to a debate in which this Committee takes part and which we should encourage, which you are encouraging, because I think it is very important that as we grapple with individual cases, individual applications, requests for British help, we should have some idea of the background and some idea of our general response to the background and I think it is part of the job of the Foreign Secretary to stimulate and take part in that debate.

253. Thank you for that general comment. Perhaps if we could apply those principles and that test straightaway to the horrors of the Balkans and ask you how you view the immediate and latest outbreak of fighting between Serbs and Croats in Krajina? Does this mean that the areas which seemed temporarily quiescent while Bosnia slaughtered itself, namely the Serbian minority areas in

The cost of printing and publishing these Minutes of Evidence is estimated by HMSO at £2,340.

[**Chairman** *Contd*]

Croatia, are now going sour again and that peace-keeping in Croatia which seemed to be holding for a moment has failed?

(Mr Hurd) You are right in saying that the calm was temporary, I think. The Committee will recognise already that that calm has always been fragile because the underlying problem of the parts of Croatia in which large numbers of Serb live have not been involved. They have been temporarily shelved under the presence of UNPROFOR I of United Nations troops in a completely separate force from UNPROFOR II in Bosnia. The Croats have forced the issue which would in any case have come out by their armed attack and capture of the Maslenica Bridge. This is dangerous because even if the Croats are correct in saying that their objective is limited, we all know that once you resort to force in this way you produce counter-reaction and you may indeed find yourself impelled to go beyond what your immediate objectives were, so it is a thoroughly dangerous situation which is why we supported the Security Council Resolution passed on this subject condemning the action, calling for withdrawal, and also dealing with the counter-reaction of Serbs in retrieving the weapons from the places where they were supposed to be safe. Two matters immediately flow from this which would have come up anyway next month when the mandate of UNPROFOR I expired: The first is the extension of that mandate, since the underlying problem has not been solved, since there would be a real danger in the absence of a mandate of a renewal of war between Serbia and Croatia. It is highly desirable the mandate should be renewed for a significant period. It is in discussion whether it should be six months or one year. The second point is the nature of the mandate. I do not want to be dogmatic about that, but I think it is clear that the mandate now in the hands of these UN forces is inadequate. It does not put them in a position to deal with the kind of problems they are now facing across the area in Croatia which they occupy. That clearly has to be looked at.

254. Going back to your earlier point about disorder, is this not an example of an area where one needs to think very clearly about what will stop the fighting? If there is no stability there, no peace to keep, then there will always be hideous problems in us signing a new mandate to peace-keeping UN forces. Does this latest outbreak not prove that these people will go on fighting and killing each other until they have a vision of a new area, not only Bosnia and Croatia, where they can live safely, where they can wake up in the morning feeling they are not going to be murdered by the next door village or area? Is this not a case for looking afresh at the whole geography of the area to see how these different forces can live in a balance of strength with each other rather than trying to divide them up and hold them apart and chop them into little villages and communities?

(Mr Hurd) Certainly, and that is of course the nature of Lord Carrington's work, and I remember saying then that the time would come when his work needed to be dusted off. The work which has been done, first by him and now by Owen and Vance, tends to be, it seems, determined as unrealistic, but then you come back to the fact that this work is needed. That work provided a way in which Serbs could live within Croatia with a decent autonomy, with a decent say over running their own lives. The alternative is to start re-drawing frontiers, but if you look at the ethnic map of Croatia, or Bosnia, or many of these parts, or many parts of the former Soviet Union, the chances of doing successfully what they tried to do in 1919, which is to re-draw the frontiers to give what one might call ethnic states, is absolutely formidable and certainly cannot be done from outside. That is why the UN, the EC and almost all those who have looked seriously at the matter come back to the existing frontiers and decent, substantial autonomy for those minorities who inevitably live within the frontiers of countries where the majority is different from them. Those two principles seem to me to be sound. You then need to go on from there to apply that in particular cases, and that was the Carrington plan for Croatia, and the Owen-Vance plan for Croatia is an attempt to move to a transition from the present situation to that ultimate objective.

Mr Harris

255. While accepting all that, how long can we sustain our present position in this? Because if the fighting continues with the intensity we saw yesterday, surely sooner or later we will be faced with a very stark choice, either we pull out completely and say "A plague on both of your houses, get on with it", or else we have to go in, we the international community, with real force to try and put an end to that fighting? Surely we cannot go on for long with our present stance, which is hoping that somehow a settlement will be reached through the talks in Geneva and elsewhere?

(Mr Hurd) And work for that settlement with pressures.

256. Yes.

(Mr Hurd) What we are attempting to do now is more sensible in the present circumstances than either washing our hands of the whole thing and letting the Serb-Croat war resume without any attempt on our part to prevent it, or, supposing that we could mobilise an international force, to impose a solution on Krajina and Croatia and remain there indefinitely to enforce that solution. It does not seem to me either of those proposals is realistic. That is why every time one looks at this problem one comes back to trying to improve, strengthen, the effort we are already making. As you know, Mr Harris, there are no British troops involved in Croatia, with the exception of the field hospital of 300 men where we are giving medical support, so we are not in the same position as the French who have front line infantry exposed and vulnerable. The problem for us is not, as it were, an immediate one.

[**Mr Harris** *Contd*]

257. It is in Bosnia.

(Mr Hurd) Yes, but you were asking I think about Croatia.

258. I was talking about the whole Yugoslavia situation.

(Mr Hurd) In Bosnia, if we are moving on to that, the position is different, and we—and others, but we have more troops in Bosnia than any other country—have a defined a role for our troops which is underwritten by the Security Council. There were many doubts about it, but so far it is actually doing good, they are actually saving lives and helping people who would otherwise die in the winter. I could give you the latest figures: our troops have so far escorted 170 convoys with 13,000 tonnes of supplies, and our civilian effort, the ODA people, have driven 90 convoys, many without escort, and have delivered over 8,000 tonnes of supplies, which is one of the few pieces of good news coming from the former Yugoslavia, and we want to continue doing that. Of course there might be circumstances in which we could not do it because of the safety of our troops, and my colleague Malcolm Rifkind has been very clear about that, and there are circumstances in which we might have to withdraw, and that is certainly true because the safety of our own troops is paramount. But at the moment they are there and they are continuing to do a very good job. But that answer also says that I do not see, we do not see, a way in which an international military force can be mobilised to impose a particular settlement on Bosnia.

259. So we hold to our present position, you do not see any change in that, and our general strategy, if it is a strategy, remains almost indefinitely?

(Mr Hurd) As long as circumstances remain as they are, as long as there is a desperate need for a humanitarian effort. The need may pass, in which case the need for our troops may pass, but as long as there is a desperate need and as long as they can help to meet that need without undue danger to themselves.

Chairman

260. I wanted to give you a chance to comment on both Bosnia and Croatia, so perhaps I can ask a Bosnian question and I know my colleagues wish to come in on that. You have talked about the Carrington plan for Croatia, but on the Owen-Vance plan for Bosnia are we not facing the same problem? Is there not a danger that the demands of that plan are unrealistic in terms of failing to recognise the desire of these peoples to be safe in their enclaves?

(Mr Hurd) They certainly desire to be safe, that the fighting should come to an end, and that is the first objective of course, the first thing to ask for, because you are not going to have any kind of constitution or provincial government or the rest of the Owen-Vance plan while the fighting is anything like at its present intensity, so that is perfectly true. If the implication behind your question is that in some way there should be a military effort by the international community to create safe enclaves, which has been thought about from time to time, again it is very difficult to conceive that troops will be there to establish by force and control by force particular areas. We do find of course that in the areas through which we escort convoys de facto we are reducing the level of violence and providing safer routes for people because as you get the convoys through you negotiate a ceasefire and the level of fighting in that area dies down—not always but it does to some extent have that effect.

261. The implication behind my question was that diplomatic pressures should be re-enforcing realistic goals rather than unrealistic ones, but I will let my colleagues develop some of these points.

(Mr Hurd) I agree with that.

Mr Lester

262. Perhaps one could approach it from a different attitude: I wanted to ask you whether any work is being done within the Security Council and within the European Community to actually deal with the question that when we put this tremendous diplomatic and humanitarian effort into a country like the former Yugoslavia, the writ simply does not run, and though one has these patient negotiations, endless ceasefires in Geneva or wherever, the participants have a hidden agenda which they do not share and therefore they go along with the negotiations as far as it suits that agenda but as soon as it does not, they break it quite freely without any by your leave and the whole thing goes back to square one. Surely one of the great frustrations is that we are moving towards some form of regional international order and one does have to have some means of, in the end, letting that writ run?

(Mr Hurd) Making that writ run.

263. Yes.

(Mr Hurd) I believe self-interest in Bosnia, and in the other surrounding problem areas of the former Yugoslavia, in the end will work for peace, because I am quite clear no one is actually going to gain satisfaction out of the continued fighting. Greater Serbia is not going to be recognised by the international community—and I am not now talking about diplomatic recognition, I am talking about trade and the ordinary contacts which people in Serbia have in all parts—and they are not going to get that without the kind of peace which is offered to them which they often, as you say, accept on paper but reject in practice. The same is true of Greater Croatia and of some of the aspirations some others have. At the end of the day, it is not going to be by fighting that they are going to get an acceptable way of life. The moment they begin to think about their economy, their prosperity, the future of their children, then they will see that the future they are condemning their children to is lounging about with a kalashnikov. It is not a way of life which people seriously think is ade-

[**Mr Lester** *Contd*]

quate for their families and their children and that is why I believe eventually self-interest under rights backs the need for agreements which are kept, but the difficulty about that position, which I think is the right one, is that it takes so long and people are always carried forward by some new rumour, some new belief that they are about to win, it is all going to fall in their place, in their lap. It is not. I think what is happening now is that the Serbs are beginning to see that and the pressure put and the policies applied from Belgrade in the last few weeks may show some glimmer of understanding of that point. To return to your alternative, Mr Lester, the imposition of agreements requires the indefinite use of force. It is the only way you can be sure that—to use your phrase—the writ runs. It involves, as indeed I see one American columnist suggests this morning, and eventually really a protection, whether over Bosnia or Croatia, Macedonia, Liberia, Somalia, Mozambique or Angola, the circumstances vary. The problem is essentially the same of the writ of the international community running and I do not actually believe in protectorates imposed and indefinitely maintained by force because I do not think the world community has the capacity to do that, so you are left with this messy unsatisfactory business of working with self interest for realistic objectives to try and get agreements to stick.

Mr Wareing

264. Can I do an unusual thing to begin with? It is unusual for me to compliment a Government Minister in the present Government on a speech that he has made, but can I compliment the Foreign Secretary on the realistic speech which he made yesterday at Chatham House, unlike some of the speeches which have been made by certain of our Members in the European Community—I am thinking of Mr van den Broek. Nevertheless, there are lessons, are there not, to learn from the mistakes that we have made and the European Community have made in the past in respect of the former Yugoslavia and perhaps most importantly of all was the mistake of recognising a part of that country as a republic whilst completely ignoring the problems that were being encountered by a large minority in that country. I am thinking of Croatia, I am thinking of the rights of the Serb minorities, and would you not agree that the problem of Krajina may not have, in fact, arisen in the way that it has if we had had a policy of saying to the former Yugoslavia, "Look, we will not recognise any republic"—and the Badinter Report I think illustrated the need for this—"which does not adhere to full human rights for its minority, whether there are Albanians in Kosovo, or there are Serbs in Zagreb or in Krajina." Maybe now we should be more evenhanded as we were before January 1992 in our attitude to Croatia and Serbia in particular. We should, in fact, would you not agree, be looking now to settle the problems of the minorities in Croatia as well as, of course, in Bosnia and Hercegovina?

(Mr Hurd) Your compliments are somewhat alarming, Mr Wareing!

265. They are well meant. I hope they do not get you deselected!

(Mr Hurd) I think Professor Hindsight is always active in these matters and covers many acres of newspapers and that is inevitable. The two Professor Hindsights accuse us of two mistakes, which, of course, contradict: There is the line of thought that it was a great mistake for the European Community ever to suppose that Yugoslavia could be held together by consent. We should have realised straightaway that the game was up, that the republics had been split up, that they need to be recognised at once. There are many learned articles to that affect. There is the opposite one which is the one you favoured, that we should have hung on to the concept of a Yugoslavia by consent for much longer and not recognised independent republics or accepted that they existed until the details of autonomy had been buttoned up. I think the difference of opinion which existed inside the Community was over a matter of months. We were not, of course, negligent. We did not forget the need to have in place decent systems of autonomy. We received, at the time you are talking about, assurances from Croatia which have been partly implemented about that. It also applies to Serbia, Mr Wareing. The same applies to the Albanian minority in Kosovo, and the Balkans would be a much safer place if Serbia showed some signs of accruing to Kosovo the kind of autonomy which it claims with the Serbs in Croatia.

Chairman

266. Can I just define the Committee's position for a second with an interjection? Professor Foresight was operating here as far as recognition of Croatia/Bosnia is concerned and we did plead very strongly in early reports that recognition would be a great mistake.

(Mr Hurd) I recall that. We were under very strong pressures from other British commentators.

Mr Wareing

267. Having looked in retrospect, so to speak, but nevertheless asking if in fact we can learn from the mistakes that I believe that we have made in the past; can I look next in the questions to you in respect of Bosnia and Slovenia and, in particular, the Vance-Owen plan. Are you really satisfied that this gives the best prospect of peace, lasting peace in Bosnia and to Slovenia because I want to bring to your attention a letter which I have in my possession which was written to the distinguished former lobby correspondent, Nora Beloff, and it reads as follows: "Many thanks for your letter. It is quite obvious that the Vance and Owen plans are unacceptable not just to the Serbs but to the Croats as well. This was perfectly clear to Cutileiro and me from the beginning. His proposals had a chance of success though they may, in the end,

[**Mr Wareing** *Contd*]

have led to partition. The real cause of all this was the premature recognition of Croatia and Slovenia." The letter is signed "Peter"—Peter Carrington. So there is quite clearly a difference of view between Lord Carrington who did such outstanding work against great difficulties and the view which is now held by Owen-Vance. Before, in fact, we try to intimidate or compel any of the parties to the negotiations in Slovenia, should we not be prepared to look at alternative plans before anybody gets the idea of requesting in military to try to solve the problem which I think you agreed cannot be solved in that way anyway?

(Mr Hurd) Lord Carrington certainly agreed with the view of this Committee. He believed it would have been sensible to hang on a bit longer before recognising Croatia and Slovenia. I believe that that difference of opinion is a matter of months because I cannot think it would have been sensible to refuse to accept, as it were, the existence of Croatia and Slovenia. Slovenia is not really a problem. The existence of Croatia: Lord Carrington accepted and indeed advocated the recognition of the Cutileiro plan, builds on the Cutileiro plan which came before, ie, it ceased to compromise between the idea of a purely unitary state and the idea of having a more sophisticated version of that original plan. So, of course, one should look at alternatives and Vance and Owen have. The Croats have now accepted, not the map, but the Vance-Owen plan, the arrangements in it because they do see it, I think, as a realistic outcome. The Bosnian Serbs have accepted it though under pressure and in Slovenia the concentration is now on the map which of course has difficulties, not least the corridor between the Serb parts of Croatia and Serbia and so on.

Mr Shore

268. What about the Moslems in Bosnia? Have they accepted that plan?

(Mr Hurd) They have not accepted the map and they are still negotiating on the constitutional arrangement.

Mr Sumberg

269. Foreign Secretary, you I am sure would agree that we have to carry the people of this country with us in foreign as in any other policy, and will be aware of the widespread feeling in Britain that we may be getting, as a country with military forces there, sucked into something which we cannot get out of. You addressed, quite rightly, in your speech the question of vital British interests, and we are coming to Iraq shortly and it seems to me that is a vital British interest because of the supply of oil, but apart from the general need to preserve the peace, and as a middle-sized power we cannot be the world's policeman any more, what is the key and vital British interest?

(Mr Hurd) We cannot be the world's policeman and nor indeed are we by a long chalk. The question is not that, but whether alongside others in a fair sharing of burdens we should take some power, according to our assets, in trying to prevent the kind of chaos and disorder which we see in several continents. In most of those cases we are not involved, though people on the inside would like us to be. In most of those cases we say no and, as I said yesterday, that will probably have to continue to be the case. I do not believe it is a British interest we should say as a matter of principle, "We are not going to take any part in any of these international exercises." Here is one which is in Europe, where there is a huge humanitarian need, and where there is a political need to prevent these conflicts in the former Yugoslavia spreading into a more general Balkan war. We felt the properly defined and limited the role which we have undertaken—diplomatic through Lord Carrington, economic sanctions and the humanitarian role of our contribution—is right and justified in the British interests. However, as you know in everything we have said, the Prime Minister has said, Malcolm Rifkind has said, we put very strict parameters around that and we have explained those parameters to our allies, which are designed to prevent the cases we are well aware of—and what you say is true—designed to prevent the sucking in process which you worry about.

270. But the problem is if they are not related strictly to vital British interests, people will start to test each involvement, "Why are you doing this here and not there?", "Isn't there a greater moral case somewhere else which you are not prepared to be involved in?", and you almost have to have a debate which is unanswerable on every world crisis.

(Mr Hurd) Exactly what you do have to do, exactly what we are doing now. We have to do that anyway because our constituents can be fiercely engaged in these matters and they say, "Why are you not doing something? Here is this mass rape and here is that and that", and we had the Chief Rabbi, for example, urging us on two days ago and drawing comparisons with the holocaust. Of course there is a debate in each case, in some cases more fiercely than in others, but there are groups of people in this Palace of Westminster, in both Houses, fiercely engaged on behalf of one side or another in most of the 25 conflicts, and they are constantly urging us to intervene, and what we must try and do—and the Committee can be of great help in this—is to set out some sort of guidelines as to when we say yes and when we say no, but the choice is there and it is going to have to be made.

Mr Gapes

271. Foreign Secretary, in your speech yesterday you referred to the decision last week to send the Ark Royal into the vicinity of the former Yugoslavia and you mentioned the French decision to send the aircraft carrier Clemenceau last week into the Adriatic, and you said in neither case was this "to extend the scope of military action, in both to reduce the risk to our troops." From what you have said earlier, can I interpret

[**Mr Gapes** *Contd*]

this as preparation for the evacuation of our troops if the situation gets out of hand?

(Mr Hurd) For their protection. I cannot answer for the French, but one of the points I was making yesterday is that in this new world situation, the interests and actions of the French and ourselves, though they vary from particular incident to particular incident, are very similar. We are comparable in many respects and we find ourselves working together perhaps more closely than ever before, not to the exclusion of other relationships, but that is a fact of the matter. As regards therefore the Ark Royal, I think my colleagues have made that clear, we are not sending the carrier with the equipment and the men on board in order to extend the parameters of our action or because we have any desire to be sucked into the conflict, but because it is conceivable that they might have to be withdrawn—and we have already covered that point—and cover would be needed while that happened, and it is conceivable they may need carrier protection while it was still possible to do their job. The other possibility exists, and can be met by re-enforcement which is on the whole sensible to have in the Adriatic, while things are in their present state, rather than here in the UK.

Mr Rowlands

272. You said you wanted advice on guidelines but before we can do that we have to work it around the assessments you are making of certain assumptions. Let us take the Owen-Vance plan, which envisages nine provinces, nine potential Krajinas, in Bosnia. Is it assumed, or have you assessed, that if they get grudging acceptance to the principle of these nine provinces these will require UN supervision in each or most of these, or UN police? When we talk of the Owen-Vance plan, are we talking about a new major role for new UN involvement in detailed parts of what was termed Bosnia with their acceptance of nine Krajinas or nine provinces?

(Mr Hurd) The first aim must be the fighting should stop on the basis of agreement on the plan, or something like that. Then the situation is changed, once that is clearly solved. There would need to be a UN involvement not as a protectorate but on the basis of helping those concerned in Bosnia to implement the plan on which they had agreed, and the nature of that involvement is far from clear, but, yes, there would need to be.

273. If it is far from clear, how can we make the assumption whether or not we are being realistic in introducing now nine provincial councils into the Bosnia situation? Given the track record so far of other areas like the Krajinas of this world or similar, will you in fact be able to carry on without a new major UN presence on the ground, policing if need be the borders and the varying factions in the population in each of these nine provincial councils?

(Mr Hurd) We are talking about an agreement and, as I have indicated before, an agreement which sticks will seek the self-interest of those who agreed. If they are simply agreeing to relieve the pressure on them for a day or two then it will break down, as it has done before, and the question will not arise. What we are looking for is an agreement between people who are weary of the fighting and do not see a prospect for themselves and their future by continuing to fight and looking for an agreement which will enable them to stop fighting without sacrificing something which they agree to be essential.

274. That was the basis of the Krajina-Serbia position, and you are saying this could be multiplied by nine?

(Mr Hurd) I am saying the basis of accepting the frontiers and autonomy within the factions is the right one, but it cannot be imposed by a protectorate, it requires an agreement, and that agreement will need to be based on people's perception of self-interest. It will need UN help but it will not need a UN protectorate because if it required that, it will not be based on agreement but force, and that is not I believe realistic, going back in a way on the argument.

Sir John Stanley

275. Could you tell us how far British policy in Bosnia is being driven by the Government's concern that if a vacuum is created in Bosnia and if international forces are withdrawn, this could lead to the possibility of a much greater involvement on the one hand by the Moslem world in supporting Moslems in Bosnia with arms supplies and finances, and also possibly greater involvement by former elements of the Soviet Union in supporting the Serbs in Bosnia?

(Mr Hurd) That is certainly possible. I think if the west, as it were, the Security Council, Vance-Owen, were to abandon our efforts and withdraw our humanitarian effort and everybody did the same, then there would be people who would, as it were, back their own friends and the likelihood of fighting, indefinite fighting, would exist because everybody would feel we have got friends, they are helping us, one more push and we are through, and the illusion that they can find answers to these problems by fighting would be perpetuated. I think that is a danger.

Mr Wareing

276. I notice in your speech yesterday you did say: "To impose and guarantee order in the former Yugoslavia would take huge forces and huge risks over an indefinite period—which no democracy could justify to its people." In an article in the International Herald Tribune on 18 January last, Mr van den Broek who is now the Foreign Affairs Commissioner in Brussels, in fact wrote: "Boutros Ghali has asked for 10,000 additional United Nations troops. That is fine, but will their mandate again be peace-keeping instead of peace-making? In the final analysis the United States may have to take the initiative again." Do you agree that you are going to come under considerable pressure

[**Mr Wareing** *Contd*]

from people like Mr van den Broek and now, from what we hear, Warren Christopher? Can you in fact say quite categorically that no matter what the pressures are you will not be asking the British democracy to intervene militarily and risk the lives of any British soldiers in Yugoslavia, other than for humanitarian causes?

(Mr Hurd) Mr van den Broek has held this position in public for a long time now, his former capacity as Dutch Minister of Foreign Affairs and it is not a position we agree with. It is certainly not a Community position because we do not believe that it is possible—I am repeating myself—to impose a peace consolidation by means of a military expedition and a protectorate. We do not think that is feasible. It is not for the United States administration, this position. What President Clinton's administration is doing, naturally enough, is to look at all the options with fresh eyes. That is the job of the administration and one can complain about that. We are in touch with them but they have not reached any conclusions yet. In answer to your specific question, yes, I think the Prime Minister and the Secretary of State for Defence and I have repeated over and over again what I told the Committee this morning. We do not intend that British troops should be used in an attempt to impose a particular political solution on Bosnia. We do not think that that is realistic or right.

Chairman: Just one or two further Balkan questions before we move over because our time, and yours even more so, is very limited. Mr Harris, a question on the sanctions aspect?

Mr Harris

277. When Mr Hogg came to the Committee in December, he said that he hoped to visit the European Community Sanctions Assistance Missions—SAMs, as they are called—in countries bordering the Danube. I do not know whether he has made that visit, but what is the Government's present assesmnent of the effectiveness or the positive non-effectiveness of equal sanctions?

(Mr Hurd) I believe they began to have an effect and then they weakened their effectiveness, particularly oil reaching Montenegro via the Adriatic before any flotillas were given the authority to stop the search. Secondly, the Danube continued to be a channel for sanctions breaking. Action has been taken in the Adriatic and I believe that situation has improved. There are still loopholes, leaks, sanctions breaking along the Danube, as we have seen in the last few days. The riparian states, Hungary, Romania, Bulgaria have taken action and we have helped them with equipment and monitoring, but clearly that is not adequate. The political directors of the 12 have been preparing a plan for a further and, I think, final round of sanctions which would involve the closing of the main road and rail crossings and the river to freight of all kinds and we will consider this among the 12 on Monday at the Foreign Affairs Council. We believe that this would be a reasonable response to further Serb intransigence at the peace table or on the ground. The Serbs have another option, of course, of actually helping the cause of peace. They are not solely responsible for the fighting, as we can see in the last few days, but we continue to believe that they are mainly responsible. So there is an option there for the intensification of sanctions which is being prepared.

278. In today's Independent, for example, there is a report that effectiveness of the blockades of Serbia is in grave doubt. Yesterday a barrage was bringing five separate shipments of oil up the Danube heading for Serbia and the report goes on to say that the captain of the tug boat pulling the barrage has threatened to blow up the cargo if force was used. Is this sort of symptomatic of widespread evasion of the sanctions and are you convinced that the unit which is there monitoring it, which I gather has 35 officials attached to it, is sufficient to prevent the breaches of sanctions?

(Mr Hurd) No, I think it is not. I think my first answer showed I am not satisfied with the present position. I think these instances arise because the riparian states are for the first time really trying to do something about it, but not yet fully effectively. We have an opportunity again on Monday because the Romanian Minister will be in Brussels for a discussion with us to make this point forcefully and I know the United States are also doing so. The fact of the matter is that those countries which wish to avoid the spread of conflict and are anxious to avert continued fighting in the Balkans should really steel themselves and apply the sanctions because there is no doubt that when they are beginning to have an effect in Belgrade they will also have an effect on Serbian policy.

Mr Rowlands

279. Part of this Committee is about to travel to Macedonia and Kosovo and I would be grateful if you could advise us, Secretary of State, about the status of Macedonia. How dangerous is it going to be if the stalemate over Macedonia continues?

(Mr Hurd) We made a bit of progress as regards Macedonia. Three points: there is now a UN battalion. I think it is at the moment still Canadian, but they will soon be replaced by Scandinavians, leaving the Canadians free, I hope, to be available for UN peace-keeping activity maybe in Sarajevo. That is there and that will act as a deterrent to adventurism against Macedonia. Secondly, at Edinburgh we agreed on an aid package. We bypassed the difficulty of our recognition and said, "Forget that. Let us get on with giving them some of the help they desperately need" and we have had a report from the Commission lately and that aid has begun to flow. Thirdly, there is a very intricate negotiation going on at the moment in New York about the admission of this country to the UN and there is agreement between the three EC Members of the Security Council, Spain, France and Britain, on how we can help solve this problem and I would hope—though not yet certain—that within the coming days that agreement can actually be reached. I do not want to go into

[**Mr Rowlands** *Contd*]

the texts but there is a greater possibility that before sorting out this problem——

280. That would be carried on in Government, would it?

(Mr Hurd) Yes, that is correct.

281. What about Kosovo?

(Mr Hurd) That is very difficult and I readily acknowledge that because Kosovo is part of Serbia and it had autonomy and the Serbs removed the autonomy, and they did so on the grounds that while they had autonomy the Albanian majority in Kosovo practised ethnic cleansing and pushed the Serbs out, and the present Serb Government is reluctant to reinstate autonomy. Fortunately there has not been violence in Kosovo but there is a continued suppression of human rights. Because it is clearly part of Serbia, and it is not seriously claimed otherwise, it is not easy for the international community to get a grip, a grasp, on this particular subject but we have made clear to the Serbs that a suppression of a rising in Kosovo would be particularly serious, and President Bush sent them a message just before Christmas and there are CSCE monitors in Kosovo and the more monitors and the greater the international presence there can be in Kosovo the better, and I therefore welcome the interest of your Committee in this.

282. Are we reasonably convinced that the Serbs have got the message that they cannot behave to the people of Kosovo in the same way they have behaved to other people in other circumstances?

(Mr Hurd) I hope so.

283. You hope so but are you reasonably confident so?

(Mr Hurd) I hope so.

Chairman: We did discuss earlier Mr Van Den Broek and the EC, and Mr Gapes now has a question.

Mr Gapes

284. Your colleague, the Defence Secretary, last week gave a speech in which he referred to the theological dispute over whether NATO or the WEU should provide a naval presence in the Adriatic, and he said that this was not an edifying experience "... and the unsatisfactory result, with both organisations duplicating each other, is not something we would wish to encourage or repeat." In your speech yesterday you referred to the responsibilities under the Treaty of Maastricht being placed on the WEU and you mentioned that we are now seeing in the Adriatic how action by the WEU can intertwine with action by NATO. I assume that is a more polite way of making the same point?

(Mr Hurd) That is correct!

285. With the development of a common foreign security policy, leading perhaps in time to a common defence, do you envisage the European Community playing a long-term role in trying to resolve the conflicts in the Balkans and South East Europe generally? How do you see that working? Do you think that would help or hinder the prospects of peace in that region?

(Mr Hurd) I am against a duplicated and confused effort. What is actually happening in the Adriatic is not ideal but it is co-ordinated and there is no actual operational difficulty. I see NATO, as I also said yesterday, actually beginning to fulfil the agreements that were reached in NATO last year about the willingness of and making available NATO assets in this kind of operation. There are NATO ships in the Adriatic and there is also a NATO AWACs exercise over Yugoslavia, and there are also parts, components, of NATO headquarters, which is why UNPROFOR II is better equipped to control than UNPROFOR I, because the UN has used certain NATO components in command for the second force. This is where NATO becomes involved. I personally think that if one got to a durable ceasefire in Bosnia and the question Mr Rowlands put to me arose, one would expect if assets of NATO could be used there I would hope they could be made available. So I do see NATO being increasingly useful in this kind of situation. The EC is not a military organisation and will not become one, and I believe that we can prevent the kind of theological—to use Malcolm's phrase—friction between the Community and NATO as we have done on the whole in Yugoslavia up to now.

Chairman: A final Balkan question on the American involvement.

Mr Sumberg

286. Foreign Secretary, we hear reports from Washington that the new Clinton Administration has been rather critical of the efforts made in Yugoslavia—I read supine was one word used—and the Americans would like to step up military commitment there.

(Mr Hurd) Whose military commitment?

287. The American military commitment, as I understand it, and they are putting pressure on others to do the same. Could your confirm or deny that that is true? What are the signals you are getting, and do you have any plans to meet with Mr Christopher to discuss these matters with the US Administration?

(Mr Hurd) The US Administration is committed to looking at this whole problem afresh and, as I said before, that is entirely reasonable, we all would do the same in their circumstances, and they are frustrated, as we all are, by the lack of progress. Like all Americans they do see this primarily as a European problem which Europeans should solve. But they have not put any proposals to us, I do not think, in fact I am sure, on that point. Yes, I am in touch with Mr Christopher and the Prime Minister is in touch with President Clinton, but they are not at the stage of having reached any conclusions and are at the stage of making assessments. I see no likelihood of American ground troops being involved in an

[**Mr Sumberg** *Contd*]
international military effort to impose a solution on any part of Yugoslavia.

288. And we are under no pressure from them for our ground troops to be increased? They are not pressing for that?

(Mr Hurd) No. No way.

Chairman: I want to build a short bridge from Bosnia and the Balkans to the Iraq crisis by a couple of questions on the general principles of UN intervention. Mr Lester?

Mr Lester

289. One could almost argue the period since the end of the Cold War at the UN has been a honeymoon period in terms of the Security Council working together in both Iraq and Somalia and in other parts of the world. But in fact there are rumblings that our involvement with the UN in Iraq and Somalia has created the idea that we are interfering in the domestic affairs of those countries. In the light of this experience, this recent experience since the end of the Cold War, how is the British Government thinking about developing the UN role in the future in terms of an agenda for peace, and how one copes with the world you described in your speech yesterday with 25 conflicts, and the ability of the Security Council to remain cohesive in terms of doing what it can about those particular issues?

(Mr Hurd) I tried to describe how the demands are piling in on the 38th floor of the UN, in the Secretary General's office, and indeed on the Security Council. Choices have to be made there, even more than they have to be made here. I believe, as I said before, that there are going to be many cases where in fact the international community is not going to be able to help those concerned on the spot to make decisive progress. Where the international community decides to come in, as it were, it needs to come in first on prevention, it needs to have its peacemakers there, to bring together the people, as for example the Secretary General tried to do the other day with the Somali leaders in Addis Ababa but do that much earlier before there is a catastrophe. Then, if that fails, decide whether or not peacekeeping is justified, who should do it, what its aims should be and get on and define them. Now the Security Council is the main body for this but it is not the only one because it is going to be possible for member states quite legally under the international law to intervene without specific authority of the United Nations in certain circumstances but the Security Council can give a unique legal authority and therefore normally now the United States and other countries go to the Security Council for such authority. The Security Council then has to work effectively. It does, I think, work effectively; the machinery, the mechanisms inside it, the way in which the Permanent Five work, the way in which the Europeans work, the way in which the United States work, the way in which the Russians and Chinese work and the way in which the other members work. All that has improved very greatly under the pressure of need. Of course it is not perfect but it is working. And pressures on it are going to remain very substantial.

290. But is there any concept of, for instance, the work of Marrack Goulding, our previous colleague and the enormous pressure he is under with a minute staff trying to operate from the 38th floor. The same thing applies to the Commission on Human Rights with a minute staff trying to deal with many complaints on human rights abuse around the world. Somebody somewhere should be thinking of what is actually needed in order for it to fulfil the functions that is being pushed on it day by day.

(Mr Hurd) The Secretary General is doing that. You mentioned the Agenda for Peace quite rightly. He was asked by us—this was a British initiative—we called a special meeting of the Security Council in January last year. Out of that came a request to the Secretary General to think exactly on the kind of questions you have put, Mr Lester. He produced his document, "Agenda for Peace". He is now acting on that. For example, the British are in direct touch with him about not creating a UN army, because neither we nor he thinks that that is needed but making it clear what kind of logistic support, what kind of assets there are here which could conceivably be called on—of course, the decision will be ours—so that he knows what is available (and other countries are doing the same)—so he has a clear idea with Goulding and the others alongside him of what might be available if the political decision were taken. On the humanitarian side, of course, he has taken up another idea of ours and he has created the Department of Humanitarian Affairs under Mr Eliasson which is designed to bring together in a crisis the work of all the different UN agencies. It is still in its relative infancy there but it is an example of how he is tying to tighten and improve the control which he can exercise of all the different activities of the UN in this new work.

Sir John Stanley

291. Foreign Secretary, in your speech yesterday you said that we must help the UN reform itself. Does your view about the desirable areas in which the UN should reform itself extend to the consideration of the membership of the Permanent Members of the Security Council? And carrying on from that is one of the factors in the British Government's position, the possibility if there were changes in the membership of the permanent membership of the Security Council which conceivably might lead to the United Kingdom losing its permanent membership, might that also result in the subsequent loss of membership of the G7 as well?

(Mr Hurd) I do not think we are in that situation, Sir John. No-one is suggesting that we should lose our permanent membership. The question is whether there should be extra permanent members and, secondly, whether there should be a European membership which is I suppose, as it were, a dilution of our membership. On that second point the

[**Sir John Stanley** *Contd*]

Treaty of Maastricht states it. We had a negotiation and you see in the relevant Article of the Treaty how that negotiation was resolved. I think that works reasonably well. We and the French are permanent members under the charter and we have our charter responsibilities and intend to go on discharging those responsibilities. But we listen to the views of our partners in the Community on particular issues and that is a reflection of the situation and works well. On the question of extending the permanent membership once that debate is open as it is there are many candidates. I do not see an early alteration of the permanent membership because it involves charter reform and that involves the unanimity of the Security Council. It is a very long road. Meanwhile, as I said before, slightly anticipating your question, what is crucial is that the Security Council now and in the next few years should operate as effectively as possible. That is crucial and that is the priority.

Chairman

292. Foreign Secretary, what we also have to anticipate, do we not, is this issue to going to come back again and again and again and it was utterly predictable it was going to arise under the new Clinton adminstration. Ought we not to, while recognising all the points you make, have our own positive view about how reform should take place otherwise we are going to lose the initiative to others?

(Mr Hurd) I think this debate is going to be a long one. It is open and we are not in the business of seeking to stifle it. It is for those who feel this is a priority in world affairs to formulate their ideas. There is another aspect of course. You have two countries of very great economic and growing political importance, who for legal and political reasons are inhibited from taking part in the kind of peace-keeping activities that we are the French take part in; I am thinking of Germany and Japan. That is another aspect which clearly is relevant. I think this will be a long time. We are not, as it were, the *demandeur*, the proposers, in this debate. We have no wish to stifle the debate. We think the crucial need is that the Security Council as at present constituted should function effectively over the coming years. We would not wish there to be distractions from that.

Mr Rowlands

293. I want to pursue a slightly different point. Is there a danger that the UN authority could be undermined by the regular appearance of double standards. To a large part of the world the inability to implement critical resolutions on Israel on the Palestinian issue, particularly the last serious one of carting off all these Palestinians and leaving them in no man's land—does lead large numbers of a significant part of the international community to believe that there is a double standard and this is going to be a westernised essentially US-led United Nations Security Council type of operation. How are we going to get over that impression? Does it seem a bit justifiable if you take some of the behaviour—and I speak as a friend of Israel—in the international community?

(Mr Hurd) I think what you say is true. There is such an accusation. Of course, in a way it arises because people tend to regard situations which are very different as if they were the same. There is not actually a very close parallel between what Saddam Hussein has been doing and what the Israelis are doing. You would accept that. Often when people talk about double standards they are, as it were, expecting us to treat different situations in the same way. I think the accusation would lie, would be to some extent valid, if we were all taking a line, "It doesn't really matter about these Palestinians, about this breach of the Fourth Convention and we don't really need to bother about it." We do have to bother about it because it is an obstacle to the peace process. The peace process is the only way in which the Arab/Israel dispute can be settled. Again, as in Yugoslavia, everybody has tried to settle these disputes by force and one gets slightly impatient with the cynical commentators who think force is the only arbitrary solution to disputes. It has been proved totally inefficient in settling them and the same would be true in Yugoslavia. These things will only be settled by a peace process. I am sorry I am going off at a tangent but it is an important point. The Security Council has to pay attention to this and we do have to say to Israel. "Look, what you are doing is wrong. It is a mistake and you need to find ways of putting it right." That remains true today in the light of the Israeli Supreme Court decision and we will have to return to this.

Mr Shore

294. But it is a very important question indeed, not only in itself but how the rest of the world perceives the so-called "double standards" of the United Nations. But is there in addition to the points that you have already made, the fact that the United Nations has only sanctioned the use of force I think in the whole post-War period on two occasions when a flagrant act of aggression against a neighbouring state has taken place; one in the case of Korea when UN observers were actually on the frontiers of North and South Korea when the North Korean invasion took place, and secondly when Iraq actually invaded and purported to absorb Kuwait. No other situation has occurred, am I not right in thinking, which has so provoked the international community to a unanimous condemnation of the act which took place and unanimous call for military action to deal with it?

(Mr Hurd) You are right as you define it. The phrase "all appropriate measures" has been used in other contexts, for example Yugoslavia in the context of humanitarian aid. But you are correct, the Security Council and the charter have singled out that act, which I mentioned again yesterday, the act of obliterating a sovereign state, one sovereign state actually committing straight forward aggres-

[**Mr Shore** *Contd*]

sion against another state it has singled out. That is perfectly true.

Mr Canavan

295. I want to ask first of all a very brief supplementary on the point raised by my colleague, Ted Rowlands. In the light of the Israeli court decision announced this morning about the 400 Palestinians who were illegally, in the eyes of international law anyway and in the eyes of the United Nations, deported by the Israeli Government to no-man's-land, will the British Government be using their so-called special relationship with the American Government to try to ensure that if Dr Boutros Ghali proposes certain UN action to be taken against Israel, including the possible use of sanctions, the American Government do not veto such action?

(Mr Hurd) We are not at that point yet, Mr Canavan, and of course I am in touch with the State Department about this, but what is needed now in the immediate future is persuasive pressure on Israel. Again it is a matter of self-interest. We have now an Israeli Government which genuinely, in my view, wants the peace process to succeed and is prepared to make compromises to do that but if that is its objective, it has to get this obstacle out of the way, it has to deal with it, has to settle this question of these Palestinians sitting in this no-man's-land because of the actions of Israel. We shall be trying to bring this persuasive pressure to bear in Israel and I believe, I hope, they will in effect be persuaded. We have an opportunity again next week because the Israeli Foreign Minister is meeting the Foreign Ministers of the 12 at the beginning of next week and we will use the occasion to make this point to him very clearly. So we are not at the stage at this time of, in my view, realistically considering sanctions against Israel, we are at the stage of showing the Israelis our opinion, that it is in their self-interest to deal with that problem so the peace process can continue.

296. It does not sound like very swift, efficient action.

(Mr Hurd) Swiftness is not always the same as efficiency.

297. You were swift enough in the situation against Iraq.

(Mr Hurd) But the situations are not the same.

298. I know they are not the same but I want to get on to that. The recent raids on Iraq have been depicted as thinly disguised American operations and there is a common perception, particularly in the Arab world, that the United Nations is being increasingly dominated by the United States, and that the British Government is being bounced by the Americans into taking precipitous and sometimes excessive military action purportedly in the name of the United Nations. What action will the British Government take to try and dispel such a perception, because it is no doubt a major obstacle to the United Nations' efforts to try and find a peaceful, lasting solution to the problem of the Gulf and indeed the rest of the Middle East?

(Mr Hurd) But it is not simply an American interest. It seems to me we have three interests as regards Iraq. One, to preserve the integrity of Kuwait; secondly, to prevent Iraq re-emerging as a threat because she possesses nuclear and chemical weapons of mass destruction; and thirdly, to deter—you cannot guarantee it but deter—her present regime from killing its own subjects whether in the north or south. All those three objectives are underwritten by the UN and they are not just American objectives, they are general objectives which are ours as well. That is why we had no difficulty in associating ourselves, indeed joining in, with the actions specifically taken in defence of those three objectives, all of which were being undermined by Saddam Hussein during a time which he thought was one of weakness and uncertainty in the western world at the end of the Bush Administration, and he was proved wrong. The kind of initiative you mentioned would, I promise you, be much stronger if we had stepped back and done nothing. Then the people who are actually afraid of Saddam Hussein will be even more afraid of him if they thought he was becoming again a threat because of the possession of weapons of mass destruction, and would have said, "What has happened? Why has everyone lost their nerve?" So I am sure in my mind we were right. Now it is not a matter, and has never been a matter throughout the Gulf War, of the President of the United States or the Pentagon lifting the telephone and saying to the allies, "Do this", that is not the nature of the relationship, that is the difference and always has been between our relationship and those in the Warsaw Pact. There are discussions and plans are made and changed and there is consultation and the records will eventually show those consultations were very detailed and complete during the episodes which you mention.

299. But if the aim was to weaken the position of Saddam Hussein then that aim has quite clearly not been achieved.

(Mr Hurd) I do not agree with that.

300. Because his standing in Iraq and the rest of the Arab world has been apparently enhanced in recent weeks.

(Mr Hurd) I do not agree.

301. Well, we will have to disagree on that, but it is very well reported by observers in the Arab world who maybe are not as biased as some advice you get from American sources.

(Mr Hurd) I received throughout the Gulf War advice from the very people you mention, Mr Canavan, and their conclusions were that the coalition is about to collapse, Saddam Hussein's prestige has never been greater. He is a loser, he lost his effort against Iran and Kuwait, he controls about half his own country, and the idea that there are huge partisans in Iraq and across the Middle East is not true. What is true, and here I would

[**Mr Canavan** *Contd*]

accept there are worries about double standards, and we have discussed that, there are worries that this is seen to be an all-American enterprise. I accept these are worries and I think they can be dealt with but I do not accept that it would have been wiser somehow to let all this pass and allow Saddam Hussein to exploit this opportunity. Our position, I promise you, would be very much weaker in the Middle East if we had allowed that to happen.

Chairman: I think we should approach this from another angle. Mr Gapes?

Mr Gapes

302. I agree with you that Saddam is a loser but in that case why is the British Government not following the logic of the position and why are we not giving more support to the Kurds and the Shias and to the Iraqi democratic opposition? Is there not a hidden agenda here, that you would prefer to keep Saddam in power because you fear the break-up of Iraq in terms of the consequences of Iranian expansion perhaps and also relations with Turkey? There is therefore a problem with the policy you have set out, the three policy objectives, and should there not be—perhaps there is—another one, and the policy objective should be to bring about democracy in Iraq? It seems to me you have another objective, which is to keep Saddam in power in a weak position in order to preserve the integrity of Iraq?

(Mr Hurd) No. Clearly it would be better if he went because the three objectives I have mentioned, which are our objectives, would be easier to realise if he was not there. It was not in any event part of our objective in the Gulf War or at any later time to say who should be the government of Iraq. We do believe in the integrity of Iraq's borders. That is to say that we believe that the splitting up of Iraq would create more problems than it would solve. That is perfectly true. We would like to see a democratic Iraq and we are in touch, of course, with democratic groups of Iraqis outside Iraq. But we are not in favour of splitting up Iraq. I do not think that would work and I do not think that would produce a good answer. We are in favour of a democratic Iraq which must involve a decent autonomy for the Kurds which is what the Kurdish leaders themselves wisely demand instead of an independent Kurdistan.

303. You do not have any other objectives about the actual internal structure of Iraq, for example, supporting the defence of autonomous Kurdish democratically-elected parliaments for the long-term and is our Government's position different to that of any of our allies? Do the French government, for example, or the Americans agree with the view that you just put forward?

(Mr Hurd) I think so. The new American administration is looking at all these matters, as I have said, with fresh eyes. I do not know what conclusions they have come to but I would be very surprised if they came to a different conclusion. We all accept the integrity of Iraq. That is not to say we do not accept there should be one Iraq but inside that Kurds and Shias should have decent rights.

Mr Canavan

304. It is just a question about the degree of consultation by the UN partners regarding military action taken in the name of the United Nations. On the 13 January in the operation against Iraq, for example, the British Government was obviously consulted there because the RAF participated but what, if any, consultation took place before the subsequent launch of around 40 Cruise missiles by the Americans which resulted in the killing of innocent civilians in places like the Al Rashid Hotel. The reason I ask is that in the aftermath of that the French and the Russians and the Arab League seemed to take the view that the Cruise missile raids were, in fact, contrary to international law and outwith the terms of the United Nations resolution whereas the British Government seems to support the Americans whole-heartedly. Why is it the British Government always seems to behave in such a servile way to the American government even when the latter takes such excessive military action resulting in the loss of innocent people living in an hotel in Baghdad or indeed on an earlier occasion when their so-called "friendly fire" resulted in the death of British soldiers?

(Mr Hurd) You misrepresent the French position. The French after the action at the UN associated themselves with it and were fully consulted. You are quoting something which was said later by a spokesman from the Elyseé which runs against what was said at the time. We took our own judgment. We were consulted. We recalled that the Security Council had determined in its statements of 8 and 11 January that Iraq was in material breach of resolution 687 and its subsequent resolutions—which the Security Council approved unanimously—and had warned Iraq that serious consequences would ensue from continued failure to comply with its obligations. I do not believe the action was disproportionate. You know what it was aimed again; it was aimed against a plant that the Iraqis had themselves admitted was producing material for their nuclear programme. Some areas had been sealed by UN inspectors and the IAEA was considering whether it should be destroyed. It seemed to me a proportionate target. It looks and sounds as if—and I have not seen an exact analysis—that one of the Cruise missiles went astray and killed innocent civilians in the Al Rashid Hotel. That clearly is to be deplored but I do not think the action as a whole can be regarded as disproportionate and if no action had been taken when Saddam Hussein in breach of his obligations was imposing conditions on the way in which UN teams could carry out this essential task of intercepting and destroying his weapon specifically, if that action has not been taken promptly then I think we would have been greatly blamed and rightly so. We would have let go of an essential constraint over that fact.

[**Mr Canavan** *Contd*]

Mr Canavan: Were you consulted in advance —

Chairman: I must give others a chance in the remaining minutes.

Sir John Stanley

305. Foreign Secretary, does not the fact that within a relatively short space of the cease fire at the end of the war against Iraq following their invasion of Kuwait, that we have had to resort again to military action against Iraq, does not that, admittedly with the benefit of hindsight, confirm that hostilities against Saddam Hussein initially were brought to a premature halt quite apart from the fact that there is still the outrageous fact that unknown numbers of Kuwaitis who were basically kidnapped from Kuwait and have disappeared and have not been returned, quite apart from other very very serious human rights violations which Saddam Hussein has not been brought to book on.

(Mr Hurd) Your second point about the Kuwaitis is entirely correct. People will argue about the first point. I was in the White House on that day and I recall vividly the conversation between President Bush and his advisers on this point before they telephoned to suggest the conclusion. Sir John, you may have read Professor's Friedman's recent work with a colleague of his on the Gulf War which deals with this point. I myself do not think that it would have been right or indeed possible to prolong hostilities to the stage of removing Saddam Hussein from Baghdad. There will be arguments about whether there should have been 24 hours more and there is an argument in service quarters. I believe we should not at that stage have changed our objectives, come to the House of Commons and Security Council and said, "We have got you all organised for a particular objective and we have achieved that and now we are going to do something else." I do not believe we would have kept the coalition together on that basis. I do not know it would have been successful because to impose a government you have to sustain it. I do not myself think that it would have been possible to carry the operation through to that extent but I do believe, as I have said, that on the three objectives I have mentioned we have got to be very rigid and strong in maintaining.

Mr Lester

306. In terms of your earlier remarks about the permanent use of force in terms of UN operations, our Committee when we reported in 1991 said that Saddam Hussein posed a continuing threat to stability in the Middle East. Unless one is going to involve the Gulf Cooperation Council in some way to take some responsibility one foresees the present situation with the constant threat of the permanent use of force by the United Nations in terms of keeping Saddam Hussein in check. Do you believe the Gulf Cooperation Council can play a role in terms of having any security in the region containing Saddam Hussein or will it always be the role of the Security Council?

(Mr Hurd) I had hoped, Mr Lester, that after the experiences in the Gulf War that the six member states of the GCC, maybe associating themselves with Egypt and Syria as they were during the War, would actually take some decisive steps for collective security. Well, they have taken some steps and there is the Damascus Declaration. There have been some moves and they are considering other moves but I do not pretend that they have put in place a collective security apparatus which they themselves would regard as adequate when faced with the threats of Saddam Hussein or with their anxieties about Iran.

307. Do you feel that the threat to Israel from Iraq still remains, or do you think the action in terms of dealing with weapons of mass destruction has dealt with that threat?

(Mr Hurd) I believe so. The Committee may just like to have the figures, because sometimes one gets the impression nothing has been done. The UN process I have described has so far supervised the destruction of 62 ballistic missiles, 32 ballistic missile warheads, 5,000 122 mm rockets and 350 aerial bombs, and that is just a selection, I could give the Committee a long list if they like, but it shows the exercise is working and I believe it is working.

Chairman: We are playing extra time and we will have one more question from Mr Wareing if you do not mind.

Mr Wareing

308. I wonder if you could tell us how you see the United Nations' continuing effort to assist and protect the Shi'ite and Kurdish populations in Iraq being carried through? How do you see the future of that particular United Nations' activity?

(Mr Hurd) There is a very substantial humanitarian effort which must continue. Emma Nicholson, the Member for Devon West, is an eloquent witness, more than a witness, a helper, as regards the south. Our own British contribution on humanitarian help to the peoples of Iraq since April 1991 is 56 million sterling, and this continues and must continue despite the difficulties of getting through. We do not believe there is a case for lifting sanctions in general, we do believe there is a case for continuing humanitarian effort to these Kurds and Shias who are particularly suffering. For the rest, we will maintain the no-fly zones. I tried to use careful words about the implementation of 688, which is the resolution which deals with Saddam Hussein's attitude towards his own people, because we cannot guarantee their safety, but we can deter Saddam, and the no-fly zones and the allied patrols over the very north and the very south of Iraq are designed, and will continue, to do that. This is satisfactory to the Turkish Government, which has again authorised the renewal of Operation "Provide Comfort" from the patrols based at Incerlik. The Turkish Government are to be applauded and congratulated on that. It was not self-evident they were doing it.

[**Mr Wareing** *Contd*]

309. Did I mishear you? You referred to Turkey, did you say, Mr Hurd, we are getting full co-operation in view of the Kurdish problem inside Turkey, from Turkey in this matter?

(Mr Hurd) Yes, we are.

310. How would you see any additional or sustained pressure being put on Saddam to ensure that he does not take the initiative in causing trouble in the future?

(Mr Hurd) It is a matter of sustained pressure—I think you have used a good phrase—and we have to sustain that pressure all the time, and we will do so. I do not think we should fall for the line that he is somehow strong and popular, it is simply naive of television cameras to wander around the streets of Baghdad putting microphones under the noses of young men and expect them, in the conditions in Iraq, to express a view and come back and say, "You see, he is very strong". This is naivety of the kind with which we were very familiar from people in Communist streets saying how strong the Communist regime was. He is a master of protecting himself; a master of getting rid of those whom he thinks might conceivably be his rivals; he is a master of self-protection, but that I think is his main achievement, the rest I think is not so realistic.

Chairman

311. Foreign Secretary, on that note of realism we must halt. I should have welcomed at the beginning the Political Director, Mr Appleyard, and the Head of the United Nations Department, Miss Evans, and I apologise for not doing so. I would like to thank all three of you for your very helpful guidance in this difficult area where developments are not clear, even to the clearest mind.

(Mr Hurd) Could I ask about your timing? When are you likely to conclude this particular bit of your work?

Chairman: Well, I think maybe with luck and a month from now. We are off to the Yugoslav region next week to look at some of these horrors first- hand and Committee Members will also be going to Cambodia and to Somalia to see UN operations first-hand. The full reply to the Agenda for Peace agenda we shall try to construct around the Easter period. Thank you very much indeed.

Printed in the United Kingdom for HMSO.
Dd.0508721, 3/93, C5, 3398/3B, 5673, 233703.

ISBN 0-10-290193-7

9 780102 901931

FOREIGN AFFAIRS COMMITTEE

THE EXPANDING ROLE OF THE UNITED NATIONS AND ITS IMPLICATIONS FOR UK POLICY

MINUTES OF EVIDENCE

Wednesday 3 February 1993

OVERSEAS DEVELOPMENT ADMINISTRATION

Rt Hon Baroness Chalker of Wallesey, MP, Mr Andrew Bearpark and Mr John Machin

FOREIGN AND COMMONWEALTH OFFICE

Miss Glynne Evans CMG and Mr Geoff Cole

Ordered by The House of Commons *to be printed*
3 February 1993

LONDON: HMSO
£5.95 net

235–vii

WEDNESDAY 3 FEBRUARY 1993

Members present:

Mr David Howell, in the Chair

Mr Dennis Canavan	Mr Ted Rowlands
Mr Mike Gapes	Mr Peter Shore
Mr David Harris	Sir John Stanley
Mr Michael Jopling	Mr David Sumberg
Mr Jim Lester	Mr Robert Wareing

Memorandum submitted by the Overseas Development Administration

THE EXPANDING ROLE OF THE UN IN HUMANITARIAN RELIEF AND THE EFFECTS ON ODA

Introduction

1. Memorandum FCO/FAC/2/92[1] provided broad details of the expansion of the work of the UN and the implications for UK policy. The Committee have asked for a further memorandum on the changing and expanding nature of the UN's role in providing humanitarian relief and how this has affected the work of the ODA. The effects the expansion of the role of the UN has had on the workload and staffing of ODA (including Emergency Aid Department) and on the FCO's Diplomatic Wing are covered in separate memoranda.

2. This memorandum takes 1987 as its starting point, that is the date the Secretary—General cited in his latest annual report when illustrating the expansion in the UN's role.

The Nature of Humanitarian Crises

3. The number and diversity of humanitarian crises has increased sharply over the last few years. Greatly enhanced media coverage has heightened public awareness of the suffering of ordinary people caught up in these crises. This has led to rising expectations about our ability to respond and the nature of that response.

4. Natural disasters—droughts, floods, earthquakes and cyclones—continue to take their toll. But an increasing number of humanitarian crises are exacerbated or caused by man-made factors. For example the suffering caused by the droughts in Somalia and Mozambique have been greatly intensified by the civil wars. Worse still, an increasing number of humanitarian crises are entirely man-made of which the former Yugoslavia is the most recent and bloody example.

5. Providing a humanitarian relief programme in an area beset by armed conflict raises very difficult operational and logistical problems. Not least amongst these is the need for those who operate the relief programme to be seen to be neutral by all sides to the conflict. Such situations also call for effective planning and coordination of the highest order. The international community has increasingly turned to the UN and its specialised agencies to play this role.

The UN's Role in Humanitarian Relief

6. There are a number of UN specialised agencies who are involved in humanitarian relief, such as the UN High Commissioner for Refugees (UNHCR), the World Health Organisation (WHO) and the UN Children's Fund (UNICEF). The problem of co-ordinating UN disaster relief has been recognised for some time. In 1971 the UN set up UNDRO (the Office of the UN Disaster Relief Co-ordinator) as a focal point. However, it had no control over the various UN relief agencies. Its role was confined to responding to natural disasters. Faced with complex emergencies the UN Secretary-General tended to appoint a senior figure on an ad hoc basis (for example Sadruddin in Iraq). Various proposals were made to improve these arrangements. The Nordic Governments in particular launched a well-informed consultation programme in 1990.

7. The response by the UN relief agencies to the Kurdish crisis in March 1991 prompted the United Kingdom to accelerate efforts to improve matters. We identified the need for a senior figure capable of co-ordinating the efforts of the heads of the various agencies, on the Secretary-General's authority, to work effectively together. This would involve pre-planning, joint evaluation of a disaster as it arose, integrated appeals for funding, and properly co-ordinated action on the ground. We proposed that the co-

[1] See HC 235-i, 1992–93.

The cost of printing and publishing these Minutes of Evidence is estimated by HMSO at £2,919.

ordinator would chair a Standing Inter-Agency Emergency Committee in Geneva and would be supported by a small secretariat based on UNDRO.

8. We also proposed that the co-ordinator should have access to a revolving emergency fund (of US$50 million), and that a register be created of UN, national and other disaster relief capabilities, on which the co-ordinator might call. The revolving fund would be available for the various UN relief agencies to draw on in an emergency so that they could set urgent relief work in train immediately. The agencies would subsequently launch appeals to donors to cover the cost of the relief programme and replenish the revolving fund.

9. The UK's proposals, which the Foreign Secretary, Mr Douglas Hurd, launched with Herr Genscher on 9 June 1991 as an Anglo/German initiative, were later adopted by the EC Twelve for action at ECOSOC in July and at the UN General Assembly 46. The London G7 Summit also endorsed it. The UN Secretary-General welcomed it. This report of 17 October envisaged a reformed UN disaster relief system and a "disaster supremo" in very similar terms to our own initiative.

10. This culminated in the creation of the UN's Department of Humanitarian Affairs (DHA) under General Assembly Resolution 461182 in December 1991. The DHA is charged with co-ordinating the work of the various relief agencies within the UN system. Mr Jan Eliasson was appointed as Head of DHA in April 1992 and he reports direct to the Secretary-General. A revolving fund of $50m has been created as described in paragraph 8.

11. The DHA, with offices in New York and Geneva, has not found it easy to coordinate the UN's response to humanitarian crises. The individual specialised agencies retain a considerable degree of autonomy and there are often sound operational reasons for giving one of them the lead role in responding to a particular humanitarian crisis. Its performance will be reviewed within the next year.

THE FINANCIAL EFFECTS ON ODA

12. The expanding role of the UN in relief programmes is mirrored by the amount of money ODA has channelled through UN agencies for disaster, refugee and other humanitarian purposes. In 1987–88 a total of £20.250m was channelled through UN agencies, by 1991–92 the figure had risen to £45.503m.[1]

13. There has also been a substantial increase in the workload in ODA's Emergency Aid Department. This extra work is partly attributable to the large increase in the number of humanitarian crises. Total expenditure more than doubled between 1987–88 and 1991–92 from £43.007m to £101.624m. Alongside this, Emergency Aid Department has also played a major part in the policy dialogue with the UN, the Red Cross, NGOs and others about disaster preparedness. This resulted, amongst other things, in ODA's new Disaster Relief Initiative.

Supplementary memorandum submitted by the Overseas Development Administration

THE EXPANDING ROLE OF THE UN: THE IMPLICATIONS FOR WORKLOADS AND THE STAFFING OF ODA

INTRODUCTION

1. Memorandum FCO/FAC/2/92 provided details of the expansion of the work of the UN and the implications for UK policy. The Committee have asked for a further memorandum on how this expansion has affected workloads and staffing levels. This memorandum relates to the ODA. The effects on the FCO's Diplomatic Wing are covered in a separate memorandum.

2. We have taken 1987 as our starting point—this is the date the Secretary-General cited in his latest annual report in order to illustrate the expansion of the UN's role.

3. Four departments in ODA have a regular interface with various parts of the UN. They are the United Nations and Commonwealth Departments (UNCD), Natural Resources and Environment Department (NRED), Aid Policy Department (APD) and Emergency Aid Department (EMAD). Other departments in ODA also have less frequent contact with various UN agencies and the expanding role of the UN has inevitably increased some of their workloads, although there have been no directly attributable increases in staffing. Senior management is also drawn into some of the more strategic issues which has similarly resulted in some increase in workloads, although again there have been no directly attributable changes in staffing.

[1] Figures showing the amount of funds channelled through UN agencies by the ODA for humanitarian purposes do not include food aid.

UNCD

4. UNCD have primary responsibility within ODA for the United Nations Development Programme (UNDP), United Nations Childrens Fund (UNICEF), Food and Agriculture Organisation (FAO) and the United Nations Industrial Development Organisation (UNIDO). They are also the lead department in dealing with reform of the UN's economic and social system, working in close collaboration with United Nations Department of the FCO's Diplomatic Wing. There have been no substantial changes in staffing levels since 1987. However, the Department has had to devote more time to UN Reform activities since the move to reform ECOSOC in the late 1980's. So far it has been possible to accommodate this within existing staff resources.

NRED

5. Since 1987 the NRED has led for ODA on global environmental issues. At that time NRED's Environment section consisted of one Grade 5 (who devoted 30 per cent of his time to environmental issues), one G7, two HEO's, one AO plus advisory support.

6. 1987 saw the publication of the Brundtland Commission's report "Our Common Future". The challenge of this report was to translate the concept of sustainable development into practice. The Brundtland report was followed by UN General Assembly decision 44/228 (December 1989) which began the preparatory process for the Conference on Environment and Development (UNCED), which took place in Rio de Janeiro in June 1992.

7. UNCED was only the start of a process. It is now for all organisations involved in the environment and development to take on board the UNCED message and embrace sustainable development, primarily through the implementation of Agenda 21 (see also under APD). NRED will continue to be heavily involved in the follow-up to UNCED and in particular in the negotiations on the ratification and implementation of global conventions agreed in Rio on Climate Change and Biological Diversity; the new Inter-Governmental Negotiating Committee (INC) on a convention for Desertification; follow-up to the Forest Principles; negotiations on the restructuring and replenishment of the Global Environment Facility, and related activities of UN agencies and the UN Environment Programme's follow-up to UNCED.

8. NRED's involvement in the UNCED process has led to an expansion of the Environment section to its present complement of one Grade 5 (who now devotes 80 per cent of his time to environmental issues) one G7, two SEOs, one HEOD, two HEOs, two EOs and four AOs plus advisory support.

APD

9. APD's central policy role brings it into contact with much of the UN system from time to time, but the work involved tends to be marginal. More central to APD are the UN Commission on Human Rights, with emphases on good government, and some of UNCTAD's work on the least developed countries. APD also has a continuing role in monitoring aid volume, in particular the UN target that donor countries should provide 0.7 per cent of their GNP in aid to developing countries. The aid volume issue comes up in a number of international fora, including the UN.

10. The most significant recent event with implications for APD's workload was the UN Conference on Environment and Development (UNCED) last June. Among the agreements and documents flowing from UNCED (see also under NRED) is Agenda 21, which in its 40 chapters sets out an agenda for the achievement of sustainable development to take us into the next century. The existing HEO(D) post in APP has been tasked with taking forward the implications of Agenda 21 for our aid programme. Monitoring and reporting to the new UN Sustainable Development Commission, established by the last General Assembly, will form a central part of this work. UNCED has generated a number of other initiatives of interest to APD, including a conference on sustainable development in small island states to be held in 1994, which are likely to place increasing demands on staff resources.

EMAD

11. The expanding role of the UN in humanitarian relief is symptomatic of the major increase in the number and diversity of humanitarian crises. It is impossible to disaggregate the increases in workload directly linked to work with UN agencies as opposed to our other means of providing humanitarian relief—for example NGO's, the Red Cross, directly managed bilateral programmes, etc.

12. That said, the number of staff employed in Emergency Aid Department has grown from 6.5 in 1987–88 to 11.5 in 1991–92 and is set to increase to 17 shortly (details are attached at Annexe A). In addition we second staff from other parts of ODA from time to time to provide extra support during major crises. And our Geographical Departments also share the burden of managing our response to some of the long running major humanitarian crises such as Iraq, Somalia and Mozambique.

Annex A

EMERGENCY AID DEPARTMENT

	Staffing Levels									
	G5	G6	G7	SEO	HEO	EO	AO	PA	Typist	Total Staff
1987/88	0.5		1		2	1	1	0.5	0.5	6.5
1989/90	0.5		1	1	2	1	2	0.5	0.5	8.5
1991/92	0.5		2	1	3	1	3	0.5	0.5	11.5
1992/93*	0.5	1	2	1	4	3	4	0.5	1	17

* In addition 1 G7 and 1 EO are seconded to Emergency Aid Dept. for the present.

Examination of Witnesses

RT HON THE BARONESS CHALKER OF WALLASEY, a Member of the House of Lords, attending by leave of that House, Minister of State, Foreign and Commonwealth Office and Minister for Overseas Development, MR ANDREW BEARPARK, Head of Emergency Aid Department, ODA, MR JOHN MACHIN, Head of United Nations and Commonwealth Department, ODA, and MR GEOFF COLE, Africa Division (Equatorial) Foreign and Commonwealth Office, examined.

MISS GLYNNE EVANS, CMG, Head of United Nations Department, Foreign and Commonwealth Office, further examined.

Chairman

312. Baroness Chalker, could we begin by welcoming you to this Committee again this morning, and thank you for giving us the time to be with us. We gather in your vast range of other ministerial duties you have been giving evidence to another committee of this Parliament in the Lords only very recently. This is obviously your heavy committee week. You have brought with you a formidable team, some of whom are familiar to us, indeed Miss Evans was before us less than a week ago and must be getting very familiar with this Committee. Would you care to introduce your other colleagues to us?

(Baroness Chalker) Thank you, Mr Chairman. On my left, as you say, is Glynne Evans, who is Head of the United Nations Department in the Diplomatic Wing of the Foreign Office; on her left is Geoff Cole, who is the Somalia Desk Officer, with special experience of Somalia in the Diplomatic Wing; on my immediate right is Andrew Bearpark, who is Head of our Emergency Aid Division in the Aid Wing, and also Head of Information; and on his right is John Machin, who is Head of our United Nations and Commonwealth Department in the Aid Wing, which looks after various UN agencies.

313. Thank you very much. I hope your colleagues, should you wish or they wish, feel ready to chip into any dialogue that develops. We will be very glad to hear their views. Could I begin, Minister, with a fairly general question, although I think we would like some quite detailed answers if they are available. With humanitarian concerns eroding national sovereignties and really changing the nature of intervention and activities by the nation states in dealing with international affairs, it seems to us that enormous new burdens are falling on your Department, and that the Development Aid administration, particularly of the advanced nations and our Overseas Development Aid administration in particular, are becoming the forward edge of foreign policy development, and of the promotion and upholding of the various nations' interests, including our own. Therefore, we naturally assume (and I think we are probably right) that this is imposing on you some very hard decisions about priorities and how you re-organise and redeploy your Department in these totally new conditions. Could you just respond to that observation, and talk to us about some of the priorities now looming up and how they are going to be addressed?

(Baroness Chalker) Mr Chairman, you really are right, rarely has the world faced quite so many crises simultaneously in quite so diverse an array of humanitarian situations. I think I would like to underline that at the outset. They are very different and you cannot have a template which will fit for all. The media particularly has made everyone much more aware of the crises. I am not saying they did not exist before, but that people have better information and the demand upon governments throughout the world and upon the United Nations is very much greater. Our priority objectives in the Aid Wing are set out in the annual FCO/ODA departmental reports. Our priorities for spending to meet these objectives and the distribution of our resources are decided annually. We have three main factors we take into account: first of all, the proportion of the expenditure which we must use to meet our firm existing commitments; that is particularly true in the case of multi-lateral aid, most of which consists of assessed or negotiated contributions, but it also applies to quite a wide range of bilateral expenditure. Development is a very long haul. Development requires us to be consistent in applying sound development strategy. Our development objectives are fairly stable from year to year. The Committee will be able to see

[**Chairman** *Contd*]

this for themselves by comparing the objectives set out in this year's departmental report, which is just about to be published, with those that were in last year's version in Command Paper 1902. What we have is a background of fixed commitments and some programmes which might take place over as long as ten years. It is into that that we have to have sufficient flexibility to meet the cost of our humanitarian assistance, and most of that is, indeed, unpredictable. We maintain a contingency reserve which enables us to respond flexibly to the unforeseen events and changes in circumstances and the humanitarian crises, but we try, through more regular programme planning, to cover some of the continuing and more predictable refugee and relief situations. In addition to the long-term development and humanitarian assistance that can be foreseen, and for which we provide support, there may be additional demands of a humanitarian need. I want to emphasise we do seek to work our programmes so that there is no trade-off between development and humanitarian assistance, and that is partly because of the forward planning we must do for long-term development assistance. It is also necessary I think to recognise that much of our development assistance is designed to prevent manmade humanitarian disasters from occurring if we can, or contain the effect of them, and contain the effect of natural disasters from wrecking the development potential of an economy. It is not all unforeseen, but the humanitarian assistance with which the public are most familiar from the media will be such things as the desperate drought in the Horn of Africa and, indeed, in Southern Africa; the situation in Iraq, looking after the Kurds in the north and trying to get help to the Shi'iahs in the south; and, of course, more recently Somalia and, indeed, ex-Yugoslavia. When we are dealing with such things as the drought we can have some forward planning, because the food and agricultural organisation of the UN and the World Food Programme do crop assessments each year. They help us to judge forward the level and the content of the needs in the year ahead. The SEPHA appeals have given us a further insight into the non-food needs. They usually come to us in December or early January and allow us to plan. The last two years, you are absolutely right, we have had disasters manmade which we could not have predicted, or certainly could not have predicted the size and the complexity of. I have already mentioned Iraq, the former Yugoslavia and, to a large extent, Somalia; plus the natural ones in sub-Saharan Africa and that Bangladesh cyclone which was really a quite terrible disaster on 29th April 1991. To the maximum extent possible we provide swift and effective help, having assessed the situation; we do not just go in with what we think they will need, we find out first. That has not undermined our basic role as an aid agency to support long-term development, and we intend that it should not, but it does mean we have to work in a flexible way; and whereas I started out the financial year 1992/93 with a budget for humanitarian aid of £85m, by the end of the year I will have spent around £160m, partly from our own contingency reserve, partly some money which we put on one side expecting a bigger bill from the European Community than we got and we had that money back and, if necessary, I go to the Treasury. But I do try to manage within my own contingency reserve as far as I am able to do so. In the coming year I shall start with a budget of £88 million and adjust it if necessary.

314. Thank you. The question we would like to probe is how you and your colleagues decide, as it were, among the demands that come flooding in. You have the United Nations with its own Department of Humanitarian Affairs, and we are going to come on to that in detail in a moment. That is a source of demand on your Department and I see that the balance flowing through your Department for United Nations humanitarian purposes has risen from about £20 million in 1987-88 to £45 million in 1991-92 and it is presumably set to head on up to the sky in the present year—or certainly to rise. How do you decide amongst all these enormous pressures driven by public concern for humanitarian requirements which are occurring in many, many parts of the globe?

(Baroness Chalker) The first thing, Chairman, is to decide what is actually needed in the specific country or areas as a result of the disaster, and that is done by assessment on the spot or by trained assessors from us or from one of the leading NGO agencies like the Red Cross, Oxfam, Save the Children, who very often have people quite able to assess on the ground what is needed. We also look at that initial stage for who has the capacity to deliver to the problem area directly and efficiently. If they have the capacity we may invite them to put a bid to us for the resources we can make available or, indeed, they are very often there before we have to ask them—we occasionally have to ask. So far as the United Nations is concerned, there are two things we would do. One is to make sure now through the Department of Humanitarian Affairs who is likely to be in the lead and could give the most help. But we have, as you well know from your earlier evidence sessions, encountered a very complex situation both in Somalia and in ex-Yugoslavia because the help that has gone there has gone by a combination of routes. When in the former Yugoslavia the United Nations decided that UNHCR because of the refugee movements must be the lead agency—that is not a concept necessarily pursued in other cases—that meant we had to work with the UNHCR because they were going to be on the ground and they were going to be funded through the United Nations. We have found it a new experience, but a valuable one, to give considerable back-up to the UNHCR by the provision of logisticians, radio operators, transport fleet managers and, indeed, many of the drivers are, of course, ODA drivers. We have more than 100 civilian staff working out of Zagreb and Metkovic on the vari-

[**Chairman** *Contd*]

ous aid convoys into Central Bosnia and also into other areas as well.

Mr Lester

315. Judging from what you said about the increase in humanitarian relief from £85 million to £160 million, it must make it very difficult for you to contemplate any expansion of longterm development aid in the sense that your overall budget is limited. I wonder if that is true. Secondly, though there is a Disaster Relief Appeal of ODA, which is very widely praised and supported, to react very quickly to emergencies, does it really mean in terms of what you said that a situation can arise where, when the money runs out, you have to refuse help either to United Nations appeals or indeed to other appeals that are really urgent?

(Baroness Chalker) I am glad to say, Mr Chairman, we have not had to refuse help. We may not have given to a United Nations agency's appeal as much as they would like to have had, that may be fair; but it may also be because we have actually assessed that we should not be putting quite so much through that particular channel for that appeal. We have, in fact, been managing extremely well but it requires very careful budgetary control, financial control, at all times. There is never a week goes by when there is not some discussion about what our forward liability may be "in the light of ..." between the Principal Finance Officer and myself. But once we have settled the PES round we know where we are for the following year and within the sorts of figures we are dealing with what else we may need to go to the Treasury for, given the potential need that we may see. Whilst, yes, of course, any minister in my position with crying demands round the world could do more if there were more money available, my job is to make sure that once that decision has been taken we get every pound of value not only for the benefit of the British taxpayer but also for the recipients out of what we do. This is why we have increasingly used certain NGOs in the disaster relief situation, because they are the most cost-effective way of getting the resources. They are often the fastest and most secure in addition to sourcing locally which can often help a local economy in the countries where we are trying to help.

316. When you negotiate the PES round, is there any relationship between the pressures, for instance, of asylum seekers and immigration from both Eastern European states and, indeed, North Africa and the size of the aid budget? Do they try and have it both ways? There is enormous pressure to try and ensure that people stay where they are best suited in their own countries—this does not just apply to Europe, it applies in Africa particularly— in regard to the actual budget you have to try and alleviate the problems which cause people to move across boundaries and borders.

(Baroness Chalker) Mr Chairman, I think Mr Lester knows well that I believe that by sound development assistance in countries that are trying hard to get their economies right and to cope with their own problems one can alleviate the pressure which is caused by refugees and displaced persons. We are seeking to draw as much knowledge from our most recent few years of experience as we can on this and, yes, more in development assistance may mean somewhat less in relief. But I am afraid it would not matter how much development assistance you put into Southern Africa, for instance: the drought which we have experienced in recent years could not have been alleviated by development assistance in its entirety. One might have got a different grain which could manage to grow without so much water, but not with no water at all—and that was the situation that we were facing. So in some cases that would be true, but by no means all, when you are dealing with these humanitarian situations.

Sir John Stanley

317. Minister, I am glad you said you do apparently continue to have access to the national contingency reserves through the Treasury, given the fact that inescapably your own departmental contingency reserve for emergency and humanitarian relief must be at the expense of the longterm expenditure on aid. Could you tell us, therefore, whether in the last year or so there have been any occasions when you have sought access to the Treasury's national reserve to deal with the humanitarian emergency demands on your Department and you have been refused, and could you cite occasions when that happened if there were any?

(Baroness Chalker) To answer, Sir John, let me say there has been no occasion when I have been refused; I have always managed to get the money. I might have liked to get rather more money than I have been able to get, and that would have been true in the case of trying to alleviate the plight of the Kurds in northern Iraq and the Shia in southern Iraq, in the case of Somalia and so on. I have never been refused, and I think this is because we try not to be unreasonable in making demands. I am always conscious of the public purse, as well as the enormous need and consequent pressure upon my Department.

Mr Wareing: I just wonder whether you feel that you are not in as strong a position as many of your colleagues in Government, by virtue of the fact that you are having to work through the FCO budget, essentially. I know the ODA has a separate budget but, nevertheless, you are not a Cabinet Minister, and many people, incidentally, thought you might have been at some point but you are not.

Mr Harris: Hoped you would be.

Mr Wareing

318. That apart, the fact that the ODA is not represented in the Cabinet, do you find that a disadvantage in the bids that you make, or would like

[**Mr Wareing** *Contd*]

to make, because, first of all, you have to consider that you are in fact a junior Minister in a sense?

(Baroness Chalker) Mr Chairman, I have to say, after nearly 14 years I do not feel very young any more, junior I may be! I can reassure Mr Wareing, I think, in this way: I have had total support from the Foreign Secretary in making what was very much an ODA bid. In many discussions with the Treasury I was leading, I was doing the talking and there has never been any downgrading, "You're the junior, you keep quiet". We have always done it as a combined effort, and the Foreign Secretary has given me excellent backing. What I think may not be known is how often the Prime Minister calls me into situations, meetings and gatherings of all sorts on issues where he believes that ODA has something to offer. If I think he should have called me in and he has not I might even been so bold occasionally to ring up and say, "Can I help?"

319. I am sure you do do that. I wonder if I could ask you about priorities. You mentioned earlier on, I noticed, the media, and we are all, as Members of Parliament, subject to that, and get letters from our constituents the moment there is a famine in Ethiopia. I think some parts of the world tend to be forgotten because the media do not treat them. I think the problems in Sudan are largely unknown or forgotten by our constituents. How far do you feel that you are media-led, and is there a need for some sort of advisory body composed of representatives of the NGOs, which could be in more or less permanent session, to give you advice, rather than perhaps waiting until the letters start to stream in and Members of Parliament like myself start asking awkward questions?

(Baroness Chalker) Mr Chairman, let me assure Mr Wareing he never really asks awkward questions, he just probes.

320. I try.

(Baroness Chalker) But that can be very helpful. I think the answer is this: the media tend to have fashions, inevitably, that is how the media works. We see far less now of work which continues to go on, for instance, in Iraq, in South Africa or in Somalia. We were giving quite a lot of money in Somalia in 1991. You would never have known it from the media, because the media were not there, they were busy covering Iraq practically the whole year. Sometimes, as I think the Red Cross said to you in an evidence session last week, it is difficult to persuade the media to go with us to see what the situation is. Frequently one could wish that they would give us more assistance. I shall be taking British Satellite Television with me to Somalia this coming weekend, but none of the others are coming with me because it is not the thing of the moment. Of course, there were crews in Bosnia last week when I was there because it was the thing of the moment. If I see or know from our Diplomatic Wing of a situation building up, where it helps I will always try to involve the media and get them to take a real interest in this. The Head of my Information Department, Mr Bearpark, spends a good deal of time briefing the media or, dare I say, from time to time correcting the media and giving the real situation on the ground. I do likewise but, obviously I cannot be everywhere at once, nor can he.

Chairman

321. Given the media interest point, which Mr Wareing rightly raised, that must be a major influence on you, but how far are your policies driven by a strategic view of the promotion of Britain's interests, both foreign policy and, indeed, commercial? Where does the input of that kind come into your Department's work?

(Baroness Chalker) As a member of the Diplomatic Wing as well as the Aid Wing of the Foreign Office, all of our decisions must fit into the context of our strategic planning for different areas of the world. That does not just take account of the consular role we must play, or the influencing role we must play either directly with that country or with our European partners in that country, but it also takes account of Britain's trade interests, Britain's involvement, maybe, for defensive purposes in that country too. It has to be a seamless whole and I must know about what is going on in other Departments in order to make the best judgement of what tactics should be deployed if something gets into trouble.

Mr Harris

322. Minister, you said earlier, and rightly so, that you are very determined to get value for money for every pound you spend. The public perception, or perhaps misconception, on a lot of these humanitarian issues, quite frankly, is that goods do not arrive where they are needed or they do not get to the people who desperately need them. Would you like to comment on that? What is the situation on the ground? For example, we are hearing now of the efforts in the former Yugoslavia and also in Africa.

(Baroness Chalker) First of all, it is very important to choose the right vehicle to deliver the assistance. I have to say that I find a number of the NGOs the most effective or, in the case of the former Yugoslavia, our own convoy drivers working with the UNHCR. What gives us very grave worry indeed is the independent people who go out with a few lorries. They simply do not understand the language usually, when it is Serbo-Croat or, indeed, the difficulties at borders or the speed with which an insecure situation becomes a disastrous situation. This is why we have always called for public donation to go through the recognised and very organised main agencies, particularly in a war situation. It is why we frequently too request public donation to be in the form of money rather than goods. You may remember at the beginning of the Kurdish crisis I think it was people in Germany who kindly donated food for the Kurds,

[**Mr Harris** *Contd*]

and they were sending food which the people, because they were Muslims, could not eat. It is no good sending old medicines that somebody has turned out of a cupboard. You have actually got to send the proper goods to do the job, which is why I emphasise the need for assessing and then for working out not only what you send but the means by which you send it. The situation in the former Yugoslavia is dangerous, but it is manageable. I spent some time with the Cheshire Regiment, and I have to say I am very proud of what the soldiers were doing, very proud indeed. I also believe that we can help in other ways to get the situation right, as we have done in central Bosnia, and that is the provision of our British military logistic team working with UNHCR. They come from UNPROFOR but they are working straight alongside. That has actually helped UNHCR to re-organise the distribution at a local level, for instance in Sarajevo, to make sure that it actually reaches the collective centres and kitchens and does not disappear en route. You can only do that with a rather formalised delivery system. I am afraid single trucks and small convoys going out could bring a lot of grief for the people who are running them, and bring a great deal more trouble for the army who are trying, through UNPROFOR, to secure a humanitarian delivery. When it comes to Africa, we are obviously not using troops to secure humanitarian deliveries but we have worked very closely through our aid agencies—the Red Cross particularly and CARE whom you also interviewed, Oxfam and others—and they are very professional in what they are doing. Whilst they have had the American Army back-up recently, they have always been very professional in what they are doing. I would not like anybody to think from what I am saying our own NGOs cannot do a very good job—they can—but it needs to be extremely well organised if the aid is to get to the end point. Ours has largely got there, that I can assure the Committee. I know of some nations that do not have the benefits of such good NGOs and they really have lost a lot along the way.

323. Your own civilian drivers must be the unsung heroes of Bosnia. The Red cross told us last week they believe very strongly in what they describe as the kitchen approach, i.e. they set up kitchens in the field and hand out the food rather than letting it go to other parties to distribute or mal-use. Do you support that approach?

(Baroness Chalker) I do entirely. My truck drivers are the unsung heroes very much in Bosnia at the moment, but I try to give them credit for what they are doing. In Africa we find that specific delivery into the village may in some cases in some situations be sufficient but in Somalia it was not going to be, because then the people running the kitchens in the village were held to ransom by the gun-toting Somali factions. That was why there we gave the fullest backing to the Red Cross that we could for the establishment of kitchens, specialist supplementary feeding centres, medical centres and so on.

Chairman: We want to come on to the specific problems in Africa and iraq and, indeed, former Yugoslavia in a minute. Perhaps we could finish on the general policy approach with a question from Mr Gapes.

Mr Gapes

324. In answer to the Chairman just now you referred to the relationship between aid policy and foreign policy. Would it be correct to say that at the end of the day foreign policy objectives and the Government's trade objectives take priority and that aid policy is subservient to that?

(Baroness Chalker) No, I do not think it would, Mr Chairman. It is frequently asserted that that is the case, but I do not believe it to be so. Provided the aid policy is presented realistically, it ranks alongside other considerations. It is sometimes difficult in specific instances to persuade people that we should not be involved in a trade situation which we may think could longterm be deleterious to the aid situation or local development situation, but by and large we have our say.

325. There are examples round the world where the Government is involved in arms contracts or is involved in particular industrial projects which it would want to pursue and they have job implications in this country and it might be difficult for relations with that government if we were going to be providing assistance to, for example, people from East Timor who are subject to Indonesian oppression or perhaps we are not pressing the Saudi Government too strongly about some issues with regard to the treatment of some of the Shia refugees from Southern Iraq who were sent to Saudi Arabia. Those are the kinds of examples I am concerned about.

(Baroness Chalker) I think they are very limited. It is perfectly true that there will always be conflicts of interest but let me say that we are most careful in the sale of arms that they are not used for internal repression. We also go to very considerable lengths to find out if there are requests for certain commodities why the requests have come in. I can remember many instances in my time in the Foreign Office where bids for goods have been refused because we did not believe the assurances that were being given by the would-be buyer. There are some very difficult human rights situations and I think this is where one comes across the most awkward situation. Where a country, let us say, in South East Asia believes that our worries are interfering in their internal affairs, that is where we have to use a great deal of persuasion to get them to see that human rights must be respected. I have been greatly helped in the last two years since we launched the Good Government Policy in this way and we now have a Human Rights Policy Unit in the Diplomatic Wing which works closely with the ODA departments

[**Mr Gapes** *Contd*]

concered. We have had a resolution through the EC Development Council on human rights and we have discussed it very fully now in the Development Assistance Committee of OECD. So this has become in recent years a very real consideration. Ten years ago it was not.

Mr Rowlands

326. Taking up the issue in Mr Gapes's question, Minister, the new experience of having considerable military cover to deliver humanitarian aid derives from the historic build-up of enormous numbers of arms. Take Somalia as a classic example where it was the subject of an arms race of some kind—there are other countries too. Are we going to see it as part of the concept of good governance of our relationships with EC policy, with United Nations policy, to make it a more and more stringent condition that longterm aid development is also going to be tied to some sort of limitation of arms budgets and arms spending which is part and parcel of the arms race, because otherwise we will just have a continuous repetition of such events as these in Somalia, where large arms were bought officially by the state and when the state disintegrated the arms got dispersed, and we have the situation of having to have a major new military presence to deliver humanitarian aid. I think the public will give great support to humanitarian situations as long as there is a policy of limiting the arms race and arms expenditure.

(Baroness Chalker) This was why I was so glad when the Prime Minister in 1991 put his initiative to the United Nations for an arms register. That has helped but it has to be made to work and, of course, one of the difficulties Mr Rowlands rightly cites is that some countries like Somalia have been building up small arms and mortars for many years—not from this country I might add—and they have been stowed away. To put it right, yes, we have made a start. The Prime Minister is determined as part of the Government's policy we shall continue to do it, but there are a lot of other people in the world who perhaps are not quite so careful.

327. Is the international community going to scrutinise collectively the arms budgets of states which are pleading for major international economic aid assistance?

(Baroness Chalker) Indeed, we already do this, Mr Chairman.

Mr Jopling

328. I just want to go back to the point you made a few moments ago about the problem of those marvellous individualistic enterprising people who take single lorry loads in. I think we have probably all had them in our constituencies. You are never going to stop them because they just feel they have to do something and they are admirable people. Is there not some way in which you could try to direct them so that they could avoid the pitfalls you quite rightly mentioned? What have you done to try to direct those people who are determined to do their thing so that they fall into the minimum number of mantraps on the way? Could you do it through Members of the House, because I think probably we have all become aware of enterprises like this in our own constituencies, or could you do it through charities or could you do it through the local press? I do not know. But it would seem to me you are not going to stop them but the thing is to try to help them as much as you possibly can to avoid the pitfalls if they insist on going.

(Baroness Chalker) Mr Chairman, Michael is absolutely right. Some of them do insist on going. We give a lot of advice and have been doing so for a very long while; so have the main aid agencies. They have appealed to people to work with them, to work through their systems, but I am afraid mavericks or people determined to go to see what it is like on the ground do not listen to that advice. The army were telling me in Bosnia last week of several very nearly hasty situations where people in fact then put our soldiers' lives at risk, because our soldiers are the ones who are going to have to go out and help them. I just appeal to Members of Parliament, both Houses and to anybody else to understand that once these people are on their own in these countries—and they frequently go without any radio contact, they lose parts of their convoy, they do not know the roads, they cannot read the language—they are putting their lives at risk, and the lives of others who they then involve. Therefore, working through the Red Cross, Save the Children, Oxfam and the others—Action Aid and CARE—there are so many good British NGOs who have learned, some of them the hard way, how to get aid through that these people who try to re-invent the wheel could cause some very great heartache in their own families and their own communities by their unprepared action.

Chairman: Could we now move from the co-ordination of individuals to the co-ordination with other nations and, indeed, co-ordination of the UN.

Mr Sumberg

329. Minister, we have talked about money, which is important, and we have talked about British initiative and so forth, but the combination with the rest of the world is truly vital, as I am sure you would agree. One of the ODA priority objectives for the aid programme into developing countries in 1992 was to improve the co-ordination of the international response to all these major emergencies overseas which we seek. I would be grateful if you could tell the Committee in what ways the ODA has helped the UN to improve its response to these sorts of emergencies?

(Baroness Chalker) Mr Chairman, whilst we have no automatic predisposition to channelling humanitarian aid through the UN, as has been evident from my earlier answers, we really do seek to help the UN agencies who are frequently given

[**Mr Sumberg** *Contd*]

these jobs to do their job as effectively as possible. We have worked with our European partners, first with the Germans and then, indeed, with the rest of the EC, to put forward the resolution that came up in the autumn of 1991 at the UN General Assembly for the formation of the Department of Humanitarian Affairs, which started in April last year, because they are charged in the role of co-ordination and facilitation amongst the UN agencies, and this was very much a gap when the flight of the Asians took place out of Iraq and Kuwait following the invasion of Saddam Hussein in 1990. The DHA is not in the business of replacing the existing UN agencies. It is not intended to control the UN agencies but to co-ordinate and to facilitate. It is beginning to help strengthen the UN agencies' response to humanitarian crises. I think they have made a tremendous effort, but that Department is small and it is extraordinarily busy. Certainly they can note successes on a special case basis, like setting up the units in Iraq and the SEPHA appeal (the Special Emergency Programme for the Horn of Africa) which I mentioned earlier, and the drought emergency programme in Southern Africa: but what has happened is that its UN Under-Secretary Jan Eliasson has, in fact, become an international humanitarian troubleshooter, so that he has not had sufficient time to give personally some of the co-ordination. He is very well aware of this. We also have an inter-agency standing committee in Geneva and that needs to be pulled in to the overall effort a lot more. The DHA have suffered some problems over staff, administrative support and resources, but there is an internal review going on at the moment, and we shall be informed of how that goes. In the 1992 General Assembly debate we had a valuable chance to consider the evolution of the DHA role. Mr Chairman, I made a speech at that session and it might be helpful to the Committee to have copies of that speech, which I will let you have. Britain is very keen to see the DHA strengthened. Their work is very valuable, but I hope that the current review will provide an opportunity for the DHA to examine its performance so far and refocus its aims and its overall strategy. Certainly they need to identify their current administrative problems and propose solutions to them. They need a re-examination of the roles of the New York and Geneva offices. The division of labour (the political labour if you like) in New York is very important, but the humanitarian co-ordination of work in Geneva is also very critical. I think Mr Eliasson needs an improved chain of command. The whole accountability of the situation is one I know he wants to improve. They further need to assess the DHA's financial position, and maximise the organisation's cost effectiveness. As I say, the direction of the DHA under Jan Eliasson, co-ordinating and facilitating the effort, is I believe a very important one, and it is certainly something on which we can build.

330. Some of us met Mr Eliasson when we were in New York last year and he was very appreciative of the assistance and help he has had from you, Minister, and from the Government. You talk about the review when you talk about the problems that it should seek to address, what particular solution is the British Government looking for in those problems? What will you be suggesting, with the review, that should come out of it at the end of the day, all the talking having stopped?

(Baroness Chalker) I think it is very difficult for us, one country, or me, a single Minister, to launch off and give the United Nations Secretary General my solutions. I think he might take exception to that. However, I am very prepared to help in any way that I can. Certainly I have encouraged the DHA to develop its relationship with the non-governmental organisations who have vast experience of delivering the goods. The DHA is not intended to be a delivery and operational agency but, as I have said, a co-ordinator and a facilitator. That means their communications have to be absolutely first-class between Geneva and New York and between all the agencies. That is why I particularly drew attention some moments ago to the inter-agency standing committee, because it is a central point for governments and non-governmental organisations, and one that we should give a lot of attention to. We are seeking to give as much support as we can to the effective implementation of the resolution from autumn 1991 in the United Nations General Assembly. What I would urge is that that resolution should be fully implemented in Geneva, and as regards this standing committee.

331. Could I just press the Minister slightly on one of the solutions. I understand your reluctance to tell the United Nations, or advise the United Nations what it should do, but I think we as a country and you as a Minister are entitled to do so because of the contribution we make. Let me test you on this one: for instance, should the DHA be given even greater control over the relevant UN agencies and, in particular, over their budgets? What should be the degree of autonomy between one and another?

(Baroness Chalker) I do not think that it is possible to impose the Department of Humanitarian Affairs, tiny as it is, above and over UN agencies. I do believe it is right and proper that the co-ordination role which was in that Resolution should be utilised to the full. what I hope will happen is that the United Nations Secretary General will himself give the fullest support to the co-ordination by the DHA in the review he is having of all the UN agencies. They can be first-class in delivery on the ground where they have resources and the planning, but I think there is overlap and I think it is on the ground that they need to concentrate their efforts. I suppose many people in my position charged with the responsibility to deliver development aid and humanitarian relief will say more work at the coalface and perhaps less in the boardroom.

Mr Lester

332. One of the things the Department sought to co-ordinate was the terms and conditions of the operational staff of the UN agencies in difficult situations. I am the last person to wish wanton loss of life or risk of loss of life, but one of the things we have evidence on, particularly in Somalia, is that there was a critical period when there was no United Nations presence for a long time when NGOs stayed there or went back very quickly, and that contributed a great deal to all that went wrong in Somalia. I fully understand people do not like risking their lives, but this does lead to a propensity of some of the UN agencies to move very quickly, as soon as there has been an incident to withdraw very quickly from the operational field.

(Baroness Chalker) Mr Chairman, Mr Lester is absolutely right. You cannot be involved—certainly not in a country like Somalia—in this whole business of relief without your operators being in some danger. We ought to be realistic about Somalia. Even though, as I said in answer to Mr Wareing earlier, the media did not pay much attention to the delivery of aid in Somalia in 1991, aid was delivered but delivered by NGOs who took the risks. But when the fighting becomes as intense as it did in November of that year, you cannot distribute —it was war there. There were two things that the United Nations could not do. One was to undertake peacekeeping on the scale necessary, and I think it has been a merciful outcome that the United States has intervened so generously because only a bilateral nation could actually push it and they are the only ones who could push it in the way they have done. The other thing the United Nations could not do was to insure its staff to work in a war zone. I realise that, while one can take out personal insurance, the premiums are enormous. I only know that because I made some inquiries before going to Bosnia, and I am very well aware that, although the NGOs have continued to work in very difficult circumstances, their capacity was very, very limited and they were a less obvious target in Somali than the United Nations have been. But the aid agencies will willingly admit they were rendered helpless for periods during the conflict. It was not that we did not want to go on helping Somalia—we did—but you just cannot get any aid into a situation where the fighting was as intense as it was after the November 1991 outbreak right through until about May of last year.

333. If you think about Afghanistan at the moment and the tragic incident there, to withdraw from Afghanistan at this stage would only be quite disastrous for the people.

(Baroness Chalker) I certainly agree. We offer sympathy to the family of the man who has given so much service, not just in Afghanistan where he lost his life this week, but it does seem tome that the aid workers who go into these situations know that that is a risk they take, just frankly as a soldier knows his life is at risk and even to some extent, I suppose, as we knew last week.

Mr Canavan

334. I would like to ask how you envisage the role of the United Nations in the provision of humanitarian relief. In your opinion, does the United Nations continue to be engaged directly in an operational capacity in all humanitarian relief work? Should its role be more that of a co-ordinator of the work of other agencies including NGOs?

(Baroness Chalker) I think, Mr Chairman, I have sought to explain that the DHA—the Department of Humanitarian Affairs—should certainly be a co-ordinator. There are some UN agencies who can with help from donors like ourselves give specific assistance, but they should also utilise the best people for the job and very often the best people for the job are, in fact, the non-governmental organisations. It is partly because those people can relate to local people so well. Now, I give another instance where relating to local people—even local fighters—works very well. That is the way in which members of the Cheshire Regiment have calmed things down in part of Central Bosnia over the last fortnight literally by being on the road blocks with Croatian or Bosnian soldiers—calming it down, creating a sense of confidence. It is creating the sense of confidence to do things in an area which is war-torn which sometimes the NGOs seem to be so much more adept at than the operators of the UN agencies. That is not a hard and fast rule. It depends on individuals and this is why we are very careful in the selection of the individuals that we send out to do jobs. So are the Red Cross; I am not sure whether they answered on this point to you last week, but we are exceptionally careful of the sorts of people we send into these situations because you can actually make a situation deteriorate if you do not have people who can cope with the deprivations which every aid worker, NGO or anybody else, feels and faces over a long period when they are trying to give aid in a very difficult situation.

335. Would you rather see an increasing role for NGOs and a corresponding decrease in the role of the United Nations in the matter of direct provision of relief?

(Baroness Chalker) I do not believe that all NGOs and no United Nations or all United Nations and no NGOs would be anything like the right thing. It goes back to what I said: whilst the co-ordination is vital and the NGOs want the co-ordination and the support, the NGOs do not want to be controlled. Now, there are some situations where there has to be a UN control, where you have got, for instance, in the former Yugoslavia UNPROFOR and there is very much a UN control. Where there is UN control it is for a good reason, it is jolly difficult to get the help through. So I believe it is right that the NGOs should retain their independence and they have a big advantage that they are not seen as—and they

[**Mr Canavan** *Contd*]

are not indeed—arms of governments or arms of the United Nations. Sometimes this creates a tension with the UN agency or indeed with the government, but, if you work closely enough with them, as my Department tries to do, you get by very well and have tremendous co-operation on a regular basis with them which does not require you to have the standing committee Mr Wareing mentioned earlier. We have regular meetings. I had one on Somalia in January and we have another when I get back. We have meetings wherever they are working alongside us and we are funding them.

336. The United Nations and its agencies has come in for some criticism on occasion regarding the humanitarian relief efforts. Some of that criticism may be deserved, some undeserved; but, for example, our Committee has been told by NGO witnesses that there was no objective evaluation of the failure of the UNHCR in Ethiopia in 1988-89 and that there never is such an analysis. How, in your opinion, could performance of the United Nations and its agencies be better monitored?

(Baroness Chalker) Mr Chairman, it is not only a question of better monitoring it is, as Mr Canavan has said, a question of better assessment. This is why I have been absolutely sure that anything we have gone into anew had to be properly assessed before we even started work. That system of assessment is now spreading. It has certainly spread to agencies which did not have it before, including some UN agencies. Some UN agencies do assess and assess well, others not so well. It is a question of manpower, womanpower and it is a question of resources and actually having the linkages in a country. It is quite difficult for a United Nations team to go in and quickly assess a situation, and it may be they should rely on other initial assessments. Thinking back to Ethiopia in the late 80s, I remember how very difficult it was to get any assessment done on the ground of what was needed in terms of relief and rehabilitation. I made several visits to Ethiopia to their RRC Committee, to go out in the field with NGOs who were working there, and it was partly because the government wanted the relief to be played in a certain way. If a UN agency, or anybody else, is obstructed by a government to the degree that there was obstruction at that time, I do not think all the blame can frankly like with the UNHCR for that period.

Mr Wareing

337. Going back to the question of the role of the United Nations vis-a-vis the NGOs, would you agree that one has to know where an NGO begins and where it ends? We were talking before about the question of individuals, very rashly sometimes but with the best of intentions, wandering off to Yugoslavia, for example. It seems to me that a distinction might be drawn between a war situation as in Yugoslavia and a disaster situation as in Bangladesh. I think the huge wagons that one sees along that road into Sarajevo (and I was there just before Christmas) with "UN" on them gives an authority that somebody with his old wagon, where he has come from England or Germany or wherever, would not have. In my opinion, that is an essential distinction. The Red Cross perhaps also carries that authority with their well known, internationally recognised insignia, but otherwise where the NGOs may only be co-ordinating, would you agree, that it is really in a situation such as Bangladesh, or where there is some natural disaster?

(Baroness Chalker) I think, Mr Chairman, that NGOs need to be co-ordinated, particularly in a war zone, by the UN if they are there. The best solution to people who want to help in a war zone where the UN are established is to approach the UN for what is needed and to deliver it to UN warehouses, and for it then to go out on the convoys, as Mr Wareing described. In the situation of a natural diaster, such as the cyclone in Bangladesh, it frankly would not have been helpful because of the level of the water, the sheer danger of the work that was being done, to have anybody other than those who were extremely tightly organised. The Bangladesh Red Crescent—backed up by the British Red Cross and other elements of the Red Cross, Save the Children, I believe, and Oxfam who were also there at the time—were also substantially backed by troops from this country, Australia and, indeed, the Bangladeshi's own army. Whilst we may be critical that they do not do things quite as we would suggest they do, you must never deny in a country which has a natural disaster the involvement of its own people to solve its problems. They may need help and then you have to work alongside them. That requires NGOs to have a good relationship with the government of that country. That does not always exist. It is a further complication for the NGOs. They are working (particularly Britain's leading NGOs) their relationships up extremely well. We do our best to help them. For instance, we provided from ODA resources an NGO co-ordinator in Bangladesh because we had repeated crises of different sorts, and it seemed sensible for them to have a channel through the British High Commission to the Bangladesh government in order to make the best of resources that we had.

Mr Jopling

338. I did go to the United Nations last week and I found a major frustration on two grounds. First of all, let us take the example of Yugoslavia. Nobody is willing to go in and make the peace, quite understandably. Yet a major frustration is the pathetic way in which United Nations embargoes and sanctions have been applied (and I am using Yugoslavia as an example), and the time I was there there were stories of barges swarming up the Danube and taking no notice of those people who invited them to stop. I came across a number of people who were saying, "What we must do is to enforce sanctions and embargoes very much better", and it is much easier to get people to send

[**Mr Jopling** *Contd*]
peacekeeping troops into surrounding countries to enforce this. I happen to be strongly in favour of enforcing sanctions infinitely better when they are applied but, of course, if you do that you do then increase very much the need for humanitarian aid both in the country concerned and in the surrounding countries, if you are stopping transshipments for instance. Has your Department thought about what might be the impact of the United Nations making sanctions and embargoes much, much more effective, especially concerned with the consequent problems of humanitarian aid which undoubtedly would come from that very worthy objective?

(Baroness Chalker) Mr Chairman, we have indeed thought about it very considerably. The Foreign Secretary himself has been discussing this with our European Community colleagues and East European countries concerned. I hope too that we will have some further positive suggestions to make to those countries who will suffer the depravations, because I can assure the Committee that we do intend to enforce still better the sanctions which have already been passed by the Security Council resolutions. I think I can only say that the depravations of a full-scale war, which would be the outcome if the hostilities did not cease, will be far worse than the depravations which will be caused by the enforcement of sanctions, which are there to deter any further expansionism on the part of any party in the area.

Chairman

339. You would apply a different standard in Iraq, would you not, from, say, Bosnia; because in Iraq the government there is demanding humanitarian help while pursuing an inhumanitarian policy?

(Baroness Chalker) Under Resolution 706 and 712, if Iraq were to comply with those, they would have no problem about getting their resources. We already make sure that help does go in, but it is in the hands of Saddam Hussein and the government of Iraq whether they have the resources and by whether they are going to follow Security Council Resolution 706 and 712. In surrounding countries, such as Jordan, Egypt and Syria, who were very severely affected at the time of the invasion and then the subsequent evacuation of Kuwait because of the United Nations sanctions, of course many donors did give resources to the governments of Jordan, Egypt and Syria to make up for the situation. But that compensation issue is a very difficult one and can be a very expensive one and we certainly would not be agreeing to do it automatically.

Chairman: Could we have a few more questions about the African operation? Mr Lester.

Mr Lester

340. As you know, Minister, what we are anxious to look at in this Committee is the effective operation of the United Nations and the Agenda for Peace. I wonder if you could say whether lessons have been learned about future United Nations operations from the United Nations peacekeeping and humanitarian intervention in Angola, for instance, where disarmament did not proceed and, therefore, the thing has fallen down; in Mozambique where many of us are concerned at the long delay in actually implementing the United Nations Resolution and are hoping that nothing breaks down there.

(Baroness Chalker) Mr Chairman, Mr Lester is absolutely right. I think we have learned an awful lot from the very sad and dangerous situation which exists in Angola still today. It was UNIVEN, the United Nations force, which created the environment for a fairly conducted election in Angola. Among the United Nations observers, British Members of your House, Mr Chairman, acted as United Nations observers there. The problem is that Unita has not respected the result of the election. So with hindsight we are all very quick now to say we should have done more to verify the demobilisation of the soldiers before the election, but at the time, remembering we still had the aftermath of Iraq on our hands, we had many problems in other parts of the world and it was not considered necessary that we should have a much larger verification of that demobilisation. We took a very pragmatic approach on the question of aid and we provided help, and the money that we provided at that time was generally well spent. There is no doubt that we could do better in providing aid in Angola but, learning from that, although it is early days for Mozambique, there will be a determination by the United Nations to demobilise the soldiers quickly, certainly before the elections. Britain has offered to train the new Mozambique Army. We hope that both sides will accept our offer. We also need to learn lessons from other places like Cambodia. I think Mr Lester will know Mr Ajello, the United Nations Special Representative in Mozambique, and Mr Bernarder, the head of UNOHAC in Mozambique, who have both worked in Cambodia so that they have direct experience. But dare I say—it is tempting fate perhaps, Mr Chairman—I have a little more hope for Mozambique than I ever had for Angola. We have to make it work. It is not a question of having hope, we are going to make it work.

341. That brings me on to the next question. You referred earlier to the American military presence in Somalia and spoke of it as being something rather worthwhile. Do you see that as a new chapter in international affairs and does that have any implications in terms of humanitarian relief operations?

(Baroness Chalker) Inevitably in a period when we have begun to go uninvited into countries as the United Nations or as part of the United Nations there are implications. I think that the Security Council is going to be extremely careful and will seek to work through Chapter 7 resolutions by persuasion. It will seek this only where

[**Mr Lester** *Contd*]

there is clearly, as in Somalia, no form of government—total anarchy and breakdown. There is not total anarchy and breakdown in Mozambique. There are some pretty horrible places but there is not total breakdown; there is a government, it is trying its best and succeeding in some places. What was done in the green areas around Maputo was quite dramatic, even while the war was going on. In other countries you have some local government working very well and I think where there is a semblance of government the United Nations needs to take great care about going in uninvited. Where there is no government, the only way to protect lives is going to be something like the operation which we have carried out over the last nine months.

Chairman

342. Would it have helped the relief operation if we had sent British troops to Somalia with the Americans—if we had had the troops, which we did not?

(Baroness Chalker) It never entered our heads because we knew we had not got the troops to send. I think in some complicated situations like Somalia it is very important to have a unified force. One of the difficulties the United Nations often comes across is trying to get people of different languages and totally different backgrounds to work together in what is a pressurised situation anyway. One only has to look at the difficulties of Sarajevo to know that, in skyscraper-tall letters is the way I think I would describe it. So, yes, of course, we could have helped in one sense but we were already helping—more than £40 million last year alone direct to Somalia, our own NGOs and our back-up. I think Somalia has had, in fact, more than enough offers of troops. It has had troops offered by many countries. The Australians are shortly to go there—indeed, some are already there to protect us this weekend. We cannot be a world policeman. We can do our best to work with the other nations to bring about peace and to keep the peace, but we cannot do it all ourselves and we should not think we can. We may get a lot of praise for what we do—that is good. We should be doing the best job we can but we should not expect to go everywhere.

Mr Rowlands

343. Going back to Mozambique, Minister, I have had longstanding contacts and connections with Mozambique, particularly through Bishop Dinis. When I met him recently I asked him the simple question "What should the international community be doing to contribute towards stabilising and developing peace?" He came up with an extraordinary suggestion, which shook me I must say. The most important thing he said was needed was to gather guns in and gather them in as rapidly as possible and he reckoned that one of the thrusts of the international aid programme, including ours, should actually be—this is the extraordinary suggestion—to buy in the guns in large quantities, destroy them and offer in return seeds, and money for seeds and development. It seemed to me a bizarre idea to spend money buying in arms, but I just wondered if it was not one of these remarkable oddball suggestions which is actually right in the situation we face in Mozambique?

(Baroness Chalker) It has been suggested, Mr Chairman, that those who hand in their arms of destruction should get food. That is fine if you can stop the supply of guns in as well. It is not enough just to buy up those that are already there; it is those that are on the way there as well—which goes back to the earlier point Mr Rowlands made. Of course, to have an effective ceasefire and lasting peace, one wants the proper control of guns and of other ammunition too. One of the first things that frequently we do—and we did not get far enough with it in Angola sadly but we are trying in Cambodia and Afghanistan through specialised agencies, private firms and so on—is de-mining because you cannot actually deliver food and humanitarian aid to many of these countries in a post-war situation until you have got the mines deactivated. That is another element too.

344. To answer my question, are we going to try something along these lines so that a lot of people will not be storing away caches of arms which will be useful in the next conflict?

(Baroness Chalker) I am very much in favour of the United Nations collecting in arms: whether it collects in arms for food or collects in arms per se would depend on the exact mandate given to those going there.

Mr Rowlands: But you will support it.

Mr Lester

345. That is paralleled in many countries. Precisely the same situation applies in Ethiopia. When we met the Foreign Minister this week he said there were too many arms in Ethiopia, too many young people carrying rifles and there was a need to get them collected. I want to ask if there is any parallel with the United Nations operation in Cambodia and if what is happening there could happen in Somalia. Perhaps quite fundamentally, how do you think the United Nations can best contribute to sustainable democratic government in Africa? We pioneered the know-how funds in dealing with Central and Eastern Europe. Would you suggest the United Nations might pioneer know-how funds on a similar basis, using the international community to assist in providing the sort of basic know-how on how to organise a state which has completely deteriorated—local government, fire, police, the things that are really important to local people?

(Baroness Chalker) There is no doubt, Mr Chairman, that our technical assistance, technical co-operation programmes in many of these countries, which are the developing country equivalent of the emergent country know-how funds, can be deployed in the way that Mr Lester has just suggested. I think that one of the most fundamental

[**Mr Lester** *Contd*]

needs to establish a sound government is going to be institution building in a country. It is also going to be straight forward teaching of how to run a civil service even. We already do a lot of that through the aid and through the head of mission schemes too. The United Nations Development Agency, UNDP, have a role here, there is no doubt about it, but they frequently will sub-contract to experts from individual member countries to do the work on the ground. It is capacity building above all that is needed. If I have a concern about Cambodia it is that, unfortunately, I do not think we have been able to do anything like sufficient capacity building in Cambodia. Even elections are no guarantee, as we saw in Angola, of peace continuing. Coming back to Mr Rowlands' question, that is why collecting in arms is not enough, even stopping the supply of new arms is not enough. The destruction of arms is also necessary, otherwise you get people simply grabbing back the arms, as happened the other day in Serbia. If I might turn to Somalia, which is the other part of Mr Lester's question, the Secretary General has made it absolutely clear that the Somalians must determine how they are going to govern themselves, but the UN will help to reinstate the structures and it can use a number of different agencies to do that, and we are already looking at how we might help them there. Of course, a precursor to doing that in Somalia will be the disarmament of Somalis. It is being discussed with the United States by the UN at the moment. There is no doubt that the US carried out a lot of successful disarmament operations, but the Somali factions have now agreed to consider the disarming of the heavy weaponry, and that is the first stage. The light weapons can be just as much killers and also need to be dealt with.

Chairman: Some more questions now on the former Yugoslavia. Mr Rowlands?

Mr Rowlands

346. Minister, the British Red Cross made some pretty tart comments on the degree of co-ordination that was taking place, particularly between the EC and the UN. If I could just read from the evidence of the organisation, they say, "In fact, there appears to be an urgent need for the UN and EC to clear their lines. Rivalries between the two have been damaging in former Yugoslavia, and with the EC Humanitarian Office (ECHO) and the UN Department of Humanitarian Affairs each newly established and seeking a role, this competition and confusion can only be detrimental to the future of victims [and the aid effort]". From your experience and from your Department's observations is that a justifiable comment on the state of play?

(Baroness Chalker) Certainly it was in October last year, Mr Chairman. When I went out to Zagreb, Split and Mostar on 1st October I was really worried at what I found there, because there was no way in which the EC in any form should, in my opinion, be trying to set up a parallel organisation with UNHCR; and yet I was actually told that baldly in a briefing in Zagreb by an EC representative. It was at that moment that I referred my anxieties to the Foreign Secretary and, indeed, the Foreign Affairs Council the following Monday in Luxembourg, and out of that came the decision to set up the European Community Task Force specially tasked to work with the UNHCR in the former Yugoslavia. It has been fortunate that a man who served us extremely well on a contract basis in northern Iraq, Dr Gilbert Greenall, gained the main position in the EC Task Force, and he has improved things greatly; but it was sad to me that there was such a demand for visibility that some members of the European Community considered having a parallel operational arm in very difficult territory. Let it not be misunderstood, the job that the EC monitoring mission has done in the former Yugoslavia has been outstanding. That was a very different, separate and not a copy example. When one goes around the warehousing which our convoys are using now, all the EC aid is very clearly labelled, and that is right, nobody disagreed with that; but there certainly should never have been, in my view, an indication that they intended to set up a parallel organisation. We did manage, in fact, to prevent that happening and wasting resources.

347. The Task Force is now working under the auspices of the UN operation?

(Baroness Chalker) Working very much with. They all rely on one another, and there is a very good team spirit working out of Zagreb now with this. I give great credit to Gilbert Greenall for the way in which he has brought the situation round. It does not mean there is not a tension there, there is a tension still.

348. Is it based on a different perception of what the problems are or what the solutions are, or just rivalry of two competing organisations?

(Baroness Chalker) Not rivalry of two competing organisations. The UNHCR have got so much to do they are not out to compete with anybody, they are out there to get on with the job. Mrs Ogata has made it absolutely clear that she wants the job well done, and they should. I have some anxieties partly because the EC Humanitarian Office has not been linked into DGI or DGVIII. It has been reporting directly to a commissioner, which means that you then do not get for future exercises, where the EC is involved, the natural progression from giving the humanitarian relief on to rehabilitation, which is so utterly critical in a country; and, therefore, it is very important that in the future the ECHO office in the EC is to work with the development aspects of the EC development assistance. That is quite separate, of course, from the giving of EC food aid, which has been well done. The division within DGVIII, headed by Anton Reitzinger who is in charge of the delivery of food aid, is exceptionally well done. Mr Rowlands put his finger on what was a problem

[**Mr Rowlands** *Contd*]

which we have overcome to a certain extent, but which we still need to work at.

349. We have committed about 70.5m of our UK aid programme to the former Yugoslavia, 23.6m we are told is provided to the UN operation side. How much has been given to the EC programmes, is that a separate allocation?

(Baroness Chalker) Yes, it is indeed a separate allocation, and I think it is £40m.

Chairman: Some final questions on two aspects, first co-ordination with the military, Sir John Stanley, and then something on the Kurds.

Sir John Stanley

350. Minister, you have referred to working with the Ministry of Defence and that obviously is likely to feature not merely in the current operation as in the former Yugoslavia but in future operations. I certainly found, when I had some responsibility, that we worked extremely well with the Foreign Office, and I had a very good relationship with your predecessor on a number of emergencies in the mid 80s. Undoubtedly at that time the PESC arrangements to cover the situations were highly unsatisfactory to both departments. I wondered whether you could tell us now whether you feel satisfied that the public expenditure cover as between the two departments has now been satisfactorily resolved and is not inhibiting either department in taking part in these humanitarian operations?

(Baroness Chalker) Mr Chairman, we value very greatly the support and the collective working that we have with the troops in the field. The military have a vital part to play in specific cases. There may be others where we should not be taking the military in, it should be NGOs or indeed the Red Cross—movements that we are using. The situation as between MoD and the Foreign Office, or specifically ODA, is that ODA pay any additional costs which MoD incur as a result or providing the humanitarian assistance. These would be extra direct costs which arise from diverting the military resources away from their primary defence tasks and which would not have been incurred had it not been for the humanitarian relief work. So additional costs do not usually include pay which would have occurred in any event or, indeed, those things which are already taken account of in the Defence Programme. We reviewed the standing agreement in 1991. We have no plans to change it. I think, however, that we should never lose sight of the very valuable training capacity which these exercises frequently give. This is something which commanders on the ground will always mention to any visiting member of either House because they feel it is so good for soldiers (who might otherwise be sitting in Germany doing valuable tasks, but nevertheless in Germany) actually to see how difficult it is to put into practice some of the things they are familiar with in better situations. So maybe we have not got it quite right yet but we keep it under review.

351. I am very familiar with the training debate that goes on between the two Departments on this subject. Of course, I would certainly accept there is training value but the Ministry of Defence has its own training budget and, if sometimes there is a call for particularly expensive things like major relief flying operations, that can very, very rapidly result in substantially greater costs. Have there been any occasions recently when you have sought additional resources from the MoD and they have not been forthcoming, either because of shortage of the available manpower/womanpower skills or because of the unavailability of the necessary finance that would fall on them?

(Baroness Chalker) Certainly there is nothing that I have sought recently from the MoD in terms of working alongside the humanitarian aid that I have been refused. They may have come up with suggestions of how we might better do the job and they have been very valuable and we welcome that very much; but on the whole I do not think there has. There are times when we make enormous demands on MoD and I am quite sure they are not very fond of us for our demands for their logisticians at the moment, but they have given them willingly and replaced them where people have to move on. We are finding it a very valuable example of Government co-operation.

352. Is it not a matter of some regret to you as Overseas Aid Minister that the British involvement with military assets in Somalia has been effectively negligible?

(Baroness Chalker) I think, as I said earlier, there are plenty of offers to the united Nations of troops for Somalia. Our troops may in this case have been better deployed as they have in the former Yugoslavia and, indeed, in other places. Let it never be forgotten that we have British troops serving in a whole range of countries, as I think the Foreign Secretary said to you just last week, and as he certainly said in his speech on the new world disorder. Just because we are not in one country with the military does not mean that the operation being done there is not good. I have to be realistic. We cannot police the whole wide world. If the Americans were willing to go in with such large resources as they have, it was better to let them do that under a unified command. I still have great anxiety about the command, communication and control—I say it C3, not C2 as the Army say, because communications are absolutely vital in places where you draw many people from many different nations.

Chairman: We are in extra time. A final question from Mr Gapes.

Mr Gapes

353. Last week the Foreign Secretary told us that the British Government had given £56 million to the peoples of Iraq since April 1991, which I work out as 50 pence per person per year for our population. Does that mean the whole of the peoples of Iraq and what proportion of that has gone

[**Mr Gapes** *Contd*]

to the Kurds? I am particularly concerned because I have seen the appeal launched by Oxfam a few months ago, the so-called Cold Front appeal about the impact of this harsh winter on areas of people forced into the mountains and I would be interested to know what plans you have to assist the Kurds. Related to that, because we are short of time I will put my second question at the same time: what is your attitude to suggestions that the sanctions on Iraq should be eased in order to make it more possible to get the assistance through, or are you going to try to find alternative ways to get the assistance through to the Kurds than going through Baghdad which I understand is done by some of the NGOs?

(Baroness Chalker) First of all, Mr Chairman, I am afraid I do not have the detailed figures but most of the assistance went to the Kurds, some went to the Shia, and we have sought to give as much assistance as we can get through. I must give due credit to the work that Emma Nicholson has done to get help through to the Shia in the south. Her support through the NGOs has been absolutely fundamental. I can certainly say that in trying to help in Iraq we have of course used many of the routes in through Turkey but have worked, as the NGOs have, alongside the United Nations at all times and, in fact, that UN/NGO co-operation has been quite a good one. When you talk about the lifting of sanctions, there indeed is no need, as I said in answer to an earlier question. If the Iraqi Government would abide by Resolutions 706 and 712 the resources would be in Iraq for the purchase of the goods that are needed.

Chairman

354. I said a final question—I am going to use the Chairman's prerogative for one final question which will be unanswerable, but what sort of operations do you see coming up next which are going to drag your Department and the MoD into the kind of activities we now find in former Yugoslavia which three years ago we would never have dreamed we would be involved in? Can you look a little into the future at world trouble spots—Central Asia?—and tell us for what problems you are preparing?

(Baroness Chalker) It is quite difficult to prepare for. As to the Central Asian Republics, of course, we are giving assistance to Nagorno Karabakh, assistance is already going internationally into Dushim Bay (?), and a lot of places I never knew existed on the map three years ago are now being dealt with by the United Nations, by the major aid donors and particularly again through the Red Cross and some other agencies. I think I was born an optimist, Mr Chairman. I cannot see any, but inevitably my job is to make sure that my Department, either along with the NGOs or in collaboration with the United Nations, and with the help very often of the MoD, is ready and that state of readiness is something I am confident we now have, which we did not have when Saddam Hussain invaded in August 1990. So we have come a long way, but I do believe we are going to see some quite severe difficulties—perhaps next winter in the former Soviet Republics.

Chairman: As you say, "be prepared" must be the motto and certainly you have explained to us how your Department is meeting these enormous challenges. We appreciate that very much indeed and are very grateful to you for helping us try to put together this jigsaw puzzle of issues related to the United Nations, its role and our role with you. Thank you very much.

Printed in the United Kingdom for HMSO.
Dd.0508726, 3/93, C6, 3398/3B, 5673, 233856.

HMSO publications are available from:

HMSO Publications Centre
(Mail, fax and telephone orders only)
PO Box 276, London, SW8 5DT
Telephone orders 071-873 9090
General enquiries 071-873 0011
(queuing system in operation for both numbers)
Fax orders 071-873 8200

HMSO Bookshops
49 High Holborn, London, WC1V 6HB
071-873 0011 Fax 071-873 8200 (counter service only)
258 Broad Street, Birmingham, B1 2HE
021-643 3740 Fax 021-643 6510
Southey House, 33 Wine Street, Bristol, BS1 2BQ
0272 264306 Fax 0272 294515
9-21 Princess Street, Manchester, M60 8AS
061-834 7201 Fax 061-833 0634
16 Arthur Street, Belfast, BT1 4GD
0232 238451 Fax 0232 235401
71 Lothian Road, Edinburgh, EH3 9AZ
031-228 4181 Fax 031-229 2734

HMSO's Accredited Agents
(see Yellow Pages)

and through good booksellers

HOUSE OF COMMONS SESSION 1992–93

FOREIGN AFFAIRS COMMITTEE

THE EXPANDING ROLE OF THE UNITED NATIONS AND ITS IMPLICATIONS FOR UK POLICY

MINUTES OF EVIDENCE

Wednesday 17 February 1993

Sir John Thomson, GCMG and Sir Crispin Tickell, GCMG, KCVO

Professor Rosalyn Higgins QC, Professor Alan James and Dr Paul Taylor

---

Ordered by The House of Commons *to be printed*
17 February 1993

LONDON: HMSO
£10.00 net

235–viii

WEDNESDAY 17 FEBRUARY 1993

Members present:

Mr David Howell, in the Chair

Mr Dennis Canavan	Mr Ted Rowlands
Mr David Harris	Mr Peter Shore
Mr Michael Jopling	Sir John Stanley
Mr Jim Lester	Mr Robert Wareing

Examination of witnesses

SIR JOHN THOMSON, GCMG, Former UK Permanent Representative to the UN; Chairman, Minority Rights Group International and SIR CRISPIN TICKELL, GCMG, KCVO, Former UK Permanent Representative to the UN; Warden, Green College, Oxford, examined.

Chairman

355. Sir John and Sir Crispin, could I begin by welcoming you here this morning and thanking you very much for sparing us your time and can I say how pleased we are as a Committee to be able to share some of your thoughts on the changing role of the United Nations and Britain's interest in these matters as part of our general inquiry. You are two very distinguished former Permanent Representatives of the United Nations. You both had the unenviable task of welcoming past members of this Committee to the United Nations and explaining to us some of the things that were going on when you were there and some of the developments that you saw lying ahead. So we have already had some preliminary thoughts and understanding of the way you see things but we would like now to explore with you the ever-changing and fast-changing scene which was given a push by Dr Boutros Boutros-Ghali's *Agenda for Peace* and see where these thoughts take us. Can I begin Sir John with you but incidentally I hope that both of you will come in as you wish without talking together because that makes it impossible for the shorthand writers—but please speak as you wish in response to the questions we are going to try to pursue answers on. What are the primary factors mediating against the greater success of the UN in the spheres in which it is operating around the world. Are there so many logistically that it cannot get its physical resources on the ground, its relief workers or blue beret troops, in the right places at the right time or is there a fundamental absence of will? Would you like to expand on that question?

(Sir John Thomson) There are so many problems; some problems get one answer and some problems get another but if I have to make a broad answer to that particular question I would say the problems are primarily political. There are plenty of logistical problems and we may get to those later but in my view the biggest problem—and if I am straying beyond the remit of the Committee you will no doubt correct me—is that the UN has hardly begun to tackle the economic and social side. That is not to say they have not been discussed for a long time and I see that as part of the cause. If one is talking about preventative diplomacy, as the Secretary-General does in his *Agenda for Peace*, and as indeed I did when I was in the Security Council when I discussed it with my colleagues at length, I think you have to come back not just to a situation which has already arisen but to the causes of the situations that come before the Security Council. In many cases I think that comes back to economic and social problems. I think there are whole areas of the Charter, chapters 9 and 10 in particular, which are not recognised as they should be as being crucial areas of the Charter and which in my view have an important political dimension and therefore a security dimension.

356. Sir Crispin, would you see it that way?

(Sir Crispin Tickell) I am not sure that I would entirely. The economic and social side is a gap, although when I had to look at it I did not come to exactly the same conclusion that it was a gap that could easily be filled or that could necessarily be filled by the UN. One of the shortcomings of the economic side of the United Nations is that the slack has been taken up by other institutions because of its failings and I would not place reform as top priority. I think the essential difficulty in the United Nations is the gap between will and means. People frequently want the UN to do things. As the Secretary-General himself has said, the UN at the moment has too much credibility, but this is not matched by the means or the willingness to carry through the will of the international community. There I draw particular attention to the failure to pay subscriptions. The various Secretaries-General have had to spend their time looking for money rather than doing what the Security Council wants them to do.

357. I think the phrase Dr Boutros-Ghali used was there was a "crisis of over-credibility" and the general feeling we certainly experienced when we visited New York that the world, having shunned the United Nations, was suddenly wanting to dump all its problems on the UN, some of which

The cost of printing and publishing these Minutes of Evidence is estimated by HMSO at £5,754.

[**Chairman** *Contd*]

of a kind that would have been regarded as domestic policy in the past. We will come to that. How do either of you see this new mood and the tendency for the United Nations really to be extended or the expectations to be extended affecting our own foreign policy here in this country. Are there pitfalls there for us or are there advantages in being an active player in an expanding area of UN activity. Sir John?

(Sir John Thomson) I think there are undoubtedly advantages for the UK. First of all we have in various ways a privileged position at the UN and therefore we have a better opportunity than some others of getting our views accepted and acted upon. We are also strong believers in the UN and it is very important for us to make the UN as operationally effective as it can be. I put that cautiously because there really is a limit on what the UN can do at any given moment or in any given field. I think that is one of the big problems, the priority problem, the problem of saying, "It is a good thing to do this," but then somebody says, "Exactly, but this is applicable in 20 different places in the world simultaneously and how are we going to do it in 20 different places?" My own view is that that should not deter us from doing it when we can.

Mr Rowlands

358. I wanted to come back to the first question, the more fundamental one. I was re-reading the marvellous history of the Mediterranean by a historian called Braudel. He was describing how the Turkish and Ottoman Empires grew. He said one of the reasons why they were in the Balkans—this is the fourteenth and fifteenth centuries—was that the Serbs, Albanians and Bulgars were all divided and then there was a division between the Orthodox Church and the Catholics. That prompted me to ask the question, where are the limits? Are we going to find a basic limitation on the UN Security Council resolutions when you come up to long-standing 500 year old divisions and problems? In some ways history will teach us to be much more cautious in our belief that we can actually create mechanistic solutions to problems which are actually long-standing or is that is very pessimistic view of the world?

(Sir Crispin Tickell) I feel in some respects, Chairman, if I answer your second question I would provide some of the reply to the first: Britain as a small and vulnerable island, heavily dependent upon overseas trade has an interest in any form of international order. We had the Pax Britannica in the nineteenth century. We had the curious Pax Americana Sovietica in the second part of this century. We do not now have any form of power that can dominate and create international order. So if it is obvious that it is a prime British interest that there should be international order, international order can only be assured, as far as we can see it now, by using the apparatus of the UN. One of the theses I would like to advance to you, Mr Chairman, in fact is that in the Charter we have all the means to do this if we want to. Answering your specific point about the problems of ingrained civil war and disturbance and differences between peoples there are, as it were, in the world a number of geological faults. All of us can determine where they are. Some of them have very long histories. It is certainly very unlikely anybody will be able to impose solutions on problems. In many cases the task is to find a kind of *modus vivendi* which can be lived with although no-one would pretend it is perfect. We can all of us think of these situations. There are several of them in different parts of the world. There are the barriers of the old Holy Roman Empire and the Byzantine Empire, barriers of belief between those of Greek Orthodox persuasion and those of Catholic persuasion, and a great many other conflicts in what was the former Yugoslavia. I think the UN has got to look for a solution which is a *modus vivendi* rather than anything which can be described as permanent. I greatly admire Mr Braudel, who beautifully analysed such issues. At the same time I do not think he would have said there was any clear solutions to these as to many other problems. The UN is the facilitator of a *modus vivendi* here as elsewhere.

Mr Lester

359. Would you, in terms of your previous answer, give any difference in interpretation in terms of the role of the Secretary-General, of the Security Council and the Assembly as opposed to the various elements of the United Nations, the different bodies, UNDP, UNHCR, UNICEF, who can come in and out of popularity according to the personality of the person running it and sometimes of course get into very great trouble when they get huge problems of refugees, for instance, for the UNHCR? Would there be any shades of your views which compared the different elements of the UN, the Assembly, the Secretary-General and the Security Council?

(Sir Crispin Tickell) The Secretary-General clearly is the most important person in the United Nations and, therefore, he has in a sense a global responsibility. His relationship with the agencies is always a delicate one by nature of the constitutions which were given the agencies when the United Nations was first set up. He has not got the power to intervene and he has not got the power to bang heads together, although many of us sometimes wish that the Secretary-General had such power. Indeed I very much hope that in the future we shall have a Secretary-General who cannot just call the heads of the agencies together from time to time, but actually invite them to do things and check up on them when they do not do them. His position is the prime mover, and I would like to see his position strengthened vis-à-vis the heads of the agencies. You see also his responsibilities when it comes to peace-making where he again will tend to be the first person who will carry something forward to find a solution, often by covert means. He has not got to do so openly. We saw that in the case of the eventual release of the hostages from the Lebanon where he and his agents played a vital

[**Mr Lester** *Contd*]

role mostly out of the public eye. So the Secretary-General has got this prime responsibility. We should give him more power to his arm to carry it out.

(Sir John Thomson) I do not entirely agree that the Secretary-General and other parts of the UN do not have the power, if they choose to use it, to bang heads of the leading agencies together. This takes me back to my answer to your first question, Mr Chairman. The Charter does provide, first of all, for the Economic and Social Council to agree concordats with each of the agencies, which it has done, and these concordats are hardly observed at all. It also provides for the agencies to submit reports to the Economic and Social Council acting under the authority of the General Assembly. I will not go on, but if I refer you to chapters 9 and 10 of the Charter, there is very considerable power there if it were used, but it is not used. All that happened during my time in the UN was that the Secretary-General chaired the ACC about twice a year of the heads of the agencies and I attended it on a couple of occasions. It was perfectly pathetic and the Secretary-General barely had the power to propose what time they were going to meet in the afternoon, but there is power there and I believe it should be exercised. On the second point which Sir Crispin raised about the Security Council and the action in peace-keeping and in peace-making, I think it has to be an interaction between the Security Council itself and the Secretary-General. The Secretary-General, as Sir Crispin said, is the most important person at the UN, but in a sense he is also the servant of the UN and of the Charter bodies in the UN of which perhaps the Security Council is the most important, or certainly the most important in security matters. I think it has to be an interaction between the Secretary-General and the Security Council and he cannot do things on his own, he cannot take action on his own. He can propose, he can behind the scenes, as Sir Crispin said, have some useful discussion, but I doubt if he can very often solve something by himself.

Mr Harris

360. When we were in the United Nations just before Christmas I think most of us gained the impression that the present Secretary-General is genuinely trying to get a grip of this huge organisation and is probably being at least on the surface somewhat more effective than some of his predecessors and I think some of us sensed a change for the better. Is that your opinion or not, or is it too early to judge? How is he doing?

(Sir John Thomson) I am not close enough to answer that question with confidence, but I must say that having had a good deal to do with the agreement that was reached on the UN budget, which was really an agreement whereby the Americans undertook to pay, not that they have done properly, in exchange for improved budgetary procedures, I personally think that not nearly enough has happened.

(Sir Crispin Tickell) I think that the last Secretary-General has been undervalued. He was a man of rare talents and I think that he is not fully appreciated for all that he achieved because he went about his business by stealth. The advantage of the new Secretary-General is that he can make his own arrangements. He can wield a new broom. Dr Boutros Boutros-Ghali has done that very effectively. So I think it reasonable that a new man should make new arrangements. I do not think in fact that they should be regarded as disrespect for the old ones, but it is a great opportunity when you start on an organisation of this kind to bring in those new arrangements and carry them through. From what I have seen so far, and, like Sir John, I am distant from the event, he looks to have done rather well. When I saw him myself in London in January he was full of optimism and determined to tackle what are the deep-seated difficulties of running the United Nations, of which perhaps the biggest one of all, as I said earlier, is this constant problem over money.

Chairman: Well, we will come to that in a moment. Perhaps we could just at this stage focus on the mechanism at the heart of the expanding system of the Security Council.

Mr Wareing

361. It is 47, nearly 48, years in fact since the United Nations came into existence. The world has changed considerably and the balance of the world, even if the Cold War had continued, has changed with the rising power of countries, for example, in the Pacific rim and yet the structure remains the same. What is your view on the discussion which is taking place on the constitution of the Security Council? Should that any longer remain in its present form or should the permanent membership of the Security Council be expanded maybe to include certain other countries that have been referred to often in comments? Have you any views on that and if you do think the permanent membership should be expanded, would you like to suggest which countries qualify?

(Sir John Thomson) My view is that although the present composition of the Security Council is not perhaps what one would ideally choose if one were starting off today, it would be a mistake to try to change it just now. The procedures for changing it are complicated, and I can spell them out if you would like, but I expect you know them. I think that it would disrupt the United Nations' work in a large number of areas, not least the Security Council area, to attempt to change it. It would be certainly very controversial. It would put the Secretary-General, in my view, in a very difficult position. He would constantly be being asked whether he thought it ought to be changed or not to be changed. It is rather difficult for him to say he has no view on the matter, but I cannot see what else he could say in the circumstances. So although I do see that there may be certain anachronisms, I think that for the sake of making the UN operate at a rather critical time, not that every time is not critical, it would be a mistake to

[**Mr Wareing** *Contd*]

plunge into the question of reform of the Security Council in the sense of its composition. Reform of the way in which the Security Council operates in other ways is another matter, but I am just talking here about the composition of the Security Council and its weighted voting.

(Sir Crispin Tickell) I do not disagree with what Sir John has said. I think there is a curious and interesting paradox. When I went to New York following Sir John in 1987 there were the beginnings of a possibility that the Security Council might be able to work for the first time as those who signed the Charter hoped it would work. While I was there I saw that the Security Council did indeed begin to work. The five permanent members used to meet together in my apartment for tea and buns following a tradition established by Sir John. For almost two years I was the chairman of the permanent five members, and in the atmosphere of a private apartment we tackled or looked at some of the problems which those five permanent members had never been willing to look at before. So you have the five permanent members working together effectively for the first time since the forties, and you have at the same time the other members of the Security Council on the one hand rather glad that the permanent members were working together but on the other hand a bit worried lest they might work too well together. Supposing in this situation you say, "Now it is working, let us change it," you would be embarking on a hazardous course because if you have got something that works very effectively for the first time I think the temptation to leave it as it is and let it work a bit longer is very great. I would not be in favour of changing the arrangements in the Security Council. At the same time I do recognise, as do we all, that the present arrangement is in some respects anachronistic. If we began to embark on the cumbersome procedure, to which Sir John referred, to change the nature of the Security Council, then we would have to consider fairly radical changes. I do not think the suggestion that I think was made by Mr Warren Christopher that Japan and Germany should join could be sustained for one minute. Once you open up the possibility of other members becoming permanent members, you would have to bring in the possibility of India, Brazil and I do not know which others are in the queue. How you are going to choose and what are the criteria you are going to establish, whether it is wealth, population, territorial area? There is an enormous number of possibilities. You will certainly find great difficulty and for that reason although I think it would be wrong to exclude the subject from debate, I do not think we should change things for the next few years. Let us make something that works well continue to work.

362. I am rather pleased to hear there is the equivalent at the UN of beer and sandwiches at Number 10! That is rather reassuring. But you know the fact of the matter is that there are greater economic powers or new economic powers now on the horizon with Germany and Japan. There are substantial, and indeed Sir Crispin has mentioned one or two other countries that may lay claim. Given your argument that the Security Council composition should remain the same is there not therefore an argument that the veto power of permanent members should in fact go? Maybe that would be a way in order to, as it were, compensate those other large countries, some of which you mentioned, from non permanent membership.

(Sir John Thomson) My view is that the veto power should not be altered. I am quite confident that the veto was essential over the last 40 years to the maintenance first of the Soviet Union in the UN and secondly of the United States. Both powers would at one time or another have left the UN but for the veto. The veto is an essential part of what the founding fathers saw as the possibility of achieving collective security. We can elaborate on that but I think the point is fundamental and fairly obvious. So I would be strongly in favour of maintaining the veto. If I may just add on the point which is referred to, of Germany and Japan and other countries. I referred also to the procedures necessary. You have to get a two-thirds majority in the General Assembly. If you are going to change the Security Council and name new permanent members you are going to have to get two-thirds majority for those. I would think perhaps it is better for me not to speculate on which countries might or might not get a two-thirds majority but I think the thought of that has in fact rather muted some of the campaigns to change the Security Council.

(Sir Crispin Tickell) I concur with what Sir John has said. I think it is the veto power which has maintained the Security Council as a serious organisation since its beginning. If it were not for the veto power it would have turned into one of those organisations that passes majorities that people take less and less notice of and it would just be yet another talking shop. I regard the veto in history and today to be indispensable to the effectiveness of the Security Council.

Mr Jopling

363. It seems to me listening to you both on changing the number of permanent members of the Security Council that the edict of Lord Melbourne, "Why not leave it well alone?" lives and is alive and kicking. But let me put it the other way round. If this Committee were in the German or Japanese parliaments I guess that we would all have a fairly good head of steam on. How long do you think those countries in particular will tolerate a system whereby they are excluded from permanent membership? I am asking you to delve into your experience on that.

(Sir John Thomson) I feel that Germany and Japan in particular have in practice achieved something rather like semi-permanent membership. I am afraid I am not up on the most recent statistics but when I left the UN I think that each of them had succeeded in getting themselves elected to the

[**Mr Jopling** *Contd*]

Security Council eight times. Given that both of them were ex-enemy powers and could not start getting elected until well into the fifties, it seems to me that they have roughly succeeded in getting themselves elected every other time. So they are on the Council very frequently. True, they are not permanent members but they have served on the Council far more often than any other countries. So I do not think that it is the case that Germany and Japan have somehow been excluded from the Security Council. What they are excluded from at present is permanent membership with the veto. I think that the veto, as Sir Crispin and I have said, is crucial but at the same time I do not particularly welcome the thought of increasing the number of veto powers.

(Sir Crispin Tickell) Yes, I agree. There is another point which needs to be made. Being a permanent member of the Security Council gives us a privileged position in New York and status that we would not otherwise have. But it is not all fun. The permanent members of the Security Council have to take up positions on almost anything that may arise in the international arena. From my experience of Japan and Germany—and I speak with three years' worth of watching them at play—they did not really want to take up positions if they thought it was going to make them unpopular. Being a permanent member cuts both ways. The permanent member has to accept it is going to be unpopular from time to time; it has to take hard decisions; above all it has to take up positions. You cannot sit back and let something happen. You have to vote one way or the other. Britain and France, although of course junior members of the grouping of five permanent members, do have interests world wide, and both of them are willing to stand up and if necessary cast a veto or at least take up positions. From my experience of the Security Council, the permanent members who do it best are those that behave like permanent members. Frankly the Germans and Japanese have not so far done so.

Mr Shore

364. Is there not an additional point too that inevitably some part of the United Nations Security Council's role deals with the enforcement of United Nations decisions and ultimately the use of force. Are Japan and Germany not still self-disqualified by their own constitutional arrangements from making any such contributions?

(Sir Crispin Tickell) I think that is an important point. But I add that until very recently there was a kind of self-denying ordinance on the part of the permanent members not to get engaged in peace-keeping operations. That has now changed. We have British troops in several parts of the world, French troops likewise and the Americans the same, but that is a new development. It did not happen before. What Mr Shore has said is a very good point. I think it is very relevant to the future.

(Sir John Thomson) Mr Chairman, might I say one more thing in response to Mr Jopling's question about how we might feel if we were sitting in Bonn or Tokyo? I think it is important to look at international machinery as a whole at the top level. The Security Council, important though it is, is not the only major piece of international machinery. I would refer, for example, to the Group of 7, which includes both Germany and Japan, and very rightly so, and, as we are very often told that the particular reasons for Germany and Japan joining the Security Council are because of their economic strength, I think that that is reflected in the Group of 7. I would like to see it reflected, as I have already indicated twice, in more activity on the economic and social side, but I would reiterate that I think the composition of the Security Council should be left as it is.

Sir John Stanley

365. Sir John, before we leave the Security Council, you said in your first answer to Mr Wareing that leaving the membership issue aside, there were other methods of working in the Security Council which you felt should be improved. Could you be more specific on that to the Committee?

(Sir John Thomson) The most important thing probably has happened already and that is what Sir Crispin was referring to the informal get-togethers of the five permanent members, but I think that there are a great many other areas in which the Security Council—I speak from personal experience which is now ten years old—could operate more effectively, especially given that the Cold War is over. I mean primarily that it could discuss, much more than it has ever done in my experience, problematic situations, in other words, discuss the way things are going and whether there is a case for some intervention (and I would like to say here that when I use the word "intervention" I do not automatically mean military intervention), whether there is a case for some intervention before a situation that very many people recognise is getting worse gets still worse. I do not think that the Security Council nearly often enough discusses things quietly without having a crisis on its agenda on which people are already divided into the reds and the blues.

(Sir Crispin Tickell) Chairman, before we leave the Security Council I wonder if I could just make two points. One is to Mr Wareing. It is often ignored that the non-aligned countries, if they get together, can exercise a sixth veto. The point that comes up quite often in the dealings of the Security Council is that the non-aligned group, which does operate as a group, can agree upon a course of action, and that in fact exercises a sixth veto. The five permanent members cannot push things through against the wishes of the non-aligned group because it can stop them in the same way as one of the five permanent members can stop something. The second point is that a lot of the best work of the Security Council is done behind closed doors. A good example of the sort of thing that Sir John found lacking when he was a permanent representative was how the Security Council dealt with Namibia, a story which on the whole still

[Sir John Stanley *Contd*]

remains to be sung. The Namibia story is a success story. The Security Council used to meet behind closed doors to try and solve the problems of Namibia. There were many difficult moments, both from the South African side and from the side of SWAPO which, you recall, was an independence movement. But we kept going, often behind closed doors and the result was that elections took place in fair circumstances, watched over by the United Nations. We now have a new independent country, ushered into existence by the Security Council acting in the sense of which Sir John was speaking.

Mr Wareing

366. I think Sir Crispin has to a large extent answered my question, but I was concerned about the fears expressed by some small and medium-sized states that they are excluded from decision-making. I think you to a large extent answered that in reference to the non-aligned movement, but I would suggest to you that even among the non-aligned countries differences of view, differences of policy and even conflict between them occur from time to time. Do you think that these fears of the small and medium-sized states are justified?

(Sir Crispin Tickell) I can only say yes, sir, to your question. It does happen. I remember that in the case of Namibia the non-aligned countries would frequently ask for an adjournment of the debate behind closed doors. They would then go out and talk to the African countries concerned. They would come back, talk among themselves and then come back to us. So there was a constant to-ing and fro-ing between the non-aligned members of the Security Council on an essentially African problem and the Africans, and then between the non-aligned countries and the permanent members. The way in which things are done may not be ideal but it works. Many of the things which are said about the Security Council about its failure to take account of things do not really stand up when you look at those things which the Security Council has successfully done. My final point is that it is very hard to invent any institution with more than 15 members which works very well. Maybe you can go up to 20, but the experience of Prime Ministers in Britain of creating Cabinets which get too big shows very well that there is a golden number and I would argue that. In many ways 15 is the golden number, and certainly I think gold can turn to tin when you go over 20 and who knows what when you go over 25.

Chairman

367. Given all the minuses as well as the pluses of permanent membership, where do either of you think the pressure is coming from, if anywhere, or is this all thought up by the media? Why did the American Secretary of State raise the issue the other day even though he went on to point out how difficult it was? Who is making the pace on this?

(Sir Crispin Tickell) The Germans and the Japanese. The Germans went very quiet on the issue when I was in New York, whereas the Japanese continued. It comes and goes and I think one or two of the bigger countries, for example, Brazil, felt that it too should be a permanent member. Indeed the Brazilian permanent representative at the time said so in terms. I had to remind him that most of the Spanish-speaking countries of Latin America might not be too happy. You can say the same when you look at the Indian sub-continent, where there is no question that India would like to be a permanent member, but then you would have to ask the Pakistanis, the Bangladeshis, the Sri Lankans and others whether they would like it to happen. So every way you go when you try to think of a different composition you run into big difficulties.

Chairman: Now, could we turn to preventative diplomacy which was mentioned a moment ago?

Sir John Stanley

368. A number of the Members of the Committee were in Macedonia last week and we saw there the first ever military deployment by the United Nations in advance of a conflict situation arising. I would like to ask you whether you see those sorts of deployments becoming much more extensive and do you believe that would be desirable if that occurred and if there is going to be a much wider role for the United Nations in preventative diplomacy, as you have both, I think, indicated may well happen, what changes do you think will be necessary within the United Nations structure to enable preventative diplomacy to be really effective?

(Sir John Thomson) You know more about Macedonia than I do, so my comment would be a general comment rather than a particular one in relation to Macedonia. I think preventative diplomacy should go back to root causes. In other words, I think we should not look at preventative diplomacy as only something that flowers when UN troops are sent off to, for example, Macedonia. I think that you would have to judge each situation upon its merits. There are very great problems about UN troops being sent to difficult parts of the world. One of these problems is the one I have already alluded to, which is if to Somalia, why not to Sudan, et cetera. Another is the terms under which they are sent and the terms of engagement, as you might call it. I think that the Secretary-General's idea of enforcement—I have forgotten the precise phrase—which he has now reformulated as peace-keeping enforcement is an interesting one. That is to say, if I understand the idea correctly, that if a cease-fire is achieved in Bosnia or wherever it may be, and then is persistently broken, which has happened on a great many occasions, that there should then be a new extension of the peace-keeping idea which would involve UN forces properly armed actually fighting, again he says, in an impartial way. This will be extremely difficult for the local commander to carry out, I think, but still one sees what he means

[Sir John Stanley *Contd]*

and I personally have felt the need for this in a great many situations. I was in Bosnia myself. I led a CSCE mission there in the summer and I did feel and have felt that since then the authority of the UN has slipped and slipped because there has been no expectation that its word will be enforced.

(Sir Crispin Tickell) I too must answer the question generally but I want, if I may, to refer to an area which the Chairman may wish to move on to later which is the question of how the United Nations best operates in using force.

Chairman

369. Yes, we will come to that.

(Sir Crispin Tickell) I will hold my fire because Sir John has made the point sufficiently. It is very interesting how the United Nations can do different things, peace-keeping, peace-enforcing, war-making, but all these things require rather different solutions. I agree with Sir John that one of the problems about the situation in Yugoslavia is really that the mandate is not very clear and many of the complaints that have been made arise from the lack of clarity in the mandate. But I will hold my views on this central subject until later.

Mr Wareing

370. There is of course a big difference, is there not Sir John, between the situation in Macedonia, that Sir John Stanley mentioned, and the problem in Bosnia. Is it not really then a matter of considering whether the United Nations looking at a possible conflict that may or may not arise, has the support or certainly not the hostility of any of the factions within a country. For example, in Macedonia I do not believe any opposition has been expressed to the United Nations' presence whereas it certainly would be if it was for any more than humanitarian purposes in Bosnia but had the United Nations gone into Bosnia Herzegovina before there had been a referendum and when the three sides, as it were, were still talking to one another in an almost civilised fashion then it may well have been possible and that would have prevented the dreadful things that have been happening over the last year in that part of the world. Is it not a matter of the UN using political sagacity in each particular case?

(Sir John Thomson) Yes, Mr Wareing I agree with you. Had the United Nations taken action around the time of the referendum we might not have seen the terrible things that have happened in Bosnia. On Macedonia I must just observe though that although my understanding is not very deep the real snag is that the great trouble that may arise in Macedonia may be sparked off in Kosovo.

Mr Jopling

371. Is there not a stage of preventive diplomacy which comes before peace-keeping or even peace-making which we have not discussed and that is the imposition of sanctions and trade embargoes and Yugoslavia is one example where the United Nations was happy to put on trade sanctions. It did it in Iraq but we know that the way these sanctions have been enforced has been wholly pathetic with tankers going up the Adriatic and barges up the Danube, planes coming in with embargo-busting material for the Muslims. Is there not a major opportunity for the United Nations to enforce sanctions infinitely better? For instance, might one not say that the moment that sanctions are applied it goes without saying that UN resources with teeth should be deployed in the surrounding countries, not in the country you are complaining about, but to monitor the enforcements and with the ability partly to enforce those sanctions themselves. Now it is much easier to do that than actually get involved with peace-making. The more effective you have been in enforcement sanctions then at the later stages, if it comes to that the job of peace-keeping is that much easier because you have enforced sanctions that much better. Of course, you will never enforce sanctions totally, nobody expects that, but compare that for instance to what has happened in Yugoslavia with regard to sanction-busting and with regard to what is really going on with Iraq over sanction-busting. Is there not a huge opportunity here to enforce sanctions much much better and therefore make peace-keeping and peace-making less likely to be necessary?

(Sir Crispin Tickell) Perhaps I can respond, Chairman, by saying there is a gradation of measures that the United Nations can take against an offending state. The first is private diplomacy in which you try by one means or another to persuade the government concerned to desist from a course of action. You then go through the process and say, "What pressures can I put?" and under article 41 of the Charter sanctions comes first after, let us say, the peace-making has failed. I think peace-making is the first thing you can do usually as privately as you can make it. When that has not succeeded you then have to consider what sanctions to impose. Imposing sanctions is quite a costly business. First it affects states around the offending state, and, secondly, it is rarely effective. In the case of Iraq sanctions had more of a chance of being successful than perhaps in other cases in which sanctions have been imposed because Iraq is heavily dependent on one export and also could be geographically corralled. Of course the main problem at that time was Jordan. Jordan claimed compensation under Article 50 in the Charter, which says that member states that are suffering particularly should be compensated. So sanctions is the second stage. When sanctions do not work you then proceed to more forceful measures. If you were to enforce sanctions you would face exactly the problem we faced on 25 August 1990 when it had become quite clear that Iraq was ignoring sanctions and that ships were getting to and fro. The first decision of the Security Council that night was indeed whether we could enforce sanctions. The passage of that resolution on the 25 August 1990 led to the later resolutions where the military operations of the coalition were authorised. This gradation of measures against a state is

[**Mr Jopling** *Contd*]

very difficult. Each stage has to be carefully considered as to whether it is going to be effective or not. I believe that sanctions are very rarely effective except over a long period of time. If they are effective, as in the case of Iraq, it is only because of Iraq's particular vulnerability to economic pressure from outside.

Mr Rowlands

372. Sir John, we are talking about general principles but you did actually say to us a minute ago if the United Nations had acted earlier the Bosnian situation would not have occurred as dramatically or tragically as it has. Are you suggesting they should have shown a large troop presence much earlier to prevent the conflict separating parties? What would the UN have done?

(Sir John Thomson) Chairman, that might be a big subject but very briefly, my view is that there were various times in the past 11 months or so when the United Nations, acting in my view preferably through NATO as a regional organisation which had the means and the logistics to take action, could have secured Sarajevo and its environs. I think that would have been a crucial point in leading to a successful political negotiation which would not have put an end to all the problems but would have put an end to the fighting.

373. A major military input, you are submitting?

(Sir John Thomson) Yes, but I am not talking about some of the huge numbers that have been used. I am not a military man and I would not want to say exactly what the numbers are, but I think some of the numbers that I have heard are enormously inflated and relate to virtually taking over the country which I regard as not possible.

Chairman: Perhaps we could now pass on to the mechanisms of the UN itself, and in particular whether it can be effective in these military or pre-military roles.

Mr Lester

374. We have been hovering around this question of peace-enforcement. Sir Crispin talked about the Namibian success and of course we have tried to repeat the Namibian formula to some extent in Mozambique and in Angola and in Cambodia and yet increasingly we see that there is a power to frustrate the role of the United Nations by those who simply go along with signing agreements and then reject them, so when we talked to Lord Owen, who has had a great deal to do with Bosnia and former Yugoslavia, he was very clear in his mind that he would like to see some version of the Military Staff Committee of the UN revived. I wonder what you feel about the arguments for a revival of the Military Staff Committee in some form and, proceeding from that one, how does one ensure an effective military operation as a result of it? A great deal has to do with the single line of command, for instance. Is the ear-marking of troops, as suggested by *Agenda for Peace*, the way in which one could actually ensure that the UN does have the potential to ensure international resolutions of the Security Council are enforced?

(Sir Crispin Tickell) Perhaps, Mr Chairman, I could say a word or two about this. It is a subject which interests me a great deal. First, I agree with Lord Owen that more could and should be made of the Military Staff Committee. The Military Staff Committee, under Article 47 of the Charter, is the chiefs of staff of the five permanent members. They meet in full only once a quarter, and constitute an instrument which has never properly been used by the United Nations. Now when the Iraq conflict erupted, it was clear to me, and to others, that the Military Staff Committee might be brought into play. It ran up against the objections of those who were frightened lest the Russians and the Chinese, who are of course members of the Military Staff Committee, might be too interested in what one or other of the other countries might be doing. So there was a lot of suspicion. At the time of the Iraqi invasion in 1990 things were less evolved than they are now and the Soviet Union was still in existence and there was a lot of suspicion. So when my Soviet colleague and I suggested a meeting of the Military Staff Committee to look at these issues we were pretty well brushed aside. Instead we had a meeting of the five permanent representatives with military advisers. It was like the Military Staff Committee, but the commissars were in charge rather than the military. We later reversed the formula and had junior military sitting around the table with senior officials from the five permanent missions and they began to look at what the Military Staff Committee might conceivably do. All this came to nothing because certain permanent members did not want to play. But I believe that it is a route that we should follow in future circumstances. The reason why we were unable to take up the Soviet suggestion that there could be a UN Naval operation in the Gulf when Iraq and Iran were fighting each other and ships risked being interfered with on the way, was simply that the mechanisms for it did not exist. As you say the chain of command, presents special difficulties. Would the Security Council be five fingers on the trigger, or fifteen fingers on the safety catch? There was a whole lot of quite obvious major problems. The important point frequently missed is that Article 47(2) of the Charter says that other members of the United Nations can be invited to join the Military Staff Committee. So had we wished to follow that route, we could have resuscitated the Military Staff Committee, and brought in the chiefs of staff of the countries principally concerned, Egypt, Jordan, and the other members of the coalition. Although I do not think that in August 1990 anyone was ready for the chiefs of staff actually to run military operations, they could have been brought in as a kind of coordinating mechanism and they could have been there to exchange intelligence and look at military options. It was not done. I suspect that if the Iraq crisis were to re-erupt next year something like that might happen. The suspicion between the per-

[**Mr Lester** *Contd*]

manent members is much less. I would have preferred it to have taken place because then the whole of Operation Desert Storm would have had more of a blue flag wrapped around it than it did, and would have looked less like a Western military intervention in the affairs of the Middle East. So the option of reviving the Military Staff Committee with other countries co-opted as desirable, seems to me, and I am sure this is also the view of Lord Owen, something we should think about in the future. We should also think about the logistical problems of how chains of command would run. Every time a crisis erupts it is no good saying, "The machinery does not exist, we have not thought about it". We need to think about it when there is no crisis and we need to work out what would happen if such things should ever happen again. It is a route which we could follow in the future and in some respects I wish we had followed in the past.

375. As to military effectiveness, for instance, in Somalia, the United Nations troops were in Somalia and people still starved, so the effectiveness until the Americans went in with Operation Restore Hope was clearly not effective and it did not achieve its role. This is where the ability to have specially-trained troops, where they are under domestic command but have signed an agreement that they will operate in international situations, is one form and, therefore, indeed the next one is that the United Nations would have its own military force which is far more difficult to conceive.

(Sir Crispin Tickell) That, if I might say so, is a slightly different case. In the case of Iraq we were considering making war to repel aggression: in the case of Somalia we were pursuing humanitarian measures with all means which were necessary. What happened in Somalia, as happened in other peace making operations was an ad hoc arrangement through one of the Under Secretaries-General reporting to the Secretary-General himself. Such operations are not in fact in the Charter, so a kind of ad hoc arrangement has grown up by which operations are conducted by the United Nations in a slightly different and non-Charter way. What I was suggesting was that we should make this more formal and use the machinery laid down in the Charter rather than use these ad hoc arrangements which, as we know from General MacKenzie, do not always work very well.

(Sir John Thomson) I think Sir Crispin has made some interesting and important points, but I would myself be a bit more cautious about the Military Staff Committee. I have a prejudice in favour of anything which is in the Charter because I wish to preserve the authority of the Charter as a whole, but, nevertheless, the Military Staff Committee has never worked and that was of course primarily because of Cold War reasons. I am not, therefore, opposed to the Military Staff Committee doing something, but what? I think the more the Military Staff Committee exercises authority generally, the less control the Secretary-General will have over its peace-keeping operations. I believe that the peace-keeping mechanism that has grown up ad hoc, as Sir Crispin says, not foreseen in the Charter, has worked pretty well and I believe it would not work better if it were constantly being overseen by the Military Staff Committee and indeed I think there would be considerable problems about lines of authority here. That is not to say that there is not something for the Military Staff Committee to do. I believe that the Secretary-General has made two or three very important proposals in his *Agenda for Peace*, although not any of them new, but it is good that he made them publicly and brought them together. One is that a pool of money should be gathered so that action can be taken much more quickly. Another is that states should really be challenged to produce statements of men and equipment that they could make instantly available if required. A third is common training. Now all those are things which I think the Military Staff Committee might very usefully concern itself with. They have the clout of the five permanent members for certain purposes. You can easily co-opt Germany and Japan. There are things that I think the Military Staff Committee can do but I would not myself like to see it agreed that the Military Staff Committee was the supreme authority for the running of various peace-keeping missions or collective security.

376. What development can you see which will actually enable the four times convoy that has gone to try to relieve Sarajevo from this wicked system of medieval siege—what will actually take that forward? Can we sit back and expect these convoys to keep on going and trying and going and trying until the people starve and nothing will get through because Serbian regulars say it will not pass?

(Sir John Thomson) Mr Chairman, if it falls to me I would say that I think action should have been taken long ago and we are now in a much more difficult situation than we need be and I would commend the idea I have already referred to of the Secretary-General's peace-keeping enforcement. I do not wish to comment on the precise details of this particular situation in Bosnia.

Chairman

377. I think we have been looking at some of these details during the last week and they are not all that clear to us but, Sir Crispin, you wanted to come in on this?

(Sir Crispin Tickell) I wanted to make a further point about the Military Staff Committee. No-one wants to upset something that works in the operation of peace-keeping, but when we move out of the area of peace-keeping into peace-enforcement then I think it is important that the Military Staff Committee should play a role. So for the moment informally and ad hoc and unsatisfactory as it is, as a peace-keeping department it is rightly under the control of the Director-General through one of his under secretaries. It is when you get into the more difficult area of peace-enforcement that I

[Chairman *Contd*]

think it is necessary. Article 46 of the Charter which says, "Plans for the application of armed force should be made by the Security Council with the assistance of the Military Staff Committee." That seems to me to put it very well because it means the political control remains with the Security Council to take measures involving the use of armed force, but it is the Military Staff Committee giving assistance which will be the instrument for it. If we are going to do that then, as I have said before, we need to do a lot more on how it would actually work. The way to begin is not by giving the Military Staff Committee a specific military function but to use it as a coordinating body looking also at intelligence.

Mr Rowlands

378. I should like to ask a question on I think it is called the new "imperial" role. I think you have stated this in the context of both Cambodia and Somalia. In your collective experience do you think this is the shape of things to come in the United Nations role in circumstances of that kind? How do you think we are going to build on the experience of Cambodia and Somalia?

(Sir John Thomson) I would like to begin by saying I think there are a number of things we can do to prevent situations getting as bad as Cambodia and Somalia. Coming back to the point I have already made, if Somalia why not the Sudan? We do have to recognise that we cannot do everything that is desirable. We do have to decide on priorities and those decisions will probably be taken broadly on political grounds with some attention to the resources available. But I do believe myself that the main area of development of UN work in the future—now I am talking about decades and not the next year or two—will be in the economic and social area and that there may be occasions on which there have to be peacekeeping forces deployed in order to provide a certain degree of safety for people who are working in the economic and social areas including NGOs. I would like to say that I believe the UN is going to have to make much more use than it does of NGOs. That is another subject. There are problems about it but I think it is an extremely important area and this is specifically provided for in the Charter in I think chapter 10. I believe that the experience of Cambodia in particular—on which I am not an expert—shows that if you are going into that sort of situation you are going to have to have taken a decision simultaneously that if it gets bad, as it did get bad in Cambodia, you are ready to go further. I think it is very dubious to take a decision to go into a bad situation with very limited resources and then to decide, "Oh, it did not work; we are going to pull out." This means, of course, an increasing doctrine of intervention—I repeat, not necessarily military intervention—and I do see a future for the UN getting more and more involved in what used to be called the "internal affairs" of various states. I am thinking very much of human rights, minority rights and various aspects of development.

(Sir Crispin Tickell) I want to add that the problem for the United Nations is that it is not equipped to take over the internal administration of a country any more than it is equipped to conduct military operations on its own at the moment. It has to delegate. In the case of Cambodia it has been a great difficulty to put together people who are willing to administer Cambodia during the election period and afterwards, supposing elections take place. We had exactly the same problem in Namibia when finding people to administer was very difficult. I think it is fair to say one of the reasons why the United Nations stopped in Iraq was that if Saddam Hussein had been removed then the United Nations would have found itself with the responsibility of having to administer Iraq and it would have had to operate in a vacuum. Just as on the military side the United Nations has not developed the mechanisms and procedures, so on the civil side it has not either. There are other difficulties of a kind which I think are not always recognised. In the event of sending administrators off to run a country you will find that their salaries and living conditions are perhaps one hundred times more affluent than those in the country concerned. They create an immense difficulty themselves. We are already seeing this in Cambodia. It is a constant issue with the United Nations. If you are going to persuade someone to come in and run a poor country you may be certain that the person concerned will soon run up an enormous amount of local resentment, and the United Nations administration could indeed become a problem in itself. So the first duty of the United Nations in such situations as Namibia and Cambodia is to educate and introduce people from that country to do the job (who should of course be doing the job anyway). This is going to be particularly evident in the case of Somalia when the United Nations pulls out. It is going to be one great dilemma. I do not know who is going to do it.

Chairman: Just as it is not equipped administratively, militarily or financially, is it equipped legally? Mr Canavan?

Mr Canavan

379. On the question of humanitarian intervention the Foreign Office Legal Counsellor told the Committee that "Operation Provide Comfort" in Northern Iraq was "in exercise of the customary international law principle of humanitarian intervention." Now the Foreign Office has been receiving some odd legal advice recently and some have said that Parliament does not have much confidence in that legal advice. I wonder whether you could tell us please how much in your opinion does the operation in Northern Iraq set a precedent for intervention and has international law developed far enough to allow any state or alliance of states to intervene on humanitarian grounds in another sovereign state?

(Sir John Thomson) I am not a lawyer and I am not going to comment on other people's legal advice.

Chairman

380. I should add that we are hoping to go on to these things in a later session this morning.

(Sir John Thomson) However, I do take the view of the Charter. In my view, the Charter enshrines two philosophies which sometimes come into conflict with each other, but which presumably the founding fathers thought were compatible. One philosophy is embodied in the phrase "sovereign equality of members" and we hear a great deal about that, especially in the UN, and it is mentioned many times a day. The other philosophy is embodied in the phrase "human rights and fundamental freedoms" which is much less referred to, but Article 55 of the Charter is very specific, that an object of the United Nations is to provide improving living standards, full employment, respect for human rights, resolving social tensions—I am not quoting exactly, it is quite a long article—so in my opinion there is ample warrant in the Charter for a degree of intervention. I do not think one has to go beyond that into other legal doctrines. Now, those passages in the Charter have not been much used and that is partly because of the Cold War and partly because of the whole process of decolonisation which has led to an intense feeling of nationalism in a great many countries in the world. Although very proud of having just become independent, the last thing they wanted to do was to think that there was some compromise in their sovereign independence, but experience is showing us that we are living more and more in an interdependent world. I think we have more or less got to the point where it is generally acknowledged that human rights is not a matter which is solely inside the domestic jurisdiction of whatever country is concerned, but it is a matter in which the international community can be legitimately interested. Therefore, I strongly believe, and repeat what I said earlier, that it is in economic and social directions, led by Article 55, that the main expansion of the UN will take place over the coming decades. I do see a continuing and developing UN activity across boundaries in areas that are, or used to be, thought to be excluded by Article 2(7), and I believe that this is right. I believe it will have to happen piecemeal and I think it cannot be taken as an absolute and we will have to go from precedent to precedent.

(Sir Crispin Tickell) I agree with what Sir John has said. There is a contradiction between Article 2(7) and the Declaration on Human Rights of 1948. What has been one of the most interesting aspects of evolution in international opinion in the last 40 years has been acceptance of the idea of human rights laid down in the Declaration. Now, the device which has been used over the years for qualifying that sovereignty in Article 2(7) has been to say that the behaviour of a government towards a minority or towards its oppressed is a threat to international peace and security, which thereby brings in the apparatus of the Security Council. It is a device, and I think one must be quite clear about it. It is a device by which 2(7) can be overridden. We have seen it not only in the case of Iraq, but also in the case of South Africa where, for example, most of the non-aligned countries were always very keen to override 2(7) when it came to their particular hates in which South Africa, the South Africa of apartheid, was concerned. So it is eroding. The concept of sovereignty was indeed laid down, as Sir John has said, but the concept of sovereignty itself is a highly rhetorical term, and everyone qualifies sovereignty in many ways, for example by being members of the United Nations. So there has been an evolution. What is interesting, I think, for students of the United Nations, and indeed for all of us, is the extent to which that evolution is taking place and, as Sir John has said, setting precedents which will be useful in the future.

Mr Wareing

381. As to some of the problems of administering an area which does not have a civil authority, and Somalia, for example, has already been mentioned, and the difficulties of the United Nations in those areas, do you, gentlemen, see any possible future in reviving the United Nations Trusteeship Council and the principle that one United Nations perhaps might have a mandate over an area such as Somalia? It seemed to work, at least to some extent, in the past particularly during the period of the League of Nations. What are your observations on that idea?

(Sir Crispin Tickell) The United Nations Trusteeship Council has now outlived its usefulness. There was one point when the Russians were proposing that it should be turned into an ecological trusteeship council, so there would be a world body to look after the environment built out of the Trusteeship Council. It was a rather interesting idea. The trouble is that it would involve Charter amendments and people are very reluctant always to consider Charter amendments. I mention it only because other people have other ideas for the use of the Trusteeship Council. If in fact there were some move to produce an organisation within the UN system which looked after humanitarian needs, you could either create something new which is probably easier because it does not mean that you have to amend the Charter or you could use the Trusteeship Council if everyone wanted to, but I do not see using that old bit of machinery because I fear it would, as I say, mean altering the Charter. The sentiment that you expressed has my warm support, but the mechanism I think would be difficult.

Mr Harris

382. Sir John, earlier you said you rather hoped the clock could have been put back and you would have liked to have seen NATO perhaps playing a role in securing Sarajevo and preventing the awful happenings there, but how do you think the UN can work more effectively with such regional organisations as NATO and indeed CSCE in these fields which is of course one of the objectives of *Agenda for Peace*?

[**Mr Harris** *Contd*]

(Sir John Thomson) I am all in favour of the regional organisations doing what their charters provide, but they have been fairly conspicuous in failing, and some regional organisations having been very much more successful, NATO being a prime example, than others. I am a little apprehensive that the Secretary-General may have put too much emphasis upon regional organisations in his *Agenda for Peace*, very understandably because the problems are so difficult to deal with that it is delightful to think of somebody else having to take the first responsibility for them. Where there is a regional organisation that is willing to act and can act effectively, the Charter certainly encourages the Security Council to stay in touch with the situation and to support the regional organisation, provided of course the regional organisation acts in accordance with the Charter and reports to the Council.

Chairman

383. Sir Christopher, did you want to add a final comment?

(Sir Crispin Tickell) Yes, I wanted to make a couple of points, but I agree with what Sir John said about regional organisations.

384. Well, I think you can now make your couple of points because I know that Sir John's time is ticking away.

(Sir Crispin Tickell) The two points I wanted to make flow from the way in which the United Nations has evolved. I have said that you can use the formula of maintenance of international peace and security to qualify the sovereignty point in Article 2(7) to protect human rights and hope to cope a bit with the human rights side but that could be qualified in other ways as well. I wanted to mention just two of them which seem to be possible points of evolution for the Security Council. One is drugs. Can we use the Security Council to help cope with the drugs business, a prime point on the global agenda of threats to the stability of states? The second is in the area of the environment. If one country is doing something which does grave damage to the interests of another, can we use the Security Council for this purpose? No-one is going to do these things in the immediate future but circumstances could arise in which the formula we have used for qualifying sovereignty in respect of human rights could be used in respect of the drugs business and the environment if one state does something of disadvantage to another. The second point arises from the accusation in the newspapers that having ignored the United Nations for an enormous amount of time (and failed to pay their subscriptions and indeed did all they could to spite the UN) the United States has suddenly taken it over. Like everyone else I greatly welcome this change in the position of the US and hope very much that President Clinton will carry this further forward so that use of the United Nations becomes one of the means of US foreign policy. But it does not mean the United States is going to dominate the United Nations. It does mean that the United Nations, if it is to continue to be a universal organisation, has to devise mechanisms by which the United States is not the only one to take effective action in peace-keeping or peace-enforcing operations.

Chairman: I think those are very good points on which to end our discussion with you. The first one of your points, Sir Crispin, points to an even faster and more extensive agenda for a re-vamped United Nations than perhaps some of us in this Committee have contemplated but we must think about these things and you have helped us to do so. I hope you will not be too late for your aeroplane, Sir John. Thank you very much.

Memorandum submitted by Professor Rosalyn Higgins QC

I. The Relationship between Peacekeeping and Sanctions

The United Nations Charter in Chapter VI provides various mechanisms for the settlement of disputes. In Chapter VII it envisages the application of enforcement measures, including the military use of force under Article 42. Arrangements for this possibility were to be concluded under Article 43. Because of the Cold War it was never possible to proceed to the Article 42 arrangements. Over Soviet opposition, the view prevailed that nonetheless the United Nations could proceed to use military action, provided it was for purposes within the Charter and of a type not dependent upon the agreements specified in Article 43. Accordingly, the concept of peacekeeping was born, first employed in its current form in the establishment of the United Nations Emergency Force in Suez in 1956. As the Secretary General made clear at the time, the deployment of peacekeeping forces would require the consent of the state to which they were sent; and UN members could not be required to contribute to them. Participation would be voluntary. Both the Secretary General in his Report and the International Court of Justice in its Advisory Opinion in the case of *Expenses of the United Nations*, left open the question of whether enforcement action under Article 42 could occur in the absence of prior agreements under Article 43.

During the Gulf conflict the Security Council authorised United Nations members, acting in coalition and under the command of the United States, to take all necessary measures to ensure compliance with its resolutions, and in particular to compel Iraqi withdrawal from Kuwait. Such action is, in my view, compatible with the text of Article 42. *An Agenda for Peace* states, however, that the Security Council has not yet used the coercive measures under Article 42.

In any event, we have arrived at the position where the Security Council has either begun to embark upon measures under Article 42 (albeit without the assistance of arrangements in place under Article 43), or is in a position politically to begin to take military measures. Peacekeeping in its old traditional sense will need to continue. Very many states have over the years assisted in UN peacekeeping and have experience to offer. Although enforcement measures will necessarily need to be led by the Permanent Members of the Security Council, widespread participation in peacekeeping should be encouraged. The different roles of peacekeeping and enforcement should be appreciated. The need to provide security to one's peacekeeping forces on the ground cannot, for example, as has been recently suggested, be a reason for deciding that enforcement is inappropriate. If enforcement is needed there is definitionally no concurrent role for peacekeeping.

II. What are the Difficulties now Facing the United Nations in establishing Credible and Effective Enforcement?

Under the United Nations Charter states may only use force in self-defence. The intended guarantee against armed attack is twofold. A state may defend itself, or call for assistance from others by way of collective self-defence. But collective security was also intended to be available from the United nations itself through the mechanisms of Chapter VII of the Charter. Under Article 39 the Security Council can decide upon measures to restore international peace and security. By virtue of Article 25, decisions of the Security Council are binding on the membership as a whole. And the Security Council can decide that the appropriate measures are economic and diplomatic sanctions under Article 41, or military action under Article 42.

In an exercise designed to see how far the Charter can be made to work effectively after the demise of the Cold War, it is well to remember that collective security guarantees are at the heart of the United Nations' role in the maintenance and restoration of peace. It was not the intention of the Charter that collective security should only be available to an attacked state if others felt that they had a direct national interest in assisting; or if it could be guaranteed that assistance would entail no harm to their soldiers; or if the political and military outcome was clear from the outset. But all of these reasons have been offered over the last weeks as to why there should be no enforcement action by the United Nations in response to illegal action in Bosnia.

Put differently, a decision to act in collective self-defence with an attacked state under Article 51 of the Charter is a judgement of national interest. So even is a decision to respond to a request from the Secretary General to offer peacekeeping forces. But the integrity of the Charter collective security system was not intended to be dependent upon states' perception of where their national interest lay. Becoming a member of the United Nations necessarily entails, at that moment, the decision that the national interest will lie in ensuring an efficacious collective security system.

Notwithstanding the end of the Cold War and abusive Soviet use of the veto, there is great uncertainty as to whether in any given case the United Nations will in fact respond to aggression with enforcement measures. The United States understandably feels that it cannot be expected to enforce the peace in every corner of the globe. The United Kingdom too emphasises the limits to the burden that it can be prepared to carry. There are two solutions. One is that realism requires that responses to international aggression be selective, and based on essentially the perceived national interest of the United States. The other is that we should move to what the Charter intended—namely, making arrangements under Article 43 for the provision by all members of forces and facilities to the Security Council, to be available on call. Only in that way can the burden of enforcing the peace really be shared.

At the moment we have the phenomenon of the key Security Council powers insisting on the one hand that they cannot alone do everything and on the other hand refusing to proceed to those intended Charter provisions which would ensure that others too have a role to play in collective security under Chapter VII. The reluctance to address this reality inevitably raises the suspicion in the minds of other United Nations members that the intention really is that enforcement measures should be applied only selectively. For one or two states to carry nearly all the burden guarantees that they retain control. But it also guarantees that collective security can only be patchily provided. The debates about the national interest, the hesitations about military overstretching, the disputes between allies as to what should or should not be done in given cases, all serves to encourage unlawfulness and aggression and not to deter it. The proposals in *An Agenda for Peace* that the Security Council initiate negotiations in accordance with Article 43, supported by the Military Staff Committee, in my view merit careful consideration.

(That being said, I do not understand the proposal made in *An Agenda for Peace* for "peace enforcement units" (p.26) that are provisional measures under Article 40 and apparently distinct from any forces that may be constituted under Article 43.)

III. The Location of Institutional Decision-Making Regarding Peace and Security

There appears at the moment to be a total fragmentation of institutional decision-making and action in relation to peace and security. The Charter provides in Chapter VIII for the pacific settlement of local disputes by regional agencies and for the utilization by the Security Council of such regional agencies for enforcement action under its authority. Past and current cooperation with regional agencies is spoken of in positive terms in *An Agenda for Peace* (p.36). In fact, the experience has been quite mixed. In some matters, such as the Western Sahara dispute, deference to regionalism has simply prevented the question from being resolved in accordance with United Nations principles. There seem at the moment to be no clear criteria as to when a situation should appropriately be dealt with by the Security Council or in a regional agency.

The Charter envisages using regional agencies both in peaceful settlement of disputes and in the enforcement of peace. But the Security Council retains the primary responsibility for international peace, and enforcement by regional agencies requires, as a matter of Charter law, authorization by the Security Council. While it is very useful for all opportunities to be taken that can lead to the resolution of international conflict, it is important that the decisions be on the basis of consideration by the Security Council as to the most appropriate means forward in particular case. What is not satisfactory is for the Security Council to fail to address a problem properly within its remit, because one or more Permanent Members believe the matter not of direct national interest. Nor should the use of force be employed by regional agencies save as part of a deliberate decision by the Security Council to delegate. Nor should paramilitary activities be engaged in by institutions which have no legal competence or infrastructure for such activities.

Which institution is dealing with a conflict at any particular moment currently often seems to be a product of political factors unrelated to the problem to be resolved. No study of the intended UN Charter relationship between the Security Council and the regional agencies under Chapter VII and Chapter VIII can explain the successive involvement in the problems of the former Yugoslavia of the European Community, the Western European Union, NATO, the Standing Conference, the Security Council, and apparently NATO again. In my view certain of these elements have been totally misconceived while others have made valuable contributions. But it is an undesirable model for the future.

IV. The Problem of Humanitarian Intervention.

A current issue of the greatest importance is whether the Security Council can intervene militarily for humanitarian purposes. Article 2(7) prohibits intervention in matters falling essentially under a state's domestic jurisdiction. But it is generally agreed that human rights are not matters of domestic concern only. The problem is a different one. Chapter VII of the Charter clearly limits the use of sanctions (economic or military) to threats to the peace, breaches of the peace, or acts of aggression. The Charter provisions on human rights are not within Chapter VII. It was not intended that military or paramilitary measures, or indeed economic sanctions, should be taken in the face of human rights violations within a country.

The United Nations has in fact a longstanding technique for dealing with this problem. When its political sense is that a human rights problem necessitates a response from the Security Council, it declares the situation one that threatens international peace. This was done in the wake of Rhodesian UDI and has been done again recently in Resolution 794(1992) authorising the United States action in Somalia. This is in my view something considerably short of any alleged legal right of intervention. The British and French action in Iraq to establish safe havens and to monitor no-fly zones was done without specific Security Council authorisation (albeit in support of policy indications that had earlier been given by the Security Council). This was because a Chinese veto would have met any suggestion to declare Iraq's treatment of the Kurds and Shias as a threat to international peace. I believe the piecemeal approach represents the best way forward. While the general principle remains that there is no right of intervention in respect of each and every human rights violation (and other mechanisms are open for redress), particularly offensive or destabilising violations may, at the discretion of the Security Council, be declared a threat to international peace, opening the way to sanctions.

V. The Problem of Financing

Whatever the nature of the response required by the United Nations, it is clear that it will never be able to realise its potential because of the deeply unsatisfactory situation over financing. The legal issues have been resolved. Many states, including the United States, are in default of their legal obligations to pay their assessed dues. The Secretary General has made (pp.41–44) certain suggestions and initiated further work. The immediate establishment of a peacekeeping fund seems necessary in the face of a failure to pay dues promptly, or at all. But that too requires an act of political will, which is unlikely to be forthcoming, for the simple reason that—in the case of the large donors at least—the problem is political rather than financial. Again, the availability of a revolving fund would represent a devolution of power.

VI. AN AGENDA FOR PEACE AND HUMAN RIGHTS

The Charter of the United Nations is predicated upon the indivisibility of international peace, human rights and social and economic progress. Some small reference is made at the outset of *An Agenda for Peace* to the question of human rights, but there no further attention is paid to the matter. Proposals for making the United Nations more efficient cannot afford to lose sight of its stated objectives—of which the securing of human rights and justice is one. Further, the denials of human rights on any large scale can be a destabilizing factor; and the pressures upon states to intervene to ameliorate such situations immediately affects the prospect for international peace.

Within the United Nations work for the promotion and protection of human rights occurs in a variety of fora. The Commission on Human Rights, a subsidiary organ of the Economic and Social Council in which member states of the United Nations are represented, places various human rights issues of current interest upon its agenda, debates them and passes resolutions. It also entrusts Special Rapporteurs to report on particular themes (for example, arbitrary executions or religious intolerance) or on particular countries. These reports provide informative and impartial factual data. The Sub-Commission on Prevention of Discrimination and Protection of Minorities, composed of experts, has used special rapporteurs to prepare important studies, ranging from administrative detention without charge or trial to the question of freedom of movement.

The last fifteen years has also seen the development of the United Nations treaty system on human rights. Very many treaties on human rights have been concluded, and some of these have relatively efficacious machinery for monitoring human rights performance. At the centre of these is the International Covenant for Civil and Political Rights, whose Committee of international experts examine state reports, and conducts a dialogue with the states concerning their performance. The Committee also has a quasi-judicial function in respect of those states who have agreed, under the Optional Protocol to the Covenant, to permit individual cases to be brought against it.

These treaty bodies, whose work is generally well regarded for its seriousness and lack of bias, are serviced by the United Nations Centre for Human Rights in Geneva. The Centre has also to look after most of the rest of the United Nations myriad activities in human rights.

It is, quite simply, extremely under resourced. The United Nations provides only 0.7 per cent of its budget for human rights activities, in spite of the general recognition of the importance of human rights work—for its own sake and because of its interconnection with security considerations—and in spite of the regard in which the treaty bodies are held. The Human Rights Centre is not only short of staff. It lacks the most basic amenities, including word processors and a fax machine. In spite of the ever increasing workload, resources can never be found for the treaty bodies to meet in more extended sessions or to have proper secretariat support. The response of governments to an *Agenda for Peace* and the preparation for the forthcoming World Conference on Human Rights should be taken as opportunities for agreeing a more realistic budget for the UN's human rights programme. If the main donor countries remain committed to zero-growth in the United Nations budget, an improved budgetary allocation for human rights can still be achieved through an internal redistribution of funds including the ending of moribund subsidiary organs.

The World Conference should also be used to rationalise the labyrithine human rights procedures within the United Nations, and in particular to deal with problems of overlap and overload within the UN treaty bodies. Detailed studies already exist as to what needs to be done.

Every effort should be made to encourage ratification of the various human rights treaties, prompt submission of the required reports thereunder, and acceptance of the optional provisions that allow for third party adjudication. The United Kingdom has not yet accepted the Optional Protocol to the International Covenant on Civil and Political Rights, though it is accepted by many of the old Council of Europe nations and by increasing numbers of the former socialist states and their successors in Eastern Europe.

The United Kingdom treats human rights as a relevant factor in determining its foreign policy and aid policy. There are no statutory provisions, nor Parliamentary procedures (whether by Select Committee scrutiny or otherwise) for this task to be performed systematically and openly. While it is understandable that in certain cases friendly concern is in fact more likely to achieve amelioration of human rights abuses than is a withdrawal of aid, there are no articulated criteria for the making of such judgements.

The findings of the Human Rights Committee on particular countries, made after detailed public examination, appear not to be routinely provided to those making decisions on foreign policy and on aid, and to be virtually unknown to the Foreign Affairs Select Committee.

Memorandum submitted by Professor Alan James

1. The writer has been a teacher of International Relations for most of his career. He was at the London School of Economics from 1957 to 1973, and has been at Keele University, as a Professor, since 1974. He has always taken a keen interest in UN peacekeeping, on which, besides much else, he has published two books—both for the [now] International Institute for Strategic Studies: *The Politics of Peacekeeping* (1969) and *Peacekeeping in International Politics* (1990). This evidence will focus on that subject and directly related matters.

2. The writer wishes strongly to endorse the UN Secretary-General's emphasis, in his *An Agenda for Peace*, on the fact that the UN is not significantly distinguishable from its member states; that what the UN can do in international relations depends almost always on the co-operation of its relevant members; and that on both political and legal grounds the Organisation does well to respect the sovereign status of its members (paras. 2, 17, and 30). The UN is nothing like a world government. It is therefore unrealistic and unwise to conceive of it as if it were.

3. For this reason it was disturbing that the Foreign Secretary was reported (*The Independent*, 19 September 1992) to have said that the UN should assume an "imperial role". It would appear from press reports that this point was not included in his speech to the General Assembly three days later. Any such call is likely to be viewed with grave suspicion by most UN members, and hence may diminish the support which the UK will obtain at the UN for its initiatives.

4. More particularly, the suggestion or even hint that peacekeeping operations could be used as a vehicle for the UN "taking over" (*ibid*) certain ill-organised states is likely to make many potential hosts think more than twice about the advisability of inviting a UN peacekeeping operation on to their soil. Any such development would be inimical to British interests. For the overall thrust of the device which has become known as peacekeeping is strongly in the direction of stability.

5. As has just been implied, and was made very clear by the Secretary-General (para. 50), successful peacekeeping rests, among other things, on the co-operation of the parties—and not least, of the host state(s). The political sensitivity of this last role is insufficiently realised in the developed states of the West—which tend to be the producers rather than the consumers of peacekeeping. For a consumer, however, a variety of possible embarrassments, international and domestic, may flow from an acceptance of peacekeepers on its territory.

6. At the international level, such a decision may underline the state's weakness; it may suggest some lack of probity; and it may raise unhappy questions about its sovereignty. In domestic terms, the presence of a peacekeeping operation may induce worries about the relations between the peacekeepers and the populace, such worries reflecting cultural or security concerns. Anxiety may also flow from the possibility that the presence of the peacekeeping body will become an issue in national politics. Above all, the host state may be troubled by the thought that the peacekeepers may not leave when asked—and may even start to throw their weight around. Remarks such as those of the Foreign Secretary referred to above do nothing to allay these anxieties.

7. Peacekeeping, therefore, from the host state's point of view is very much the lesser of the possible evils. However, it can also offer marked advantages to the host, as well as to the wider international society. Testimony to this is found in the huge relative increase in the number of UN operations in the last four or five years. However, it would be a great mistake to assume that peacekeeping is something in the nature of a panacea, or that it opens the way to a much better-ordered world.

8. This last remark is especially apposite in that recently-established UN peacekeeping operations have overwhelmingly involved activity within a single national jurisdiction rather than at the border, whether de facto or de jure, between two states. For, as both past and present peacekeeping missions of an internal kind suggest, the very contexts to which they go may exhibit or generate obstacles to their success.

9. The basic reason for this is that a mission with an internal mandate can easily find itself having to act in a situation which is extremely complex and, seemingly, in perpetual motion. This is because the peacekeepers may be directly exposed to the play of politics in the jurisdiction in question. Inherently, politics is an ongoing activity in which the ultimate stakes are high—the seat of government, no less, with all that that may entail by way of power, perks, and prestige. In such a context, some of the local partic-

ipants may well see the work of the peacekeeping mission as assisting their cause; others as obstructing it. They will respond accordingly.

10. It must be emphasised that such reactions are entirely compatible with the very best efforts of the peacekeepers to act strictly in accord with their mandate. But the execution of that mandate may, willy nilly, have an impact, of one sort or another, on the domestic balance of forces (in which, it may be added, some outsiders may also display a keen interest). And the direction of that impact may change with the changing situation. It is for reasons of this kind that internal peacekeeping can become a politically controversial business.

11. For example, the UN's supervision of a self-determination exercise may be upset by one of the parties deciding that the stakes are too high to be left to the ballot box. The UN's ambitious plan for "transition assistance" in Namibia in 1989–90, for example, almost came off the rails before it had started as a large body of Namibian fighters unexpectedly came into the territory from Angola. The UN peacekeeping mission in Western Sahara, which is supposed to have organised a referendum last January, seems to have run into the sand—perhaps because of Morocco's determination to ensure that the referendum is held only on a basis which ensures her success.

12. Correspondingly, a UN operation to watch over promises to end intervention may instead find itself watching continued intervention—as happened in respect of the Afghan-Pakistani agreement of 1988. Thus the peacekeeping side of the UN mission was wound up in 1990.

13. Likewise, missions to assist a process of national reconciliation (the lack of which has had international repercussions) may find little market for their wares. Currently (the end of October 1992) there are reports in the press, by no means for the first time, of the substantial problems which such UN operations are meeting in Angola, Cambodia, El Salvador, Mozambique, and Somalia. It might also be noted that the UN-supervised election in Haiti (1990–91) was followed within a few months by the elected President being ousted by the military.

14. Another possible role for an internal peacekeeping mission is simply to try to hold the political ring—to keep the situation on ice—in the hope of encouraging a reconciling agreement. The UN Force which has been in South Lebanon since 1978 has almost throughout been partly oriented in this direction. Similarly, the UN's protection of certain Serbian enclaves in Croatia, together with some of the tasks which the London Conference of August 1992 envisaged in Bosnia for the UN Force, have a ring-holding character. In all three contexts considerable difficulties have been encountered.

15. None of these remarks are meant to imply either that internal peacekeeping is always unsuccessful or that such an enterprise has little value. In recent years the UN has successfully watched over the withdrawal of Soviet troops from Afghanistan, Cuban troops from Angola, and an election in Nicaragua, and has provided valuable help to the wider peace process in Central America. It is also the case that almost all of the operations referred to in previous paragraphs have had positive political aspects as well as problems—not to mention the valuable humanitarian work which many of them have done. While, therefore, such peacekeeping activity may, by its nature, be difficult, frustrating, and even dangerous, it has also proved its worth as a means of channelling acceptable third-party assistance to internal problems which are causing upsets on the external scene.

16. The point of the critical comments, rather, is to emphasise that too much must not be expected of UN peacekeeping, especially in its present, largely internal, phase. Ever since the UN's establishment, both enthusiasm for and pessimism about the contribution it can make to international peace have exhibited disproportionate tendencies. At the moment there is perhaps a somewhat inflated measure of enthusiasm. Undoubtedly, the end of the Cold War has opened many possibilities for the Organisation in the area of peacekeeping, as in other fields. But this is not a road to the relatively easy eradication of international trouble spots. And it would be a great pity if subsequent disillusion resulted in a downplaying of the UN's potential. Peacekeeping, notwithstanding its in-built limitations, should be carefully nurtured.

17. One response to the sort of difficulties which internal peacekeeping operations have experienced is to urge that a tougher line be taken (which would turn them into something other than peacekeeping bodies). Armed force, it is sometimes suggested, should be threatened or used when that seems necessary to ensure the execution of the peacekeeping mandate. It is thought that this would be a grave mistake. Quite apart from the fact that it would raise all the apprehensions on the part of the host (and potential hosts) which have already been referred to, such a line of advocacy appears grossly to underestimate the difficulty of implementing, by force, an internal mandate.

18. It is by no means a straightforward task successfully to bang the heads together of deeply suspicious and hostile internal factions—even if a significant measure of force is available. Nor is it any easier

to pave the way to victory for the one of them who may be deemed to be legitimate—or even just to keep each of them in check. It is also possible, given the casualties that such efforts would probably entail, that it would be difficult to secure, or retain, the necessary troops to act in these ways on behalf of the UN.

19. At this juncture it is worth drawing attention to the two occasions on which internal peacekeeping missions did, arguably, go beyond the parameters of peacekeeping. In the Congo (now Zaire) in the early 1960s the events which led to the overthrow of the left-wing premier (and the subsequent efforts to conciliate the internal factions) led to huge suspicion of the UN operation in many parts of Africa and beyond. And the later forceful moves against the secessionist Province of Katanga led to much disquiet elsewhere, not least in Britain.

20. A non-UN peacekeeping force was despatched to Lebanon in 1982 to assist the Government in its efforts to restore its authority. However, before long the civil war was resumed. The American and French (unlike the Italian and British) contingents came to be seen as assisting the Government's forces; those two contingents then took large casualties; and the Force made an inglorious departure in 1984, with the civil war still raging.

21. These comments underline the fact that peacekeeping, as that concept has come to be understood, cannot create the conditions for its own success. It is a secondary activity, in the sense that it depends on the co-operation of others—the primary actors in the dispute in question. This is not to underestimate peacekeeping's importance. As in other walks of life, impartial and non-threatening third-party help can be of enormous value, and perhaps even essential, in resolving or containing a problem. But if the primary actors do not wish or cannot be persuaded to resolve or contain it, pacific third parties can have little to offer. And even if they change their spots and bring a bludgeon to the issue (by virtue of which they would have thrown off the mantle of peacekeeping), they may find it of little utility in internal situations.

22. Forceful activity of the sort which has just been discussed must be distinguished from the use of force by peacekeepers in self defence, either of themselves or their positions. A distinction must also be drawn between both such uses of force and its use for humanitarian purposes. It may be that the UN will sometimes wish, as now in Bosnia and Somalia, to use force to ensure the passage of food and medicine to civilians. It must be pointed out, however, that from the angle of one or more of the contestants the dividing line between humanitarian and political activity may be very thin, or even non-existent. The UN could therefore, through its humanitarian efforts, be seen as effectively taking sides in the conflict—with all the physical and political hazards which that may well entail.

23. Taking sides in a conflict is also involved in some aspects of what the UN Secretary-General calls preventive diplomacy (paras. 28 and 32). For the placing of a UN presence on one side only of a threatened border clearly lines up the UN on that side. It may be that that is precisely what the UN wishes to do. But if the threat is serious, it should be recognised that an effective response requires a willingness to use armed force should the border be breached—as in Korea in 1950. This sort of activity is therefore far removed from what has come to be called peacekeeping, inasmuch as it is neither impartial nor non-threatening. This point must not be obscured by the emollient associations of the phrase "preventive diplomacy", and its discussion alongside quite different methods of contributing to the maintenance of peace.

24. There is, in fact, no real half-way house between peacekeeping and enforcement, either in an internal or in a border context. It has been suggested that internal enforcement is enormously hard to execute. At a border enforcement is certainly possible—provided that the UN's member states are willing to put enough deterrent force in the field, and use it should an attack nevertheless occur—or mobilise such a force in response to aggression. The Secretary-General refers to this possibility under the heading of "peacemaking" (para. 43). Again, neither the heading nor the adjacent discussion should mislead as to what is envisaged. It is far removed from what is known as peacekeeping.

25. It may be doubted, however, whether there will be many cases where aggression is clear cut and the international response to it unambiguous. In other words, situations like that which developed in and in relation to Kuwait in 1990–91 are likely to be rare.

26. It is therefore probable that peacekeeping will remain the UN's chief direct contribution to the maintenance of international peace. It is perhaps also probable that major demands on the UN in this respect will be of an internal kind. Some such situations—where there is no real peace to be kept—may well seem rather unsuitable for peacekeeping. But the UN finds it hard to say "no" to such requests. This makes it particularly important that while the UN does what it can, there should be no misunderstandings about what it can achieve. Peacekeeping is one of the more interesting and promising international

developments of the twentieth century. But it cannot erase the political characteristics of the contexts in which it operates. And it is only when the pre-existing political grain is favourable that peacekeeping will be able to help in stabilising or settling international problems.

Memorandum submitted by Paul Taylor, Senior Lecturer, London School of Economics

REACTIONS TO THE AGENDA FOR PEACE: THE FUTURE OF UN ARRANGEMENTS FOR THE MAINTENANCE OF INTERNATIONAL PEACE AND SECURITY

(The following is developed from the author's concluding section to Paul Taylor and A J R Groom, *The UN and the Gulf WAR*, R.I.I.A, Discussion Paper 38, February 1992.)

For many people, including President Bush, the experience of the United Nations in the Gulf represented a transition from a period of relative ineffectiveness in the area of international security, to one of solid achievement. The success in the Gulf should not be underestimated, but a sober assessment of the use made of the United Nations by the great Powers reveals some grounds for concern. The New World Order, if there is to be one, should be accompanied by appropriate adjustments in the working arrangements of the world organisation.

The Heads of State and Government of Security Council members met in January 1992 to discuss the way forwards. They asked the Secretary General to prepare a report and this appeared in the summer of 1992 under the title of *Agenda for Peace*. What follows is a reaction to this document in the light of the recent experience of the UN, particularly as regards the Gulf and Yugoslavia crises. It was not thought necessary to repeat what the Secretary General has proposed, but to outline problems, general patterns of development, and priorities.

INSTITUTIONAL CHANGES AND IMPLICATIONS

The Gulf crisis was a success for the Powers but less so for the United Nations. Although the action then was legitimised through the organisation, it was not based on Chapter VII procedures as set out in specific detail in the Charter. It did, perhaps, reflect the spirit of 1945 of great Power dominance within the setting of the Charter, but the war was managed outside. Furthermore it depended very much on improvisation by the great Powers—finding ways of building from what the Charter said when this was impracticable in the much changed world of the 1990s compared with 1945. On the positive side, the Charter proved flexible enough to allow this development, and it permitted the necessary adjustment in procedures.

The worrying thing is that to the extent that it depended on a chance coincidence of favourable circumstances in the positions of the permanent members of the Security Council, there was but a small legacy of experience which could be built on for the future and which would make it more likely that the same firm response would be met by any state which contemplated aggression. Of course, it has happened once and could happen again, and that thought must in future be in the mind of the prospective malefactor; but a weakening of great Power resolve would not be balanced by any countervailing enhancement of the inducements to act deriving from the institution's arrangements. Hence the need to reconsider these, and—to borrow a phrase from the European Community—to manufacture an *acquis communautaire*.

One effect is that the success of the P5 has led to changes in the pattern of work of the Security Council, and, indeed, of the General Assembly, which have caused the developing countries to fear that they are being excluded from the key decisions of the organisation. The Security Council has changed from being a forum for adversarial ideological debate and acute political confrontation, to being a ratifying chamber for decisions the major outlines of which have been agreed elsewhere. The sessions have become rather short and focussed strictly upon getting through an agenda formed largely by the P5. The Resolution which ended the Iran-Iraq war took 5 months of negotiation outside the Council but only about 15 minutes to approve in it. There may well have been consultations with the non-permanent members before then but nevertheless the small and medium-sized states have begun to fear that they are spectators at the world organisation rather than participants. This is not just a view expressed by members of the non-aligned movement: the medium-sized and smaller developed states have expressed it too. Is it the necessary price of a more active and effective organisation?

It is necessary to find ways of mitigating this problem, without losing the very positive contributions of the emergence of P5 and of the great Power consensus on which it is based. As John Thomson put it: "While still under the influence of a victorious Security Council operation, the international community needs to increase expectations of a repeat performance. To a great extent this depends upon the US playing as a member of the Security Council team rather than as its owner".[1] Ways need to be found to bridge the gap between the great Powers and the others.

[1] The Guardian, 28.II.91.

CONSULTATIONS FOR PEACE

A way of reconciling the practical requirement for effective command and control of forces acting in the name of the UN, and the need to involve the organisation through the Council and such institutions as the Military Staff Committee, must be found. It is simply not acceptable to declare, as did one official, that the Military Staff Committee was 'flaky', and that such involvement did not suit those who contributed the bulk of the forces. In any case there would be very few occasions on which the scale of force required in the Gulf would be necessary—or available.

A possible way to a satisfactory compromise between the need for effectiveness and the need for involvement is to go in precisely the opposite direction from that followed in the Gulf crisis with regard to activating Articles 43 to 47. That would involve the members of the Security Council together in concluding agreements for a United Nations force on a permanent basis i.e. before the event, and setting up on this basis a small rapid deployment force under the control of a commander, and staff, appointed by the Military Staff Committee, and approved by the Security Council.[1] If such a force had been available and moved to Kuwait if necessary in 1990 it might have had the same deterrent effect as the small British force sent there in analogous circumstances some thirty years earlier. Such a force could also be used for what the Secretary-General has called Peace Enforcement, that is, to reinforce cease fires, and to act in other circumstances where the mission of peace keeping forces might be exceeded.

The Military Staff Committee would be the overseer of such an organisation, being the body to which the commander would be answerable in the event of action, and would approve strategies and contingencies, and would in turn be answerable to the Security Council. It need not be responsible for the hands-on command of such a force, and details of the arrangement could be modified, for instance to give a more immediate role to the Security Council.

What is sought is an arrangement which would be effective, allowing a degree of initiative on the part of the Great Powers, and at the same time encourage consultation with all the members of the Council in the event of a crisis. It should be stressed again that success in the Gulf depended on the unique military power of the US, and that this is likely to be scaled down in the years to come. Indeed one US officer pointed out that had the crisis happened even a year later the response would probably not have been what it was. We need to find ways of enhancing the capacity of the organisation to compensate for this decline.

This arrangement does not go beyond the present terms of the Charter, but rather returns to the original interpretation of it, in that it involves a permanent force. The Charter may also be interpreted as meaning that a force could be recreated whenever a crisis arises. It has the advantage of involving the non-permanent members of the Council, and possibly other major military Powers, in the negotiations required to establish the new force before it is required, and in determining the circumstances in which it might be used; they will feel that UN procedures are being used and that they are not excluded. Such a force could be identified in various ways; probably the most practical first step would be to earmark contingents of national forces, to train them for UN use, be it traditional peace-keeping, humanitarian aid or enforcement, and to arrange exercises under the UN command. They would not, however, be under full time UN command: the model would be that of NATO in peace time.

At the same time there is little or no risk for the permanent members, as they retain the veto, and the right to reject arrangements which look impossible. The existence of the force is however likely to increase the status of the non-permanent members of Council, as they will have a part in deciding about its use; it may also, by existing, create a self-fulfilling prophecy in making its use seem more acceptable. At the same time the option remains open for the P5 to act under Article 51, as in the Gulf, if they think it necessary, and establish co-operative arrangements with the UN force if that seems desirable.

A RANGE OF UN RESPONSES: PEACE-KEEPING TO ENFORCEMENT

There should be a spectrum of security capability available to the United Nations, from very lightly armed observer and other special duty missions—such as those to help "alleviate suffering"—through police forces for helping to maintain law and order, to peace-keeping, peace enforcement and full enforcement under Chapter VII. Sir Anthony Parsons had it right when he wrote that "the traditional form of UN peacekeeping, namely lightly armed forces removable at the whim of the parties to the dispute, will not do".[2] Other kinds of forces, and levels of military preparedness and capability, are required.

[1] See the leading article recommending this course of action in the *Financial Times*, 25.III.91.

[2] Sir Anthony Parsons, "A need the UN can meet", *The Times,* 9.VIII.90. See also his "The United Nations after the Gulf War, *The Round Table*, 1991, 319, pp.265–273.

But there is still a great need for interpositionary forces, which may be more lightly, or defensively armed, than those concerned with enforcement, and, as the Secretary-General has said, this may be the time to reduce the amount of ad hocery connected with them, and further to professionalise the institutions and arrangements on which they depend. As already argued this means agreements with states about the allocation of troops and equipment which involve a commitment for them to provide these as and when necesssary. It has been said that the part of the Secretariat involved with peace-keeping forces should be more than "a corner grocery shop undertaking"[1], which implies a need for more involvement by high level military staff on a permanent basis.

There is a need to go beyond the improvisational methods which were seen by Dag Hammarskjold as the only way of arranging matters in view of the tensions between the East and West. The end of the Cold War significantly increased the likelihood that peace- keeping forces would be used in a wider range of disputes, and this is illustrated by the setting up of 13 such forces since 1987. In this case too, however, the Military Staff Committee could be more involved in providing advice, and the Security Council in providing a forum in which representatives of the various groups of states could be involved through the non-permanent members.

The logic behind the Secretary-General's arguments in *Agenda for Peace* about the differing command structures was not clear. His view was that as the enforcement procedures are under Chapter V1I the Charter's stipulations about the Military Staff Committee (MSC) should apply. But the MSC should not have a role with regard to peacekeeping forces, or the new peace-enforcement forces, which should be authorised by the Security Council, but under the command of the Secretary-General. The present writer would prefer to involve the MSC in the range of activities which involve military personnel acting in the framework of a UN mandate: it should have overall responsibility for the forces, under the Security Council, though hands-on command could be through an individual appointed by the MSC, or by a coalition of states, in the case of enforcement, or the Secretary-General for other activities involving military personnel.

But it is hard to find arguments against the Secretary-General's view that a range of improvements in areas affecting peace-keeping should be introduced, especially with regard to logistics, equipment, personnel and finance. As he pointed out these problems could be corrected "if member states so wished and were ready to make the necessary resources available". There was a need for a prepositioned stock of equipment, as delays often arose out of the need to order and supply scarce items in the event of a crisis. Too few people were trained for the special tasks encountered in the course of peace-keeping; in particular police personnel of the right calibre and training were hard to find. There had also been serious problems with the financing of the peace-keeping activities, and the Secretary-General clearly had fears that the UN could move towards bankruptcy, as had been threatened in the mid 1960s as a result of the Congo crisis.

In 1992 the Secretary-General was deeply concerned about the relationship between the regional and global organisations in the context of the Balkans problem. How far should regional agencies undertake peace keeping or enforcement duties *on behalf of* the global organisation? The point was stressed, as under Chapter VIII, that enforcement was under the control of the UN, but the mechanisms for ensuring this, if it was actually carried out by the regional organisation, remained to be discussed. (More of this below)

FINANCIAL ASPECTS

It should be recognised that in 1992 the financial problems of the UN were extremely serious, and large sums of money were owed, around $805 million on the peace keeping fund and $1.05 billion on the regular budget. There were three reasons for such debts. First some states, such as the US, had not paid in full for policy reasons, and because of a disagreement between the Administration and the Congress.[2] The US was far and away the largest debtor, owing a total of $863 million—45 per cent of the total debt of all states to the UN in April 1992. Secondly some states, though apparently willing to pay, simply did not have the resources; these included Russia and other East European states. Thirdly were states which had not paid, or appeared as non-payers, because of administrative delay, or because of a mismatch in budgetary cycles. The British had a significant debt on the peace-keeping side during 1992, despite their support for more peace-keeping actions in various parts of the world.

Of the $805 million unpaid on the peace-keeping account in April 1992, the US owed $308.3 million, the Russian Federation $203 million, France $25.1 million, Britain $17.5 million and the Chinese $3.0 million. It was hardly surprising that the Secretary-General should be concerned in *Agenda for Peace* to find ways of correcting this problem and avoiding its recurrence. Hence his proposals for the setting up of various modest funds, for being allowed to borrow in the market, and to be allocated a capital fund

[1] Interview with an American official, New York, September, 1990.

[2] See Paul Taylor, "Financing the United Nations System", *Review of International Studies*, October, 1991.

which could provide earnings to the UN in its own right. In the meantime, it was understandable that he should insist that states should guarantee in advance their payments for the support of peace-keeping operations to which they were contributing in Yugoslavia.

Boutros-Ghali added a point of crucial importance: that the financial pain could be considerably eased by providing funding out of the states defence, rather than foreign affairs budgets. An important principle here, not explicitly discussed by the Secretary-General, was that spending for UN security purposes is not something which is a luxury over and above national defence, but is part and parcel of the same thing. This is a function of the increasing interdependence of international society. Keeping peace-keeping and enforcement expenditure out of defence budgets is a measure of states' indifference to more distant security risks, and indicates a failure to understand the changing reality of international society. Peace is indeed becoming indivisible.

THE FOURTH PHASE OF UN PEACE AND SECURITY ACTIVITIES.

These adjustments are, however, only aspects of what could be called a fourth phase in the development of the role of global international organisation in the area of international peace and security. In the first phase the international organisation, the League of Nations, acted as a fire brigade, responding when war broke out. In a second, the organisation was given a more permanent watching mandate with the main institutions, such as the Security Council, being permanent ones; the fire brigade was permanently on stand by. In a third phase, the peace-keeping forces were developed, which were based on what was described as Chapter 6½, being intended not to impose a settlement, but to stop the parties to it from trying to settle it by force. In the fourth phase the organisation could get much more actively and closely involved in monitoring international developments, in surveying troop movements on a day-to-day basis, acquiring information about any development which could lead to the use of violence, including the recording of arms transfers.

Some movement in this direction had already taken place in the section of the Secretariat administered in the early 1990s by James Jonah, but this operation needed to be considerably expanded, particularly to include improved facilities for analysing the information which came in. The CSCE process developed out of the Helsinki Final Act of 1975, and the Charter of Paris of 1990, also moved in this direction in the European context.

There were many ideas about how to increase the flow of information, and the various activities under this heading identified by the Secretary General were appropriate. He placed them under the heading of preventive diplomacy, and included measures to build confidence, fact finding, early warning, preventive deployment and demilitarised zones. As already mentioned, the regional agencies were seen to have an important contribution to make in this area, especially with regard to fact finding, and mediation, and as agencies for the collection and location of resources for peace keeping. But he rightly stressed that the Security Council had and would continue to have primary responsibility for maintaining international peace and security. Regional organisations could, however, lighten the burden of the Council and "contribute to a deeper sense of participation, consensus and democratisation in international affairs".

With regard to preventive diplomacy a few points could be added to the Report. Use could be made of satellites, even of commercial satellites, to provide early warning, and some authorities have proposed that early warning and fact finding would be much assisted by agreeing among the member states a network of treaties to guarantee a right of access to their territories for UN inspectors.

As the Secretary-General pointed out, however, the threats to security which were revealed could relate to economic or social conditions, and in this event it would be very helpful if he himself, or another office, such as a reformed Economic and Social Committee, could "draw upon the resources of all agencies and programmes concerned" in the affected areas. At the moment lead co-ordinators tended to emerge in a rather ad hoc fashion—UNDRO in Iraq and UNHCR in Yugoslavia, and the operations remained too fragmented. This relates, of course, to a long standing problem in the United Nations system—its decentralised character and the weakness of the central institutions with regard to co-ordination in the economic and social areas. In the view of the present writer attention should be turned once again, despite the understandable *ennuie* of officials, to finding ways of putting this problem right.

The fourth phase would be characterised by the Security Council's having much improved access to information concerning security questions through an office under the Secretary-General, and an enhanced capacity for analysing that information. There would be a kind of **Global Watch** on security risks, set up alongside a capacity for a more rapid response over a much wider range of circumstances.

Before the Gulf crisis it was said that there had been only two occasions in the history of the United Nations when the Secretary-General and the Council did not have very adequate knowledge of a developing crisis; the Cyprus crisis of 1974, and the Falklands/Malvinas crisis of 1982. This may or may not be the case but it misses the point. This is to combine a certainty in the mind of a potential aggressor that whatever is contemplated is seen clearly by the global organisation, and that there is an instrument available and working which could respond quickly. At the moment this middle level response is absent. The power of the great Powers is needed, and their co-operation is essential. But most crises will not need the massive escalation which seemed necessary in the Gulf and in the routine of the organisation's dealings with transgressors a lesser response may be all that is required.

CONCLUSIONS

The above arguments suggest a number of areas of reform where attention should be focussed.

1. The area of reforming the finances of the UN should perhaps have the highest priority. There are real dangers here of enfeebling the organisation, and even leading it into what in effect would be bankruptcy, precisely at a time when it seemed to have a promising future.

2. The setting in place of more permanent resources, human and otherwise, for peace keeping forces, should also have a very high priority. They are being used more and more, and the present writer was much struck by the US official's indictment, mentioned above, of the present arrangements. Despite the impressive, dedicated work of the officials concerned, the UN needs more than "a corner grocery shop" at this stage in its evolution.

3. The range of security activities and their various command and control structures needs to be reviewed. The idea of adding peace-enforcement units to the existing range is a very good one. When these arrangements are considered attention should be given to ways of reconciling the need for effective leadership, and the natural reluctance of the leading states to give control of their armies to international officers, and the need to involve as far as possible non-permanent members of the Security Council, and others, and the international organisation's own mechanisms, like the MSC, in decision-making. There are three linked imperatives here which have to be reconciled; to make the UN stronger, to do this without alienating less powerful member states, and to ensure continuing leadership through P5.

4. It would not be difficult or expensive to strengthen significantly the surveillance and information gathering and analysing role of the UN, but this would have major implications. For the first time real progress could be made towards creating doubts in the minds of potential malefactors that they were seen, that the attention of the world was upon them, and that their intentions were understood. This would be a qualitative change in the role of the mechanisms for the maintenance of international peace and security. If crime thrives behind a veil of secrecy, to help to penetrate this would be for the good.

Examination of witnesses

PROFESSOR ROSALYN HIGGINS, QC, Professor of International Law, London School of Economics, University of London; UK Member on the Human Rights Committee under the International Covenant on Civil and Political Rights, PROFESSOR ALAN JAMES, Research Professor of International Relations, Keele University, and DR PAUL TAYLOR, Department of International Relations, London School of Economics, examined.

Chairman

385. I think we will push ahead with the second part of our session this morning and warmly welcome Professor Rosalyn Higgins, Professor Alan James and Dr Paul Taylor, all distinguished professors if I have my terminology right. Dr Taylor is from the Department of International Relations at the London School of Economics. Professor James is a Research Professor of International Relations at Keele University and Professor Higgins is Professor of International Law at the London School of Economics and University of London. I think I have got that right—forgive me if I have not. We are extremely honoured to have your expertise available this morning. I would really like to continue with some of the questions you may or may not have heard us asking the previous witnesses. I wonder if we could begin almost where we left off with Sir John Thomson and Sir Crispin Tickell. Sir John was depicting the situation facing the new United Nations as one in which there is a sort of polarity of principles between sovereignty rights on the one hand and human rights and we were talking about drug enforcement and the environment and ecological problems on the other: one in effect saying, "Keep out of the affairs of nation states," and the other saying, "Plunge right into the very heart of nation states," Going into the area of human rights could be set to raise issues without end because there are so many infringements of human rights let alone human duties and obligations which are probably more important. Could I ask each of you to begin with where you see this polarity, this choice, looming up for the UN and how you think the UN is going to undertake these operations given the pressure for increased intervention within states in all sorts of areas?

(Dr Taylor) If I start the ball rolling by stressing that I am not a lawyer but it does seem to me that there is a sense in which 2(7) of the Charter

[Chairman *Contd*]

has been interpreted in a particularly hard way, that in previous periods in fact the right of intervention was not so firmly stressed. The British in the early nineteenth century, for instance, did intervene in a sense in that they inspected shipping when they thought the rules about the abolition of slavery were being infringed. After the First World War there were conditions in the treaties about the rights of minorities which of course were frequently not respected. The complaint then was there should be more intervention to protect the right of minorities rather than less. This is not something new and in the past there has been a rather softer position. It seems to me that there has been a certain relaxation of the hard view of 2(7) over the past few years particularly in Resolution 688. I think also in the General Assembly resolutions approved in December last year you will find some softening of the language. I think the wording is that normally the primary responsibility of states should be respected and that in principle this should be done. So while agreeing that there are risks (and I must be very careful about the risks) I think that on the whole it points towards a somewhat more relaxed attitude towards intervention in certain very extreme circumstances involving infringements of human rights.

386. Professor Higgins, your very interesting paper which you kindly submitted to the Committee addresses this issue amongst others. Would you like to expand?

(Professor Higgins) Yes. I apologise for the fact that I have almost no voice. I think the issue from the legal point of view is as follows: that it has been accepted since the beginning of the Charter that human rights are not a question of domestic jurisdiction, therefore intervention in the lay sense of the term, resolutions directed towards human rights—economic action and diplomatic action—has always been accepted as lawful. The issue is a rather different one. It is whether one can engage in intervention in the sense of enforcement measures. That is the legal problem because under the Charter, Articles 41 and 42, enforcement measures, whether economic or military, are reserved for threats to and breaches of the peace. So one has to do exactly as Sir Crispin has explained. One has to square the circle by finding a human rights angle to constitute a threat to international peace if one actually physically wants to intervene or mount sanctions. That is one point. The second point is that humanitarian intervention is something different again. Humanitarian intervention is not about the promotion of human rights in the broad sense of the term but about saving lives that are imminently about to be lost and that is indeed part of the general international law and it has been a rather controversial principle as to whether physical intervention by states is allowed in support of that. Our view in the Gulf was that the general principle, coupled with the previous resolution that required states to support the position of the Shiahs, the Kurds, allowed it. My final point is if we move towards enforcing human rights through the Security Council, it is extremely important it be seen to be done even-handedly and not selectively.

387. Which, if I may say so, raises a whole lot of further questions we would like to pursue, but perhaps, Professor James, you would like to comment on the opening point.

(Professor James) Thank you, Mr Chairman. I think I would generally, while recognising the polarity to which you referred, urge a cautious approach to such interventions on political grounds simply because states are so very sensitive to anything which smacks of such quasi-government—the UN, through the members of the Security Council, taking it upon themselves to intervene and saying what should or should not be done. Clearly there will be some situations, in extreme humanitarian needs, for example, where this might be called for and would be widely accepted. But I do think that one has to be cautious in this respect. And I would link it, if I might, Chairman, with the wider issue of peace-keeping inasmuch as if the UN becomes more interventionist, I wonder whether this might have an unfortunate fall-out on the readiness of states to play host to peace-keeping operations for fear that the operations might in the end, as it were, get tougher with the states. And it would be a very unfortunate thing if the states were less willing to play host to these valuable operations which have developed over the last 30 or 40 years.

388. We are going to come in a moment to how the UN might mobilise peace-keeping or peace-making forces in the next question, but really what you said already raises the question before that which is how does one begin to define human rights issues within states in what Professor Higgins has rightly said must be an even-handed way? One can think of a dozen situations in which a state may regard a situation as one requiring force to maintain its internal stability and uphold the rule of law for the vast majority, but a tiny minority may feel that they are having their fundamental human rights flouted. Does the outside agency of the United Nations arrive to support that tiny minority and are they prepared to argue their case against the indignant cries of the majority who say, "These are not human rights; these are opportunities to destabilise our state. Go away"? How are we going to deal with that kind of situation? It is happening at this moment in Bosnia.

(Professor James) I do not really know how one can deal with it. All I think I can say is that I agree very much with your comment. I think one has to distinguish between the integrity of the UN, the impartiality of the actor, and the impact of the actor on the situation. And as you rightly say, the actor does have an impact and, therefore, will be seen as partial even if the actor itself is trying to behave impartially. How one deals with that, I just do not know. I imagine that one just has to take it on a case-by-case basis and consider each issue as it arises.

Mr Lester

389. I would just like to cite a couple of examples to see how in terms of human rights one would judge the situation today. Do you really think that Cambodia under Pol Pot was a situation in which the UN should have intervened rather than have everyone sit on their hands while a million people were slaughtered and the current situation in Burma where you had democratic elections which have been totally frustrated by human rights violations, causing reports to the United Nations but again in a very ineffective way? They are a couple of examples of where the UN tries to do something, but has proved to be quite ineffective.

(Dr Taylor) I think that obviously this is an extremely difficult situation in which it is really quite hard to set out in advance the principles which could justify intervention on human rights grounds in particular cases. I think that one is left in a situation of having to say that one has to find some way of relying on procedures which embody the authority of the UN. In reading through the various submissions to this Committee, the one I particularly liked was the one produced by the Development Studies Association where the person writing that I think did stress the need for Security Council authority and he also made the point that there should be clear evidence of massive and immediate threat to human rights and also talked about the need to place this under the jurisdiction of the International Court of Justice. Now, I understand that one immediately then gets into other problems and the Security Council at the moment is not subject to such jurisdiction. On the other hand, there is a pattern, there is an example there, because the European Community institutions, which are in some ways loosely comparable, are subject to a judicial regime.

Chairman

390. Professor Higgins, would you like to comment?

(Professor Higgins) I would like to, thank you very much. In certain major human rights violations, such as Bosnia, there clearly is, without any doubt, a violation of international peace and security so one is already within the parameters of permissible intervention. It is simply a question of political judgment as to whether one wishes to. In cases such as Burma you have important human rights violations but not huge loss of life and you do not for the moment have anything that objectively looks like a major threat to international peace. Then you have your third category of Cambodia which was destabilising to the region with major huge loss of life and, in my opinion, in that latter case the United Nations should have intervened. In the Burma-type case the Security Council is right to work through the human rights organs and that brings me to a second point, which is that if the Security Council is going to intervene for a human rights question, I agree also that there should be objective verification of the type of violation, just as one had Ambassador Mazowiecki reporting on behalf of the Commission on Human Rights to the Security Council regarding the situation in Bosnia. My third point is that the International Court of Justice is there to settle international disputes and not to second-guess the Security Council's appreciation as to whether international peace, which is the triggering requirement, is threatened.

391. Did you want to say a word, Professor James?

(Professor James) Yes, briefly, Chairman. Certainly Cambodia and Pol Pot if ever there was a case, I suppose, that was a case where one might have said that yes, the UN should go in. But one still has to take account of the political problems which that would have given rise to at that time and also which would have led to the case discussed earlier this morning of the UN taking over the administration of the country. And that, as I think was commented earlier, is not the easiest of tasks.

Mr Rowlands

392. One other criterion for intervention is where the actions of a government or authorities within one state create a large refugee problem which inevitably does have effect on the wider community than just itself. Would that not be a reasonable, justifiable criterion to use in the case of justifying intervention?

(Professor Higgins) That, Mr Chairman, is exactly what the introductory clauses to the Somalia resolution say, that this is not a case, as has been portrayed in the press, of the UN deciding to go in on a matter which it perceives as purely internal and that it has a significant refugee problem and has the internationalisation of the issue as the grounds for going in.

393. That would be consistent with the UN Charter and that is justifiable within the UN Charter terms?

(Professor Higgins) Yes.

Mr Jopling

394. When you are talking about peace-keeping and peace-enforcement roles, looking at Dr Taylor's paper, as I read it he is suggesting that peace-keeping and now peace-enforcement processes which should be authorised by the Security Council should be under the command of the Secretary-General. The question I want to ask is why do you feel that the Secretary-General should be in charge rather than that the forces should be contracted out to regional organisations or to member states whether it be NATO or as we had in the alliance in the Gulf. If the Secretary-General has to be in command, how do you believe the United Nations' Secretariat's capacity to run a military operation should be and could be strengthened given the shortcomings of the Military Staff Committee?

[**Mr Jopling** *Contd*]

(Dr Taylor) It seems to me that firstly the experience in Yugoslavia is that the closer you get to enforcement (I agree we are not yet at that point but we have moved towards more active forms of peace-keeping) as one moves that way it becomes clearer that only the UN can exercise the authority to sanction such forms of more active military intervention. That is something more regional organisations cannot do. One ends up in a situation in which regional organisations are really acting as the agent of the global organisations. I am saying that I think the experience of Yugoslavia is that at the end of the day only the UN has the authority to provide the sanctions for more active forms of military intervention. As regards the role of the Secretary-General I think the point there is that with regard to peace-keeping, that peace-keeping usually is part of a process for encouraging negotiations between the parties to a dispute. It implies mediation and negotiation. I think that is something that the experience of the Secretary-General is very useful for. That is an area where the UN has acquired significant experience over the years.

(Professor Higgins) My view would be that first of all we have to distinguish between peace-keeping and enforcement and if we are talking about peace-keeping that peace-keeping has to be authorised by an appropriate UN organ. But in my view because it is consent-based it can also be taken on by a regional organisation. So depending which is the authorised body so is the chain of command; and the day to day running of UN operations have traditionally been for practical purposes in the hands of the Secretary-General but the policy control has been that of the authorising organ, most usually the Security Council. The regional practice has been frankly very disappointing so far as enforcement is concerned. We are only at the beginnings of those possibilities so it is all out there for argument and I would have thought, as we heard here earlier this morning, that planning and strategic targeting should be done by the Military Staff Committee, the policy control by the Security Council but again the day to day command structure should still be in the hands of the Secretary-General.

395. So during the Gulf Storm operations, as I think it was Sir Crispin Tickell who told us, that he felt that various military options and the intelligence should have been sifted by the Military Staff Committee, maybe with the co-option of some of the other member states and alliances. Would the Americans not have had apoplexy over a Committee of that sort having access to the planning and the operations and the discussions about intelligence?

(Professor Higgins) I am sure that that is right and this was a dilemma I tried to point out in my memorandum, that on the one hand the United States wants to keep these matters to itself both to be able to choose when to act and to keep the military intelligence under its control and on the other hand it appreciates it is not able to act anywhere and increasingly criticises others for not also acting and we have to find a way though this impasse.

Chairman: I find it as we discuss it more and more difficult to find the dividing line between peace-keeping and the enforcement of peace-keeping and the relief and help of the people caught up in the whole process but Mr Canavan has some further questions on this.

Mr Canavan

396. Yes our Committee was told by the Foreign Office Legal Adviser that the "Operation Provide Comfort" in Northern Iraq was carried out in exercise of the customary international law principle of humanitarian intervention." I wonder if you could tell us is this principle defined in detail somewhere and has international law developed far enough to allow any state or alliance of states to intervene on humanitarian grounds in another sovereign state?

(Professor Higgins) As it is a legal question perhaps I might try and answer. I think in fairness it has to be said that the international principle of humanitarian intervention has always been controversial. It is nowhere written down. Some states have over the years taken the view there is the entitlement so to act. Others have taken the view that because it is open to abuse and because it necessarily involves the territorial integrity of another state it may not be done. There are simply different views on that but it is certainly a perfectly respectable view held by many states. What we do know, as I said before, we believe that is coupled with a call in a previous resolution from the Security Council for the process to lend every support to these suffering from major human rights' violations in Iraq, namely the Kurds and the Shiahs. Those two were put together to authorise the UK and French intervention. Of course, it would have been better as UN intervention but the prospect of the Chinese veto meant that that could never happen.

397. Did the humanitarian intervention in Northern Iraq set a precedent in any way?

(Professor Higgins) Only in the sense that everything that goes before is invoked after but one always has to look to see if the facts are analogous.

398. Professor James, you said in your memorandum that "the dividing line between humanitarian and political activity may be very thin, or even non-existent." How can the United Nations avoid the danger in distributing humanitarian assistance, of appearing to take sides in a conflict?

(Professor James) I think that in some circumstances it is very hard to do that because the one side will feel that the other side is being assisted by the purely humanitarian aid which goes to that side in the shape of food and medical supplies and so on. I think this is just one of the conundrums one has to solve. Sometimes the United Nations will feel that the political situation is too politically touchy to become involved. In other situations it

[**Mr Canavan** *Contd*]

will say, "Come what may we will do it and it does not matter what the parties think." Therefore it comes back to the political background, what is the political support for any particular proposed operation? If the support is there, fine, the UN may decide to go ahead—by which I mean the political support amongst the membership of the UN in particular and perhaps the NATO members.

399. Just one further question. Can abuse of human rights be ample justification for the humanitarian grounds under international law and do you think this is also political justification?

(Dr Taylor) If I could have a go at that. It seems to me that this relates to the fact that there are various situations where in fact contested sovereignty might be argued. There are clearly cases where it looks as if the sovereign state exists and the vast majority of other states do recognise the existence of that state. But there are also cases when internal authority seems to have broken down and there is, in fact, a dispute about whether such a territory retains settlement and whether it retains sovereignty. It seems to me that there are really practical problems that occur when you have contested sovereignty, as in Somalia, as to whether particular organisations, as happened in Somalia with UNDP, say that they have a particular sum of money which they cannot use in Somalia for relief purposes because it was down for development purposes and in agreement with the Government of Somalia. The issues, it seems to me, are somewhat different and indeed in some ways more complicated where you get contested sovereignty and that in fact might point then to the need to consider the processes by which states are recognised (at the moment they are recognised, I suppose, individually and separately) and by which they might be de-recognised by states.

(Professor James) If I could just comment on that, certainly there are occasions when internal authority totally breaks down. But what strikes me as very interesting is that where that has occurred, and it occurs very rarely—but I am thinking particularly of the Congo in 1960 and the Lebanon ever since, I suppose, about 1976 until quite recently—the international community, by which I mean the member states of the UN, are most reluctant and in fact have not in these cases, nor have they in the case of Somalia, said that the state has ceased to exist. There is still the notion of the state there and, therefore, the idea that one should respect the state even though you cannot really find anyone who is exercising authority on behalf of the state. I imagine that that flows from certain very difficult consequences which would arise where one would say the state had disappeared as distinct from the locus of the government within the state.

Mr Rowlands

400. Do quite a lot of these problems and conflicts arise because frankly the boundaries which create these states were often artificially drawn and I am remembering a bit about the creation of Iraq, as we know it today, where really there was not any justification for the particular boundaries? In the case of the Somalis they are a great nomadic people and never really understood historically the boundary line and their claim on neighbouring states is based on traditional nomadic movements. If it is a case where you have got a conflict like that, has the United Nations not tried to engineer plebiscites on ideas of trying to genuinely reconstruct some of these boundaries rather than let them think that they are rigid for ever and that we must fight to protect them and, therefore, stand by them in international law and everything else?

(Professor Higgins) There is a clear principle that goes with a Latin tag of *uti possidetis*, which is that however purely an administrative convenience the old boundaries were, the new states wished those boundaries to be retained upon their independence. That was confirmed even for Africa by the newly-independent African states in Cairo in 1964 and there is a very interesting speech by the Egyptian delegate at the time, one Boutros-Ghali, pointing to the fact that were the boundaries to be withdrawn to make them objectively more sensible, that would simply open up another vast range of problems, so that the clear principle has been—and this has been confirmed by the arbitration commission supporting the Vance/Owen endeavour in Bosnia—that boundaries today may only be changed by negotiation, but never by the use of force. So they are not sacrosanct for ever, but their arbitrariness, insofar as that exists, is not a reason for using force to change them.

401. I am not thinking of using force; I am thinking of trying to engineer it. If I remember my historical knowledge, after 1918 there was a series of plebiscites to try to draw boundaries in central Europe, among others, was there not? I am thinking that although I understand that principle very well, as many of these boundaries are now the cause of very serious considerable conflict with large refugee movements, creating humanitarian problems and leading to UN intervention, I wonder whether it is time to think about it.

(Professor Higgins) But negotiated solutions are always desirable and I am very doubtful about the utility of plebiscites here. May I give you an example? Quite far removed from any area we have been looking at, Quebec recently has, as you know, been considering whether to have a referendum on secession, and the Quebec Parliament has been concerned about the position of the Indians within Quebec territory. Would the plebiscite ask the people of Quebec about redrawing the boundary or would it ask the Indians, who are happy to be an anglophone minority within the federal unit but not within a small francophone unit? Would they then get the plebiscite and to what unit do you reduce the plebiscite option?

Chairman

402. And yet in the Western Sahara, for example, the UN has proposed some kind of plebiscite

[**Chairman** *Contd*]

which immediately raised the issue you have touched upon as to who is to vote in this plebiscite.

(Professor Higgins) That, Chairman, if I may say so, is an entirely different issue. The International Court was asked years ago what should happen at the moment of decolonisation of the Western Sahara. It said the people as a whole should be asked as to what they wanted to do with their future and the Morocco invasion has until this moment prevented that happening. The debate now, Morocco having at last given way, is about whether people are being moved in to pack the election.

(Dr Taylor) Could I add a further point about the relationship between sovereignty and intervention? There are, I think, two issues here. One is the extent to which the conditions attached to sovereignty might be reinterpreted, and one refers to 688, but the other issue is really how far sovereignty might in some sense be evaded and intervention carried out on that basis because there are some illustrations of that. For instance, in the case of Somalia the non-governmental organisations have had a very strong presence there and in fact complained very strongly that they were there and that the UN was not, but there are also some organisations of the UN which in fact have a somewhat softer approach towards sovereignty and I think particularly of UNICEF which does not have in its charter the requirement that it has to get the formal consent of states to intervene. Obviously if the state deliberately and specifically excludes UNICEF then they cannot intervene, but there is a kind of, I suppose, non-dissent procedure that UNICEF has occasionally acted on. It was, for instance, present in Cambodia for a while, before Oxfam became involved, in a very quiet way acting and without attracting the opposition of the Vietnamese in that particular state. My point is that it is not just what you do given sovereignty, but it may be that another kind of question should be how can some of the implications at least of sovereignty occasionally be evaded. Now, one could not mount the kind of massive intervention which has now taken place in Somalia on that basis, but some kind of intervention could take place on that basis.

Mr Rowlands

403. That does logically lead on to the next question we want to ask you and that is about what the Foreign Secretary, for shorthand purposes, called the "imperial role" of the United Nations, and I can think of this in the context of Somalia, Cambodia and possibly Angola. What conclusion do you draw about this experience and its application to future UN development?

(Professor James) I think that one must be extremely hesitant about pursuing this particular line because an imperial role implies that you go in and take over in a manner in which people once called imperialists used to do. This has become very unpopular in the world and is still unpopular, I think, throughout the Third World and not just throughout the Third World either. I believe it was a member of the Government who said not long ago that we were not looking for international help in respect of Northern Ireland. There is a desire on the part of states generally to handle their own affairs and I think this business of imperial roles is extremely sensitive and could cause all sorts of problems. Therefore my view is that one should not be thinking in these concepts. Certainly one should be thinking what one could do to help states, maybe persuading them to accept help. But the idea that the UN should suddenly be transformed into a quasi imperial body does not strike me as a very good idea and a bad idea, I think, from the point of view of the further development of the UN.

(Dr Taylor) I think once again there are complications involved in this. I agree completely with what Alan has said but again thinking of Somalia and a number of the non governmental organisations, I think particularly Save the Children are really quite unhappy about the intervention of the Americans. One of the reasons for that was that they thought they were really building up the authorities that were already there. It is very important I think to try to keep what exists and to develop on that basis and it is very dangerous to move in from the outside and to try to impose some kind of administrative authority or regime from outside. So one thinks of an arrangement whereby there is international help but international help very much to encourage those local authorities that have survived and still exist.

404. It was not working, was it. The relief was not getting to people and whatever dangers there are are not the dangers to life much greater?

(Dr Taylor) Yes, I do agree but nevertheless one must still I think point to the danger of certain things being missing when intervention on that scale takes place particularly the dangers when local authority structures are missing. I think there is some evidence of that in Somalia. I am not denying your point at all. Obviously at the end of the day if human life is indeed under grave threat sacrifices have to be made in other areas but there are ways of building up administration that are not just a matter of the UN acting as a kind of trustee and moving in. It is also important to try to build up structures that have survived and even in Somalia local structures have survived.

Mr Lester

405. Is there not a formidable administration problem anyway in the UN attempting that for first of all in administration terms if people are seconded to a country like Cambodia it can affect their career because they have no place to come back to. Frequently, as I understand it, they have to re-apply for a job within their particular organisation and even more significantly in the case of Cambodia I believe there are only three Khmer speakers in the whole of the UN. How on earth you can help run a country without speaking the basic language, I do not know.

[**Mr Lester** *Contd*]

(Dr Taylor) I think that is right.

(Professor Higgins) I agree with the view one has to be extremely cautious about the imperial role. I simply wanted to add I believe there will still be from time to time very exceptional occasions where for a short-time it may be warranted and there has been past experience of it in Western Iran. In the blue prints set up in Trieste we do have assurances by the International court that it is within the competence of the UN if there is a real breakdown of international peace.

Mr Rowlands

406. I think two of the three actually were rather cautious and critical. Compared to what has happened to somewhere like Cambodia or Somalia almost anything is better than what has been happening surely. Is it not a rather fantastically imaginative concept to try to set up in Cambodia a system by which people can actually come to ballot boxes and try to define how they want to be governed and really is that not a rather a noble principle rather than the cautious and rather critical observations you have made about it?

(Professor James) In the case of Cambodia I would just say that agreement arises out of the agreements with the local authorities which were reached with some difficulty a couple of years ago. Therefore there is a difference in principle between going in as the UN has gone in with its Transition Authority and the sort of situation where the UN takes the initiative and decides it is going to go into country X. I would certainly agree with Professor Higgins. There are exceptions but my approach would be that the exceptions prove the rule rather than seeing the exceptions as building up a different rule.

Sir John Stanley

407. We discussed the general principles of the extending role of the UN in the preventative diplomacy area but there is one specific policy proposition that has been put to us by the British Government, namely that the Secretary-General should make greater use of Article 99 which says that the Secretary-General may bring to the attention of the Security Council any matter which in his opinion may strengthen the maintenance of international peace and security. Could we have your views as to whether as the Secretary-General's staff and office and the UN Secretariat is currently set up whether it is actually feasible for him to make greater use of Article 99 or whether the implications of him being able to make greater use of Article 99 would be that he would have to have very much greater access to the intelligence information of the national governments and particularly the five permanent members of the Security Council?

(Professor James) Well, Chairman, I am sure there are always improvements that could be made to the UN Secretariat. But I would have thought that in many cases it is not a lack of intelligence which is the problem but the political difficulties which would arise if article 99 is utilised because in the first place all the Secretary-General can do is propose; the Security Council has to dispose—to decide to discuss the matter. And this takes me on, if I may, to the more general issue perhaps of preventative diplomacy which was raised and this is an enormously sensitive issue in as much as states are not keen on having their affairs discussed in the light of the possible development of crises. Therefore while I see the preventative diplomacy comments and suggestions as a nice idea in theory I see all sorts of difficulties in practice simply because of the way in which the world is structured.

(Dr Taylor) I think that I would disagree slightly with one of the points there. I think this point was also made a little earlier today that there is a case for strengthening the procedures by which the UN and its political sections assembles and obtains information about crises. I think it would have some success. I think the word "globalwatch" is sometimes used in this context. It covers a very wide range of ways of proceeding. One of them, of course, is the use of monitors. Another element is the arms register and there is technology available that could greatly strengthen that. Another one would be the use of various kinds of surveillance procedures. The point has also been put to me by the ambassador of another country to the UN that there might be a case for having a system of treaties which would facilitate the movement of UN monitors to spots where there might be trouble. That would have two advantages it seems to me. One is it would provide the kind of early warning system that the ex ambassadors this morning referred to which I think is a very useful thing but it would also have a second advantage that it would provide potential miscreants with certainty that they are being seen, that they are being watched. So whilst I agree that there has to be intelligence available (the intelligence is the point that has been made) there are very few cases of use of force about which nothing was known, nevertheless I still think that there are strong arguments in favour of strengthening a range of early warning information gathering and intelligence collecting procedures in this context.

Mr Jopling

408. I do not want to repeat what I said at some length to the previous witnesses about the desirability of enforcing sanctions and trade embargoes very much more effectively but it seemed to me that the answer I got then was too loose. To use the words that Professor James first used, "nice idea in theory but much more difficult in practice", can I get any enthusiasm from any of the three of you about the desirability of changing the present pathetic way in which sanctions are enforced or not enforced. Is there not something here we can do and can I have some enthusiasm?

(Professor James) I think, Chairman, my response would be it would depend on the particular case as to whether there was enthusiasm on my own personal part. But on the more general issue

[**Mr Jopling** *Contd*]

there are, as I think the previous witnesses suggested, considerable difficulties in the way of (a) making sanctions effective and (b) there are problems of the overspill effect of sanctions on particular states whose trade diminishes markedly perhaps on account of sanctions being imposed—and I do not think that one has been sorted out adequately yet, so there is scope for more thinking about this. Again I would relate the very general issue to the political background. I think one has to look at the political disposition in any particular case to see whether sanctions are likely to be successful. But I imagine that as in some other areas it is only perhaps worth having a go at them if one thinks that they are going to be successful.

(Dr Taylor) If I may add another point to that, I think that the point was also stressed this morning that sanctions should be seen as part of the spectrum of pressures on states and that there are sometimes arguments in favour of trying a relatively unsupervised system of sanctions first, but very much retaining the possibility of moving to more effective supervision and possibly even military supervision, and this happened in the case of the Gulf with Resolution 665. It is also beginning to happen, I think, in the case of Yugoslavia. So much depends upon the political circumstances, but there is a case for having a process of increasing pressures upon the problem states, so I would not say that the use of the military to impose sanctions should be excluded, by no means, but I am saying that maybe it has value at a particular stage in the process of increasing pressures on miscreant states.

Mr Lester

409. Professor Higgins, you were very critical of the UN's record in upholding human rights and I think all of us who have looked at it will accept that the organisation is under-resourced and also that their resolutions are often ignored or, at best, they move very slowly to correct any situations. You suggested that there are moribund subsidiary organisations of the UN which could be wound up to provide more resources for human rights work, and we would be interested in your views on that, and also how could human rights work in the UN be better integrated into the overall work of the organisation and even, dare one use the word, enforced in terms of action?

(Professor Higgins) If I may take those separately, the Council for Namibia continued its life even when Namibia became independent. The Special Committee Against Apartheid continues but does nothing very much. There is the Commission Against Apartheid in Sports and that continues doing nothing very significant. The Committee on the Exercise of Inalienable Rights of Palestinian People continues, although that question is dealt with elsewhere amply within the UN system. I am not denying the importance of the question, but it is dealt with in duplicate and triplicate. Various regional commissions, the various regional economic commissions within the UN do almost nothing. All of these bodies, because the participants in them enjoy them, go on meeting. The Human Rights Treaty system is actually very efficacious. It does not enforce by military means, but through its constant monitoring and its cajoling and suggesting to the states who feel able to participate. You can point to tangible results, but it is absolutely starved of resources.

Chairman

410. You are critical, Professor Higgins, about the role within this country and indeed within this Parliament and indeed even within this Committee, the role that we play in pursuing being informed about human rights abuses. Is that entirely fair? Do you think maybe some of the problem lies in the fact that "human rights" are not a wide enough definition to describe the proper state of freedom of the human soul and there are also obligations and duties and if you concentrate solely on rights you get not a totally full picture of the way in which a democracy should develop?

(Professor Higgins) I had in mind not that this Committee should be addressing itself to the full way in which democracy should develop in any particular country, and of course I accept what you say about the need for the total picture, but it is our foreign policy that human rights should play a part in our decisions about aid of various sorts and political support. My impression is that this, though very seriously meant, is not done in a very systematised way and that possibly a committee such as this could, as is done, for example, in the United States Congress, look in a rather regular way at the reports which come in, for example, from bodies such as mine, the Committee on Human Rights, which report on particular countries, to then ask government, "Well, where does this leave you on your aid programmes? Is this one where you think you do want to continue with aid, notwithstanding this report and, if so, why, or is this report putting this country into the category that you will withdraw either aid generally or military aid?" The work is not done, it is my impression, very systematically.

Mr Canavan

411. Does the United Nations have the right under international law to override the court decisions of member states concerning alleged human rights violations? For example, the Israeli Supreme Court recently took a view that it was perfectly legal under Israeli law to expel these 400 Palestinians into no man's land and there seems to be a strong body of opinion that they were contravening international law and certainly contravening a United Nations resolution so what could and should the United Nations do in a situation like that?

(Professor Higgins) A decision of a national court is in no way binding as such upon the Security Council. The Security Council should be looking at the issue of whether the particular matter threatens international peace. That is what the Security Council is there for. Sometimes, as an

[**Mr Canavan** *Contd*]

incidental in that task, it pronounces upon legal matters and I think lawyers have become a little concerned at the extent to which the Security Council has taken on this quasi-judicial role. It has done it rather generously in the Gulf, pronouncing upon all sorts of legal matters which normally you would expect a tribunal to pronounce upon. If the Security Council does feel that a further view on the lawfulness of the expulsion of the Hamas is needed rather than the mere fact that their expulsion has jeopardised international peace, which is actually enough for the Security Council, then it could ask for an advisory opinion of the International Court of Justice.

Mr Rowlands

412. You heard, when listening to Sir John Thomson earlier on, he actually said that in his view one should have intervened earlier to secure Sarajevo, for example, and intervene by military means. Given the situation, would that have been within international law of the United Nations justifiable? Would it have been possible and feasible?

(Professor Higgins) In my opinion, it would have been. Once we engaged in our perhaps premature recognition of Croatia and Bosnia we had international states and international states that were being invaded, and if the United Nations had decided that the appropriate way to deal with that was through the use of force, that would be entirely within its competence under Article 42 and I personally—and this is a personal, political, not a legal, view—I am among those who believe that action should have been taken very much earlier.

413. So you said "invaded". That means that the Bosnian Serbs were invading their own territory. How can you call it an invasion?

(Professor Higgins) My understanding of these events is that at all times, particularly in the early phases, the Bosnian Serbs were assisted materially and militarily from Belgrade Serbia.

414. That would constitute an intervention. The term that is used frequently in the House of Commons, "civil war", is not an accurate description?

(Professor Higgins) There are obviously strong civil war elements but it is not only a civil war. I feel the constant reiteration of that term avoids our own recognition and avoids the military consequences we want to avoid.

Mr Jopling

415. According to the CVs I have got Professor Higgins in the only lawyer so I suppose this question is put to you. Can you tell us what the legal problems would be with regard to bringing alleged war criminals in the former Yugoslavia before a war crimes tribunal and court and can you tell us how it would operate and how you would see the difficulties could be overcome and who would be the personnel who headed the cases?

(Professor Higgins) Could I begin by saying that there does already exist in place and there is operating a War Crimes Commission under the presidency of Professor Karlshoven, a very eminent Dutch military international lawyer, which is now the repository of all the dreadful information coming in from the component parts of the former Yugoslavia. They are doing all the fact-finding and assessing and they will be making proposals. Where war crimes are concerned there is in principle universal jurisdiction, that is to say actually any state in the world could establish a tribunal. It would obviously be much more desirable if it were established not by a single state, not perhaps even solely by the states who have military presence, but perhaps by a body representing the membership of the Security Council as a whole. If there is an even wider representative body such a body would have jurisdiction. Of course the great dilemma has been that the persons concerned we would at the end of the day wish to bring in front of a tribunal are exactly the persons that at the moment one has been treating with in the on-going role in conferences in Geneva and elsewhere because we have not been sure in which direction we want to move.

Chairman

416. What would be the route of authority of this process? One thinks back to Nuremburg and the allies who formed a tribunal and tried the other side who lost the war. It was a straight forward point whether it satisfied international law correctly, I do not know. But what would be the legal internal basis of such a Commission if some of these monsters from Serbia, for instance, were being tried?

(Professor Higgins) It goes back to this point of the basis of criminal jurisdiction. International law allows criminal jurisdiction to be exercised in respect of war crimes. That is exactly the basis of our recently acted upon jurisdiction under our War Crimes Act 1991. Those events occurred abroad by persons who were not nationals at the time. International law allows that. Of course, one could, and it would be better, to move to a permanent standing international criminal court, with the responsibility to take away this flavour of victors' justice. This is being looked at by the International Law Commission at the moment which has just been asked by the General Assembly to draw up a state for a possible such body.

417. That is very helpful. Now a final question to all three of our distinguished witnesses on a matter that we dealt with with the ambassadors earlier. This brings us back to the central mechanism of the UN, namely the Security Council. We have got effectively the sort of issue we have been discussing with the prospect of advanced involvement in the domestic affairs of nations over human rights, drugs, the environment and heaven knows what else as well. Given that the workload is going to increase, how can the capacity be reformed and improved to deal with it?

[**Chairman** *Contd*]

(Professor James) In general terms I would agree with the comment which was made earlier, I believe by Sir John Thomson, that certainly if we were starting from scratch one would not set up the Security Council in its present form. But given the situation that we are in, it is enormously difficult to do anything about its constitution because of the veto which the five permanent members have over the amendment of the Charter. And, of course, they need to get a two-thirds majority vote in the Assembly for any amendments to the Charter. I suspect that for a little while we have to live with what we have got. In terms of its efficiency, I would think there that the onus rests not on the United Nations as such, but upon the member states, the members of the Security Council. It is up to them to ensure that their delegations, their representation in New York are sufficient to cope with, as you say, the very increased burden which is falling on the Security Council at the present time and which may well continue so to fall.

(Dr Taylor) I agree with that.

(Professor Higgins) I would simply say I think there is a case for beginning to think seriously about some common training and some stand-by forces and I think the Security Council, which has operated rather effectively since the Gulf mostly through private meetings and then public approval for what has been agreed in private, the Security Council must now take great pains to make sure that not only do the five consult the ten, which I think happens, but to do it visibly and they must make great efforts to ensure that what is targeted for enforcement action, whether for violations of the peace or for human rights, is done in the most even-handed way possible, otherwise all the potential will be lost to us and the Security Council and the UN will start to be seen not any more as the creature of the Cold War but as the creature of one of the major powers.

418. That is the point that concerns us really. It is, is it not, a question of legitimacy and if the UN is going to involve itself in more active or sensitive and intimate and internal situations, it is all the more important that it has a democratic legitimacy from the nations of the earth?

(Professor Higgins) Yes.

Chairman: I think we are trying to see ways in which the Boutros-Ghali *Agenda for Peace* can go forward in that direction without rendering it a totally ineffective body. I think if we may end on that note, we really have completed our questions. I, on behalf of the Committee, Professor Higgins, would like to say that we appreciate both you coming and Dr Taylor and Professor James and we are very grateful to you for your wisdom in casting some more light on this vast and complex issue. Thank you very much.

Printed in the United Kingdom for HMSO.
Dd.0508829, 4/92, C6, 3398/3B, 5673, 238361.

ISBN 0-10-297393-8

9 780102 973938

HOUSE OF COMMONS SESSION 1992–93

FOREIGN AFFAIRS COMMITTEE

THE EXPANDING ROLE OF THE UNITED NATIONS AND ITS IMPLICATIONS FOR UK POLICY

MINUTES OF EVIDENCE

Tuesday 23 February 1993

Mr Mohammed Sahnoun

Ordered by The House of Commons *to be printed*
23 February 1993

LONDON: HMSO
£4.95 net

235–ix

TUESDAY 23 FEBRUARY 1993

Members present:

Mr Dennis Canavan
Mr David Harris
Mr Jim Lester
Sir John Stanley
Mr David Sumberg

In the absence of the Chairman, Sir John Stanley was called to the Chair

Examination of witness

MR MOHAMMED SAHNOUN, formerly UN Secretary General's Special Representative in Somalia, examined.

Sir John Stanley

419. Mr Sahnoun, thank you very much indeed for joining the Foreign Affairs Committee this afternoon. We have a slight dilemma at the moment because we have just started on the floor of the House of Commons a major debate on a subject directly related to this Committee's inquiry into the wider role of the United Nations, a debate on international peacekeeping, and our Chairman, David Howell, is in the Chamber at the moment and may wish to speak. So some of our Committee is there but other members of the Committee are, of course, here. We are very grateful to you for coming to join us today to act as a witness in our inquiry into the wider role of the United Nations. May we start with your involvement in Somalia which is of particular interest to us not least as some members of the Committee are going to be travelling to Somalia this coming weekend. Could you first give us your own view as to why it took the United Nations so long to become re-involved in Somalia notwithstanding the observable evidence of the desperate conditions there and what, in your view, were the factors which finally did precipitate re-involvement by the United Nations.

(Mr Sahnoun) Mr Chairman, members of the Committee, thank you for the privilege to address you and answer—or try to answer—some of your queries. I think it is long overdue to have an investigation of the United Nations system. I think it has been largely done up to now by governments, by think-tanks, sometimes by the institution itself, but maybe not enough by the parliaments. I think this is an important contribution of your own Committee. If I am not mistaken, it will be the first time there has been such an attempt to investigate the United Nations system and see how to improve its efficiency. You want to know why, in my view, there was such a long delay before the United Nations responded to the crisis situation in Somalia. I wish I could give you a clear answer. I think certainly part of it is inherent in the system, in the way it responds. I think very often at the level of the Secretariat they think they should wait for the political wing of the system, for the Security Council or the General Assembly to make the move, or for a specific state or government to intervene and put the problem before them before they act. I think this is something which should certainly change. I think there is ample margin of manoeuvre which is given to the Secretary-General within the Charter to initiate steps which are not necessarily going to be in contradiction to his mandate. I think that is something which should be strengthened really in the United Nations system—the preventive approach, the need for the Secretary General to move as quickly as he can when he senses there are the ingredients of a very serious crisis somewhere, whether it is a political or humanitarian crisis, and he should therefore organise himself; because there is some indication that the Secretary-General after the meeting of the Security Council Summit which was held (and I think that was a wonderful thing to do when your Prime Minister John Major, invited the Secretary General to organise a summit in January 1992) had a mandate to go through the United Nations system and explain the shortcomings and propose some plans, and he proposed some plans dealing with that. I think that is an aspect which should certainly be very, very seriously considered. It is right that in Somalia in fact we should have been intervening in 1988 even when Siad Barre was in power, after the revolution occurred in Somalia and the town of Hargeisa was purely and simply demolished. It was bombed by air and in other ways and there was no intervention. In 1989 when again the crisis deepened there was not any intervention—in 1990 again. In January 1991 the government collapsed and left Mogadishu, there was no government in the country; yet there was no intervention on the part of the United Nations. There were some attempts from neighbouring states to intervene, Djibouti, for instance. I spoke with the President and the Foreign Minister of Djibouti; they told me of the attempts they had made to try to organise some kind of conference. In fact, they told me they even tried to contact the United Nations Secretary-General to send an emissary; they talked with the representative of the United Nations in Djibouti to get him to send a message to New York to ask for support from the United Nations Secretariat for a conference they hoped to organise between the different factions in 1992. The response from the United Nations was negative. In fact, I interviewed the United Nations

The cost of printing and publishing these Minutes of Evidence is estimated by HMSO at £2,919.

[**Sir John Stanley** *Contd*]

representative in Djibouti, who was no longer in Djibouti, but in post in New York, and he told me exactly what happened. He did indeed convey the message from the Government of Djibouti to the Secretariat but the Secretariat said, "No, we have no mandate, it is too tough a question, we can't involve ourselves in it". So this shows there is in a sense a lack of a very clear perception of the mandate of the Secretary-General, how he should and can intervene in a situation before the crisis has become very acute: sending good people there to try to put some pressure on the government in place, trying to gather some support on the part of neighbouring countries, trying to mobilise the regional organisations, and so on. These are steps which can be taken at least without even having a mandate from the Security Council to undertake. I think that has been lacking and it should be improved. That was the whole problem with Somalia. It is really a matter of timing. The delay was largely the cause of so many deaths and I think that should be corrected very quickly. The United Nations should be in a sense like a fire brigade, ready to undertake an operation which is not necessarily going to resolve the problem but which will at least check it, or contain it, before it gets worse. That is unfortunately not very much built into the system now.

Mr Lester

420. That is a very interesting technical reason why the United Nations did not operate, Mr Sahnoun. We have also heard that there was great difficult in persuading anybody of your seniority actually to go to Mogadishu and operate on the ground. To what extent do you think there was a personnel problem as well as a technical problem?

(Mr Sahnoun) In a sense I would call it a management problem—technical or personnel, if you want, but it is really a management problem. It is true that the Secretary-General does not always have the quality of human resources which is needed for quick intervention, timely intervention, thorough intervention, and with the necessary political will. Unfortunately that is indeed missing. Now, we will discuss this if you want to, and I am sure there will be other opportunities for you to go into it, but the whole question of staffing within the United Nations is to be reviewed. Most of the staffing of the United Nations was done during the Cold War with of course governments pressuring the Secretariat to hire the people and not necessarily for the Secretariat to find the best people, the best committed and the best ready to make sacrifices when it comes to undertaking a wonderful operation like multilateral intervention in a crisis situation and helping the people. That is why if you have a balance sheet of what happened in Somalia you will notice that the NGOs, the non-governmental organisations, the International Red Cross, Save the Children, Irish Concern—and I should pay tribute to both Save the Children and Irish Concern who have made sacrifices including the loss of wonderful people whom I have known, both Save the Children at the beginning of the year and Irish Concern only a few days ago—these are the quality of people which are needed in the UN. These are the kind of people, committed people, who are ready to go and not wait for the necessary minimum accommodation, the minimum comfort and conditions to be able to intervene. So the UN people who went there before did not even stay in Mogadishu; they spent a few hours in Mogadishu and went back to Nairobi. When I went there and tried to have a meeting of the UN agencies concerned in Mogadishu, one meeting, just during a day, I could not get them to come from Nairobi to Mogadishu because of course they feared for their safety. I understand that because they have not been recruited for that job; they have been recruited for some kind of prestige position, I suppose, so that has to be certainly investigated.

Sir John Stanley: You have already touched on your own involvement and we would like to ask you a number of questions about your own experience and your own role while you were in Somalia.

Mr Canavan

421. Mr Sahnoun, could you explain to the Committee the circumstances of your appointment by the Secretary-General and what you considered your task in Somalia to be?

(Mr Sahnoun) I was called by the Secretary-General first to undertake a fact-finding mission in March and I had a technical team which was sent by the Security Council there to undertake their investigation. I spent a few days there and helped them actually get the agreement from the faction chiefs for a UN presence in Somalia. Then I was appointed as Special Representative at the end of April after the Security Council took the decision on the need to have UNOSOM, to have a United Nations presence in Somalia. What I thought was my duty was really to first of all try to help the humanitarian operation to be undertaken in the best conditions possible and therefore, I spent a lot of time trying to smooth relations between the NGOs who were there and the Somali environment and also get the UN agencies to come to Somalia and work because at the time I was there, only one organisation, which is UNICEF, was in Somalia, so we needed to have the other organisations, such as the World Food Programme, we needed to have WHO, we needed to have ILO, we needed to have FAO, we needed to have all the agencies. I referred before to the attempt to have a meeting with these agencies which failed at the beginning and then only came later. After attempting to convince the leadership to help them move a little faster on this issue and having failed to have that kind of response, I had to go public and that kind of public criticism was resented by the Secretary-General and that is why I had to leave my job. I do not know whether I have answered your question, but of course the other important objective of my work was to help the political solution or to put in place a process for the political solution not only for the reconciliation, and there is a lot of talk about reconciliation, but for a polit-

[**Mr Canavan** *Contd*]

ical solution. This is not only the kind of national reconciliation which may be visible, may be spectacular with people around a table signing a document, and which you can achieve maybe with some arm-twisting, something like that. The real problem is how to stabilise the situation inside the country in the different regions going from what I call the bottom up, to stabilise the situation at the local communities, stabilise the situation in the different regions and then get these regions to work together and check and neutralise the warlords and the faction chiefs. I think that is my *démarche*, my approach, and we were making some very good progress because of the good contact which I had with the elders and which helped me very much check the position of the faction chiefs or the warlords, as you might call them.

422. So before you actually took up the job, did you have a considerable degree of consultation with UN agencies and NGOs before you took up the job?

(Mr Sahnoun) Yes. First of all, I should tell you very briefly of my background. I lived in the Horn of Africa and I was the Assistant Secretary-General of the Organisation of African Unity in Addis Ababa for almost ten years and I knew the region well and that is the reason why Boutros Ghali has asked me to undertake this job. He himself was a lecturer at the university in Cairo and he used to come to Addis Ababa and I knew him from that time, which is more than 25 years, so it was because of my knowledge of the area that I was asked to undertake this job. I did have indeed a very, very thorough kind of contact with the different agencies inside Somalia, outside Somalia, and I went to Nairobi, I went to Geneva, and I met with the leaders of the different agencies and I organised the first conference of the donor countries in Geneva which I think produced the first plan for Somalia, the comprehensive plan for Somalia.

423. Once you actually started working in Somalia, what was your relationship with those UN agencies which were already working there and what was your relationship with the military command of UNOSOM? How exactly did that chain of command work in practice?

(Mr Sahnoun) The relations with the different agencies were good. I must say of course I did try to provide the leadership, and I was sometimes maybe a little tough with them, but I think I certainly had a much better relationship with the NGOs and with the ICRC than with the UN agencies, and they realised that I was trying to help to create conditions for humanitarian action. Now, of course the UN agencies being not yet at the time as fully involved as we would have wished—not only I myself, but the NGOs because they provide the logistics for the NGOs and, therefore, we needed them to be there, so I have been critical. Now, the people in the field in Mogadishu, I think, had great respect for my approach and certainly tried to co-operate and they did not always have the support of their own headquarters, so, generally speaking, my relations were good, certainly very good with the NGOs, and maybe a little critical of the UN agencies.

424. What about the military command?

(Mr Sahnoun) There were very good relations. I was critical of also the slow response, but that is not for the military leadership in Mogadishu, but the slow response in terms of bringing in the troops. I had been able to negotiate the agreement with the faction chiefs to bring the UN force into Somalia and I was the one who negotiated with the different faction warlords, if you want to call them that, and they all signed and agreed, including General Aideed, who was considered to be the one who most objected to the presence of the UN force. They agreed that the Pakistani force of 500 should come. The agreement was signed between General Aideed, the other factions and myself at the beginning of August, but the Pakistani troops who were supposed to be the first troops to come in did not come until the beginning of October. It took two months for the United Nations to bring in 500 troops. I was indeed critical of that fact, because between the time they signed the agreement with me and the beginning of October things had changed. Things change very quickly—in the terrain, in the minds of the people. If the Pakistani forces had come one week after we signed, or ten days after, it would have made a big difference.

425. What about your relationship with the various political factions and the warlords in Somalia? Can you tell us something about that please?

(Mr Sahnoun) I was very clear with them as to what were the objectives and the objectives that I mentioned to them were to help the grass roots, to help the people in the communities, to create a political structure. It is very important. I was very clear as to the need for them to be political leaders and not militia leaders. I stated, "You have to understand that one day or another you will have to give up arms. If you want to be political leaders do not think about weapons and arms any more. If you are political leaders then you can play a role but you cannot be both military militia leaders and political leaders—you will have to choose". Sometimes these relations were tense but I had an excellent relationship with the elders of some of them and this undermined their authority. They were a bit nervous about it but there was little they could do because the elders had a very great impact on their own troops and, therefore, they knew of this very good relationship I had with the elders. Even if they did not like it, they respected me and respected the fact that I understood the problems and understood Somalia and understood how to go about it in the sense of giving the means to the local communities to be able to build a new Somalia, a new system, a new administration, a new government. That is extremely important. It is a civil society in a sense. That was one of the objectives I had in mind: how to help the local communities strengthen their own communities

[**Mr Canavan** *Contd*]

because there was no civil society. In most developing countries and in many developed countries, when you have had that long dictatorship you never have a civil society, only an artificial civil society, a one-party system. You have a front, you call it a civil society, but the front is artificial, you do not have rules. I was also trying to work with merchants. The thing I proposed to the United Nations agencies was that we would have a food programme and monetarise part of the assistance, part of the humanitarian assistance, and work with the emergency services so that the merchants could have a percentage of the food coming in there. With the money we got from the merchants we could pay some of the Somali doctors and Somali nurses, who are working practically without being paid. In that sense you can involve them in the security of the operation. Of course, there are good and bad merchants. I am not saying they are all good. There are some who speculate, some who try to, but there are some good, conscientious merchants if you could find them and try to make them in a sense the core of this civil society. I was trying to get their co-operation but they quickly saw that the humanitarian operation was done in such a way that it threatened their interest and they would themselves pay people to go and loot the humanitarian aid so that they could get money for food. Not all did that but some did, and the good merchants, those willing to co-operate, were complaining and telling us "You should help us, we want to get rid of these people who are making bad publicity for us. We would like to be able to work with you but we have to be able to continue our business and then participate in the building of Somalia". So I think that kind of comprehensive strategy was also missing. It has been missing.

Mr Canavan: You have received considerable praise from various organisations, including the International Committee of the Red Cross, Save the Children Fund, and other NGOs——

Mr Lester

426. And our own Foreign Secretary.

(Mr Sahnoun) I am very grateful for that.

Mr Canavan

427. ——for greatly improving the United Nations response to the crisis in Somalia. What do you think was different in your approach to the problems of Somalia that led to this improvement, that led to a greater degree of success in the United Nations' work there?

(Mr Sahnoun) Well, I think one difference in approach was that I did spend a lot of time talking to Somalis, whether they were the faction chiefs, the political leaders, women's organisations. I must underline here that the women in Somalia are very powerful and much more powerful than one would think. They can be powerful within the markets, within the families, within the societies, and I did have very good relations with some of their leaders. In fact, they were the ones who helped me make some of the contacts with the elders and this was not easy, because the elders are in their tribal villages and not in Mogadishu. In a sense their structure is in the original tribal villages and it was very much thanks to some of these women leaders that I was able to make contact with them. Also, I was very much ready to meet NGOs; whenever they had problems they would come and I would try to resolve the problem right away. I think that helped very much. I can give you a number of cases where I had to intervene but it would be too long. I think the fact that I tried also to work with the local communities and tried to build from the bottom up was important. There was the fact that I also proposed that we should try to stabilise the different regions. In fact, I was the one who proposed that we should have four zones and have the four ports, Kismayu, Mogadishu, Bosaso and Berbera—in a sense strategic points for our political and humanitarian action. I later also made proposals about the whole region of the South West, the Rahanwein area where most of the suffering has occurred. This is the area about Bardera. All the scenes you have seen of people dying are in that area. These are wonderful people. Unfortunately their area was a battlefield between the tribes to the north of their region and the tribes to the south of their region and they suffered a lot there. So I also proposed that there should be a region there for them and that we should stabilise the situation, get the regions to work together in a kind of federative system until they realise or feel they should create a new united system or united structure. I must underline the fact that I feel the neglect with which the multilateral intervention, United Nations and all, has treated the whole area of Somaliland in the north-west is extremely serious and I think it is certainly an object of great concern. These people have suffered a lot. Many people who look at the pictures think that Mogadishu has been terribly destroyed. It is true the centre of Mogadishu has been. I understand you are going to visit it. You will, of course, be shocked to see downtown Mogadishu which was a beautiful little town with Italian, Arabic, African, British, Portuguese influences, completely destroyed. It was really a jewel which has disappeared. But as to destruction of cities as a whole, Hargeisa has been much more destroyed, it has been totally destroyed. There are areas in Mogadishu which are still intact; where the United Nations is there are villas which have been left intact. But Somaliland has been terribly destroyed, there is clearly terrible psychological shock amongst the people. That is why they do not want to have any relations with Mogadishu. I have been able to talk to them and I have been able to have several meetings with them, meeting with the elders, meeting with the political leaders and trying to convince them that the process of secession, if that is their goal, has to take time and they have to first see whether they can be convinced that they can stay within maybe a federal system, but then if they are not convinced, they should then try to convince the others that they should seek a way

[**Mr Canavan** *Contd*]

and realise it takes time to do it, and I think that should be left open to them. These people have terrible wounds and you have to understand them and, therefore, I did share, I did understand their concern and I think that in a sense also within Somaliland the people knew that I understood their problems and I think that helped very much to keep them patient. I said, "Listen, you cannot expect now the *de jure* recognition from anyone. Nobody is going to grant you *de jure* recognition, but if you are able to give the necessary basis for recognition of some kind of autonomy, people will then maybe walk with you a distance, but you have to go through some kind of process", and they agreed. The leaders agreed, the elders agreed, but they were afraid of their rank and file. They were afraid of the people because the people wanted secession and they asked me to go and talk to the people through the radio and so on which I did, which I tried to do, but I had to leave unfortunately.

Mr Lester

428. One of the substantial criticisms you made is the long delay in bringing in the Pakistan troops, having agreed to actually have them deployed. Could you draw any lessons from that about the wider role of troops in the UN, for instance, in Mozambique where there is a great deal of criticism of the slow build-up of the UN operation having got a ceasefire and having wanted to move things along like they did in Namibia and indeed in Cambodia where there was a very long build-up, and whether there are any lessons we should reflect to our own government about the preparedness of units which could be mobilised very much more quickly and, therefore, very much more effectively in the future?

(Mr Sahnoun) Well, of course it is something which I again might be assisting in and it is really very much a question of management. I feel that a lot is being said about the financial needs of the United Nations, about the structure and it is true, there are problems, financial problems, there are structural problems which can be improved upon, but I think the question is really a question of management. It took one week in the Congo crisis to bring the troops into the Congo in the early 1960s, and it took us two months to bring in 500 Pakistani troops, so I really have no answer except that I think the people who were in charge to create, to provide the necessary logistics, to manage the necessary logistical support maybe did not, and, as General MacKenzie of Canada said, "If you call the UN after five o'clock in the afternoon, you will not find anybody answering the phone", that is his statement, but I think it is a question really of management. I do not know whether in New York they perceived the urgency of the need to have these troops to come very quickly and, believe me, they would have made a difference because they were expected and people had signed and had agreed and they were expecting them and they could have come there. In fact I even went on the radio and I said, "These are your brothers coming and you should wait for them. They are coming to help you", and so on. There was a lot of sympathy for them if they had come as early as August, but coming two months later meanwhile of course looting had become a tradition and criminality had increased and cynicism had increased and the leaders, the faction leaders had lost authority to sub-marginal groups and so on, so the situation had deteriorated and, therefore, they could not do the job.

Sir John Stanley: Mr Sahnoun, clearly in these situations a critical relationship is the one between the Secretary-General and the leading UN person on the ground in the country involved. Mr Sumberg has some questions about that relationship as far as the Secretary-General and yourself is concerned.

Mr Sumberg

429. Mr Sahnoun, I would like to look at the circumstances surrounding your resignation because that might be very helpful to us in understanding how the United Nations is working. You were quoted in *The Guardian* newspaper here in this country as saying, "You can't work in Somalia without the support of New York". First of all, I suppose I should ask you whether that is a correct attribution, and whether you did in fact say that and whether you stand by those words and, if you do, which I gather from your nod to me that you do, I wonder if you could tell us really what the fault was and, in particular in relation to the Secretary-General, what were the grounds of your disagreement with Mr Boutros-Ghali which led to your resignation?

(Mr Sahnoun) I would like you to really understand that I would not want, not at all really, in any way whatsoever to give the impression that I retain some kind of grievance. I feel I have done my duty and am absolutely satisfied as far as my conscience is concerned and because of the support I received from the NGOs and a number of governments it has been confirmed that I have done what I felt my conscience dictated to me and I do not have any kind of acrimony. I do regret having to leave Somalia and I do wish I could have continued and I did write to the Secretary-General in my letter of resignation that I wanted to remain there as the special envoy dealing with the two, and I put it very clearly, the two thorniest questions, that is the security of the humanitarian operation and national reconciliation or the peace process, which is probably the way to put it. I did say that I wanted to continue to do that. I said, "I do not want to be the manager of the day-to-day activities because apparently New York is understanding that job as staff work for somebody and I am not staff". I was a retired diplomat and I was asked to do this job and I did say to the Secretary-General when he asked me to do the job, "I do not want to be staff of the UN" and he said, "No, the UN needs you and we want you to do the job", so it was very clear that it was political work which I was undertaking. Suddenly, but gradually, I was seeing that it was not anymore political and I was

[**Mr Sumberg** *Contd*]

given instructions almost like a civil servant, so it just could not work and that is really basically it. I did tell all the friends who came to see me when they heard that I was resigning, the NGOs, Save the Children especially, who came to see me, I told them, "I am going to lose credibility". The only way I could get through with these faction chiefs, these warlords, was because I could speak with the authority of the international community behind me. I could tell them, "It is going to be this way", or not, and that is what made them accept some of their worries about some of the conditions I was asking for and working for. I said, "That credibility, now I have lost it" because of the letter which I received from the Secretary-General asking me not to criticise publicly the work of some of the agencies and also asking me why did I organise a meeting of the intellectuals, Somali intellectuals which was a very important meeting which I was able to organise. Anyway I think it is the case. The main fact is that indeed there was, I felt, a kind of trust gap between New York and my function and, therefore, I drew the conclusion and I, as I said, wanted the status of my work to be changed and that was not accepted, so in fact I told the Secretary-General in my letter that I did not want to be a liability for him, he is in charge and one should accept his instructions.

430. Do you think some pressure was being put on the Secretary-General to take that view and, if so, where was that pressure coming from?

(Mr Sahnoun) I am not in a position to say whether there were instructions and where these instructions came from. I am not informed of that. I hear rumours, but I do not think I can give the necessary credibility by——

431. Because there was clearly a difference of opinion between the Secretary-General and yourself as to what your exact role was and a misunderstanding, if you like. You went out with a certain belief that you had established with the Secretary-General of what you would do and then after you got there and were doing it, a changed perception of your job emerged. I am really trying to find out why that changed perception occurred.

(Mr Sahnoun) I wish I could give an explanation. I did explain that lately I was in Washington with the new Administration and they wanted input on my part on the situation there and how to work for a political process. I did underline that I feel it might be useful if the Special Representative (whoever that is going to be because I understand my successor is resigning) should try to go back to the suggestion I made and have a difference between the political role of the Special Envoy and the manager or co-ordinator, the one who has to do the day-to-day work, the management. I think the political aspect of the role should be detached from that of the man in charge—the way Cyrus Vance is undertaking his mission, for instance, in Yugoslavia, or David Owen. They are not special representatives sitting there all the time managing the day-to-day operation; they are trying to resolve the political issue. I think Somalia needs somebody who could devote his time to that kind of specific action.

432. Looking back, would you say in criticism of the Secretary General and the Secretariat in New York you had inadequate support from them for the work you were doing?

(Mr Sahnoun) I did not have the necessary understanding, yes—you can call it the necessary support, yes.

433. Lack of backing for what you were trying to achieve?

(Mr Sahnoun) Yes.

434. How effective do you think the lines of communication are in general and between New York and Geneva and Somalia with regard to getting the perception of what New York requires done in Somalia? How good are those lines of communication? If they are not good, what do we need to do to put them right?

(Mr Sahnoun) I think it depends very much on the personality of the people who are in charge and on whether they want to make the necessary direct contact and so on, whether they rely on the bureaucracy or feel they should directly approach the heads of agencies. I think it really depends very much on personality itself. When I arrived in Mogadishu one of the problems I found was the very real feud between the International Committee of the Red Cross on the one hand and a United Nations agency on the other. They were fighting each other because they considered they had the same constituency with other donor countries. Sometimes this rivalry of "I am doing better" and so on is very detrimental to the humanitarian action. Sometimes they were overbidding each other in Somalia in terms of recruiting or paying rents or paying the staff and so on. So I had to be very, very tough to stop this thing and I had to go to New York and tell Boutros-Ghali about the decision. He gave me a letter which I took with me to the President of the Red Cross in Geneva. I spoke to him and said "We have to stop this kind of feud, that is not the way you convince the donor countries that you are doing a good job. Do it, and then people will see." So I think this is really much more a question of personalities. Now, of course, as I said, there are some inbuilt habits and the routine approach and so on which have to be changed. We were in the Cold War situation but we are not any more in a Cold War situation. Many of the staff there are still reacting with this kind of Cold War mentality: what should I do, what should I not do? This can create problems for others. That has to be changed. We have to realise there is now a larger consensus on the need for multilateral intervention in a crisis situation. The political will is there. Therefore, there should be a little more dynamism, more commitment on the part of the staff; but maybe the staff itself has to change. The other thing which I think is extremely important is that more and more reliance on the

[**Mr Sumberg** *Contd*]

NGOs should be perceived as positive on the part of the United Nations agencies, not as competition. I think they should be considered as a spearhead of our humanitarian action. They are the people who have staff there, they have the people who can go and take risks if necessary, who commit themselves to work in the bush and so on. The United Nations is much more providing the logistics. So I think that should be recognised and accepted as an established situation. In fact, some kind of document should be written to say these things very clearly within the United Nations system. The NGOs have decentralisation and more efficiency. I think there should not be opposition in the perception of their work, they should see each other as complementary.

Sir John Stanley

435. Just before you finish this series of questions on your own role in Somalia, could I ask you, in view of the evidence we have had from a number of quarters, if in dealing with these very severe humanitarian crises the right course might well be for the United Nations to appoint a single representative who would have overall authority to bring together all types of United Nations operations in the country concerned? Do you think that that is the right course in principle for the United Nations to follow? If so, do you think it is actually achievable against the way in which the United Nations is at present structured with so many semi-independent agencies?

(Mr Sahnoun) In a sense, Mr Chairman, you are asking a question about co-ordination and the need for co-ordination of the different humanitarian agencies. I think co-ordination has to be done. I think it is important because sometimes there is overlapping; sometimes, as I said, there is competition which when it is healthy is fine but sometimes there are antagonisms which one should resolve. There are problems with the environment which should be perceived as common and treated as the same. I think there are a number of things which really need some kind of co-ordination but co-ordination should be perceived as a service, not perceived as a control. It should be perceived as a means to achieve something with co-operation. I think co-ordination should respect decentralisation, co-ordination should respect the mandate of each organisation. They have been working within that mandate for years and years. You cannot oblige them to change their mandate. I think co-ordination should provide information, co-ordination should get people together regularly so that they can explain the problems they have with the environment, so that the co-ordinator would attempt to resolve these problems when they cannot do it. I think co-ordination is also sometimes helping to provide the logistical support. There are transport problems. When I was there Save the Children in Northern Somalia complained at one time that the plane provided by the British Government for transport was going to be stopped. So I talked with the British Government and tried to convince them that it should be maintained, and I think it was maintained. So co-ordination is important, I think, but it should be perceived really as being to help the needs of the people, not to try to regulate the work or try to impose itself. That is what happens sometimes. To create a new agency which is going to superimpose itself on the other agencies would be wrong; to say to people "I am here to help you, to provide services which you need" can certainly be very helpful.

Sir John Stanley: Can we turn now to the dimension of the United Nations involvement where there is a requirement for military protection. Mr Harris has questions on that.

Mr Harris

436. In conditions of armed conflict, how can the United Nations give its humanitarian aid and operate military protection without becoming a party to the actual fighting? Do you think it is easier to deliver aid in conflict situations with or without military back-up? Does that depend on the circumstances?

(Mr Sahnoun) Military intervention is a very delicate matter, a very difficult question. We hear a lot of discussion of the need to have earmarked forces and troops and so on. I think if we are not careful we might be creating more problems for ourselves. There is no doubt that the need of punctual, efficient intervention is sometimes there and I think it should be perceived as that. Certainly when I myself saw the failure of our operation in Somalia, I wrote an article in *The Los Angeles Times* saying that we should welcome the offer made by the US Administration to send troops together with other countries to Somalia. I saw it really much more as a surgical operation, not something which should be a standard operation. It was needed and it was important because, as I said, there are the Hawiya people, the people between the two rivers, the Shebelle River and the Giuba River, and these are the people who were suffering and they were dying by hundreds a day. The need for intervention was there and I supported it, but I think if that is going to persist or to perpetuate or to last too long, it will be counterproductive and it will create a lot of problems, psychological problems, habit-forming problems, all kinds of problems are going to occur and the relations with the environment will be tougher and tougher and you will see there will be more difficulties and then when they withdraw they will leave maybe a much more chaotic situation, so that is why it is a very delicate matter and should be perceived as such. That is why I said that if the 500 Pakistani troops had come when they were called for in August, they might have, and I am not absolutely certain, but there is good ground, this is my belief, they might have made the later intervention of 25,000 or 30,000 troops unnecessary. It might have been so, so that is what I mean about the timeliness and the need to intervene at the right time with some understanding for the environment which I had achieved and the people had agreed. They realised the need for that, even

[**Mr Harris** *Contd*]

the faction chiefs because I was saying to them, "The problem is with the people, these looters whom you cannot control and these 500 Pakistanis will help you control them", and they welcomed it and they said yes and Aideed signed, all of them signed the agreement for these 500 to come. I think the protection for humanitarian action is sometimes important and you realise now why the NGOs were in the beginning very resentful of the presence of large numbers of troops because they did realise the danger which I was talking about which can occur when the troops stay too long, but I did make them understand that we needed these 500 to come for the specific purpose which was to protect the humanitarian action with the understanding of the environment.

Mr Lester

437. Is not one of the problems though of not having that protection the rather offensive action necessary for NGOs to conduct their responsibilities of having to pay protection money to actually be protected in Mogadishu or wherever by one or other of the factions? I recognise it is a very imperfect world, but that is one of the concerns which many of us felt, that the only way they could operate was to pay protection money to one or other of the factions in order to operate.

(Mr Sahnoun) That is again why I felt we should have these troops and they were not large numbers of troops, they were small numbers of troops, and they were supposed to control the situation in Mogadishu, in the airport, in the port and along the way to the distribution centres. I felt they were enough, yes, certainly, but now let me say also something concerning some of the dispositions which some of the NGOs and the UN agencies have undertaken. We pay the price of a long delay in not responding to Somalia. We pay the price of pouring so many arms into Somalia. The Somali situation in a sense is unique in that in five years, I think, if I am not mistaken, between 1982 and 1987, or six years, the US military aid was something like $500 million. It is a tremendous amount of money and think of what the Russians have done in the ten or nine years when they were there with all the arms which found their way into the hands of the people there. The situation was extremely difficult in Somalia and because of this long delay in responding to the situation, the situation got out of hand. In this kind of environment the NGOs and the UN agencies working in the humanitarian action had to think of formulae of this kind, like having some armed people to help, and at the time they were not very highly paid. Then of course, as I said, there was the lack of co-ordination, the overbidding, and I suffered from it and I do not need to enter into the details, but I can tell you stories about rents sky-rocketing because of the overbidding and so on, and that is the environment.

438. Turning to the lessons we should learn from your experience, you have spoken very highly about the work of the NGOs and they certainly spoke very highly about your operation. Should there be or do you think it is always necessary for the UN to be a lead agent or do you think that the NGOs could in some circumstances take the lead or do you think that given the political job you describe which is vitally important below that one could appoint an NGO or NGOs to carry out the humanitarian functions, not necessarily with the UN taking the lead?

(Mr Sahnoun) It is a difficult question to answer because for the people, for the country, what is the nature of the organisation, whether it is an organisation which has an official recognition which is an organisation which is sent out by governments or whether it is an organisation which is independent from government and it is sent there by its constitution which can include of course government sources and governments, but, therefore, is not perceived as a political organisation and might not be respected as much as the UN. The UN has of course its presence, its legal position, that it represents a number of governments and I think that kind of umbrella is helpful in negotiations. Now, when it comes to the work being done, I think the UN should recognise, as I say again, the role of the NGOs, respect it, give it a higher status, co-ordinate with them as much as possible and help them because if it was not for the ICRC and some of the NGOs, I think we would have more people who would have died of hunger and hunger-related diseases in Somalia by far.

439. Could I confirm also that you suggested in terms of management of personnel then the UN could learn a lot from the way the NGOs operate in terms of the rules of security and personnel and motivation in terms of actually operating on the ground in difficult circumstances?

(Mr Sahnoun) Yes, definitely.

Sir John Stanley

440. We have some questions about the UN staff, but just before we come to that, there is one remaining question on the military side I would like to ask you. Were you personally supportive of the US Government's decision to intervene militarily in Somalia when that decision was taken? Do you think that was the right thing for the US Government to have done?

(Mr Sahnoun) As I mentioned before, yes, I think it was a surgical operation and I think it was needed because there was obviously a failure on the part of the UN and the whole population was threatened. I think there was a real, maybe the word is too strong, but almost genocide which was occurring within the Hawiya people who, as I said, are the farmers. These are the peaceful people and these people do not have a self-defence system and they did not have militias like the others and, therefore, their area was a battlefield and that is where the suffering was occurring and that is where the children were dying. I think we needed a surgical operation, but a surgical operation, like every surgical operation, has to be quick and it has

[Sir John Stanley *Contd***]**

to be thorough and it has to become not a long treatment because that can be counter-productive.

Mr Sumberg

441. When we were in New York we talked a little bit with the people we met about how staff were recruited in the United Nations and trying to get the best quality of people there. I wonder if, in light of your experience, you could give us a line as to how the United Nations could improve the calibre of staff who are sent into the field in humanitarian measures of this sort?

(Mr Sahnoun) I think one of the things which could be done would be to look within the NGOs and see whether the NGOs can provide on a contract basis some of their staff to operate within the region. There was this idea of creating a voluntary corps within the United Nations which has not been very successful so far. But certainly there are many people who have worked within NGOs who can only work with NGOs for short periods because the NGOs do not pay them usually for their work but just pay their expenses, and therefore they would have to sacrifice a job or sacrifice studies. I think the United Nations should elaborate a system whereby they can recruit the staff, get from the NGOs an indication of the quality of these people, and try to use as many as they could at least until a renewal of the staffing within the United Nations has occurred. As I said, a lot of it has been conditioned by the Cold War situation and, therefore, there should be new criteria for recruitment within the United Nations in the future. I think people should be asked whether they are ready to accept hard accommodation, difficult conditions of life, not only when it comes to humanitarian action in work but also in peacekeeping or peacemaking. Peacemaking is very important. How many people are ready to go and be able to work within a country which is in a crisis situation, to do specific political work but stay there while the detail of this political action is undertaken through discussions, shuttling between the country and New York or other countries separately, trying to get the co-operation of regional organisations and neighbouring countries? This has not been undertaken in Somalia. In fact, there was quite a lack of support from neighbouring countries. Yet today Ethiopia is instrumental in the process of national reconciliation. But when I arrived there they were feeling so resentful of the United Nations that, in fact, they were advising the Somali faction not to accept a United Nations presence. I had to go to Addis Ababa, Asmera, Nairobi, Djibouti and Khartoum to talk to them and persuade them that the United Nations is working for the Horn of Africa. They said to me very clearly, "Why didn't you get concerned up to now? We have never been asked for anything. You were the first one to come and ask for our advice". I said, "We cannot solve the problem without you". It was because of that I finally got their involvement. I think there should be staff there. They should be staff who are ready to go and work with, as I said, the civil society, work with different kinds of elite, work with the women's associations, work with the merchants and so on. So there are people who should certainly be used for that. Maybe there is a need for training for that.

442. You see that being done from the NGOs initially, not by United Nations people but through the NGOs on a short-term basis? You see that as the way to tackle it?

(Mr Sahnoun) At the beginning of the process, until the staff has been changed within the United Nations, until new staff have been recruited on the basis of new criteria.

443. Do you see any danger in that relationship of accountability in the sense that the people you are talking about would presumably be accountable to the NGOs and not accountable, for example, to the Security Council or the General Assembly or the United Nations generally?

(Mr Sahnoun) You have raised this problem of accountability, and that is really basic to United Nations action and I think practically it is very little contemplated today. We do not know why there was no intervention. I did ask. This is one of the problems I had. There should be an investigation as to why for a whole year (let us forget about 1988, 1989, 1990) from January 1991, when the Siad Barre Government collapsed and left Mogadishu, the country was without government. Why from January 1991 until January 1992 was there no United Nations intervention within Somalia, no political attempt to resolve the problem? There were only the NGOs. I ask for accountability. Somebody should be accountable to the international community, whether it is the executive body or staff; somebody should say why there was no intervention. People knew there was a crisis there. Unfortunately there is no accountability to date, I think, within the United Nations.

444. Whom do you blame for that lack of response? Do you believe it was the fault of the Secretary-General?

(Mr Sahnoun) I think it is the Secretary General, the Secretariat, the Council, the leadership of the United Nations, both the political and administrative leadership of the United Nations. Both should require better accountability.

445. So accountability is a factor but also management. Do you believe it is possible for the United Nations to have an efficient management which can respond effectively and quickly and properly to a whole range of complex emergencies? It is difficult. You spotlighted the difficulty of dealing with one emergency—it is reasonable to suppose there may well be several emergencies. How can the United Nations construct a management team and the ability to respond to emergencies throughout the world in an effective way? How can that be done? What do we have to do to achieve that?

[**Mr Sumberg** *Contd*]

(Mr Sahnoun) I do believe that we need a total and thorough assessment of the situation now in the post-Cold War period. I think we have not done it. I think there was a good step taken when the Security Council met at summit level in January last year, and I think it should be pursued by thorough assessment of the situation now and looking into the accountability and criteria for the staffing and so on. I think there should be a new assessment of past failure, past shortcomings, and a new mandate given to the United Nations. I think the situation has changed and we are bound to have more crises of an intrastate nature—not inter-state, not between states. I think the whole concept of authority should now be looked at and the concept of intervention. Of course, it was a handicap to the intervention of the Secretary General sometimes that the Security Council saw the situation as of an internal nature, but we are bound to have moral issues, moral problems. Should we, because of the concept of sovereignty, remain absent? I think not. I think we should in the community of nations, just as in society, look at our responsibilities. You intervene when your neighbour is beating his spouse or is undertaking child abuse; you are responsible, you have to break his door down, if necessary, to stop that, or call the police. It is the same with the community of nations. I think the Cold War prevented that. The Cold War was a situation where each big power thought about the domino theory; no international intervention should come within the camp of which you were not in control. That situation is now past. We have to look at every possibility and I think there are articles in the Charter which, of course, make it a bit difficult. Countries, rightly so sometimes, say "Be careful. National integration is a long process, you cannot use a conflict situation to intervene, you are preventing us from undertaking national integration." But, provided there are safeguards—and safeguards are the democratic process, the protection of minority rights, and so on—if these safeguards are there, okay, you can give clout to the people for national integration. When these safeguards are not there, when whole populations are victims of starvation and so on, you cannot remain idle; you have to create the necessary mechanism to intervene. There is the conference on human rights, the Declaration on Human Rights of the General Assembly, some articles within the Charter itself which actually give a base for a new understanding of the concept of sovereignty and the need for that. I think the whole thing has to be reviewed certainly and I am glad your Committee has undertaken this investigation and I think you should be commended for it certainly.

446. One of the problems with all these situations is that they are not very safe places and there is a security danger to those who are operating there on behalf of the UN or on behalf of anybody else and, as you know, in Somalia several UN agencies moved their resident representatives in Somalia to Nairobi in Kenya due to the security situation. Now, did you persuade any of those representatives to return to Mogadishu or did you try or did you feel that was right that they should do and do different agencies have different rules governing security? How do you see this security perception in these difficult jobs people do in these situations?

(Mr Sahnoun) Yes, of course again here I think we do have to deal with the understanding of people and of staff of the work when they are recruited. Certainly there is a different perception of security in the NGOs who usually feel that there are security conditions after a certain point and that this security is being endangered and they themselves give the freedom, liberty to their staff to withdraw from a situation when they feel that their security is in question. The UN system is different. The UN system is there because they have security insurance and so on, so it is the insurance companies sometimes which establish security criteria so you have this problem to deal with. I did try to get a meeting, and I mentioned it, to get a meeting in Mogadishu and at the beginning it was very difficult. In fact the representatives of these agencies did not want to come and gradually they finally were able to come, but your own Foreign Secretary when he came to Somalia realised when he visited the "hurt" centres that there was a lack of some basic medical items. He enquired why and he was told that one specific agency was not there which was supposed to provide these medical things and I think he mentioned it in his press conference. So yes, of course again, as I said, it is an understanding of security at the time people are recruited. If someone who has been a civil servant in this country and has left his job thinking that he is going to the UN for a higher position but with the same kind of conditions in terms of security, he is not going to easily accept the risk in confronting a risky situation, so I think this is a matter for the management to resolve and see that criteria are established for the recruitment of people who are going to be called on to undertake the kind of operation, not all the staff because for the people who are going to stay in New York it is fine, but the people who are going to work in the field should be given a very clear understanding of the criteria.

Sir John Stanley: We have taken of course a close interest in the new Department of Humanitarian Affairs and we have seen Mr Eliasson and his team in New York and also his team in Geneva and Mr Canavan has some questions on that.

Mr Canavan

447. It has been suggested to the Committee that there are certain areas where there is a multiplicity of UN agencies in operation and that there would be some advantage, in fact a need for one single person to be in charge of the whole operation, as it were, and that that person should be either the Secretary-General's special representative or the representative of the Department of Humanitarian Affairs. I would like to ask your

[**Mr Canavan** *Contd*]

opinion on that and what should be the relationship between the Secretary-General's special envoy in a country and the DHA co-ordinator?

(Mr Sahnoun) I think from my experience in Somalia it is very important that the special representative and the co-ordinator for humanitarian assistance work very closely. I think the co-ordinator should work under the leadership of the special representative because co-ordination, at least in the case of Somalia, has a lot to do with a political situation. Co-ordination is resolving a lot of problems between the agencies, the NGOs and the Somali environment and that kind of solution which we have to undertake can only be undertaken by somebody who has a political hat on. A co-ordinator of humanitarian assistance would not have that kind of authority and, therefore, he needs to have the help of the special representative. It is exactly the same structure which you have in New York with the Secretary-General who has under him the political department, the humanitarian assistance department, the peace-keeping department and the other departments which are not necessarily concerned. These are the people and they should co-ordinate with the special representative and I think again co-ordination on the part of the representative of the humanitarian assistance department or the Department for Humanitarian Affairs should be understood as being service-orientated, not as control because you will run into serious problems in confrontation with other agencies who do not want to be controlled by a superimposed agency, whether you call it the DHA or otherwise. You have to have an understanding that they continue to fulfil their mandate, but they have to be present every day at the meetings, co-ordinating meetings, and they have to explain the problems that they have to the other NGOs. If there are some contradictions or overlapping they should be stated, they should air their grievances and the co-ordinator should try to resolve these problems; I think that is the way it should be undertaken. If the DHA understand their role as being a new agency which is going to have branches everywhere and so on, I think it would be a mistake; I think it should be understood as a real co-ordinator, as a chief of orchestra, as somebody who does not have to play all the instruments or think that he plays better than somebody else, but I think he should understand that the man who is playing the violin is a good violinist and he should only know how to harmonise between him and somebody else. This is an analogy which I used when I was there because there were problems between the co-ordinator of humanitarian assistance and some of the NGOs, because sometimes they wanted to do the job of other agencies and I said, "No, that is not your role" or thinking that you are going to have better visibility by bringing more public relations in and talking about your work as co-ordinator to the public relations department or to the press and that is not the way that you do it. I think that is the way I understand co-ordination. It is really a service, and it is not control.

448. If the Department of Humanitarian Affairs had been in existence earlier, do you think that the crisis in Somalia might have been handled differently?

(Mr Sahnoun) I doubt it. I think it is much more a political action than purely an absence of the Department of Humanitarian Affairs. Now, all the agencies have left Somalia and there was an organisation called UNDRO, the United Nations Disaster Relief Organisation, which was in Geneva and was a UN disaster relief organisation, as the name indicates, and it did not intervene in Somalia, so I am not sure that the DHA would have made a big change. I have sympathy with the question, but I am not sure it would have made a big change.

Sir John Stanley

449. Could I just ask you finally, Mr Sahnoun, just in a nutshell from this immense experience and invaluable experience that you have had in this desperate position in Somalia, what would you say, just very briefly, are the key lessons to be learned by the UN and the international community from the UN's involvement in Somalia or lack of involvement?

(Mr Sahnoun) I think the most important matter which in a sense was there all through the questions you have asked is the need for the UN to first of all be timely in its intervention, that we should really avoid the kind of delay we have experienced in Somalia. That is disastrous. I think it should be investigated. I think we should know why we did not respond and we should draw the lessons from this so that we cannot repeat this mistake. I think it is important that, whenever the United Nations or the international community undertake action, it has a clear comprehensive strategy. It is not just going into an area and reacting and responding and trying to find some kind of solution, like having national reconciliation—after that, what is going to happen? I think there should be a very clear strategy. Very often this comprehensive strategy is not there. There should be certainly a very, very important emphasis put on prevention. I think it is absolutely vital. That would spare wasting time and also save human lives. I think prevention is vital. Prevention has to be efficient. There are several aspects you could develop there, not only the need for the Secretary-General as soon as he knows there are really the ingredients of a crisis somewhere to send some high profile personalities there, get some governments to put pressure on the parties concerned, and if necessary undertake some kind of sanctions which do not require a resolution through the Security Council. There could be a kind of consensus between the different states, especially members of the Security Council, and especially Permanent Members of the Security Council. Some kind of clear message could be sent, by a statement of the President of the Security Council, to the specific parties concerned, that enough is enough and that there would be tough decisions which would be taken. I think there should be mobilisation of all the countries concerned—the neighbouring states, mobilisation of regional organisations concerned,

[**Sir John Stanley** *Contd*]

and so on. That is something which the United Nations can undertake, of course informing the Security Council members, the parties and so on. It should be capable of intervening very quickly. Then we would spare the cost which we have to assume afterwards and we would spare human lives.

450. Thank you very much indeed, Mr Sahnoun. It has been a most illuminating session for the Committee. We are very grateful to you for travelling to see us. Thank you very much for coming to be with us today.

(Mr Sahnoun) Thank you for your patience.

Printed in the United Kingdom for HMSO.
Dd.0508834, 4/93, C6, 3398/3B, 5673, 238548.

HMSO publications are available from:

HMSO Publications Centre
(Mail, fax and telephone orders only)
PO Box 276, London, SW8 5DT
Telephone orders 071-873 9090
General enquiries 071-873 0011
(queuing system in operation for both numbers)
Fax orders 071-873 8200

HMSO Bookshops
49 High Holborn, London, WC1V 6HB
071-873 0011 Fax 071-873 8200 (counter service only)
258 Broad Street, Birmingham, B1 2HE
021-643 3740 Fax 021-643 6510
Southey House, 33 Wine Street, Bristol, BS1 2BQ
0272 264306 Fax 0272 294515
9-21 Princess Street, Manchester, M60 8AS
061-834 7201 Fax 061-833 0634
16 Arthur Street, Belfast, BT1 4GD
0232 238451 Fax 0232 235401
71 Lothian Road, Edinburgh, EH3 9AZ
031-228 4181 Fax 031-229 2734

HMSO's Accredited Agents
(see Yellow Pages)

and through good booksellers

ISBN 0-10-297793-3

HOUSE OF COMMONS SESSION 1992–93

FOREIGN AFFAIRS COMMITTEE

THE EXPANDING ROLE OF THE UNITED NATIONS AND ITS IMPLICATIONS FOR UK POLICY

MINUTES OF EVIDENCE

Thursday 11 March 1993

MINISTRY OF DEFENCE

Mr Bill Reeves, Air Vice Marshal Nigel Baldwin, CBE and Colonel Austin Thorp, MBE

FOREIGN AND COMMONWEALTH OFFICE

Ms Glynne Evans, CMG

Ordered by The House of Commons *to be printed*
11 March 1993

LONDON: HMSO
£5.95 net

235–x

THURSDAY 11 MARCH 1993

Members present:

Mr David Howell, in the Chair

Mr Mike Gapes
Mr David Harris
Mr Michael Jopling
Mr Jim Lester
Mr Ted Rowlands
Mr David Sumberg
Mr Robert Wareing

Examination of witnesses

MR BILL REEVES, Assistant Under Secretary of State (Commitments), AIR VICE MARSHAL NIGEL BALDWIN, CBE, Assistant Chief of Defence Staff (Overseas), COLONEL AUSTIN THORP, MBE, Directorate of Military Operations, Ministry of Defence, examined. MISS GLYNNE EVANS, CMG, Head of United Nations Department, Foreign and Commonwealth Office, further examined.

Chairman

451. Could I begin be welcoming, on behalf of the Committee, our witnesses this morning: Mr Reeves, Assistant Under Secretary of State, Air Vice Marshal Baldwin, Assistant Chief of Defence Staff, Colonel Thorp, Directorate of Military Operations, and Miss Glynne Evans, Head of the UN Department, Foreign and Commonwealth Office. We are extremely grateful to you for taking time to come before us this morning and to help us in preparing our report on the changing role of the United Nations and this country's interests and concerns in relation to that. We are very grateful to you for agreeing to answer some questions which we would like to put to you. I gather, Miss Evans, that you have to head for the direction of the former Yugoslavia rather promptly. I would like to try to end this session at 12.15, though I cannot guarantee it—your answers may be too interesting! I will remember about releasing you at 12.15, should we overrun. Lady and gentlemen, could I begin with a fairly obvious but fundamental question based on the fact that the demands for UN or UN-blessed forces to fulfil peacekeeping in various forms seem to be escalating very rapidly. We now have the Secretary-General seeking apparently 28,000 troops to replace the withdrawing Americans in Somalia for UNOSOM II. Estimates of the troops needed to police the Vance-Owen plan—if such a thing was agreed in Bosnia—range from 25,000 up to enormous numbers, and of course there are current demands for UN forces in Mozambique, Angola, quite aside from all the outstanding demands on UN troops in all the areas of long-running troubles such as Cyprus, the Lebanon and so on. All this confronts us as Members of Parliament and this Committee with the prospect of huge additional demands on those countries and the military establishments of those countries who are prepared to contribute to the peacekeeping operations of the world. Our first question is, given these future and existing demands, will the UK be in a position to contribute troops to further UN operations round the world? Also, if I may add to that question, if we are able to meet these demands, what are the implications for the restructuring of our own armed forces? Those are big questions, I am afraid, but perhaps we should set these at the beginning. Who would like to catch the ball first? Mr Reeves?

(Mr Reeves) Thank you, Chairman. I think there is one point to make at the outset, which is that Ministers will be selective as to which of these demands they wish to meet in the future, as they have been in the past. You may recall, Chairman, the words of my Secretary of State on Tuesday apropros Somalia at Question Time, where he said, "We could have sent a battalion if we had thought it appropriate. We decided that the best contribution that we could make to Somalia was with RAF Hercules." So that was an instance where a deliberate decision was taken not to send ground troops, because Ministers decided to sit this one out. Therefore, it does not follow that because demand is increasing, every demand will be met. Nevertheless, you are absolutely right, there will be, we can foresee, demands which it will be very difficult *not* to meet. Perhaps I could put it in the context of what is happening to the armed forces. They are going through quite a radical process of reduction and restructuring as a result of the Options for Change decisions taken by Ministers in 1990. If I can quote figures for the Army, which is the Service most involved in peacekeeping (though of course the other Services are also involved in different ways), the Army is moving from a strength of 156,000 in 1990 to 119,000 in 1995, and it is about halfway through this reduction. The same is happening to the other Services. The policy aim, of course, is smaller forces, better equipped, properly trained and housed and well motivated; they have to be flexible and mobile and able to contribute in NATO and if necessary elsewhere. The forward planning for the armed forces is based on three defence roles which were set out in last year's White Paper. Perhaps I could briefly run over them. The first is to ensure the protection and security of the United Kingdom and our dependent territories even where there is no major external threat. The second is to insure against any major external threat to the United Kingdom and our allies. The third role—Defence Role 3—is to contribute to promoting the United Kingdom's

The cost of printing and publishing these Minutes of Evidence is estimated by HMSO at £2,919.

[**Chairman** *Contd*]

wider security interests through the maintenance of international peace and stability. That third role is the role—a very broad one—which embraces peacekeeping as well as other things. The basis of planning on which we work is that there are no armed forces dedicated to Defence Role 3. When this role needs to be put into operation forces are drawn from those planned for the other roles. I think it is fair to say that the broad size and shape of the force structure which will emerge from the Options for Change exercise has not so far been a constraint on our ability to provide troops for peacekeeping, and we would not expect it to be so in the long term. That said, of course, there is a transitional problem of achieving the restructuring which is planned, the amalgamation of regiments and that sort of thing, and that imposes a turbulence which is in fact going on now and will continue for the next year or two. So there is a transitional problem. However, I repeat, the availability of forces has not so far been a constraint on our ability to respond to demands of this kind when Ministers wish to do so.

452. I do not know, Air Vice Marshal Baldwin or Colonel Thorp, if you would like to chip in, as it were, on these questions. Please do not hesitate to do so. I will not press you unless you have something to contribute. Is there something you want to say on those opening general points?

(Colonel Thorp) I would only emphasise the importance of the transitional phase over the next 12 months. There are something like 28,000 trooops involved in amalgamations, unit moves and so on, to get them into the configuration and the place that they will be required to be in on 1 April 1995. That obviously is a constraint on our ability to generate forces, because they cannot be moving and reorganising as well as being on operations.

453. I suppose the question that follows, Mr Reeves, from your opening comment (which was extremely clear), is that although we are in transition is the strategic aim—namely, to concentrate on items 1 and 2 in your list and, as it were, meet the needs of item 3, international peacekeeping, as they arise—the right balance, or might it not be necessary, looking into the long-term future, which is always uncertain, to plan our armed forces on the assumption that it is item 3 which will be the big source of demand and the troubles all round the world in the post Cold War era, and item 2, combining with our allies to fulfil NATO-type tasks, will be the lesser demand? Might that not indicate that we should indeed construct the shaping of future forces in the realisation that the demands of peacekeeping round the world are going to be the main, most regular and insistent demand on our armed forces?

(Mr Reeves) Realistically, what you say, Chairman, may be true that peacekeeping is likely or liable to make the biggest demands on the armed forces for operations, and indeed we would hope that that *were* true, because the other two aims, concerned with the security of the United Kingdom and defence against external threat, must surely be regarded as more fundamental and, in a last resort, more important because they touch on the safety of the country and its people. So planning must always be directed primarily to those roles, but that by no means excludes the possibility or likelihood that forces prepared and trained for those roles will in practice spend a great deal of their time on Defence Role 3, peacekeeping and that kind of thing.

Mr Wareing

454. In view of the fact that the Foreign Secretary has referred to the new world disorder and the fact that the nuclear threat from the old Cold War possible adversaries seems at the very least to have diminished, would not now be the time to look again at Options for Change? Bearing in mind what the Chairman has said about the importance of the peacekeeping role of the United Nations, is it not important that we should? Would you agree that it is far better to look to the building up of our infantry regiments rather than, in fact, spending excessive money on nuclear arms such as Trident? What would your reaction be to that? The Secretary of State for Foreign Affairs has looked at the overall picture. What would your response be?

(Mr Reeves) I am sure the Cabinet in taking their decisions on Options for Change had the overall picture very much in mind, and their concern was to provide a range of capabilities—the nuclear deterrent, provision for the effective defence of the United Kingdom, provision for garrisons where these remain in overseas places, to play our full part in the defence of Europe, to have maritime strength in the Atlantic, and to be ready also for the unexpected under Defence Role 3. I am sure this balance is essential, but I think the implication of your question, Mr Wareing, that these two things are mutually exclusive, is one I would like to take issue with, because our experience has been in peacekeeping that well trained regular forces of the highest capability with the best equipment available are, in fact, precisely what you need for peacekeeping, and I think our experience in Bosnia has demonstrated that up to the hilt.

455. Yes, but what I am getting at is this: I was in Somalia along with my colleague Mr Rowlands last week and on a significant number of occasions the question arose as to the absence of a British battalion in Somalia. It does seem to me that our influence on the political decision-making depends far more on our being seen on the ground as the Australians and Canadians are in that part of the world than on our nuclear pretensions, if I can put it that way. It does seem to me hardly likely that Trident is going to be very useful in Somalia or Bosnia or Angola, but indeed the actual on-the-ground presence of a cohesive, well-disciplined—and that is what they are—British force would

[**Mr Wareing** *Contd*]

enhance Britain's role in foreign policy decision-making within the international community.

(Mr Reeves) I believe our role is already a very powerful one. Miss Evans can speak to that. Certainly it is true that no one would envisage employing Trident missiles in Somalia or even Bosnia. That is not to say that they have not a very important purpose to fulfil. I am quite certain they have. But, as I said earlier, a deliberate decision was taken that we would not send a battalion to Somalia, that we would contribute in other ways, we would send 2 RAF Hercules. We did, and a very valuable contribution they made. I think this decision was taken against the background of a great many other things we were doing. It should be borne in mind that the number of men we have committed to peacekeeping operations has almost quintupled over the last couple of years, from 800 two years ago to 3,700 odd now. I am including in that figure something like 2,800 for the two operations in former Yugoslavia. That in itself is a low figure because, if you take into account things like the maritime patrol in the Adriatic, airborne early warning and many other things we do, one is talking of very nearly 6,000 British servicemen employed in that theatre. So we are doing a great deal. Just to go over the places where we are employed on peacekeeping: Cyprus, the Western Sahara, the boundary of Iraq and Kuwait, Cambodia and, of course, above all the two operations in former Yugoslavia. The United States themselves do not at this moment have troops on the ground in former Yugoslavia. We do. So there is a parallel there with Somalia. We cannot and should not be everywhere. I do believe Ministers would always wish to be discriminating in what they take on. Our inability—not inability, our decision—not to contribute a battalion did not impede the operation in Somalia in any way. It was very well manned by other people.

Mr Rowlands

456. Could I pursue this point because I was with Mr Wareing in Somalia. I know these are political ministerial decisions. Let us explore the criteria and rationale behind the deployment we have in Somalia. We were in Baidoa, where last August 6,000 bodies were picked up on the streets in one month alone, and saw nobody dying of starvation there as a result of the 1st US Marines and now the Australian battalion there. They are going to pull out and the biggest challenge to peacekeeping, a new challenge of a particular kind, is going to arise as a result of this because United Nations peacekeeping is going behind what is already a very successful military emergency mission. We get the impression that what is needed is frankly the skills and professionalism of Western NATO forces to make UNOSOM II. Given our own particular special connections with British Somaliland, I wondered what rationale and criteria were used to say, no, we are not going to make any commitment in the case of Somalia?

(Mr Reeves) I am not sure whether this question of a decision is liable to be reopened, I suspect not, but the counter-argument one would hear, Mr Rowlands, is that Yugoslavia, unlike Somalia, is actually on our doorstep and it is specially incumbent on European nations to do something about the problems of that place. That is an argument one hears and I think it is bound to have significance.

Mr Rowlands: Somalia was not on the United States' doorstep.

Mr Lester

457. They were having an election.

(Mr Reeves) I must say for the record the United States does contribute to the airlift for Sarajevo just as we do with our RAF Hercules, but they are not there on the ground.

Mr Rowlands

458. On what rationale are these political judgments and decisions by Ministers based? Have officials a set of criteria to advise ministers on where they should deploy and how they should deploy with the growing United Nations demand?

(Mr Reeves) Of course, the military advice is available, the diplomatic advice is available; in the last resort I think it has to be a political judgment by Ministers of priorities. That will always be so.

Mr Lester

459. We were in Cambodia last week and were, therefore, able to see some of our military people there. I wanted to ask about the sort of lessons we have been learning. You say our troops are not dedicated to the third role you listed, but I wondered if you could say anything about whether they are actually trained in order to take part in these operations because the lessons we perceived were, first and foremost, that quality troops count a great deal more than those who have not got the training. There are special problems of multi-lingual 35-nation operations which again would need special training for those participating. Possibly the most important thing is the speed of reaction. We have evidence to show that in Somalia, for instance, if the 500 Pakistani troops had been able to get into Somalia within a week or two weeks of being asked, then perhaps we would not have needed 26,000 American troops to put it right subsequently, because it took two months to get those troops on the ground. Are the lessons we are investigating in this Committee, as it involves peacekeeping, being passed on and learned, or perhaps you are ahead of us in terms of making sure those units we have possibly earmarked for this type of operation are in a position to act very quickly and have some familiarisation with what it is like to do one of these operations.

(Air Vice Marshal Baldwin) If I can react to that, I am delighted to hear you emphasise—as indeed we would—about the value of, in this case, our all-professional forces and the skills which we all know they have. They are well-disciplined troops. We would say that they are well-disciplined troops trained for high-intensity operations—those

[**Mr Lester** *Contd*]

Defence Roles 1 and 2—and they are very well suited for peacekeepers. In fact I think we would assert that they are best suited for peacekeepers. As you probably know, we would not advocate in the British military a stand-alone United Nations force and assert our way of doing it, but we are of course unique in the world because we do have all-professional forces. As you know, very few nations have that. As far as training is concerned, if I take the case of our people in Cambodia, I think we would probably break our training up into three areas. Firstly, if we are going to send individuals or a very small package of people to staff posts, in that case they are hardly trained but they are briefed almost man to man or individually, not least by my colleague on my right and by headquarters UK LF. If we are talking about people deploying for duties as military observers, liaison officers or ceasefire monitors, UK LF have developed training packages which I think are about five days in length. We have had that under way for some time, so we have a disciplined approach to that element. Then the third one is something like Bosnia where we have taken a whole formed unit called the Cheshires, for the sake of this point, with many hundreds of men. They were trained over a long period for a specific training directive, and the training is designed to meet the particular priorities of that mission. They had five weeks of pre-Bosnia training. I know that Colonel Thorp on my right can add to that, should you wish. As far as feedback is concerned, we do have a circular feedback mechanism, in that we receive reports from all our officers acting as the COMBRIT forces wherever they are, whatever their rank. Some of them are relatively junior, as you know, such as lieutenant colonel. These provide valuable feedback to us in the Ministry and to UK Land Forces Headquarters Wilton and also Royal Air Force Headquarters Strike Command and, of course, my colleagues at Fleet. They are very interested in what is going on in Cambodia, as you know. The nature of the reports varies enormously from Minurso in Western Sahara in one extreme to Bosnia. We are developing all the time, because DR3 is a relatively new interest, as you have quite rightly focussed on. So far we have been mostly involved, in my life in the Ministry, in DR1 and DR2. Now this is changing in the last few months almost, but certainly less than two years. We are shifting the whole focus of this. If I may digress for a second, I spoke to a colleague of mine who is the Commandant of the Joint Service Defence College at Greenwich only yesterday to put him on the spot and say "How much is the UN training in your organisation of high-grade officers, lieutenant colonels, at Greenwich, the Joint Service Defence College? How much training are you doing on the United Nations? Is it fashionable?" "Of course, it's expanding all the time. A day does not go past," he said, "without some element of feedback from perhaps a visiting speaker, perhaps the Chief of the General Staff lectures to the course and there are questions on this." There are a large number of questions, as you can imagine, I am sure, these days, whether it is on Bosnia or whether it is on Cambodia. So although the syllabus of many of our staff college courses has increased dramatically from half a day's training three to five years ago to perhaps three or four days' training now a year, so there has been an increase, but not very much, in the United Nations itself. The work of the United Nations is impacting on and influencing the day-to-day work of our colleges to a tremendous extent. I suspect that it will increasingly do so as the headlines direct us to do just that.

Mr Gapes

460. Mr Reeves, taking you back to Somalia, you made reference to the distinction between countries being in Europe or not being in Europe. Could you then explain why the French, the Italians, the Belgians feel a desire to be involved in the Somalia operation? Could it be that the real reason is more to do with the way in which the Somalia operation was set up; that it was established by the Americans almost unilaterally and then got authorisation and did not come in in the same way as Cambodia or former Yugoslavia? I know that you already gave evidence to the Defence Committee in January, where you said that it came up at a time when we had already made a pretty large commitment to former Yugoslavia. Is it that because of the reorganisation of our forces, which has already been referred to by Colonel Thorp, there is not a possibility to have the resources available at this time for Somalia, or is it more a political problem? Could you enlarge on the reasons, please?

(Mr Reeves) It is certainly true that the requirement for a force for Somalia came up at a time when we had just made a large deployment to Bosnia, and you can never be sure what other demands there may be from that quarter. It did seem sensible to draw breath at the point that the Somalia operation came up, to take stock, to observe, as we did, that this operation was going to be well manned by other nations, the United States and others who wished to contribute. The decision was that since that was going well, there was no strong reason for a ground contribution, although an air contribution was made, to show willing. I think this was a sensible, pragmatic decision. I do not think it owed very much really to the way it came up. I do not think that that made any difference at all.

Mr Gapes: So you are satisfied that this operation is, as you put it, well manned?

Mr Rowlands: Is UNOSOM II going to be well manned? That is the question.

Mr Gapes

461. The British contribution could not have made it, or will not make it in the future, a better operation than it might otherwise be?

(Mr Reeves) I believe that it was a successful operation at the time and it did not suffer from lack of resources. I think that perhaps you are beginning to ask a different question.

[**Mr Gapes** *Contd*]

462. I am asking you about your role now. Given that you have had time to draw breath, as you put it, maybe it is time to consider what contribution we could make alongside the other European countries which are already planning to be engaged in the second phase?

(Mr Reeves) Each country has to make its national choice of what it wishes to get involved in, and the choices of different nations will be different. I do not think there is any need for uniformity for uniformity's sake, which you seem to be implying, Mr Gapes.

463. It is not uniformity, it is just that if there is a European contribution of Italy as a former colonial country involved in that region, why on earth can Britain not play a role, when it is clear that humanitarian needs are very, very great and that once the American presence is withdrawn there is going to be a danger of some kind of vacuum, unless there is a very strong operation in the future?

(Mr Reeves) We are delivering humanitarian aid or facilitating the delivery of humanitarian aid in Bosnia: the Italians are not. So there is a certain symmetry in their participating in Somalia when we are not.

Chairman: Given that the context that we cannot do everything and be everywhere is the one that you have given the Committee, I think we will leave it there for the moment. Maybe we will come back to that. I would like to turn the discussion onto the more precise mechanics of what is happening now and how we organise ourselves vis-à-vis the UN authorities. Could I ask Mr Sumberg to ask particularly about military advice to the UK mission in New York.

Mr Sumberg

464. We went to New York, met the mission there and had some very valuable meetings. I wonder if you could tell the Committee how the advice from the Ministry of Defence on military matters is channelled to New York? Does all information and advice and so forth go via the Foreign and Commonwealth Office, to the military adviser at the UK mission, or does it go direct to the UN secretariat's peacekeeping section?

(Mr Reeves) The Mission is the channel. Miss Evans can speak on this in a moment, but as far as the link between the mission and the Ministry of Defence is concerned, of course, the formal reporting chain is from the Mission to the Foreign and Commonwealth Office and specifically to the United Nations Department of which Miss Evans is the head. The Military Adviser whom you probably met is a Colonel who is a member of the mission and as such his reporting chain is to the FCO. That said, it will be obvious that his day-to-day links with the Ministry of Defence are very extensive indeed and the channel of communication between us and him is a very important one and a very heavily used one. If we wish to communicate with the United Nations, it will be through the Mission. Can I ask Miss Evans if she wishes to add anything?

(Miss Evans) Mr Chairman, the Committee, as you say, met our military adviser who was appointed at Sir David Hannay's initiative last year. He is his normal point of contact on military issues with the United Nations Secretariat, particularly with the Department of Peacekeeping Affairs and the Field Operations Division. There is in a sense a circle. If you have seen, as Mr Wareing said, the evidence given by Mr Reeves to the Select Committee on Defence, he mentioned there that liaison between the Foreign Office and the Ministry of Defence was very close indeed on these matters. So that in preparing instructions and advice for Sir David Hannay on any peacekeeping matters, including military aspects, that will take into account very detailed systematic and regular discussions with the MoD which we send to Sir David Hannay. He then reflects that, either at his own level or through the military adviser, in contacts with the Secretariat.

465. Within what you have said, that is the principal role you see of the military adviser at the Mission?

(Miss Evans) It is a two-way role. He on the one hand will pass on instructions and views from London and on the other hand will inform us—and he plays a very valuable role in informing us—on developments in the United Nations and the United Nations Secretariat. There is a growing volume of business, there is a very on-going role. He is an extremely busy officer, as I am sure you found.

466. Given the volume of business, should we have more military advisers there? Is he capable on his own of doing that job which you describe or does he need someone, or more than someone, to help?

(Miss Evans) At the moment there are only possibly not as many as 20 countries who have military advisers accredited to their Missions in New York. I am not aware of any who have more than one. The staffing of the Mission, of course, is something that is kept constantly under review. They have just been subject to inspection. While Colonel Manners-Smith is a busy officer, we are not under the impression that he is totally overburdened. He is also supported by other desk officers who are subject desk officers for Cambodia, for ex-Yugoslavia and so on. He does not carry the whole burden himself. His speciality is military advice.

467. The load is reasonable at the moment and you would be happy with it?

(Miss Evans) I think it is for Sir David Hannay to judge that and we have not had any suggestion that he needs more reinforcement on that side.

Mr Jopling

468. Did Sir David Hannay ask for extra military staff and, if so, what reaction have you given?

[**Mr Jopling** *Contd*]

(Miss Evans) He has not asked for extra military staff but perhaps this is really for Mr Reeves to say. There is, of course, at the same time an on-going dialogue from capitals with New York. I leave that for Mr Reeves to respond.

(Mr Reeves) We have no perception in the Ministry of Defence that Colonel Manners-Smith, busy though he certainly is, is so overloaded that he cannot give us the service we would seek from him in terms of keeping us informed and conveying our views through the channels I described or directly. But if there were to be such a perception in future, I am quite sure a reinforcement would be provided.

Chairman: What about the military capability within the United Nations. We would like now to look at your judgment of that.

Mr Jopling

469. I think Mr Reeves and Colonel Thorp appeared before the Defence Committee recently. Reading that, I think you said that the United Nations was principally a political organisation and there was only a modest military staffing element. You said that that presented problems in view of the expansion of the United Nations tasks. Could you tell us just what is the military input within the United Nations itself and at what rank it is there to provide military advice to the Secretary-General and—what I was really looking for—how many people to offer military advice are there in his office? We shall come in a short time to questions about the military staffing, but what I am talking about is the military element in Mr Boutros-Ghali's office. Do you believe the amount and quality of that advice is enough, given the multitude of different roles which the United Nations now has round the world?

(Mr Reeves) I will ask Air Marshal Baldwin in a moment to give the detail of how many people and of what kind the Secretary-General has to give him military advice, and when he does that I will answer your question on how things might be improved. The basic chain of command is the Secretary-General at the top, reporting to him the Under Secretary-General for Peacekeeping, now Mr Kofi Annan and reporting to him, the Secretary-General's Military Adviser who at present is Brigadier General Baril, a Canadian. Air Marshal Baldwin will now describe the detail.

(Air Marshal Baldwin) General Baril is now a Brigadier General, shortly to be a Major General. He heads a small team of colonels, 8 of them, seconded from national military services, and these 8 officers are the focal points for liaison purposes on military aspects of individual missions. They serve the political officers within the Department of Peacekeeping Operations as well as liaison with the permanent missions of Member States. There are more than 20, as we just heard from Miss Evans—the figure is 22—military advisers now. There were 8 18 months ago, it has grown to 22 as of the end of last week. The United Kingdom itself reappointed a military adviser—the good colonel we have been talking about—after an interval of 28 years in May of last year, and he works to Sir David Hannay, as you heard. Now, in addition to the Secretary General's military advisers—the good General Baril and his team of 8 colonels—there are additionally 39 military officers currently serving in the United Nations Secretariat and they are as follows: a stand-by planning team with 7, 2 specialist advisers, 8 involved in the UN special mission in Iraq inspector function; there is the Mozambique planning team which has 3, a field operations division—I will come back to that in a second—19, totalling 38, and there are two United Kingdom officers at present in the Field Operations Division, a lieutenant commander Royal Navy who heads the logistics unit in the Logistics and Communications Section responsible for logistics planning and co-ordination for United Nations peacekeeping, and other missions and continuing provision and support to on-going missions; then we have an Army major who is a finance officer in the Field Finance and Budget Section. The United Nations has recently asked us if we will extend these officers' secondments, which are six months at the moment, not least so that their familiarity with United Nations staff procedures can be exploited. We are looking at that at the moment. I must not say that we will automatically extend them—I do not know, but we are looking at it, and if this is agreed and it is the case, then the major, the finance man, will be appointed Deputy Head of the Field Finance Section. Then finally the United Kingdom also provides one of two specialist advisers so far appointed—a third, a police adviser, is expected shortly—and this is a retired Royal Engineers brigadier who took up the appointment as the Secretary-General's adviser in August last year. As well as developing detailed plans for mine clearance in a particular mission area he is looking at the need for a coherent approach to mine clearance across all United Nations agencies. The other United Nations specialist adviser already appointed is a Swedish colonel responsible for training and doctrine.

470. Could you please just give us the nationalities of the 8 colonels who are one below the Canadian general?

(Air Marshal Baldwin) Somewhere here I have them.

Mr Jopling: When you find it perhaps you could catch the Chairman's eye.

Chairman

471. Or leave us a note.[1]

(Air Marshal Baldwin) I will indeed.

(Mr Reeves) You asked about the future, Mr Jopling. One has to tread carefully here because it is after all the United Nations organisation that one is talking about; but I think it is fair to say that they themselves recognise that with the great expansion in their own peacekeeping activities over

[1] The 8 Colonels who work to the Canadian General are provided by; Argentina, Canada, 2 by France, Finland, Malaysia, Sweden and the United Kingdom.

[**Chairman** *Contd*]

the last few years, a quintupling of the number of men on the ground in the various peacekeeping operations, their organisation has been subjected to stress and strain and may well need to be developed. I do not think the United Nations themselves would dispute that. There are a number of possibilities which have been mooted. I think that if we were advising them we would suggest that the best buy, so to speak, would be to develop a military policy and planning cell manned by seconded Service officers from the nations, with a number of functions—preparing advice for the Secretary-General on all kinds of operations, all aspects of United Nations operations, developing contingency plans, assessing national capabilities, making proposals for force requirements, command and control, logistics, rules of engagement, training needs, liaising with nations and regional bodies, 24-hour support for current operations and so on and so forth; the kind of military role analogous to the sort of thing which goes on in national ministries of defence. I think that if our advice were sought, we would encourage the United Nations to explore that avenue.

Mr Jopling

472. Can I ask, if the Secretary-General decided that he wished to have a significantly higher military presence in his office from the one which the Air Vice Marshal has described to us, he would come to the British Government wanting more of our people. Would we be prepared, are we ready, to send more people? Can I link that question with another rather deeper one which follows what Mr Boutros-Ghali told us in November, that there were only a limited number of countries where he felt he could reliably go in order to find peacekeeping forces? We may come on to this with regard to our experience in Cambodia and the Bulgarian detachment later this morning, but would it be also true to say in realism—and I do not think we asked Mr Boutros-Ghali—that there are probably only a limited number of nations to which he could go to get competent military staff of the sort that the Air Vice Marshal has described to us?

(Mr Reeves) You are inviting me to tread on dangerous ground, Mr Jopling!

473. That is what we are here for!

(Mr Reeves) I must be careful what I am saying. I will ask Miss Evans to comment in a moment, but I am sure that if such a request were to go from the Secretary-General for military assistance it would be addressed to a number of nations, not simply to us, and I would be very surprised if Ministers did not wish to respond helpfully to such an approach. As regards the calibre of forces, you are quoting the words of the Secretary-General. I think we would certainly agree that the quality of troop contributors is apt to be variable, but there are important political considerations and considerations of political balance which necessarily play a part in the establishment of the military forces needed for peacekeeping, and I am sure that the same considerations would apply to headquarters. So I do not think it would be likely—Miss Evans may wish to comment on this—that that kind of request would be addressed to the stronger brethren alone, but that is my surmise. Perhaps I may ask Miss Evans to comment.

Chairman

474. Miss Evans, can you help us?

(Miss Evans) Perhaps I may make two comments. As Mr Reeves has pointed out, the Secretary-General is the servant of 179 nations and he cannot afford to be seen unduly to favour a limited number among those, so he has to create a delicate balance in his headquarters staff which reflects both expertise and equitable and geographical balance. It is a particular matter of sensitivity among the non-aligned nations, many of whom have been traditional troop contributors and quite successful across the years, who do not wish to be excluded either from headquarters posts or from future operations. One has seen some of this in the discussions in the Security Council and indeed on the Agenda for Peace. The kind of points just made by Mr Reeves in answer to your question, of course, are a matter of constant comment and discussion in New York. It is generally recognised, not least by the Secretary-General, that he does need to enhance his capability for military planning. There are various internal studies going on. We stay in close touch with the secretariat behind the scenes. We hope we are able to offer them some useful advice from time to time, and we hope that some positive recommendations will come forth which balance the two factors of expertise and equity in geographical terms.

Mr Rowlands

475. The one message which we had all week last week in Somalia, from General Johnston down, was that the UN is going to have to think differently about the character and nature of its military operations, it is going to have to think operationally; that the ethos has to change, in a sense, I think is the message we were getting; that the UN has to think like a superpower because it is now embarking on peacekeeping operations of a particularly difficult and complex kind, and that really there is need, not just for more people, but actually almost a change of thought and attitude. Do you share that feeling?

(Mr Reeves) I would certainly share the feeling that the challenges which United Nations peacekeepers have to face are much more demanding than they used to be. The types of activity they are called upon to undertake are much more varied than they used to be. So in that sense I would agree that there is a need for even greater professionalism than you have at the moment. Where I might hesitate is over the possible implication in your question that we might be straying too far from peacekeeping towards peacemaking—if that *was* an implication (maybe it was not).

[**Mr Rowlands** *Contd*]

476. It is an area which this Committee has been looking at as well, where one boundary ends and another one starts.

(Mr Reeves) That takes you into quite difficult territory, and it raises the question of how far that is an activity which ought to be undertaken.

477. If it is, though, you would certainly have to think differently in operational terms?

(Mr Reeves) Yes, that would be an even more severe challenge to those commanding and organising the force than peacekeeping as we know it today.

Chairman: Could we have a question on intelligence aspects of the military effort. Mr Harris?

Mr Harris

478. Mr Reeves, you said that if you were advising the Secretary-General you would be very happy to put forward the best-buy package on which you were planning your policy. Would enhancement of military intelligence capability form part of that package? Those of us who went to Croatia a few weeks back were very struck to learn that apparently in Croatia and former Yugoslavia there is no United Nations military intelligence capability as such and they were really, it seemed to us, living off the scraps of intelligence which they gathered in almost casual conversations with our own forces and various other people, but there did not seem to be a coherent intelligence effort. I do not know if that is the case, but that is what we were told. Do you see the United Nations having in these sensitive areas its own intelligence capability, or do you think there is scope for the Secretary-General to be allowed access to the military intelligence of member states?

(Mr Reeves) The concept of intelligence is a difficult one for the United Nations because of its connotations, because of its implication that there is somewhere an enemy, and in peacekeeping there is not an enemy. So the United Nations has difficulty with the word and the concept. On the other hand, it must be obvious that to run an operation of the kind which you have in Bosnia, for example, or Cambodia, you need information about what is happening, and if you give the task a different name—call it the collection of military information—you may find that this is necessarily the lifeblood of what the force commander is doing. Certainly from the point of view of force contributors, troop contributors, it must necessarily be an essential part of what they are doing, and it is certainly the case that national forces will, in gathering information about what is going on on the ground, share that information with their command. If we take Bosnia as an example, the British Force is reporting to the UN Commander, General Morillon, in his headquarters at Kiseljak. Obviously there must be a very important reporting line there. Does that answer the question?

479. I think it does. Perhaps I could ask about a different aspect of the same subject in the area of preventive diplomacy which might be somewhat different from the situation at least in Bosnia now where people are actually on the ground. Do you think it is feasible that the Secretary-General could have access to, shall we say, military information rather than military intelligence sources of Member States or do you think that is probably a sensitive area? If that is going too far, should he be able to plug in, say, to our intelligence system in areas where we think perhaps there is a danger emerging?

(Miss Evans) I think, Mr Harris, as you say, this is a sensitive area. It is difficult to envisage the United Nations Secretary-General formally being given any kind of intelligence capability for all the political reasons Mr Reeves has mentioned. It is always open to him, if he wishes to know more about a particular area, to approach Member States who might be in a position to help him. If I might just recall perhaps, when General Mackenzie, the former Force Commander Sarajevo, spoke in London, he was asked about the problem of military intelligence and he said, in fact, people organise themselves on the ground pragmatically. You are not allowed to call it intelligence, it is called information. The soldiers get round and get on with the job and sometimes, of course, commanders such as himself who have access to national sources continue to have that access and use it sensibly. That is not an answer to your question but I thought it might be a useful quotation.

Mr Harris: Thank you.

Chairman: Could we now look at the Military Staff Committee itself which, of course, has been a dormant organisation, but somebody suggested it should now be revived. Mr Wareing.

Mr Wareing

480. It does seem to many people that the military response, when necessary, by the United Nations has been rather haphazard and not really noted for cohesion. Both Lord Owen and Sir Crispin Tickell when they gave evidence to this Committee argued fairly strongly that the Military Staff Committee should now be revived in some form. Whilst one understands the difficulties there will have been during the Cold War period, there does seem now to be some reason for looking at this. What is the view of the Ministry of Defence on this proposal?

(Mr Reeves) Our view, Mr Wareing, I think, is to side with the other witnesses who appeared before this Committee who have suggested that to resuscitate the Military Staff Committee would be a "worst buy" rather than a "best buy". The Military Staff Committee was provided for in Article 47 of the Charter which prescribed that it should consist of the Chiefs of Staff of Permanent Members of the Security Council or their representatives. It does, in fact, meet, I understand, on a fortnightly basis. Our own representative is a member of the British Defence Staff in Washington who goes to New York for these occasions, but the business, I understand, is fairly perfunctory and mainly concerned with arranging the next meeting. So the bed is, so to speak, kept warm but no sub-

[**Mr Wareing** *Contd*]

stantive business is done. The Committee was devised at the time when it was thought the United Nations might develop standing forces of its own and in that context I think perhaps the idea made sense; but of course it has not come to fruition, I do not believe it ever will come to fruition, it is not something we would recommend. So that would seem to us the wrong sort of body to have to direct military operations. Politically it would be difficult. The idea that five Permanent Members of the United Nations should have their military advisers as a kind of military directorate for the United Nations as a whole might not be pleasing to some other members, and it would also be practically difficult to establish the kind of military bureaucracy to support this. I have already argued that there should be a stronger, if you like, military bureaucracy, military advice in the form of the planning cell I recommended, but if one were to make a reality of the Military Staff Committee it would require, I think, bigger support than that and we would regard this as rather wasteful as well as inappropriate. So we favour going down a different path to build up the military advice available directly to the Secretary-General, but not to impose a top hamper of Chiefs of Staff.

481. But the alternative to that seems to me to be rather less effective, because we seem to respond to conflicts as they occur and you may have a different view of this, but it does seem to me also that where there is a cohesive unified military command, such as the Americans are able to provide now in Somalia, the United Nations is more effective. It may be that we should not dismiss out of hand in any case the possibility of a cohesive United Nations force in the future. It may take time to come, but maybe we should be working towards the day when there would be recruitment of a United Nations force, like but not exactly in the same way as the French Foreign Legion recruits from all nationalities. Is this not something to be looking forward to in the future?

(Mr Reeves) It is an interesting idea, but I think an expensive one to bring about, because what you say, Mr Wareing, implies recruiting a force, equipping it, giving it logistic infrastructure such as a national force would require. This would be a very expensive operation indeed. It would be much cheaper to draw on national forces as need arises. You mentioned the absence of planning. I think Miss Evans can speak to that further if you wish, but you have introduced, I think, a very important point here in your reference to the United States and the command it can provide. I think that is the notion that the scale of a peacekeeping operation makes a very big difference, and there does come a point, I believe, where, if a peacekeeping operation is big enough, it may actually be too difficult for the United Nations to handle or command directly. If I can give an illustration of this—it is not a perfect illustration by any means—let us take Desert Storm, the operation to liberate Kuwait. That was not peacekeeping, I concede, but it was an operation which took place under the authority of the United Nations. It would have been inconceivable, I think, that the United Nations themselves could command such an operation, and inevitably it was a task delegated to a coalition of nations. I believe that was the only way it could be done. You are suggesting, I think, that the United Nations might develop a capability to deal with the very biggest operations. I am not sure that that is a path they are likely to go down.

482. Even if the United Nations itself does not become the superpower that my colleagues mentioned before—a possible superpower policing the world—even with the earmarking of troops by individual Member States, it does seem to me there needs to be an on-going military command instead of having to respond every time there is a crisis by creating a new military command there in each particular case. In any case, no matter what your own feeling is, Mr Reeves, has the Defence Ministry in any way got any contingency plans just in case the Military Staff Committee were revived?

(Mr Reeves) The Defence Staff look at all kinds of contingencies all the time. Maybe my military colleagues can say more about this. I would say that the situations where peacekeeping forces may be needed may be foreseeable in a broad political sense—Miss Evans can speak to this and can describe the kind of contingency planning that the FCO undertake—but they are probably rather difficult to plan for in a military sense, because you may not know when or in what form the crisis will arise. Could I ask Miss Evans first to comment, then to be followed by my military colleagues.

Chairman

483. Could I follow Mr Wareing's question by saying that, of course, the Ministry of Defence is against the earmarking idea and in fact sent a "No, no" return to Secretary-General Boutros-Ghali when he sent a round-robin in 1990 asking countries whether they would earmark troops. That is still the position, is it?

(Mr Reeves) You express it rather negatively, Chairman! We do not regard earmarking as efficient, for the very simple reason that if each nation earmarks troops and declares them to the United Nations, the aggregate of all those declarations is likely to be a rather shapeless force in a military sense. We believe it is much more logical to say that *most* of our armed forces—obviously not the Trident submarines—are, in principle, available for peacekeeping, subject to the other commitments they may have. If every nation made that kind of declaration it would be quite easy for the United Nations to mix and match the kind of force it needs to establish for a particular operation. So we believe that our approach is really much more constructive than the one requested.

484. I am sorry, I interrupted. Miss Evans was going to speak.

(Miss Evans) If I may add on that last point, I think the Secretary-General himself has now

[**Chairman** *Contd*]

moved away from the concept of earmarking, as represented in the 1990 questionnaire, towards a concept of what you might call a greater visibility of what forces can be made available and within what sort of time period. The question I was going to answer was on planning. In the Foreign Office our planning staff, in consultation with regional departments, do, by definition, keep potential flashpoints under review both as regards the medium and the long term, and we pass the fruits of those assessments to other Whitehall departments and to the Cabinet Office. We in my department look at these with a beady eye as to whether or not they might have a United Nations application. As you will have heard from previous evidence given to the Committee, one of the strands one is trying to develop now is preventive diplomacy. In other words, before you go down the road of a military route, what are the alternatives, is it not better to pre-empt something which is going to descend into conflict, by some suitable diplomatic measures, rather than automatically assume that a military answer is necessarily the right one? Indeed, the Foreign Secretary, in a speech only last week, did make this point rather clearly and also noted that he had discussed this very theme with the Secretary-General. He said that there needed to be a rigorous analysis of risks and benefit, and that the international community must not lurch into enterprises the objective, scope and duration of which have not been thought through. I think that in his evidence he himself did very much stress preventive diplomacy. Perhaps I might mention the example of Macedonia and the UN battalion deployed to Macedonia as a first-ever example of such preventive deployment, as a model which may have future possible application.

Mr Wareing

485. That is a decision, of course, which can quite easily be taken by the Security Council. The whole issue of preventive diplomacy is a matter of politics rather than military action. What troubles me really is that whilst the mechanism is there in New York for dealing with political decision-making, when it comes to military operations there is not anything that really co-ordinates matters, and we wait for a conflict to arise, then we respond. It may be that the Third World countries, which perhaps are inadequately equipped to provide for United Nations peacekeeping, will look askance if every time something arises in the world it is left to one or two nations, particularly to the United States, as well as they have performed in Somalia. There is this feeling that it is the half-a-dozen powers capable of going into the field now which will indeed dominate the world as the world peace force.

(Miss Evans) I think you have Somalia again in mind there. As I recall, Sir David Hannay did talk in his evidence about the delays in getting the operation on the ground. I think this relates perhaps to another area, if I might momentarily stray, which is the humanitarian side and the need for a great deal of very systematic contingency planning when you see a humanitarian emergency in the making. This was precisely the thought which underlay the British and Anglo-German initiative on humanitarian affairs a year ago which led to the creation of a department of humanitarian affairs and a co-ordinator. In a sense, had that operation existed a few years ago—this is speculation—perhaps there could have been a more systematic, integrated, humanitarian approach in Somalia before the circumstances deteriorated. That is not an answer to your question, but it is, I think, part of one of the facets which is worth bearing in mind.

Chairman: I think we want to come on to this whole question of military interrelationship with humanitarian tasks in a moment. However, perhaps we could stay with the military for a moment and, having asked about staffing and staff officers, ask about generals and force commanders.

Mr Sumberg

486. I wonder if you can tell us how the commanders of the UN peacekeeping forces are appointed? For instance, is the MoD routinely consulted by the FCO about these appointments?

(Miss Evans) The force commanders are selected by the Secretary-General and have hitherto been drawn from officers from among the traditional troop contributors who have been those who have contributed battalions and have experience. Quite apart from his military qualities, it is a cardinal rule that he must be acceptable to the parties on the ground. The Secretary-General would normally notify the Security Council rather than consult them. By definition, in the past the five permanent members of the Security Council who did not take part in UN peacekepping until UNICOM, with the exception of UNFICYP, have never held commands and have therefore not been involved in that particular process. The only senior command held by a member of the permanent five has been that of the theatre commander in Bosnia, General Morillon. This, of course, may change as the contingents for making up the bulk of the UN peacekeeping forces change in their nature and nationality. Those who have the largest troop commitments, as the Committee knows, are firstly France, and currently the UK is second. But I would not wish to speculate. A state would be consulted. If the Secretary-General thought that a particular state was appropriate for a particular operation they would be consulted, as would the parties to the conflict or the situation on the ground.

487. So are you saying that the matter has not arisen, or does not arise, of consultation between the two departments of state? It has not arisen or would not arise? Which is it?

(Miss Evans) I am saying we, the United Kingdom, would not expect to be involved in the selection of the force commander because that is very much the Secretary-General's own decision which he takes on the basis of military advice available to him and the political circumstances of

[**Mr Sumberg** *Contd*]

the country where the force commander would be deployed. We would certainly be informed.

488. He takes it within his own department without reference to Member States and their national governments?

(Miss Evans) He would take it within his department, consulting the states concerned. As you will know, he has just selected a Turkish general to be the force commander for UNOSOM II. In that process I have no doubt he would have consulted the President of the United States as being directly relevant and the Turkish Government, by definition, and possibly some of the OAU states taking a particular interest in Somalia.

489. To press the point slightly, if he had consulted the British Government, presumably the Foreign Office, would there then have been an intercommunication between the Foreign Office and the Ministry of Defence on that consultation?

(Miss Evans) Absolutely, as with all other aspects.

490. Can you tell us how the United Kingdom, any government department, MoD or FCO, are involved in the preparation for the sending of peacekeeping forces to areas in conflict, whether or not we are involved indirectly, whether or not British troops are involved? How is the United Kingdom involved, if at all, in the whole preparation of the enterprise?

(Miss Evans) The steps are that the Security Council would pass a resolution inviting the Secretary-General to prepare a report on the possible despatch of the mission. The Secretary-General would send one or more reconnaissance missions to the area which could involve a potential force commander or other senior officers for a possible headquarters. It would also bring in representatives of Field Operations Division and those bits of the United Nations Secretariat that are responsible for supporting the force in the field. It would almost certainly include representatives from actual or potential troop contribution nations. The fruits of that technical mission would be incorporated into a further report to the Security Council and once the Council took a decision the process of deployment would begin. As has been noted earlier, it is rather a slow process because even after the resolution has been adopted the budget for the operation then has to be put to the United Nations budgetary authorities. Behind the scenes, and at the same time, the United Nations Secretary-General and his staff would consult those nations who they believed were willing and had the capacity to contribute to that force. It would be an interactive process. They would ask Ruritania, "Could you provide a logistics battalion?", Ruritania might say, "We can't do so, but we might be able to provide X", and in the light of that interactive process they would see what the components of the corps would be, the formal Orbat (order of battle) of the force. The formal components would also be presented to the Security Council for approval.

Chairman

491. Who would advise on the rules of engagement for peacekeeping forces in the field? Obviously the Security Council makes final decisions on this, but who sets out the menu, who gives the military and expert input to what choices of rules of engagement should be presented to the permanent representatives?

(Miss Evans) The United Nations rules of engagement are basically an internal document prepared by the military staff, I think, and they have more or less a standard model which would then be adjusted according to the demands of a particular operation in consultation with the force commander. They would not normally be put to the Security Council for approval because they are by definition confidential and internal.

492. But surely when the other day, for instance—February 19, I think—the Security Council enlarged the mandate of United Nations troops in Bosnia somewhat, so that they could perhaps have a more effective role in opening roads and so on, that must have involved a revision of the rules of engagement.

(Miss Evans) Mr Chairman, in Croatia?

493. In Bosnia, the February 19 position, the decision of the Security Council to enlarge the mandate of United Nations troops.

(Mr Reeves) That rings no bells, Chairman.

494. I am going on reports in the newspapers; perhaps nothing happened.

(Miss Evans) There has been no change in the mandate since the adoption of 776.

495. No upgrade of the rules of engagement—from now on you can force your way down the road rather than merely return fire?

(Mr Reeves) No, the mission has not changed at all.

Chairman: Then we have been reading misleading newspaper reports—not for the first time!

Mr Rowlands

496. I am sorry to harp on Somalia, it may be *sui generis*, to borrow the Foreign Office phrase. There again we found almost an obsession about the importance of maintaining nothing less than the existing rules of engagement that the present coalition forces have for UNOSOM II. How would that be decided and who would decide whether the new UNOSOM II forces were going to have at least the same rules of engagement as those that exist for the present forces in Somalia?

(Miss Evans) The Secretary-General's report on Somalia on UNOSOM II which has just been published does make clear that it should be a Chapter VII operation, which points to robust rules of engagement. I do not know how—I am not famil-

[**Mr Rowlands** *Contd*]

iar with the rules of engagement in Somalia—they would be adjusted. This would be an internal process between the United Nations Secretary-General, as I say, and the force commander. But it would be a Chapter VII exercise. This, I think, would prove your point, Mr Rowlands, that it would be a robust outlook.

497. On behalf of the 358 workers in the field in Somalia, let alone the forces, nothing less than what they have got would do because everybody believes the thing could unravel if they were not. How does one get that message across?

(Miss Evans) I think the Secretary-General has very well taken that point. That is why he has proposed an operation under Chapter VII of the Charter.

(Mr Reeves) You occasionally get differences of perception. For example, I recall when UNPROFOR II, the force in Bosnia, was being set up in the summer the concern of the United Nations High Commissioner for Refugees was rather the opposite, that they did not want this to be too robust, or too military. So obviously circumstances alter cases.

Mr Rowlands: Yes, okay, but you have a successful military mercy mission in operation in Somalia at present; it would be disastrous for the concept of United Nations peacekeeping if as a consequence of any alterations or changes the thing would unravel under the auspices of the United Nations. This is a concern we picked up very forcefully when we were there.

Chairman: Could we turn to costs and resources, the root of a great deal of these matters. Mr Gapes.

Mr Gapes

498. Could you explain to us the exact financial relationship between the Foreign Office and MoD votes with regard to accounting for the costs of British military contributions in United Nations peacekeeping? I understand—perhaps you will correct me—that costs appear on the MoD votes but there is also a payment from the Foreign Office to MoD and there is also a payment from the United Nations which I have been told is $998 per man per month from the United Nations to countries which contribute to a particular United Nations operation, but that in our case that is not sufficient to cover the costs of our own contribution. Could you give us some information about that?

(Mr Reeves) Certainly, Mr Gapes. I will begin by taking the Ministry of Defence end of it, so to speak, and then move to Miss Evans. As you say, in the first instance the expenditure connected with deploying the Armed Forces is charged to the Ministry of Defence Votes, like any other activity. That is the only way it can be done. However, Vote responsibility for all international peacekeeping operations rests with the FCO. The reasons for this convention are that the defence budget exists to meet the costs of national defence, whereas military involvement in peacekeeping is in support of foreign policy objectives; and that the way that the budgetary system is organised, financial responsibility is aligned with policy responsibility, and that makes it appropriate for the FCO to pay. Therefore, where we incur the initial expenditure, the FCO reimburse us. There may be, depending on the case, a separate financial transaction involving the United Nations. I may say, though, that this is not the case at the moment for UNPROFOR II which at the moment is being paid for by national contributors. Perhaps I may ask Miss Evans to extend this reply.

(Miss Evans) I think that there is not much more to say, other than to say that there is indeed a claim on our budget for international peacekeeping. If the FCO budget is insufficient to meet such claims, in so far as this expenditure is unforeseen, mechanisms exist to enable us to make a claim on reserve. With regard to reimbursement for UN operations to which we have deployed forces, as Mr Reeves says, this does not apply either to offset our contribution in UNFICYP or Bosnia. The pattern is that we would prepare returns and put them to the UN Secretariat. These cover not only the $998 per man per month but also some equipment costs which are deemed to be UN reimbursable. This is, of course, a matter for negotiation with the secretariat. We do not have much experience of this, because our previous peacekeeping experience with Cyprus we financed ourselves. However, in the case of Namibia we did have components there which were UN-reimbursable, and we duly negotiated with the UN secretariat and received some return quite speedily.

499. When that money is reimbursed, where does it go to? Does it go to the MoD, does it go to the Foreign Office, does it go to the Consolidated Fund? What happens to it?

(Miss Evans) I cannot answer that very precisely because, as I say, we rather lack experience. I believe it ends up with the Treasury sooner or later. The sheer mechanism of how it gets there I am afraid I cannot say.

500. So the expenditure comes out of an FCO budget head, yet the money which comes back from the UN does not come back to the Foreign Office, is that right?

(Miss Evans) It will depend on the timing of its reimbursement, on whether it is something which is unforeseen expenditure, has been the subject of a claim on the reserve or has been within the FCO expenditure budget for that year. As I say, since the last time it has happened was a long time ago, I am afraid I am not able to answer with any great precision.

501. Would you think that that is a sensible arrangement?

(Miss Evans) To be reimbursed?

502. No, how it is reimbursed.

(Miss Evans) In terms of how the UN does it, or whether it goes to the Treasury?

[**Mr Gapes** *Contd*]

503. How it is dealt with within our own Government.

(Mr Reeves) I think it is perfectly logical, Mr Gapes. The Ministry of Defence pays out in the first instance and receives money from the FCO, because the activity is in support of a Foreign Office objective. Any money obtained from the United Nations certainly does not come to the MoD because we have already been paid, it comes either to the FCO or, depending on the timing, it may go to the Consolidated Fund, I imagine. It is a perfectly logical financial chain.

Mr Jopling

504. It is *not* logical, if I may say so, because it is exactly the way the Common Agricultural Policy works! What the Treasury say is that you must do this out of your budget, and you are not allowed to say, "Yes, we're trying to do it out of our budget, but of course we do get some reimbursement which reduces the costs." What the Treasury do is that they charge you for anything you spend and they take back any reimbursements. It is not logical at all, it is a disgrace!

(Mr Reeves) From the Ministry of Defence's point of view it is fairly satisfactory.

Chairman

505. Perhaps we could ask a broader question about the whole way in which these resource allocations are made. We are moving into a world, as we discussed, where peacekeeping is becoming a mixture of mobilising emergency aid, as we will be discussing in a minute, on humanitarian grounds, and preventive diplomacy which is peacekeeping and maybe a well-honed military intelligence for the deployment of troops on the ground in various roles. Are you satisfied that within the Whitehall machine the increasing co-ordination this is going to require between the Foreign and Commonwealth Office, the ODA (which is part of the FCO) and the MoD, so that one can put in and use overall resources in the right way, in the right situation, is a sufficiently well-developed piece of machinery?

(Mr Reeves) I think the co-ordination machinery is extremely well developed, Chairman. Of course, at its apex are the Cabinet and the Ministerial Committee on Defence and Overseas Policy controlling all these things, where all these interests are represented, but at official level the co-ordination is very close indeed. In the case of a large and difficult operation like Bosnia it is daily, and there is cross-membership of the various committees in either department. For example, Miss Evans is frequently to be seen at our Ministry of Defence meetings on Bosnia, and I and my staff are frequently to be seen in the FCO at their meetings. So the dialogue is very, very close indeed. The ODA are brought in, the Treasury are brought in.

506. What I was getting at, as was Mr Wareing earlier, is that one battalion may cost less than a weapons programme, and the Foreign Secretary said recently in the House of Commons that one ambassador costs less than a battalion. Are these opportunity costs weighed up sufficiently carefully before we plunge into these totally novel kinds of operations around the world?

(Mr Reeves) I am not quite sure what the implication of the Foreign Secretary's remark was. Of course, as you know well, Chairman, the PES mechanism exists to deal with precisely this kind of task of establishing financial priorities.

Mr Jopling

507. Can I revert to costs. We came across quite a serious problem in Cambodia last week with regard to the payment by the UN of $998 per man per month. The problem there is that some troops from some detachments I understand have not been paid for six months and have been behaving in a disgraceful way which reflects that, because their government has pocketed the money and not paid the troops. Are there any moves that you are aware of going on to try to rearrange this system so that there is some sort of a guarantee that troops on the ground will be paid?

(Mr Reeves) That is certainly not a problem which has ever occurred to British troops, I am sure.

508. Naturally, of course not. I am not suggesting that.

(Mr Reeves) I simply do not know what the answer to that is. Perhaps I could ask Miss Evans whether she can throw light on this.

(Miss Evans) I have not before heard this story, but reimbursement is not something that is actual, it does take place much later. I think that whatever governments are responsible, the odds are that they have not yet themselves received their payments from the UN. All governments who deploy forces are supposed to deploy them adequately provisioned and equipped when they have formed battalions, and then, of course, they receive reimbursement. It may be that some of the poorer countries have found the obligation rather onerous. As I say, I have not heard this story before.

(Air Vice Marshal Baldwin) I do not have personal experience of this, but my deputy, an Army brigadier, went out and only just preceded you, I think, and he certainly did not come back with any concerns, to put your mind at rest about British servicemen anyway.

509. I am not suggesting that for a moment.

(Air Vice Marshal Baldwin) My own predecessor, General Harley, who went out to visit our people there in the autumn reported back to the Chief of Defence Staff that all the servicemen he spoke to agreed that the United Nations subsistence allowance of $145 a day (this was October last year) more than covered their expenses, even allowing for regular telephone calls to the UK for those who could get to telephones. Doubtless in their conversations there was a soldier or two who said, "I could do with some more money," and

[Mr Jopling *Contd*]

"I'm not being looked after as well as the Ruritanians," but we are not conscious of any problem at the moment.

Mr Jopling: I was not for a moment suggesting that. I was referring to other detachments.

Chairman: Are there any other questions on costs from my colleagues?

Mr Rowlands

510. We talked earlier, Mr Reeves, about the close working interdepartmental relationship on Bosnia and planning the costs etc. Are you making assumptions on contingency plans that the costs in Bosnia are going to rise subsequent to the Americans going there?

(Mr Reeves) What developments do you have in mind?

511. The possibility that the Owen-Vance plan might come into force with 25,000 to 30,000 plus.

(Mr Reeves) That, of course, would require a decision by Ministers which has not yet been taken. There is as yet no Owen-Vance agreement. Negotiations are intensive at the moment. Ministers have not taken a view on participation. You probably heard the words of my Secretary of State on Tuesday when he said, "We are prepared to give serious consideration to the help that we could give if a genuine ceasefire were delivered on the ground in Bosnia, but any proposals for a combat role do not accord with the policy of Her Majesty's Government." I think if and when the Owen-Vance process results in an agreement we would have to look at it very carefully to see whether those tests for British involvement were met.

512. Referring to earlier questions based on the point that, because of the special European connection, Bosnia attracted the contribution of Britain, do you think it is going to be politically realistic to walk away from that situation and not play a very much larger role?

(Mr Reeves) It is not a question of walking away. We are undertaking a role at the moment which we have no plan to discontinue. As long as the need for escort for humanitarian aid or greater security in which aid can be delivered by others exists, I imagine our operation would continue. What you are talking about is a completely new kind of operation on a much bigger scale and, as I say, Ministers have not addressed this yet and in any case there is no agreement as yet.

Chairman: Mr Reeves, this is a completely new kind of operation. We mentioned earlier the question of training for it, but what other experience are we accumulating?

Mr Rowlands

513. Contacts I have had with the Army and military personnel getting involved in these roles suggest this is a very different animal to the layman from the traditional soldier or military man. It is a very sophisticated political role offering a political feel to the subject. That struck us forcefully in Somalia. Are we gathering experience, knowledge, expertise as we get more and more involved in the United Nations and are we using that resource in either training processes or in thinking through creative development of military personnel within the process?

(Mr Reeves) The answer is yes, Mr Rowlands. Could I ask both my military colleagues in turn to comment?

(Air Marshal Baldwin) Perhaps I could answer the question by starting with the way it begins, the selection of people, because much of this is very new to us, if you put the Cyprus experience to one side, in the last couple of years. The selection for United Nations posts as far as British military are concerned depends very much on own background and experience but as a general principle we seek volunteers and normally get them. Those who have been to Cambodia, for example, have seen the excellent Royal Engineers, with a lieutenant colonel running the mine-clearing operation out there. He was a volunteer for that post who had been seeking the post—we interviewed him three weeks ago—for over nine months. The appointments are in the Military Secretary's Department and, indeed, other services try to identify individuals who are suitable. We recognise that an international environment demands particular attributes—confidence, personality, initiative, all of those good military qualities. Language is important and particularly relevant to United Nations appointees, we would assert. We tend to be careful to send high-grade individuals which is borne out by the many plaudits we get about their performance. Time and time again our people excel. So far as career progression is concerned, which may be behind your question, although we will always argue in the military that selection for promotion is on merit, it is more how you do the job than the job you have got or have been given. It is how you perform a specific job. Most of these United Nations jobs, of course, are only to my view admittedly for six months or so. That is a relatively short time for officers' careers. Nevertheless, there is a formal report mechanism on those officers in terms of their own career and we would expect everyone—indeed, they do—to report not just in writing, but literally to their masters when they come back, so we can pluck from them their experiences both as individuals and for information feedback to the circular training machine. Although we are not complacent about it, I would like to give you the impression that we are conscious that (a) we send people of high quality and (b) there are some very unusual ones amongst them as well, and we seek to draw everything we can from them, not just when they get back but also in the capacity of a pastoral role I have hinted at earlier on this morning where, for example, officers work for me and my predecessor, the Chief of the General Staff, not constantly but mixing our people. So they are not forgotten. I think if I have given you something there to hang on, perhaps Colonel Thorp, who is much more expert than I

[Mr Rowlands *Contd*]

am as far as the Army is concerned, might like to add.

(Colonel Thorp) I think we are fortunate in the Services in that we still attract highly motivated and very high quality officers and soldiers. They develop throughout their careers, particularly junior ranks, into NCOs who are the envy of the world's armies. You commented on their political awareness. International affairs and regional studies are quite a substantial proportion of promotion exams, staff college courses and an officer's education—which goes on throughout his career—and indeed that is one of the benefits of having comparatively large numbers of foreign students attending places like the staff college and staff college run courses and so on. We have a very structured and quite formal mechanism for learning the lessons of the work that our officers and soldiers are currently doing, of assessing it, formalising it in terms of doctrine, which as far as the Army is concerned is what we teach, incorporating the lessons into our training and disseminating it as quickly as possible. In that context our interest is not only in what we are doing but, for example, we have a programme of exchanging liaison officers with those other troop contributors in Bosnia. We observe each other's training methods and we generally try to pool all the information we can get our hands on because we need other people's experiences from which we can also learn.

Chairman: Now the question of the military role in sanctions. Mr Jopling.

Mr Jopling

514. To add to Mr Rowlands' point, I listened to what the Air Marshal said about careers for those who serve. Really what he said did not lie alongside the experience we had in Cambodia last week. Let me say we found the British officers we met admirable, but I remember saying goodbye and thank you to two of them and I said, "I hope this sort of service is good for your careers", and they said, "Well, no, as a matter of fact it isn't—it is rather the opposite." I said, "Why is that, because you are doing a wonderful job", and they said, "The difficulty is we don't have a senior officer who can authoritatively report on us." We raised this with the Australian general at a later meeting and I think he rather acknowledged that this was so, because sometimes maybe the reports of some of the senior officers who may be reporting perhaps do not carry quite as much weight as if they had been made by British officers who were familiar with the standards of the British military forces. I am just wondering if anything can be done to ensure somehow that service of this sort is not a minus in terms of a career?

(Air Vice Marshal Baldwin) Perhaps you will allow me a few minutes to speak on this, because it is very close to home, not least because one of my colonels is the first or the second reporting officer of some of the officers you have been talking about, so it literally comes through me. I can say in a general sense, having spent four years in the last 11 years working with another country's military, that we all, not suffer, but we are all conscious of the fact that reporting standards vary across services. We all in our baggage worry about whether our own masters acknowledge the fact that that inevitably happens. All I will say is that swings and roundabouts over a long career, generally speaking, the good get through. I come back to the six-month point I was making to Mr Rowlands. This is a relatively short period in an officer's career. All personnel, including those people you saw in Cambodia, do get a report at the end of their six months which is in addition to the traditional annual reporting mechanism in the British services. Clearly the laid-down reporting system for officers in all three services is to their respective personnel branches. My own colonel who has a responsibility for such people prepares reports on all Royal Navy commanders, lieutenant commanders and wing commanders from notes made by the UNTAC commanders. Then in addition to that we have to rely to a certain extent on the impressions gained by our own officers who, in the pastoral role I have mentioned, look at this. Equally, and perhaps more importantly, there is, I assure you, constant dialogue going on, whether it is written or telephonic increasingly these days. A day will not go past without one of my officers talking to one of those people you have met, and in a managerial sense an impression is being gained all the time that will help to write what I would hope—because most of the people we are talking about are Army overseas—is reflected by appointment and selection boards. Finally, I reiterate, it is how you do in our business rather than the process itself which is critically important. We are fairly confident—more than fairly confident—overall of our reporting chains and mechanisms which are constantly being looked at. So I am disappointed to hear the reaction which that particular officer gave to you. We will have to wait and see. I personally gained a very high impression of that particular officer. I suspect you did too. Let us wait and see what happens to him.

Chairman: Perhaps we could turn to sanctions now.

Mr Jopling: I wonder if you could tell us how important you see the role of sanctions in the future? Of course, you will never make sanctions 100 per cent effective, but would you not agree that there is a great opportunity and a great need to make sanctions infinitely more effective? With regard to former Yugoslavia, I had a Question down for the Foreign Secretary not very long ago with regard to how many tankers had got into that area through the Adriatic and how many barges had gone up the Danube, how many Iranian aircraft had been seen flying into the territory. We all know that there has been sanctions busting. Is it not possible for the United Nations to devise for the future a much better way of ensuring that sanctions are much more effective, whether it is by deploying military or policing forces in surrounding states at the point of the imposition of sanctions? Are there not ways that we could save ourselves having to deploy military forces in places

[**Mr Jopling** *Contd*]
like Yugoslavia, by imposing sanctions, making them much more effective and putting on pressure that way, before you had to put troops on the ground?

Chairman

515. If Miss Evans is going to answer on this she should do so now, because in two minutes we are going to release her. Would you like a last answer before you leave for Zagreb, Miss Evans?

(Miss Evans) Thank you, Mr Chairman. I think I am going to be glad that I am going to be stopped by the clock, as it were, as it is a very big question! As a starting point, clearly where a sanctions regime is adopted it must be seen to be effective. I think that you yourselves have heard from the Foreign Secretary about the various measures which we have been instrumental in promoting in the UN and through the European Community and the CSCE, in particular in the case of ex-Yugoslavia, to make the sanctions bite more. The appointment of a sanctions co-ordinator as an overall supremo who would have the dual role of being a force to persuade those states principally involved, neighbouring states, riparian states, to comply with their obligations, to give them the kind of advice that sometimes they genuinely need, and to act as a continuing focus of pressure, was something that was very much a British initiative. The sanctions co-ordinator has now been adopted, and the Foreign Secretary saw him in Brussels only last week. We were also instrumental during the British presidency in establishing the sanctions assistance missions in the neighbouring countries and have indeed contributed a team of customs officers who man the SAM in Hungary. These are innovative ideas; they have not before been done in any sanctions regime, and the various results are reported back to the UN sanctions team on ex-Yugoslavia. In present circumstances it is the UN, through the Sanctions Committee, which is responsible for the effective implementation of sanctions. By definition, they play a diplomatic role, but it is not one to be underestimated, it is a focus of pressure. It is also a focus of embarrassment. This is one of the prime roles that any evidence of sanctions we receive, any information that may not amount to evidence, is brought to the attention of the committee and the committee would invite the state identified to explain what it is about. That degree of attention can be unwelcome and can produce results. So progressively and step by step we have been, with partners and through the UN, trying to tighten the sanctions regime as far as possible. I will leave Mr Reeves to talk about the military aspects, but that is as far as the civilians are concerned.

Chairman: Thank you. I think we must now release you to get your aeroplane. We have a few more questions, although we are a little over time, on the crucial area of military involvement in humanitarian operations, if we could put some questions to our remaining witnesses on those.

Mr Sumberg

516. If, as Miss Evans just said, UN sanctions must be effective, then UN humanitarian assistance must be as effective as we can make it. Mrs Ogata, the UN High Commissioner for Refugees, has stated that she would prefer all aid to be transported by the military in their own vehicles, as this would be safer than having civilian drivers accompanied by military vehicles. Would the Ministry of Defence be prepared to take over the delivery of aid in this way on these sorts of missions?

(Mr Reeves) I am not sure that the quotation from Mrs Ogata which you have just made, Mr Sumberg, is her position today. I think she said that at a time when she was quite depressed about the problems of delivering aid in Bosnia, and she later, I think, cheered up a bit. I do not think that she is now proposing that the *modus operandi* of aid delivery should be changed in Bosnia. I will ask Colonel Thorp to enlarge on this in a moment, but what our forces in Bosnia have tried to do and, I think, succeeded in doing to a very large extent, is not so much to escort aid deliveries as to create an atmosphere of security and confidence in the area where they operate which would enable others to deliver the aid. This is sometimes an uphill task because there has been fighting in those areas, of course, but it is one on the whole that they have been able to discharge with success, and I would not myself see a need to change the way they are working. That said, let me turn to the military expert, Colonel Thorp, who lives with this problem day to day.

Chairman

517. We did have evidence that, I think, the Belgian and Dutch military operations did involve carrying civilian aid and reference was also made to our operations in Northern Iraq where I think the military involvement in aid was greater than it is in Bosnia.

(Colonel Thorp) We have no intrinsic objection to carrying aid and in certain circumstances we have done so. It might help if I just explained, first of all, the concept which is to proceed by consent with the military in support of the UNHCR. Because of the UNHCR-led operation, it became apparent very early on in the experience in Bosnia that proceeding by consent was much easier if you did not have to cross the front lines where consent tended to break down because the perception of the parties was that one was delivering sustenance to their enemies. That led the UNHCR to develop a concept whereby they now deliver aid to Central Bosnia from Split, to Eastern Bosnia from Belgrade and to Northern and Western Bosnia from Zagreb, thereby in most instances avoiding crossing front lines. The UNHCR has warehouses distributed throughout Bosnia and the people who run those warehouses are responsible for assessing the needs of the local refugee communities and demanding the appropriate aid, whether it be food, medical supplies, housing materials and so on. In our area of Bosnia that process of importing aid

[**Chairman** *Contd*]

and assessing the overall need is brought together at the UNHCR main office in Metkovitch and they devise a monthly convoy plan to deliver that aid from Split up to their warehouses. They decide which of those convoys requires escorts and, in the case of those that they assess do need escorts because they are going to particularly difficult or dangerous areas, joint planning then takes place and the convoy is escorted. Generally, if it runs into trouble—and there have been some well-publicised incidents on television—it may either sit it out until it can get through or it comes back and tries to complete the operation the next day. Clearly the major difficulties have occurred where you have enclaves like you do in Eastern Bosnia which are entirely surrounded and to which you can only get through enemy territory. In those instances consent has sometimes been difficult to obtain, and sometimes impossible.

Mr Sumberg

518. Now, one way, I suppose, of avoiding those problems on the ground which you mentioned is to send the aid by air and that is what the United States has been doing recently. I wonder if from your experience of what is happening on the ground, as it were, you could tell us how effective that air delivery of aid has so far been. Has it got to the people it was intended for?

(Mr Reeves) Mr Sumberg, I think the answer is that some of it has and some of it has not. By the end of last week the Americans had undertaken 10 sorties and dropped 60 pallets. It is very hard to know how many of these landed in Muslim areas, the Muslims being those for whom they were intended, and how many did not. It could be in the region of fifty-fifty and, of course, dropping in that way is quite a difficult operation. It is important to avoid built-up areas, which limits the way the drops are conducted, and also the front lines are liable to shift. But one can say that they succeeded in delivering a lot of aid to the right side of the line. That said, the Muslims had difficulty in recovering some of it because of the progress of the battle. So it did good, but it is a somewhat expensive way of giving aid.

519. Presumably if 50 per cent at best has gone to the right side of the line, 50 per cent has gone to the wrong side of the line?

(Mr Reeves) I said fifty-fifty. One can only make a very rough assessment. I am offering that as a best assessment.

520. Some part of it got to the wrong side of the line?

(Mr Reeves) That is right.

521. Is this the sort of operation that you think is an effective way of delivering aid?

(Mr Reeves) Well, it was a desperate situation. It was clear from reports that that was one part of Bosnia which aid had not been able to reach. I think we entirely applaud the American attempt to do something about it. It was not something we wished to join in because, of course, we are delivering aid on the ground and have been doing so since November. We are also delivering aid by air to Sarajevo and have been doing that since July, so we are in the air delivery business; but that is not air drops, that is landing the Hercules aircraft in Sarajevo. So I think in an extreme situation it was something that was sensible to attempt but very difficult to execute.

522. You would like to see the Americans therefore continue that operation?

(Mr Reeves) Yes, indeed. They have made a judgment that it is a worthwhile thing to do; others may join in—we wish them success.

523. But not us?

(Mr Reeves) Not us.

(Colonel Thorp) I would just add to that that I think you need to recognise that the airlift operations, both of them into Sarajevo and Eastern Bosnia, have both political and military purposes. The vast majority of the aid that reaches Sarajevo reaches it overland but the air effort continues in circumstances when passage by land is no longer possible and, of course, it has an important political signal to send.

Chairman: Here we are getting into the fascinating ares of political motives involved in the humanitarian aid and it raises many difficulties. Mr Rowlands, a final question.

Mr Rowlands

524. In light of the experience we have had in trying to deliver humanitarian aid with British troops in Bosnia, would you now wish to try to alter the terms of either the rules of engagement or the way in which are troops have been allowed to operate?

(Mr Reeves) In terms of the rules of engagement, I do not think—subject to any comments Colonel Thorp may make—Ministers would envisage changes, because the mandate and the Ministerial decision to commit troops were both based on the intention to deliver aid by negotiation of safe passage; there was to be no fighting of the aid through. I do not believe Ministers would wish to cross this bridge even if it were desirable. I do not think it is desirable or necessary anyway, because in general aid delivery has succeeded very well and in our area we are pleased with that operation. Can I ask Colonel Thorp to add to that?

(Colonel Thorp) I think it has been a very effective operation to date. We have delivered something over 24,000 tonnes of aid. We have most mercifully only suffered one soldier killed and a number of others with minor injuries. The rules of engagement are more than adequate to allow our soldiers to defend themselves if they are attacked and they have done so on a number of occasions. I think it has been an extremely effective operation, albeit it has not been as belligerent as some would wish. But we are content at the moment with the way that is going.

Chairman: Clearly, gentlemen, we are all on a huge learning curve in these novel world conditions, but we do admire the dedication with which you and your Ministry and other officials are addressing these new challenges. We are extremely grateful to you for stressing some of your problems and some of your thoughts with us this morning and helping us in our own work. Thank you very much indeed for coming. We are very grateful to you.

Printed in the United Kingdom for HMSO.
Dd.0508886, 4/93, C6, 3398/3B, 5673, 240750.

HMSO publications are available from:

HMSO Publications Centre
(Mail, fax and telephone orders only)
PO Box 276, London, SW8 5DT
Telephone orders 071-873 9090
General enquiries 071-873 0011
(queuing system in operation for both numbers)
Fax orders 071-873 8200

HMSO Bookshops
49 High Holborn, London, WC1V 6HB
071-873 0011 Fax 071-873 8200 (counter service only)
258 Broad Street, Birmingham, B1 2HE
021-643 3740 Fax 021-643 6510
Southey House, 33 Wine Street, Bristol, BS1 2BQ
0272 264306 Fax 0272 294515
9-21 Princess Street, Manchester, M60 8AS
061-834 7201 Fax 061-833 0634
16 Arthur Street, Belfast, BT1 4GD
0232 238451 Fax 0232 235401
71 Lothian Road, Edinburgh, EH3 9AZ
031-228 4181 Fax 031-229 2734

HMSO's Accredited Agents
(see Yellow Pages)

and through good booksellers

HOUSE OF COMMONS SESSION 1992–93

FOREIGN AFFAIRS COMMITTEE

THE EXPANDING ROLE OF THE UNITED NATIONS AND ITS IMPLICATIONS FOR UK POLICY

MINUTES OF EVIDENCE

Wednesday 5 May 1993

<u>FOREIGN AND COMMONWEALTH OFFICE</u>

Rt Hon Douglas Hurd CBE MP, Mr Alan Charlton and Mr Paul Level CMG

Ordered by The House of Commons *to be printed*
5 May 1993

LONDON: HMSO
£5.10 net

235–xi

WEDNESDAY 5 MAY 1993

Members present:

Mr David Howell, in the Chair

Mr Dennis Canavan	Mr Ted Rowlands
Mr Mike Gapes	Mr Peter Shore
Mr David Harris	Sir John Stanley
Mr Michael Jopling	Mr David Sumberg
Mr Jim Lester	Mr Robert Wareing

Examination of witnesses

RT HON DOUGLAS HURD CBE, a Member of the House, Secretary of State for Foreign and Commonwealth Affairs, further examined. MR ALAN CHARLTON, Head of Eastern Adriatic Department, and MR PAUL LEVER CMG, Assistant Under Secretary of State, Arms Control, Foreign and Commonwealth Office, examined.

Chairman

525. Foreign Secretary, could I begin by welcoming you here this morning together with Mr Lever and Mr Charlton. We are extremely grateful to you at a time of unparalleled business for the opportunity to share some of your thoughts with us on the developing situation in the former Yugoslavia. This is not just because obviously we, like you, want to help allay the very widespread concerns about the developing crisis, but also because we value your help in completing our inquiries on the role, the ever-expanding and changing role of the United Nations, and this nation's interest in an attitude to that changing role, so that is the background to our discussions today. Could we, Foreign Secretary, therefore, begin with the immediate events in the former Yugoslavia and try and set them in some kind of context. I want to ask first how you would answer the question about the United Kingdom's actual short and longer-term policy interests in this area and explain to many people around why we are so involved and apparently getting more involved in the area and where this is going to lead us to.

(Mr Hurd) The British interest has been quite rightly discussed and analysed whenever the House has discussed this matter. It is a British interest that there should not be a widespread Balkan war, therefore, that the existing fighting should be, so far as is possible, contained. It is a British interest as part of our membership of not just the European Community, but also NATO, the Security Council of the UN and the other bodies, international bodies to which we belong that this particularly savage fighting should be influenced by us towards an end and it is a British interest, I think, in responding to the wishes of the House and of our constituents that we should play our part in actually relieving suffering, keeping people alive who would otherwise die of hunger and disease. So those are three, I think, British interests which we are serving and ought to continue to serve.

526. Can I just press you a little further again in the name of those who say, "Why are we getting dragged in at each stage apparently against our previous predictions and our will?", and who might say, "Well, there have been endless Balkan wars". A hundred years ago there were Balkan wars before 1914 and even in the apparent peaceful period before the second world war there were hideous conflicts going on. Why is it different now and why is it our concern that these people should fight and kill each other, other than the totally understandable humanitarian concern that suffering and even more genocide are horrific things to see, but in terms of our policy why do we not just stand back from an area where they have always been fighting each other?

(Mr Hurd) Of course it would not be entirely true to say that they have always been fighting each other. There is a long tradition of Balkan fighting from which we have not managed to stand aloof. Indeed the worst war in our whole history arose out of Balkan fighting and that is why I put first in our objectives as a British interest to prevent the fighting which has been going on in the former Yugoslavia spreading until it becomes a major Balkan war. I think that is a very clear British interest. Of course it is true, as I said, when we had what I thought was a rather high quality debate last week on this subject on the floor of the House, this is not the only conflict of this kind going on or even the most tragic in the world, so we do need to look at it, as your Committee is, against a background of world disorder and Britain's place in that. We have a particular interest, I think, in preventing a wider Balkan war and one has to take account, without letting it dominate policy, of the fact that people in this country have witnessed day by day and night by night from Bosnia horrors and tragedies of an intensity and a frequency which has not been true of the other trouble spots, so, as I say, I do not think that should dominate the policy, but it certainly affects the attitude of the House of Commons and is bound to affect the attitude of the Government.

Mr Harris

527. Do you feel, Foreign Secretary, sometimes that events are just pulling us further and further

The cost of printing and publishing these Minutes of Evidence is estimated by HMSO at £2,340.

[Mr Harris *Contd*]

in, the events and media coverage of those events, and indeed pressure from America and that it is really all outside our own control?

(Mr Hurd) No, I do not think that at all. If you look at the steps we have taken and agreed to, first of all the diplomatic steps, the creation of the framework of the London Conference and out of which the Vance-Owen plan arrived, the economic steps, the sanctions, the humanitarian operation which has been highly successful and, I think, more successful than probably most of us would have expected at the time, and I remember having some quite difficult questions from this Committee and certainly on the floor of the House on this point, but I think that operation, that decision, has justified itself. Now, we may be on the edge of further decisions. We have to make sure that they are related to reality, that is to say, that we can play a part in them which is realistic in terms of our resources and in terms of objectives which are defined. We are at the moment at a stage of a fork in the road as regards Bosnia. Either the Athens agreement is implemented which would be the best course, in which case we have a set of decisions to take as Britain and as an international community about how to make that agreement stick, or it may collapse, go the way of earlier agreements, in which case we are back with the options which the House discussed last Thursday. So we are at a fork in the road, but in either case there will be decisions for this country to take not alone, but with others, and we have to make sure that they are realistic and they are within the bounds of what we can do and that they have objectives which are reasonable and attainable. They will not be without risk, but we have to make sure and do our best to make sure that they are realistic and attainable.

Mr Lester

528. Is not part of the problem, Foreign Secretary, the difference in appreciation between those who feel that it is a tripartite civil war and, when we had the Foreign Minister from Bosnia here only last week, it was suggested that it is aggression by Serbia from another recognised nation state? I wondered in terms of the tensions within Bosnia what diplomatic feedback you have had from the Islamic states as to which of the two or a combination of the two was the current appreciation?

(Mr Hurd) Well, certainly it is true that Islamic states take your second view, I do not say exclusively, but they are alarmed and angry at what they see as basically aggression against Muslims. It clearly is not a religious matter and I have seen no suggestion that really religious feelings are involved on one side or the other, but it is certainly true that the chief sufferers from the conflict are people who have the Muslim faith and your assumption is correct that this is causing strong feeling through the Muslim world.

Mr Sumberg

529. You talked, Foreign Secretary, about the British interest and referred to the role our troops are playing, and I think that does give us a very close interest in what is going on. What concerns me very much, however, is, if the conflict is escalated from outside and, in particular, if air strikes come, will you confirm that the presence of the British troops in their present form would not remain, they would be removed from the scene; because it seems to me that their lives would be in unacceptable danger?

(Mr Hurd) There are a number of military options which have been considered which might create risk for our troops, and indeed the troops of other European countries helping in the conflict. We, like the French (and this was affirmed last night in conversations here with the French Prime Minister), are clear that if any such options were to be decided upon our first concern would have to be the safety of our own troops and taking the necessary dispositions to ensure that as best we could. None of these things, nor their presence, are risk-free, as we have seen. I used the phrase I think in the House of "putting them at serious risk". It is our first priority to make sure they are not put at undue or serious risk as a result of any further decisions which are taken by the international community, that is quite right.

Mr Shore

530. Foreign Secretary, you drew a parallel for us with the importance of Sarajevo in 1914 at the beginning of your remarks, but surely one of the great achievements of diplomacy, internationally and within Europe, is that the conflict in old Yugoslavia has not become, as it were, a cockpit for rival powers fighting with each other or seeking to exploit the situation. This, I think, is a very admirable feature of the modern world, that that temptation to try to exploit the situation has been resisted. The other point surely is this, that because it is not a clear act of aggression, but the disintegration of a previously existing state, we really have not got clear the rules of conduct which are expected for the rest of the international community. Kuwait and Iraq was a very simple case, in a sense, it was an obvious invasion of one state by another and one knew what to do. In this state you have had disintegration with, quite frankly, atrocities and outrages being committed by all three communities. Is this not among the very special difficulties and exceptional circumstances of this issue?

(Mr Hurd) Exactly, I follow you on all your points. We have managed, not least through co-operation between the members of the 12, to avoid that kind of backing of rival groups which, in my view, caused so much harm in the Balkans in earlier times of conflict. We have not been able from outside to settle the matter, but it has always, in my view, been an unrealistic expectation from outside that you could. What we have managed to avoid is that degree of rivalry of backing different groups. You are perfectly right, indeed most of the tragedies now going on in the world are tragedies within countries where, up to about ten years ago, the orthodox response would have been, "Well, it's

[**Mr Shore** *Contd*]
nothing to do with the rest of the world. Get on with it"; but, first in Somalia and now in other places, we see that that is no longer acceptable, and that the international community is increasingly deciding to take a hand. The trouble if it takes a hand too late is that it can only take a hand at great cost and danger. I think inexorably what we are being pushed to—and this is a wider point but is perhaps of interest to your Committee—is a system by which these matters are tackled earlier at a diplomatic stage, even though they do relate to internal matters, and I think of the Sudan and what is happening there. I am wandering, Chairman, but I agree with Mr Shore.

Mr Rowlands

531. You were asked a question by Mr Lester earlier on about the Islamic attitude. I just wondered about your attitude. Is this a tripartite civil war or is it an act of Serbian aggression against the nation state?

(Mr Hurd) It is certainly a tripartite civil war in the sense that a great majority of those fighting are Bosnians, Bosnian Serbs, Bosnian Croats and Bosnian Muslims. There is no doubt that the civil war originated and, to a considerable extent, is sustained by Belgrade, by Serbia. Croatia joined in to a certain extent, but the main share of the responsibility for the international aspect of it lies with Serbia.

532. You said there were no religious connotations, but is it a mere coincidence, therefore, that you have got a Christian Croatia, a Muslim Bosnia and a Serbian Orthodox and historically they do follow religious divisions?

(Mr Hurd) They do. The community divisions follow religious lines, but it is not really a war of fighting about religion.

Chairman: If we could move on from the general context to the specific questions on the agreements and plan such as they are for the future. Mr Lester?

Mr Lester

533. Does the Vance-Owen plan have a future? What changes to the plan were agreed in Athens last weekend which make it more acceptable?

(Mr Hurd) I think the main change which occurred in Athens was that Mr Milosevic decided to put his weight behind the plan. That was the main change. As I understand, there were no changes in the plan. There were clarifications about certain points about the corridor across the northern part of Bosnia and the way in which transit traffic might pass from one Serb province to another. As I understand it, there was no change in the map or the documents. The change was in the attitude of Mr Milosevic.

534. Did he agree that Bosnia would be governed in the future from Sarajevo and by whom, or has that part of the discussion not developed?

(Mr Hurd) He agreed to the concept of a Bosnia within existing frontiers, but organised into provinces. That is what the map is about, as you know, organised into provinces with a high degree of autonomy.

535. Is the UN, in effect, setting up a protectorate?

(Mr Hurd) No, it is not setting up a protectorate. The idea would be that Bosnia would continue as a sovereign state, not a protectorate, but that the implementation of the plan would be safeguarded by United Nations' or by international action on the ground. That is the essence of the Vance-Owen plan.

536. To what extent then have the troop figures that have been widely reported been worked into this plan, in the sense if that is not a protectorate with all those soldiers then what is their role?

(Mr Hurd) Their role is to help implement the cease-fire and the return of peace. They would, for example, monitor the cease-fire, patrol lines of conflict, supervise the withdrawal of forces and heavy weapons and supervise access routes. Would it save a little time, Chairman, if I expanded on this a little bit at this stage?

Chairman

537. It would be helpful.

(Mr Hurd) A lot of work is going forward on this, and has been for some time, but was rather put in abeyance because the prospects for peace looked so scant. That work is now being resumed at New York, in the UN and at NATO. What is envisaged is an operation which would follow, first of all, a resolution of the Security Council which would welcome the agreement and ask the Secretary-General to prepare a plan for its implementation. There would then be a period during which the Secretary-General would work out with NATO, and that is established, such a plan and send it to the Security Council which would then, if it agreed, endorse it. We are talking about an operation under the overall political authority of the UN. That would be its legal base and the Secretary-General has already appointed a special representative, Mr Stoltenberg. The Committee already knows Mr Stoltenberg. He was the Norwegian Minister for Defence, Foreign Minister and UN High Commissioner for Refugees, so his range of experience is exactly right for this job and I welcome his appointment. What remains to be worked out is the relationship with NATO because it is quite clear to us and to others that this operation needs the efficiency of execution that only a NATO command structure can provide and this has not happened before. This is NATO actually operating at the request of the United Nations. It is a very significant development indeed, but there are detailed aspects of it on which there is not yet agreement. It is called C2 Command and Control—and there is not yet complete agreement, so that needs to be worked out. We would envisage it being financed on a UN basis with the United Kingdom share being 6.3 per cent. Troop contributions have not been decided and there has

[Chairman *Contd*]

been no decision as regards a United Kingdom possible contribution. Clearly from our point of view we would need to be sure of the UN political authority, the base in international law, we would need to be sure of the efficiency of command arrangements organised by NATO, we would need, I think, to be clear that there were going to be United States troops on the ground, and we would need to be clear that the terms of reference, the definition, the objective of the plan was realistic. None of those things is certain at the moment, but I think perhaps I have said enough to show the lines on which work is going on and where it is actually happening.

Chairman: That is very helpful and we will take the opportunity, Foreign Secretary, of following up on this particular aspect now, although obviously other questions arise, not least the question of whose backing this plan has at the United Nations and how that is working and we will come back to that in a moment, but if we can perhaps follow up on these issues you have raised.

Mr Jopling

538. Foreign Secretary, whilst I do not want in any way to belittle the potential prize which comes from Vance-Owen if it does succeed in stopping the fighting, would you not agree that history has taught us that settlements of this sort which are imposed from outside are nothing like as likely to be as effective as settlements which are internal and it is clear from looking at the way Bosnia is proposed to be carved up that there will be a myriad of flashpoints? How possible do you feel it would be, assuming Vance-Owen works and sticks, that if it is possible in the future to get amendments to Vance-Owen which are agreed and proposed locally by the, general term, "three communities" that as a matter of principle Vance-Owen can be modified provided there are locally agreed amendments which do tend to reduce those flashpoints which are bound to be created by this rather hotch-potch plan on the map?

(Mr Hurd) I entirely agree with that. We should never say, David Owen has never said, Cyrus Vance has never said, that this is some sort of Holy Writ which cannot be altered; of course you are perfectly right. It just is, I think, the only way, the only route by which this fighting can come to an end. The alternative favoured by so-called realists is simply to attempt a partition and have a greater Croatia and a greater Serbia and a small or smallish Muslim area. I do not think there is a basis for agreement there. The ethnic map, even after the so-called ethnic cleansing, the ethnic map of Bosnia is a nightmare. It does not lend itself to the tidy borders and that is why the international community has all the way through thought that the only way for peace is to accept there is a country called Bosnia with its existing borders and work out how the communities inside it could live together, but you are perfectly right, there can be nothing immortal about the actual lines and they must be capable of local adjustment and negotiation and agreement.

Sir John Stanley

539. Foreign Secretary, as we know, the new Clinton Administration initially poured cold water on the Owen-Vance plan and critically important diplomatic momentum was lost. Do you now judge that the American Administration is firmly behind Owen-Vance and not merely diplomatically, but has it also accepted the likely military implications which you have just referred to, that there will be a requirement for the major parties, including the United States, to make some deployment of ground forces in the former Yugoslavia?

(Mr Hurd) For a long time the United States has accepted the Vance-Owen process, ie, this is the route through which peace can be achieved. I think they accept the document signed in Athens, subject to Michael Jopling's qualification, that they must be capable of adjustment by agreement. I do not think there is any longer a great difficulty about that. I cannot put words or decisions into President Clinton's mouth, but I think from our discussions with the Americans which were very prolonged on Sunday it is very clear that they understand that this exercise down the peace route, as it were, this international exercise we have been talking about for the last five minutes, is going to require American participation on the ground here and he has not taken any decision about that any more than we have, but I think that assumption is becoming clear.

Chairman

540. Just very quickly, Foreign Secretary, I think this is a question people will ask: do you see these troops as enforcing the Vance-Owen plan or simply policing it when, by some miraculous way, the Bosnian Serbs have withdrawn from the areas they have captured and the Croatians ditto? Are we going to be putting our troops or American troops into an area where the bullets have not stopped flying?

(Mr Hurd) Well, we certainly would not be putting our troops in, and I do not think anybody would be, to push Serbs out of areas which they have to vacate under the Vance-Owen plan. The Vance-Owen plan has to be followed and one main feature of the plan is of course that the Serbs have to withdraw from quite a lot of territory on which they are now sitting and of course that cannot be accomplished by force, and it is not part of the plan that they should do that, and the results should then be policed. One cannot of course guarantee a bullet-free situation. That would be unrealistic, but we are not talking about an operation of enforcing the Vance-Owen plan by pushing the Serbs out of areas which they now occupy. A central part of the plan is that they would withdraw by agreement from those areas.

Mr Canavan

541. Secretary of State, could you tell us please how realistic is the plan for a supervised withdrawal and dismantling of heavy artillery and supposing the forces refused to co-operate with

[Mr Canavan *Contd*]

disarmament in this way, would this scupper the Vance-Owen plan completely?

(Mr Hurd) Well, the plan is still being worked out. The work that I talked about at the UN and NATO has not yet resulted, for example, in rules of engagement, which you are talking about, Mr Canavan, and it really is the rules of engagement, the rules under which the troops are operating. That is a crucial point which I should have mentioned before, but that is still being worked out and it is still being worked out within the framework I have just described. It is not their job to move in and enforce a plan; it is their job to monitor the success of the plan which is in operation.

542. And will the United Kingdom put in more troops even if the fighting has not stopped?

(Mr Hurd) No, I think it is clear we have taken no decisions about putting in troops other than those we have there now, nor have we taken any decision about altering the mandate of the troops who are now there. In neither case have we taken a decision, but we are not contemplating and the plan does not contemplate a decision to fight one's way in, and fight one's way in through armed opposition.

543. What happens if the worst comes to the worst and the fighting continues and the UN troops, including British troops, get dragged into the fighting more and more and there are casualties? If it becomes clear that the political and military objectives of the whole operation just appear unattainable, is there a way out? Is there some contingency plan at all?

(Mr Hurd) There would have to be a way out, that is certainly true, what Warren Christopher called an "exit strategy". Of course, in any such operation you have to envisage the possibility that the operation becomes impossible. We are not envisaging, I repeat, the deployment of troops into a war. The fighting would have, effectively, to have stopped; that, I think, is common ground. We are not proposing to fight our way into imposing a peace settlement, that is not the purpose. I do not think any of the potential troop contributors or the Secretary General of the UN, or anybody else, see it in that way.

544. Do you have a timescale in mind whereby after a certain period of time you will assess or reassess the situation to see whether the military and political objectives are attainable or otherwise?

(Mr Hurd) I think it would have to be continuous assessment.

Mr Wareing

545. May I preface my question by declaring an interest, in that I was invited by President Cosic to visit Yugoslavia this last weekend. I took up that invitation but did not see the President because he was suddenly called to this conference in Athens. I did in fact take the opportunity to look in on District 3 on the map. This is the area in which there is to be a corridor. I wanted to perhaps share with the Foreign Secretary what in fact I found there. This area, it is alleged, was invaded by HOS troops, who support the Ustashe (and the "Ustashe" word is scrawled in the derelict buildings in the area), as early as September 1991, and was followed up by a further invasion in March 1992. It was before Bosnia was actually recognised by the international community. I witnessed a mass grave where bodies were being exhumed, allegedly of Serbs and possibly Muslims who had been murdered by the HOS people when they were in the area. I actually witnessed two bodies being discovered. It was like discovering Belsen and I can imagine how British troops felt at that time. The local people, when you talk to them, say there is no way in which they could possibly stay in District 3. Although UNPROFOR and the International Red Cross have been informed about the events I am relating, nobody has been to the area. It does seem to me that the success of the Vance-Owen plan can only come about if there is support from local people. Do you think it is wise to rush too speedily with the plan, or should we not make haste slowly? I know we want to end the terrible war and the atrocities committed by all sides as fast as possible, but should we not explore areas such as region three (and I am sure there are others in contention too) before we press on with threats of more sanctions, and particularly of military intervention? I am very, very pleased that you have had a much more restrained view about it, it would seem to me, than, for example, the Americans.

(Mr Hurd) I hope that I have said enough previously to the Committee and to the House to show that personally I am very cautious down both these roads—the road towards implementing Vance-Owen where, I believe, preparation is needed. If you followed, Mr Wareing, the steps that I sketched, which is what seems to us sensible, you see that there is time. On the other hand, we are at risk all the time from renewed hostilities. This plan needs to develop and keep a certain impetus so that people can see that steps are actually being taken to establish peace, otherwise the background that you sketched, of massacre and countermassacre, accusation and counteraction, will lead again to fresh fighting, whether in the corridor or in East Bosnia or in other parts of the former Yugoslavia. It does need a certain impetus, of course it does, to be properly prepared if it is going to be properly executed. On your sanctions and other points, this is really down the other road of the fork, where the plan collapses. Sanctions we are agreed on—we have to make them work. The co-operation building between the Americans and Europeans on that is promising. On the other options, military or semi-military options which we discussed successfully in the House last week, the position remains exactly as I said it then. We are not excluding those options, and the Committee knows and, I think to some extent, shares the reserves we have expressed in private and public both about generalised air strikes and about changing the arms embargo. The discussions with

[**Mr Wareing** *Contd*]

Warren Christopher which he is conducting right across Europe will take the rest of this week. We have covered these options but we have not resolved them.

Mr Rowlands

546. I need to clarify the situation, if I may, Secretary of State. Let us look at the processes by which the troops carry out their functions, the role they are playing and how it happens. Shall I take it as correct that the first that is going to happen is that a large new deployment of troops under UN supervision, or under UN resolutions, will go in to control the truce lines, the cease-fire lines when the war stops. Is that the first process?

(Mr Hurd) No, the first process is reaching agreement inside the international communities as to how this would work. I sketched the amount of work which remains to be done, not just between NATO and the UN, because an important point which I left out is the importance of including troops from countries which are non-NATO—the Russians, for example; but not only the Russians, there is a Nordic battalion already in Macedonia and a country like Sweden is very important and effective in this kind of operation. It is not just NATO troops, there has to be room for non-NATO troops, and the command structures have to allow for that. I am sorry, that was something I had forgotten. There has to be preparation and there has to be NATO agreement, and in our view there have to be two Security Council resolutions, one before the preparation of the treaty and the other after.

547. After that Security Council resolution is agreed, the first major deployment of troops will be along the cease-fire lines as they stand when the war stops, or when the Vance-Owen agreement is introduced. Is that right?

(Mr Hurd) There have been no decisions about operational deployment, but the aim of the force would be to help keep the peace. We are presuming there is a peace, that basically the fighting has stopped.

548. The first major additional deployment of troops—and it might be more British or United States troops on the ground—would be to, as it were, patrol the cease-fire lines?

(Mr Hurd) That is correct.

549. What happens after that is, you have said they are not there to enforce the Vance-Owen plan, and while the cease-fire is held one hopes that there will be a demilitarisation taking place, with guns and heavy artillery etc. That is stage two, is that right?

(Mr Hurd) I do not know what the timing of these different stages would be, but the role would include supervising withdrawal of forces in areas in which they need to vacate under the plan, and supervising access routes. For example, the plan conceives that there would be this corridor, not part of a Serbian province, in which there was access for traffic across another province between the Serb province, Serbia and, indeed, Krajina. That arrangement would be supervised by the international community. They would have this range of tasks, correct.

550. But again it would be very much in the context of voluntary agreements that are on the ground and in place?

(Mr Hurd) Correct.

551. And then at some future date presumably, and we do not know, it could be months, it could be much longer and it will be interesting to see what timescale one is envisaging, the situation arises on the ground where you can have your nine provinces, is it then envisaged that these troops will then move to guarantee, as it were, the internal boundaries of the Vance-Owen plan?

(Mr Hurd) Certainly it is not envisaged they will be there indefinitely.

552. Over what period of time?

(Mr Hurd) Their role would be more or less the one which you have defined.

553. I am not sure you have accepted the third part of my definition.

(Mr Hurd) No, I have not. I am accepting your first part.

554. What I am really getting down to is whether behind this there is going to be an international guarantee, UN-backed, for military troops on the ground for the internal administrative borders of the Vance-Owen plan. Is the international community going to guarantee the Vance-Owen plan to that extent?

(Mr Hurd) The international community will need, between the first and second Security Council resolutions, to work out what it says about the end game and it has not yet done so. I do not see an international force staying in Bosnia indefinitely, for your last purpose of the definition. I think that is unrealistic. I think that the contributors and the Security Council and NATO, if this agreement holds, if this agreement begins to work, will want to do its best to give the agreement a shove forward, to give it a help, to give it a period of time during which it can establish itself. I do not think and I have not heard anyone envisaging a longer or a more permanent operation than that and that has certainly not been envisaged, but one cannot, perhaps to anticipate your next question, one cannot, I think, put a timescale on it exactly at this moment, but I think Mr Canavan—I think it was Mr Canavan—was right and one would all the time have to be looking. The situation might deteriorate, might become impossible—that is one scenario—or it might prosper to the extent also that the operation could be withdrawn because it was no longer needed and all of that would have to be, I would think, regularly reviewed, as it is in other peace-keeping operations. Most other UN peace-

[**Mr Rowlands** *Contd*]

keeping operations have a review clause and a review time in them.

555. I think I would like to pursue one more question because I am trying to clarify it. To what extent is the international community going to underpin the Vance-Owen plan? That is really what is behind my question. Is the Bosnian Government and all the people who have signed it and who are going to agree to sign it, are they making an assumption that there is going to be an international endorsement and a guaranteeing of not just the external boundaries of the Bosnian state, but actually the internal Vance-Owen arrangements? That might not be done by extensive numbers of troops, but is there going to be, as it were, a guarantee which, if it broke down, would trigger off some form of international support and sustain it?

(Mr Hurd) You are pushing me beyond what has been agreed or even so far considered in detail, but it is a perfectly fair question. I do not myself see (this is a personal answer) that the international community can guarantee every detail of internal arrangements for ever. I see this operation, as I said, of giving a boost, giving an impetus to an admittedly difficult and complicated plan which has taken hold, ie, you do not start giving this impetus until you can see that the prospects of success are good, so it has taken hold, you want to give it a boost, you want to give it a period to establish itself, but that is different from what you are trying to lead me to further than that, quite understandably, into some sort of permanent guarantee of the internal arrangements of Bosnia. I do not think that is realistic to the international community and I doubt if the main troop contributors or the Secretary General would want to do that, and obviously it goes beyond what has happened in other countries.

Mr Canavan

556. You said, Secretary of State, that the command structures will have to allow for participation of non-NATO troops. Could you elaborate on that? Will the troops be under the command of NATO or the UN or some hybrid kind of command structure?

(Mr Hurd) Well, this is a point of discussion at the moment. You have seen the Secretary-General yesterday produced what is called a "non-paper" which touched on these points, but the exact nature of the command structure has to be worked out, but it includes overall political authority of the UN and the effective operational command structure of NATO and I think troop contributors who are non-NATO accept both of those, but the exact relationship, say, between Mr Stoltenberg and the NATO command structure, that is what is being discussed and worked out at the moment. Mr Rowlands was questioning me on the extent of the military involvement and I should have added that this military exercise, an exercise of soldiers, would be accompanied under the Vance-Owen plan by a civilian political process helping to restore law and order and civil administration on the basis agreed in Vance-Owen, so we are not just talking about a military operation.

557. Is there any difference of opinion amongst members of the Security Council about the format of the command structure?

(Mr Hurd) Yes.

558. The Americans in particular seem to be very reluctant to have their troops under UN command, despite the fact that they will be presumably wearing blue berets.

(Mr Hurd) There are differences of opinion, Mr Canavan, that is perfectly right, and the British Government came to the conclusion after our discussions on this over the weekend that these differences could be undone. They are not crucial and they are not differences of principle.

Sir John Stanley

559. Foreign Secretary, you made it clear in your answers that the UN military force will have no peace-enforcement role and, therefore, it will not have any remit to make certain that the Owen plan is implemented, particularly in relation to withdrawal from territory which is being occupied by those who no longer have it under the plan. Could you tell us against that background what is the basis for your confidence that military deployment of that sort is actually going to produce the withdrawals which are going to be required under the plan?

(Mr Hurd) The force would supervise withdrawal, but I do not think it would be deployed until it is clear withdrawal is under way. There is an agreement and the force is not acting in substitution for agreement and it would not begin unless and until it was clear that the agreement was actually being operated by those who have signed it. The whole thing may, as previous agreements have done, still evaporate and that is why we still need also to think down the other track, but if it were clearly being operated, the withdrawals were taking place, the will to execute what has been signed is clearly present, then troops could be there to supervise and monitor its effectiveness. That is the consequence.

Chairman: We have talked about Mr Milosevic maybe backing the plan and we will see who else will back it, but there is a question of the Security Council powers and their role.

Mr Gapes

560. Foreign Secretary, you said very early on in your remarks that it was important to make sure that further decisions are related to reality. Could you tell us your assessment of the pressure in the statements made by President Clinton and his Administration about possible air strikes or lifting of the arms embargo on the Bosnian Muslims? Would you say that those decisions would be related to reality if they were to be taken today?

[**Mr Gapes** *Contd*]

(Mr Hurd) They are not going to be taken today.

561. Well, even next week.

(Mr Hurd) What struck me very much and has struck me all the way through this is the way in which the Clinton Administration coming into office with a perfectly understandable wish to do better than the rest of us or than their predecessors, is tackling this in a way which has been very realistic both in the statements of February and in the consultations that Warren Christopher is now having across Europe. They are not rushing into these things and they are analysing them and discussing them. Of course as they discuss them the difficulties emerge and become clear, so I am not critical of the way in which they have set about this. I think given their position, given what they have said before, the way they have set about it is a realistic one and I do not believe they will take decisions which are unrealistic.

562. You have had long discussions with Secretary of State Christopher. Did you tell him that lifting the arms embargo would be to level the killing field? If you did, what was his reaction?

(Mr Hurd) The argument is widely shared, not just in the House of Commons but among the others, against altering the arms embargo in order, in theory, to supply arms to the Muslims but in practice to the Croats as well, and in practice also to the Serbs. The arguments against that are well known. Yes, we did cover this ground, but in terms which are pretty familiar to you, Mr Gapes, and it is one of the options which we discussed.

563. It is also reported that the United States is at this moment having personnel in the former Yugoslavia preparing the sites for air attacks to highlight where would be the appropriate place. Do you think the American administration is currently still considering air attacks in the near future if, for example, the meeting in Pale today rejects the Vance-Owen proposal, or if, in a few days' time, it becomes clear that on the ground the Bosnian Serbs, whatever they vote today, are not implementing it in reality?

(Mr Hurd) There are a lot of options, military and what I call semi-military, the arms embargo, which are still being considered. They are still being considered and they are part of Warren Christopher's consultations. There are several options, all of which I think were mentioned in last Thursday's debate. I think it is highly unlikely that the United States would undertake any of these options unilaterally or in the next few days.

Chairman

564. How much have you had in your mind during all the debates of options, Foreign Secretary, that if these threats are made to sound credible by detailed preparation then they do have some deterrent effect? Do you see the deterrent concept as operating in this area?

(Mr Hurd) Yes, I think so to some extent. I think that people will argue the reasoning behind Mr Milosevic's stand at Athens, and I think that the intensification of sanctions was part of that, and it may be your argument was also part of it.

Mr Sumberg

565. When the Bosnian Foreign Minister came to see us he told us that he thought the obstacle to lifting the embargo on the arms to the Bosnian Muslims was the British Government. You have talked about the discussions which have taken place between you and Warren Christopher, and all the options being discussed, and I wonder if you could share with us where is the push coming from? Is the United States still trying to convince Britain and France that in fact the arms embargo should be lifted, and are we resisting that? Is that really Warren Christopher's mission? I am sure there is general discussion, but what was the thrust of the United States' intention?

(Mr Hurd) On the arms embargo, I do not need to repeat our views, I see the attraction of providing arms for that community, that government, which is manifestly inferior in terms not of men but of equipment. Everyone can see the initial attraction about that. That option I think runs the risk perhaps more than others not just of inflaming the fighting but of spreading the war. When you begin to ask the questions about: how the arms would reach them; what is the position of Croatia; would you be supplying arms to enable Muslims to fight Croats, and Croats to fight Muslims; how does that relate to the humanitarian effort and the position of British and other troops; these are the kinds of questions which need to be asked. They do not dispose of the argument, but they are questions which have to be asked. Our reserves about this are very widely shared. The Bosnian Foreign Minister is wrong in supposing otherwise. Anywhere he went, any discussions he had with the Co-Chairmen, Cyrus Vance and David Owen, would show him the extent of the reserves and anxiety about this option. It is still being considered, because there are arguments in favour of it and there are adherents of it, particularly in the United States. Other options are also being considered. The United States has not taken decisions. Most of these options require a change in the attitude of the Security Council, and the arms embargo certainly is one. That is the position. These things have not been excluded, and they have not been decided on either by the United States or anybody else.

Mr Gapes

566. You have said something about the American attitude, but what about the Russians, are they really committed to the Vance-Owen plan, or are they just going along with it because they do not want to offend the Americans?

(Mr Hurd) I talked to the Russian Foreign Minister yesterday; he has kept in very close touch with me, and I with him. No, he (fortified I think by the referendum result) has played, in my view, a very constructive part in supporting the Vance-

[**Mr Gapes** *Contd*]

Owen plan, and in bringing the Serbian government to the position they are now in. Russian co-operation in this remains important, and that is not just our view but the Americans' view, and co-operation has been forthcoming, and that is why Warren Christopher is in Moscow at present, today.

567. Would you see that Russian co-operation continuing if it came to air strikes or a strong military action in the next few weeks?

(Mr Hurd) I cannot say. I could not speculate on that.

568. Can I ask you then about the other members of the Security Council. You have mentioned France who are clearly very close to our own position. What about China? Could you say something about the Chinese attitude, and also the non-permanent members?

(Mr Hurd) The British, French and Spanish are the three EC members of the Security Council who have worked extremely closely together, and our views are just about—just about—identical; there are nuances from time to time, but considering the speed of events the three of us work very closely together. The Chinese take an attitude of abstention; that is the way they vote and that is the way they speak. They have not opposed anything, but they are not enthusiastic participators in any of these matters. The non-aligned tend to put the stress on the need to stop aggression, influenced of course by the Islamic worries we were talking about earlier. On the whole their attitude is in that direction.

569. Is there any desire amongst the Muslim members, for example Pakistan and Morocco, to support the lifting of the arms embargo within the Security Council?

(Mr Hurd) That has not been pushed to a proposal or vote so I cannot really say, although I would expect their sympathies would lie that way.

Chairman

570. How are the Japanese reacting, given that they are going to have to pay for a large percentage of this astronomically expensive operation?

(Mr Hurd) Japan is increasingly keen to be seen to perform as an effective international player. They have played a very helpful part, and I am sure they will continue to do so. They have their problems about contributing troops—that is a very different question—but on their attitude on the Security Council they work closely with the rest of us.

Chairman: Could we return again to the situation on the ground and how, in detail, things are going to unfold in the next few days. Mr Wareing?

Mr Wareing

571. Could I relate to you that I saw ten members of the Bosnian Serb Parliament at the weekend, and I can only say that if Mr Milosevic persuades them to accept the Owen-Vance plan as it stands now his persuasive powers must be almost miraculous. That is my view. Because trying to persuade them is difficult. I must say that I have some understanding, having looked at Sector 3 as I said before. Do you expect that Parliament to support Mr Karadzic today, or do you have my reservations?

(Mr Hurd) I really have no prediction to make to the Committee about that. It is not an elected parliament,[1] nobody elected them, they do not represent anybody and I do not know how they will operate, but the signatures on the plan are those of the Serbian President, President Milosevic, and Mr Karadzic on behalf of the Bosnian Serbs, and we would expect them to carry out those undertakings which they have signed.

572. Do you think there is a likelihood that the signature and perhaps the endorsement of the Bosnian Serb "Parliament" will lead to an end of the fighting on the ground or do you think it might have the reverse effect because when the Croats and the Muslims signed the plan, it was a prelude to the opening of the fighting around Vitez and some of those horrible events we saw on our television screens? Is it not possible that the signing of that plan could actually lead to further conflict in the immediate future?

(Mr Hurd) One could always argue that about any step, about all the steps we have been considering, about all the options. What is certain is that if there were no efforts towards agreement or no efforts towards making peace, the fighting would continue, in my view, more or less indefinitely, so there are uncertainties down every path; Mr Wareing is perfectly right. The certainty is that if nothing is done the fighting will continue indefinitely.

573. Should there not perhaps be, as I said before, in making haste slowly, should there not be some preliminaries? For example, I would think that the presence of UNPROFOR troops in a combat in Sector 3, just as an example, that might make the plan much more digestible in that case to the Serbs, but there would be parts of Bosnia-Herzegovina where the Muslims and even the Croats would be concerned about the plan.

(Mr Hurd) I cannot answer for Sector 3. You have been there, Mr Wareing, and I have not. Of course I agree that the plan requires preparation if it is to be effective on the ground and the procedures have to allow for that, I agree with you.

574. I want to, as it were, pursue this point about, if you like, preventive diplomacy in implementing the plan, which I think has many faults, and I think many people believe it too, but would it not be wise to take up, I believe, Mr Karadzic's offer that the United Nations' monitors be sited at every airfield, at every command post of all three

[1] *Note by witness*: It is true that the Bosnian Serb assembly is self-appointed as is the Bosnian Serb republic. Its members were however elected in 1990 to the all-Bosnian assembly.

[**Mr Wareing** *Contd*]

factions in Bosnia-Herzegovina to make sure that the ceasefire holds and, furthermore, would it not make much more sense to have an UNPROFOR presence along the line of the Drina river which forms the border, as you know, for most of its length, even than the very costly operation along the River Danube, which would be much more effective, less costly and, I would suggest, would actually seal the possibility of arms coming across the bridges and, unlike air strikes, would not in fact prevent humanitarian aid crossing those bridges into Bosnia? What do you feel about that?

(Mr Hurd) This idea of putting monitors on the main crossing points between Serbia and the Serbian-inhabited parts of Bosnia is not a new idea. I always thought it was quite unrealistic when President Milosevic was clearly helping the Bosnian Serbs because his agreement to that would not be forthcoming or could not be effective on the ground, but the idea now seems a more realistic one in view of the attitude of Mr Milosevic and we are examining with others whether that could in fact be a helpful part of it. That is to say, if clearly he is now going to interrupt any help which has been given in the past, then the monitoring of that process becomes more possible than it would have been when his consent clearly was not available, but anyway that does seem to be one of the possibilities that can now be explored and we are exploring.

575. Is it a possibility that you personally would support?

(Mr Hurd) Let us have it evaluated.

Mr Rowlands

576. If I can follow Mr Wareing's line of questioning, you said earlier in an answer that you did not know how representative the Bosnian Serb Parliament is and whom they represented. If they do not represent the actual fighters on the ground, particularly those who have fought a particularly torrid war to basically carve up most of what is Sector 5 on the original Owen-Vance plan and to conceive the political geography of that drive to extend the basic Serbian border even if it is not formally said to be the objective further westwards, do you believe that, having fought all this, they are going to withdraw gracefully? I can see them saying, "Right, we will finish fighting and we will sit tight for the moment", but do the troops go in along the present ceasefire line, as it were, or do we have to, as you said to Sir John Stanley, see witness of a really significant shift and movement of Bosnian Serbs from the area they have spent the last three or four months fighting line by line, ditch by ditch to obtain?

(Mr Hurd) I think we would have to be clear that the plan was being implemented not just by votes in the so-called Parliament or by signatures on a bit of paper, but by local commanders because, as I have said, it is not part of the concept of the operation that they will be there to push these commanders by force out of the hills and villages which they have occupied which are not there under the Vance-Owen plan and they would have to be clearly withdrawing.

577. Not fighting, but clearly withdrawing?

(Mr Hurd) Yes, that would be my feeling, that would be right, but these are the definitions of mission. The areas into which you are quite reasonably pressing me are exactly the areas in which the NATO and UN work is now going ahead.

Chairman

578. If some local commanders and local warlords do agree to withdraw and others do not agree either to withdraw or to stop fighting, will we still try and go ahead with the plan?

(Mr Hurd) It is not all going to happen at once, is it?

579. No.

(Mr Hurd) It is not going to happen in every area simultaneously. I think it is going to be, let us face it, an untidy, messy, imperfect situation because there is not any longer—perhaps there never was—total effective chain of command between someone sitting in Belgrade or someone even sitting in Serbian-inhabited Bosnia and every commander on every hillside, of course not, so one will have to make judgments.

Mr Harris

580. Foreign Secretary, you have just said with absolute accuracy that it is a messy, imperfect situation, but are we going into this with our eyes open? What evaluations have been done about the number of troops which will be needed? Have you got an estimate you could give to the Committee of how many troops will be needed and how many we are prepared to contribute? Have you got an estimate of the possible cost over the next twelve months of mounting what must be a huge and massive and complicated operation? Can you give the Committee any idea at all of this and also could you say what you think the effect is going to be on the overall work of the United Nations because it seems to me here again the United Nations is about to embark on this vast operation when it has already mounted a number of other large operations in different parts of the world? Do we know where we are going, both in the case of Bosnia and in the case of the future development of the United Nations which is what this Committee is enquiring into?

(Mr Hurd) Before decisions are taken on the deployment of British troops in a new role, agreement has to have been reached on size, finance and command and control, which we started out on, in a way which is absolutely crucial. This is going to be, if it is going to make any sense or have any competence as far as we are concerned, a NATO-run operation. It is going to be NATO in action. Now, we of course have always prided ourselves on our participation in NATO, in the new rapid reaction arrangements, for example. Numbers, you have seen, Mr Harris, numbers speculated about in

[**Mr Harris** *Contd*]

the press, but numbers are not yet fixed. Finance I mentioned. We envisage UN financing with the United Kingdom producing 6.3 per cent of the cost, but of course the total of what that 6.3 per cent amounts to depends on the numbers, and command and control we have discussed. There are many uncertainties and we are not going to take, and nor I imagine is anybody else, decisions on contributions until these uncertainties have been ironed out. Your wider question is one which I am very glad the Committee has concentrated on. I have already started and will go on trying to get discussion in this country and elsewhere focused on these points, which is the role of the UN in this kind of situation. There are twelve or 13 at the moment and many more possible places where this kind of choice, varying from time to time, will face the United Nations. The UN has to be realistic about what it can do and what it cannot do, who it uses, its relationship with NATO now being worked out for this one, and is that a valid one in the future? How about the OAU and four or five such cases in Africa? How about the former Soviet Union, and three or four such cases in the Soviet Union? These are the realities of the world situation. The Russians may be calling a ministerial meeting of the Security Council to discuss these points before the end of their presidency of the Council this month. We are beginning to work out our response to Agenda for Peace. We are beginning to spell out in public our views on the questions which arise. You are perfectly right, the choices facing us in Bosnia if this agreement holds have an impact, a relevance and importance for the whole future of the UN, what it does, what it can afford to do and at what stage it begins to take a hand in these kinds of tragedies. It is the biggest question facing our foreign policy.

Chairman

581. That Security Council meeting you have just mentioned may happen before the end of the month would really be a strategic gathering, comparable to the one the British initiated back in January of a year ago?

(Mr Hurd) That is the Russian idea, although there are various complications about it. I am not certain that it will happen, but it just illustrates the point that the Russians, like ourselves, think that this has to be discussed and tackled strategically.

Mr Lester

582. One of the fundamental things that we have discovered in our inquiries so far is that where, under the UN arrangements, people are not disarmed, as for instance in Angola and Cambodia, all the resolutions fall to the ground, in the sense that it makes the whole operation infinitely more difficult. In Somalia we are actually into the business of peace enforcement, possibly because you are dealing with a different level of military activity. Surely this is really the crunch point. It has a direct relationship to Bosnia. If we cannot get disarmament, the heavy artillery and the rest, all the best proposals and the Security Council resolutions become almost unworkable?

(Mr Hurd) That is right. That is why the Vance-Owen plan does spend a good deal of time particularly on heavy weapons. I think this is right. In Somalia you were dealing with quite a different situation. You were dealing with gangs really. They had grand names, but they were basically gangs. It is a different situation in Bosnia, and indeed in Cambodia.

583. We can take on gangs but not anything much bigger?

(Mr Hurd) We are talking about realism.

Mr Gapes

584. Can I take you back to events of the last year. Can I ask you, why has it taken so long before effective sanctions were agreed by the Security Council? Original sanctions came into effect in May 1992, but clearly they were not successful. It is only now that Mr Milosevic has shifted his position. Is that due to the new sanctions, or to the possible military threats? Why has it taken so long to get to that position?

(Mr Hurd) The original sanctions have certainly had a very powerful effect on the Serb economy. They have run it down to a disastrous level. There are an increasing number of reports which show that this has had an impact. I cannot peer into people's motives and decide what mixture of pressures produced a change, if it is durable and has produced change in Serb attitudes, but I am certain that existing sanctions played a part. Since last Monday they should amount to a great deal more. We have spent a lot of time with Warren Christopher on Sunday night on these issues, and how we build up sanctions assistance missions in Rumania, Hungary, Bulgaria, Croatia, Macedonia and the Ukraine; and how we deal with the financial problems. There has been quite effective action taken in Cyprus in the last few weeks, Cyprus having been until recently, I believe, the main place where illegal trade was certainly being financed. It is quite effective action taken there by the Cypriot authorities after discussion with others. So this is moving. Of course, the Security Council being what it is with the Russian veto, it has to move at a rate, and the resolutions have to be acquiesced to by Russia, and they have to move at a rate which the Russians are content with. The Russians did, with difficulty, agree before the referendum to this very substantial tightening of sanctions. I do not think they have done so before.

585. What about the existing sanctions, because there are goods on sale in shops in this country at the moment which are labelled "Made in Yugoslavia", and, as I understand it, there have been no prosecutions of any British firms at all, because I asked a question this week and was told there have been no prosecutions whatsoever of any British company for breaching those sanctions in the last year. How effective are our own enforcement procedures?

[**Mr Gapes** *Contd*]

(Mr Hurd) Yugoslavia is a place which covers a good many territories, not all of which are subject to sanctions. If there are particulars you would like to let me have then please do so.

Sir John Stanley

586. Foreign Secretary, just continuing on sanctions. The withdrawal strategy obviously rests considerably on hope and trust and obviously we hope that is going to be fulfilled, particularly having renounced any use of a military enforcement option. Against that background sanctions may become of the utmost importance in the withdrawal context. Can you give us an assurance that, so far as the British Government is concerned, its position will be that sanctions should not be lifted once withdrawal starts, but only once withdrawal has been completed to the boundaries laid down in the Owen-Vance plan?

(Mr Hurd) You are quite right, I agree with the analysis and with the conclusions.

Mr Jopling

587. In the past everyone has rather wrung their hands and said that sanctions never work and they are not effective, but you may remember I have been critical in the past about the way that the sanctions against former Yugoslavia have been enforced and now we are told it is all going to be stepped up to a blockade, which I personally welcome very much. Do you think the international community has learnt anything over the last few months in that in future, where there is a dispute of the sort we see so often, that when the United Nations says, "We will have sanctions", understanding they will never be 100 per cent. efficient, there is huge scope for making them very, very much more efficient than they have been in the past. Can we not move to the blockade situation at the beginning, police it properly and make the best use of what should be a very positive weapon?

(Mr Hurd) That is the ideal but, of course, we are dealing with a large number of countries whose economies are pretty fragile and which are quite hard-hit by the process you describe, and I read out some just now some of the places where we have sanctions assistance missions. At the beginning there was a question as to whether the sanctions resolution overrode the Danube Conventions. It was established beyond doubt that they do. Then there are the questions of administration; what you actually do when trains and boats carrying illegal cargo present themselves; the documents look all right, but how do you check that what actually happens is what is written in the document which is presented to you at the port of entry? These are the kinds of questions which are gradually being sorted out. We have, and are building up these pressures until they amount to a blockade. I think full American participation in that is going to be very helpful. It also needs the Russians, Ukrainians and many others. There is no difference of policy now about this, it is just a matter of cutting through all these bureaucratic and other difficulties.

Chairman: Perhaps we could end, Foreign Secretary, where we came in at the beginning, and that is with the horrific bloodshed and blood soaked sieges which have been so vividly portrayed on the media, and whether, amidst all this uncertainty about the next stage and whether the fighting will stop or not, we as a national community can produce some safety and some likelihood of minimising further horrors like Srebrenica?

Mr Sumberg

588. When the Iraq war ended the Prime Minister rightly got a great deal of credit for the creation of the safe havens for the Kurds and the suggestion is now being made that perhaps something similar could operate in some of these Muslim enclaves. Do you see a role, Foreign Secretary, for that if we can get a more peaceful atmosphere? In other words, there will be a permanent deployment of troops to protect these areas for the years to come because it seems to me that if we hope for the best that after one year or two years all will be peace and it is really only hoping for the best and that we have to see, if we want to make the peace last, a permanent deployment to try and protect the lives of those who will be under threat perhaps for many years to come?

(Mr Hurd) I think there is scope for expanding the safe havens concept and Srebrenica is in effect now a safe area. That is to say, the safety of the people who live in it is for the time being assured by the Canadian presence. There were reports yesterday of an attack on Zepa, another of these townships. We have not been able to get confirmation. The report was made and it was denied. The UN are trying to get monitors into Zepa today. They have agreement that it will be permitted, and let us see that it actually is. In Gorazde we have Mr Hollingworth, or Mr Hollingworth was there. There has been a UN presence there. If that can be established and gradually built up, it has the effect you describe. Tuzla is rather bigger. It is not cut off and convoys of food are reaching Tuzla from Belgrade all the time so that is a slightly different situation, but the concept of the safe havens and safe places negotiated on the ground and gradually built up, the safety of them built up, is, I think, well worth trying.

Mr Rowlands

589. Secretary of State, you have just said that safe havens was another breakthrough in international community terms.

(Mr Hurd) I do not think so.

590. Well, I think you did anyway. It is another interesting precedent which has been created in a previous situation which we are building on. You have talked about the role of NATO could be breaking new ground in terms of UN international community relations. Do you think, to come back to the point I have been asking fairly continuously during the course of this morning, that when we

[**Mr Rowlands** *Contd*]

look on this experience it will also be that the international community through the UN has gone further than just defining the recognition of external borders and it is actually going to end up by underpinning in some way or another the internal arrangements of the nation state and this will also be in a way a major precedent or a new precedent in the whole development of a new order?

(Mr Hurd) Well, I do not think it will do so in detail or permanently, Mr Rowlands. I just do not think that is possible in practice, but there is no doubt that if this begins to happen it will be, along with Cambodia, a first. I think the Somali exercise is rather different, do you not think, but I think that Cambodia really comes first in time. This Bosnia operation, if it happens, and I am very cautious about it for the reasons that the Committee has teased out of me, but if it happens it will be, yes.

591. How will we translate that experience to the possible next killing field which is Kosovo?

(Mr Hurd) Well, I do not think one can extend these things to other cases. I think the last time I gave evidence to the Committee I compared Bosnia to a fire surrounded by heaps of combustible material. In that interval the combustible material has not actually gone up in flames, but one of the heaps of combustible material is Kosovo. It is a different situation legally and on the ground, but I think Mr Milosevic, as everybody, is well aware of the combustible nature of it. My attention has been drawn to Namibia. In a way Namibia was a first. It was a bit easier because the fighting had died down, but the UN did really prepare and set out the independence of Namibia and had a force there. It was relatively easy compared with the other two we have been mentioning. The history books will find that as a precedent.

Mr Gapes

592. We have spent a great deal of time talking about action against the Bosnian Serbs or Serbia, can I take you to a question of what the Croats have been doing, in particular effectively a third of Bosnia that has been annexed with the same currency and so on. Are there any plans to put pressure on the Croatian government to force them to recognise and protect the Muslim minority in those areas? We have had reports this morning about what is happening in Mostar and various other places, and also this so-called Sector 10 of the Vance-Owen plan, which is a mixed Croat-Muslim area. Is that really realistic, given what has been happening in recent weeks? Are we in fact going to be into a partitioning of that, or some kind of safe haven to protect minorities in that area?

(Mr Hurd) The plan is signed by and applies to the Croats as to others. Their signature is on it.

593. Is their signature worth anything in reality on the ground?

(Mr Hurd) I do not want to start weighing the worth of the signatures on that bit of paper, that would be very rash. What counts is the test you have just described: what actually happens on the ground. The Bosnian Croats have their obligations under the documents they have signed, just as the Serbs and Muslims do. As regards sector ten, you are right, it is a mixed province, but the provisions for it are there.

Mr Jopling

594. Foreign Secretary, continuing on the thought about what lessons have been learned over this tragedy, I wonder if you would care to speculate on how less difficult the problem might have been if we had not been dragged, I may say against this Committee's recommendation, into recognising some of the states in the former Yugoslavia? Do you believe that if a similar situation happens around the world in the future, as it may well, that as a consequence of what has gone on in Yugoslavia there will be a much greater reluctance in the future to rush in and recognise individual bits of a former state as new nations, as we did, I think in the view of this Committee, tragically so far as Croatia in particular was concerned?

(Mr Hurd) The view of the Committee is as you have stated it, and I know that. I think a pause is needed before that can be assessed. I have never quite understood the argument which says that the tragedy in Bosnia could have been avoided if we had not recognised Croatia so soon. There is an argument pushed with just about an equal force by other people that our main error was hanging on to the idea of Yugoslavia too long. The idea of Yugoslavia by consent, which is clearly, in my view, the best answer, would have been the best answer. We did cling on to this for some time, and this did lead us to delay recognition long past the time when Lady Thatcher, the Germans, Austrians and many others thought we should have recognised Croatia. We did not, and then eventually we did, and we were much criticised, both for doing it too early and for doing it too late. I do not myself think (and one can argue the case for this month or that month) that a delay of a few months would have had a decisive effect either on Croatia or on Bosnia. It would have become increasingly unreal because these countries evidently existed. They have made arrangements, professions, about their treatment of their minorities. I do not myself think that the weapon of recognition, or the withholding of recognition, would have had a powerful effect on what actually followed on the ground. This is going to be a fertile argument for historians. As regards the future, the name of the game is reality. You have to reckon with what you are actually dealing with on the ground. You can hope that countries are not going to disintegrate, just as I hope that Yugoslavia, by consent, would be possible; but there comes a stage when you are pretty paralysed unless you are actually dealing with and prepared to recognise the people on the ground. So reality has to be the main guide in this matter.

Mr Wareing

595. Really on the back of Mr Gapes' question, the question of Croatia, it does seem to me that

[**Mr Wareing** *Contd*]

very, very little pressure is in fact put on Croatia particularly about the activities of HOS in Bosnia-Herzegovina. The military adviser to David Owen told Members of the Committee when we were in Geneva that they were a major problem and I wonder whether you know anything about the deployment of HOS. What part of Croatian-held territory is under their control because they are accused as the ones perpetrating many of the atrocities from that particular angle and President Tudjman's attack, as it were, on Krajina recently seems to have been all too quickly forgotten and this may be a bad omen for the future of the Vance-Owen plan. Would you like to cast your observations on that?

(Mr Hurd) I do not think the Croats carry the main responsibility for the war in Bosnia, but there is no doubt that Croats have committed atrocities and there is no doubt that Croatia has helped the Bosnian Croats and we are well aware of the activities you talk about, but the solution is the same one. They have signed the agreement and they have to be held to the agreement. There is no way through different for them than for the others. The two have accepted that there is a country called Bosnia-Herzegovina with the frontiers which are there on the map. They are entitled to interest themselves in the way in which the Croat community inside that country can live, its provinces, et cetera, et cetera, but that is it.

Mr Lester

596. Foreign Secretary, you talk about reality and the problems on the ground. Surely the great reality to many people in Bosnia-Herzegovina is to become refugees in their own country and I would just ask that in terms of the implementation of the Vance-Owen plan one is very mindful of the fact that there are refugees from all three communities in different parts of that country and that we do not forget them.

(Mr Hurd) I entirely agree with that and we have not really tackled the humanitarian side in this. If I may give the Committee the latest figures, we have been the first to respond to the latest UN appeal designed to help refugees and others with a further commitment to 15 million sterling, and an immediate cash contribution of £8 million. That brings the total United Kingdom humanitarian aid to ex-Yugoslavia of over £92 million. That is partly bilateral and partly through the EC. We are now concentrating on seed. Seed potatoes are going from Scotland to Bosnia through the ODA programme because they now need to move from simply keeping themselves alive to actually preparing for the next winter. The humanitarian work on escorting the convoys has been extremely successful. Of course it has been risky; we have lost one man and there have been many dangers for the troops and for the civilian drivers, one of whom was injured the other day, but I hope that the Committee in all this discussion will not forget what British people have been doing in this time much more successfully than was anticipated in helping to keep people alive.

Chairman: I think that is a realistic, if not a sobering, note on which to end. Thank you very much indeed, Foreign Secretary, for your patience in answering all our questions. This is a situation in which things are changing hour by hour and day by day and we wish you well in steering through the very tricky waters ahead.

Printed in the United Kingdom for HMSO.
Dd 5060879, 5/93, C6, 3398/3B, 5673, 246505.

HMSO publications are available from:

HMSO Publications Centre
(Mail, fax and telephone orders only)
PO Box 276, London, SW8 5DT
Telephone orders 071-873 9090
General enquiries 071-873 0011
(queuing system in operation for both numbers)
Fax orders 071-873 8200

HMSO Bookshops
49 High Holborn, London, WC1V 6HB
071-873 0011 Fax 071-873 8200 (counter service only)
258 Broad Street, Birmingham, B1 2HE
021-643 3740 Fax 021-643 6510
Southey House, 33 Wine Street, Bristol, BS1 2BQ
0272 264306 Fax 0272 294515
9-21 Princess Street, Manchester, M60 8AS
061-834 7201 Fax 061-833 0634
16 Arthur Street, Belfast, BT1 4GD
0232 238451 Fax 0232 235401
71 Lothian Road, Edinburgh, EH3 9AZ
031-228 4181 Fax 031-229 2734

HMSO's Accredited Agents
(see Yellow Pages)

and through good booksellers

FOREIGN AFFAIRS COMMITTEE

APPENDICES TO THE MINUTES OF EVIDENCE

APPENDICES TO THE MINUTES OF EVIDENCE

APPENDIX 1

[This appendix reproduces the second part of the evidence given by the Foreign Secretary on 12 October 1992, which covered the role of the United Nations. The first part of the evidence (QQ 1–50) concerned the Committee's inquiry into Europe after Maastricht and is published with the First Report, Session 1992–93 (HC 205)]

MONDAY 12 OCTOBER 1992

Members present:

Mr David Howell, in the Chair

Mr Dennis Canavan	Mr Ted Rowlands
Mr Mike Gapes	Sir John Stanley
Mr David Harris	Mr David Sumberg
Mr Jim Lester	Mr Robert Wareing

Examination of witnesses

RT HON DOUGLAS HURD, CBE, a Member of the House, Secretary of State for Foreign and Commonwealth Affairs; MR LEN APPLEYARD CMG, Political Director; MR MICHAEL ARTHUR CMG, Head, European Community Department (Internal); MR MARTIN EATON, Deputy Legal Adviser; and MS GLYNNE EVANS CMG, Head, United Nations Policy Unit, Foreign and Commonwealth Office, examined.

* * *

Chairman

51. Now, Secretary of State, if we could take a deep breath and leave Maastricht and all its works and turn to the developing role of the United Nations which is the subject of an inquiry this Committee is launching upon, resting our questioning very much on the Secretary-General's paper, *Agenda for Peace*. We also have a very helpful memorandum from your office, the Foreign Office, and a list of other papers. I think you are going to be joined at this stage by some new colleagues.

(Mr Hurd) Yes. Can I introduce Glynne Evans who is in charge of our United Nations policy and that is it.

52. Foreign Secretary, may I begin with a general question. A view emerges that the United Nations today is over-burdened with over 11 military or UN-blessed operations around the world and under-financed. You have made some very interesting comments about how you think the United Nations might develop to carry all these new burdens. How do you see this debate continuing and what are the main issues in it?

(Mr Hurd) The UN is certainly increasingly burdened. To say over-burdened is to suggest it should not be doing some of the things it is doing, but I think if you look at the peace-keeping operations now in place, it is hard to question the need for them. That it is under-financed is absolutely clear. It is owed $1.5 billion in outstanding assessed contributions and the Secretary-General is entirely right in saying that these debts, this underpayment, has to be dealt with if he and his operations are to have any hope of success, but there are wider issues which I have tried to tackle, Mr Chairman, and about which the Committee may want to ask questions, but as the Cold War came to an end, the number of disputes which the UN could reasonably be asked to intervene in has very substantially picked up and this trend may continue. It is very hard for the UN to say no to pressing requests of this kind. It means a greater degree of intervention in the internal affairs of countries which would not have been thought conceivable 20 years ago. It means demands for money and, to some extent, men which the UN has difficulty in meeting, and this is the strain, this is the point which I have been trying to draw attention to.

Chairman: Thank you for that introduction and I wonder if we could bridge the discussion between what we were talking about earlier and the UN's role by looking at regional conflicts and particularly the regional conflict in the former Yugoslavia where the UN is now involved, but the EC thought it had a role either as an agent of the UN or indeed an independent role in its Community garb.

Mr Sumberg

53. Foreign Secretary, I am looking at your memorandum which you kindly sent us and paragraph 8, headed "Preventive diplomacy", highlights the role of the EC Monitoring Mission in the former Yugoslavia and states that such "preventive diplomacy is far more effective than the most successful peacekeeping or peacemaking operation which inevitably must follow the outbreak of vio-

[**Mr Sumberg** *Contd*]

lence". I wonder if you would like to tell the Committee what you think the Monitoring Mission in the former Yugoslavia has so far achieved because it is a criticism made that this form of preventive diplomacy has totally failed there given the scale of the fighting, given the horrendous stories that we hear, and I wonder if you would like to set out perhaps for the Committee what its successes have been since it has been established.

(Mr Hurd) The Monitoring Mission is a relatively small part of the total EC effort. The Monitoring Mission is a number of individuals, unarmed individuals, who are stationed mainly in Croatia and whom I have seen in action, and other Members may have too, and they are creating the kind of conditions in Croatia, village by village, which enable people to go back to their homes and to enable the UN force in other parts of Croatia to contain what might otherwise be a disastrous breakdown of the ceasefire and we mention them in the memorandum because they are part of the effort, but they are only part of it. The framework we now have for trying to achieve or to help people of Yugoslavia to settlements is an EC/UN framework and it is now very elaborate and energetic, with David Owen, Lord Owen, on behalf of the EC, and Cyrus Vance, on behalf of the UN, working day in and day out in the republics and in Geneva to bring people together and stop the fighting. We have moved to that and after a period during which we simply tried to achieve ceasefires, and we did on paper but they were not implemented in practice. We came to the conclusion at the London conference in August that what was needed was a continuous effort and a framework. You are perfectly right that that has not yet produced in Bosnia the stopping of fighting or the conditions of a political settlement. It has produced, together with sanctions, a powerful debate in Belgrade and some signs of movement as between Serbia and Croatia and may lead to demilitarisation. There are other examples of progress which is beginning alongside, and perhaps more stark in the coming weeks is the humanitarian one in which the EC also is the greatest provider and help, out of which comes the decision of some EC members (Britain, France and Spain alongside Canada) to send troops to escort humanitarian convoys. There is political and humanitarian effort, both of which Member States and the Community as a whole are deeply involved with.

54. You see the deployment of those UK troops purely to escort those convoys and nothing further than that?

(Mr Hurd) That is their mandate.

55. You do not see the danger of them being drawn into the fighting? How do you see that being prevented? They may start with that objective, I accept, but the danger is that they will be drawn further into it?

(Mr Hurd) Of course, there are dangers. When the other Committee cross-examined the Minister of State about this two weeks ago when the House debated it on the Friday of the recall I think these dangers were admitted. They exist and we have to provide against them as best we can by a proper command structure, by a proper back-up and proper rules of engagement enabling proper self-defence. These are all essential matters for the Ministry of Defence but of course they are of great interest to me as well. It would be possible, I suppose, to have said some weeks ago that these difficulties and risks are so great that we are not going to do anything about it, and we are not going to take part in this enterprise at all. This is a choice which will confront Britain over and over again if my analysis is correct. Over and over again we will be faced with this choice: are we a middle-sized power seeking to retain a seat as a permanent member of the Security Council, seeking to exercise responsible action in the world in a way which I think most of our constituents would want? If we are in this new world then this would involve taking this kind of decision, and not pretending it is risk-free. If we are not then it will be for others. When our troops are deployed the French will still have many more troops in the former Yugoslavia than we have. They have taken casualties already. It will be for them and others to take up the role. There is a particular problem about Germany which does not do this, which, for reasons of its past and its constitution, believes at the moment that it is debarred from making a positive choice, and a somewhat similar problem with Japan; and both those countries, which would purely in 1992 terms be highly qualified to take part, are wrestling with their constitutions and their own policies. I would guess that before a very long time both of them will be able to make a positive choice in circumstances where that seems to be sensible, i.e. to dispose of the past as far as that is concerned. That does not necessarily make our problem any easier. We will have this recurring choice, and it will be very difficult for all governments but that is the nature of the choice.

Mr Wareing

56. Is it not the fact that we are now debating this question of military intervention, albeit for humanitarian aid needs, and in this illustration of the fact that preventative diplomacy has broken down, and that this arises out of the premature recognition of the Yugoslavian republics of Croatia and Slovenia, but particularly Croatia, and really in order to save the expense of the United Nations in the future and to save the cost in human lives that we should really be looking for a package, a political solution rather than a military solution, that will recognise the needs of the Serbian minority? It does seem to me that the extremists who have led this conflict in Bosnia Herzegovina are really in the hands of these extremists? They are really the outcome of our fail-

[**Mr Wareing** *Contd*]

ure to give support to more moderate elements. It was notable to me that David Owen, who I had fears of as being appointed to his particular post, nevertheless came out with the expressed opinion that we should be doing all we can now to support the federal government in Belgrade whose Prime Minister, Mr Panic, appears to be in a more reconciliatory mood than some of the people we have had to deal with in that part of the world. I wonder whether the Foreign Secretary would like to say something about that. May I just also say, before he answers, that I have to declare an interest because I recently visited Yugoslavia and Serbia and was assisted in doing so during the recess by the Federal Assembly in Belgrade. I should say that last year I visited under different auspices.

(Mr Hurd) I am sure that there is not going to be a militarily composed solution in Bosnia, or Kosovo if it comes to that, or anywhere else. I am certain of that. If that is so, leaving aside the humanitarian problem which is huge, then we have to keep up the pressures and the talks designed to produce political settlement a way in which these different problems, and there are about half a dozen in Yugoslavia, can be peacefully settled. That is what the Owen/Vance, EC/UN framework is about. Of course, that does involve listening to and trying to help those, particularly in Serbia and Montenegro, who are arguing for what we would regard as a saner policy. I have had several discussions with Mr Panic and Mr Owen. What we should not do, in my view, is relax the existing pressures on Serbia and Montenegro, the pressures of sanctions which are clearly having some effect, before we are clear that the saner policies are prevailing. We are not clear of that. What is actually happening now in Bosnia, at the instance of the Bosnian Serbs, is plain contrary to what was undertaken in London by Mr Panic. I am not accusing him of deceit because I do not think that is the right accusation; but what is clear is that he does not control all those who are responsible for continuing the fighting.

Chairman: I want to keep the discussion today on the UN involvement, because these other aspects are absolutely crucial but ones I do not think we can spend time on today. You said, Foreign Secretary, that we are bound to be drawn again and again into these sorts of situations where there is a demand for troops under the auspices of the UN to go on being involved in humanitarian work. Dr Boutros-Ghali in the *Agenda for Peace* is suggesting a wider agenda which is not merely peacekeeping and humanitarian work but peacemaking. Could we just ask you about that.

Mr Lester

57. Foreign Secretary, could I say before that, when you talked about the United Nations having more responsibility and people not funding it, surely the same thing applies to your own budget in terms of the same numbers and disasters which we were asked to co-operate and assist with, the troops that we are now putting into Bosnia at a cost of £90–100m coming out of your budget. One of the things that has been suggested in the *Agenda for Peace* is that that sort of operation should come out of the defence budget in any national government, which is far more considerable by a factor of about five or ten as far as our own budget is concerned. Should those things not go together in the sense of the increased requirement and where the funding comes from?

(Mr Hurd) Well, you can argue this, Mr Lester. I think these kind of activities are a function of our international relations. It is very hard to foresee them in advance on a three-year cycle, which we have for the public expenditure reviews, and, therefore, if whenever something of any size comes up, of course there have to be discussions with the Treasury, whoever carries the load of this budget, so I do not think this question of budget attribution is of huge substantial importance. The basic question which will confront governments from time to time is whether Britain is going to take the risk of involving itself in a particular UN operation or not and the question of finance is of course an important part of that, but I do not think the decision will revolve really on what comes out of the Defence or the Foreign Office budgets. We are very good at this. We have, as Sir John knows, highly professional task forces with a lot of experience in this kind of thing. We are going to be sought after again and again and again and of course we cannot do everything, nor can we leave people indefinitely in places because we have other responsibilities, but this pressure is, I think, already mounting and I think it is going to be quite severe and I think it does require a great deal of thought on our part, but also on the part of the whole international community, as the Secretary-General's *Agenda for Peace* paper proves.

58. The reason for my question about budgets was to try and find out why we seem less enthusiastic about the Secretary-General's proposals for UN peace enforcement units to be deployed following a ceasefire in any conflict. I am assuming we are willing to collaborate with other countries in planning crisis management and intelligence for peacekeeping and a joint training of troops available for peacekeeping duties as proposed at the UN General Assembly by President Bush, but one detects the thinking and the movement of international opinion from peacekeeping to peace-enforcement which is something we are moving towards in both Somalia and indeed in Bosnia and I just thought perhaps it was because of the inordinate costs of these operations, as seen from the costs of Cambodia, the participation in that operation, that makes us less than willing to take a lead in what must be the way in which the UN proceeds.

(Mr Hurd) Of course cost comes into it, and I am not denying that. What I was questioning was whether the budget attribution of the departments is the key. Clearly of course cost comes into it. What the Secretary-General was insisting on in

[**Mr Lester** *Contd*]
Bosnia is that those who contribute should actually pay and it should not fall on the UN budget as a whole. We are talking, we have begun discussions with the Secretary-General's military experts at a high professional military level to establish what UN needs are under the heading of *Agenda for Peace* and how we can best respond to them. We think that this is the stage for some rather detailed discussion on these comments before we start uttering about them so that is in hand. I would not accept that we are laggard in this. If you include the troops we have decided to send to Bosnia, we will be the third largest troop contributor, and that is worldwide. France and Canada come ahead of us. So we cannot be described as laggard and when you think of the commitments we have particularly in Northern Ireland which are not parallelled in other countries, I think it is a very substantial effort.

Chairman: Well, again it is not just a question of even peacemaking but increasing involvement in internal disputes as well.

Mr Canavan

59. Secretary of State, I understand that during a recent television broadcast you said that the United Nations should play an "imperial" role. Was that not an unfortunate choice of phrase or what exactly do you mean by it and is your view shared by other members of the United Nations?

(Mr Hurd) It was not a broadcast, but it was actually a speech to the Young Conservatives of West Oxfordshire and nor was it saying that this is what ought to happen. It was saying what is happening and I deliberately used the word "imperial" in the hope, which was justified, that it would make people sit up a bit. That is what is happening. If you go to Somalia today you find the collapse of everything which comes under the heading of "public service" and you find Ambassador Sahnoun, the representative of the Secretary-General, trying skilfully with a lot of non-governmental organisations to substitute for those services. No one will ever call him the Governor of Somalia or the High Commissioner and no one will ever call those others District Commissioners. Because the world has changed, these titles are no longer acceptable, but if you actually think about what he is attempting to do, he is perforce trying to provide some sort of government for that country. You could describe it in different ways, but it is what is traditionally called an "imperial" role. Now, that goes much wider, as you have said, Mr Chairman, than preventive diplomacy or indeed peacemaking. It involves the provision of every public service and that is what the different agencies of the UN with a lot of help from Member States are in fact going to do and that is what they are setting their hand to doing with the help of the NGOs in Somalia, which is the worst case. There are other cases which are teetering, but which have not yet fallen into that position. Preventive diplomacy of the kind we have seen in Mozambique where it has been up to now, touch wood, successful may have rescued that country from some similar situation.

60. Yes, but bearing in mind the exploitation and injustice associated with Britain's imperial past, it would suggest, with respect, it is not the most diplomatic phrase for a British Foreign Secretary to use.

(Mr Hurd) We will change places for the time being, Mr Canavan. You be an expert on that and I will be the expert on trying to stimulate discussion on something which is actually happening in the world and which I think is very important, so I do not regret that at all.

Chairman

61. You are clearly succeeding in that, Foreign Secretary, but can I ask with this very interesting opening up of minds, does it lead to the thought of UN mandates and trusteeships? Are we beginning to look into a world where the only governing framework available, let us say for the Balkans or for Somalia, will be one which has a UN authority in it?

(Mr Hurd) I think Mr Canavan is right to this extent: that as the UN perforce, when all other exercises have failed, perforce takes over this duty, it cannot actually be put back into either colonial terms or even the mandate terms, and I think you are right in implying that. You have to find a new way of describing it and doing it, but you actually have to do it and you have to finance it. Someone has suggested a UN protectorate over Bosnia. Again I do not think that is the right way of describing it and there is a legitimate government in Bosnia, but it is going to need, on the humanitarian side and on the diplomatic side, the kind of help from the international community which will go very far.

Mr Canavan

62. Well, whatever justification there might be for intervening in certain situations, is there not a danger here of perceptions, for example, in the under-developed south that there is a new imperialism on the part of the rich north, albeit under the cloak of the United Nations and they might see it differently from us as, for example, many of the Arab peoples perceived the intervention during the Gulf war.

(Mr Hurd) What the Arab peoples are urging is greater intervention in Yugoslavia, the Muslim people are urging that, so it varies of course case by case, but it is important that the Security Council, which is the key body here, should operate in cases where the case is absolutely proven. There can be no adventurism on this front, I agree with you, but actually the reluctance of Member States to get involved is very great and they often get involved when the countries concerned, for

[**Mr Canavan** *Contd*]

example, Mozambique, Angola, and so on, actually ask for such help.

Chairman: We have talked about peacekeeping, peacemaking, peacebuilding and interventions of the kind which may or may not have a imperialist flavour, but so much of the poor south is going to be driven by appalling suffering and humanitarian motives.

Sir John Stanley

63. I would like to ask a question in terms of the specific context of Somalia. Foreign Secretary, I think that most people would acknowledge, you possibly may have a little difficulty in doing so, that the international community response to the Somalian tragedy was needlessly delayed, and that over a period of a year or more, when the appalling suffering was evident on television screens, newspapers and was totally known worldwide, the international community was not able to produce any real response. I do not single out the United Nations in this, I think it applies equally to governments around the world, and I would have to say our own. I would put it to you that to justify the delayed response in terms of the security position is not a sufficient justification, because the security position when the international community moved was basically no better than over the period when the delay took place. I would like to ask you to share with us your views as to the lessons that have been learnt by the British Government, and possibly the United Nations as well, as to how we can respond more speedily and without the appalling delays that undoubtedly did take place in dealing with the Somalian tragedy?

(Mr Hurd) I think this does follow very much Mr Canavan's line of questioning. We must accept that there was excessive slowness, although I think our own part in providing supplies and seeking to get them in was good. Why was there the slowness? Because of the basic feeling in the United Nations that the internal affairs of Somalia were Somalia's business. It had been a colony shared between Italy and Britain; it was independent, and the UN had no basis, as it were, to fight its way in and make sure that the supplies which were being allocated actually reached the people in being. You will find that reluctance because of the background. I think the lesson is that that reluctance has to be overcome soon, but it does involve risks. When I was in Mogadishu it had just been announced that there was going to be not just the 500 Pakistanis that are there now but about another 3,000 troops in the rest of the country arriving from the UN in order to secure that supplies actually reached the people in need up and down the country. We were met by a demonstration against this, organised by the warlords. The British Government is not actually sending troops to Somalia; the Belgian Government is. They face this question: are you actually going to hold back the sending of your troops until there is some semblance of a ceasefire on the ground, or are you going to fight your way in? If you fight your way in, how many of your troops are going to be killed in a country of which Belgium has heard very little until recently? How long are you going to stay there? That is the lesson from Somalia and the lesson I was trying to draw in these speeches, that we have got to be prepared, and we have got to be more active in trying to prevent this situation coming about, but more prepared to take the necessary risks if and when it does.

Chairman: Mr Gapes is going to have the last questions this morning, and although they are going to be very much central questions about future inquiries, they are questions about the structure of the UN itself and how best it is going to be equipped to play all these roles we have discussed today.

Mr Gapes

64. Foreign Secretary, what is the attitude of the Government to proposals for restructuring and changing the composition of the Security Council? Last month the German Foreign Minister said that Germany should stake a claim for a seat as a permanent member. Would you be in favour of that? Would you alternatively be prepared to move towards a rotation of the British and French seats on behalf of the European Community's political union? Do you support the Japanese membership, and there are a number of other suggestions, and also the whole question of the role of the permanent members and the veto? Is it suitable in the post-cold war world that the British Government will ever want to use its veto again, or will we only do so as part of a European collective foreign policy decision?

(Mr Hurd) As you rightly said, Mr Gapes, there are a lot of ideas in this field, and the difficulty about changing the composition of the Security Council is that it involves revising the Charter. That is an extraordinarily difficult operation. Certain ideas, such as the ones you have mentioned, will certainly produce other ideas from people who say, "If it is going to be discussed, we have to be represented. We have to be there. We are not going to allow one, two or three extra permanent members because, clearly, that would be unrepresentative. We have to be there too". This process has hardly started, and would be immensely time-consuming and difficult. So we are not persuaded of the case for seeking to reform the Security Council. We think that would create more controversy at a time when the body is actually functioning pretty well. The corollary though is that the members of the Security Council, particularly the permanent members, have to do a great deal of listening in order to justify their position. That leads on to the second part of your question which we discussed in the run up to Maastricht: this is the question about Europe's views. We and the French achieved what I think is a good outcome, which corresponds to what is actually happening now with Maastricht. The Member States

[**Mr Gapes** *Contd*]
which are also members of the UN Security Council will keep the other Member States fully informed. Permanent members ensure the defence of the positions and interests without prejudice to their responsibilities under the provisions of the Charter. That means that we continue to do our job as the Charter provides but we do try and seek out, before we speak about it, the views of our partners. That is happening all the time. You have a discussion such as we had exactly a week ago in the Foreign Affairs Council at which the permanent members and the elected members of the Council belonging to the Community listened to and saw the views of the others. They are not bound, but in practice in Yugoslav cases this works pretty well, and we are acting in effect on behalf of the 12 although, legally speaking, we are not bound and we certainly could exercise our veto. We have not done so since December 1989, but I certainly would not want to give the Committee any assurance that we would not do so in the future; we have the right to do so.

65. Could I ask you about the item you referred to earlier on when you referred to $1.6 billion unpaid contributions to the United Nations. The Secretary General's report to the General Assembly last month refers to the fact that "the financial foundations of the organisation daily grow weaker debilitating political will and practical will and new and essential activities". What is Her Majesty's Government doing to press those countries which owe money to the United Nations, particularly the United States, to pay their back contributions? Have you got any suggestions as to how this financial crisis at the UN can be resolved?

(Mr Hurd) They should pay, Mr Gapes, that is quite right, and we should urge them to do so. When the Committee releases me, I shall go and talk to the Russian Foreign Minister and urge him to do that himself. $524 million is the United States, $138 million Russia, South Africa $49 million, Brazil $33 million, and the Ukraine $17 million. I think those are the principal ones outstanding. All EC members have paid their contributions to the regular budget in full. We have tried, the British try to pay our assessed contributions on time and in full and encourage other members to do the same, but it is very important. People know the background to the American problem and it is the result of an argument between their administration and Congress and I think whatever the result of the election on November 3, the President will have to, and will wish to, tackle this problem and clear it up because I do not think the United States can reconcile its position in the world today with the existence of these debts.

Chairman: Foreign Secretary, this has been a marathon session but then you have a marathon job and we are extremely grateful to you for answering our many questions this morning and sharing some of your thoughts about a very complex future both at the European Community and at the United Nations levels and the international order which we grope towards in the future, so could I thank you very much indeed for coming to us during the recess. Thank you, Mr Arthur, Mr Appleyard, Mr Eaton and Ms Evans as well. We are most grateful to you.

APPENDIX 2

Memorandum by Gwyn Prins, Director, Global Security Programme, University of Cambridge

AGENDA FOR PEACE: QUESTIONS FOR BRITAIN

During the 1992–3 Parliamentary Session, decisions will be made that could determine Britain's position in the world for the next generation. So this should be a time of clear and concentrated political discussion in the country: but instead the whole situation is wreathed in irony and vagueness. On the one hand, the name of the Maastricht Treaty is well known, even if the contents are opaque to popular perception, and ratification is not in much doubt unless the vote becomes a tactical domestic issue, unrelated to the substantive matter. On the other, also published this year, stands Boutros Boutros Ghali's *Agenda for Peace*. Its contents are barely discussed. It is quite unclear what position Britain will take on the renovation of the United Nations yet the issue is as important if not more so than our regional arrangements.

Will Britain miss the boat both regionally and globally? We might. It would not be without precedent. But in the autumn of 1992, the signs are that we are more likely to miss the boat in the latter case than the former. Yet, I would argue, it should not be so; it need not be so, and with sufficient political will, there are opportunities for Britain where national and global interests harmonise, which could be richly productive if seized in time. In this Memorandum, I shall touch first upon the central issue of sovereignty which creates difficulty in both the regional and global spheres. Then I will argue that while *Agenda for Peace* should be welcomed, it does not represent new thinking. I will suggest that the United Nations stands in potentially serious jeopardy if a different way to that which is currently being pursued is not found in which to develop a new approach to peace building. Thirdly, I will indicate three areas where action is required both by the international organisation and by individual national members before, finally, suggesting four areas of opportunity where, by the exercise of selfish altruism, Britain could assist in the vital task of developing policy and procedures for global security while at the same time deriving national benefit.

1. Sensitivities about Sovereignty

In the debate about Europe and in the pursuit of global security through the agency of the United Nations, the central issue is the same. It is the issue of sovereignty and the constraints upon it. At Maastricht, the FCO expertly and successfully caused the general inscription of the principle of "subsidiarity", and promoted a narrow construction of the term. This was not at all the intention of the original promoters of the Treaty; yet, as the Secretary of State for Foreign Affairs has observed in an understandably exasperated manner in recent weeks, opponents of the Treaty seem simply not to understand that much of what they seek has been already obtained. We now experience a muddied debate about whether "subsidiarity" is a good or a bad thing. It is a meaningless debate; for subsidiarity (like market management) is appropriate in some circumstance but not in others. Responding to the shock of the Danish referendum, the European Commission quickly adopted a different phrase for a more flexible approach. It described "pooled sovereignty" to signify changed circumstances which in certain arena demand collective, pan-European action—for example on environmental matters—whereas some which are of local impact may be decided locally. In contrast, in the United Nations arena, the debate about sovereignty has been approached from a different direction to that of domestic management in a common European house. The revolutions of 1989 give strength to the criterion of "good governance". This, rightly, began to judge the right of rulers to rule by criteria to do with their human rights records and democratic credentials. This was a welcome development, and the universalisation of the Helsinki process. It has been followed in the last 18 months or so by a further stage. This was given substance in the adoption by the General Assembly in early 1992 of an extended definition of global security which embraces potential threats that arise not from identifiable human agency but as a consequence of mismanagement of humankind's relations with the natural world, producing pollution and environmental stress. This expanded definition is touched upon in paragraphs 11, 12 and 13 of *Agenda for Peace*.

Just as the "subsidiarity" debate has produced tensions in Europe, so has the increasingly clear articulation of constraints upon sovereignty in the UN context; for the fundamental position of sovereign independence of member states is implicitly challenged. This challenge is clearly visible but is not addressed directly in *Agenda for Peace*, where, in one sentence we read, "The foundation-stone of this work is and must remain the state. Respect for its fundamental sovereignty and integrity are crucial to any common international progress," and in the next without comment, except a *non sequitur* "however", "The time of absolute and exclusive sovereignty, however (*sic*) has passed; its theory was never matched by reality." Both statements are obviously true. The challenge is to address the tension between them. There is, of course, no such thing as unfettered sovereign power in a world of globalised manufacture, trade and communication where transnational corporations conduct 70 per cent of world trade and own 25 per cent of the world's productive assets.[1] In Britain, I know of only one political attempt thus far to grasp this nettle. The Liberal Democrat Working Party under the Chairmanship of Dr William Wallace in its Report *Beyond the Nation State* calls explicitly for the inscription of criteria associated with the breach of human rights which might legitimate and trigger intervention in the internal affairs of a member state by the global community. The thorny (or rather, leafy) issue of contending rights in the remaining tropical rainforest is angrily in dispute, and was conspicuously unresolved at the Rio Earth Summit. In neither the regional nor the global arena can these issues be dodged.

2. Not New Thinking, but Welcome all the same

Agenda for Peace sets down an indication of the enlarged security arena but then proceeds to discuss it in terms which are principally those of internal institutional reform. These are necessary I do not deny, but the discussion on its own is insufficient. The Secretary General is keen to engage the interest of member nations in thinking about practical ways to increase the provision both of funds and of forces for United Nations Peace Keeping Operations (PKOs); so in UN terms the document is about new or extended interpretations of Chapter VI and VII, and principally VII, of the UN Charter.

The debate is necessary but *Agenda for Peace* does not prosecute it with sufficient rigour. There are three sets of issues raised by the question of a larger role for the UN in peace-keeping, peace-building and peace-making. The first, already signalled, is the need for **explicit new criteria for the breaching of sovereignty**. The second is the issue of **the relations between large and smaller powers in PKOs**. The third is **consideration of ways in which the Military Staff Committee could be used in such operations**. Each of these is strongly controversial.

The fact that the latter two pose difficulties contributes to the jeopardy into which the UN is now moving. For many years since the mid 1950s UN policy has been to draw principally upon smaller nations to provide contingents for PKOs. This was for obvious reasons during the years of the Cold

[1] "On-going and future research: Transnational corporations and issues relating to the environment," United Nations Commission on Trans-National Corporations, Meeting of 5–14 April 1989, p.5 mss.

War. But this ended with the passing of the Cold War, and Operation Desert Storm was an example of a different sort of UN operation, much closer to the first model set during the Korean emergency. I would argue that it is not necessarily a helpful precedent. In particular, one of the lessons of Desert Storm was that the United Nations as an organisation was simply technically incompetent to exercise an effective countervailing voice in relations with the principal military powers conducting operations on its behalf *ad hoc*. Such influence could only be provided through a thorough renovation of the provisions under Article 47 of the Military Staff Committee. Yet many members of the Security Council whose Chiefs of Staff would under Article 47(2) form that Committee are strongly but quietly opposed to attempts to give it teeth, eyes or muscles. These countries include France, China and Britain. The position of the United States is at present unclear, and is, of course, crucial.

The main thrust of US policy as practised since 1989 was expressed by the Permanent Representative to the North Atlantic Council just after the Gulf war.

> ... nations will continue to play independent roles for national purposes or objectives for which collective efforts are not feasible. At the moment, it looks as if some peacekeeping and most or all power projection functions fall into this category. Certainly power projection is a role NATO has never assumed. It is a role for which the CSCE is not chartered. It is a role the EC is not ready for. And it is a role that the WEU has yet to assume. Those nations that have the capability and inclination for this mission will, for a time at least, likely continue to perform it nationally or in such *ad hoc* coalitions of nations as are put together for particular efforts.[1]

In contrast, in a speech to the UN General Assembly on 21 September 1992, President Bush announced firm backing for the *Agenda for Peace* approach. He suggested that concrete proposals be developed in five areas: National provision on short notice of specially trained peacekeeping forces; joint training (for which he offered US facilities); adequate logistic support; development of planning, crisis management and intelligence capabilities (for both of which he offered US facilities[2]) and provision of "adequate, equitable financing".

But these are words only, so far; action on this five point agenda would have serious military and cost implications for the USA. And all is in limbo until after the election. What I now see happening is the worst of ways forward. The Balkan crisis gives rise to calls for strengthening the United Nations role and I would argue that this is precisely *not* the sort of context in which to try to develop new policy or new forms of operation.

Historically, UN land operations have been the moments which have brought the whole United Nations organisation into greatest jeopardy. This was so in Korea and again in the Congo. The Balkans crisis might easily go to the bad in this way. Let us recollect that its origins lay in a monumental failure of EC foreign policy when, against their better judgement, the British and French failed to dissuade or prevent the German presidency from promoting recognition of Croatia. This was followed by a prolonged failure of regional response in which none of the regional European institutions appeared to be able to prescribe ways of reacting to the Balkan crisis, still less actually doing so, which served to hearten the territorial aspirations of Serbs and Croatia. This failure led to an enlarging United Nations role whose rationale was in part to paper over European deficiencies; and that has led in turn to a form of military intervention which is, for many reasons, both politically and militarily, precarious. But the die is cast. Convoys will roll and, I predict, will require tactical air power on a substantial scale. This can only be provided, in my understanding, either from NATO bases in Italy and/or from American carriers operating in adjacent waters. In either event, this escalation makes the operation *de facto* a NATO operation; and viewed from the perspective of most of humanity who do not inhabit the rich world and its alliances, such a solution, coming hard on the heels of Desert Storm, and after the tensions between rich and poor at the Rio Earth Summit in June and in contrast to the laggardly response to the Somali disaster, tends to confirm the view of the poor that they stand excluded and that the United Nations as policeman is the United States and its proximate allies in thin disguise. I have no crystal ball when I look at Balkan affairs. I only suggest that prudence and humility dictate that we observe very closely and learn the lessons of this precarious period in the post-Cold War era; that we try to minimise the risks of fundamental breakdown either in that region or in the operation of the PKO and that we as quickly as possible begin to undertake that new thinking which *Agenda for Peace* calls for but does not itself undertake.

3. Three Essential Elements for New Thinking

a) It is not very surprising that *Agenda for Peace* is strongly preocccupied with the problem of money. At the end of 1991, member states owed the United Nations more than $US816 million: $439 million for the regular budget and $377 million for PKOs. Of this, the United States owed more than $266 million to the regular budget and $141 million for PKOs, which is half of the total debt. That is what an American President would have to place on the table to give sub-

[1] William Taft, speech to the International Institute of Strategic Studies, 8 February 1991.

[2] "... we will work with the United Nations to best employ our considerable lift, logistics, communications and intelligence capabilities to support peacekeeping operations." Bush speech to the UN General Assembly, official text, USIS, p.4.

stance to Mr Bush's words. The Secretary General proposes in *Agenda for Peace* a number of devices including the creation of a $1 billion Peace Endowment Fund, the proceeds of whose investments could be used to initiate peace-keeping operations and other activities, and the charging of interest on amounts of assessed contributions not paid on time (rather in the way that the Inland Revenue operates). Clearly these are sensible measures, but do not answer the full scale of the need. This is for a new initiative not so much from the UN as from the *member states.* Member states have to work out new ways in which to provide money to the UN which conform with their own internalised national goals. In the areas of PKOs, one way forward is that used in the Gulf where forces were assembled *ad hoc* and various non-combatant states were persuaded to make contributions This is not a satisfactory general solution. Another way forward is through the provision of standing forces to the United Nations and this appears to be a route that will be developed; it is certainly explicit in the Bush speech.

But it carries with it important implications that in the British case, have been first explored by G W Hopkinson who as the Head of the Defence Arms Control Unit in MOD led the MOD position in the Conventional Forces negotiations and has undertaken this work on a personal basis, in his ensuing sabbatical in the Global Security Programme in Cambridge.[1] Mr Hopkinson suggests that a country such as Britain, which has an imperial past but plainly cannot afford either an imperial present or imperial future in its ambitions or in the scale of its forces, may, nonetheless, wish to continue to maintain forces and make contributions to international peace-keeping beyond the scale which the size and importance of the economy strictly justify. Indeed, there are good reasons why Britain should continue to do this as I will explain in the final section. However, Hopkinson observes, if such expenditures are to be made and if they involve maintaining a security establishment larger than that which can be justified on purely national grounds, then thought should be given to how that surplus be funded. In particular, if, for example, maintenance of power projection forces or certain types of army units can only be justified in terms of UN operations, then should the cost of those operation be set against the national contribution or should they be paid for by claims upon new UN funds such as those proposed in *Agenda for Peace?* I urge that this be an issue for conversation between this Committee and those on Treasury and Defence matters.

b) Whilst money is important, that sort of new thinking is in the realm of accountancy rather than strategy. And in that latter realm, the question which is raised but left unexplored in *Agenda for Peace* is what to do about the Military Staff Committee. The issue is sensitive for two reasons. Firstly, the Security Council powers, including Britain, are not enthusiastic about the surrender of authority to the MSC which would be the consequence of boosting its infrastructure. Secondly, making the MSC competent touches a raw nerve in the United Nations world because it means stating that competence rather than representation shall be the over-riding criterion. The fudge which has for many years filled the UN administration with representative quotas of less than optimally efficient administrators is brought into question. In fact, I think that the "competence vs representation" issue has been raised inevitably as a result of the "good governance" debate. It may be possible to employ forces on the Pearson principle from smaller nations, but the logic for creating the MSC in the form specified in the sleeping clauses of the Charter in Chapter VII is the same logic of *realpolitik* which led to the creation of the Security Council in the first place, and should be followed.

More serious is the difficulty posed by the reluctance of the major powers. This may be abated if there is a clearer understanding of what in fact the MSC would—and would not—do. Taking the Gulf operation as an example, it is evident that the Secretary General was unable to enter into an informed debate with the Coalition commanders because he lacked not so much command authority as intelligence and communication facility and, of course, the financial power to provide and design forces as required. Therefore, creation of a United Nations Command Centre and necessary ancillary backup to the MSC seems to me prudent and desirable. The sentence quoted in footnote 2, p.235 is much to be welcomed, if acted upon. Furthermore, having regard to my remarks above about the dangers of trying to make up such policy and institutions on the back of an operation such as that in the Balkans, I think it would be far more sensible to do this design and planning work in a clearer context. That is why the Cambridge Global Security Programme is in October 1992 commencing, with the assistance of the Royal Navy, and others, a two year study on the potentials for awakening the Chapter VII powers in the maritime realm and particularly with regard to global security problems of a longer term variety. A more detailed paper on these issues has already been tabled for the use of Members of the Committee.[2]

However, new thinking on the MSC is not in itself sufficient. Global security research has, starting in the field of environmental security, been in recent years stressing increasingly the cyclical

[1] G W Hopkinson, *Changing Options: British Defence & Global Security*, Global Security Programme Occasional Paper, June 1992.

[2] G Prins, "The United Nations and Peace-Keeping in the Post Cold War World: The Case of Naval Power", *Bulletin of Peace Proposals*, Vol 22, No 2, June 1991.

relationship between poverty, conflict, environmental degradation and further conflict. The need to recognise such interlinkages was signalled in the General Assembly definition of global security and inscribed powerfully in the "Rio institutions" that were agreed at the Earth Summit in June. In particular, creation of a Sustainable Development Commission to be derived from the ECOSOC (Economic and Social Committee) areas of the UN Charter make this clear. The MSC must therefore be able to liaise and communicate with these new instruments. Marrack Goulding's terms of reference may include this: but manifestly it will be through the Private Office of the Secretary General that such liaison between Heads of Departments will occur on a regular basis. To date, I am not aware that the need for such communication has led to appropriate organisational responses within the UN.

c) The sensitive issues of sovereignty and subsidiarity with which this issue is shot through mean that member states themselves have, at root, to decide in the international sphere how much sovereignty they are prepared to pool. Paradoxically, I think this should be a less difficult issue than when approached in the European context. The experience of NATO and the developing ideas for the Western European Union mean that in the traditional security field this is one place where countries, and this country in particular, are well familiar with pooling sovereignty. Accordingly, the challenge here is to clarify rapidly relations between regional and global institutions. The Balkans mess is a dreadful warning to Europe of what happens if such lines of thought are not clear.

4. Opportunities for Britain

For historical and technical reasons, Britain is well positioned to be pro-active in fostering the new thinking called for but not produced in *Agenda for Peace*. I see four areas in which it would be in the country's interests to take an active lead. These areas are discrete but in an obvious manner interlinked.

— **Strategic thinking**. Britain could seek with other Security Council members, and the support of friends in the General Assembly consensus for the establishment of an Expert Working Group to refine the definition of global security. The great danger of this term is that as it comes into more general currency it means everything and nothing. (It was awareness of this possibility which caused us in Cambridge to choose Global Security as the title for the new Programme, which I direct, precisely to attempt, pre-emptively, to prevent the dissolution of meaning which we now see around us!). The New York based organisation Parliamentarians for Global Action has, I believe, already gone some way in preparing the ground for such an endeavour; but it requires a decisive push by a prominent country, which could be Britain.

— In the area of **broad strategic planning**, Britain has an opportunity to capitalise upon the forward position taken by the Prime Minister at the end of the Rio Conference. On that occasion, he undertook to convene in 1993 a follow-up conference on technological transfer between the rich and poor worlds. This is a key area which crosses many of the sources of conflict and contains within it many of the instruments that can remove the sources of conflict. It would be a great service if this conference could be used to get a grip on the institutional response to the circular interconnections of global security problems. Bush's offer of the re-tasking of the US Arms Control and Disarmament Agency towards military conversion should be taken up.

— **Detailed strategic planning** needs to be addressed as a matter of urgency, and from several fronts simultaneously. In the policy studies and academic communities, several attempts are now being made to grip these matters, some, such as the Cambridge GSP work, in close liaison with colleagues in the strategic concepts staffs of our own and other armed forces, and in NATO. Britain is uniquely positioned to take a lead here. We could take a forward position as a Security Council member in winning support for the preparation of the necessary logistic and C^3I (Command, Control, Communication and Intelligence) infrastructure of the MSC. Britain's Commonwealth contacts and diplomatic expertise are not to be scorned, as in some quarters is it fashionable to do. They give the country demonstrable leverage which could, in this issue, be used to good effect. Furthermore, the central position which Britain has in NATO, especially with command of the Rapid Deployment Force, and the depth of experience in our armed forces, make this a logical issue for us to promote. I have several times in this Memorandum alluded to the danger that UN PKOs could easily come to be seen as US dominated, Rich World operations, and indeed become so. Britain is excellently placed to help avert that outcome.

— *Agenda for Peace* believes, rightly I think, that **national/regional/global differences of interest** will become more, not less acute. How will this express itself? One predictable way will be through demands for Britain and France to surrender their Security Council seats. Whether or not that is appropriate, I do not believe in musical chairs because it would be a wasteful diversion of energy. But how will this be avoided? By Britain and France making serious efforts to promote and lead reform in the areas, such as peace-keeping, where it is urgently required. That also includes promotion of new thinking on national funding of PKOs, as described above.

CONCLUSION

There are concrete tasks to be undertaken to provide the new thinking and actions for which *Agenda for Peace* calls. These tasks will be addressed one way or another. If Britain hangs back from the process, there will be political costs and a further erosion of influence. But these tasks should be politically congenial to Britain; and the country is well placed to give a lead. If it does so, there could be commensurate benefits. It would be a pity if Britain missed this boat.

APPENDIX 3

Memorandum by the World Disarmament Campaign UK

We are pleased to offer our views on Dr Boutros-Ghali's "An Agenda for Peace". We welcomed the Prime Minister's initiative in convening the meeting of the Security Council at heads of state level in January '92. It paved the way for the Secretary-General to formulate imaginative proposals for strengthening the UN which are equally welcome. The earlier report of the independent and prestigious Stockholm Initiative on Global Governance also made positive proposals in relation to the UN: they too merit consideration by your Committee.

WDC (UK) was born to keep alive the prophetic Final Document of the UN's SSDI of 1978 and is aimed at ensuring that the General Assembly fulfils its mandate for disarmament and the rejection of war given by the consensus resolutions of SSDI, article 26 of the Charter and numerous subsequent resolutions.

For this reason we are disappointed to find that "*An Agenda for Peace*" for some unexplained reason makes no reference to the importance of world disarmament or the equally vital need to enlarge upon the framework of the UN's forthcoming Register of Arms Transfers. We have submitted comments on this question to officials of the Foreign Office, MOD, the UN Conference on Disarmament, Geneva, and others (see annex p.253).

The Secretary-General's proposals to strengthen the UN in efforts to settle international disputes; prevent conflicts; and to participate in preventative diplomacy, peacemaking, peace-keeping and post-conflict re-settlement are fully supported. But we are painfully aware that the safety of military and civilian personnel assigned to these tasks under the UN flag is greatly jeopardised by the ready availability of all types of weapons in a grossly over-militarised world. The General Assembly has evidently not recognised that the Charter envisages that UN policing and peace-keeping under Articles 42 and 43 will take place in a world that has been significantly disarmed under Article 26.

Experience in the former Yugoslavia and other areas of violent internal conflict has shown the need for UN forces, mandated by the Security Council on behalf of the international community, to be able to intervene militarily to prevent genocide and the slaughter of innocent civilians, and in areas such as Somalia to re-establish basic administrative structures. We do not wish to see the present UN, which is dominated by one powerful and influential superpower, given free rein to impose terms for internal settlements. We are sure that the Charter's rigid insistence on impartiality and respect for sovereignty, however politically and morally intolerable a member state may be, needs to be revised. This brings into question the limited and out-of-date make-up of the Security Council, the injustice of the power of veto, which is much resented, and the need for its decisions and actions to accord with the wishes and interests of the broad international community. We hope HMG will use all the international influence that it still retains to seek such revision of the Charter as will make the implementation of the UN's peace-keeping and other roles more effective and more generally acceptable.

None of the proposals made in the Report will stand much chance of success unless they are adequately and promptly funded. We are dismayed at the poor response of the wealthier member states to the Secretary-General's continuous pleas for funds; the failure of HMG to pledge any contribution specifically for the UN's World Disarmament Campaign of education, information and promotion of public awareness in relation to disarmament has long been an embarrassment to all who have to explain British policies abroad. We agree with the Secretary-General that the sharp contrast between the costs of UN peace-keeping and the awful alternative, war, would be merely farcical were the consequences not so damaging to global stability. We welcome the suggestion, therefore, that the cost of allocating personnel, equipment and logistics on stand-by to the UN should be debited to the Defence budget.

We urge your committee to take up the challenges contained in the Report to make the UN an effective institution of world governance. The Stockholm Initiative has proposed a new World Summit and the Secretary-General has recommended further high-level meetings of the Security Council. In addition, we welcome the new independent international commission on global co-operation and governance, which has been set up following the Stockholm Initiative, under the co-chairmanship of Ingvar Carlsson of Sweden and Shridath Ramphal of Guyana. We hope HMG may be persuaded to take the lead in implementing the above proposals.

Annex

UN REGISTER OF CONVENTIONAL ARMS RESOLUTION 46/36 L

At its Annual General Meeting in May 1992, the World Disarmament Campaign (UK) unanimously carried the following resolution—

"The World Disarmament Campaign (UK) commends the United Nations General Assembly for adopting at its 46th Session resolutions 46/36H and 46/36L as first steps to the registration and control of legitimate international transfers of arms and to the eradication of illicit and covert trading in arms.

"It regrets, however, that member states are requested to provide data for the proposed Register of Conventional Arms on a post factum and voluntary basis; that the absence of advance notice of transfer precludes any preventive action; that the Register is limited to specific categories of higher calibre weapons; that the first annual registration is not required until 30 April 1993; and that the Register is open for consultation only by representatives of member states.

"It therefore respectfully urges the Secretary-General and the Conference on Disarmament earnestly and speedily to rectify these shortcomings and to establish effective procedures for independent documentary inspection and investigation to verify that data provided for the Register is accurate, comprehensive and complete."

The comments and suggestions which follow are offered in elaboration. They arise from an earnest wish to see the Register operating successfully as a key factor in controlling the international arms trade, and minimising the military provisions of member states under United Nations governance.

Resolution Para. 7: Annex Para. 2(c)

1. The annual return of data for the Register is merely voluntary. The intention to "prevent the excessive and destabilising accumulation of arms" will only be achieved if all member states participate fully: compliance with the terms of the Register will need to be mandatory, preferably under a treaty.

2. The notification of existing holdings and procurements of the specified weapons should also be compulsory.

3. If politicians, the public and ngo's are to exercise any restraint on arms transfers, *prior* notification and announcement is essential, preferably no later than the signing of a contract. It would also be of value if all applications to the Department of Trade and Industry for export licences were given full publicity.

Resolution Para. 8

4. We welcome the direction to the Conference on Disarmament to consider the elaboration of technical procedures and adjustments for effective operation and *early* expansion of the scope of the Register.

5. The data returned by member states must be accurate comprehensive and verifiable. Weapons need to be described with the fullest details, e.g., particulars of supplier, carrier and receiver: declared value, invoiced price, weight and dimensions. The value will be necessary if a levy is to be imposed on arms transfers.

6. Full particulars should be required to be entered on export and import licences, bills of lading, cargo manifests, advice and delivery notes, end-use certificates, etc.

7. Transparency would be increased if all specified weapons were required to be included in the export and import statistics of the member states involved.

8. Clear definitions will be needed of the precise *time* of exportation and importation, especially in relation to part-consignments.

9. Penalties should be prescribed by participating member states for non-compliance or breaches of the relevant law and regulations by exporters, agents and others. Offences should be publicised to alert public opinion.

10. Adequate provision is necessary for *independent* verification and monitoring of arms transfers, preferably by an effectively staffed and adequately financed United Nations agency. This could involve satellite surveillance and promiscuous spot checks on movements and deposits of weapons.

11. Spot verifications should be comprehensive and cover, as appropriate, the examination of import/export documents, correspondence, orders, delivery records and books or records of account indicating all payments, receipts and other financial transactions.

12. End-use certificates could be verified and attested by foreign Customs, or by embassies or consulates of the supplying state.

13. The general control of arms transfers should be undertaken with full co-operation by the Ministry of Defence, Department of Trade and Industry, HM Customs, the Police, Interpol and other investigative agencies. It would be of value to require that all exports and imports of weapons under licence are produced for Customs examination, preferably at a few designated ports or airports.

14. Information on the procedures established by member states should be exchanged and discussed with others to their mutual advantage and, where practicable, co-ordinated through UN agencies; MTCR, ICAO, International Maritime Organisation and other relevant international bodies.

RESOLUTION PARA. 8: ANNEX PARA. 2(A)

15. It is most important that the range of weapons specified is extended to include components, production technology and dual-use equipment.

16. The smaller arms and shoulder-launched missiles that are readily available in the Third World, and now in central and East European conflicts call for special control of both overt and covert transfers.

17. The proposed Convention on Chemical Weapons would be strengthened if chemical weapons, associated equipment and chemical precursors were included in the list of specified weapons.

RESOLUTION PARA. 8: ANNEX PARAS. 4 AND 5

18. For transparency to produce results the Register needs to be open to public scrutiny. This would counter the often unwarranted secrecy in relations to arms questions imposed on grounds of national security.

19. Maximum openness in relation to all arms transfers, procurements, deployments, etc. would enable parliament to scrutinise and question arms export criteria and to monitor administrative controls. The public could similarly exercise the democratic right to question, make representations and exercise political pressure.

APPENDIX 4

Letter to the Clerk of the Committee from Brigadier Michael Harbottle OBE (Ret), Director, Centre for International Peacebuilding

I was recently invited to submit to the United Nations Association of Great Britain and Northern Ireland my comments on the United Nations Secretary General's *AGENDA FOR PEACE* to be included in its planned submission to your Committee, as part of the feedback that I believe the Committee had requested.

As a former Chief of Staff of the United Nations Peacekeeping Force in Cyprus and an author of a number of books on the subject of United Nations Peacekeeping, I made a fairly comprehensive response. Subsequently in conversation with Sam Daws of the Association it was clear that only selected extracts from my response would be included as a part of a collection of overall comments. Since I was anxious that the comments I had made should be available to the Committee I asked for, and got, their (UNA) agreement to submit my comments in full to the Committee. I am therefore enclosing them in the annex attached for the consideration of the Committee.

I hope that this is not a presumption on my part but will assist the Committee when they come to consider the United Kingdom's response to *AGENDA FOR PEACE*.

Annex

AGENDA FOR PEACE—UK GOVERNMENT'S RESPONSE

COMMENT

Peacebuilding: Ch. VI

The Secretary General refers to peacebuilding as being a post-conflict process for dealing with the many problems of reconstruction and rehabilitation of economic and social structures. My comment is that peacebuilding is the third dimension, with peacemaking and peacekeeping, of the peaceful settlement of disputes. It is required in the preventative diplomacy of the pre-conflict phase; it is performed by the UN peacekeepers as an important part of their role in working to restore, maintain and ensure the civil human rights of the people in the conflict area, freedom of movement and their right to normal existence. Peacebuilding is all embracing and should not be limited. It is important that this is understood by HMG and defined clearly as such.

Peacemaking and Peacekeeping: Chs. IV and V

Both with peacemaking and peacekeeping, definitions are confused and are sometimes used synonomously. *Peacemaking* is the diplomatic and political initiative for bringing about a solution to the disagreements which brought about the conflict in the first place. It involves mediation, conciliation, negotiation, and arbitration too so long as it does not constitute coercion and enforced acceptance of imposed solutions.

Peacekeeping is the third party intervention by the military to *assist* in bringing about the end of the fighting; the end of the manifest violence. Peacekeeping cannot resolve the conflict, only the manifest violence. Peacekeeping is quite different from peace enforcement and the differentiation must be clearly understood and defined. It would be a constructive initiative were HMG to work for a clarification and a definition of both to be inserted into Chapter VII.

Article 2(7): Para 30

The current debate about the validity of the UN's intervention in Iraq and the former Yugoslavia appears to ignore the fundamental authority of the Security Council to maintain international peace and security. Under the provisions of Article 39, the Council is empowered to take measures to maintain international peace and security wherever a threat to it exists. There are no exceptions. Article 2(7) has a qualifying final sentence which states that the provisions of this Article will not be allowed to prejudice the application of Chapter VII. The actions of Saddam Hussein against the Kurds and the Shiites, and the war in former Yugoslavia, would seem clearly to constitute threats to international peace and security and therefore there should be no argument against the UN's intervention. I suggest that HMG should endorse this interpretation of the validity of the UN acting within sovereign boundaries when the international threat is seen to exist.

Humanitarian Assistance: Para 29

This has been a part of most past UN operations. Yugoslavia is the first time that a Humanitarian Relief Operation has been conducted on its own. Inevitably it is vulnerable to interference, even of an extreme nature as in Yugoslavia. Essentially therefore, it needs the protection necessary for it to fulfil its mandate. It should therefore be supported by a peacekeeping operation which would provide the safe conduct it needs. Humanitarian assistance is likely to become an integral part of any operation since it is in essence a peacebuilding process. Consideration therefore should be given to it being conducted as a joint military-civilian operation, as was done in the Congo (ONUC) in the 1960s.

Use of Force: Para 42

Surprisingly, no mention is made in *Agenda for Peace* of the use of force in peacekeeping operations. The principle of using force only in self defence is, I believe, well understood. However, it should be clearly defined and recognised. I have been amazed by the indecision which has been shown regarding this automatic right of peacekeepers to use force when attacked, or threatened with attack, either to their persons, their positions, *or their physical ability to carry out their mandate.* It has always been the accepted provision for a peacekeeping operation and is part of its Standing Operating Procedures. It does not require a special Security Council resolution and uncertainty diminishes the protection and confidence of the UN soldiers. HMG should press for the need to establish broad "rules of engagement" which can be adapted for specific operational circumstances.

Military Staff Committee: Para 43

I do not entirely agree that the MSC, if reactivated, should not be involved in the planning of peacekeeping operations. If the MSC were to be designated as an advisory planning group, it would be quite reasonable for it to help plan such operations, assisted by representatives of states who have a first hand knowledge of the countries or regions where a conflict, or a potential conflict, exists. This would ensure that all factors affecting the successful conduct of the UN intervention would be considered.

Finance: Ch. IX

The chronic financial situation in the UN makes it extremely questionable how long the UN will be able to mount and sustain its peacekeeping operations. I propose that besides making a firm commitment to provide military/naval/air units or contingents for UN peacekeeping, HMG should set an example by accepting to bear the costs of their participation. If this example were accepted and followed by other member states, it would greatly reduce the financial burden of the UN. To cover the cost to UK, I suggest that a regular budgetting should be included in MOD's annual budget to offset any extra expenditure which otherwise would be incurred.

I appreciate that this could exclude the smaller member states and the poorer ones from participating, but assistance could be given to those countries of the Third World which have the manpower and which have already proved themselves adept at peacekeeping, viz. India.

APPENDIX 5

Memorandum by Anne Bennett, Secretary, UN Committee, Quaker Peace & Service

AGENDA FOR PEACE

The Religious Society of Friends (Quakers) with their long tradition of opposition to the use of force, have consistently supported national and international institutions which seek alternatives to the use of violence to resolve conflicts. The ending of the Cold War has provided new opportunities for the United Nations to utilise its skills of preventive diplomacy and peacemaking and earned considerable respect for its effectiveness in these processes.

We welcome Agenda for Peace and the discussion it will provoke. Meeting violence with violence is rarely effective in the long term and it is important to extend and develop the Secretary General's role (and that of the UN as a whole) in peace making/peace keeping.

However, we have some concerns about the implications for the UN as it develops this role. It has to be realistic about what it can offer, ensure that it does not over extend itself or raise unrealistic expectations. A secure financial base is crucial. The UN must have the human and financial resources it needs to take the work forward.

We are also concerned about the possibility that increased military involvement could undermine the UN's major role, to act as a mediator in disputes. We have misgivings about providing the UN with "heavily armed" units for peace enforcement, especially as it is implied that the credibility of the UN might depend on the existance of such armed units. We suggest that the authority of the UN should be based on trust developed by the consistent pursuit of peace, the improvement of the conditions of human life and the promotion of human rights. There is also concern that the UN could be influenced by member states or alliances, with their own agendas, to participate in wars under the UN banner.

We welcome the proposal to strengthen and utilise the International Court of Justice. We hope that the Security Council will take a more active role in areas of arms control, non proliferation and disarmament. Agenda for Peace requires the UN to possess the capacity to effectively monitor and prevent the escalation of disputes into full-scale conflicts. This monitoring relies heavily on the UN and its agencies, on regional organisations and non-governmental organisations. It is of critical importance that the relationship between these component parts are maintained and strengthened. This requires their ongoing commitment to the future opportunities for the UN to promote preventive diplomacy, peace keeping, peace building and peace making.

The UN has considerable potential. We hope that this will be fully supported by the UK Government. Sustainable peace is vital for the survival of the planet.

APPENDIX 6

Memorandum by A J R Groom, Professor of International Relations, University of Kent at Canterbury

INTRODUCTION

1. The comments which follow arise from the recent report of the UN's Secretary General entitled "*An Agenda for Peace*" and Mr Boutros-Ghali's report to the General Assembly of September 1992. The comments are not intended to be comprehensive, nor to be restricted solely to the agenda as set by the Secretary-General.

THE IMPLICATIONS OF ACTIVISM

2. The founding fathers of the UN were careful to write into the Charter Article 2.7 which safeguards the domestic jurisdiction of States. Domestic jurisdiction is now under some pressure from the intrusive activity of various international bodies and especially of UN bodies. An obvious example is that of the Security Council with the leading role played by the permanent five (P5), who have acted as a directing group since 1986 when Sir John Thomson, the then British Ambassador brought his four fellow Ambassadors together in the context of the war between Iran and Iraq. The role of the P5 has been particularly important in the case of the Kuwait crisis, but it has also been concerned with Namibia, Cambodia and Afghanistan, as well as other conflicts.

3. One area in which the P5 has acted as a background legitimiser is that of humanitarian intervention in Iraq. Initially in the North, but also now in the South, Iraq is the object of a muscular humanitarian intervention, backed as it is by French, British and US air patrols in the North acting as a deterrent to Iraqi misdemeanours and the few hundred UN guards on the ground who act as a moral witness. The work of the humanitarian agencies, both UN and NCO, on the ground has therefore been given a highly political character. This sort of muscled humanitarian intervention is usually necessitated by calamity which has been brought about by a massive abuse of human rights. We can therefore see a link between the need for muscled humanitarian intervention and human rights.

4. In another dimension, namely that of economic and financial affairs, the IMF and the World Bank, as UN Specialised Agencies, and the G7 have all undertaken a directing role which in many cases prejudices seriously the domestic jurisdiction of states. In short, their economic policies are subject to the approval of the major Powers through one or all of these institutions.

5. The activities of P5, the IMF, the World Bank and the humanitarian bodies constitute a significant intrusion in the domestic jurisdiction of some states. It is not only Iraq that is fearful and it is not only Iraq that has much to hide. The activism of the leading members of the UN system, of which the UK is one, in these matters is therefore inciting a reaction. It is a moot point the extent to which the P5 may be able to carry China with them in the Security Council.

6. There is a hostile reaction on the part of some states because they have things to hide. There is a growing anxiety on the part of other states because they fear that the major Powers are acting in a very roughshod manner over the sensibilities of smaller Powers and taking into account insufficiently their views and interests. There is a concern among others about the double standards of such interventions. In short, there is an urgent need to get our double standards right. However, it is not likely that the UK will join with others to intervene in all disputes in the same category. Consider for example the different reactions to the occupation and annexation of Kuwait by Iraq, and that of Timor by Indonesia, not to mention ambivalence towards the Israeli occupation of the West Bank and Gaza and annexation of East Jerusalem.

7. I would recommend that the Committee give serious attention to the implications of the intrusive activities of UN agencies on the domestic jurisdiction of states. It needs to consider carefully when such intrusion should take place, by whom, in what way, over which range of issues.

8. The anxiety of some states over such intrusion is partly a reflection of their concern over the nature of the agenda, of what is tantamount to global riot control. The agenda of the West includes arms control, particularly over nuclear weapons, terrorism, drugs, refugees, human rights, AIDS, and a gamut of factors linked with the environment, not to mention traditional concerns about aggression, civil wars and wars of secession. This agenda is that of the developed Western countries who back, on the whole, the intrusive activism of the UN system. But such activities can only be fully effective if they represent a broad consensus. Otherwise, there is likely to be a strong reaction led by countries such as China and India, with the support of other major regional Powers such as Nigeria, Brazil and Indonesia. Their objections may be somewhat mollified if the agenda of global riot control is broadened to include matters of their interest, such as the whole question of development on a global scale and the assymetries and inequities of the present world economy. An example of the growing irritation can be found in reaction to some of the environmental measures proposed by the developed countries and resisted by the developing countries. It is not that they are against global riot control, since they have much to gain

from it too, but that they need to ensure that the agenda reflects the full gamut of everybody's interests, and not just that of the powerful few who have come, in effect, to control international organisations such as the UN.

9. The question of intrusion and reactions to it is important when seen in the context of an increased access by many small groups to effective means of coercion. Western society is open, complex and interdependent. It is also liberal and rich. It is therefore highly vulnerable. It can only counteract threats to its security, broadly defined, by restricting its liberal basis or sacrificing a significant potential for economic development. On the other hand, small determined groups who fear that they have nothing to lose, can cause maximum disruption at very little cost, particularly if they are unconcerned about their own safety and well-being. If they have nothing to lose they may be so unconcerned. In the UK framework we can see this in the current disruptions caused by bomb explosions and bomb scares in the London area. It is not hard to see analogies on the global scale. One act of terror against US and French forces in the Lebanon caused those countries to withdraw from the multinational force. The ability of local commanders to scupper agreements in the former Yugoslavia is another such example. Similar instances can be found in economic and social systems. Thus, if those beyond the pale cannot be defeated or contained at a minimal cost, then they can make their voices felt. Those therefore, who see intrusive activity of the P5, the IMF or whatever as a panacea for global riot control without a strong element of consensus, may find that they are in for a rude shock. Access to effective means of coercion is much more widespread because of the nature of the contemporary world, than was previously the case.

10. This thought relates to the Secretary-General's' conception of peace enforcement, which is perhaps best seen as Chapter 6¾ of the UN Charter. Chapter 6 deals with pacific settlement of disputes. Chapter 7 deals with acts of aggression etc. Chapter 6½ deals with traditional peace-keeping and the Secretary-General wishes to look towards the notion of peace enforcement, which does not yet fall under Chapter 7. It is not likely that those on the ground will accept clear-cut distinctions between Chapter 6½, peace enforcement and Chapter 7. It can only work if it is accepted, and if it is accepted then Chapter 6½, that is, traditional peace-keeping will suffice. Otherwise, there is likely to be a phenomenon of Vietnamisation, as the UN is dragged into a quagmire, which like the Congo could lead to prejudicing the very existence of the organisation. To be sure UN intervention in conflicts needs to be pro-active, and indeed preventive and possibly preemptive, but there should be a major gap between traditional peace-keeping based upon the consent of the parties, including non-state parties, impartiality and no enforcement on the one hand, and full-scale enforcement on the other.

11. One final aspect of the intrusive activities of the UN, particularly through the Security Council and the P5, is the growth of tension between the Secretary-General and the P5. The Secretary-General's role is ambivalent. He is the chief administrative officer of the organisation, and as such has to implement the wishes of the organisation, especially those of the Security Council when they are made clear explicitly in the form of a Resolution backed by the P5. On the other hand, the Secretary-General is an actor, and under Article 99 he has the right to bring the Security Council into session, when he believes that there is a political need to do so. He therefore has both an administrative and a political role which are now coming increasingly into conflict.

12. In the past Secretaries-General have adopted an even-handed position between members in dispute. They are, after all, the Secretary-General of the whole organisation. Indeed, one of the major functions of the Secretary-General has been this mediatory role. However, matters changed, particularly in the context of the Kuwait crisis, where the enforcement measures meant that the Secretary-General should be the Chief Administrative Officer of an organisation which was taking enforcement measures against a member state. Mr Perez de Cuéllar found this change of role difficult to handle. Mr Boutros-Ghali likewise, appears to be taking initiatives which emphasise his political role, sometimes in a manner which rubs up against his administrative functions as the Chief Administrative Officer of the organisation. The role of the Secretary-General, an activist himself, in an organisation which is also active at the behest of others requires exploration. Hence, there is a tension between the two functions of the Secretary-General and that tension is likely to give rise to difficulties between the Secretary-General and those in the system who are taking a lead, notably the P5 in the context of global riot control.

Enfranchisement of Relevant Actors

13. In his presentations the Secretary-General makes clear his view that states and sovereignty are prime elements of the UN and global political systems, yet the first words of the UN Charter are "We the peoples . . .". However nowhere in the Charter, except for Article 71, do other actors come in with a central role. This absence of other important non-state actors is a significant weakness of the UN system. If we consider the agenda of global riot control, which is in effect the agenda of the UN system mentioned above, then in many of these activities non-state actors are crucial. This is particularly the case in humanitarian questions, and in those concerned with human rights, as well as with development issues. It is almost ludicrous to consider global economic development without enfranchising multinational co-operations, irrespective of whether they are seen to be benign or malign in their behaviour regarding development goals. Nor can it be said that governments adequately reflect the views and the actions of

these actors. It is patently not necessarily true what Charles Wilson said when he remarked that "what is good for General Motors, is good for the United States". Moreover, multinational corporations, churches, terrorist movements, Greenpeace, Amnesty International, the drug barons, both legal and illegal, all command important resources and the loyalties of significant numbers of individuals or groups. Because such actors have an effect on matters within the domain of the United Nations, they have to be enfranchised in a more systematic and effective manner than is at present the case.

14. One way in which some progress has been made in this direction is through the holding of large conferences on a particular theme, in which the central bodies of the UN, the Specialised Agencies and non-state actors participate in an interactive manner whatever the formal differences. The first time this occurred was in the context of the UN Conference on the Environment, held in Stockholm in 1972, and it has been a feature of such large global conferences ever since, whether dealing with women, population, habitat, disarmament, or the environment. The number of such conferences over the last two decades is more than 200, and this represents a development of the UN system in a little-publicised, but effective manner. It is however, but a step in the right direction and not the answer to a serious lacuna in the system, namely how to enfranchise non-state actors who are important for the concerns of the UN system.

FINANCE

15. It is no longer sufficient to shrug-off the UN's financial problems as something which is inevitable and can be lived with. The Secretary-General rightly points to the vast expansion of activity and to the chronic problems of cash flow and the absence of capital. The present situation is such that it is no longer a question of whether the system will break down, but when it will break down. In this matter the position of the United States is inexcusable. Decisions are now taken on a consensus basis and therefore, the United States has an effective veto. The United States can therefore, in effect, call the tune, but it is refusing to pay the piper. It is therefore important that other members put intense pressure on the United States to pay, no matter what the internal difficulties the United States has got itself into are, and a situation for doing this presents itself with the change of administration, whoever is the winner in the present US elections. The same argument holds with Russia, but should be kept in abeyance until such time as Russia is in a position to pay. In the meantime, it is in the interest of other Powers who get so many benefits from the system, to increase their contribution. Japan and Germany have already acted in this manner, and it is up to other members of the EC and in particular those who have structural privileges in the system, such as Britain and France, to increase their contribution. Given the range of activities of the UN system, and its benefits to Britain and the calamities that would occur, should that system collapse, such an increased contribution is surely in Britain's interest.

TRAINING OF PERSONNEL

16. It is widely acknowledged that in the past too great an emphasis has been put on the geographical distribution of posts in the secretariat and not enough on the efficiency of members of the international Civil Service. To some degree, geographical distribution may enable on the job training of individuals from countries where such training would otherwise not be available, however, this is not the point of the system. Moreover, the actual training of many personnel is not suited to many of the new roles, particularly in the area of peace and security, which they are being called upon to fulfil. The argument applies therefore a *fortiori* if the UN develops proactive measures in the area of prevention of conflict along the lines envisaged by the UN Secretary-General.

17. As an academic discipline, International Relations is now 70 years old and it has a lot to offer by way of training to international Civil Servants. More particularly, in the area of conflict research a useful corpus of knowledge has emerged and there are an increasing number of postgraduate courses in the field. While many institutions may have a prejudice against such professional academic training, because they wish to institutionalise and socialise their personnel themselves without the let or hindrance of an academic background in the field, nevertheless this argument does not abnegate the value of such training in terms of effectiveness of the individual. But what of academic research? The role of the academic is to act as a discussant for the policy maker, whether in a Foreign Office, or in an international secretariat. Usually the academic does not have the sort of information available that is required for day-to-day decision making. The academic's role therefore, is to provide a framework, to give a sense of perspective, and above all, to challenge assumptions: in short, the discussant's role. In the areas where the UN Secretary-General wishes to develop the organisation's activities, that is, in the area generally of conflict settlement and conflict resolution there is now, as indicated above, a substantial corpus of worthwhile research. This is particularly true in the areas of mediation and facilitation in conflicts, of both an international and an inter-communal character. There has been little interaction between UN practitioners and academics in these fields, and there ought to be more to their mutual benefit.

A BRAIN?

18. About a quarter of a century ago Sir Robert Jackson, in his review of the UN system, raised the question about whether or not it had a brain, and found that it did not. That is still the case despite the Secretary-General's efforts at co-ordination and this is also true in particular areas such as the develop-

ment of peace-keeping and the like, as described by the Secretary-General in his report. It could be that such a central brain is not possible, even in the area of the peace activities of the UN, and it might even not be desirable. What is clear is that it does not exist, although if the activities of the Security Council and of the Secretary-General could be integrated, despite the tensions described above as well as linked to the academic world through a discussant role, then such a locus of ideas and practice might be possible. On the other hand, the more likely is the creation of such a locus, the more some member states would be fearful of it. Being as it may, the left hand needs better to know what the right hand is doing in peace and security affairs. For example, the appointment by Mr Perez de Cuéllar of at least six special representatives with different but overlapping functions in the context of the Kuwait crisis was clearly dysfunctional and the system needs to be so organised that such dysfunctionalities are eliminated.

CAVEAT

19. In recent years the author has, with Paul Taylor, undertaken a number of studies of the UN system including a substantial study of Britain and the United Nations, as well as of the diplomacy of the Kuwait crisis. In his submission to the Committee, Dr Paul Taylor will draw upon the authors' joint conclusions. In addition, the author of this submission has made a speciality of conflict research, including the practical application of theory to practice in facilitation meetings in actual international and intercommunal conflicts.

APPENDIX 7

Memorandum by the Christian Fellowship Trust (CFT)/Namibia Christian Exchange (NCE)

THE UN IN NAMIBIA AND SOUTH AFRICA.

During Namibia's transition to Independence under Security Council Resolution 435, the Namibia Christian Exchange (a sub committee of CFT) was closely involved in sending a number of independent observers to Namibia under the auspices of the British Council of Churches "Namibia Group". The observers included church delegations, eminent people, MPs and Human Rights lawyers.

Under SCR 435 the task of the UN was to ensure the early Independence of Namibia through free and fair elections. When the UN first arrived in Namibia in April 1989 there was great enthusiasm in the country which rapidly turned to dismay as the UN was seen to be inefficient in carrying out its functions. The Special Representative was perceived to be negotiating, not supervising and controlling, free and fair elections.

At the start of the 435 process there were many criticisms of the UN both in the country and by independent observers. This was due to several factors; a lack of resources, poor briefing and an infra-structure dependent on the South Africans. NCE, at the invitation of the Council of Churches in Namibia, sent two observers, Peter Pike MP and John Macdonald QC in May 1989. Many of the problems which were present then are described in their report (see Annex 1). Gradually more personnel arrived, the UN team became more efficient and independent of the South Africans and many of the recommendations by independent observers were taken on board. By the time of the elections in November 1989; the UN had regained the confidence of the country, the violence was greatly reduced and the elections could be pronounced free and fair. As the Committee heard in its evidence from Sir David Hannay on October 27, Namibia is now used as a model of successful UN involvement. However, this was only after considerable pressure from other bodies.

In 1990 and 1992 the Christian Fellowship Trust helped to arrange two International Commission of Jurists missions to South Africa. These resulted in two reports; "Signposts to Peace" and "Agenda for Peace".

Both these missions to South Africa were at the request of NGOs, churches and Human Rights organisations working in Natal in areas torn apart by violence. Both the reports recommended the need for international monitors in South Africa. In 1989, the report, "Signposts to Peace" suggested the UN model in El Salvador (see Annex 2). Apart from the people in Natal affected by the violence there was no recognisable response to these recommendations. In March 1992, a similar recommendation, based on research by people in South Africa, had a dramatic effect. (see Annex 3) The report, "Agenda for Peace" had worldwide coverage and was used in the UN during the debate on Security Council Resolution 765 in July 1 1992.

SCR 765 resulted in Cyrus Vance visiting South Africa in August 1992 as the Secretary-General's Special Representative. His report formed the basis for SCR 772 which, "authorised the Secretary-General to deploy, as a matter of urgency UN observers in South Africa to help reinforce the mechanisms established by the 1991 National Peace Accord. The mechanisms are aimed at ending the violence, and facilitating socio-economic development and reconstruction in that country."

The Secretary-General was to determine the number of observers as he deemed necessary, consulting the Council from time to time. The first number was 50 observers of whom 33 are now deployed in the country.

Initial response from the people most closely affected by the violence, is delight that the UN (and other international monitors) are in the country. In Kwa Machu in Natal, where an Inkatha rally was thought likely to provoke considerable violence, the presence of UN monitors at the meetings before hand resulted in concessions being made that would not have been accepted had the UN had not been there. During the rally itself the presence of the UN was felt to have helped enormously in reducing tension. This has been the case in several other places. However, as reported by IDASA (Institute for a Democratic Alternative in South Africa) the UN, unlike other larger missions, went into South Africa, "without doing a thorough job of developing a mandate and *modus vivendi* which is goal oriented. It assumed the National Peace Accord was an adequate treaty based framework and that its structures had an adequate infrastructural base. Because of this, the mission got off on a poor footing and will constantly have to re-negotiate its role. As it has no timetable or destination it runs the risk of an ongoing and painful sojurn in the country, prey to the changing political landscape."[1]

An example of the inadequacies of the UN role occured at Richmond/Phateni on October 18 and was reported by an international observer sent from the Ecumenical Monitoring Programme in South Africa (EMPSA)[2]. The UN monitors were transported to the area of potential violence in an armoured SAP troop carrier and remained on a hillside watching events through binoculars while other independent monitors from NGOs were on the ground providing a visible presence and helping to reduce tension. When questioned about this afterwards, the UN explained that they have to take the advice of the Regional Disputes Resolution Committee who could not guarantee their safety on the ground. Reports from Natal say that the UN are extremely reluctant to involve themselves *in situ* with any of the parties or to intervene in any way.[3]

There are only 33 monitors at present. This is not nearly enough to cover the areas affected by the violence and many of them do not have practical or professional training in policing etc. being desk bound people from the UN in New York. The ICJ report recommended 100 professional monitors backed up by an average of 3 support staff for each professional and providing their own infra-structure. This was the result of considerable research by people in the field. In his recommendations to Cyrus Vance, Nelson Mandela stressed the need for an adequate, and not merely symbolic, number of UN monitors, having freedom of movement and the independent resources to act as the "eyes" of the international community. He recommended 400–450 observers.

At present in South Africa, although there is a welcome for the UN there is great concern that there are **not nearly enough of them** and if they want to "get to grips" with the problems they will have to step up the numbers of monitors considerably. At the moment their activity is limited by having to be attached to Local Dispute Resolution Committees. In many areas these are not established or have failed because one of the parties has pulled out for example, Inkatha Freedom party in Natal, the Ciskei Administration in the Eastern Cape.

Increasingly, the concern is not only about the violence, but simultaneously the preparations for elections. Across large areas of the country, especially the homelands, there is a complete lack of freedom for political activity; with harrassment of political opponents, the use of headmen to bribe and control people and the exclusion for some political parties of any facilities. For example, the ANC have been told the hall in Esikaweni in Natal has been block booked by Inkatha for 4 months.[4]

If the UN is to be, "seized of the matter of South Africa until a democratic, non racial and united South Africa is established" (SCR 772) then the following urgent action must be taken:

— the number of monitors must be greatly increased;

— they must be professional with practical experience in the field (this is very much the case of the Commonwealth observers who have just arrived)

— they should be allocated to specific areas, so they build up local knowledge.

— they should have their own infra-structure and jurisdiction

— they must monitor, and not just observe the activities of the security forces and the Political Parties, against the provisions of the National Peace Accord and they must act firmly where these are being broken

[1] Letter from IDASA October 27 1992.
[2] Report from Network of Independent Monitors.
[3] Report from Phateni by EMPSA monitor. EMPSA is an independent international monitoring programme established by the churches in South Africa.
[4] Weekly Mail October 25th.

— they should address the question of elections as well as the violence.

The Secretary-General's optimistic report, "*An Agenda for Peace*" is to be warmly welcomed. However, if people in troubled areas are not to be disullusioned, the International community must ensure that adequate resources are available to properly perform the assigned task. The apparent tragedy in Southern Africa appears to be that even when the task is done and elections are declared "free and fair" as in Angola, the results can be manipulated to retain power and so destroy people's belief in democracy.

1 Namibia–Report of a visit by Peter Pike MP, John Macdonald QC and Alison Harvey. May 28–June 2 1989

2 "Signposts to Peace" International Commission of Jurists. October 1990

3 "Agenda for Peace" International Commission of Jurists. June 1992

Additional information from South Africa from: Legal Resources Centre (Durban), Diakonia (Durban), PACSA (Pietermaritzburg), Human Resources Centre (Durban) IDASA (Durban)

Annex 1

Extract from "Namibia" a report by John Macdonald QC, Peter Pike MP and Alison Harvey

THE ROLE OF THE UNITED NATIONS: TO SUPERVISE AND CONTROL FREE AND FAIR ELECTIONS

34. Wherever we went we were told that the United Nations actions in Namibia had been too weak. There was criticism of the decision taken by the Special Representative on 1 April to unleash South African troops, but that was not what was uppermost in people's minds. They were concerned that Untag appears to be negotiating with the South Africans instead of supervising the election process. The students at the Pauline Lutheran Seminary at Otjimbingwe made it very clear that they want the United Nations to give a lead, so did the villagers in the north, so did Untag workers in the field. The general feeling was summed up for us in the United Nations building in Windhoek in these words: "The United Nations is behaving as though it represents the weakest of the Front Line States. We don't. We represent the World."

35. We believe it is essential that the United Nations not only stands firm but is seen to stand firm. The mandate of the Special representative of the Secretary General is clearly stated in Resolution 435. It is: **"to ensure the early independence of Namibia through free and fair elections under the supervision and control of the United Nations."**

36. We have been encouraged by the Amnesty, the first stage of the repeal of the discriminatory laws, and the safe return of the first refugees. We are particularly heartened by the amnesty. This was agreed while we were in Windhoek. Mr Martti Ahtisarri must have been very tempted to settle for something less, to keep the 435 process moving forward. The South Africans were proposing that the amnesty for criminal offences should only apply until a specified number of days after the election. The United Nations could have said that that went further than the South Africans had ever gone before and that it should have been accepted. It is greatly to Mr Ahtisarri's credit that he did not make this mistake. We think this is important because it will have strengthened the position of those in the Secretariat who have been insisting that the United Nation's role is to supervise and control the election not to negotiate with the South Africans.

37. The next test will be the registration of electors. The regulations the Administrator-General has proposed are a virtual reprint of the rules of the unfortunate 1978 election This will not do. As an absolute minimum there must be one national registration roll, listing the names of all registered voters in alphabetical order by district, which is published throughout the country. The districts must not be defined as the old ethnic areas. The Untag monitors must also have a specified place in the legal framework so that they have real authority. Comments on the draft rules were invited from interested parties. We have studied the comments of Swapo, the Churches, The Trades Unions and the Lawyers Committee For Civil Rights Under The Law. They are sensible and constructive. United Nations legal advisors believe 80 per cent of them should be accepted. We agree. The South Africans refuse to say which of the recommendations they accept and which they reject. South Africa must not be allowed to get away with this. If the Administrator-General persists in his indefensible attitude the Special Representative must make it clear to the Namibian people and to the rest of the World that the Registration proposals do not provide the basis for a full and fair election. The South African government would then have to decide whether it wants the road to stop there.

38. The United Nations will have to be equally resolute over the rules for the election itself. It is indeed foolish to consider one without the other. The rules must be practical fair and based on experi-

ence in other democratic elections. A ✓ on ballot papers will lead to much less abuse than a X. If a cross is used to mark a ballot paper there is a danger that some voters will think that it should be placed opposite the candidate the voter wants to vote against. Votes should be counted and declared locally. The votes should be counted over as short a period as possible. There is much to be learned from the successful elections in Zimbabwe.

39. The United Nations must recruit its election monitors without further delay. They must all be able to speak English fluently and as many as possible should also speak Dutch or Afrikaans. They must all have had practical experience of running elections.

40. We believe the United Nations is in a strong position. Carl von Hirschberg told us that the South African Government wants the 435 process to succeed. We believe him. We think the return of the refugees is a clear sign that South Africa is serious. We have no doubt however that they will argue strongly for rules which favour their allies. Carl von Hirschberg told us that they do not want Swapo to obtain a two thirds majority.

41. There is no need for the United Nations to compromise on the framework of the laws for the elections, and they must not do so. Even those who are nervous about a Swapo victory in the election should recognise that one of the worst outcomes would be for Swapo to be denied a clear majority by a rigged electoral law. **The November elections will be a precedent for elections in an independent Namibia. A new nation should start with the best possible election law.**

42. We hope the United Nations will find a new confidence. We think they need to explain much more forcefully to the people of Namibia what they are doing.

43. One of the most important functions which the United Nations can perform is to supply accurate and impartial information about what is going on. We think the United Nations should make maximum use of local radio and television programmes. They should go further than that. They should he broadcasting their own programmes throughout the country in the local languages as well as English. Mr Martti Ahtisarri and his senior advisors should appear regularly on television and radio and take the people of Namibia into their confidence.

44. We saw Mr Ahtisarri for 45 minutes and were able to put our main concerns to him.

How the United Kingdom can Help

45. We are very grateful to the members of the United Kingdom Liaison Office in Namibia who went out of their way to assist us. We saw most of Roger Clark who impressed us greatly. He has an open mind and is taking great trouble to ascertain the views of a wide cross section of Namibians.

46. Peter Wallace, the head of the mission, cautioned us against accepting everything the Churches say at face value. We think this was well intentioned advice, and was no doubt given because rumour is rife. We think that everyone reporting events in Namibia needs to check information they are given rigorously. We stressed the importance of this to Church leaders and we are satisfied that they are taking great care in what they report.

47. It is clear that the Church leaders and the teachers are the community leaders. Many of them are members of Swapo. They are quite open about it. This does not mean that they are partisan or that they abuse their position. The thing which impressed and encouraged us most about our visit to Namibia was the very high calibre and integrity of the religious and community leaders we met at parish level. We would expect that the South Africa secret service would attempt to disparage church leaders at all levels. We think it is important to be alert to this. We think the Churches will provide the backbone of the new Namibia. We trust that the United Kingdom government will be sensitive to this.

48. The United Nations has to stand firm, something which would come naturally to our Prime Minister. We are all convinced that Mrs Thatcher made a great impression on Mr Ahtisarri when she was in Namibia in April. We have no doubt that he would greatly value any advice she might give.

Recommendations

49. We would give the following advice:—

(1) The United Nations must make clear that its mandate is to supervise and control free and fair elections, its function is not to negotiate with South Africa.

(2) The proposals for Registration put forward by the Administrator-General are unacceptable and do not provide a basis for free and fair elections. The registration proclamation must take account of the submission made by Swapo, the Trades Unions, the Churches and the Lawyers Committee for Civil Rights Under the Law which have been accepted by Kwame Opoku, the United Nations legal advisor.

(3) The electoral law must be practical, fair and based on the Zimbabwe experience.

(4) The United Nations must recruit sufficient election monitors now. It is vital that there should be sufficient United Nations monitors to check every stage of the election process. All monitors must speak English fluently and as many as possible Dutch or Afrikaans or another local language.

(5) The Election monitors must have had practical experience of running elections. The United Kingdom should offer to make available the computers which will be needed and the son of experts it provided to supervise the Zimbabwean election.

(6) The United Nations should use television and radio as much as possible to explain what Untag is doing to the Namibian people. The United Nations should broadcast its own regular news service throughout Namibia.

(7) The BBC should institute a special broadcasting service for Namibia in addition to the Africa Service, and we would hope to see more British journalists living in Namibia.

(8) The Proclamation setting up the O'Linn Commission is unsatisfactory and needs substantial amendment. The O'Linn Commission cannot discharge the United Nations role and is no substitute for effective action by Untag.

(9) An experienced policeman, who is competent and fair, and is not from the counter insurgency unit or the secret police, should be appointed to command the police in the north.

(10) United Nations police monitors should accompany all police patrols. There should be one South African and one UN vehicle on every patrol. If necessary the number of Untag police should be increased above 1,000 already agreed. The police must all speak English fluently and if possible Dutch or Afrikaans or a local language.

Annex 2

Extract from "Sign Posts to Peace" Dec. 1990

4. AN INTERNATIONAL MONITORING AGENCY

In the Central American country of El Salvador, a civil war between a guerilla movement and the right wing government has during the last ten years claimed more than 70,000 lives. However, the parties to this conflict have recently, with the assistance of the good offices of the Secretary General of the United Nations, embarked on a series of meetings in order to explore the prospects for a peaceful settlement. This has in itself been considered an important development, taking into account the bitter polarization between the parties and the fact that the government—and the Salvadoran army—earlier on many occasions have dismissed the UN as a left wing agency.

The obstacles to a peaceful development in the Salvadoran conflict are in some ways similar to those prevailing in South Africa. Over the years, there have been massive human rights violations, primarily against the civilian population. While it is true that such abuses have been carried out at the hands of both parties to the conflict, the atrocities perpetrated by the Salvadoran army and police are by far the worst and most numerous. So called death squads, with links too the army and the police, have over the years abducted, mutilated and killed thousands of union leaders, priests, academics, journalists, human rights advocates and others suspected of left-leaning political sympathies. And by using political influence, threats and intimidation against the judicial system, the police and the army has then effectively prevented the perpetrators from being brought to justice. As a result, a total lack of confidence on part of the general public in relation to the law enforcement agencies and the judicial system has developed.

One of the main issues in the Salvadoran peace talks have been the human rights situation and how to create future sage-guards, acceptable to both sides, against such lawlessness as has been existing in the past. It seems clear that without reasonable such safe-guards there will be no peace. At the same time it is obvious that the present strong position of the army and the police prevents any major short term restructuring of these establishments, however badly needed.

In this situation the parties to the Salvadoran peace talks have on 26 July 1990 entered an "Agreement on Human Rights". This agreement starts with a wide commitment in the matter of human rights which are understood, in the context of this agreement, to be those recognized by the Salvadorian legal system, including the treaties to which El Salvador is a party, and by the declarations and principles concerning human rights and humanitarian law adopted by the United Nations and the Organization of American States.

The agreement includes the commitment to take immediate action to prevent any attack on the life, integrity, security and freedom of the person, and the commitment to climinate every practice that involves missing persons, abduction or torture.

A central part of the agreement is a construction for international verification of the compliance of the human rights commitments. In the field of human rights, this is something entirely new. Under the agreement a United Nations Verification Mission will be set up, starting from the cessation of the armed confrontation. This mission will have a devote special attention to observance of the right to life, to the integrity and security of the person, to the due process of law, to freedom of the person, to freedom of expression and to freedom of association. In that context, efforts will be made above all to clarify any situation that appears to reveal a systematic practice of violation of human rights and, in such a case, to recommend to the Party which the matter concerns the appropriate measure for eliminating that practice.

A Director appointed by the Secretary-General of the United Nations will be in charge of the Mission. The Director will work in close co-operation with organizations and entitles on present human rights in El Salvador. It will also count on the support of specialized advisers. Moreover, the Mission will include as many verification personnel as may be necessary. The Mission will be given wide powers to take whatever action it may deem appropriate for promoting and protecting human rights, as part of the intention to promote the respect and guarantee of such rights in El Salvador and to contribute towards improving those situations in which such respect and guarantee are not duly observed.

Included among the foregoing powers are the powers to receive accusations of violations of human rights; freely to visit any place; to interview any person freely and privately; to collect all relevant information by whatever means it may deem appropriate; to submit recommendations to the Parties; to consult the Attorney General of the Republic; and to publish its reports, conclusions and recommendations.

As stated above, the conflict in El Salvador contains elements which can also be recognized as obstacles to peace in Natal and Transvaal. One such element is the almost total lack of confidence on part of the population in the affected areas in the police force and its ability to maintain law and order in an impartial manner. The same lack of confidence also affects the prosecutors and the courts. What are people to believe when notorious killers are not prosecuted at all or else released on symbolic bail, pending a trial which never happens? If the law enforcement agencies prove incapable to provide security and maintain law and order, then people will arm themselves, for defence purposes or in order to carry out their own law enforcement.

It is our view that a human rights agreement, similar to that of El Salvador, would prove beneficial to the present unrest situation. Such an agreement should involve all three parties in the conflict, namely the government, ANC and Inkatha. Both top ANC leaders and Chief Minister Buthelezi have reacted favourably to this proposal. If the United Nations is not acceptable some other international organization could be entrusted with the task of organizing and running the verification mission.

15. Finally we suggest that the South African Government should invite a team of international monitors, perhaps drawn from The USA, Commonwealth Countries or the EEC to monitor on a continuing basis the law enforcement agencies and to report direct to the State President. The Monitors would need to have power to summon witnesses and require the production of documents. This proposal is based on the United Nations experience in El Salvador which we have discussed above. It will take time to implement. The International Commission of Jurists will therefore maintain its interest in Natal. The situation in South Africa is changing from week to week. It is therefore valuable for those who have studies the problem in depth to continue to do so. The Foreign Minister told us that we would be welcome to come back again. We would like to accept his invitation and return in 1991.

Annex 3

Extract from "Agenda for Peace" IC 3 March 1990

5. RECOMMENDATIONS

International Monitors

1.1. We suggest that Codesa should invite a team of international monitors, perhaps drawn from the EEC, the Organisation of African Unity, Commonwealth Countries and the USA to monitor, on a continuing basis, the law enforcement agencies. The team should report direct to Codesa, or to a special commission appointed by Codesa, until the interim government is constituted.

1.2. We envisage that the team would monitor the performance of the law enforcement agencies against the codes of conduct in the Peace Accord. We also think they should monitor the performance of the political organisations and the other signatories of the Peace Accord.

1.3. We suggest that the team be led by a Head of Mission who would be a person with an established record in human rights. The head of mission would be assisted by regional co-ordinators, human rights investigators, police and military liaison officers and political advisers. We anticipate that a majority of the investigators would be lawyers or have appropriate police experience. We think a team of 100 monitors, with an average of three backup staff to each monitor, would be sufficient. The head of mission would have to be a person who was acceptable to all parties in South Africa.

1.4. The Mission would have its headquarters in Johannesburg, regional offices in Durban, Cape Town and Port Elizabeth and additional offices in Soweto and Pietermaritzburg. It would hold regular surgeries in the townships where violence is a problem. We envisage that the team would work in close co-operation with the Goldstone Commission, and Dispute Resolution Committees. It would provide a point of reference for everyone who is concerned about the violence.

1.5. It would be essential to equip the team with a reliable communications system to enhance its effectiveness and the security of its functions and personnel and adequate transport resources would be required to give it mobility essential for its effective operation. To give some idea of the cost of the proposal: The total cost of the United Nations mission to El Salvador, which was of a comparable size, for an initial period of 12 months including the initial major procurements of vehicles and communication equipment was budgeted in April 1991 at 32 million US dollars.

1.6. We suggest that the EEC, the OAU or the Commonwealth Secretariat should be invited to undertake a feasibility study as soon as possible. The International Commission of Jurists will do everything it can to assist such an initiative. The study would be designed in particular to ensure that such a mission would have full access to the people and information it would need, with suitable procedures for securing such access in case of difficulty, perhaps through the Goldstone Commission or the Regional Dispute Resolution Committees.

ELECTION MONITORS

2. We believe that South Africans should consider inviting an international election monitoring team to supervise the run up to the elections, as well as the election process itself. Such a monitoring team should report direct to Codesa or to a special commission appointed by Codesa until the interim government is constituted. It could have a stabilising effect out of all proportion to its number. We believe the international community would be eager to provide this help.

THE SECURITY FORCES

3.1. We think senior civilian administrators should be introduced into the South African Police force at all levels.

APPENDIX 8

Memorandum by the United Nations Association

SUMMARY OF RECOMMENDATIONS

The United Nations Association (UK) warmly welcomes the publication of "An Agenda For Peace" as an historic contribution to the essential on-going debate on the UN's future role.

Priority must always be given to the prevention of conflict. Criteria to allow UN fact-finding and humanitarian assistance without State consent should be elaborated and agreed.

The UN must develop an effective early warning capacity using Satellite technology and the monitoring of political and social developments by UN Personnel in the Field. Regional organisations should play an enhanced fact-finding role and co-operation with NGOs be developed. The analysis of information should take place through a Centre for conflict prevention within the UN Secretariat.

We support the preventive deployment of UN Personnel.

We welcome the UK's acceptance of the compulsory jurisdiction of the International Court of Justice. We urge that the UK withdraw its reserved right to terminate ICJ jurisdiction and that it contribute annually (both financially and technically) in enabling poorer countries to bring cases to the Court.

We recommend that sanctions against those who disregard judgements of the Court are introduced.

A mechanism must be introduced to ensure that adequate compensation goes to neighbouring States most effected by the imposition of UN sanctions.

We recommend the activation of the Military Staff Committee to advise on the military aspects of proposed or on-going enforcement action, and for the strategic direction of troops under Chapter VII.

The UK should ear-mark personnel and logistics as specified under Article 43 of the Charter.

The military advice to the UN Secretary-General should be enhanced through increasing the complement of military advisors within the UN Secretariat in New York.

We support the concept of Peace Enforcement Units as long as their mandate is agreed before the start of each operation.

The UK should augment the training it provides to UN peace-keepers and nominate a specific UK Peace-Keeping Headquarters.

The UK should establish a separate peace-keeping department within the MoD, and emphasize logistical support and language training in contributions to UN Peace-Keeping Operations.

The Field Operations Division in New York should become part of the Office For Peace-Keeping Operations. The Secretary-General should be allowed to place contracts without competitive bidding in exceptional circumstances.

We support the establishment of a substantially resourced Peace-Keeping Reserve Fund.

We urge that a working group be set up by the Treasury, FCO and MoD to study the mechanics of paying for UN peace-keeping from the defence rather from the foreign affairs budget.

The UK Government should send a delegation to President Clinton to exert diplomatic pressure on the United States for immediate payment of remaining US arrears to the UN.

New measures should be introduced to punish those in arrears and to provide incentives for prompt payment.

We welcome the forthcoming review of the Scale of Assessments of members contributions to the UN. We do not support a reduced assessment for the United States if this places an increased burden on poorer states.

The International Advisory Group on UN Financing should examine proposals for:

1. levying of taxes on international goods and services (other than the proposal made on arms);
2. a surcharge on international communications or mail;
3. fees for use of international water-ways, in addition to a levy on air travel;
4. part of profits from the exploitation of resources from the sea bed to go to the UN;
5. the surrendering of a percentage of member's national taxes.

We congratulate the UK on its good current record in meeting its assessed contributions to the UN. It should always pay its dues on time, should pay its outstanding peace-keeping arrears relating to the ONUCA operation, and should provide substantial assistance to the UN Information Centre in London.

The UK must take the initiative in defining the nature and timing of Security Council Reform. It should work for the eventual abolition of the veto, and a representative Council which avoids selectivity.

The UK should take the lead in addressing arms transfers through unilateral restraint on arms sales, whilst pursuing multilateral arrangements; by strengthening the UN Register and through reducing demand by supporting regional confidence-building measures.

1 Introduction

1.1 The Security Council Summit of 31 January 1992 requested that UN Secretary-General Dr Boutros-Ghali prepare an analysis and recommendations on strengthening UN preventive diplomacy, peacemaking and peace-keeping. This resulted in the publication in June 1992 of the document "*An Agenda for Peace*" (hereafter "the Report").

1.2 The United Nations Association (UK) warmly welcomes the publication of the Report as an historic contribution to the debate over how the UN can be equipped to prevent and resolve conflicts in this post-Cold War era. We congratulate the Secretary-General and the other members of the drafting committee for producing recommendations which are far-reaching yet politically achievable.

1.3 This submission by UNA-UK to the House of Commons Select Committee on Foreign Affairs (hereafter "the Committee") focuses on specific recommendations that we would urge the UK Government to undertake. The submission follows the chapter structure of the Report itself. UNA-UK would be pleased to submit more detailed memoranda to the Select Committee on aspects of the Report during the course of its enquiry.

A CRITIQUE OF THE REPORT

2 DEFINITIONS

2.1 We would caution against any wider acceptance of the definition of peacemaking given in the report. "Peacemaking" is defined as "*essentially* through . . . peaceful means" [emphasis added], and later in the report the Chapter on Peacemaking contains sections on the Use of Military Force and Peace-Enforcement Units. Thus there is no clear differentiation between the types of action envisaged in Article 33 of the UN Charter[1] and Chapter VII military enforcement. This must be seen against a background of the increased use of the term "Peacemaking" by some Permanent Five Governments to refer purely to military enforcement activities.

2.2 While we welcome the integration of peace-keeping activities with those of preventive diplomacy and peace-building (e.g. in mine clearance and election monitoring), we firmly wish to see the distinct identity and peaceful and neutral characteristics of UN peace-keeping maintained.

2.3 It should be noted that the definition of Peace-keeping contained in the Report uses the phrase "*hitherto* with the consent of all the parties concerned" [emphasis added]. Previously consent was considered an "essential characteristic"[2] of UN Peace-Keeping. The use of "hitherto" thus opens the way for a significant departure in peace-keeping practice. This raises important issues about the safety of peace-keepers deployed on operations where consent has not been given, and issues of the criteria for such "intervention". This issue is raised later in this Report under section 23.5.3.

3 PREVENTIVE DIPLOMACY

3.1 Priority must always be given to the prevention of conflict. In this context we welcome the holding of the proposed "Round Table on the Preventive Diplomacy of the UN" to be hosted by International Alert and the United Nations University in New York in January 1993.

4 Fact Finding and Humanitarian Assistance

4.1 UN Fact-Finding continues to require State consent. This was explicitly recognised as a requirement by the General Assembly last January[3]. The emphasis that the Secretary-General places on State consent for humanitarian assistance (Para 30) rests jointly on a particular reading of the Charter, and on the annex to General Assembly Resolution 46/182 of 19 December 1991. It is arguable that there is a right in customary international law for a State to provide limited humanitarian aid to the people of another without its consent[4], and if this is accepted it would appear illogical not to permit such assistance under the auspices of the United Nations. The precedent set by Resolution 688 in this respect should be noted.

5 Early Warning

5.1 The information gathering capacity of the UN Secretary-General is key to the fulfilment of Article 99 of the charter. The Office for Research and the Collection of Information (ORCI) was inadequate for this task and was disbanded in the restructuring of the secretariat in March 1992. The job of processing information relating to the early warning of conflicts has fallen for the present to the two Under-Secretaries-General in the Department for Political Affairs. The utilisation of modern computer, satellite and communications technology by the Secretariat is essential in developing an effective early warning capacity.

5.2 Recommendation: an integrated approach is needed towards information gathering. A comprehensive system of observing military movements (using UN satellites or satellites belonging to member States) is needed. This should take account of the UN study undertaken on a proposed International Satellite Monitoring Agency (ISMA[5]). This must be complemented by the monitoring of the political, ethnic, nationalist and religious developments that increasingly lie at the heart of conflicts. This latter task could be under-

[1] Article 33 of the UN Charter states that parties should first "seek a solution by negotiation, enquiry, mediation, conciliation, arbitration, judicial settlement, resort to regional arrangements, or peaceful means of their own choice."

[2] Goulding, M (1991) "The Evolving role of UN Peace-keeping Operations" in *The Singapore Symposium—The Changing Role of the UN in Conflict Resolution and Peace-keeping* (United Nations Department of Public Information, 13–15 March 1991) p.20.

[3] Declaration on Fact-Finding by the United Nations in the Field of International Peace and Security (GA Res.46/59, 17 January 1992).

[4] See the *Nicaragua Case*, 1986 *ICJ Rep.* 14 at para. 243.

[5] UN Document A/AC.206/14.

taken on an individual country basis by UN Resident Representatives who are already present in most developing countries[1], and on a regional basis by the 68 UN Information Centres, which previously reported daily or weekly to ORCI. The potential role of NGOs in the early warning of conflict should be developed. On the analysis side the current interim measures are not working adequately. We would recommend the setting up of a Centre for the analysis of information on incipient conflicts (effectively an enlarged, restructured ORCI) to be accountable to either the Secretary-General's office or to the Department for Political Affairs. The Centre would require substantial additional funding, and should include in its functions the 24 hour a day (rather than 8 hours under ORCI) monitoring of the world media.

6 Preventive Deployment

6.1 We fully support the proposals in this section. If the forces deployed in this capacity are not to be heavily armed, the Security Council must make explicit that action under Chapter VII of the Charter would follow if the Preventive Deployment line were breached.

7 PEACEMAKING

8 The World Court

8.1 We welcome the fact that the UK is one of the 53[2] States which recognise the Court's compulsory jurisdiction under Article 36(2) of the Court's Statute. This recognition is on the basis of reciprocity and with certain exclusions, including those relating to certain disputes with members of the Commonwealth. The British Declaration under Article 36(2) also reserves the right to terminate our acceptance at any time. UNA-UK welcomes the proposal that all States should accept the general jurisdiction of the ICJ, without reservation, by the year 2000. Nevertheless, certain types of disputes might be better dealt with in other fora (e.g. investment disputes could be taken to the Washington-based International Centre for the Settlement of Investment Disputes) and this should be borne in mind.

8.2 Recommendation: that the UK takes steps to withdraw its reserved right to terminate its acceptance of ICJ jurisdiction at any time.[3]

8.3 We are also pleased that the UK is one of the 34 states that have contributed to the Trust Fund to assist countries in taking cases to the Court. However the total contributed to date by all States since the Fund's inception on 1 November 1989 is only $583,705 (as of 7 October 1992), a tiny sum when bringing just one case to the Court can easily cost $1 million dollars.

8.4 Recommendation: that the UK, which has only contributed once to the Fund, in 1990, should follow.the example of France and contribute annually.[4]

8.5 Since up until now most States have only been engaged in at most one case every couple of decades, there has been no effective "learning curve" for Government officials preparing for cases.

8.6 Recommendation: that the UK also enhances the technical assistance which it provides developing countries in the preparation of cases. The Chinese government has done valuable work in this field, hosting its second "Symposium on Developing Countries and International Law" in August 1992.[5]

8.7 Even States that accept ICJ jurisdiction do not always fully implement the judgements of the Court.

8.8 Recommendation: that consideration is given to procedures for introducing sanctions where the judgements of the Court are disregarded.

9 Sanctions and Special Economic Problems

9.1 While there is considerable discussion in the Report on the various contingencies for the use of military forces, there is virtually no discussion of methods short of military force. In particular the Report fails to address how political and economic sanctions can be used more effectively as a peacekeeping and peacemaking measure.

9.2 The imposition of sanctions needs more UN resources, both for compensating neighbouring States most affected and ensuring that sanctions are effectively applied. When sanctions are imposed on a State,

[1] The majority of conflicts (using the SIPRI definition) take place in or between developing countries.

[2] 53 countries at the time of the Report of the ICJ to the 46th session of the General Assembly (A/46/4, p3).

[3] This proviso is contained in Paragraph 2 of the British Declaration under ICJ Article 36(2) (ICJ Statutes I.4 p25).

[4] See Report of the International Court of Justice to the 47th Session of the General Assembly: "Secretary-General's Trust Fund to Assist States in the Settlement of Disputes through the International Court of Justice—Report of the Secretary-General" (A/47/444 7 October 1992).

[5] See "United Nations Decade of International Law—Note verbale dated 6 October 1992 from the Permanent Representative of China to the United Nations addressed to the Secretary-General" (SIXTH COMMITTEE A/C.6/47/6 9 October 1992)

then UN inspectors—essentially UN customs officials—should be put in place at all the customs posts between that State and neighbouring States. There are currently no effective penalties imposed on a State which allows sanctions to be breached, with the result that sanctions (such as those currently in force against Serbia and Montenegro) frequently fail to be respected.

9.3 Recommendation: that the Special Committee on the Charter of the United Nations and on the Role of the Organisation continue its work on the implementation of the provisions of the Charter related to assistance to third parties affected by sanctions[1]. The Special Committee should particularly address the lack of machinery guaranteeing an adequate response to Article 50 of the Charter. The UN Secretary-General should be asked to set up a study of ways in which sanctions could be made more effective, to include consideration of UN custom posts in neighbouring states.

10 Use of Military Force

10.1 Here the Secretary-General proposes that States provide troops to the UN on a permanent basis, as foreseen in Article 43 of the Charter, and that the (if necessary augmented) Military Staff Committee be used to support negotiations for securing agreements to effect this.

10.2 The Secretary-General argues that there should be at least three designated types of military personnel; those who may eventually be constituted under Article 43 to deal with acts of aggression, those to be used in peace-enforcement units to be utilised as a provisional measure under Article 40 of the Charter, and those personnel whom Governments agree to put on stand-by for peace-keeping operations. In addition, a number of further potential roles are mentioned for the military under other sections of the Report—their use in preventive deployment, along borders and demilitarised zones (paragraphs 28 to 33), humanitarian assistance (paragraph 29) and post-conflict peace-building in the areas of mine clearing etc. (paragraph 58).

10.3 The Report gives far less thought to the political control of troops to be deployed under the UN or the necessary military "command and control" that is needed. Annex 1 by Admiral Sir James Eberle GCB, LLD, contains a detailed analysis of the key military issues. In addition to the recommendations contained in this Annex we wish to make the following points:

10.4 The potential for military enforcement by the UN is at present a necessary element of conflict prevention and resolution. However, we firmly believe that military action undertaken to enforce international law must have direct political and military Security Council supervision. Since the primary raison d'etre of the UN is "to end the scourge of war", military enforcement should, wherever possible, only be used as a very last resort.

10.5 Sir Brian Urquhart, former UN Under-Secretary-General for Special Political Affairs has raised questions about the failure of the Security Council to exhaust non-military avenues prior to the Persian Gulf War of 1991. He asserts that in relation to Article 41 of the Charter, "no determination about the adequacy of sanctions was ever made by the Council"[2]. Others assert that the determination of inadequacy was implicit in Security Council Resolution No.678. Whatever the truth in this case, it is essential that all other avenues are exhausted and are seen to be exhausted before military enforcement occurs in future.

10.6 Recommendation: UNA-UK supports the activation of the Military Staff Committee. We believe that its membership would need to include representatives from all fifteen members of the Security Council. The chief role of the Military Staff Committee should be to advise on the military aspects of proposed or on-going enforcement action undertaken under the auspices of Chapter VII of the Charter, and to provide the strategic direction of troops engaged in such action.

10.7 Recommendation: UNA-UK supports proposals for the ear-marking of troops, as specified under Article 43 of the Charter. The UK should identify troops and logistical support which would be available for such duties.

10.8 Recommendation: For peace-keeping, peace-building and preventive deployment operations the military advice available to the UN Secretary-General, the Under-Secretary-General for Peace-Keeping Operations and the Under-Secretaries-General for Political Affairs should be strengthened. This should be done by increasing the complement of military advisors within the UN Secretariat in New York.

[1] The Special Committee on the Charter has already undertaken important work on this subject: see Working Paper A/AC.182/L.73 entitled "Implementation of the Provisions of the Charter of the United Nations related to assistance to third states affected by the application of sanctions under Chapter VII of the Charter", and the Report of the Special Committee on the Charter to the General Assembly (A/47/33).

[2] Urquhart, B (1991) "Learning from the Gulf" in Bustelo, MR and Alston P *Whose New World Order: What role for the United Nations?* (Federation Press, Australia 1991).

10.9 We welcome the UK's appointment of Colonel Tim Manners-Smith as a military advisor on peace-keeping operations to the UK Permanent Mission to the UN in New York.

11 Peace-Enforcement Units

We welcome the idea of Peace-Enforcement Units to operate as a provisional measure under Article 40 of the Charter. Their mandate and how heavily armed they will be must be agreed before the start of each operation.

12 PEACE-KEEPING

13 Personnel and Training

13.1 Specialised training for peace-keeping is necessary because the attitudes, methods and tactics of peace-keeping are significantly different from those in conventional military doctrine. Many UN peace-keepers enter field operations without such essential training. There is currently no international UN training programme for peace-keepers. The closest approximation to this is the series of seminars and materials sponsored by the International Peace Academy. Meanwhile most training (if it happens at all) takes place in national military establishments. The Nordics currently lead the way in joint multinational training exercises, while the Canadian Contingent to the UN Force in Cyprus (UNFICYP) are preparing a detailed training package in mediation skills to be used as a two and a half week preparation for Canadian soldiers who are to be deployed on peace-keeping duties.[1] The United States recently promised to establish a permanent peace-keeping curriculum in U.S. military schools and "to make available our bases and facilities for multinational training and field exercises".[2] However these proposals may not be implemented with the recent change in the US administration.[3]

13.2 Recommendation: that the UK should review the training it provides at Staff Colleges. Since there is a current reluctance to earmark particular troops for peace-keeping operations, the UK should provide courses in peace-keeping as an integral element of every soldier's training. A peace-keeping headquarters should be nominated, to establish and provide such training.

13.3 The UK, along with many other countries, also fails adequately to de-brief soldiers who have completed their tour of peace-keeping duty. This can all too easily lead to a constant re-inventing of the wheel with each new UN operation. The UN work-load of the Secretariat Overseas Commitments in the Ministry of Defence has dramatically increased over recent years.

13.4 Recommendation: it would now appear useful to establish a separate department concerned solely with the deployment of UK troops in UN operations within the MoD. This should liaise closely with the FCO UN Department and oversee both the de-briefing of British troops on return from the field and the establishment of adequate training at staff colleges, or through a new peace-keeping headquarters.

13.5 On the "theory" side, the 1992 Defence White Paper provides a new three point framework for Britain's defence roles. The third of these is now defined as: "to contribute to promoting the United Kingdom's wider security interests through the maintenance of international peace and stability". In elaborating how this role could be carried out, a reference is made to peace-keeping and the White Paper states that "military operations could be conducted by . . . the UN or *ad hoc* coalitions under UN or CSCE auspices". We welcome this more explicit mention of peace-keeping and the United Nations, but we need to go much further in integrating this thinking into the Armed Services.

13.6 Recommendation: the United Kingdom's practical contribution to UN Peace-Keeping should emphasise logistical support, an area of national expertise. The cuts in military expenditure enacted in "Options For Change" have not decreased our ability to provide such support. The UK should also respond to the Secretary-General's request for language training—but not just for police contingents. English is used as the *lingua franca* of the majority of the current UN Peace-Keeping operations and we have valuable experience in this field.

---

[1] The Mediation Training Package is being prepared by Major D.M. Last for Lieutenant Colonel M.D. Capstick, Commanding Officer, 1st Regiment, Royal Canadian Horse Artillery, Canadian Contingent, United Nations Force in Cyprus, c/o CFPO 5001, Belleville, Ontario, KOK 3RO, CANADA.

[2] Text of George Bush's speech to the General Assembly on 21st September 1992 in "Bush announces initiatives to meet global challenges" (United States Information Service, 23 September 1992 p4).

[3] The military base singled out by Bush as an example of those that would be made available for multinational training and field exercises was Fort Dix in New Jersey. Ruth Marcus of the Washington post has pointed out that Active-duty basic training at Fort Dix ended in August as part of pentagon cutbacks, and that New Jersey was a target state for the Republican Party. (Marcus, R "Bush endorses expansion of UN peace-Keeping Role" in *The Washington Post* 22 September 1992 p15) Occurring just weeks before the US presidential Election, this promise must therefore be seen in the context of other pledges aimed primarily at US domestic voters.

14 Logistics

14.1 One of the main complaints from UN Peace-Keepers in the field concerns the way logistical support is provided. Currently the Field Operations Division (FOD), which is part of the Office of General Services, an administrative unit, provides such support. As F.T. Liu[1] points out, this has two negative effects: it plays down the importance of logistical support which is an essential element of peace-keeping operations and it weakens the control of the Secretary-General in the field.

14.2 Recommendation: that the office responsible for the organisation and direction of peace-keeping operations should also deal with the logistical support of such operations; thus the FOD should be significantly strengthened and incorporated into the Office For Peace-Keeping Operations.

14.3 A recurrent logistical problem in UN Peace-Keeping operations results from the fact that components frequently come from more than one country with the resulting diversity causing confusion and reducing efficiency. There is clearly a balance needed between broad participation in UN operations for reasons of political necessity, and cost-effectiveness in economies of scale and uniformity of logistical support. Frequent problems have arisen over the rules for competitive tendering in the procurement of peace-keeping equipment. A larger stock of basic UN equipment should be maintained at the UN depot in Pisa, Italy.

14.4 Recommendation: we support the request of the Secretary-General that he be allowed to place contracts without competitive bidding in exceptional circumstances. A study should be undertaken on how to provide more uniform logistical support in new peace-keeping operations while maintaining the participation (and financial burden sharing) of a broad spectrum of States.

15 POST-CONFLICT PEACE-BUILDING

15.1 We welcome the inclusion of post-conflict peace-building on a par with conflict prevention, peacemaking, peace-keeping and peace enforcement. However the section on peace-building in the Report simply reflects and describes what are in effect current developments in UN peace-keeping and development assistance, without making further recommendations.

15.2 The debate over peace-building raises crucial wider issues of the relationship between social and economic development and the prevention and resolution of conflicts. Conflicts are rarely solely the product of the ambitions of ruthless leaders; they arise when the basic needs of a population are not met. These needs include both the physical (food, water, shelter, etc) and the need for security and identity. Thus effective peace-building must take place before as well as after conflict. Greater recognition is needed of the role of sustainable development and environmental protection in conflict prevention, and the Security Council must recognise that solutions to conflicts necessitate an integrated approach of development assistance alongside attempts to curb and stop physical violent conflict.

15.3 Valuable work on the issue of peace-building is to be undertaken by UNESCO. On 28 October 1992 the Executive board of UNESCO agreed to establish an action programme[2] to operate in areas where United Nations peace-keeping forces are deployed or where conflicts might arise. The UNESCO Director-General will consult with experts and submit the proposals and costing of the programme to the 141st session of the UNESCO Executive Board in May 1993. All member states of UNESCO are invited to participate in planning the programme.

15.4 In agreeing to the proposal the Executive Board recommended that an International Centre to implement the programme for a culture of peace, under the joint control of UNESCO and the UN security Council, be established. This centre would also co-ordinate the creation of an international network of specialists in social sciences, which would form an early warning system for the prevention of violence.

15.5 Recommendation: that the UK support the UNESCO study on mechanisms for expanding the work of the UN in pre-[3] and post-conflict peace-building. This study should also address the integration of sustainable development and environmental priorities agreed in Agenda 21 at UNCED, with a long term global strategy for conflict prevention, highlighting the institutional co-ordination needed within the UN system. The UK should re-join UNESCO without delay and play a full part in shaping this important work.

16 Co-operation with Regional Arrangements and Organisations

16.1 We believe that it is vital to strengthen the capacity of regional security arrangements to prevent and resolve conflicts. Such arrangements should evolve in conformity with the provisions of Chapter VIII of the Charter. The respective roles of the European Community and the Conference on Security and

[1] Liu, F.T. (1990) "United Nations Peacekeeping: Management and Operations" (International Peace Academy Occasional Paper on peace-keeping No.4,) p11.

[2] UNESCOPRESSE "UNESCO to launch action programme for a culture of Peace" 4 November 1992.

[3] This idea was raised in a letter addressed to the Secretary-General dated 26 May 1992 (A/47/232, S/24025) from the representative of 12 Latin American States. They stated that "we believe that the time has come for the United Nations to undertake the task of "preventative peace-building" (p5).

Co-operation in Europe in the former Yugoslavia and the roles of the Organisation of African Unity, the Arab League and Organisation of Islamic Conferences in Somalia have highlighted the need for a practical division of competence and responsibility between the UN and regional arrangements, while maintaining the flexibility necessary to respond to developing political circumstances.[1]

16.2 The provisions of the Charter which define the de jure relationship between the UN and regional organisations appear under Chapter VI (Article 33) and Chapter VIII (Articles 52–54). These contain four important elements; that States should settle disputes through regional arrangements before referring them to the Security Council; that the Security Council may in turn utilise such arrangements for the settlement of local disputes; that regional arrangements shall only undertake enforcement action with Security Council authorisation; and that the Security Council shall be kept fully informed of activities undertaken or contemplated by regional arrangements for the maintenance of peace and security.

16.3 In practice, however, the experience of regional organisations in conflict prevention and settlement has not been an impressive one. This has reflected inadequate resources, inadequate mechanisms to tackle conflicts once they arise and Superpower domination within regions. Thus attempts by the Organisation of African Unity to launch a peace-keeping force in Chad in 1981 were a fiasco through lack of experience and resources. Similarly the CSCE was totally ill-equipped to tackle the escalating crisis in former Yugoslavia.

16.4 Superpower domination in certain regional organisations has meant that the Security Council has at times not been kept informed, and has been supplied solely with "after the fact" perfunctory accounts of action taken on a regional level.

16.5 Recommendation: useful proposals have emerged on the implementation of Chapter VIII provisions from the work of the Special Committee on the Charter of the Organisation and on Strenthening the Role of the Organisation. These include the need for regional organisations to create mechanisms for the collection and analysis of information about disputes; the strengthening of early warning mechanisms; the training of military and civilian observers and regional peace-keeping forces; and better co-ordination with the UN Secretariat. We support these proposals, but would go further. In the field of preventive diplomacy we would like to see the establishment of impartial "ombuds" panels[2] in each region who could undertake regional fact-finding missions. Such panels would collaborate with the UN Secretary-General's Staff reflecting the collaboration with regional organisations envisaged in the December 1991 Declaration on Fact-Finding adopted by the General Assembly.

16.6 The main obstacle to regional peace-keeping is resources. Since most conflicts occur within and between developing countries, the most demand for such regional forces will fall most on the regions least able to afford them.

16.7 Recommendation: that a mechanism be established to allow a proportion of the UN's Peace-Keeping Reserve Fund to be allocated for the use of regional organisations on approval of the Security Council.

17 FINANCING

18 The Current Situation

18.1 As the UN faces unprecedented demands, "a chasm has developed between the tasks entrusted to this Organisation and the financial means provided to it". The UN was owed a total of $US 500,607,665 outstanding on its regular budget (all figures as of 31 December 1992), with $US 561,950,627 owed in total for UN peace-keeping. It was recently necessary for the Secretary-General to borrow from the UN peace-keeping account to pay ordinary UN staff salaries.

19 The Secretary-General's Proposals

19.1 We fully support almost all of Dr Boutros-Ghali's proposals contained in the section on Financing. We are very pleased that the Humanitarian Revolving Fund has already been implemented and hope that his other recommendations are swiftly adopted. We are sceptical of the idea of a levy on arms sales linked to a UN arms register. At a time when countries need to be encouraged to participate in such a register it seems inappropriate to increase the cost of their doing so.

[1] For a detailed analysis of this issue see Daws, S (1992) "Global and Regional security compatibility in the 1990s—Extending Mechanisms for Co-operation between the UN and Regional Bodies in Preventive Diplomacy and Conflict Management" Paper presented to the International Symposium on Prospects of Reform of the United Nations System, Rome, Italy 15–17 May 1992. Mimeo (Societa Italiana Per L'Organizzazione Internationale, Rome).

[2] This suggestion was made by Erskine Childers in a paper entitled "UN Mechanisms for Intervention and Prospects for Reform" prepared for "The Challenge to Intervene Conference", organised by the Life and Peace Institute, Sigtuna, Sweden, 25–26th May 1992.

20 Our Proposals

20.1 While supporting the modest proposals contained in the Report, we believe that more radical steps are needed to address the present financial crisis.

20.2 We support the immediate establishment of a Peace-Keeping Reserve Fund. However this requires more than the $US50 million start-up capital recommended in the Report.

20.3 Recommendation: UNA-UK supports the suggestion recently made at the General Assembly that the outstanding balances from the UNTAG and UNIMOG peace-keeping operations (a total of $US 60 million) are used to establish the Reserve Fund. We are cautious of, but do not reject outright, the suggestion that $90 million of regular budget and peace-keeping arrears be added to this Fund (and thus be effectively ear-marked rather than be owed to the Capital Fund). This would produce a start-up Reserve Fund of $US150 million but may mark a dangerous precedent, allowing those in arrears more say over where their money goes than those who pay on time.

20.4 We broadly support the Secretary-General's suggestion that peace-keeping operations be paid from States' defence rather than foreign affairs budgets. One argument cited against the adoption of this measure in the UK is that the FCO may have less incentive to bring diplomatic disputes to a quick conclusion if they do not have to foot the on-going peace-keeping bill. We do not believe that this would be the case. While it is true that the threatened withdrawal of peace-keeping troops can at times be used as a diplomatic weapon to help force a swift diplomatic solution (for example the current developments in Cyprus), MoD payment for peace-keeping need not hinder this potential diplomatic weapon. We believe that a shift in payment from the FCO to the MoD would be a significant step in recognising that national defence should increasingly (in this post-Cold War era) contribute to global collective security, and play a role in upholding and enforcing international law through the United Nations.

20.5 Recommendation: that the Treasury, the Foreign and Commonwealth Office and the Ministry of Defence set up a working group to study the mechanics of paying for UN peace-keeping from the defence budget with a view to implementing the recommendation of the UN Secretary-General.

20.6 The major financial problem facing the UN remains the substantial arrears of certain States. In particular the Russian Federation and the United States remain substantial debtors to the organisation. The Russian Federation inherited the debts of the former Soviet Union and does face some genuine difficulties in paying its arrears. In the first two weeks of November 1992 the United States contributed substantially to paying off the majority of its peace-keeping arrears and part of its arrears to the regular budget, leaving total US arrears of approximately $US380 million. In September 1992[1] Bill Clinton advocated paying the US debts to the UN in full, and we hope that this will be enacted now that he has been elected.

20.7 Recommendation: while welcoming the recent partial payment of arrears by the United States, the Select Committee should nevertheless strongly criticise the present failure of the US Government to pay its UN dues. The UK Government, as a close political ally of the United States, should send a high level delegation to President Clinton to exert diplomatic pressure for immediate US payment of UN dues outstanding.

20.8 The current financial contribution of States to the UN is tiny when compared to their existing defence budgets (see Annex 3 for comparisons for Security Council members).

20.9 Recommendation: in the long term, the financial contribution of States to the UN System needs to be substantially increased.

20.10 The existing provisions in the Charter to address payment arrears (Article 19) have proved inadequate. A number of States simply remain just less than two years in arrears to maintain their General Assembly vote.

20.11 Recommendation: that new measures are introduced to punish those in arrears and to provide incentives for prompt payment. We particularly support the incentive schemes currently operating in the ILO and WHO. We support the Canadian resolution (currently in draft form) to introduce such a scheme for General Assembly members.

20.12 Recommendation: we welcome the fact that the UN Committee on Contributions will be undertaking a comprehensive review of the Scale of Assessments of members' contributions to the UN . This should receive input from the International Advisory Group on United Nations financing recently established by the Secretary-General.

20.13 In this context we do not support a reduction in the 25 per cent assessed contribution of the United States if this places an increased burden on poorer States. The levels of assessed contributions are based on

[1] In a speech to the UNA of the USA.

a capacity to pay and technically on this basis the US should be paying 32 per cent of the total UN budget. Its capped assessment of 25 per cent means that the US is currently assessed at a lower rate than all other UN members in proportion to its capacity to pay.

20.14 Recommendation: the International Advisory Group on UN Financing should also examine the following proposals:[1]

1. **levying of taxes on international goods and services (other than the proposal made on arms);**
2. **a surcharge on international communications or mail;**
3. **fees for use of international water-ways, in addition to a levy on air travel;**
4. **part of profits from the exploitation of resources from the sea bed to go to the UN;**
5. **the surrendering of a percentage of each member's national taxes.**

21 The UK's Record

21.1 The UK has a good current record in meeting its assessed contributions to the UN. It is presently up to date in contributions to the regular budget and in its peace-keeping dues with the exception of ONUCA (see Annex 2).

21.2 We pay one third of our regular budget each January and two-thirds in April because of the timing of our fiscal year. This is done in UN parlance with the "understanding and acknowledgement" of the UN but not with its "agreement", since we are thereby technically in partial arrears for four months of each year.

21.3 Recommendation: We commend the UK Government on its good payment record, but we urge it to always pay its UN dues on time (usually on January 1). This would help remove any UK reluctance to support the introduction of incentive schemes which may penalise existing UK payment practice.

21.4 The present UK arrears to ONUCA result from the fact that the assessment letter seeking contributions from member states for the period November 1991 to April 1992 was issued in mid-January, one day before the operation was terminated by the Security Council. In these circumstances, the UK decided that it would pay part of the assessed dues on a pro-rata basis and transferred $US300,000 to the UN, leaving a balance of $US420,000 outstanding. The majority of ONUCA's assets were transferred to the ONUSAL operation, the mandate of which is likely to be extended beyond this Autumn.

21.5 Recommendation: that when the UN Secretariat provides revised estimates for the ONUSAL operation, the UK should pay in full its outstanding arrears.

21.6 The UK has played a constructive role in advocating greater transparency in UN finances, and now that this is bearing fruit it will be easier to identify and put pressure on those in arrears.

21.7 One major disappointment is that the United Kingdom is one of the few host Governments which does not give its UN Information Centre (UNIC) substantial assistance to enable it to carry out its indispensable work. At the same time it is noted that UNIC, which faces an increasing work burden, particularly now that the United Nations is an explicit part of the National Curriculum, is chronically understaffed.

21.8 Recommendation: that the UK Government follow the example of most UNIC host Governments and provide substantial assistance to fund the work of the UNIC currently based at 20 Buckingham Gate, London SW1E 6LB. This funding should include appropriate and long-term rent-free premises.

22 ISSUES NOT ADEQUATELY ADDRESSED IN THE REPORT

22.1 The changing post-Cold War context raises three key areas not comprehensively covered by the Report that must be addressed. These are the composition of the Security Council,[2] the international arms trade, and evolving an appropriate UN response to intra-national conflict.

23 Composition of the Security Council

23.1 The current composition of the Security Council does not reflect the economic, political and military realities of the 1990s. Challenges to the present composition come from both the industrialised

[1] These recommendations are based on the Article by Simon Duke "The UN Finance crisis: A History and Analysis" In International Relations Vol X August 1992.

[2] Significantly the Security Council Summit statement of 31st January 1992 restricted the remit of the Secretary-General's recommendations to staying "within the framework and provisions of the Charter". Thus the Report does not address issues of Security Council reform. See United Nations Security Council "Note by the President of the Security Council" 31 January 1992 (S/23500) p3.

North and an increasing number of countries of the South. Japan has recently launched a diplomatic campaign for Permanent Membership and this year's General Assembly has seen leading members of the Group of 77 developing countries advocating change. The South has largely lost the influence that it wielded as a result of the Cold War division in the Council, and now is concerned at the implications of an invigorated and consensual Permanent Five willing to take a more interventionist approach.

23.2 The exact "package" of any change in Security Council composition needs to be carefully crafted. While Germany and Japan are obvious candidates if the reconciliation of economic with political power is desired, this would further imbalance the Permanent Membership towards the industrialised North. Adding leading powers from the South, for example, India, Brazil and Nigeria to the Council on a permanent basis would improve the geographical spread but the choice of particular countries could be contentious for their respective regional neighbours.

23.3 A compromise suggested by Sir Anthony Parsons would see the Council expanded to 20 members including Germany and Japan, but with regional seats for Latin America, Africa and Asia; each to remain empty until regional agreement had been reached for how the seat would be occupied. It should be noted that any move towards seats for regional oganisations (for example OAU, OAS, etc) would accentuate existing pressure for the UK, France (and indeed Germany) to be replaced by EC representation.

23.4 Enlarging Security Council membership also raises the issue of Permanent Member veto. Consideration could be given to a parallel approach; giving new entrants Permanent Membership without a veto in parallel with agreement from the Permanent Five that they would agree to a graduated phasing out of the veto.

23.5 Recommendation: in response to these developments, we believe that the UK Government should have a four-fold strategy:

1. **to recognise that "seeking to retain"[1] our Permanent Seat on the Security Council requires a greater UK role in maintaining international peace and security through the United Nations.**

We make a valuable contribution to the Council through the experience of our diplomats, our world-wide diplomatic outreach (in part a product of our colonial past, our Commonwealth commitments and our role in European Organisations) and our drafting ability in English (often by default the *lingua franca* of the UN). If the UK Government wishes to justify our continued position on the Council we must give substantial additional financial and political support to the UN;

2. **to work for reductions to and the eventual elimination of the power of veto in the Security Council, enshrined in Article 27 (3) of the Charter.**

This could be through a graduated timetabled phasing out of the power of veto based on a series of agreements covering the areas of dispute on which the Permanent Five would refrain from veto use;

3. **to seek to ensure that the issues considered by the Security Council are chosen and prioritised on the basis of the need to uphold and enforce international law, to maintain and strengthen international peace and security and to meet human need.**

Thus selectivity reflecting the strategic, political or economic interests of the current Permanent Members should not dominate over the duty of the Security Council under Article 24 of the Charter to act on behalf of all members of the United Nations. Annex 2 contains an analysis of Security Council action with respect to current conflicts. This illustrates the need for explicit criteria to guide Security Council involvement in conflicts.

4. **to take the initiative and play an active role in defining the nature and timing of future Security Council reform.**

In doing this the Government should bear in mind:

i) that changes to Security Council composition should be undertaken as part of a wider package of Charter amendment. This could define the updated roles of the UN General Assembly, Secretary-General, Security Council, Specialised Agencies and Regional Bodies; and establish relationships and reporting responsibilities appropriate to the. changing nature of international relations and the increasing demands upon the United Nations;

ii) that arguments for an enlargement of the Council are given weight by the precedent of the enlargement of 1963 when Council membership grew to reflect a rapid increase in UN members resulting from de-colonisation. Arguments for a proportional relationship between General

[1] Rt Hon Douglas Hurd CBE, MP, Secretary of State for Foreign and Commonwealth Affairs, recently acknowledged that "we are a middle-ranking power *seeking to retain* a seat as a permanent member of the Security Council" [emphasis added] in answer to a question while giving evidence to the Select Committee on Foreign Affairs Monday 12th October 1992 (Ev. p.229, Q55).

Assembly and Security Council membership are strengthened by Article 24 [1] which states that the Council "acts on behalf" of all members of the UN;

iii) that changes to the composition of the Council on the grounds of more equitable geographic, economic, political or military representation, may reduce the consensual nature and hence the "efficiency" of the Council. Delays in reform can only be justified on such grounds of increased efficiency if rigorous steps are taken to prevent the potential selectivity outlined in Point 3 and to ensure regular and detailed consultation with Member States not represented on the Council.

24 The International Arms Trade

24.1 The Permanent Five members of the UN Security Council account for approximately 80 per cent[1] of the world's arms sales. Concerted Permanent Five action therefore lies at the heart of successful curbs to the arms trade. There have been two recent important developments in this field. First, the UN General Assembly approved a resolution on 9 December 1991[2] setting up a UN Conventional Arms Register. Second, meetings of the Permanent Five have taken place (parallel to but outside the UN framework) with a view to establishing voluntary guidelines for all conventional arms transfers and setting up a procedure for notification and consultation about planned sales to the Middle East.

24.2 The UK, the world's fourth largest arms exporter during the period 1981–90, was the driving force behind the General Assembly resolution. The idea behind the UN Register is that promotion of transparency will encourage restraint in the arms trade, prevent transfers which might destabilise a region and alleviate tensions caused by lack of information. UNA-UK supports any action to generate greater transparency in arms transfers but transparency must go hand in hand with moves to curb arms sales. The current Register is a valuable first step and we particularly welcome the appointment of Colonel Terence Taylor as UK Expert on the Register. Nevertheless, the Register needs strengthening in four significant areas. First, it is limited to just seven categories of conventional weapons.[3] Secondly, it only requires "available background information" regarding military holdings and procurement through national production, advantaging major suppliers. Thirdly, it is based on the voluntary submission of data, with no independent monitoring of submissions. Since there are no penalties for States which fail to submit their first annual report by 30 April 1993, or which submit incomplete reports, buyers and sellers may collude in secrecy when it suits them. Fourthly, it may not have the support of all the Permanent Five members; China did not participate in the General Assembly vote. The Resolution did make clear that the Register will continue to develop, and a Panel of Experts has been asked to prepare a Report on including further categories of equipment and actual data on existing military holdings and procurement.

24.3 Meetings of the Permanent Five have taken place since the end of the Persian Gulf conflict. They agreed to notify each other when transferring certain weapons to the Middle East, and set an objective of a Middle East zone free of weapons of mass destruction. The basis of the Permanent Five agreements has not been on limiting arms transfers *per se*, but rather in not upsetting bilateral or regional power balances. The flaw here is that the notion of regional balance lies at the root of the arms race since each State tends to measure itself against the combined strength of several different potential adversaries. In the two years since Iraq's invasion of Kuwait the United States received arms orders worth approximately $US 28.5bn from the Middle East. The principle client was Saudi Arabia with orders of more than $US 17bn—and that was before former US President Bush approved the sale of 72 F-15 fighter jets in September 1992. The need for foreign exchange has increased pressure on the Russian Federation to export ex-Soviet military hardware; it continues to supply arms to Iran and remains the world's second biggest arms supplier. The UK's sales to the Middle East in 1990–92 came to $US 4bn.

24.4 The recent revelations concerning the supply of machine tools by Matrix Churchill destined for use in Iraq's defence procurement programme between 1988 and 1990[4] starkly raise the potential consequences of our participation in the sale of arms—that they will be used against our own citizens. Such a clear cut repercussion is rare—a central difficulty in addressing the arms trade is that the profit resulting from arms sales accrues to specific supplier countries and firms while the losses (in decreased global security, the reduced budget available for social expenditure in recipient country, and the destruction that results from the use of the arms) are usually borne in a more diffuse way.

24.5 Thus we believe that concentration on increased transparency and regional power balance is an inadequate response to the growing problem of conventional weapon proliferation. Action must be taken to prevent arms transfers, not just to measure them and promote their increase in a "balanced" fashion. Curbs on the supply of arms must go in tandem with reduced demand. This can be achieved in part through regional confidence building measures (such as those pioneered by the Conference on Security and Co-operation in Europe) and regional arms limitation agreements.

[1] Figure derived from the SIPRI Armaments and Disarmament Handbook 1992 (SIPRI, Stockholm, 1992).

[2] (UN General Assembly Resolution: A/Res/46/36 "Transparency in Armaments").

[3] The seven categories addressed by the UN Register are battle tanks, armoured combat vehicles, large calibre artillery systems, combat aircraft, attack helicopters, warships and missiles or missile systems.

[4] see Daily Telegraph (10 November 1992) "Inquiry urged after collapse of arms trial" by John Steele and Philip Johnston p1.

24.6 Recommendation: the UK should take the lead in addressing arms transfers through unilateral restraint on the sale of arms (backed up by an enhanced defence diversification programme), while actively pursuing multilateral arrangements; by strengthening the existing military holdings, procurement and enforcement elements of the UN Register and by strengthening regional confidence-building measures to lessen the demand for arms.

25 UN Response to Intra-national Conflicts

25.1 We welcome the recognition in the Report that "the time of absolute and exclusive sovereignty . . . has passed" (paragraph 17). However the Report does not effectively address the issue of how UN mechanisms from fact-finding to humanitarian assistance should be developed to match the increased role of the UN in what were hitherto seen as internal affairs of States. Most of the wars occurring in the world at present are internal (see Annex 2). There have also been recent precedents which have helped to redefine what constitutes "essentially the domestic jurisdiction of States" (Article 2 [7]). These include responses to apartheid in the 1960s, Security Council Resolution 688 to establish "Safe Havens for the Kurds in Northern Iraq" and on activities in Somalia and in the former Yugoslavia. Thus both the potential and need for UN action in intra-state matters has increased.

25.2 Recommendation: that the Security Council set up a working group to establish criteria and mechanisms to co-ordinate effective and appropriate UN action in response to intra-national conflicts, and humanitarian and human rights crises. Utmost care should be taken to avoid selective interference in a country's internal affairs or the promotion of UN intervention in the pursuit of narrow Foreign policy goals.

Annex 1

Military Aspects of "An Agenda For Peace"

By Admiral Sir James Eberle. GCB, LLD. Former National and NATO Commander in Chief and Director, Royal Institute of International Affairs, London. Advisor on military issues to the UNA-UK United Nations and Conflict Programme.

1. The United Nations has been involved in "Peace-Keeping", an operation requiring the deployment of armed forces from the international community, for some forty years. It is not a task that was enunciated in the Charter. As the report by Dr Boutros-Ghali says (Paragraph 46) "Peace-keeping can rightly be called the invention of the United Nations". "Action with respect of breaches of the peace and acts of aggression" was addressed in Chapter VII of the Charter, and has come to be described as "peacemaking". The broad principle that differentiated these two forms of action was that peace-keeping required the consent of all the parties concerned. Peacemaking did not.

2. The world has, however, moved on, and this simple differentiation no longer suffices. The report attempts to define three terms—Preventive Diplomacy—Peacemaking—and peace-keeping (Paragraph 20). Significantly, the definition of Peace-keeping includes the phrase "*hitherto* with the consent of all the parties concerned". However, within the report, the use of military forces is envisaged in:—

preventative diplomacy (Paragraph 31)
peacemaking (Paragraph 42)
peace-keeping (Paragraph 50)
peace enforcement (Paragraph 44)
peace building (Paragraph 55)

There should now also be added the role of protection of humanitarian assistance. The part that can be played by units of the armed forces in the relief of natural disasters should not be overlooked.

Concepts

3. Whilst it can be well argued that there are important theoretical and conceptual differences in the definition of these various roles, the practical complexity of today's issues is such that in operational terms, there will seldom be clear dividing lines between them. Preventive deployments may turn to enforcement operations (Desert Shield/Storm); peace building should be part of peace-keeping (Cambodia); peace-keeping operations of very different natures may proceed in closely proximate areas (Croatia/Bosnia); what is peace-keeping when there is no legitimate government to give its consent (Somalia)?

4. These complexities arise not only through the developing nature of conflict itself, in which historical, ethnic, religious, economic and political issues are closely interwoven, but also through change in the perception of the responsibilities of the international community in respect of human rights and the rights of minorities, responsibilities that were in the past, and in many cases still are, considered to be

matters "within the domestic jurisdiction" (Article 2 [7] of the Charter) of a member state. They are further complicated by the impact of modern weapon technology that has put the ability to inflict severe damage on an opponent within the hands of both the professional and amateur warrior alike.

COMMAND AND CONTROL

5. The result of these complexities is that it is often no longer feasible to give clear political directives to the military commanders; nor is the commander able to establish a single military aim. Often it will be impossible to determine who is "the enemy", when clearly there is one, because you are being shot at! To cope successfully with such situations, there needs to be a high degree of professionalism in the operational management of the forces which are engaged, a high degree of flexibility in their use, and the ability to respond rapidly to changing circumstances in their task. None of these characteristics are now evident in the present organisation for either the political direction or the military command and control of UN forces.

6. I believe it is difficult to overstate the importance of early action to achieve improvements in this respect. There is evident reluctance of the public and in many countries, including Britain, to send their, soldiers to risk their lives in far off regions, in which there is no readily discernable national interest. And yet, there is widespread acknowledgement that, as members of the international community, we all have responsibilities for doing everything that we can to prevent parts of the world sinking into anarchy and chaos, with the attendant misery and suffering that is inflicted on innocent men, women and children; and the danger of horizontal escalation. This reluctance is undoubtedly re-enforced when casualties are incurred, as inevitably they will be. If such casualties are seen to be the result of mismanagement, of conditions in which "our boys" were not given a fair chance to defend themselves, or of situations in which sound military judgement was over-ridden by political expediency, then reluctance is most likely to turn to outright opposition. Such opposition could make the United Nations impotent.

7. The line of political direction from the UN may seem at first glance to be clear and simple. It runs from the Security Council, through the Secretary-General, and the Under Secretary for Peace-keeping Operations to the senior UN representative in the field. But I believe this is misleading. The complexities arise out of the multitude of other agencies, of the UN, of national governments, of regional organisations and of non-governmental organisations that are part of the action. Improvements have been made to try to ensure better co-ordination between civil agencies. But much more needs to be done if full co-ordination, including co-ordination with the military is to be achieved in New York, Geneva, and in the field.

8. A particular facet of such co-ordination is related to the balance of roles that might be played by regional security organisations. This subject is addressed in Chapter 7 of the Report, in which the importance of the UN maintaining close relationships with the various regional organisations is stressed. However the report deliberately refrains from trying to set forth a formal pattern of relationships (Paragraph 64). If the UN is to be successful in the deployment of military forces in support of international peace and security, it is vital that there is a clear understanding of "who does what", and where authority and responsibility properly lies. A case study of the interaction of the EC, WEU, NATO, CSCE and the UN in the former Yugoslavia might provide useful lessons in this respect.

9. The lines of military command are far from clear. There is no available senior military "element" in New York to whom UN Field Commanders can be responsible, from whom they can seek advice, to whom they can refer their military problems or by whom they can expect reasonable co-ordination of the overall effort. Thus in the former Yugoslavia, the military headquarters in Zagreb, and that in Sarajevo, are reported to find it difficult to acknowledge each others missions.

10. The tasks in support of the UN military units in the field that require to be carried out in New York can be listed as follows:—

a) to give general military advice to the Security Council and the Secretary-General.

b) to provide military advice to UN Commanders in the field.

c) To co-ordinate inputs from national military intelligence sources relative to potential conflict areas.

d) to maintain records of the status of forces that are earmarked by nations for UN assignment (see Paragraph 13)

e) to prepare and maintain outline contingency plans for UN deployments.

f) to provide advice to nations on training for UN operations.

g) to advise on the establishment of, and changes in, the "rules of engagement".

h) to maintain standard operating procedures for UN operations.

i) to co-ordinate certain logistic planning, control and operational functions—including transportation and communications.

j) to act as a repository for the collective experience of the military aspects of UN operations.

11. To fulfil these tasks, it is necessary to set up a military planning cell for the UN in New York. What is to be avoided is for this cell to be seen as some sort of embryo of a "UN Ministry of Defence"; or yet as an operational military headquarters. What is required is the means to carry out those military tasks that can only be done successfully at the highest level in order to achieve the flexibility and rapid command response at the highest level that are vital to the effectiveness of UN military deployments, in whatever role. The organisation also needs to recognise that every UN operation has its own particular and special characteristics, that require it to be treated on a separate but co-ordinated basis. UN operations cannot successfully be forced into a single mould.

12. How this military planning cell (or International Military Support Staff—IMSS) is integrated into the UN's New York headquarters is an important and politically sensitive issue. There is a *prima facie* case that it should serve the Military Staff Committee (MSC), which would need to be enlarged (probably to include a representative of all the fifteen member states of the Security Council), since the Charter charges the MSC with the "strategic direction of any armed forces placed at the disposal of the Security Council" (Article 47 [3]). However, the military cell could be integrated with the operations staff of the Security Council; or come under the direction of the Under-Secretary-General for Political Affairs. This issue requires further detailed study. Action to set up the IMSS need not however, await the result of this study.

THE PROVISION OF FORCES

13. The comments in Paragraph 42 of "An Agenda for Peace", which call for the full implementation of the Article 43 commitments of the Charter, whereby nations are asked to make available armed forces to the Security Council for its use have given rise to widespread support for what are referred to as "UN Standing Forces". Experience in other fields has shown that such forces are very expensive to maintain; and discourage flexibility. In the, UN context, it would also be extremely difficult to agree their size and composition. What is required is for nations to commit themselves to the provision of "earmarked capabilities". Such earmarking of general and specialist military capabilities, at various levels of notice, would provide the IMSS with the ability to create "a la carte forces" rapidly and flexibly to suit various and changing situations. It is important that the IMSS should have good knowledge of the capabilities, the state of training and the degree of inter-operability with forces of other nations (including problems of language) of which they are capable. The deployment of ill equipped, badly disciplined or poorly trained units into the field may well prove a significant handicap to the achievement of the aim. Nor can the need for sophisticated equipments be discounted. Success in UN peace-keeping is unlikely now to be achieved with just a display of sound sense, sensitivity and side arms.

14. However high the standards of the troops in the field, success is unlikely to be achieved without good command, control, communication, co-operation and information. In the UN context, the acknowledged vital importance of C31 in war is replaced by the similarly vital importance of C41 in peace-keeping. This requires a "worked up" multi-national headquarters, into which all the various military *and civil* functions can be moulded.

15. It is unrealistic to expect officers and officials, brought together at short notice in unfamiliar circumstances, to function as an efficient and effective command and control team. There is thus a strong case for the provision of a limited number of UN field headquarters units which would be assigned to the UN on a semi-permanent basis. They would be available "on call" to undertake operational assignments on behalf of the UN. Their composition and location would require detailed study. They could be based on existing national military headquarters units that would provide the skeleton structure and appropriate communication support to which would be attached military and civil staff from other countries and agencies. They would act under the authority of the IMSS. Initially and occasionally, the whole HQ staff would be brought together to conduct a UN staff exercise; and from time to time, if operational requirements permitted, undertake an exercise deployment. The headquarters would, over time, build up its own experience and expertise.

16. The undoubted success of the international nature of the many multi-national NATO headquarters has, to a significant extent, resulted from the foresight of General Eisenhower who, as SACEUR, set up the NATO Defence College (NDC) in order to provide a corps of military and civil officers to fill senior NATO appointments who had been trained in a NATO environment. Facilities of the NDC have now been extended to members of the former Warsaw Pact Countries in order to contribute to overcoming the divisions of Europe. The possibility of further extending the concept of the NDC to that of a UNDC, aimed at providing civil and military officers trained for UN headquarters duties seems to merit further study.

COSTS

17. There is ample evidence that the present system of UN procurement and of UN field payments requires review. The reports proposal (paragraph 53) that there should be pre-positioned stocks of basic peace-keeping equipment needs to be further studied. A system that all costs should lie where they fall, as is suggested for air and sea lift capacity (paragraph 54), would clearly be the most simple to operate. Unhappily though, it would deter the less well off nations from offering forces for UN operations; and might inhibit the success of an operation in which no nation was readily willing to "pick up the tab" for an essential provision. There is no simple solution. But a detailed independent review of present procedures and practices is called for.

CONCLUSIONS

18. From the above considerations, the following recommendations for action by the British Government, can be drawn:

- **a) The concept of earmarking appropriate national and civil "capabilities" for UN operations should be encouraged.**
- **b) The possibility of setting up semi-permanently assigned multi-national UN Field headquarters units, including civil and military functions, should be examined.**
- **c) The means of setting up in New York of an International Military Support Staff (IMSS) should be progressed as a matter of urgency.**
- **d) A study of how the IMSS be fitted into the UN New York headquarters should be investigated.**
- **e) The possible establishment of a UN Defence College for the training of senior civil and military personnel in UN peace-keeping should be investigated.**
- **f) An independent review of the present policy and practice of costing, procurement and payment for UN peace-keeping operations should be initiated.**
- **g) The appropriate balance of roles for regional security organisations with respect to the global security responsibilities of the Security council should be the subject of further examination.**

Annex 2

CRITERIA FOR UN SECURITY COUNCIL ACTION WITH REGARD TO ARMED CONFLICTS.

Prepared by Professor Frank Blackaby, Former Director of SIPRI, Stockholm.

"The principles of the Charter must be applied consistently, not selectively, for if the perception should be of the latter, trust will wane and with it the moral authority which is the greatest and most unique quality of that instrument", Dr Boutros Boutros-Ghali, *An Agenda for Peace*, para. 82.

The purpose of this exercise is to take one of the standard lists of world major armed conflicts, and set out whether or not there has been any UN involvement. The resultant list raises questions about the criteria for Security Council intervention in a given conflict.

The list of major armed conflicts is the one prepared by the Department of Peace and Conflict Research, Uppsala University, Sweden. It is published each year in the SIPRI Yearbook of World Armaments and Disarmament. The latest version, in the SIPRI 1992 Yearbook, is for major armed conflicts in 1991.

The definition used is as follows: "A major armed conflict is characterised by prolonged combat between the military forces of two or more Governments or of one Government and at least one organised armed group, involving the use of weapons and incurring battle-related deaths of at least 1,000 persons." The figure of 1,000 is the cumulative total of deaths from the beginning of the conflict. The 1991 list includes those conflicts which were judged to be ongoing in that year.

Note that this definition of conflict includes those which are internal, within states. Para 7 of Article 2 of the Charter is relevant here: "Nothing in the present Charter shall authorise the United Nations to intervene in matters which are essentially within the domestic jurisdiction of any state or shall require the Members to submit such matters to settlement under the present Charter . . ." However there has been recent reinterpretation of Article 2(7), most notably when the UN Security Council approved military action to help protect the Kurds and the Shi'ites within Iraq.

The Uppsala group lists ongoing major conflicts in 1991 in 30 locations. This appendix follows the Uppsala list; notes the nature of the conflict where necessary; and notes the nature of UN involvement. The section in the SIPRI Yearbook gives full details of the nature of each conflict.

Major Armed Conflicts	*UN involvement*
Europe	
1 UK/Northern Ireland. Govt. vs. IRA and UDA. Internal.	Nil.
2 Yugoslavia. Debatable whether the conflict in Bosnia should be labelled internal or external	Security Council resolutions. UN Protection Force I (UNPROFOR I) initially on Croatian-Serbian border. UNPROFOR II—humanitarian relief within Bosnia.
Middle East	
3 Iran. Iranian Government vs. Mujahideen Khalq. Internal.	Nil.
4 Iraq. Iraqi Government vs.Kurdistan Front, and Shiia Muslim revolt, led by SAIRI (Supreme Assembly of Islamic Revolution in Iraq). Internal	Approval to coalition to prohibit and interdict Iraqi flights over areas in both North and South. Internal.
5 Iraq-Kuwait, and multinational force. Included here, because the war was in 1991.	UN involvement extensive. Note UNIKOM, an unarmed force patrolling the demilitarised zone on the Iraq-Kuwait border.
6 Israel-Palestine. Internal?	Security Council resolutions. UN Deployments: UN Truce Supervision Organisation in Jerusalem (UNTSO). UN Disengagement Observer Force (UNDOF) on Golan Heights. UN Interim Force in Lebanon (UNIFIL). UN in the refugee camps. No UN forces in Gaza or West Bank.
7 Turkey. Turkish Govt. vs. PKK (Kurdish Workers' Party). Internal (although now may be spreading to Northern Iraq).	Nil.
South Asia	
8 Afghanistan. Combat between Mujahideen groups. Internal	There were earlier UN peace plans. No UN forces.
9 Bangladesh. Govt. vs. JSS/SB These are Buddhist Mongol people of the Chittagong Hill Tracts. Internal.	Nil.
10 India. Govt. vs. various groups: ULFA; Naxalites; Sikh militants; Kashmir militants. Internal (except for Kashmir issue.)	UN Military Observer Group in India and Pakistan (UNMOGIP), in Jammu and Kashmir. No UN involvement in internal conflict.
11 Myanmar. Govt. vs. a number of dissident organisations: KNU; KIA; NMSP; RSO. Internal.	Nil.
12 Sri Lanka. Govt. vs. Tamil Tigers. Internal.	Nil.

Major Armed Conflicts	*UN involvement*
Pacific Asia	
13 Cambodia. Govt vs. a coalition of three groups. Internal.	UN Transitional Authority in Cambodia (UNTAC): 15–20 thousand civil and military personnel who are to oversee the administration of the country until a new Government is elected UN role includes peace-keeping; disarming the factions; refugee repatriation; setting up and supervising elections etc.
14 Indonesia. Govt. vs. Fretelin and others. Internal (except that UN General Assembly has not recognised the annexation of East Timor).	Nil.
15 Phillipines. Govt. vs. New People's Army. Internal.	Nil.
Africa	
16 Angola. Govt. vs. UNITA. Internal.	A UN verification operation has joined in the observing of the cease-fire and elections (UNAVEM-2). UNAVEM-l was to verify the withdrawal of Cuban forces.
17 Chad. Govt. vs. Forces of Habre. Internal.	Nil.
18 Ethiopia. Clashes between some of the armed opposition groups formed in the Mengistu era. Internal.	Relief only.
19 Liberia. Clashes between NPFL and INPFL (Independent NPFL). Internal.	Nil. Peacekeeping was left to ECOWAS (Economic Community of West African States and their peace-keeping force ECOMOG (ECOWAS Monitoring Group)
20 Morocco/Western Sahara. Govt. vs. Polisario. External, since the issue was whether Western Sahara should be independent or integrated with Morocco.	SC agreed to establish a UN mission for the Referendum in Western Sahara (MINURSO).
21 Mozambique. Govt.vs. Renamo. Internal.	Somewhat marginal presence in negotiations on peace accord brokered by Italians. UN and OAU to supervise elections to be held within a year of the signing of a peace agreement. UN military observers now expected.
22 Rwanda. Govt. vs. Rwandan Patriotic Front (RPF), Internal.	Nil. The OAU provided a cease-fire monitoring group.
23 Somalia. Fighting between factions. Internal.	UN Operation in Somalia (UNOSOM). Essentially a relief operation: but 3,000 military (of which only some have arrived) are to give protection to relief convoys.
24 South Africa. "Armed Struggle" Govt. and ANC now suspended. Combat between Inkhatha and ANC, and possibly dissident South African security forces and ANC. Internal.	Past sanctions between resolutions. There is a UN Observer presence in South Africa.

Major Armed Conflicts	*UN involvement*
25 Sudan. Govt. vs. two factions of SPLA (Sudan People's Liberation Army); also combat between the two factions. Internal.	Attempts at relief only. Some mediation efforts by OAU.
26 Uganda. Govt. vs. UPA (Uganda People's Army) and UPDCA (Uganda People's Christian Democratic Army).	Nil.
Central and South America	
27 Colombia. Govt. vs. FARC Fuerzas Armadas Revolucionarias de Colombia) and ELN (Ejercito de Liberacion Nacional). Internal.	Nil.
28 EL Salvador. (Should not now be considered an on-going conflict: included because of UN involvement). Govt. vs. FMLN (Farabundo Marti Front for National Liberation). Internal.	Mediation by UN Secretary-General. ONUSAL created —UN Observer Mission to El Salvador—to monitor agreements on human rights between Govt. and FMLN.
29 Guatemala. Govt. vs. URNG (Guatemalan National Revolutionary Unity). Internal.	Nil. Attempts at a peace process made by Guatemalan National Commission for Reconciliation (CNR)
30 Peru. Govt. vs. Sendero Luminoso. Internal.	Nil.

Annex 3

CONTRIBUTIONS AND ARREARS OF MEMBERS OF THE SECURITY COUNCIL TO THE REGULAR UN BUDGET[1]
STATES LISTED WILL BE COUNCIL MEMBERS FROM 1ST JANUARY 1993

UN Security Council Members	*1992 Scale of Assessment (%)*	*Regular fees Payable for 1992 ($US)*	*Amount paid in 1992 ($US)*	*Total arrears (all years) to date ($US)*
Permanent Members				
France	6.00	59,088,830	59,088,830	0
China	0.77	7,583,066	7,583,066	0
UK	5.02	49,437,654	49,437,654	0
Russia	9.41	92,670,982	28,580,000	110,110,295
USA	25.00	298,619,001	325,495,230	239,531,646
Non Permanent Members				
Cape Verde	0.01	98,482	111,233	79,380
Japan	12.45	122,609,322	122,609,322	0
Morocco	0.03	295,443	283,142	12,301
Brazil	1.59	15,658,539	4,465,801	29,016,698
Pakistan	0.06	590,888	590,888	0
New Zealand	0.24	2,363,553	2,363,553	0
Spain	1.98	19,499,313	19,499,313	0
Venezuela	0.49	4,825,587	4,825,587	0
Djibouti	0.01	98,482	50,000	164,923
Hungary	0.18	1,772,664	1,772,664	1,115,853

1 Derived from Annex II of UN Secretariat Document "Status of Contributions as at 30 September 1992" (ST/ADM/SER.B/387 6 October 1992

1992 DEFENCE BUDGET OF SECURITY COUNCIL MEMBERS[1]

China $US 6.76bn	Cape Verde (Figure not available)	Djibouti $US 5.18m
France $US 34.91bn	Hungary $US 1.16bn[2]	Brazil $US 2.12bn
UK $US 41.20bn	New Zealand $US 663.40m	Pakistan $US 3.29bn
Russia $US 133.70bn[3]	Spain $US 7.4lbn	Morocco $US 1.13bn
USA $US 282.60bn	Venezuela $US 1.62bn[4]	Japan $US 34.30bn

1 Derived from the International Institute for Strategic Studies (IISS) "The Military Balance 1992–1993" (Brassey's, 1992)
2 Does not include costs incurred by Yugoslavian crisis.
3 This is the official figure for the Russian Federation for 1991; an estimate for 1992 was not available. Commentators have estimated the real 1991 figure to be $US 237.99bn [International Institute for Strategic Studies (IISS) "The Military Balance 1992–1993" (Brassey's 1992) p92].
4 1991 figure, 1992 figures not available.

Annex 4

OUTSTANDING UN PEACE-KEEPING CONTRIBUTIONS[1]

Peace-Keeping Mission	*UK Total Assessed Contribution Outstanding at 31 December 1992 ($US)*	*Total Outstanding Contributions from all Members at 31 December 1992 ($US)*
United Nations Interim Force in Lebanon (UNIFIL)	0	228,129,748
United Nations Iran-Iraq Military Observer Group (UNIMOG)	0	1,059,832
United Nations Angola Verification Mission (UNAVEM AND UNAVEM II)	0	21,708,447
United Nations Transition Assistance Group (UNTAG)	0	–6,576,770 (in credit)
United Nations Observer Group in Central America(ONUCA)	424,660	12,716,027
United Nations Iraq-Kuwait Observation Mission (UNIKOM)	0	23,204,901
United Nations Mission For The Referendum in Western Sahara (MINURSO)	0	20,966,298
United Nations Observer Mission in El Salvador (ONUSAL)	0	11,593,125
United Nations Advance Mission in Cambodia (UNAMIC)	0	4,843,331
United Nations Transitional Authority in Cambodia (UNTAC)	0	163,561,700
United Nations Protection Force (UNPROFOR) (Croatia/Bosnia)	0	61,520,498
United Nations Emergency Force (1973) (UNEF) and the United Nations Disengagement Observer Force (UNDOF)	0	19,223,490
TOTAL OUTSTANDING	424,660	561,950,627

[1] Derived from UN Secretariat document "Status of Contributions As At 30 September 1992" (ST/ADM/SER.B/387 6 October 1992). Since this date the United States has paid a substantial proportion of its peace-keeping arrears.

Contributors to the Preparation of this Memorandum

MEMBERS OF UNA'S EXPERT ROUNDTABLE ON "AN AGENDA FOR PEACE":

Michael Aaronson—Director Overseas Department, Save the Children Fund.
Professor Frank Blackaby—Former Director of SIPRI, Stockholm
Dr Olivia Bosch—Programme Manager, Mountbatten Centre, Department of Politics, University of Southampton
Professor Adam Curle—Emeritus Professor of Peace Studies, University of Bradford
Myriel Davies MBE—Deputy Director of UNA-UK
Sam Daws—Head of Research, UN and Conflict Programme, UNA-UK
Jane Drake—Research Assistant, UN and Conflict Programme, UNA-UK
Admiral Sir James Eberle GCB, LLD—Former National and NATO Commander in Chief and Director, Royal Institute of International Affairs, London
Lord David Ennals—Vice-Chair of UNA-UK
Nicholas Gillett—Trustee, John Bright MP Trust Fund
Malcolm Harper—Director of UNA-UK
Keith Bindell—Presenter, Media Watch, BBC World Service
Suzanne Long—Policy, Information and Research Officer, UNA-UK
Sir Hugh Rossi—Chairman of UNA-UK

Mr David Travers—Director of Graduate Studies, Department of Politics and International Relations, University of Lancaster
Graeme Warner—Director, United Nations Information Centre, London
Dr Peter Willetts—Department of International Relations, City University, London

OTHERS INDIVIDUALS WHO HAVE SUBMITTED WRITTEN COMMENTS:

Sydney Bailey—Quaker expert on UN affairs
Anne Bennett—Secretary, UN Committee, Quaker Peace and Service, London
Dr Geoff Berridge—Reader in Politics, University of Leicester
Reverend Keith Clements—Co-ordinating Secretary for International Affairs, Council of Churches for Britain and Ireland
Colonel Richard Connaughton, Consultant
Bill Davies—Secretary, UNA-Wales, Welsh Centre for International Affairs
Scilla Elworthy—Director, Oxford Research Group
Professor William Gutteridge—Executive Director of the Research Institute for the Study of Conflict and Terrorism
Brigadier Michael Harbottle—Director of The Centre for International Peacebuilding
Roger Harrison—Oxford UNA and World Disarmament Campaign
Dr Derek Heater—Former Dean of the Faculty of Social and Cultural Studies, Brighton Polytechnic
Edmund Ions—Former Reader in Politics, York University
Bruce Kent—President, International Peace Bureau, Geneva
Dr Lorna Lloyd—Department of International Studies, Keele University
Dr Nigel White—Lecturer in Law, University of Nottingham

OTHERS WHO HAVE CONTRIBUTED FORMALLY OR INVORMALLY TO THE PREPARATION OF THIS MEMORANDUM:

Ken Aldred—Secretary General, Peace Through NATO
Margaret Aldred—Director of Defence Policy, MoD
Bronwyn Brady—Associate for European Affairs, British-American Security Information Council, London
Stephen Bridges, UN Department, FCO
Ann Feltham, Co-ordinator, Campaign Against the Arms Trade, London
Colonel Chen Feng—Military Attache, Embassy of the People's Republic of China, London
Martin Howard—Secretariat Overseas Commitments, MoD
Sally Morphet—Head of International Section, Research and Analysis Department, FCO
Helen Leigh Phippard—Department of Political Studies, Queen Mary and Westfield College

THIS MEMORANDUM IS A SUBMISSION BY THE UNITED NATIONS ASSOCIATION (UK). IT WAS RESEARCHED AND COMPILED BY SAM DAWS, HEAD OF THE UN AND CONFLICT PROGRAMME OF UNA, AND DOES NOT NECESSARILY REFLECT THE VIEWS OF THOSE LISTED ABOVE, WHO HAVE GENEROUSLY CONTRIBUTED TO ITS PREPARATION.

APPENDIX 9

Memorandum by the Development Studies Association

INTRODUCTION

This memorandum is submitted by the Development Studies Association (DSA) a charitable organisation representing academics and practitioners involved in the study of development and the practical application of development assistance. Membership is drawn from academic institutions and development agencies in the United Kingdom and the Republic of Ireland.

Some of the DSA's Members have formed a Study Group to look at the relationships between conflict and development. It is in that context that we have come to address the issue of the capacity and authority of the United Nations in the provision of humanitarian assistance. The memorandum comes with the endorsement of three past Presidents of the Development Studies Association (Professor H W Singer, Dr Tony Killick and Dr Frances Stewart) and has been written by the current President (Martin Griffiths) and Peter Roth, barrister.

Recent developments in Somalia and in Mozambique have drawn our attention to deficiencies in the United Nations system, leading to unnecessary deaths as a result of avoidable delays in responding to these crises.

In particular, we believe that reform is required in two areas. *Firstly*, there is a need to improve the capacity within the United Nations system to respond both rapidly and effectively to humanitarian needs. *Secondly*, it is necessary to clarify the legal basis upon which the United Nations can intervene to provide assistance, in particular when there is no sovereign request and when the government of the affected state may itself be responsible for the crisis.

We have treated these two areas in two separate sections below.

1. The Operational Issues

1.1 In early 1992 the office of the United Nations Resident Co-ordinator in Turkey issued a memorandum which sought to analyse the difficulties faced by the different parts of the UN System in responding to the influx of Kurds from northern Iraq[1]. This memorandum made no reference to the new post of Undersecretary-General for Humanitarian Affairs, to be filled by Mr Jan Eliasson from March 1 1992.[2] But the problems it identified within the system added powerful arguments in support of the new post.

1.2 The memorandum identified the following problems:

— an absence of effective leadership from UN Headquarters. Different missions visited the country, issuing different instructions which were not sufficiently derived from the field experience of the United Nations agencies in Turkey.

— the UN Resident Co-ordinator did not have the authority to co-ordinate the actions of the different agencies. The memorandum states that "without clearcut authority and accountability at field level, the United Nations system will be condemned to committing the same mistakes . . . . In times of emergency and crises United Nations Agencies must put aside their coveted independence in order to more efficiently pursue a common aim." For example, "efforts to develop an overall integrated manpower needs table for the whole UN System in Turkey did not prove possible."

— United Nations staff lacked the necessary experience and training to respond well. This was compounded by inadequate support facilities, the whole betraying a basic lack of preparedness in the system.

1.3 It could have been hoped that the appointment of Mr Eliasson would lead to an improvement in the system to address these problems. Unfortunately, seven months on, similar problems are being encountered in Somalia and Mozambique. These cases are reviewed below, and their analysis leads us to make the recommendations for further reforms in the United Nations structure outlined in para 6.2 at the end of this section of the submission.

2. Somalia

2. It is not our intention here to rehearse in detail the passage of events which have combined to create the tragedy of Somalia. Others are better placed to do so—notably Save the Children Fund, and the International Committee of the Red Cross, whose witness has proved so significant in mobilising international awareness. It is, however, necessary to provide a brief summary of United Nations action if we are to deduce some lessons regarding their capacity to respond to such crises.

2.2 We propose therefore to provide a brief overview of events in the south of Somalia during 1992 and then move on to a more detailed analysis of particular difficulties faced by the United Nations in the north of the country.

The United Nations in Somalia

2.3 The United Nations withdrew its staff from Somalia in January 1991, judging that conditions there were too dangerous. One agency, UNICEF, returned on 24 December 1991 to set up a small office in Mogadishu. In the intervening period, security had deteriorated and non-governmental organisations had in particular called for a resumption of United Nations assistance during the last two months of 1991, the period of the greatest destruction in southern Somalia. Eventually, at the end of 1991 James Jonah, the Undersecretary-General for Political Affairs visited Mogadishu. His report resulted in a Security Council Resolution[3] which called for more urgent action, but which did nothing to ensure that humanitarian aid could be effectively distributed: See para. 10.6 below. This at a time when agencies were already calling for a policy of massive infusion of food aid *as a means* of reducing the insecurity.

2.4 The period from January to March of 1992 was absorbed in the efforts of the United Nations to secure a ceasefire, with agreement finally reached on 3 March. The first shipment of food did not reach Mogadishu until the beginning of May, when 5,000 tons was delivered by the World Food Programme to Mogadishu port; its distribution was immediately hampered by the (by then) well established pattern of

[1] "An analysis of the UN System's response in Turkey to the humanitarian problems resulting from the Gulf Crisis". An updated memorandum from the office of the UN Resident Co-ordinator in Ankara.

[2] The office was created pursuant to UN Security Council Resolution 46/182 of 19 December 1991: See para. 10.5 below.

[3] Security Council Resolution 733, 23 January 1992.

looting amongst a population accustomed to the desperate hunt for food. Meanwhile, as a result of the establishment of the Department of Humanitarian Affairs (DHA), co-ordination of United Nations operations in Somalia had been assigned to Ambassador Sahnoun. In April, the United Nations agreed a plan of operations apparently designed to cover a 6–9 month period totalling $23 million and including the deployment of 550 military personnel.

2.5 By late July, with the continued insecurity in Somalia and the inevitable consequent deterioration in food distribution and availability, the Secretary-General returned to the Security Council, this time in a mood of anger contrasting the international response to Somalia with that to Yugoslavia, which he described as "a rich man's war." A United Nations Technical mission arrived in Mogadishu on 7 August. This mission reported back at the end of August, recommending an increase in military protection (eventually set at 3,500 personnel), an upgrading of relief deliveries, and other measures to improve local security. The report, crucially, recommended that "In the event that no agreement is reached the United Nations should be prepared to do so without the consent of the parties .... The essential point is that the international community cannot stand idly and witness the unnecessary loss of human life in Somalia".[1] This represented a very considerable shift from the position taken in January where, it seems, the agreement of the parties was considered a necessary condition precedent to humanitarian action.

2.6 In the interim, a highly visible US airlift of food supplies had been put into place on 21 August, with President Bush authorising (on August 14) the delivery of 145,000 tons of food. This occurred at a time of significantly increased media coverage of Somalia, and the concomitant opportunities for non-governmental organisations to make very public their profound disappointment in the belated international response to a situation which had been predicted.

2.7 On October 12 the United Nations finally presented their 100-Day Plan for Somalia in Geneva, its essential recommendations flowing from the visit of the "technical mission" in early August. A sum of $82.7 million was now recommended as necessary, a very significant increase on earlier estimations of need.

2.8 The energy and commitment of Ambassador Sahnoun—and perhaps, in particular, his openness to criticism of United Nations operations—has done something to restore the credibility of the United Nations in Somalia. It is therefore all the more disappointing that Ambassador Sahnoun's open style appears to have led to his resignation. This will have sent a very depressing signal to those concerned not just with the fate of Somalia but also with those who wish to see a greater public accountability within the United Nations.

The United Nations in the North of Somalia

2.9 At the beginning of 1992, United nations staff were withdrawn from the north of Somalia for security reasons. Representatives of two agencies (UNICEF & UNHCR) operated from bases in Djibouti until June when they returned to Hargeisa. In the intervening period they provided some assistance, principally through NGOs working in the north. UNICEF provided essential drugs through NGOs and also directly to local Health Units; UNICEF also financed the rehabilitation of some water supplies, for example in Berbera. UNHCR's remit was to provide for the rehabilitation of refugees returning from Ethiopia, but mainly focussed on mine clearance through the work of RIMFIRE, an international NGO. In addition, up until May UNHCR operated an air service from Djibouti. This was stopped in May and did not resume until September.

2.10 In June, UNICEF and UNHCR moved back to Hargeisa following the launching of the United Nations' 90-day Plan for the whole country. They continued their assistance previously managed from Djibouti, but with the advantage of having in place international staff who could make operational decisions and convert resources.

2.11 In September, these two agencies were joined by UNDP and UNOSOM. The former was at first unclear about its task but devoted itself to the valuable task of pooling information on security, and providing a liaison with the authorities in Hargeisa for NGOs and UN agencies working in Somaliland. UNOSOM's role was to manage the deployment of troops, facilitate peace talks, and to provide security for UN and NGO work. The latter overlapped with the task taken up by UNDP.

— WFP had maintained a presence in the north throughout the period although, like UNICEF and UNHCR, it had been obliged to withdraw its international staff to Djibouti for the period from January to June 1992. FAO have, to date, had no presence in the north despite the fact that assistance to livestock and to agricultural production was vital for both the local economy and for the maintenance of the fragile security in the area. A response to a request for assistance to FAO for $5,000 worth of veterinary drugs by ActionAid was delayed for 2 months and resulted in a consignment worth only £150.

[1] *Financial Times*, 26 August 1992, p.1.

— The absence of UN staff on the ground in the north for a large part of 1992 led to problems in deploying effective assistance, due to lack of local knowledge and a lack of local decision-making. In addition, UN agencies did not feel able to relate to the authorities in Hargeisa—UNICEF's drugs assistance, for example, had to bypass the "Ministry" in Hargeisa and be provided directly to local MCH centres. We understand that this concern not to deal directly with a Government not yet internationally recognised, has recently given way to a more pragmatic approach allowing for direct contact. It is a pity that this pragmatism could not have been in place sooner.

— Deployment by the United Nations of air support and co-ordination of security information has been of real value. It is therefore, also, disappointing that more of this nature has not been effected and that for example UNHCR stopped the operation of its aircraft from May to September.

— Co-ordination between the United Nations agencies has not been easy. UNDP's mandate overlaps with that of UNOSOM, and is made all the more problematic by the fact that UNDP—with no office in Mogadishu—reports directly to Nairobi. All United Nations relief operations in Somalia (and in the north) are, in theory at least, co-ordinated by the office of the DHA through their representative in Mogadishu, Mr David Bassiouni. But it is not clear what executive authority, if any, he has over UN agencies and how relief work is matched with the political work of the Secretary-General's Representative, Mr Ismat Kittani (formerly Mr Sahnoun).

2.12 The United Nations record in the north illustrates the difficulties faced by the UN system: lack of clear lines of control and accountability; difficulties in working where no recognised sovereign Government exists; lack of experienced staff on the ground. It also shows that, despite the valuable work of NGOs, there is a need for a United Nations presence in such circumstances, not least in the provision of logistic support and security co-ordination.

3. Conclusions to be Drawn from United Nations Operations in Somalia

3.1 The United Nations experienced difficulty in responding to a rapidly deteriorating situation. At the beginning of 1992 they focussed their efforts on achieving a ceasefire instead of also giving priority to the moving of significant amounts of food into the country. By early February both Save the Children Fund and the International Committee of the Red Cross had already concluded that the priority need was to "flood the country with food", and that this would itself lead to an improvement in security[1]. The decision in late August to provide assistance even without the consent of the parties was an implicit recognition of the deficiencies in the earlier policy.

3.2 The absence of United Nations staff either from the country at all or, subsequently, from parts of the country resulted in an inevitable lack of local knowledge which inhibited their efforts to make sense of local circumstances and then to act upon them. This was due largely, to United Nations regulations concerning the security of their own personnel. The more risk-taking approach of the Red Cross and the NGOs seems, with hindsight, to have been more effective. If changes in UN regulations had been considered impractical then it would at least have made sense for the United Nations to have done more to avail themselves of agencies working in Somalia as partners and proxies, and put United Nations assistance through these agencies.

3.3 There appear to have been considerable delays between the visits of survey missions and the provision of assistance. One of the key differences between relief work and development work is the requirement in the former case to move very swiftly from the survey stage to action. This means that action is almost inevitably taken with what a development worker would consider inadequate information. Either the United Nations procedures (for obtaining approval for funds and then actually for their expenditure) are too slow *or* United Nations staff did not adequately perceive the need for urgent action. This is therefore either a problem of procedure or of human skills and experience or both.

3.4 There was a problem of co-ordination between United Nations agencies. The Undersecretary-General for Humanitarian Affairs has no power to enforce the co-ordination of United Nations operations, particularly because he has no financial control over the specialised agencies. It is difficult, in practice, to see how he may adequately link and co-ordinate the work of the different agencies without being given more authority. In addition, the co-ordinating role of the UN Resident Representative (again without executive authority) causes confusion when, in particular crises, the DHA deploys its own staff. This confusion was apparent to other organisations in Somalia and we have anecdotal evidence that it was confusing to UNDP staff as well.

3.5 There were continuing difficulties posed by the United Nations' desire to seek sovereign requests for their assistance. One consequence was that some $68 million of relief funds were not distributed for

[1] As reported at the time to one of the authors of this Memorandum by the Overseas Director of Save the Children Fund, and by Michael Veuthey, Head of Division of International Organisations, International Committee of the Red Cross.

months for lack of signed consent from the Somali government to its dispersal.[1] There appeared to be a lack of clarity within the United Nations as to how to manage relations with local authorities when there is either no sovereign Government, or when there is a Government (as in the north) but which is not recognised. Mr Eliasson has spoken of the advantage of leaving the issue of sovereignty and the humanitarian response in times where it is lacking as a "grey area", thus allowing in each case for United Nations diplomatic work to establish a particular *modus operandi*.[2] That the UN Undersecretary-General should express such an opinion may reflect the practical reality of the situation but is an indictment of an alarming lack of clarity in international law. We address that issue in the second part of this Memorandum. The effect of this approach on the ground is to cause uncertainty and confusion that can delay the distribution of vital relief.

3.6 Few organisations welcome public discussion of their problems. Such discussion is nevertheless an essential part of a learning process which improves its operations. In public organisations it should also form part of its accountability. Ambassador Sahnoun's public openness to criticisms of the United Nations operations—and indeed his willingness to contribute to them—were undoubtedly hard for others within the system to accept. But they did a great deal to restore much needed credibility. It is, therefore, a particularly bad sign that Ambassador Sahnoun's approach led to his resignation.

4. MOZAMBIQUE

4.1 We do not propose to deal at length with the case of Mozambique, but some reference to it may add some depth to the discussion of United Nations operations in Somalia. We deal here with the difficulties faced by the United Nations in responding to the drought in Mozambique.[3]

4.2 By the end of February 1992 all the signs of crop failure in the southern provinces of Mozambique (Sofala, Manica, Gaza, Maputo and Inhambane) had been registered and recognised by the Government and by the United Nations agencies. The early warning system established with the assistance of the United Nations—and FAO in particular—and managed by the Government had worked well, and the potential extent of emergency food requirements had been identified.[4]

4.3 From early March, United Nations agencies in Maputo began to make urgent calls upon the international community to alert it to Mozambique's needs. These calls became formalised in two separate but linked appeals in mid-May, one by the Mozambican Government and the other on behalf of the SADCC countries by the United Nations.

4.4 The early action of the United Nations in identifying a need, and then with reasonable dispatch in calling on the assistance of donors is to be commended. And indeed these actions produced positive results, with adequate consignments of emergency food a id being shipped to the ports of Maputo, Beira and Nacala.

4.5 Unfortunately action at the international level by the United Nations was not matched in efficiency by action at country level. From March the United Nations agencies in Maputo began to work on the necessary administrative and logistical details of a co-ordinated plan for the distribution of food, and its supplementation with water supply projects and, where necessary, supplementary feeding. A plan drawing together these elements was to be produced by the end of May.[5] It was naturally of considerable interest to the NGOs in Mozambique, which would then be in a position to make their own complementary dispositions. Unfortunately, such a plan, at the time of writing of this submission, has not yet been produced.

4.6 On 2 October Charles Lamouniere from the office of the DHA was despatched from Geneva "to devise a more effective response to the emergency situation and to expedite the opening of the land corridors for relief supplies".[6] Following on his visit an Interim Special Co-ordinator reporting through the DHA's office to the Secretary-General was appointed, taking over the overall responsibility from the UNDP Resident Co-ordinator.

4.7 The conflict with RENAMO added markedly to the complications of the task facing the United Nations. Indeed, it is probably true that the appointment of a Special Co-ordinator has as much to do with the United Nations' role in monitoring the demobilisation process as it has to do with dissatisfaction at progress towards planning relief operations. Nevertheless, after RENAMO and the Government

[1] *Observer*, 6 September 1992, p.2.
[2] A remark made to one of the authors of this Memorandum on February 26 1992.
[3] The account presented of Mozambique is principally drawn from the experiences there of ACTIONAID and its staff. One of the authors of this Memorandum is the Director of ACTIONAID; he visited the country from 1–11 May 1992.
[4] See, for example, the summary description of requirements included in a report by Reg Green of the Institute of Development Studies, entitled "Sound the Tocsin, Drought in South and Southern Africa 11991/3".
[5] This was confirmed by Mark Latham, WFP Representative in Maputo during the visit to Mozambique referred to in footnote 3 above.
[6] *Guardian*, 2 October 1992.

of Mozambique had agreed in mid-July to allow the passage of food to RENAMO areas there was a gap of three months before the first convoy departed on October 8. The intervening period had partly been taken up with negotiations to overcome RENAMO's insistence that all food be airlifted. It is possible to argue—with hindsight—that it would have been more effective to airlift food, even at an enhanced cost, in order to prevent people from moving to food distribution points and thus being unable to plant seeds for the next year's crop.

4.8 There is some evidence to suggest a reluctance on the part of the United Nations to use information provided by NGOs. Medecins Sans Frontieres, for example, provided the UN Resident Co-ordinator's office with details of their survey of NGOs which were working, particularly in the sectors of health, water supply and supplementary feeding. This information was provided by MSF in early September but has yet to be used or incorporated into United Nations operational intelligence.

5. Conclusions Drawn from Operations in Mozambique

5.1 The heads of the United Nations agencies in Maputo earned a great deal of respect from their efforts in drawing international attention to the situation in Mozambique. Individually, there is little doubt that they were skilled and committed officials. However, they failed to produce effective results. It is difficult to be precise about the reasons for this, as United Nations officials in Maputo have been reticent (in discussion with the NGO representatives) on this point. Yet, the delay in producing a plan, the visit of Mr Lamouniere, and the appointment of a Special Co-ordinator all suggest that the problem identified in Turkey, namely the absence of a system of control to reinforce the coordinating function of the United Nations Resident Co-ordinator, was replicated in Mozambique.

5.2 In addition, there was a failure to create an effective partnership with NGOs, particularly in relation to the acquisition, analysis and use of information on needs and the operational deployment of NGO staff. This was not due to a lack of understanding or of respect for the work of NGOs, but seems to have been more as a result of difficulties in creating a focal point for such information within the UN System.

6. Recommendations

6.1 In both cases presented—Somalia and Mozambique—we suggest there are indications that the UN System is having considerable difficulty in acting in a co-ordinated, timely and effective manner. It will always be difficult to act with expedition and without error in situations of such complexity and confusion. And it would be wrong to deduce a too easy condemnation of some of the actors. Rather one should learn from these experiences to improve future operations of the United Nations.

6.2 We *recommend* that the following issues need to be addressed:

(a) There needs to be a requirement for humanitarian response from the United Nations, rather than a discretion for this. We discuss the legal basis under the UN Charter for that requirement. The Undersecretary-General for Humanitarian Affairs should, on a regular basis, report on his record in fulfilling this requirement and this report should include reasons for inaction as well as analysis of action.

(b) It is axiomatic that effective co-ordination necessarily entails giving adequate authority to the co-ordinator. The Undersecretary-General should therefore be given the resources to enable him to carry out his co-ordination role. This should include financial control over the actions of the specialised agencies; executive authority over their operations pursuant upon a declaration of a "state of emergency" in a particular case by the Secretary-General; and financial reserves to enable the Undersecretary-General to make forward commitments on his own discretion, assessable on the member states, up to an agreed limit. It is clear, also, that prompt payment of assessed contributions by member states is a prerequisite for effective United Nations action.

(c) In preparing plans for an operational response to humanitarian crises, the United Nations, through the DHA, should take into account all assistance likely to be received whether through multilateral, bilateral or non-official sources. The Undersecretary-General would be greatly assisted in working with host Governments to dovetail this assistance if contributions to multilateral aid could be provided at an early and assured stage. The experience of the International Emergency Food Reserve (IEFR) of the FAO/World Food Programme shows that bilateral donor decisions continue to vitiate the effectiveness of the Reserve as a mechanism for early response to crisis.

(d) To reinforce the capacity of the UN System to make effective judgments, the Undersecretary-General must be entrusted with a cadre of staff, who should be trained and become experienced in the particular exigencies of emergency operations, notwithstanding that they may be deployed as between the specialised agencies; the responsibility for their rapid deployment should be at his behest and under his control.

(e) To promote and encourage the dissemination of good practice in emergency response, the Undersecretary-General should be required to review and evaluate, on a formal basis and with external assistance, all major operations in which his Office is involved, and to report the results.

(f) There is a need for more active use of the information on needs and resources generated by NGOs, and for this to be matched with information generated by the UN System and host Governments. The Undersecretary-General should be mandated to improve and, where necessary, develop such complementary early-warning systems in countries he judges to be vulnerable to crisis.

(g) The Undersecretary-General should take a primary responsibility for making effective the operational and financial links between the United Nations, NGOs and the Red Cross as well as bilateral aid agencies engaged in emergency relief. It is likely that this will be an increasingly important aspect of the international community's response. A proactive involvement by Mr Eliasson, to include investment in training, staff development as well as operational partnerships would go a long way to improving the United Nations' reputation, and its effectiveness on the ground. It may be that a future pattern of emergency response would include a co-ordinating role by the DHA with the operational work being carried out by inter-governmental and non-governmental organisations rather than by United Nations Specialised Agencies.

6.3 Many of these recommendations reflect those put forward by Sir Brian Urquhart and Erskine Childers.[1] Insofar as our proposals differ, they press the case for greater authority over the specialised agencies of the UN System than is comprehended by mere co-ordination. They also move in favour of greater public accountability of the humanitarian operations of the UN System. Finally, they suggest that the DHA take primary responsibility for relations with inter-governmental and non-governmental organisations. We have not included the Urquhart/Childers proposal that the DHA be headed by a Deputy Secretary-General rather than an Under Secretary-General, as we do not feel competent to judge upon the difference this might bring to the authority of this Office. Clearly, if it would significantly add to his authority and enable him to carry out the tasks already assigned to him, and the added responsibilities for control recommended above, then we would support such a change.

6.4 These proposals recognise the need for clarity in the respective roles of the various actors within the UN System, the importance of delegation combined with accountability, the essential requirement of staff development and the basic premise that without adequate funds *in hand* the System is unable to function.

6.5 These responsibilities can only be carried out if the Undersecretary-General is provided with the resources, and the political support, necessary for the task. Finally, the effectiveness of his operation, and of the UN response generally depends upon clarification and strengthening of the legal basis of the United Nations' right to intervene.

7. The Legal Issues

7.1 This section considers the legal role of the United Nations in providing humanitarian relief. By "humanitarian relief" is meant the provision and distribution of food, medical care and shelter to the victims of natural disasters or political emergencies, including internal conflict. Indeed the distinction between natural and man-made disasters is not absolute: for example, a government may for political reasons exacerbate a famine by impeding food distribution. Moreover, relief may be closely linked with prevention, in particular where a government is responsible for gross human rights violations that give rise to the need for humanitarian assistance. These aspects are also considered accordingly.

8. The Primacy of the United Nations

8.1 The rights and obligations of states are governed by international law. The Charter of the United Nations is "the basic legal instrument of the international community" and the principles of the Charter are regarded as generally applicable in international relations.[2]

8.2 The purposes and principles of the United Nations Organisation are set out in Articles 1 and 2 of the Charter. Article 2(1) states that the Organisation is based on "the sovereign equality of all its Members." Articles 2(4) and (7) are central to the concerns addressed by this Memorandum:

> "(4) All Members shall refrain in their international relations from the threat or use of force against the territorial integrity or political independence of any State, or in any other manner inconsistent with the Purposes of the United Nations.
>
> "(7) Nothing contained in the present Charter shall authorise the United Nations to intervene in matters which are essentially within the domestic jurisdiction of any State or shall require the

[1] "Towards a More Effective United Nations" by Brian Urquhart & Erskine Childers, Development Dialogue 1991:1–2.

[2] R. Jennings and A. Watts (eds) *Oppenheim's International Law* (9th ed.) 1992, p.31.

Members to submit such matters to settlement under the present Charter; but this principle shall not prejudice the application of enforcement measures under Chapter VII."[1]

8.3 At the same time, Article 1 expresses, as one of the purposes of the United Nations, the achievement of international co-operation in solving international problems of a humanitarian character and in promoting respect for human rights. This is reiterated in Articles 55(c) and 56:

> "55. ... the United Nations shall promote ..... universal respect for, and observance of, human rights and fundamental freedoms without distinction as to race, sex, language, or religion."
>
> "56. All Members pledge themselves to take joint and separate action in co-operation with the Organisation for the achievement of the purposes set forth in Article 55."

8.4 The reference to "domestic jurisdiction" in Article 2(7) has not precluded the United Nations from considering human rights abuses within Member States. The adoption of the Universal Declaration of Human Rights (a resolution of the General Assembly in 1948), the Genocide Convention (1948) and the two International Covenants on Human Rights (1966; in force 1976) has demonstrated that violation of human rights is not, under international law, a matter solely within a state's domestic jurisdiction. The practice of the United Nations has involved consideration of denial of human rights, racial discrimination, apartheid and internal strife in such countries as the Congo, Rhodesia, South Africa and Lebanon. The International Court of Justice has stated that in contemporary international law certain obligations, including the prohibition of genocide and "the principles and rules concerning the basic rights of the human person" are obligations owed to the international community as a whole.[2]

9. THE DOCTRINE OF HUMANITARIAN INTERVENTION

9.1 By the end of the 19th century, international law had broadly accepted a doctrine of humanitarian intervention, whereby one or more states had the right forcibly to intervene on the territory of another state to curb widespread abuse of human rights. Indeed, support for such a limit to state sovereignty can be found in the earliest writings on international law.[3] In the course of the 19th century, the Great Powers threatened or carried out intervention in a number of cases on the stated grounds of protecting religious or ethnic minorities facing massacre or brutal repression. Many of these cases concerned the conduct of the Ottoman Turks, in Greece (1827–30); Crete (1866), and Bosnia Herzegovina and Bulgaria (1876). In 1860, after the massacre of thousands of Christians in Syria, France was expressly authorised by a protocol between the Great Powers to intervene to halt the bloodshed and 6,000 French troops landed in Syria for this purpose.[4] Based on such precedents, Judge Sir Hersch Lauterpacht wrote in his authoritative edition of *Oppenheim's International Law*:[5]

> "There is general agreement that, by virtue of its personal and territorial supremacy, a State can treat its nationals according to discretion. But there is a substantial body of opinion and of practice in support of the view that there are limits to that discretion and that when a State renders itself guilty of cruelties against and persecution of its nationals in such a way as to deny their fundamental rights and to shock the conscience of mankind, intervention in the interest of humanity is legally permissible."

9.2 However, even as regards the period before World War I, the existence of a right of humanitarian intervention was not universally accepted. Since the establishment of the United Nations, there has been much argument among jurists as to whether any such right survived the prohibition on the use of force in Article 2(4) of the Charter. Evidence of a persisting right of humanitarian intervention has been claimed on the basis of such incidents as the rescue of 2,000 foreign hostages of many nationalities from the Congo in 1964 (an action carried out by Belgian troops, in US planes, using British bases); the invasion of East Pakistan by India in 1971 following mass killings and rape of East Bengalis by the Pakistani army; and the invasion of Uganda by Tanzanian troops in 1979 supporting Ugandan exiles to overthrow Idi Amin, who was responsible for large scale executions of Ugandan citizens. But significantly, in none of these cases did the intervening states seek to justify their action on the basis of a right of humanitarian intervention. Instead, they asserted the legality of their action on the right of self-defence which is expressly reserved under Article 51 of the Charter and which is claimed to cover the rescue of nationals

---

[1] Chapter VII concerns action by the Security Council with respect to threats to the peace and acts of aggression. See para 11.4 below.

[2] The Barcelona Traction Case [1970] ICJ Rep. 3, paras.33–34; and see Rodley, "Human Rights and Humanitarian Intervention: The Case Law of the World Court" (1989) 38 *ICLQ* 321 (discussing also the Nicaragua Case).

[3] E.g. Grotius, the "father" of international law, wrote: "Certainly it is undoubted that ever since civil societies were formed, the ruler of each claimed some especial right over his own subjects ... [But] ... if a tyrant ... practices attrocities towards his subjects, which no just man can approve, the right of human social connexion is not cut off in such case." Qu. in Fonteyne, "The Customary International Law Doctrine of Humanitarian Intervention: Its Current Validity under the UN Charter" (1974) 4 *Ca.W.Int.L.J.* 203, 214.

[4] The various incidents are described in Fonteyne, loc.cit.; and Franck and Rodley, "After Bangladesh: The Law of Humanitarian Intervention by Military Force" (1973) 67 *Am.J.Int.L.* 276.

[5] 8th ed., 1955 p. 312. The new 9th (1992) edition is more qualified as regards unilateral intervention in the light of recent practice but recognises a right of collective intervention: at pp.442–44.

of the intervening state.[1] It is notable that recently Mr Douglas Hurd claimed that the imposition by the UK, US and France of a "no-fly zone" to protect the Marsh Arabs in southern Iraq was justified not by a UN Resolution but on the principle of "extreme humanitarian need" under international law.[2] But across the whole spectrum of precedents from the early 19th to the late 20th centuries, many of the incidents of unilateral or multilateral intervention can be criticised as based on political motives of self interest rather than purely humanitarian objectives.[3] Any such right of intervention carries the danger of the wolf in Good Samaritan's clothing.

9.3 Those who claimed that the right survived in the post-Charter period largely did so on the grounds that the United Nations showed itself paralysed even in extreme humanitarian crises. The genocide by the Khmer Rouge of between one and three million people in Kampuchea in the mid-1970s, the massacre of hundreds of thousands of Ibos in Nigeria in 1968, and the famine that claimed about a million lives in Ethiopia in 1984–86 (to which the Mengistu regime substantially contributed) were a powerful indictment of inaction by the United Nations.[4] However, there had also been many instances before the creation of the United Nations when states failed to intervene to prevent massive human rights violations: the Armenian massacres of 1914–19 are perhaps the most striking of many examples. The preponderant opinion has been that Article 2(4) of the Charter imposes an absolute prohibition on the unilateral use of force, save in the particular case of self-defence and subject, perhaps, to recognised grounds of mitigation if such intervention is directed at the relief of humanitarian need.[5] Observations in the International Court's judgment in the *Nicaragua* case provide support to that view.[6]

9.4 This does not mean that international law is insensitive to large-scale human suffering, or subordinates it to state sovereignty. The substantial development of international human rights law shows the opposite. It means rather that an effective mechanism for intervention for humanitarian purposes must be developed within the framework of the United Nations. That intervention can take various forms. It may be by the United Nations directly; by a Member State or States acting under UN authority; by a regional organisation reporting to the United Nations; or by non-governmental humanitarian organisations with UN protection.

10. The United Nations and Humaritarian Relief

10.1 The collective interventions undertaken by the United Nations were largely to carry out a peace-keeping role in situations of armed conflict.[7] In Korea, and now the Gulf crisis, the United Nations went further and authorised intervention to repel invasion of an independent State. But the United Nations has been notably cautious as regards the development of any right to provide humanitarian relief and assistance. In 1988 and 1990, largely on the initiative of France, this issue was addressed in resolutions of the General Assembly. Resolution 43/131 of 8 December 1988 on "Humanitarian assistance to victims of natural disasters and similar emergency situations" stressed the importance of humanitarian relief and the role of inter-governmental and non-governmental organisations working with humanitarian motives. Resolution 45/100 of 14 December 1990 went slightly further in its emphasis on access for relief supplies, including the establishment of relief corridors. But those Resolutions did not expressly cover non-natural (that is political) disasters. And they reaffirmed the sovereignty of the States affected and "their primary role in the initiation, organisation, co-ordination and implementation of humanitarian assistance within their respective territories."

10.2 Despite their incantation of strong concern about the victims of disasters and the need for rapid relief, the Resolutions fall far short of establishing any right to provide relief, the "*droit d'ingerence*" for which some French campaigners and scholars had championed.[8] It may be that the reference to "primary role" leaves scope for the argument that when the affected state is unable to carry out that task (for example because of lack of resources or political division) inter-governmental organisations and NGOs have a right to step in to fill the void. But that was left unclear and the weight of the text is against any right to intervene without the consent of the affected states. These Resolutions served to bring the issue

[1] Whether that right allows armed intervention in another state for the rescue of nationals of the intervening state is itself a matter of controversy that need not be discussed here.

[2] BBC Radio 4, "Today" programme, 19 August 1992. President Bush justified the action on the basis of SC Res.688: see below.

[3] See for example Franck and Rodley, *loc.cit.*

[4] Reisman, "Humanitarian Intervention to Protect the Ibos" [a petition to the United Nations] in R.Lillich (ed.) *Humanitarian Intervention and the United Nations,* 1973; Bazyler, "Reexamining the Doctrine of Humanitarian Intervention in Light of the Atrocities in Kampuchea and Ethiopia" (1987) 23 *Stan.J.Int.L.* 547.

[5] Proponents of a continuing right to humanitarian intervention were largely American scholars: see in general R. Lillich, *op.cit.* Their views did not command international consensus, either among jurists or at the United Nations: see Brownlie, "Thoughts on Kind-Hearted Gunmen", *ibid.* at 139; Akehurst, "Humanitarian Intervention" in H. Bull (ed.) *Intervention in World Politics* (1984) at 95. For a summary, see Beyerlin, "Humanitarian Intervention" in R. Bernhardt (ed.) *Encyclopaedia of Public International Law*, Inst. 13 (1982).

[6] *Case Concerning Military and Paramilitary Activities in and against Nicaragua, Merits* [1986] ICJ Rep. 14.

[7] See Luard, "Collective Intervention" in H. Bull, *op.cit.*

[8] This literally translates as a "right to interfere", but is effectively used to mean a right to intervene [on humanitarian grounds]. See Bettati, "Un Droit d'Ingerence?' (1991) 95 *Rev.Gen.Dr.Int.Pub.* 639. He notes that the original proposal covered all political disasters but this was amended as a compromise to obtain acceptance of the Resolution.

of a general "right to humanitarian assistance" onto the United Nations agenda; but they also demonstrated how much further it needed to be developed.

10.3 Security Council Resolution 688 of 5 April 1991 regarding the Iraqi civilian population was therefore a major departure. Although it reiterated the almost ritual reference to states' right of sovereignty, it *insisted* that Iraq allow "immediate access by international humanitarian organisations to all those in need of assistance in all parts of Iraq" (para. 3). And it requested the Secretary-General to "use all resources at his disposal" to address the critical needs of the refugees (para. 5) and *demanded* that Iraq co-operate (para. 7). It was on the basis of this Resolution that US, British and French troops were later deployed to ensure the effectiveness of the "safe havens" created for the Kurds and to protect the distribution of relief supplies.

10.4 In terms of the United Nations' attitude to a right of humanitarian intervention, SC Resolution 688 is undoubtedly of great significance. But is it to be a precedent for the future or the exception that proves the rule? China, which has consistently objected to a United Nations right to intervene in the affairs of Member States on human rights or humanitarian grounds, abstained (along with India) and of course has a right of veto. Cuba, Yemen and Zimbabwe voted against. The Resolution and relief action that followed can be seen as driven by wholly unusual circumstances in that the plight of the Kurds in northern Iraq was in part the aftermath of the military operation against Saddam Hussein's regime by, in particular, the United States, Britain and France, and that President Bush had arguably encouraged the Kurds to rebel. Therefore it does not necessarily signal a redefinition of the notion of sovereignty to take account of a right to bring humanitarian relief.[1] Two subsequent developments give little cause for optimism.

(a) General Assembly Res. 46/182

10.5 This Resolution, adopted on 19 December 1991, is entitled "Strengthening of the co-ordination of humanitarian emergency assistance of the United Nations". It was under the ambit of this Resolution that the post of a UN Emergency Relief Co-ordinator, restyled as Undersecretary-General for Humanitarian Affairs was established. That was undoubtedly a significant advance, as discussed in the first part of this Memorandum. However the wording of the provisions concerning intervention was the subject of intense negotiation.[2] In the final text, the General Assembly came out firmly against a right of non-consensual intervention. The "Guiding Principles" in the annex to the Resolution accordingly state, in paragraph 3:

> "The sovereignty, territorial integrity and national unity of States must be fully respected in accordance with the Charter of the United Nations. In this context, humanitarian assistance should be provided with the consent of the affected country and in principle on the basis of an appeal by the affected country."

The ambiguity in the final phrase gives perhaps some modest opportunity for development.

(b) Security Council Res. 733 (Somalia)

10.6 The displacement of population and wholesale famine in Somalia, while the country is devastated by civil war and lawful governmental authority disintegrates, represents a humanitarian disaster of a massive scale. Unless adequate relief is provided and effectively distributed there will be a considerable increase in the number of avoidable deaths. However, armed gangs and members of both government and rebel forces have frustrated efforts at distribution and members of NGOs working on humanitarian relief have been killed. The emergence of this catastrophe has been clear to NGOs and observers since late 1991 (see para. 2.3 above). On 23 January 1992 the Security Council adopted Resolution 733. This imposed an arms embargo on Somalia (para. 5) and called for a cease-fire (para. 4). But as regards the humanitarian assistance that was so desperately needed, the Resolution requested "the Secretary-General to undertake the necessary actions to increase humanitarian assistance" (para. 2) and merely asked that a commitment be sought from the parties to the conflict to permit the distribution of humanitarian assistance (para. 3); and urged that they should ensure the safety of personnel providing such assistance (para. 8). The contrast with SC Resolution 688 on Iraq is striking, particularly when regard is paid to the coded nuances embedded in the wording of United Nation Resolutions. It was not until 24 April 1992 that the Security Council finally decided, by Resolution 751, to establish a UN operation in Somalia and agreed in principle to the deployment of a security force. Moreover, the situation in Somalia was considered by the Security Council at the request of what was left of the Somali government. If no such request had been forthcoming, it seems unlikely that even this action would have been taken. The practical effect could be seen both in the inadequacy of the United Nations relief effort, and in the delay in the distribution of relief funds (see para 3.5 above).

---

[1] See Mayall, "Non-intervention, self-determination and the 'new world order' " (1991) 67 *Int. Affairs* 421.

[2] The GA proceedings are described and analysed in Scheffer, "Towards a Modern Doctrine of Humanitarian Intervention", (1992) *U.Toledo L.Rev.* 253, 280–83.

11. An Agenda for the Future

Peaceable Intervention

11.1 If consent from the affected state is a requirement for the provision of humanitarian relief, that requirement should be satisfied, where the recognised government is not in control of certain areas, by consent from the power in effective control of the area where relief is to be distributed. That is the position under the common Article 3 of the four Geneva Conventions that govern the activity of the Red Cross and "impartial humanitarian bod(ies)" in cases of armed conflict.[1] It should apply to humanitarian relief by the United Nations. It is of importance because many of the humanitarian disasters in the contemporary world occur in circumstances of internal conflict. Recognition of this principle would mean that a government would not have the opportunity to withhold consent to the distribution of relief to areas in rebel hands; and that distribution of supplies to those areas would not be seen as violation of the sovereignty of the recognised government.

11.2 However, in the last resort, consent to humanitarian relief should not be necessary. The proper approach should be to focus on the need of the population: it is their right to receive humanitarian assistance that is critical, not a right of any outside organisation, state or agency to provide it. That right is a concomitant of the rights enshrined in the Universal Declaration of Human Rights: the rights to life and to a standard of living adequate for food, clothing, housing and medical care.[2] The primary obligation to provide such assistance indeed rests on the effective authority of the territory concerned. But if that authority is unable or unwilling to do so, only outside agencies can satisfy the need. Often the government or authority will consent to, or indeed request, such assistance. But where it does not, Peaceable intervention on humanitarian grounds should not be regarded as an infringement of sovereignty. If the government or effective authority acquiesces in the provision of assistance, there should be no problem. But if it expressly objects, the United Nations, through the Security Council, should be able to authorise the provision and distribution of relief.

Forcible Intervention

11.3 This Memorandum has concentrated on the problem of humanitarian relief and the position regarding intervention by force was described because it forms an essential part of the development of international law in this area. However, in the practical concerns of relief agencies, the two are not discrete subjects. NGOs and aid workers sometimes require personal protection; food and medical supplies may need to be guarded. Moreover, large-scale human rights violations and the need for humanitarian relief are often connected. The former are frequently the result of conduct or policies pursued by the government or effective power in the affected territory. And the government may seek to prevent distribution of food to certain parts of the country as deliberate policy in periods of internal conflict: this occurred in Ethiopia in 1984–86, and Sudan in 1986–88.

11.4 As explained above, the preferred view is that unilateral humanitarian intervention, in the sense of intervention by one state by force to curb human rights abuses in another state, was prohibited under the Charter. The consequence should be not that the right to intervene on humanitarian grounds, previously recognised by customary international law, was abolished altogether but that it is vested in the United Nations. The United Nations has so far largely failed to assume this role, hampered by a broad concept of unqualified sovereignty. The same basis for United Nations intervention to curb extreme human rights violations applies to intervention to ensure the provision of humanitarian assistance. But if this is a task for the United Nations, where is the necessary authority found in the Charter? The only basis for enforcement measures is in Chapter VII of the Charter, which concerns "Action with Respect to Threats to Peace, Breaches of the Peace, and Acts of Aggression." It is this Chapter which is expressly reserved in the "domestic jurisdiction provision under Article 2(7): see para. 8.2 above. The concept of a "threat to international peace and security", within the terms of Chapter VII, has been used elastically in the past to justify the imposition of sanctions against Rhodesia and South Africa.[3] SC Resolutions 688 and 733 significantly include a finding of such a threat in the situations in Iraq and Somalia. Indeed, large-scale human rights abuses and extreme humanitarian need can properly be regarded as a threat to international peace and security. They lead to massive refugee problems; threaten to involve neighbouring states; and can create substantial economic distortion in the development of the region.

11.5 Accordingly, what is needed is to develop objective criteria for the exercise of such enforcement measures to ensure that the strictly humanitarian purpose is preserved. That is particularly important in view of the suspicion of any form of intervention felt by Third World countries, with their colonial heritage, as evidenced in the debate over GA Resolution 46/182. Paradoxically, the requirement is all the greater since the end of the Cold War, which has brought a shift in power to the United States within the

---

[1] Article 3 is exceptional in the Geneva Conventions (1949) in its application to armed conflict not of an international character.

[2] Arts. 3 and 25. See also the International Covenants on Civil and political Rights; and on Economic, Social and Cultural Rights (1966, in force 1976).

[3] See Fifoot, "Functions and powers, and interventions: UN action in respect of human rights and humanitarian intervention" in N Rodley (ed.) *To Loose the Bands of Wickedness* (1992)

United Nations. Previously the United Nations was often stunted in its activity by the East-West confrontation. Now the Security Council could become an instrument to further the policies of the permanent members, and in particular the United States, and thereby lose the respect of the Third World.

11.6 Articulation of those requirements can effectively draw on the criteria developed by jurists to control and define the unilateral right of humanitarian intervention.[1] Four considerations should apply where military force is required for non-consensual intervention:

(a) There should be an immediate and widespread threat to human life or other fundamental human rights. It should not matter whether that danger arises through massacre, starvation, disease or extreme brutality. The concept of fundamental human rights can be justified, for example, by reference to the Genocide Convention (1948) and common article 3 of the Geneva Conventions (1949).

(b) Whenever practicable, attempts should first be made to persuade the government or effective power to halt its abuses or guarantee the safety of humanitarian relief. Only if the government or power is unable or unwilling to take the necessary steps or to accept the offer of outside assistance should non-consensual intervention be undertaken. The proviso of practicability has regard to the circumstance where there may be no effective authority. This reflects the established international law principle of exhaustion of remedies.

(c) The scale and duration of the intervention should be limited to the achievement of the humanitarian purpose. Once the humanitarian purpose is achieved, the intervening forces should withdraw. This draws on the principle of proportionality, well-recognised in international law.

(d) The activities should regularly be reported to the UN Secretary-General or his appointed official for reference to the Security Council. When the intervention is carried out by forces under UN command, that requirement is superfluous. It is relevant where forces of Member States carry out the intervention under UN authority, as with the "safe havens" in northern Iraq, or where a regional organization carries out collective intervention, such as ECOWAS in Liberia.

11.7 By the recognition of such criteria the United Nations would have a basis to determine that intervention is appropriate and an affected state would have a basis for challenge to intervention as unlawful. Such a challenge is capable of adjudication by the International Court of Justice, which can order provisional measures to preserve a state's rights pending a final judgement.[2] The Court can, where necessary, give such a decision quickly and its new President, Sir Robert Jennings, recently expressed the hope that the Court would become more directly involved in the central functions of United Nations, "working in harness" with the political organs as international law is increasingly relevant to many situations.[3] The procedural mechanisms of the United Nations also need development, for example to enable monitoring by UN officials of potential trouble-spots so that preventative action can be taken and made effective before a crisis turns into a catastrophe.

Development of the United Nations and International Law

11.8 Not all the principles set out above can be regarded as presently accepted, so as to form part of customary international law. But international law is not frozen, but develops through the practice of nations accepted as lawful, the recognition given to general principles of law found in developed legal systems and the writings of jurists that command particular respect. The United Nations provides its Member States with the opportunity to develop international law through collective decision and conduct. The Charter is not a statute of precisely specified rules and obligations but expresses more general principles and competing values. It is, as one distinguished commentator has observed, "like every constitutional instrument, continuously interpreted, moulded and adapted to meet the interests of the parties"[4]. The issues addressed in this Memorandum sometimes appear to require a balance between sovereignty and the international obligations to uphold human rights. But that is a false antithesis. In the interdependent world of the end of the 20th century, sovereign identity within the community of nations involves not only accountability for human rights violations but acceptance of the community's right to enforce this obligation. The development and furtherance of that concept lies at the heart of the new agenda of the United Nations in the world after the Cold War.

11.9 The need to develop the United Nations and enhance its effectiveness has been widely acknowledged and the end of the Cold War presents a particular opportunity to achieve that end. There have been some encouraging recent signs of a willingness to confront the challenge. At the G–7 Economic Summit in London on 16 July 1991, the leaders of the world's most powerful industrialized nations called

[1] See especially Lillich, "Forcible Self-Help by States to Protect Human Rights" (1967) 53 *Iowa L. Rev.* 325; Moore, "The Control of Foreign Intervention in Internal Conflict", (1969) 9 *Vga.J.Int.L.* 205; Bazyler, *loc.cit.*

[2] Statute of the International Court of Justice, Art.41

[3] Address to the General Assembly by Sir Robert Jennings on the Report of the International Court of Justice (1991), repr. in (1992) 86 *Am.J.Int.L.*249.

[4] O. Schachter, *International Law in Theory and Practice* (1991) pp.118–19. Prof. Schachter was for many years legal adviser to the UN Secretary-General.

for improvement in the way the resources of the United Nations and support from donor countries and NGOs can be mobilized to meet urgent humanitarian crises. Noting the exceptional action taken following SC Resolution 688, they declared:

> "We urge the UN and its affiliated agencies to be ready to consider similar action in the future if the circumstances require it. The international community cannot stand idly by in cases where widespread human suffering from famine, war, oppression, refugee flows, disease or flood reaches urgent and overwhelming proportions."[1]

The statement at the end of the Summit Meeting of Heads of State and Government of the members of the Security Council on 31 January 1992 noted the momentous changes taking place and continued:[2]

> "The international community ... faces new challenges in the search for peace. All Member States expect the United Nations to play a central role at this crucial stage. The members of the Council stress the importance of strengthening and improving the United Nations to increase its effectiveness. They are determined to assume fully their responsibilities within the United Nations Organization within the framework of the Charter.
>
> "The absence of war and military conflicts amongst States does not in itself ensure international peace and security. The non-military sources of instability in the economic, social, humanitarian and ecological fields have become threats to peace and security. The United Nations membership as a whole, working through the appropriate bodies, needs to give the highest priority to the solution of these matters."

And the outgoing UN Secretary-General, J Perez de Cuéllar, speaking at the University of Bordeaux on 22 April 1991, stressed the need to develop, by common consent, international law that is the foundation of the United Nations to make it more effective in international relations. Referring explicitly to the question of a right of intervention, he asked:[3]

> "Has not a balance been established between the right of States, as confirmed by the Charter, and the right of the individual, as confirmed by the Universal Declaration of Human Rights? We are clearly witnessing what is probably an irresistible shift in public attitudes towards the belief that the defence of the oppressed in the name of morality should prevail over frontiers and legal documents.
>
> "This shift is of the utmost importance ... We must now ponder this issue in a manner that is at once prudent and bold. In a prudent manner, because the principles of sovereignty cannot be radically challenged without international chaos quickly ensuing. In a bold manner, because we have probably reached a stage in the ethical and psychological evolution of Western civilisation in which the massive and deliberate violation of human rights will no longer be tolerated."

12. Summary

12.1 There is an urgent need for effective recognition and exercise of the right to humanitarian relief within the terms of the UN Charter. It should form part of the principles of international peace and collective security, and the respect for basic human rights, that are fundamental to the Charter. Before the establishment of the United Nations, a right of humanitarian intervention by one or several states in cases of extreme human need was claimed and broadly accepted under international law. That right should be regarded as subsumed within, and not extinguished by, the UN Charter. Although exercise of that right through the United Nations was largely stifled during the Cold War, the United Nations has now entered a new era when it can, and should, fulfil that role. In this regard, the establishment of "safe havens" for the Kurds in northern Iraq and the terms of Security Council Resolution 688 form an important precedent.

12.2 The United Nations has failed adequately to address the problem of lack of consent by the affected state within whose borders the need for relief arises. The right of victims to receive humanitarian relief from neutral, non-governmental agencies, and the corresponding duty of states to grant access, needs to be recognised. Criteria for humanitarian intervention by the United Nations, whether by forces under its command or authority granted to member states, need to be developed, lest the United Nations be perceived, in particular by the less developed states, to be acting in the interests of the powers dominant in the Security Council and not on the basis of the common interest of the international community. These objectives can be achieved within the existing Charter but they require a strengthening of the United Nations and refinement of international law and state practice. In circumstances of extreme humanitarian need or gross violations of fundamental human rights, the sovereignty of an individual state must yield to the state's obligation to the international community.

---

1 Qu. in *Oppenheim's International Law* (9th ed. 1992) p.442 n.18.

2 Security Council Summit Statement Concerning the Council's Responsibility in the Maintenance of International Peace and Security, (1992) 31 ILM 758.

3 Address of J Perez de Cuéller at the University of Bordeaux on 22 April 1991, UN Press Release SG/SM/4560.

13. Conclusions

13.1 The two sections of this Memorandum have discussed separate but ultimately related issues. The first section has identified, through two examples, particular problems within the structure of the United Nations in providing timely and effective assistance. We have deliberately kept separate, and thus within the two sections, our recommendations on steps that might be taken. The second has argued that there is scope for greater clarity, and indeed for an advance in thinking, on the legal aspects relating to the rights and responsibilities of the United Nations in providing humanitarian relief in circumstances where a sovereign request for assistance is not, for a number of reasons, forthcoming.

13.2 The assumption which underlies our approach throughout this submission is a desire to improve and extend the capacity of the United Nations to provide humanitarian assistance. The organisation has great expectations laid upon it. If we are to avoid the adverse and destructive impact which would inevitably ensue if the United Nations were to fail to meet these new challenges, then we must give it the necessary resources, legitamacy and mandate. The United Nations represents our best hopes for the future; we must not let it down.

APPENDIX 10

Memorandum by Christian Aid

Introduction

1. First of all, the Committee's decision to examine the United Nations and the United Kingdom's role within it is very appropriate at this time. New responsibilities are being accepted by the United Nations and it is more than ever important that it should conduct its political and humanitarian activities in a manner which inspires trust, not only in its efficiency, but in the Organisation's capacity to represent the international community as a whole.

2. Christian Aid works in a number of areas which the Committee may examine in the course of its work. They include Somalia, Iraq, Sudan, Eritrea, Cambodia, Central America, Mozambique, Angola. As you may be aware, Christian Aid does not employ British or expatriate staff abroad and works instead through local organisations and churches. Our perceptions of the work of United Nations' agencies therefore reflects the experience of our partners as well as our own.

3. If the Committee would like to consult us about our experience of United Nations' operations in any of the above countries (or others in which we have a programme) we would be happy to provide such information. Our overall view is that it is difficult to generalise on the basis of particular country experiences, because these so frequently have exceptional characteristics. It is very difficult, for example, to compare the situations in Somalia, Iraq and Cambodia. For this reason, we feel it may be more helpful to respond in greater detail when the Committee has set its working agenda.

General Concerns

4. We share a number of the concerns that will have been raised by other development agencies in their submissions to the Committee. We believe that:

— ways must be found to deliver aid to populations that are not protected by their own governments;

— the existing early-warning and response system should be implemented effectively so that aid can be delivered where it is needed and in time—thereby saving many lives and very large sums of money;

— it will be helpful to improve co-ordination of the work of the United Nations' humanitarian agencies;

— some agencies need to be reformed, so that they will deliver their services less expensively, more professionally, and in ways that are more respectful of local conditions and indigenous organisations;

— there is an urgent need, already recognised by the outgoing Secretary-General, to review the financing of United Nations' activities, including the funding of its humanitarian operations, because the present arrangements are insecure and insufficient, and tend to multiply inefficiencies. If the United Nations is to fulfil its essential functions, as defined by Dr Boutros Boutros-Ghali, it must be funded adequately and reliably.

Accountability

5. We would like to use this opportunity to raise broader issues of public accountability, which are of special concern to some of our partners in countries of the South. This matter is addressed by Dr

Boutros Boutros-Ghali in his *Agenda for Peace*, where he discusses the importance of democracy. We do not believe that a reformed United Nations will fulfil its mandate unless it is better able to represent the world's people, however indirectly. If some present trends continue, we believe that confidence and trust in the United Nations will continue to evaporate in many parts of the South.

6. The reform process initiated by the Secretary-General has extended the peacekeeping role of the United Nations and has rationalised, to increase their efficiency, the structures of its social and economic organisations. The first process has reinforced and extended the authority of the Security Council. The second has reduced the autonomy (and power) of the United Nations' economic and social organisations. We do not comment on the utility of these reforms, but note that their political effect is to increase those instruments of the United Nations where the influence of the industrial powers is greatest, while reducing the power of those which are of the most direct service to the majority of the world's (poorer) States.

7. Though the United Nations' power to intervene in relation to peace-keeping has been reinforced, in practice key Security Council Members (including the United Kingdom) have been unwilling to renounce operational control over their forces to the Secretary General. There have continued to be delays, too, in funding such operations. Once again, we are not in a position to judge the technical merits of these decisions, but we note that the political effect is to maintain or increase the independent power of Permanent Members of the Security Council (and the major powers) in relation to the Secretary General—whose powers have historically been weak.

8. While the powers of the Security Council have been augmented, those of the General Assembly have not. This has further reduced the accountability of the Security Council—and of the permanent Members who dominate its deliberations—to the General Assembly and to the international community. There is a "democratic deficit" at the heart of the UN system which the current reform process, and the new demands placed upon the United Nations, are widening. More and more, our partners in the South are asking whether the United Nations represents the international community of nations or the Great Powers.

9. The primacy accorded by the United Nations to the nation State, which is apparently re-affirmed by *Agenda for Peace*, compounds these problems of accountability whenever a Government which is the subject of United Nations' action does not represent its people, and whenever United Nations intervention also reflects the interests of the Permanent Members of the Security Council. It is at present almost impossible for the United Nations to take adequate formal account of points of view that are not represented by States. This does not reflect the pluralist character of modern societies, a fact recognised both by the Secretary General (who speaks of a multi-polar world) and by OECD governments, which have emphasised the importance of civil institutions and pluralist democracy in relation to good government.

10. This imbalance is reflected in other ways. One function of the United Nations is to be the ultimate arbiter and mediator in world affairs. This role requires punctilious neutrality and is personified by the Secretary General who is a servant of the international community. At the same time, the United Nations is a forum of nations, in which governments regulate their relations in terms of self-interest. These are two different functions, which reflect the relationship between law and power: on one hand, the universal principles of the Charter and on the other the interactions of realpolitik. Both probably play a necessary role, but we fear that the universal principles of the Charter are at present under-represented in relation to the exercise of power by governments.

11. In short, a balance should be restored between the United Nations' role as a supreme representative of the world's peoples and its role as an international instrument for the world's States. We do not claim to know exactly how this balance should be restored, but unless the force of international law is seen to be exercised neutrally and to be an adequate counterweight to the interests of governments within the United Nations system, the Organisation's credibility will decline. This would have serious implications in view of the very important tasks which the United Nations must address—ranging from peace-keeping and mediation to action on the environment, drugs and world poverty.

12. Among the issues that should be addressed, we suggest that:

- Operations of United Nations organisations should become more accountable at all levels.
- At local level, one step would be to introduce independent evaluation of United Nations projects.
- At international level, steps should be taken to ensure that the Security Council is accountable to international opinion. We believe it will not be sufficient merely to add new members to the Council, though the removal of the veto might help. The Security Council's relations with the General Assembly, and also perhaps with the Secretary General, need review.
- The contribution of independent opinion to the United Nations should be enlarged. This may involve strengthening the influence of bodies of experts, such as the Human Rights Committee; and multiplying the opportunities for UN bodies to take evidence from non-official organisa-

tions (on the model of the Decolonisation Committee and the Human Rights Commission Hearings).

— Financing of the United Nations, and its operational activities, should be placed on an orderly footing. Without denying the reasonable rights of donors to proper accountability, steps should be taken to distance the financing process from decision-making in the United Nations, so that the principal donors are not seen to exercise undue political leverage on the operations of the United Nations because of their wealth.

— We welcome the appointment of a Co-ordinator for Humanitarian Affairs. At local and at operational level, we hope that UN institutions will see the value of co-operating closely with non-governmental bodies in their peace-keeping and reconciliation activities as well as in their humanitarian and development programmes. The latter are vital elements of the United Nations' overall function. They need to be given adequate recognition and financial support by the international community if we are to deal with the global problems that face us.

CONCLUSION

We would not wish to give the impression that we are over-critical of the United Nations. It operates frequently in very difficult circumstances; its humanitarian assistance saves millions of lives; its diplomacy has protected millions from the threat of war. The quality of performance is uneven, however, and reform is necessary. The primary responsibility for setting the United Nations on a stable footing for the 21st century lies with the industrialised powers. They have a twin responsibility which they alone can fulfil: to finance the United Nations adequately so that it can carry out the tasks entrusted to it; and to share power within the United Nations in ways that ensure that it is representative of and accountable to world opinion. We recognise the difficulty of this task, which will require considerable wisdom and tolerance from governments. We believe it is essential to the credibility and effectiveness of the United Nations and other international institutions.

APPENDIX 11

Memorandum by Dr David Norris, Department of Slavonic Studies, Nottingham University

EC-UN OPERATIONS IN FORMER YUGOSLAVIA

Two broad areas for consideration are outlined below regarding EC-UN operations in former Yugoslavia. The first concerns the situation in Bosnia, and the second concerns the long-term objective of stability in the region.

BOSNIA

Liaison and communication:

1. Distribution of humanitarian aid is hampered by difficult terrain and continual danger at the front line. It appears impossible to gain access via main roads for convoys. All warring sides wish to involve EC–UN forces on their side and are capable of firing on them to provoke their involvement.

2. Commanders on the ground sometimes seem to have problems in comprehending the complexity of the divisions and fragile alliances between the warring sides. Language barriers and cultural differences also make communication more difficult.

3. Practical problems of liaison and communication could receive more attention assuming that the operations will continue for some time to come.

Refugee crisis:

4. In addition to the use of convoys to protect humanitarian aid EC-UN operations have considered problems of civilians caught up in the fighting. They have failed to get their member states to agree a co-ordinated approach to the refugee crisis. A variety of options are available:

(a) extra finance for Croatia and Slovenia to take more refugees

(b) the creation of safe havens within Bosnia

(c) a quota system for the West to distribute the refugee burden abroad.

5. The options do not preclude each other. Issues of principle under discussion at the moment which reject any attempt to deal with the crisis in a manner which might appear to complete policies of ethnic cleansing have to be balanced against the demand to save civilian lives.

6. A co-ordinated and orderly movement of refugees to safety is preferable to the present situation. Many civilians are moving themselves without informing the authorities. Such independent actions add to the difficulty of ever re-establishing civilians back in their home areas. Co-ordinated movement of refugees is a more sensible way of controlling numbers and destination points in order to return refugees home following hostilities. There is no evidence that such refugees are economic migrants.

Military intervention:

7. The sphere of EC-UN operations is limited to avoid military intervention. It is not obvious that military intervention in Bosnia would accomplish any immediate aims to stop the war or stop policies of ethnic cleansing.

8. There is no long term advantage to be gained from changing this policy. The military option linked to handing administration over to Bosnian authorities would imply support for one or other of the warring parties. However, not one of the Bosnian leaders has shown any reason to be entrusted to work for long term stability above the narrow interests of his own national group.

9. The patient line of negotiation pursued by Lord Owen and Cyrus Vance is the one most likely to bear fruit. It is becoming increasingly clear that EC-UN involvement in Bosnia will have to be maintained through any transitional phase relating to the organisation of Bosnia as either a unitary state or its division into cantons.

STABILITY IN THE REGION

Application of domestic criteria in determining policy:

10. From June 1991 when Croatia and Slovenia declared their independence the approach of EC member states has often been dictated by the relationships amongst the member states rather than the divisions between the Balkan states.

11. For example, during 1991 the EC refused to recognise Slovenia and Croatia without a political settlement. In order to preserve a united front when some states (notably Germany) decided that they would recognise Croatia and Slovenia unilaterally the EC announced its recognition of those two states on 16 January 1992.

12. Recognition became such an important issue for domestic reasons that Croatia was recognised on 16 January despite the fact that the EC received a report on 15 January from its own commission to examine the human rights policies of the republics requesting recognition in which it was recommended that Croatia not be recognised.

13. The EC states are not alone in not taking as their first concern the needs of the Balkan states. The United States reiterated its stand that no republic of former Yugoslavia be granted international recognition without a political settlement on 17 January. More than one commentator has interpreted the abrupt change in American policy later in 1992 as part of the Presidential election strategy.

14. The governments of the new states have great problems in interpreting the intentions of the EC and UN in the face of such abrupt changes in policy. Local politicians are constantly trying to see if they have backing from abroad. Backing from abroad plays a very strong psychological role amongst the populations of the new states as they try to discover a new collective identity in the ideological vacuum of post-communist Yugoslavia.

Recognition of states and the need for a politically negotiated settlement:

15. EC-UN operations have sometimes sent the wrong signal to the warring parties in former Yugoslavia. In June 1991 EC member states insisted that there would be no international recognition of new states without a political settlement.

16. However, recognition followed without a political settlement when hostilities had already begun in both Croatia in January and Bosnia in April. Recognition during hostilities encouraged Croatian and Bosnian politicians to expect armed intervention on their side.

17. International recognition of Bosnia on 6 April was misinterpreted as it is the same date on which Hitler bombed Belgrade. It appeared that a green light was being given to the non-Serbian faction in Bosnia. President Izetbegović immediately forgot the agreement on cantonization which had been agreed with Mate Boban and Radovan Karadžić in March.

18. International recognition was based on the self-determination of territories. From the beginning EC-UN operations failed to take into account competing historical and national claims to these territories. By default, recognition of the territory of Croatia denied the right to self-determination of the Serbs in Croatia. A similar situation arose in Bosnia. The recognition of these territories may have been the

most practical solution to be followed, but the issue of territorial (or state) rights and those of the national groups living there could have been taken as the basis for negotiations before recognition.

19. EC-UN decisions to recognise Yugoslavia's former republics as sovereign states has created an unfortunate precedent. Statehood was recognised during hostilities which themselves were evidence of a grave lack of democratic consensus. In such a situation the competence and legitimacy of those governments would normally be considered questionable.

20. The end of negotiations is not in sight. EC-UN operations still have a large responsibility in settlements for Croatia (timing of handing back Krajina and Slavonia to Croatian administration) and Bosnia (the future distribution of power in Bosnia). Similar problems arise in Serbia and Macedonia where there are concentrated national minorities. Packages which link the different problems within some kind of principled framework show a concern for the region as a whole and inject greater coherency. EC-UN operations tend to have focused on one area at a time, whereas the issues are linked over the whole of former Yugoslavia.

Introduction of sanctions:

21. Sanctions against Serbia and Montenegro do not seem to have had any results. The war in Bosnia has not been stopped, tension remains high in Kosovo and Macedonia, the Serbian (as opposed to Yugoslav) government have not recognised the frontiers of new states. These are presumably some of the political goals of sanctions.

22. Sanctions are influencing the voting intentions of some of the electorate to back the evolving Panić/Ćosić programme in the forthcoming elections. But, they are also hardening support for Milošević because of the apparent lack of success at the agreements given by Panić and Ćosić over, for example, recognition of Croatian and Bosnian frontiers. It appears that concessions are being given for nothing in return.

23. No concessions over sanctions are a logical policy in EC-UN operations since their political objectives have not been won in full. However, it can be argued that it is not in Milošević's electoral interest for sanctions to be lifted in the short term. Hence, Milošević has recently become more vocal in his backing of the Serbs in Bosnia and Croatia. It is difficult not to see this as a calculated move on his part in the approach to elections. Sanctions run the risk of being counter-productive to their political objectives.

24. Panić has proposed that some sanctions be lifted on humanitarian grounds for a period of time to cover the coming elections, to be followed by a thorough review of the situation by the UN with the option of re-imposing sanctions. The proposal is potentially embarrassing if the UN decides to re-impose all sanctions against Serbia and Montengro, but the consequences of an outright Milošević victory have two worrying aspects. His victory will further fragment the democratic opposition and Montenegro has threatened to withdraw from the new Yugoslav federation if Milošević wins. Such a move on the part of Montenegro threatens to spread the conflict in former Yugoslavia wider still.

25. It is difficult to see how sanctions can achieve their political objectives. It might be more effective to consider exactly whose interests are now at stake in relation to the political objectives of sanctions and to target those interests rather than rely on blanket or indiscriminate sanctions.

26. There are indications that certain private banks are involved with Serbian political circles in Serbia, Bosnia and Croatia (Krajina). The largest of these banks are "Dafinament banka" and "Jugoskandik". They are also behind much of the sanctions busting, having recently begun to buy petrol stations. Given the finance required to run sanctions busting on the present scale, it is most likely that financial institutions abroad are unknowingly involved. The prevention of such resources reaching Serbia would guarantee quicker success in the political objectives of sanctions than the present indiscriminate policy.

Sanctions busting and the black market:

27. There is no evidence to suggest that the Serbian economy is experiencing an up-turn because of sanctions busting. Profits from these activities appear to benefit only the private companies involved. The two main banks are strengthening their hold over the running of the black economy in Belgrade.

28. These banks control the black economy operating in Serbia at present. They control the black market exchange rates through releasing foreign currency and then buying it back on the streets. They offer 10 per cent interest rates on Deutschemark savings (100 marks per month on savings of 1,000 marks). Savers exchange their marks for dinars to supplement their income. The recent devaluation of the dinar by 275 per cent only resulted in a corresponding shift in the black market rates since the banks' ability to control the flow of deutschemarks allows them to control the price.

29. Sanctions busting from Belgrade is further proof of the increasing power of the black economy and the corresponding damage being done to the social fabric with its long lasting consequences. This state of affairs also threatens long term stability in the region.

Conclusion:

30. EC-UN forces are operating in exceptionally difficult and frustrating circumstances. Atrocities being committed in Bosnia are repeated by all sides according to reports from Helsinki Watch. Leaders on all levels are willing to say one thing and pursue contrary policies.

31. EC-UN operations are not the cause of the conflicts in former Yugoslavia but have in some cases intensified those conflicts by their inconsistencies and sending of the wrong signals. The pressure from home electorates on governments abroad to act demands more than the patient and time-consuming process of negotiation.

32. Bosnian Moslem forces will accept arms from the Islamic countries if they proceed to break the arms embargo around Bosnia from 15 January 1993. This does not mean an extension of Islamic influence in Bosnia but it will lead to further deterioration in the region, particularly with regard to relations between Croats and Moslems in Bosnia.

33. The lack of democratic consensus in Croatia and Bosnia is mirrored in Serbia. The possibility of civil war there cannot be ruled out. EC-UN operations and the weakening of Serbia will not add to stability in the region. Stability requires stable state structures.

34. It seems unlikely that strong state structures can be founded which are based on the equal rights of all citizens. In a very real sense it is this inability which is the cause of many of the problems in the Balkans. International institutions which can guarantee rights of national minorities and the status of autonomous areas established according to a formula to be agreed have to be put into place.

35. EC-UN operations, in order to see through the establishment of stability in the region as whole, will have to continue for years to come. Part of that process includes rebuilding confidence in the offices of EC-UN operations before EC-UN negotiators can begin to help the communities in the region to find common ground for negotiations.

APPENDIX 12

Memorandum by Professor Adam Roberts, FBA, Montague Burton Professor of International Relations, University of Oxford

PROBLEMS FACING THE UNITED NATIONS IN THE FIELD OF INTERNATIONAL SECURITY

Since about 1987, and more markedly since 1989–91, there has been much optimism about the present and future contribution of the United Nations in the field of international security, and an impressive growth in demands for the UN's services. While the UN deserves strong support, its role in the security field faces excessive demands and numerous difficulties. It needs a coherent rationale. This memorandum in part a constructive critique of *An Agenda for Peace*. That document, though admirable in many ways, does have faults, and is too optimistic.

An Agenda for Peace presents a general view of the UN as a near-failure in the Cold War years, and as now having a much better prospect of success.[1] However, it was precisely in the 40 years from 1945 that the UN established its position as the first truly universal organisation of states, and developed many important techniques, principles and practices. Moreover, with the Cold War now over, the UN faces many serious problems in the security field. While many such problems are well identified in *An Agenda for Peace*, some are not.

Ten propositions are advanced here about the UN's role in the field of international security:

1. The UN is seriously overloaded.
2. This overload has happened for good and enduring reasons.
3. A debatable assumption which informs *An Agenda for Peace* is that there is agreement among the major powers about the basis of international security, and a strong shared interest in seeing to the implementation of international norms.

---

[1] Boutros Boutros-Ghali, *An Agenda for Peace*, UN doc. A/47/277 of 17 June 1992, paras. 2, 3, 75 and 76. However, in his 1992 annual report he subsequently gave credit to the success of member states in keeping the Charter vision alive during the Cold War decades. "Report of the Secretary-General on the Work of the Organization", UN doc. A/47/1 of 11 Sept. 1992, para. 2.

4. The veto system, though open to criticisms, has served some useful purposes. Change in the composition of the Security Council should not necessarily involve abandonment of the veto.

5. There are good reasons why enforcement actions take the form of authorised actions by individual states or groups of states, rather than coming under direct UN command as per a literal reading of the UN Charter.

6. The forms of action used in support of UN positions pose problems. There is a tendency to rely on relatively low-risk methods of remote control, including economic sanctions, whose efficacy is debatable.

7. Many actions by the UN, especially interventions in a country without the consent of all parties concerned, are bound to run into serious local opposition. Sometimes there may be a need to take the controversial step of setting up a trustee-type administration under UN auspices.

8. While the UN's role is increasing, there is no prospect of a general system of collective security emerging. Eleven basic questions about collective security are outlined.

9. Recognizing the seriousness of the problem of overload, the UN is seeking to operate alongside regional organisations. Such organisations, including NATO, need to respond positively. However, it is doubtful whether most regional organisations have the reputation, the universality, and the range of skills of the UN itself.

10. The UN Security Council, the UN Secretariat, and UN members need to address a number of other issues urgently if the organisation is not to repeat some of the errors of the recent past, and is to be equipped to address future tasks.

These ten propositions, each discussed in a separate section below, are in no way intended as criticism of an increased emphasis on the UN in UK foreign policy. Rather they constitute a plea for sober assessment of both the merits and defects of the UN's increased role; for constructive thought about some of the difficult issues it has exposed; and for not hastily abandoning traditional approaches to international relations, many of which continue to have validity.

The precise implications of these propositions for policy are not explored in detail, but are fairly obvious in some cases. If there is a characteristic British view of international relations, its less deplorable features include a respect for historical continuities, an acceptance that there are cultures different from our own, and an emphasis on interest as a guide to the actions of states. Of course, interest can be defined in many ways, and can encompass an interest in the success of international norms and organizations. However, the elements of the "British" view of international relations identified here do lead to a degree of healthy scepticism about certain ideas of "new world order". In the end, the UN's greatest contribution to international security may lie in actions outside the scope of this memorandum. In particular, the UN's strikingly increased commitment to democracy, if it assists democratic development around the world, could help reduce risks of war.[1]

THE TEN PROPOSITIONS IN DETAIL

1. Overload of UN

Peacekeeping and humanitarian responsibilities in a wide range of countries are over-stretching the capacities of the UN Security Council and the UN Secretariat. The capacity of UN bodies and member states to think effectively about so wide a range of problems, to manage so many operations, and to keep them on a sound financial footing, is in doubt.

That there is some degree of overload is accepted in the UN Secretariat. Boutros-Ghali has spoken of "the tumult of demands" placed on the UN, and of a "crisis of expectations".[2] He also said in his letter of 30 November 1992 about Somalia: "The Secretariat, already overstretched in managing greatly enlarged peace-keeping commitments, does not at present have the capacity to command and control an enforcement action of the size and urgency required by the present crisis in Somalia."[3]

It is sometimes suggested that a solution to the problem of overload is to put more resources, including of troops and of money, into the hands of the UN on a sensible regular basis. This would reduce the hand-to-mouth element which is a feature of the way the UN is forced to run peacekeeping operations. An organization which scarcely possesses a blue beret, yet is in such demand to provide forces, is remarkable even by the standards of the paradox-ridden subject of International Relations. It is not surprising that *An Agenda for Peace* emphasises additional resources.[4]

[1] On democracy, see *Agenda for Peace*, paras. 9 and 81–2.

[2] *1992 Annual Report*, para. 44.

[3] Letter dated 29 November 1992 from the Secretary-General Addressed to the President of the Security Council, UN doc. S/24868 of 30 Nov. 1992, p. 6.

[4] *Agenda for Peace*, paras. 51–4 and 69–73. The question of additional military resources being put directly at the UN's disposal is discussed further in Section 5 below.

So far, there is not much sign that dramatically increased resources will be available to the UN on a permanent basis. Even if they were, would that solve the major problems of overload? If the Security Council had troops permanently available, and if it had fewer worries about the financing of new activities, that would facilitate the running of peacekeeping or other military operations. However, there would also be a risk that even more tasks would be thrown at the UN; and the overload of the Secretariat might become more rather than less serious.

In any case, a major feature of the overload problem has to do, not with resources, so much as with the inherently difficult nature of the problems being tackled. There are problems in international relations that are not soluble through the application of resources from outside. One of the challenges facing the UN Security Council is to find some means of dealing with what may become an increasingly familiar challenge: states using the UN as a "dustbin" into which they can throw urgent and difficult problems which they cannot tackle by themselves.

The overload of the UN is likely to have three serious consequences: (a) Some of the operations in which the UN is heavily engaged may end in controversy, recrimination and failure. (b) The UN members most involved in these operations may become tired of their heavy responsibilities. (c) The financial basis of peacekeeping and other UN operations, weak at the best of times, may become even more difficult.

2. Reasons for Overload

The reasons why the UN has been in such heavy demand to deal with wars, civil wars, and other crises are numerous and persuasive. Whatever difficulties the UN may face in the coming years, these reasons will not suddenly disappear. They include:

(a) *The impressive record of the UN in the years 1987–92 has created expectations of the organization.* The UN has contributed to the settlement of numerous regional conflicts, including the Iran-Iraq war, the South African presence in Namibia, the Soviet presence in Afghanistan, and the Vietnamese presence in Cambodia. It provided a framework for the expulsion of Iraq from Kuwait.

(b) *Given the choice. most states contemplating the use of force beyond their borders prefer to do it in a multilateral, and preferably UN, context.* Such an approach to the use of force helps to neutralise internal political opposition, to increase the chances of acquiring useful allies, to reassure the international community than an operation has limited and acceptable goals, and to reduce the risk of large-scale force being used by adversaries or rival powers.

(c) *There is no immediate prospect of diminution of the sources of conflict in the world.* In particular, the collapse of large multi-national states and empires always causes severe problems, including a revival of ancient ethnic, religious or other animosities, and the absence of fully legitimate political systems, regimes, and state frontiers. Ex-Yugoslavia and the ex-USSR are merely the two most conspicuous contemporary examples. In both these cases, the taboo against changing the old "colonial" frontiers has been undermined much more quickly and seriously than it was in post-colonial states in Africa and elsewhere in the decades after European decolonization.

(d) *The UN has some notable advantages in tackling security problems which most regional organizations lack.* These are discussed further in Section 9 below.

One conclusion inescapably follows. Whatever setbacks the UN suffers in the next few years, it will continue to have great demands placed upon it, and states will in many cases want some degree of UN legitimation for uses of force beyond their borders.

3. Assumption of Harmony Among the Major Powers

An Agenda for Peace seems to be based on an assumption, however qualified, that the member states, including the major powers, are in substantial agreement with each other on central security issues:

> The manifest desire of the membership to work together is a new source of strength in our common endeavour. Success is far from certain, however ...
>
> Even as the issues between States north and south grow more acute, and call for attention at the highest levels of government, the improvement in relations between States east and west affords new possibilities, some already realized, to meet successfully threats to common security.[1]

It is undeniable, and very welcome, that there is more agreement among states about international security issues now than there was during the Cold War. However, there remain fundamental differences of both interest and perception.

[1] *Agenda for Peace*, paras. 6 and 8.

An Agenda for Peace says virtually nothing about interest as an explanation of state behaviour; and what it says about the sources of conflict applies more to post-decolonisation problems than to traditional rivalries between great powers.[1] This apparent under-estimation of national interest could lead to excessive expectations as regards possible action by major states to enforce the international order.

There are also differences in perceptions about the fundamental nature of world politics. Some states view colonial domination or a more loosely defined imperialism as the worst problems faced in international relations; others see civil war as the supremely dangerous threat; yet others, including the UK and USA, tend to view aggressive conquest and international war as the central problems.

Even among the member states of the European Community, fundamental differences of perspective on international problems are evident. For example, Germany has drawn from its history the lesson that the age of the warring nation-state has to yield to participation in a larger framework; while the UK has learned from its history that it must retain a degree of autonomy so it can be in a position to look after its interests, defend vulnerable states, maintain a balance in Europe, and uphold international principles.

There are also serious differences of perception and interest among the five permanent members of the UN Security Council. One should not necessarily expect relations between major powers to be good, and it is important to understand that there may be perfectly valid reasons why various countries perceive major security problems differently. The different perceptions of major powers may yet prove serious, for example, in respect of Yugoslavia: in particular, Russia's traditional friendship with Serbia may already have led Russia to take a different view regarding sanctions and military policy. Moreover, China's world-view, although undergoing important changes, retains distinctive elements which could put it at odds with other Security Council members.

4. The Veto in the Security Council

An Agenda for Peace, understandably, says little about the veto and about permanent membership of the Security Council, but it may well err in its implication that the era of veto use is largely behind us.[2]

The Security Council's structure and decision-making procedures, especially the existence of the veto in the hands of the permanent five, are a matter of intense controversy, and would plainly not command the consent of all states in anything like all likely or imaginable international crises. The veto system privileges a particular group of states, including of course the UK, in a way that is bound to be contentious; and it is widely perceived as having held the UN back from fulfilling its functions in the Cold War years.

Yet the veto has merits as well as faults: it reduces the risk of power and law wandering off on divergent paths; it has helped to get and keep the major powers within a UN framework when they would otherwise have either not joined it in the first place or else deserted it; it may have saved the UN from involvement in impossible missions; and it may have contributed to a sense of responsibility and a habit of careful consultation among the permanent five. In short, the veto can be viewed as one factor which has made for the superiority of the UN's decision-making procedures over those of its predecessor the League of Nations, and over many regional organisations.

There are bound to be pressures for the modification or abandonment of the veto. The procedures governing the matter of Charter amendment make any change affecting this power difficult.[3] Yet some change will eventually have to come, especially if the UN Security Council gets committed to an unsuccessful policy and its wisdom is thus called into question. UN decision-making needs to command broad political assent around the world if it is to be effective. If there is change, it should probably not involve complete abandonment of the veto system, but rather some change in the composition of the Security Council along one of the several lines which have been widely canvassed.[4]

5. Enforcement Actions: Authorised or under UN Command?

The question of how enforcement actions are organized is central to almost all discussions of the UN's future role. It brings out a conflict between "Charter fundamentalists", who would like such actions to be organized precisely in accord with the UN Charter, and those with a more "common law" approach, who believe the most important guide is the UN's actual practice.

The discussion of enforcement actions in *An Agenda for Peace* reflects a curious use of terminology which has developed at the UN. Matters relating to the Charter's Chapter VII (that is Articles 39–51, on "Action with Respect to Threats to the Peace, Breaches of the Peace, and Acts of Aggression") only fea-

[1] *Agenda for Peace*, esp. paras. 5, 8 and 11–13.

[2] *Agenda for Peace, paras.* 14 and 15.

[3] The UN Charter, Article 108, stipulates that amendments must be adopted by two thirds of the members of the General Assembly; and be ratified, in accord with their respective constitutional processes, by two thirds of members of the UN, including all the permanent members of the Security Council.

[4] Note particularly Bill Clinton's statement: "Japan and Germany should be made permanent members of the UN Security Council."—Address to Foreign Policy Association, 1 Apr. 1992.

ture as part of a larger section entitled "Peacemaking".[1] This may appear particularly odd in view of the definition of "peacemaking" earlier in *An Agenda for Peace* as: "action to bring hostile parties to agreement, essentially through such peaceful means as those foreseen in Chapter VI of the Charter of the United Nations."[2] Part of the explanation may lie in the ambiguity of the word "essentially". However, there remains something half-ominous, half-ludicrous, about the UN's role in war-making being subsumed under the label of "peacemaking".

In this notably unsystematic framework, *An Agenda for Peace* advances the idea that the UN Security Council might have forces available on a permanent basis as one means of increasing its credibility and its power to deter. It envisages that the UN Security Council might authorise preventive military deployments, and that member states might "undertake to make armed forces, assistance and facilities available to the Security Council ... not only on an *ad hoc* basis but on a permanent basis ... .The ready availability of armed forces on call could serve, in itself, as a means of deterring breaches of the peace since a potential aggressor would know that the Council had at its disposal a means of response."[3]

The major powers have reacted to these proposals with circumspection and silence. *An Agenda for Peace* offers no serious discussion of the reasons why states have traditionally been nervous about the idea of making armed forces available to the UN on a permanent basis. These reasons include a natural concern about the command of troops being put into the hands of an international body which might employ them, risking their lives, in a cause which was distant from home, or controversial there. States may well prefer a situation in which the provision of military force for UN activities is managed in an *ad hoc* manner, giving them a greater degree of control over events. Such a view is not surprising. Rightly or wrongly, states guard their power jealously, including their power to decide the exact circumstances in which their armed forces will or will not be used. Just as the power of national governments needs to be subject to constraints both internal and external, so the UN itself, even the Security Council, is far from infallible: in principle, some limitations on its power may not be a bad thing.

At this stage, therefore, full-time and large-scale allocation of forces to the UN in advance of any crisis is improbable. However, earmarking of national military units for possible UN use is realistic. More important than this may be the training of national forces in international military co-operation: such training has taken place within NATO, and proved to be of great value in the Gulf crisis of 1990–91. There could also be possibilities for improving the military advice available at UN Headquarters, and for better preparation of national armies in the range of problems liable to be encountered in UN-related actions.

An Agenda for Peace contains no discussion of the possible merits, as well as defects, of the system which (with variations) has emerged in respect of Korea in 1950–53, Iraq in 1990–91, and now in Somalia in 1992: a system by which the UN authorises military action which is then under the control of a state or group of states. There are some advantages in such an arrangement. It reflects the reality that not all states feel equally involved in every enforcement action. Moreover, military action requires an extremely close relation between intelligence gathering and action, a smoothly functioning decision-making machine, and forces with some experience of working with each other in performing dangerous and complex tasks. These things are more likely to be achieved through existing national armed forces, alliances, and military relationships, than they are within the structure of a UN command. As habits of co-operation between armed forces develop, and as the UN itself grows, the scope for action directly under the UN's command may increase: but it must inevitably be a slow process.

One statement on the use of military forces under UN control is bound to be seen as evidence of a kind of international discrimination underlying the whole *Agenda for Peace* project:

> Forces under Article 43 may perhaps never be sufficiently large or well enough equipped to deal with a threat from a major army equipped with sophisticated weapons. They would be useful, however, in meeting any threat posed by a military force of a lesser order.[4]

This can easily be interpreted as evidence that the UN is ready to use force against Third World countries, not against major powers. However, from the context, it appears possible that this statement is merely an implicit admission that when there is a threat from a major army, the powers might indeed have to resort, as in Desert Storm, to the idea of authorised action, as distinct from direct UN command.

Experience does seem to show that mobilizing for collective security only works when one power takes the lead. But that same power may, as a result of the effort, be reluctant to continue taking the entire burden of collective security. After the Korean War, the US tried to set up regional alliances to reduce its own direct commitments. After the 1991 Gulf War, the US was manifestly reluctant to get entangled in

---

1 *Agenda for Peace*, paras. 41–44. Similarly, the structure of the Secretary-General's 1992 annual report is such that there is no thorough treatment of issues to do with enforcement actions. See *1992 Annual Report*, paras. 8 and 9.

2 *Agenda for Peace*, para. 20. The Charter's Chapter VI is on "Pacific Settlement of Disputes".

3 *Agenda for Peace*, para. 43.

4 *Agenda for Peace*, para. 43.

the quagmire of Iraq, and nervous about underwriting all security arrangements in the area. The desire to limit the degree of US involvement is likely to remain strong under President Clinton.

Could the UN Military Staff Committee, if life were breathed into it, usefully take on the role of co-ordinating military enforcement action under the Security Council? The idea that such a disparate international committee might be in charge of military operations has attracted little interest; and the Military Staff Committee is only touched on incidentally in *Agenda for Peace*.[1] For the foreseeable future, there is no point in thinking of the Military Staff Committee as a commanding body for major military action. However, there may be more modest tasks which it, or some other body, could and should perform: including, for example, the development of rules of engagement, the harmonization of laws of war rules as they affect multilateral forces, and the tendering of military advice on a wide range of issues.

6. Avoidance of Risky and Committing Action

The major powers, especially the USA, which have had a principal role in carrying out UN Security Council mandates, have been understandably nervous about taking action which involves a high risk of casualties and failure. This caution was evident even in the case which might seem to be an exception, namely Operation Desert Storm. In the planning of this action, the extreme care taken to minimise coalition casualties was sensible, even commendable. However, the UN may face—may indeed be facing—some problems which require risky and committing action if there is to be a chance of tackling them effectively.

Member states involved in UN-related military actions tend to operate by methods of remote control (economic sanctions, air exclusion zones, arms embargoes, attempts to broker cease-fires) or limited involvement (peacekeeping, observer, and humanitarian activities). Such methods may or may not be appropriate in particular circumstances. They sometimes work, or at least may be one factor assisting a solution to a crisis. They are undoubtedly reinforced by the UN's high reputation. However, the record of such methods of remote control and limited involvement is patchy.

This is particularly true of economic sanctions. The only aspect of economic sanctions discussed in *An Agenda for Peace* is the special economic problems which they may create for certain states.[2] This is an important issue, but hardly the central one so far as their place in UN actions against breaches of the peace are concerned. Economic sanctions raise five other major problems which need more careful discussion than they have had at the UN or elsewhere.

(a) Economic sanctions may be ineffective in the obvious sense that there are always some sanctions-busters;

(b) Sanctions, even if they are 100 per cent effective in stopping all trade, may still be 0 per cent effective in bringing about a change of policy in the target state;

(c) Sanctions are liable to hurt the innocent in the target state before the guilty; and

(d) Sanctions may, like some forms of strategic bombing, have the perverse effect of making the inhabitants of a country more rather than less dependent on their government.

(e) The timing and mode, of transition from economic sanctions to military action is liable to be intensely controversial, as witness the debates on this matter in the 1990–91 Gulf Crisis.

In short, sanctions are a blunt, unreliable, and controversial instrument. Their historical record is poor, and has not yet been improved by their application against Iraq since August 1990 and against Serbia and Montenegro since May 1992. Nonetheless, they have value in some crises as a declaration of intent; and they can sometimes be effective when used in a discriminate way, or on an issue on which the target state can be flexible.

More thought is needed on other measures short of military force which can be employed in particular crises. The sanctions provisions of the Charter should not be allowed to become a straightjacket forcing the Security Council into a Pavlovian reaction, and preventing creative thought about a range of methods which might be appropriate to the particular situation.

In general, some of the methods which have up to now been used in implementation of UN policies bring to mind the Chinese proverb quoted by Chou En–lai in an interview with a Yugoslav journalist in 1971: "Distant waters do not quench fire."[3]

[1] *Agenda for Peace*, para. 43.
[2] *Agenda for Peace*, para. 41.
[3] Chou En-lai, interview with Dara Janekovic published in *Vjiesnik*, Zagreb, 28 Aug. 1971.

7. Controversial Character of Many UN Interventions

Many crises call for intervention by the UN on the ground in one way or another—whether in peacekeeping, humanitarian, observer, administrative, or combat mode. While such interventions are often justified, some are bound to be strongly opposed locally, by those who see their interests or dignity threatened; or who condemn the UN for not taking a particular action that seems to them to be self-evidently needed. The fact that the mission of UN forces has to be the subject of advance international agreement seriously reduces their flexibility in fast-changing situations, and may further stimulate opposition.

An Agenda for Peace foreshadows a much more active UN role, not least in the area of peacekeeping, which it famously defines as "the deployment of a United Nations presence in the field, hitherto with the consent of all the parties concerned ..."[1] This phrase has caused controversy, but it is only realistic to work on the assumption that some UN actions, particularly in situations of chaos and collapse of state authority, may have to take place without consent. What is more worrying is that these and other actions may be opposed. The key question of safety of UN personnel is discussed, but only in very general terms.[2]

A special risk arises where a situation seems to call for different kinds of action at the same time. There are obvious hazards in having peacekeepers and/or humanitarian relief workers in a country at the same time as UN-related military action is taken there. The fate of the US-led Multinational Force in Lebanon in the early 1980s is a warning of the terrible risks which can face peacekeepers when they slowly get associated with, or involved in, controversial policies and military actions, and then become a target for retaliation. The UN Secretariat is well aware of this problem, to which there is no general solution. It is not surprising that in the Yugoslav crisis some states, including the UK, have expressed reservations about that kind of dual UN role.

Some crises may require not just the placing large numbers of troops in hostile territory, but also the establishment of a trustee-type administration to replace a system of government which has broken down. The admirable anti-colonial instincts of both the UN and the USA have contributed to a reluctance to envisage such a role, yet the logic of involvement in fractured societies may sometimes point in that direction. The responsibilities laid down for UNTAC in the 1991 Paris Agreements on Cambodia are one example of a trend towards more direct (in this case awkwardly shared) involvement in governmental functions.[3] Such action may be needed, but is bound to breed local opposition: the UN and its members have to be prepared to stay on in some very rough situations.

8. Collective Security

Is it possible to say that out of the rubble of the Cold War a system of collective security is emerging? The term "collective security" appears in *An Agenda for Peace*, but is not extensively discussed there.[4] It has also been used by Bill Clinton.[5] The term normally refers to a system in which each state in the system accepts that the security of one is the concern of all, and agrees to join in a collective response to aggression. In this sense it is distinct from systems of alliance security, in which groups of states ally with each other, principally against possible external threats.

Ideas of "collective security" have been in circulation since the very beginnings of the modern states system, and were indeed aired at the negotiations which led to the 1648 Peace of Westphalia. However, all proposals for collective security have to be tested against eleven basic questions, some of which have already been touched upon, and which can be briefly enumerated as follows.[6]

Question 1. Whose collective security? Does the system protect only certain powers or types of power? Are there countries which, for whatever reason, feel excluded from its benefits, or even threatened by it? The anxieties expressed by some Third World countries regarding the concept of the "New World Order", while they have not yet crystallised into definite opposition to any specific UN action, are evidence of concern on this point.

Question 2. What is the unit (regional or global) within which a system of collective security operates? Although the UN system is the first truly global international system, and although it involves virtually

1 *Agenda for Peace*, para. 20.
2 *Agenda for Peace*, paras. 66–8.
3 Text of the Paris Agreements of 23 Oct. 1991 on a Comprehensive Political Settlement of the Cambodia Conflict is in UN doc. A/46/608–S/23177 of 30 Oct. 1991.
4 *Agenda for Peace*, paras. 42 and 63.
5 "The world stands on the brink of an era of unprecedented opportunity, a time when the nations of the world can begin to realize the goals of collective security, sustainable development, and respect for human rights . . ."—Statement by Bill Clinton to UNA-USA, 9 Oct. 1992.
6 The following enumeration of questions relating to collective security systems is adapted from that in Andrew Hurrell's excellent article "Collective Security and International Order Revisited", *International Relations*, London, Mar. 1992. An exploration of how some of these questions relate to the current position of the UN can be found in my chapter "The New Face of the United Nations", in the forthcoming edition of *Brassey's Year Book*.

all countries in the world subscribing to a common set of principles, it is still not self-evident that the same principles and practices regarding international order are applied consistently to different regions; or that collective security could operative as effectively for East Timor or Tibet as for Kuwait. Yet the political price of apparent inconsistency could be high.

Question 3. Against which types of threat is a system of collective security intended to operate? Does it apply equally to massive aggression and annexation; cross-border incursions; acts of terrorism; human rights violations within a state; and the collapse of state structures under assault from internal opposition? In 1991 and 1992, inspired partly by the "safe havens" in northern Iraq, and partly by a trend of opinion, admittedly far from universal, in favour of democracy, there was increased advocacy within the UN system of some right of intervention in states even in the absence of a formal invitation. This remained a deeply contentious issue, and served as a reminder that the ends toward which collective security efforts might be directed are not fixed.

In 1990–1, when supporting the policies of the powers seeking to reverse the occupation of Kuwait, many people (including myself) argued that it was the particularly egregious nature of the Iraqi invasion, occupation and annexation of Kuwait which justified the coalition's response. The fact that this argument was so widely used perhaps underlines the point that in cases where aggression is not so blatant, it might be much harder to secure an international military response: a state might have to look after its own interests.

Question 4. What is the decision-making procedure by which threats are identified and action decided upon? Is it a majority of states; unanimity among a small concert of major states; a key role for one major power; or a key role for a Secretary-General figure? Whatever the answer, the decision-making procedure is bound to be controversial, as the contemporary discussion of the veto (discussed above in Section 4) and of the US role in the UN shows.

Question 5. By what means is collective security enforced? (for example denial of recognition; economic sanctions; use of major military force.) Traditionally, in the League of Nations era and again in the UN, collective security has been envisaged as operating, at least initially, through such forms of pressure as international condemnation backed by economic sanctions, whose effectiveness was questioned in Section 6 above. Even if the international community agrees on the ends of policy, the choice of means is likely to be controversial.

Question 6. Who commands a collective military action? The concerns expressed about US leadership of UN actions (whether in the Gulf in 1990–91 or in Somalia in 1992–93) illustrate the complexity of the problem. To some, the US role appears as a threat, as evidence that the UN has been hi-jacked by the USA. To others, especially Americans, the responsibilities of the white man's burden seem daunting.

Question 7. How collective does enforcement have to be? Is complete unanimity impossible to attain, especially in the case of military action? Is there still space for some states to be neutral? In practice there has never been, on the global level, a truly "collective" case (let alone system) of collective security. In the Gulf Crisis of 1990–91, the key UN Security Council resolution avoided calling on all states to take military action. Instead, it merely authorised "member states co-operating with the Government of Kuwait" to use a degree of force.[1] This wording allowed continued space for neutrality or non-belligerency in this conflict. It marks an interesting and realistic interpretation of some over-optimistic provisions in Chapter VII of the UN Charter.

Question 8. How can a system of collective security actively deter a particular threat to a particular country? In the wake of the 1991 Gulf War, there was much discussion as to how, in future, threats of invasion could be deterred before disaster struck: this was one context for "preventive deployment" envisaged in *An Agenda for Peace*.[2] Yet in practice the idea of such "preventive deployment" is fraught with difficulty. There is the risk that large numbers of states would request it; that it would be insufficient to discourage aggression; and that it might be used by a government as a means of avoiding serious moves towards its own defence, or towards conciliation with adversaries. Yet despite all these difficulties, there are possibilities here. There may also be some residual deterrent value in the lessons of Korea 1950–53 and Kuwait 1990–91: twice, under UN auspices, the USA has led coalitions which have gone to the defence of invaded states to which the US was not bound by formal alliance commitments, and in which it had no troops deployed at the time. This curious fact may not be entirely lost on future would-be aggressors.

Question 9. Can a collective security system have forces available on a permanent basis and under a centralised command? This remains, as indicated in Section 5 above, a touchy question. If such forces and command structure were in place, they would begin to transform a collective security system into something more centralised.

[1] Security Council Resolution 678 of 29 Nov. 1990.

[2] *Agenda for Peace*, paras. 28–32.

Question 10. Are international forces acting on behalf of the international community subject to the same rules of restraint based on the laws of war (jus in bello) as ordinary belligerents in an inter-state war? There is little serious dissent from the proposition that certain rules of restraint do apply to all the forces involved in collective security actions. However, the application of such rules presents special problems in a large *ad hoc* multi-national coalition typical of a collective security action, for several reasons. First, different partners may have different national standards, and be bound by different treaties. Second, the perceived legitimacy of an operation, and the maintenance of coalition unity, may depend on a public perception that warlike actions will be restrained in certain ways. Third, those rules based on an assumption that neutrality requires impartiality may conflict with the obligations of all states, including neutrals, to support the principles, purposes, and even actions of the UN. Fourth, economic sanctions, which often hit the innocent along with the guilty, may conflict with certain underlying principles of the laws of war. Fifth, the question of possible trials in respect of war crimes often arises in large coalition actions against a state perceived in some sense as an outlaw; which in turn raises the question of whether it is time for the establishment of an International Criminal Court (which might also have some other functions—for example in relation to terrorism and drugs).

The UN Security Council might usefully devote more consistent attention to laws of war matters than it has in the past, including in the Gulf Crisis of 1990–91. *An Agenda for Peace* avoids the subject entirely—an interesting example of the way in which laws of war matters, actively pursued in many parts of the UN system, are treated fitfully in those parts of the UN most directly involved in the management of international security. The UN risks getting a bad reputation if the Security Council (as over Iraq in 1990–91, and over Yugoslavia in 1992–93) makes loud warning statements about violations of the laws of war, and then fails to follow them up with action.

Question 11. Who pays for collective security? The question of burden-sharing in international security matters generally is notoriously complex, as shown by the experience of NATO, of UN peacekeeping, and of the US-led operations in the 1990–91 Gulf Crisis and in Somalia in 1992–93. In September 1992, unpaid contributions towards UN peacekeeping operations stood at US $844 million; and the annual cost of peacekeeping activities may now be close to $3,000 million.[1] If any of the current peacekeeping operations goes badly wrong, there could be great difficulty in securing payment. Bill Clinton has repeatedly called for new agreements for the sharing of costs of maintaining peace.[2]

*****

These eleven questions, taken together, are not intended to lead to the conclusion that there can never be any such thing as collective security. Rather, they suggest a more modest conclusion: collective security may properly be considered, not as a general system of international security, but rather as a form of action which is mobilised occasionally, and imperfectly. Its most common use may be in response to especially glaring aggressive actions by military powers of the second rank. It is not a complete substitute for national or alliance defence efforts.

9. *Regional Organisations*

Recognizing that the UN risks being seriously overloaded, much thought has been given to the question of co-operation with regional arrangements and organisations.[3] However, the UN has often and with some success sought to encourage the handling of a crisis by regional bodies, only to find that important aspects of the problem remained on its own shoulders. *An Agenda for Peace* is particularly interesting for its open acceptance that there has to be a partnership between regional organisations and the UN, not a shuffling off of responsibilities between them.

Suggesting an enlarged role for regional organisations is easier said than done. Such organisations have a bewildering variety of purposes and memberships, and they often have great difficulty in reaching decisions and in taking action. Many regional bodies are widely seen as too partial to one particular power. It is often far from self-evident which regional body should have the principal role in addressing a given problem.

Some of these difficulties are particularly evident in Europe, where there is a proliferation of regional bodies. In the security field, CSCE and NATO are the two main ones, though the EC and WEU have played key roles on occasions. NATO could perhaps do more than it has done in the recent past to develop a role as a regional organisation with a close relationship to the UN. Such an approach would hardly be new: the 1949 Treaty of Washington, which led to the creation of NATO, put much emphasis on the UN.[4] NATO had an important role in a number of ways in the UN-authorised 1991 Gulf War.[5]

---

[1] *1992 Annual Report*, paras, 18 and 46.

[2] Bill Clinton, "A New Covenant for American Security", *Harvard International Review*, Summer 1992. See also his call for the US apportionment of UN peacekeeping costs to be reduced from 30.4 to 25 per cent, in his 9 Oct. 1992 statement to UNA-USA.

[3] UN Charter, Chapter VIII; and *Agenda for Peace*, paras. 60–65.

[4] The North Atlantic Treaty, Washington DC, 4 Apr. 1949, preamble and Arts. 1, 5 and 7.

[5] See Jonathan T. Howe, "NATO and the Gulf Crisis", *Survival*, International Institute for Strategic Studies, London, vol. xxxiii, no. 3, May/June 1991, pp. 246–59.

However, the connection between NATO and the UN has not been adequately articulated. Curiously, while the major document on NATO's post-Cold War role, the Rome Declaration of November 1991, contains extensive reference to the CSCE, it says little on the UN.[1] The crisis in Yugoslavia has since forced attention on the subject.[2]

The UN does have certain advantages compared to many regional organisations. *(1)* It has remarkable powers to act, laid down in the Charter. *(2)* It has a procedure capable of reaching tough and controversial decisions fast—namely the structure and voting system of the Security Council. *(3)* It has an unrivalled reputation for impartial "good offices" under the Secretary–General, and also for peacekeeping.

10. Other Issues to be Addressed

If the UN is to avoid some of the more obvious hazards of the activist path onto which it has been directed, then its member states and its principal organs (especially the Secretariat, and the Security Council) need to consider a number of additional but related issues:

(a) *The sheer difficulty of operating in conditions of deeply engrained ethnic/communal conflict.* It would be a tragedy if the United Nations, at the point when it has some chance of increasing its role in international relations, were to be damaged by the combined forces of ethnicity and communal hatred.[3] *Agenda for Peace* has wisely warned that there are limits beyond which self-determination should not be taken.[4] But it says little about the special problems of peacekeeping, humanitarian aid, enforcement and other tasks in bitter ethnic conflicts where there are no front lines.

The power of ethnic/communal divisions merits a more careful and judicious use of the word "nation" than in most contemporary usage, whether at the UN or in the UK. The sentimental assumption that all states are "nations" is built in to such terms as "United Nations" and 'international'. Where possible, we should use more neutral terms such as "state" or "country", especially when speaking of the majority of states which are hardly coterminous with a single "nation".

(b) *The criteria used in recognizing political entities as states. and in favouring their admission to the United Nations.* When the UN admits member states, it is in fact conferring a particularly important form of recognition on them, and it is also implicitly underwriting the inviolability of their frontiers. Yet the UN does not appear to be taking sufficient account of traditional criteria for recognition, which include careful consideration as to whether a state really exists and coheres as a political and social entity. Many European states, including the UK, also appeared to forget these traditional criteria in some of their recent acts of recognition. If the result is that we enter into risky security commitments for states which never really cohered internally, public support for action in a UN framework could be weakened.

(c) *The appropriateness to situations of internal conflict of certain principles derived from inter-state relations. including the principle that the changing of frontiers by force can never be accepted.* This principle, which is very important in contemporary international relations, has been frequently reiterated by the international community in connection with the Yugoslav crisis.[5] It has relevance, not just because the crisis has partly the character of conflict between states, but also because worrying precedents could be set by successful grabs for territory on largely ethnic grounds. Yet there must be a question as to whether it is wise to express this legal principle so forcefully in circumstances where the existing "frontiers" lack legitimacy, where there are such deep- seated ethnic problems, and where almost any imaginable outcome will involve some degree of recognition of changing these frontiers by force.

(d) *A philosophy to inform disarmament efforts in the post-Cold War era.* The UN's Office for Disarmament Affairs has in the past three years made significant moves towards a more realistic

[1] The Rome Declaration on Peace and Co-operation, issued by the Heads of State and Government participating in the meeting of the North Atlantic Council in Rome on 7–8 November 1991, contains one passing reference to the UN in para. (in connection with the arms transfer register). The Alliance's New Strategic Concept, a lengthy document agreed at the same meeting, did envisage in para. 42 that "Allies could, further, be called upon to contribute to global stability and peace by providing forces for United Nations missions." Texts in *NATO Review*, Brussels, vol. 39, no. 6, Dec. 1991, pp. 19–32.

[2] See the brief para. 13 on the UN in the communiqué of the ministerial meeting of the North Atlantic Council, Oslo, 4 June 1992. Text in *NATO Review*, vol. 40, no. 3, June 1992, pp. 30–2. See also the references to UN peacekeeping in the communiqué, and in the statement on former Yugoslavia, issued by the North Atlantic Council, Brussels, 17 Dec. 1992. Text in *NATO Review*, vol. 40, no. 6, Dec. 1992, pp. 28–32.

[3] On the importance of ethnic issues in today's world, and the limits of the doctrine of national self-determination, see the forthcoming book by Senator Daniel Patrick Moynihan, *Pandaemonium: Ethnicity in International Politics*, Oxford University Press, 1993.

[4] *Agenda for Peace*, para. 17.

[5] See for example, the Declaration of 3 Sept. 1991 of the CSCE states; SC Res. 713 of 25 Sept. 1991, and numerous subsequent Security Council resolutions; the Statement on the Situation in Yugoslavia, issued by the North Atlantic Council meeting in Rome, 7–8 Nov. 1991, para. 2; and the Statement of Principles adopted on 26 Aug. 1992 by the London Conference on the Former Socialist Federal Republic of Yugoslavia, para ii.

and less propagandistic approach to the subject, but nothing like a philosophy on the place of arms control and disarmament in contemporary international relations has yet emerged. The rationales for arms reductions, for control of arms transfers, and for nuclear non-proliferation efforts, all need to be carefully examined and refined. This is especially important in view of the common fears of a discriminatory system of arms control, the influence of ideas about "common security", and the possible military requirements of the UN itself.

(e) *A centre for the study of international security problems.* While there are several admirable research and training institutions associated with the UN, a strengthening of professional study of UN-related international security problems is badly needed. A centre for the study of international security problems, dealing particularly with UN-related issues, could have several functions in the post-Cold War era: as an institutional memory, a place of serious scholarly study, a focus for reflection, a forum for informed consideration of policy options, and a centre for training of senior officers and officials on a multi-national basis. Such a centre could be a useful means of enhancing the professionalism of those serving the UN.

APPENDIX 13

Memorandum by the Foreign and Commonwealth Office

THE EXPANDING ROLE OF THE UN: IMPLICATIONS FOR WORKLOAD AND STAFFING OF THE FCO

Introduction

1. Our earlier Memorandum[1] provided details of the expansion of the work of the UN and the implications for UK policy. The committee have asked for a further memorandum on the effect this expansion has had on FCO staffing and workload. This memorandum is confined to the FCO's Diplomatic Wing. The implications for ODA will be covered in a separate memorandum.

2. The Secretary-General in his latest annual report took 1987 and the end of the Cold War as a starting point to illustrate the expansion in the UN's role. We have therefore used this date as our base point.

3. The end of the Cold War has brought into high relief the role of the UN, and raised expectations of its ability to address major problems, whether security, political, economic or humanitarian, to potentially unrealistic levels. The role of the Security Council in addressing international problems from Africa to Asia with legal powers to take action is at one end of the spectrum. The new role of the UN High Commissioner for Refugees (UNHCR) in coping with mass displacement and migration throughout the world is at another. In between come disarmament, economic development in the Third World and global environmental issues, as well as increased emphasis on human rights and drugs.

4. The Foreign and Commonwealth Office has responsibility for the overall co-ordination of policy towards the UN. The expansion in UN activity has implications for the FCO as a whole. This memorandum concentrates on the main UN policy areas which are the responsibility of United Nations Department (UND), Arms Control and Disarmament Department, Environment, Science and Energy Department, Human Rights Policy Unit and UK Missions in New York, Geneva and Vienna.

UND

5. UND is organized into seven separate sections (see organogram, p.320). There are few areas which have not been affected by the expanding role of the UN.

Political Section

6. The Political Section provides policy advice on the Security Council and the UN General Assembly and on political issues before other UN bodies including the elections of a UN Secretary General. There has been a significant increase in co-ordination with EC partners on areas of common interest including a joint input to the Secretary General's report "Agenda for Peace". This reflects both increased activity at the UN, and enhanced political co-operation among the Twelve. The rise in Security Council activity (26 Security Council resolutions passed on Iraq and 30 on former Yugoslavia) has placed the section under increasing pressure. The section also takes much of the weight of increased Parliamentary and public interest in UN affairs. It is responsible for relations with the United Nations Association. Staffing in the Section has not been increased although its workload has been restructured with a devolution of peacekeeping to a separate section in 1991. The section is headed by a DS5 supported by a DS7/8, a DS9 and a DS10.

---

[1] See evidence p.1.

PEACE-KEEPING

7. There has been a dramatic increase both in the number of peace-keeping operations and the level of involvement of UK forces within them in recent years. Since 1988 14 new operations have been launched compared to 13 in the preceding 40 years.

During this period UK involvement in peace-keeping has also increased. We are now the second largest troop contributor after France, with some 3,756 personnel on the ground in five different operations. Peace-keeping section is responsible for policy on the launching and financing of all new UN peace-keeping operations. When British forces are deployed, it is involved in the necessary briefing, co-ordination etc with MOD and with key military personnel.

8. Until January 1991 responsibility for peace-keeping lay with a DS9 Officer working in the Political Section. In January 1991 responsibility for peace-keeping was transferred to the Finance and Administration Section which was re-named Peace-keeping, Finance and Administration Section. The Head of Section was upgraded from DS7 to DS5. In September 1992 with the increased workload, a separate peace-keeping section was formed headed by a DS5, assisted by a DS9. In November 1992 an additional DS9 was attached to the Section to deal exclusively with peace-keeping finance.

UN FINANCES

9. UND is responsible for co-ordinating UK policy on budgetary and financial questions in the UN in consultation with other Whitehall Ministries, particularly the Treasury. To keep pace with increased activity within the UN and the level of FCO payments and developments on the peace-keeping side, a separate DS7 position covering UN finances and administration was established. This officer liaises closely with Specialised Agencies and Peace-keeping Section.

ECONOMIC AND SOCIAL

10. The UK has been in the vanguard in pressing for reform of the economic and social sectors of the UN and has made a major input to the policy of the EC Twelve on these issues (particularly in the successful reform of the Economic and Social Council in 1991/2). The section works closely with the ODA, in particular on reform of the development and operational aspects of the UN, and the department takes the chair in a Whitehall inter-departmental group which considers reform in the UN social and economic sectors and financial questions, as well as on UN institutional aspects of follow up to the Rio Conference on the Environment. The section also handles UN social policy and the preparations for the World Social Summit in 1995. It was responsible for co-ordination of the Whitehall effort in following up the recommendations and report called for by the World Summit for Children in 1991. The DS5 Head of Section is both Head of ECOSOC Section and of Sanctions Unit (cf. below). He is assisted by a DS9 on the ECOSOC side and a DS9 on Sanctions (a new post established in 1991) and supported by a DS10.

SANCTIONS

11. Before August 1990 the only UN sanctions regime was that applied against South Africa. Since then comprehensive economic sanctions have been imposed against Iraq and Serbia/Montenegro and more limited measures including arms embargoes against Libya, the whole of former Yugoslavia, Somalia, Liberia and the Khmer Rouge. UND has led on the formulation and implementation of all relevant UN sanctions resolutions. In liaison with other government Departments such as the DTI, the department is also responsible for monitoring compliance with the sanctions regimes, both through the relevant UN Sanctions Committees and within the UK. This includes processing applications by other UK companies for permission to trade with embargoed countries, forwarding the applications to the Sanctions Committees where appropriate. In 1992 UND dealt with 2,438 applications relating to Iraq, and 880 to Serbia and Montenegro.

HUMANITARIAN

12. The Humanitarian Section was created in 1990 in recognition of the growing importance of policy on humanitarian issues. The section deals with policy towards UNHCR, the International Committee of the Red Cross, including international humanitarian law, and international refugee and migration policy including the Geneva Inter-Governmental Consultations and the International Organisation for Migration. The UK has taken the lead internationally in mobilizing opinion for a more effective UN response to international humanitarian crises. It was a British initiative in 1991 (later to become an Anglo/German and EC initiative) which led to the establishment in the UN of the first Under Secretary General for Humanitarian Affairs and Department of Humanitarian Affairs in 1992. The section works closely with the ODA on the humanitarian aspects of such crises as the Gulf and the former Yugoslavia and Somalia. This takes up to 80 per cent of the section's time. The public interest generated by these humanitarian emergencies, and the growth of several hundred per cent in associated parliamentary tasks—MPs' letters, Parliamentary Questions etc, has led to increased work for the Section.

13. The section was initially staffed in 1990 by a DS7/8, a DS9 and a DS10. In September 1991, the section was boosted with a DS5 Head of Section and the appointment of an additional DS9 officer. In

September 1992, because of the sustained heavy workload, a third DS9 officer joined the section on a temporary basis bringing the total strength to five.

SPECIALISED AGENCIES

14. This Section is responsible for the co-ordination with other Whitehall Departments of policies towards certain specialized agencies (for example with the ODA on UNICEF and FAO, with the Department of Employment on the ILO, and with the Department of Health and ODA on the WHO). The UK is a member of all UN specialized agencies except UNESCO. The Section is headed by a DS6, supported by a DS10. The DS6 is also charged with monitoring progress towards reform. If the UK decided to rejoin UNESCO, there would be resource implications for the Section and, perhaps in Paris.

15. Until June 1992, UND was also responsible for UN and some other aspects of human rights policy. Since then, all human rights work has been handled by a separate Department (the Human Rights Policy Unit) headed by a DS4 (see para 17–20 below).

WORKLOAD

16. Most of the increases in staff mentioned above followed an internal FCO review of UND in 1991. This review concluded that events in the UN had significantly increased the department's workload and that this burden was unlikely to diminish in the near future. This has proved to be the case. Most members of staff work long hours. Total overtime worked in 1992 by UND staff (not including the Head of Department) was 4,439 hours.

HUMAN RIGHTS POLICY UNIT

17. Human Rights Policy Unit has responsibility for human rights within the UN system (Human Rights Commission, Human Rights Committee) the Council of Europe and the CSCE. Since 1987 the number of Special Rapporteurs investigating alleged human rights abuses in a particular country (for example Iraq), or a particular theme (for example torture), has more than doubled (from fourteen to thirty). In addition the number of human rights treaty monitoring bodies, the expert supervisory bodies established pursuant to human rights treaties adopted within the UN system, has risen from three to six. As one of the main objectives of the UN, the promotion and protection of human rights has increased in importance as the UN's international role has expanded during the past few years.

18. The UK is actively involved in all United Nations human rights bodies, particularly the Third Committee of the UN General Assembly and the UN Commission on Human Rights, to which we were re-elected in 1991 after a one year absence. The UK is also represented on the Sub-Commission on the Prevention of Discrimination and the Protection of Minorities and on two of the Treaty Monitoring Bodies; the Human Rights Committee, the overseeing body of the International Covenant on Civil and Political Rights, and the Committee on the Elimination of Racial Discrimination, the overseeing body of the Convention on the Elimination of all Forms of Racial Discrimination. The UK will also play an active role in the World Conference on Human Rights to be held in Vienna in June 1993. The Conference will address, inter alia, the problems of implementing existing human rights instruments, and explore ways of improving existing human rights mechanisms.

19. The UK has, since 1987, ratified three further UN human rights treaties, two of which have been extended to the Crown Dependencies and Dependent Territories, adding considerably to the work required to fulfil reporting obligations. Increased EC cooperation on human rights in the UN has also added to the workload. With the expansion of human rights work within the United Nations, it has become necessary for staff to spend more time assisting UK delegations to international human rights fora overseas. In practice, at any one time, one officer from the Human Rights Policy Unit is almost permanently away from London.

20. The Unit consists of eleven staff, of whom four work full-time on UN human rights issues. The latter were transferred from UND when the Human Rights Policy Unit was set up, and the number of officers working on UN human rights issues has remained unchanged.

ENVIRONMENT, SCIENCE AND ENERGY DEPARTMENT

21. Although FCO staff have for many years dealt with international environment issues, a reorganisation took place in April 1990 to create an Environment, Science and Energy Department which could devote more attention and resources to the environment. At the start Environment Section had four desk officers (2 x DS6, 1 x DS7, 1 x DS9) and a DS10 Section Clerk.

22. The environment, and its links with sustainable development, has become an increasing focus of international concern, culminating in the UN Conference on Environment and Development in Rio de Janeiro in June 1992.

23. The UN General Assembly in Autumn 1992 endorsed the results of United Nations Conference on Environment and Development and provided for an institutional framework, the Sustainable Development Commission, to co-ordinate the follow-up to the agreements reached at the United Nations Conference on Environment and Development. The UK has been actively involved both within the EC (particularly during the Presidency) and more widely preparing for, participating in and following-up United Nations Conference of Environment and Development.

24. Establishing and maintaining an effective international system for global protection is a continuing process as agreements, once achieved, need to be updated, monitored and implemented. The degree of international cooperation required to implement the Rio agreements is very high and will impose a significant burden on Environment, Science and Energy Department over the next few years. The UK has taken the lead in the EC and G7, and in the wider body of the UN General Assembly.

25. Taking forward the agreements reached at Rio involves Whitehall Departments (especially the DOE, ODA and FCO) in a heavy programme of follow-up action. The FCO, through Environment, Science and Energy Department and UND, take the lead on the international institutional aspects. The Environment Section of Environment, Science and Energy Department is also closely involved in concerting a Government line on the Climate Change and Biodiversity Conventions signed at Rio, and in the international negotiations leading to ratification and implementation. It is also involved in international negotiations which may lead to further conventions on desertification and tropical forests. Work at desk level on the follow-up to the agreements reached at Rio is handled by the DS5 Head of Environment Section, a DS6, and a DS7 with other members of the Section being involved as necessary depending on the volume of work. The DS4 Head of Department also devotes a substantial proportion of her time to the supervision of work on the environment (up to 70 per cent during the preparations for United Nations Conference on Environment and Development).

26. The Environment Section was reinforced during the initial United Nations Conference on Environment and Development preparation phase by the upgrading of one of the DS6 posts to DS5, and the appointment of an additional DS7, and a DS10 reinforced in January 1992 by 2 DS9s and a DS10 who formed a unit to deal with the administrative arrangements for the UK United Nations Conference on Environment and Development Delegation. These included the drawing up the UK Delegation budget, liaison with the British Consulate in Rio de Janeiro, making travel arrangements, and answering public enquiries. This unit was disbanded in July 1992 (and the staff transferred out of the Department). In the immediate run-up to United Nations Conference on Environment and Development the Head of Department, a DS5, a DS7, three DS9s and a DS10 dealt solely with the Conference. The Assistant Head of Department also became more closely involved and "anchored" for the FCO in London while United Nations Conference on Environment and Development took place. Other members of the Section (1 x DS6, 1 x DS7, 1 x DS9 (supernumerary) and 2 x DS10) did some United Nations Conference on Environment and Development related work but were not directly involved in preparations for the Conference. Work on follow-up to United Nations Conference on Environment and Development will remain a dominant aspect of the Department's work.

Arms Control and Disarmament

27. The UN plays a significant role in the field of arms control and disarmament and in the drive for openness in military and weapons matters. It does this through the First Committee of United Nations General Assembly, the UN Disarmament Commission (the UN's deliberating body for arms control and disarmament), and the Conference on Disarmament, a permanent, autonomous negotiating forum which reports directly to the United Nations General Assembly First Committee. There have been three Special Sessions of United Nations General Assembly, in 1978, 1982, and 1988, devoted to disarmament, and the United Nations General Assembly First Committee will exceptionally reconvene in March this year for further consideration of the multilateral arms control and disarmament machinery. The UK plays an active role in all these fora.

28. Recent initiatives by the UN Secretary General in his Reports on "New Dimensions on Arms Regulation in Disarmament in the Post-Cold War Era" have required extensive liaison with EC Partners in producing common replies on the issues raised. In 1992 these and the regular issues of UN disarmament work were covered by one DS7D desk officer in Arms Control and Disarmament Department with half a DS10, supported by specialized input from Desk Officers in other departments dealing with defence and security issues.

29. In December 1991, following the Prime Minister's initiative at the European Council in April 1991, the United Nations General Assembly voted to set up at the UN a universal register of conventional arms transfers. The register came into effect in January 1992 and requests all party states to provide the UN Secretary-General annually with information on their imports and exports of certain major weapons systems. The first reporting is required in April covering imports and exports in 1992. Work to establish the register has been a major task for the Conventional Arms Transfers Section in Non-Proliferation and Defence Department. The Section set up in 1991 comprises one DS5 and one DS9.

30. Agreement at United Nations General Assembly in November 1992 on the Chemical Weapons Convention will allow room on the CD agenda for other disarmament issues to be negotiated and may also permit cuts in the staffing of UKDis Geneva. But it also creates obligations for the setting up and manning of the Chemical Weapons Convention Secretariat to bring the Convention into effect. This will require a DS5 UK representative in the Embassy in The Hague.

31. An important, recent UN Disarmament activity is the work of the UN Special Commission, established under UN SCR 687, calling for the elimination of Iraq's capabilities in nuclear and other weapons of mass destruction. Significant progress has been achieved. However much remains to be done both to complete the programme of elimination and also to verify Iraq's future compliance with its obligation not to use, develop, construct or acquire weapons of mass destruction. A Section was set up in Arms Control and Disarmament Department in July 1991, staffed by a DS5 and DS10, to meet the resultant workload in the FCO.

UKMIS New York

32. The expansion in the work of the Security Council has had a significant effect on the workload of the UK Mission in New York. The UN Secretary-General drew attention in his annual report in 1992 to the extraordinary expansion in the responsibility of the United Nations. As an illustration he gave figures for meetings of the Security Council: in 1987 there were 49 Security Council meetings and 43 Consultations of the Whole; in the final seven months of 1992 alone there were 81 meetings and 49 Consultations of the Whole. The Security Council passed 14 resolutions in 1987 and 74 in 1992. The increase in Security Council business and in consultations among informal Council groupings has placed enormous strain on staff resources in UKMis New York which have remained largely unchanged since the days of the Cold War. The Gulf, Yugoslavia and Somalia are major areas of attention, with continuing work on other issues such as Cambodia, South Africa and Cyprus. The proliferation of ethnic and other disputes in Eastern Europe, the former Soviet Union, Africa and the Middle East, together with the increasing tendency of all parties to disputes to look to the UN, mean that demands on the mission are likely to continue to increase. Work on the proliferating number of Security Council Sanctions Committees and in support of the growing UK contribution to UN peacekeeping operations is particularly time consuming. In 1987 there were 31 UK-based staff in New York. In 1992 an additional four staff (Military Adviser, DS8, DS9 and Secretary) were provided, initially on a temporary basis.

33. The need for scrutiny of the financial management of the UN has grown substantially, as has the role of the UN's financial watch-dog body, the Advisory Committee for Administrative and Budgetary Questions. The UK is represented on the Advisory Committee for Administrative and Budgetary Questions by the Financial Counsellor (DS4) at UKMis New York. It is expected that the Committee will be in session for 8 months in 1993, a substantial increase from the 6 months in 1992 and the previous average of 4 months per year. The Financial Counsellor is expected to combine his responsibilities as a member of the Advisory Committee for Administrative and Budgetary Questions with his normal duties of representing the UK on the Fifth Committee. On the Economic and Social side the Mission is also under pressure on a wide front. The decision to locate the Sustainable Development Department in New York will impose an additional workload.

34. Of the P5 members in New York our mission is the smallest. Nevertheless the reputation of our mission is high and it makes an effective contribution to maintaining the UK's position as a member of the Permanent Five. Staff work into the night and at weekends on a regular basis. FCO Inspectors will visit New York in February to assess the case for an increase in staff to cope with the additional workload.

UKMIS Geneva

35. The Commission for Human Rights, International Committee of the Red Cross and UNHCR are all based in Geneva as well as five Specialized Agencies. Following an initial meeting in London the International Conference on Former Yugoslavia is now also based in Geneva. The increased focus on humanitarian and human rights questions particularly in the former Yugoslavia has resulted in a significant increase in workload for our Mission in Geneva. There are few signs that the expansion of work by the UN and related agencies on humanitarian issues and human rights is likely to abate in the near future.

36. In the meantime UKMis Geneva has had to re-assign staff resources to cope. They have reduced staff (by one DS6) working on United Nations Conference on Trade and Development and the UN Economic Commission for Europe. In 1991 a new DS5 post was added to deal with environmental issues. The Legal Adviser to both UKMis Geneva and the UK Delegation to the Disarmament Conference now devotes the majority of his time to human rights, thus freeing one DS5 to work exclusively on humanitarian issues. The current UK Permanent Representative in Geneva is also, with effect from 1992, the UK representative on the Commission for Human Rights (until 1992, this post was held by an outside expert).

UKMIS VIENNA

37. Our Mission in Vienna has probably been least affected by the expanding role of the UN, although the developing role of the IAEA, in particular in relation to Iraq, has increased the workload. The IAEA has had to devote more time to issues of safeguards, non-proliferation, nuclear safety and liability. Staffing at UKMis Vienna has remained unchanged since 1987.

CONCLUSION

38. The increased workload for the FCO and overseas posts flowing from the expanded work of the UN has been absorbed through small increases in staff in UND and UKMis New York (under 10 per cent in each case) and a reallocation and in some instances an intensification of effort elsewhere (for example a significant increase in staff in Environment, Science and Energy Department).

39. The increased workload stemming from greater UN activity has been set against other demands on FCO resources in the annual Top Management Round, the Diplomatic Wing's basic planning and resource allocation process. In response to changing priorities, since 1990, posts have been closed at Monrovia, Brazzaville, Libreville and Edmonton; posts at Damascus, Tehran and Phnom Penh have been reopened and new posts have been opened in Tallinn, Riga, Vilnius, Kiev, St Petersburg, Alma Ata, Zagreb and Ljubljana. This has been achieved without increasing overall manpower numbers. The resource allocation process is supplemented by regular staff inspections to ensure that departments and posts have the appropriate staff establishment to cope with current requirements. As noted in paragraph 34, UKMis New York is being inspected in February 1993.

DIPLOMATIC SERVICE/HOME CIVIL SERVICE: GRADE EQUIVALENTS

DS 4	—	HCS 5
DS 5S	—	HCS 6
DS 5	—	HCS 7
DS 6	—	SEO
DS 7	—	HEO
DS 8	—	AT
DS 9	—	EO
DS 10	—	AO

UND STRUCTURE

Head of Department (DS 4)—PA

Assistant Head (DS 5S)

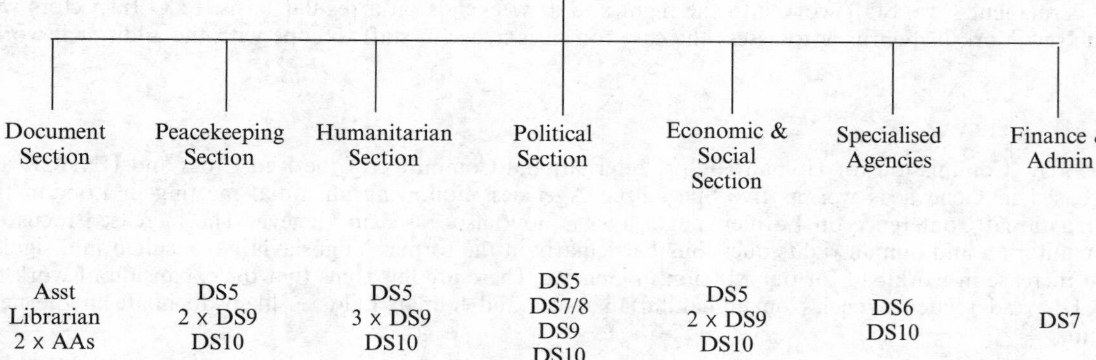

Support Staff
2 x Secretaries (S2)
2 x AAs

APPENDIX 14

Memorandum by the Foreign and Commonwealth Office

BRITISH PERMANENT MEMBERSHIP OF THE UN SECURITY COUNCIL AND BRITAIN'S GLOBAL INTERESTS

1. Britain is a member of over 80 international organizations. Britain holds a unique position as a member of the European Community, NATO, Group of Seven and Commonwealth as well as a permanent member of the Security Council.

SECURITY COUNCIL

2. The United Nations was set up in 1945; it grew out of the victorious war-time alliance. Under the Charter, the Security Council was given primary responsibility for maintaining international peace and security. For much of the Cold War, super-power rivalry prevented the Council from acting effectively. With the end of the Cold War, the authority of the United Nations, and in particular the unique legal powers of the Security Council, have become more important.

3. Permanent membership of the Security Council enables us to protect Britain's interests. In the past, for example, we were able quickly to get Security Council condemnation of Argentina's invasion of the Falkland Islands. Britain was instrumental in the drafting of the 12 Resolutions condemning Iraq's invasion of Kuwait and authorizing action to expel Iraq. The last time we had to use the veto in defence of a specifically British interest was in June 1982.

Although we would hope never to have to do so again, it might be necessary if the international situation were to deteriorate. The world environment is now generally more benign, but we cannot take that for granted; and we still have to deal with the exceptions. Our permanent membership automatically gives Britain a central place in any discussion of UN reform.

International Peace-keeping

4. In its first 40 years, the Security Council authorised 13 peace-keeping operations; in the last four years, it has authorised 14 more. As of March 1993, Britain is the second largest troop contributor (after France) to UN peace-keeping operations. Britain is participating in UN peace-keeping and monitoring operations in Cyprus (UNFICYP), Western Sahara (MINURSO), Cambodia (UNTAC) and Yugoslavia (UNPROFOR).

5. Britain is one of the guarantor powers in *Cyprus*. The United Nations has been involved continuously there since the outbreak of inter-communal violence in 1963. The UN has provided a peace-keeping force and acted as a forum for negotiations between the two sides.

6. The Security Council authorised coalition action to expel *Iraq* from Kuwait. The international community is still coping with the aftermath of the war. Helping to enforce the No Fly Zone in northern Iraq, the RAF have eight Jaguar aircraft supported by two VC10 K-tankers based at Incirlik in Turkey. Covering southern Iraq, there are six Tornado GRI aircraft and one Victor tanker. Since April 1991, Britain has given £56½ million for humanitarian aid to the people of North and South Iraq. About £28 million has gone direct to northern Iraq; much of the rest has gone to UN agencies and the International Committee of the Red Cross for distribution in northern and southern Iraq.

7. Britain is providing the biggest contingent of troops in *Bosnia* of any UN country. By 18 March, our troops had escorted 337 UNHCR convoys carrying 28,560 tonnes of food and medicines. In 398 flights since July last year, the RAF had airlifted nearly 5,500 tonnes of supplies into Sarajevo. The ODA's civilian drivers had carried some 20,000 tonnes in over 200 convoys. Britain has also provided monitors for the European Community Monitoring Mission in Slovenia and Croatia.

8. In *Somalia*, Britain supported Security Council Resolution 794 providing for all necessary means to be used to create a secure environment for relief operations. The Unified Task Force (UNITAF), led by United States, has secured relief centres; aid is flowing. Although Britain is not involved on the ground, the RAF helped with the airlift. Britain remains the second largest aid donor in Somalia.

UN Budget

9. Britain pays 5.02 per cent of the *United Nations* general budget ($49.4m in 1992; the estimate for 1993 is about $55m). This does not include contributions to peace-keeping operations, to which Britain paid 6.1 per cent in 1992 (approx £90m); this will rise to 6.5 per cent in 1993. Including contributions to agencies, Britain paid a total of about £250m to the UN in 1991–92.

10. Britain's permanent membership of the Security Council does not add to our financial contribution to the UN, apart from the 1.353 per cent peace-keeping supplement which we and the other four perma-

nent members pay. The advantages of permanent membership include influence on the size and remit of peace-keeping operations, which justifies this extra contribution.

Enlargement of the Security Council

11. There is *no* pressure for Britain to give up its permanent seat. The Treaty of Maastricht establishes in a satisfactory way the position of Britain and France as members of the European Community who are also permanent members of the Security Council. The Treaty recognizes our responsibilities under the Charter, and we accept the need to take the views of our partners into account as we fulfil those responsibilities.

12. The debate about Security Council membership is about possible additions to the permanent membership to reflect changes in the world since 1945. We want discussion to take account of the following factors:

(i) it is impossible to imagine a solution which would satisfy all aspirations; debate is therefore likely to be long;

(ii) a simple proposition to add Germany and Japan to the list of permanent members could not survive without others from other continents putting forward their claims;

(iii) permanent membership carries certain obligations, new permanent members should not face constitutional constraints on contributing troops to the full range of UN peace-keeping operations;

(iv) discussion should not frustrate or undermine the efforts of the Security Council to deal with problems of the moment. The Security Council has never been more in demand. It must be able to do its job effectively without too many distractions.

Security Council: Priorities

13. As a permanent member, Britain helps set the Security Council agenda. Here, we need to learn three main lessons from experience since the end of the Cold War:

(i) it is better to move early to avert a disaster than to clear up its consequences. An ambassador costs less than an infantry battalion, and peace-keeping costs less than war. The UN and the international community must make a concerted effort to solve international disputes before they reach the point of armed conflict. The UN has perhaps not done enough in this crucial area in the past. But the preventive deployment of troops to Macedonia and the despatch of fact finding missions to the Former Soviet Union are steps in the right direction. We must build on this in future;

(ii) there has to be an equitable sharing of burdens in any substantial international enterprise;

(iii) there has to be a disciplined analysis of risks and benefits. The international community should not lurch into enterprises, the scope and duration of which have not been thought through.

If we ourselves follow these principles and encourage others to do so, then we may together case by case cope with at least some of the problems of world disorder.

BRITAIN'S GLOBAL INTERESTS

14. There is a solid British interest in Britain helping the Security Council fulfil its remit to maintain international peace and security. We are, more than almost any other, a trading nation; conflict and chaos are enemies to trade and thus to our prosperity.

Trade

15. Measured by GDP, Britain has the sixth largest economy in the world. Britain accounts for about 5 per cent of world output (using a Purchasing Power Parities exchange rate, slightly less than France and Italy). The United States accounts for over 28 per cent, Japan for over 16 per cent and Germany about 7 per cent. In the 1980s Britain's economy grew at an average rate of 2.7 per cent per year; the US (3.2 per cent), Germany (2.2 per cent), France (2.2 per cent), Italy (2.4 per cent), Japan (4.1 per cent).

16. Britain ranks fifth in the world for international trade. Exports account for 18 per cent of GDP (compared with 9 per cent for Japan and 7 per cent for the United States). Britain is either the largest market or largest supplier of 14 countries (or in three cases both—Ireland, Cyprus and Kenya). There are a further 33 countries for whom Britain is the second or third largest trading partner.

Investment

17. British companies' investments are world-wide. In 1991 the stock of *direct investment abroad* amounted to £129.6 billion compared to £8.8 billion in 1970. In the USA, the stock of British investment is now estimated at £45 billion, 28 per cent of all foreign investment there. Britain is the largest foreign

investor in the US. US assets account for 38 per cent of British overseas investment compared to 28 per cent in 1981. EC assets account for 24 per cent of the total.

18. *Inward direct investment* (cumulative stock) in 1991 amounted to £127 billion, increased from £4.9 billion in 1970. The UK is the second largest recipient of Japanese direct investment (12 per cent of Japanese direct investment abroad in 1990, a book value of £5.7bn), and the largest recipient of US direct investment (16.1 per cent in 1990, book value of $45bn).

Defence

19. Britain is serious about collective security. The Defence budget is 3.9 per cent of GDP, £23.5 billion in 1993–4. 95 per cent of British defence expenditure is on NATO commitments. Britain's budget in 1991 was the third largest in NATO, after the United States and Germany. We are one of five nuclear weapons states (the other four are the other four permanent members of the Security Council).

Overseas Aid

20. In 1990 (the latest year for comparative figures) Britain spent £1.569bn ($2.65bn) on overseas aid—the sixth largest aid donor in the OECD behind the US, Japan, France, Germany and Italy. Britain had aid programmes to more countries (128) than most other donors; only Germany, Japan and France have programmes in a larger number of countries.

Britons Abroad

21. About 7.9 million British nationals live abroad. Of these, up to 2 million are in Australia, over 1 million in Canada, roughly 750,000 in South Africa and about 650,000 in the USA. There are about 475,000 British nationals in other EC countries. In 1990 British residents took over 20 million overseas *holidays*, the majority in the EC. The total number of visits abroad, including business trips and visits to relatives was 31.2 million.

CONCLUSION

22. The maintenance of the international rule of law through the United Nations is important for Britain because of our global interests. The Security Council is central to our global objectives; our permanent seat is central to Britain's influence. When you consider all the criteria by which permanent membership could be judged, Britain scores well. (The exception is size of population, where Britain ranks nineteenth in the world). As a permanent member, Britain helps set the Security Council agenda. Permanent membership would also help us to protect British interests if the world situation again deteriorated. As long as Britain has significant global interests, it is to Britain's advantage to keep its permanent membership of the Security Council. As long as Britain continues to act like a permanent member, it is in the UN's interest that we should remain on the Security Council.

APPENDIX 15

Memorandum by the Foreign and Commonwealth Office

IRAQ: UN SPECIAL COMMISSION/INTERNATIONAL ATOMIC ENERGY AGENCY DESTRUCTION ACTIVITIES: SUMMARY

Inspectors have so far supervised the destruction of:

Ballistic Missiles and Supergun

62 ballistic missiles
10 ballistic missile launchers
18 fixed scud launch pads
32 ballistic missile warheads
127 missile storage support vehicles
Tons of rocket fuel
Assembled 350mm supergun
Components for 350mm and 1,000mm superguns
1 tonne of supergun propellant
54 items of ballistic missile production equipment
10 buildings related to ballistic missile production

Chemical Weapons

The number and quantity of munitions and agent destroyed by the Special Commission as of 14 December 1992 were in the order of:

— 12,000 empty munitions;

— 5,000 sarin filled 122mm. rockets, including motors and warheads;

— 350 R.400 aerial bombs;

— 44,500 litres of GB/GF

— 120 litres of GB;

— 5,000 litres of D4;

— 1,100 litres of dichlorethane;

— 16.5 tons of thiodiglycol;

— 5.5 tons of mustard agent.

Nuclear

— hot cells and manipulators and glove boxes at Tuwaitha have been destroyed.

— fresh nuclear fuel has been removed from Iraq and returned to Russia

— EMIS (that is calutrons) equipment has been destroyed as well as a considerable number of centrifuge components.

— the principle buildings at the A1 Atheer weaponisation facility (8 buildings covering a surface of approximately 35,000 square metres and 26 major equipment items, some consisting of several components).

— the large bunker at the A1 Hatteen site was filled with concrete and scrap iron to prevent its further use (350 cubic metres of concrete were poured), as the use of explosives in this case was judged to be impractical. The bunker's high protective berm was levelled.

— the EMIS site at Tarmiya and Ash Sharqat. At Tarmiya all of the EMIS production buildings and associated electrical power distribution capability have been destroyed. The same action has been taken at Ash Sharqat.

Iraq claims to have destroyed:

89 ballistic missiles
24,470 chemical munitions
200 tonnes and 3,000 litres of chemical precursors
"various quantities" of imported and locally made parts for the Scud missile airframe, motor and guidance system
25 ancillary vehicles for the Scud missile system
5 decoy launchers
4 test and launch vehicles
100 tonnes of maraging steel
1,000's of aluminium forgings

20 January 1993

APPENDIX 16

Memorandum by Oxfam

NOTE TO THE COMMITTEE IN ADVANCE OF THEIR VISIT TO SOMALIA[1] ON ISSUES OF IMMEDIATE HUMANITARIAN CONCERN

BACKGROUND

From 9–19 February 1993 David Bryer, Director of Oxfam, accompanied by John Magrath, Oxfam's Press Office Manager, visited Somalia to assess the situation and Oxfam's work there. They interviewed Mr Kittani, Special Representative of the UN Secretary General; Ambassador Robert Oakley, US Ambassador; Colonels Kevin Kennedy and Bob Macpherson, responsible for UNOSOM-NGO liaison; Prof. Warfa, working on peace and reconciliation issues for UNOSOM; and representatives of Unicef, ICRC, Goal, Irish Concern and World Concern. They visited Mogadishu North and Oxfam health and agricultural projects in the Lower Shabelle river valley.

[1] The Committee visited Somalia on 2–4 March 1993.

CONCLUSIONS

The following is a summary of our main general conclusions:

1. The importance of what has happened and what still needs to happen in Somalia is recognised by all parties. They see it as a test case for similar interventions in the future in terms of setting new principles by which to operate and in terms of setting up new structures. In particular it is a test for the UN. It is also seen by many NGOs as an opportunity to expand and to experiment. There is a reasonable degree of optimism that the changeover from UNITAF to UNOSOM 2 operations will take place smoothly and that UNOSOM 2 will be fully functioning from about April.

2. The relative effectiveness of the co-ordination between the military and humanitarian sides of the operation has not, we think, been sufficiently recognised. Co-ordination is not perfect; nevertheless, considerable efforts have been made, regular and seemingly effective meetings happen and an effective structure has been put in place in the form of the Humanitarian Operations Centre of UNOSOM. A high and perhaps surprising degree of respect has grown up between most military and most NGOs. It is vital that these structures continue and are strengthened after the transition from UNITAF to UNOSOM 2. One challenge will be to co-ordinate the activities of the many NGOs which have been coming and continue to come into the country as security gets better.

3. The military and humanitarian operations have had a high degree of success in delivering aid along main routes and to and from principal centres. But numbers have not been sufficient to guard all humanitarian staff and locations so the degree of insecurity for NGO and UN humanitarian staff has increased. Furthermore, military forces are not trained to act as police. The establishment of a police force will be important as will the next steps of establishing a prison service and judicial system. In terms of numbers it is clear that UNITAF succeeded in its objectives by use of overwhelming force, but insecurity still persists. UNOSOM 2 will have to continue to fulfil those objectives and operate a "law and order" role while the police are established plus go into "Somaliland" to fulfil a similar role there, although it should be recognised that elders in Somaliland have had more success than in other regions of Somalia. It is our worry that incoming forces (25,000 strong) will be spread too thinly, particularly by the move into the north.

4. There is strong consensus among all people spoken to that disarming and the threat of disarming has enabled the military and humanitarian operations to succeed. Disarming is seen as the key to the next step, which is to advance the political process. Without disarming, powerful warlords will continue to be excessively powerful and other, more representative, groups will be afraid to emerge. Disarming will be enormously difficult and may never remove more than a fraction of the weaponry in Somalia. Nevertheless, it is seen as crucial that the process continues and continues visibly. One difficulty is that the most visible guns belong to guards who accompany NGOs (although not employed by NGOs) and it is these weapons which have been frequently confiscated; given increased insecurity this makes it impossible for NGOs to travel around. Systems have been put in place to enable NGOs to carry or reclaim guns, but these are still operated rather arbitarily depending on the interpretation of individual soldiers or commanders or of particular national forces.

5. It seems clear that the UNOSOM 2 force will have the necessary mandate to operate in a similar manner to the UNITAF force, that is to make peace and to act forcefully when required. The continued presence of some US forces may be important both symbolically and practically, both to supply logistics and communications and to act as a rapid reaction force in case of serious unrest.

6. It will be very important that Kittani and Oakley are replaced by equally senior and adept people. There is also general agreement that the civilian side of the UNOSOM 2 operation will need further strengthening and that more expert managers, administrators and operational staff are needed. The emphasis should very much be on getting the right persons for the job, from wherever they exist, whether they be from within the UN or from governments or from NGOs. This might mean by-passing normal lines of seniority or of reporting. Also, aid agencies now provide employment for many trained Somalia staff—agronomists, logisticians, managers—but in the long term these people will be needed and should be enabled to go back into government and civil administration.

7. While the military and humanitarian sides of the operation have gone well, there has been much less progress on the political restructuring of Somalia. The UN and US have firm commitments to the widest possible political participation, but this cannot be hurried. There is also the difficult question of whether the faction leaders should have any place in the political process and if so, what. Furthermore, given the desire for wide participation, many Somali leaders have suddenly emerged whose ability to represent anyone but themselves must be in doubt. It is likely that the March 15 peace conference, if it takes place, can only be seen as a further step in a process which might take many years. It is also significant that progress so far has happened after the judicious and appropriately timed use of military force by the US. Whether this "judicious force" will be a tactic employable by UNOSOM 2 is doubtful although a contin-

uing process of disarming must continue. Finally, it seems that the US at least would want to see a federal, regional structure emerging similar to that which existed before Siad Barre came to power.

8. The UN appeal for Somalia should also only be seen as a first step. Its production was criticised by some, who felt it would be largely a list of what NGOs were doing and a wish list of what they wanted to do. However, it seems likely that the final version may be at least the start of a proper plan, setting up a framework for rehabilitation and be rather more forward-looking, more comprehensive and more realistic. However there is a lack of long-term planning for the future. Given the level of political uncertainty this is perhaps understandable but there are certain areas for example long-term food security, basic health provision, where planning could start now. Such planning could and should involve, right from the start, the many expert Somalis who could contribute. This would also contribute to an atmosphere conducive to political progress. There is also an urgent need to gather basic information and to standardise that information for example on health.

9. A major next step, and one desired and requested by many Somalis, is to enable displaced people to return to their homes and fields. Developing the infrastructure to enable that return must have high priority. It should be at the same time be recognised that this will create arguments (and therefore potential violence) over land tenure and the possession of houses. But there are also 800,000 Somali refugees in neighbouring countries. They must be allowed/enabled to return, but to yield to pressure for them to return too soon might overwhelm the infrastructure. Finding the right balance will be difficult but important.

10. Rehabilitation of pastoralists as opposed to agriculturalists will be more difficult but must be explored.

11. The lack of a banking system is causing nightmares for NGOs.

20 February 1993

APPENDIX 17

Letter to the Clerk of the Committee from Lord Gladwyn, GCMG, GCVO, CB

May I refer to the copy that was sent to me of Sir Anthony Parsons' paper on Reform of the United Nations?[1]

I note he is in favour of enlarging the Security Council to twenty by the inclusion (as Permanent Members) of Germany and Japan and a representative of Africa, Latin America and (another) representative of Asia, all possessing, presumably, the power of veto. At the same time he appears to doubt whether this will be possible because of "rivalries"—a doubt which, as will be seen from my letter to the *Independent* (Feb. 3) I myself strongly share.

Unlike Sir Anthony, I also fear that a Security Council of (at least) twenty would probably be so "unwieldy" as to be inoperable. Nor do I think that "divisionism" will diminish in the New World. Indeed it will probably be increased!

I hold these views reluctantly and only hope I may be wrong, as the present system is obviously out of date and should be reformed somehow. Perhaps a temporary way out might lie in some enlargement of and changes in the operation of the Military Staff Committee?

I hope in any case that you will put this letter before your Committee for consideration.

APPENDIX 18

Memorandum by Sir Michael Marshall DL MP, President of the Council of the Inter-Parliamentary Union

Since the Presidential statement by the Prime Minister at the UN Security Council Summit in New York on 31 January 1992, we and the IPU Secretariat in Geneva have had regular exchanges with the UN Secretary General and his staff. These discussions have been principally concerned with an examination of how parliamentarians might assist the United Nations in performing the ever more numerous and difficult tasks imposed upon them.

---

[1] Published in *International Relations,* December 1992.

We have established that parliamentarians have a useful role to play both in preventive diplomacy and post-conflict peace-building. While such activities are not confined to those directed centrally or at national or regional level by the IPU, the present note summarises the Union's experience to date recognising that British as well as other European parliamentarians have been prominent in such work.

The main areas of co-operation are electoral observation, and the joint IPU/UNDP project to provide technical assistance to emerging Parliaments. In addition, the work of the IPU's Committee on the Human Rights of Parliamentarians is linked closely with the activities of the United Nations Human Rights Commission. That the IPU has a unique role not only in preventive diplomacy but also in peace-making, was pointed out by the Secretary of State in the House on 4 March 1992, when he said that the IPU "is an important element in preventing conflicts reaching the stage of war".

The participation of parliamentarians in the work of the United Nations was also welcomed by the Minister of State, the Hon Douglas Hogg, in the Commons on 28 October 1992. He noted that there are particular areas in which the extensive experience and tradition of democracy of Members of the House can be of benefit. He commented that the Government remained willing to assist Members of the House to participate in such areas and he added that the Foreign and Commonwealth Office arranged an annual visit for Members of Parliament to the UN General Assembly.

These visits play an invaluable part in increasing the understanding of the work of the United Nations. However they fail to take full advantage of the opportunities afforded in two important respects. First, there is little or no attempt made to ensure that British parliamentarians are put in touch with their counterparts from other countries at the UN. There are always a significant number of such representatives present during the General Assembly attached to their national delegations. One obvious opportunity of meeting would be to plan the visits to coincide with the UN/IPU Day in New York in early or mid October when senior members of the UN Secretariat cover a number of current themes for parliamentarians of all nationalities.

Second, when delegations visiting the United Nations through the Foreign Office return to Westminster their report back session has, historically, been purely an internal debate with Government. In February 1993, a combined visit of both those selected through the Foreign Office and the usual channels, together with 4 MPs selected by the IPU (12 in all) took part in a visit to the UN. Through the initiative of the Chairman of the British Group IPU a report back session was organised which attracted the interest of Members of both Houses and demonstrated the way in which Members of Parliament are increasingly concerned with practical aspects of support for the UN including finance and resources. It is suggested that such report back sessions for Parliament as a whole should become standard practice for future visits.

Finally, it is to be hoped that publication of the Select Committee's report may provide an opportunity for parliamentary debate on a wide-ranging basis which might include contributions from the relatively large but largely unidentified number of Members who have had the opportunity of observing UN work at first hand in recent years.

APPENDIX 19

Memorandum by Professor P J Rowe, Faculty of Law, University of Liverpool

LEGAL PROBLEMS ASSOCIATED WITH AN INTERNATIONAL WAR CRIMES TRIBUNAL

I was requested to consider the above topic in the light of the *ad hoc* tribunal established by Security Council Resolution 808 (22 February 1993) for the prosecution of persons responsible for serious violations of international humanitarian law committed in the territory of the former Yugoslavia since 1991.

It will be recalled that there have been earlier war crimes trials. By the Treaty of Versailles in 1919 the German Government recognised the right of the allied and associated powers to bring before military tribunals persons accused of having committed acts in violation of the laws and customs of war. The allies asked for the surrender of 896 persons for trial but the German Government, unwilling to comply with this request, proposed trying themselves some of the persons named. Between 1921 and 1922 trials were held under German law in Leipzig, which resulted in the conviction of only 13 defendants. Many of the sentences were deemed to be inadequate and a number of those convicted were able to escape from prison shortly after their conviction[1].

The International Military Tribunal at Nuremberg was established by the London Agreement of 8 August 1945 'for the just and prompt trial and punishment of the major war criminals of the European

[1] *History of the United Nations War Crimes Commission and the Development of the Laws of War* HMSO (1948) at pp 46–52.

Axis.' The Charter of the Tribunal set out the charges that might be brought, which included crimes against humanity (in Article 6) and emphasised that there could be individual responsibility in respect of the acts charged. It also declared (in Article 8) that superior orders would not relieve a defendant of responsibility but could be considered in mitigation. Article 12 indicated that the Tribunal could try a defendant in his absence and Article 16 set out the procedure to ensure that a defendant received a fair trial. The Tribunal was not bound by 'technical rules of evidence' but was able to admit any evidence which it deemed to be probative (Article 19). There was no review or appeal from the findings or sentence (Article 26). Twenty two defendants were tried (Bormann in his absence); 19 were convicted and 3 acquitted.

A similar (although not identical) procedure was adopted for the trial of major Japanese alleged war criminals. One commentator described the difficulties involved as follows

> "Rapid demobilization and repatriation of ex-POWs, witnesses and evidence scattered literally throughout the world, wholesale destruction of key documents by Japanese, incredible difficulties in identifying, locating and apprehending suspects in Japan proper and East Asia and other factors combined to render nearly impossible the tasks given to Allied prosecutors. Any attempt to abide meticulously by strict evidentiary rules applicable to municipal courts would have precluded the majority of war crimes trials and delayed interminably those deemed triable."[1]

All 25 defendants were found guilty, 7 were sentenced to death, the remainder to imprisonment.

In addition to these international military tribunals a number of States conducted their own war crimes trials. The United Kingdom did so under a Royal Warrant, dated 14 June 1945. Under it a Military Court could be convened to try an alleged "violation of the laws and usages of war committed during any war in which His Majesty has been or may be engaged at any time since the 2 September 1939." A large number of trials were conducted under this Warrant and by other States. By 1948, a total of 24,760 accused persons had been tried by various States, of whom 1,999 had been sentenced to death.[2]

Individual States have tried their own citizens for crimes that were, in effect, war crimes. The trial of Lieutenant Calley for his involvement in the deaths of South Vietnamese civilians was perhaps the best, but not the only, example of a soldier being charged with offences relating to the conduct of a modern armed conflict.[3] Indeed, the basic structure of the Geneva Conventions, 1949 and the First Additional Protocol of 1977 is for the trial of grave breaches of the Conventions or of the Protocol to be held before national courts under national law[4]. The United Kingdom has implemented this provision in the 1949 Conventions (but has not ratified the Additional Protocol of 1977) in the form of S.1 of the Geneva Conventions Act 1957, which makes it an offence for any person, whatever his nationality, to commit, in the United Kingdom or elsewhere, a grave breach of the 1949 Conventions.

A New International Criminal Court

The Report of the International Law Commission in 1992 contains a report of a Working Group on the question of an international criminal jurisdiction[5]. It proposes the establishment of such a court by treaty, having jurisdiction over private persons for crimes of an international character only where these are *defined in specified treaties*. These would clearly include serious war crimes defined in treaties and would therefore exclude such charges as crimes against humanity. The Working Group conclude by stating that a further mandate from the General Assembly is required in order to proceed further by compiling a draft statute.

Resolution 808 (22 February 1993)

It will be recalled that by this resolution the Security Council decided that an international tribunal should be established for the prosecution of persons responsible for serious violations of international humanitarian law committed in the territory of the former Yugoslavia since 1991.

By Security Council Resolution 780 (6 October 1992) the Secretary General was requested to establish an impartial Commission of Experts with a view to providing him with its conclusion on the evidence of grave breaches of the Geneva Conventions and other violations of international humanitarian law com-

[1] P. Piccigallo, *The Japanese on Trial, Allied War Crimes Operations in the East, 1945–51* University of Texas, p.13.

[2] *Op. cit.* note 1, at p. 518. For trials under the Royal Warrant see (now Brigadier) A.P.V.Rogers, *The Royal Warrant and War Crimes* (1990) 39 I.C.L.Q. 800.

[3] Calley was charged with murder and related offences under the Uniform Code of Military Justice and not with having committed a war crime. It is not thought appropriate to discuss here the effect of the War Crimes Act 1991. For a good account see Greenwood in Fox and Meyer (eds.), *Effecting Compliance, Vol. II, Armed Conflict and the New Law*, British Institute of International and Comparative Law (1993), Chapter 12.

[4] The preference for the trial before national courts of crimes having an international dimension is not confined to war crimes in the form of grave breaches of the Geneva Conventions 1949. It includes, for instance, the hijacking offences and the dealing in narcotics.

[5] This followed a General Assembly Resolution, 46/54 (9 December 1991), although the issue of the creation of such a court can be traced back to 1948, Resolution 260B, 9 December 1948.

mitted in the territory of the former Yugoslavia. Professor Frits Kalshoven (The Netherlands) was appointed as Chairman.

On 16 December 1992 Mr Vance, Co-Chairman of the International Conference on the Former Yugoslavia, expressed the view that

> "Lord Owen and I believe that atrocities committed in the former Yugoslavia are unacceptable, and persons guilty (sic) of war crimes should be brought to justice. We, therefore, recommend the establishment of an international criminal court."[1]

Whilst the trial of alleged war criminals can be supported as a means of enforcing the laws of war and of giving substance to the principle stated in Security Council resolutions that 'persons who commit or order the commission of grave breaches of the Conventions are individually responsible in respect of such breaches' there are, nevertheless, some difficult legal issues involved. It can hardly be disputed that "Whatever the precise structure of the court ... it must guarantee due process, independence and impartiality in its procedures." These words are taken from the Report of the International Law Commission's Working Group on the establishment of an international criminal court, referred to above. Moreover, a competent defence lawyer may make serious challenge to the court's jurisdiction and procedures, which must be capable of withstanding such attack.

The principal legal difficulties may be considered to be the following.

(a) Can a charge of war crimes be brought in respect of activities in the former Yugoslavia?

The concept of the "war crime" has been developed as a result of activities committed during a war or an international armed conflict *between States*. All the war crimes trials discussed above have been of this type. There is therefore no precedent for the trial by an international tribunal of a person for committing "offences" during a civil war or a non-international armed conflict. Where trials have taken place they have been in respect of crimes under the law of the territory concerned. In addition, the laws of war make a very clear distinction between an international and a non-international armed conflict. The Geneva Conventions 1949 and the First Additional Protocol of 1977 only apply to cases of "declared war or of any other armed conflict which may arise between *two or more of the High Contracting Parties*."[2]

In a non-international armed conflict there are relatively few treaty provisions. Common Article 3 of the Geneva Conventions 1949 lays down some minimum standards and Additional Protocol II of 1977 will also apply. In these provisions there is no concept of the grave breach or any mention of war crimes. It was assumed that only the law of the territory would apply since an armed conflict of this type would *ipso facto* not involve the armed forces of any other State. Common Article 3 goes on to direct that

> The Parties to the conflict should further endeavour to bring into force, by means of special agreements, all or part of the other provisions of the [Conventions]. The application of the preceding provisions shall not affect the legal status of the Parties to the conflict.

Such agreements have been concluded. On 27 November 1991 a Memorandum of Understanding was signed between representatives of Yugoslavia and Croatia, setting out the treatment to be accorded to the wounded and sick, captured combatants, the protection of the civilian population against certain consequences of hostilities and the conduct of hostilities. On 22 May 1992 a similar agreement was concluded by representatives of the President of the Republic of Bosnia-Herzegovina, the President of the Serbian Democratic Party, the President of the Party of Democratic Action and the President of the Croatian Democratic Community. This agreement stated that

> The Parties agree that, without any prejudice to the legal status of the parties to the conflict or to the international law of armed conflict in force, [they will apply the following rules]

Yugoslavia was a Party to the Geneva Conventions 1949 and the Additional Protocols of 1977; Bosnia-Herzegovina acceded to them on 31 December 1992, Croatia on 11 May 1992, Serbia claims the treaty obligations of Yugoslavia and Slovenia acceded on 26 March 1992. In addition, the Genocide Convention 1948 declares that murder and other serious crimes committed with intent to destroy in whole, or in part, a national, ethnical, racial or religious group is a crime under international law.

The status of the conflict in Bosnia-Herzegovina would appear to be of a non-international kind. It is difficult to argue that it is an armed conflict between States, which would bring into operation the 1949 Geneva Conventions and the First Additional Protocol of 1977. Moreover, the Agreement of 22 May 1992 is specifically stated to be without prejudice to the status of the Parties or to the international law of armed conflict in force. It is instructive to note that Security Council Resolution 770 (6 October 1992)

[1] S/25221 (2 February 1993) p.8. The Interim Report of the Commission of Experts, established pursuant to Security Council Resolution 780,S/25274 (10 February 1993) concludes that 'a decision [to establish an ad hoc international tribunal] would be consistent with the direction of its work' (p.20).

[2] Article 2 common to all the 1949 Conventions and Article 1(3) of the Additional Protocol of 1977.

referred to "grave breaches" of the Geneva Conventions 1949 (relevant only to international armed conflict) whereas Resolution 808 (22 February 1993) used the term, "serious violations of international humanitarian law".

If the armed conflict in Bosnia-Herzegovina is properly characterised as a non-international armed conflict common Article 3 to the Geneva Conventions 1949 (prohibiting in respect of those not taking an active part in hostilities, violence to life and person, the taking of hostages and outrages upon personal dignity, in particular, humiliating and degrading treatment) would apply. So also would Additional Protocol II of 1977 dealing with a non-international armed conflict, from the date of accession by Bosnia-Herzegovina, of both the 1949 Conventions and the Protocol, namely 31 December 1992. The Genocide Convention 1948 may also have effect in the territory of Bosnia-Herzegovina if that State had become a Party to it,[1] If this is the correct legal basis of the armed conflict there is no room for the formal application of the Geneva Conventions of 1949, save for common Article 3, and therefore of the grave breach (or war crimes) provisions.

Can a counter argument be presented? The Commission of Experts in their report of 26 January 1993[2] thought so. It argued that

> The Commission is of the opinion ... that the character and complexity of the armed conflicts concerned, combined with the web of agreements on humanitarian issues the parties have concluded among themselves, justify an approach whereby it applies the law applicable in international armed conflicts to to the entirety of the armed conflicts in the territory of the former Yugoslavia.

It may be concluded that the opinion of the Commission of Experts may be open to strenuous challenge by defence counsel in a trial of a defendant for a breach of the international law of armed conflict. Counsel would be likely to put the prosecution to proof that an international armed conflict was in existence at the time the alleged crime was committed. This may require, for instance, proof that the armed forces of Serbia or Croatia were engaged in combat with Bosnian Government forces or that the Bosnian Serbs and Croats were controlled directly by these States.

(b) Could a defendant be charged with crimes against humanity?

Article 6(c) of the Charter of the International Military Tribunal set out the terms of the charge of crimes against humanity as to include acts such as murder and other inhumane acts committed against any civilian population, before or after the war. The Nuremberg Tribunal held, however, that "it only had jurisdiction over crimes against humanity committed after the beginning of the war or if penetrated before, in pursuance of a policy of initiation and preparation of a war of aggression."[3] It will be noted that the thrust of the Nuremberg judgment concerning crimes against humanity was in respect of such crimes committed during an international armed conflict. The mere fact that the International Military Tribunal limited itself, in effect, to the trial of crimes against humanity during the war is not conclusive authority that these offences can be tried by an international court only if committed during an international armed conflict. Indeed, the Commission of Experts takes the view that crimes against humanity [include] gross violations of fundamental rules of humanitarian and human rights law committed by persons demonstrably linked to a party to the conflict, as part of an official policy based on discrimination against an identifiable group of persons, irrespective of war and the nationality of the victim.

Should the conflict in Bosnia-Herzegovina not be classified as an international armed conflict there is little direct precedent for the framing of charges of crimes against humanity when the perpetrator and the victim are both nationals of the same State.

(c) Could a charge be brought under the Genocide Convention 1948?

There would appear to be little difficulty in framing a charge under this Convention. Article 6 directs that

> Persons charged with genocide ... shall be tried by a competent tribunal of the State in the territory of which the act was committed, or by such international penal tribunal as may have jurisdiction with respect to those Contracting Parties which shall have accepted its jurisdiction.

[1] Which is not known at the time of writing. It may be argued, however, that the 1948 Convention reflects customary international law but it does not automatically follow from this that an individual may be liable before an international court for acts of genocide. Although the basis of a number of charges at the International Military Tribunal in Nuremberg was customary international law all offences were linked (eventually) to an international armed conflict.

[2] Included with S/25274(10 February 1993).

[3] Woetzel, *The Nuremberg Trials in International Law*, (1962) p.173; Schwelb, *Crimes against Humanity* (1946) XXIII BYIL 178. Sixteen defendants were convicted of crimes against humanity (2 were convicted on this charge only) at Nuremberg. Adolf Eichmann was tried before the District Court of Jerusalem under Israeli law (the Israeli Nazi and Nazi Collaborators (Punishment) Law of 1951) for war crimes and crimes against humanity. He was convicted and sentenced to death.

Such a charge has the advantage of a clear definition of the prohibited acts and the necessary intention; it is specifically stated to apply in peace and war and is described in Article 1 as a crime under international law. Most of the acts alleged to have been committed in Bosnia-Herzegovina, such as mass rape and 'ethnic cleansing', would appear to have been committed with the requisite intent.

(d) Could Bosnia-Herzegovina try those who may have committed crimes?

In a non-international armed conflict States have jurisdiction to try offences committed within their own territories. A charge could be brought under the criminal law of Bosnia-Herzegovina. Indeed, it is reported in The Times of 13 March 1993 that

> Bosnia's first war crimes trial opened in Sarajevo yesterday, with the military prosecutor seeking the death penalty for Boris Herak, 21, and Sretko Damjanovic, 30, two former Serb soldiers accused of atrocities.

It would appear from a report in the New York Times of 27 November 1992 that Herak is a Bosnian national, although fighting for the Serb nationalists. If convicted (he has apparently confessed in great detail to his crimes) the principle of double jeopardy may, in practice,[1] prevent the international war crimes tribunal trying him in respect of the same offences. In an international armed conflict a decision of the Privy Council in 1968 considers that

> It would be an illegitimate extension of established practice to read [national law] as referring to members of regular forces fighting in enemy country. Members of such forces are not subject to domestic criminal law. If they were so subject, they would be committing crimes from murder downwards in fighting against their enemy in the ordinary course of carrying out their recognised military duties.[2]

Members of such forces would, of course, be liable for any war crimes (as defined under international law) that they might commit. They would also be entitled to remain, even if convicted, prisoners of war under Geneva Convention III of 1949.[3]

If this decision is a correct interpretation of the relationship between international and national law in respect of crimes committed during an international armed conflict the conclusion must be drawn that by trying Herak and Damjanovic under the criminal law of Bosnia–Herzegovina the authorities there do not understand the conflict to be of an international character.

(e) Should the international tribunal apply *national rather than international law*?

This is a possibility. It could apply the criminal law of Bosnia Herzegovina if the alleged crime was committed on the territory of that State. The CSCE proposal was to this effect. It would mean that a defendant would be tried under the relevant national law, which has implemented the international law of war crimes and crimes against humanity.[4] It may be argued, however, that this approach would not produce the same deterrent or precedential effect as liability directly under international law.

(f) Should the general principles of the laws of evidence normally applying to a criminal trial under national law be applicable before an international criminal tribunal?

It will be recalled that the Charter of the International Tribunal at Nuremberg directed that the Tribunal would not be bound by any technical rules of evidence but would admit any evidence that it considered probative.[5] There is here a conflict of goals. On the one hand, the exclusion of evidence that might be unreliable (such as oral hearsay or disputed identification evidence) or unduly prejudicial (such

[1] In A.P. v. Italy, Doc. A/43/40 the Human Rights Committee observed that Article 14(7) of the 1966 Covenant on Civil and Political Rights 'prohibits double jeopardy only with regard to an offence adjudicated in a given State.' It is difficult to envisage the international tribunal dealing with a defendant who had been tried and convicted by a national court. Suppose he had been sentenced to death? A Commission of Italian Jurists, in their Report to the Secretary General of the United Nations, S/25300 (17 February), indicated that the international tribunal should he able to try such defendants but 'take into consideration penalties inflicted by a national jurisdiction for the same crime and already served.'

[2] Public Prosecutor v. Koi [1968] 1 All ER 419,427. There was a powerful dissent from Lord Guest and Sir Garfield Barwick.

[3] This is the effect of Article 85 of this Convention. Yugoslavia did not enter a reservation to this Article, unlike a number of former Soviet allied States. It is assumed that upon its own ratification of the Geneva Conventions, Bosnia-Herzegovina undertook the same obligations as the former Yugoslavia.

[4] Letter dated l8 February from the Permanent Representative of Sweden (Chair of the CSCE) to the U.N. addressed to the Secretary General, S/25307, para.5. Adolf Eichmann was tried by an Israeli court under an Israeli law which had incorporated the international law of war crimes and crimes against humanity, see p. 316, footnote 3.

[5] The trials held under the Royal Warrant of 14 June 1945 were conducted on a similar basis. Paragraph 8 directed the Military Court to take 'into consideration any oral statement or document appearing on the face of it to be authentic, provided the statement or document appears to the Court to be of assistance in proving or disproving the charge, notwithstanding that such a statement or document would not be admissible in a [court-martial]' This principle is not maintained in the War Crimes Act 1991. The Hetherington/Chalmers Report of their war Crimes Inquiry. Cm 744, showed how changes. particularly in respect to the admissibility of hearsay evidence, would make the admissibility of evidence in a British court less difficult.

as the admissibility of offences committed which are not the subject of the charge) go to ensure that the defendant receives a fair trial. On the other, an international criminal tribunal may, if it applied the 'technical' rules of evidence find that it cannot produce sufficient evidence judged by these rules to justify a conviction. A compromise will have to be reached between these two goals. It is, perhaps, interesting to note that Herak, on trial in Sarajevo, claims that 'he was beaten and tortured into confessing to Bosnian authorities' (The Times, 13 March 1993).

There is a gathering storm of evidence of criminal acts committed in Bosnia-Herzegovina. The final report of the investigative mission into the treatment of Muslim women in the former Yugoslavia, headed by Dame Ann Warburton[1] concluded that rape is part of a pattern of abuse, usually perpetrated with the conscious intention of demoralizing and terrorizing communities, driving them from their home regions and demonstrating the power of the invading (sic) forces.

The mission heard direct testimonies from a small number of victims but was unable to gain access to eastern Bosnia-Herzegovina. The Commission of Experts has developed a database and methodology for gathering and investigating evidence. The Report on the situation of human rights in the territory of the former Yugoslavia submitted by Mr. Tadeusz Mazowiecki contains a detailed account of human rights breaches drawn from witness testimony.[2] An independent prosecutor would need, in due course, to sift these accounts to determine whether the evidence is of such a type that the Tribunal might rely upon it.

(g) What rights should the defendant be given?

The Charter of the International Military Tribunal at Nuremberg set this out in Article 16. It provided for an indictment containing full particulars of the offence charged to be delivered to the defendant within a reasonable time of the trial, the right to legal representation, to present evidence and to cross-examine prosecution witnesses. It is inconceivable that an international tribunal would not accord a defendant the rights given in the 1966 International Covenant on Civil and Political Rights (to which Yugoslavia was a Party). Article 14 provides

> All persons shall be equal before the courts and tribunals . . . everyone shall be entitled to a fair and public hearing by a competent, independent and impartial tribunal established by law . . . Everyone charged with a criminal offence shall have the right to be presumed innocent until proved guilty according to law ... to be tried *in his presence* to have legal assistance assigned to him, to examine the witnesses against him, not to be compelled to testify against himself or to confess guilt.

Whether the international tribunal should be able to try a person in his absence gives rise to problems similar to those discussed in relation to the applicability of the 'technical' rules of evidence.[3] An unwillingness to do so may make it difficult to prosecute those who may be involved in the chain of actions preceding the commission of the act concerned. Thus, the prosecution of an individual for ordering, being a secondary party to, or a superior who fails to prevent, a particular act may be more difficult, although not impossible. It is distinctly possible that one or more defendants, against whom a prosecutor may have sufficient evidence to prefer a charge, will not be within the jurisdiction of the tribunal. It may be that the right course to adopt is to try that individual in his absence. If his presence is known extradition might be sought on the basis that in handing a suspect over to the tribunal the State concerned would be complying with the determination of the Security Council in Resolution 880 (1993) that the situation constitutes a threat to international peace and security.[4]

(h) What trial procedure should be applied?

This would need to be formulated as precisely as possible in a statute of the court.[5] It would need to include the question of sentencing powers. Where would any period of imprisonment be served? Would there be a "special prison" on the Nuremberg model or would prisoners be required to serve their sentences in the prisons of States? The French Committee of Jurists preferred the latter approach, which would be under the direction of the tribunal. The Commission of Italian Jurists considered it to be "primarily the responsibility of the competent organs of the State in whose territory the crimes are committed to enforce . . . penalties inflicted by the Court." Again, would the death penalty be available? The

---

[1] S/25240(3 February 1993).

[2] E/CN.4/1993/50 (10 February 1993). Security Council Resolutions 771 and 780 called upon States to make available to it substantiated information in their possession.

[3] The Report of the Working Group on the question of an international criminal court, *op cit.*, does not recommend the trial of a defendant in his absence, p.184. At Nuremberg Bormann was tried in his absence. The Human Rights Committee in the case of Mbenge v Zaire, Doc.A/38/40, took the view that the due process provisions in Article 14 of the 1966 Covenant on Civil and Political Rights cannot 'be construed as invariably rendering proceedings *in absentia* inadmissible irrespective of the reasons for the accused person's absence.'

[4] There is a full discussion of the possibilities in the Report of the Committee of French Jurists, S/25266 (10 February 1993). This report was published 12 days before Security Council Resolution 880.

[5] See the detailed suggestions in S/25266(10 February 1993) Report of the Committee of French Jurists. Detailed matters are also discussed in the Working Group of the International Law Commission, *op cit.*

same bodies were clearly of the opinion that it should not. Article 15 of the 1966 Covenant on Civil and Political Rights prohibits

> a heavier penalty than the one that was applicable at the time when the criminal offence was committed.

Legal argument can be expected if the statute prescribes the death penalty which may, in particular, consider the relationship between Article 15(1) and 15(2).

(j) Could a defendant argue that trial before an international criminal court would be retroactive and thereby infringe the principle of *nullum crimen sine lege*?

There can be little doubt that the acts a defendant before the court may be alleged to have committed would have been criminal acts, whether under the law of Bosnia-Herzegovina or under international law at the time they took place. These acts would not fall foul of Article 15 of the 1966 Covenant which provides that

> No one shall be held guilty of any criminal offence on account of any act or omission which did not constitute a criminal offence, under national or international law, at the time when it was committed.

Retroactive jurisdiction (as contrasted with retroactive criminality) is not prohibited. This was also the position taken by the Hetherington/Chalmers Report in 1989, which led to the War Crimes Act 1991.[1]

(k) Would appeal be possible? If so to which body?

Article 26 of the Charter of the International Military Tribunal stated that the judgment of the Tribunal would be final and not subject to review. Article 14 of the 1966 Covenant directs that

> Everyone convicted of a crime shall have the right to his conviction and sentence being reviewed by a higher tribunal according to law.

The Committee of French Jurists considered all the options for review, including the International Court of Justice and concluded that 'it would probably be better to envisage the establishment of a special court for the revision of judgments of the Tribunal.' The Italian Commission of Jurists and the CSCE report also took this view.

(l) What defences could be advanced?

Superior orders. Although Article 8 of the Charter of the International Tribunal at Nuremberg stressed that superior orders would not relieve a defendant of liability, but could only be pleaded by way of mitigation the position was adopted that a superior order would not relieve of liability if, in the circumstances at the time, it was possible for him not to comply with the order.[3] Different considerations might apply if a defendant was himself threatened there and then with death if he did not, for instance, carry out the orders of a superior to rape one or more victims. Where the order was to kill a civilian not taking part in the hostilities there is some doubt whether an immediate threat of death from the superior would merely go to the mitigation of punishment of the killer.[4]

There is no doubt that the person who ordered the offence to be committed would be liable for it to the same extent as the subordinate who carried it out.

(m) Could the leaders be liable for crimes not specifically ordered by them?

General Yamashita was held liable by a U.S. war crimes tribunal for failing to act in the knowledge that the troops under his command were committing war crimes against the civilian population in the Phillipines.[5] Article 86(2) of the First Additional Protocol imposes liability on the commander if he knew, or had information which should have enabled him to conclude in the circumstances at the time, that a breach was being committed or was going to be commited and he did not take all feasible measures within his power to prevent or repress the breach. This is relied on by the Commission of Experts as the

---

[1] *Report of the War Crimes Inquiry* Cm 744. Note also the effect of Article 7(2) of the European Convention on Human Rights 1950, which is similar.

[2] It should be noted that Article 29 of the same provided that if fresh evidence became available after conviction it could only be used by the prosecution to found a fresh charge against a defendant It is difficult to imagine that a similar provision would be applied by a modem international military tribunal.

[3] This is the effect of Article 4 of the Draft Code of Offences Against the Peace and Security of Mankind, 1954, prepared by the International Law Commission. It is stated in similar terms by the Commission of Experts established by Security Council Resolution 780(1992) at p.16, by the Committee of French Jurists (1993) at p.25 as the Nuremberg principles and by the Commission of Italian Jurists in their draft Article 5(2). Article 2(3) of the Convention Against Torture 1984 concludes that 'An order from a superior officer or a public authority may not be invoked as a justification of torture.'

[4] See *Manual of Military Law Part III*, HMSO (1958) para. 629. This would not amount to a defence under English law.

[5] (1945) 327 U.S. 1.

basis of command responsibility. There may be a number of difficulties in respect of activities taking place in Bosnia-Herzegovina, apart from the issue addressed earlier as to whether the Protocol applies at all. Is there a real command structure so that those who carry out the acts are indeed the subordinates of the superiors, who may be charged? Can the 'superiors' enforce discipline on their 'subordinates'? If the superiors knew that rape was being carried out on a systematic basis what 'feasible measures within their powers' could they take to prevent or repress the breach? In an international armed conflict this becomes less of a problem since the armed forces of States will normally have an established form of military discipline.

APPENDIX 20

Letter to the Chairman of the Committee from Yousuf Jama Ali Duhul

My letter to the UN Secretary-General (attached as an Annex) may supplement the evidence on Somalia given by Mr Sahnoun to your Committee.

As a concerned Somali, I solicit your help in the Somali people's search for a way out of their present misfortune. Such a solution has to be based on the customary consenus. That is why the appropriate beginning is for the West to recognize *de facto* the governments of the two territorial entities in which effective governmental authorities have been constituted—namely, the Republic of Somaliland and the Somali North-Eastern State. The rest of Somalia should, at the same time, be assisted in the formation of comparable governments. It would thereafter be for the resulting Somali governments to agree, through the usual process of consensus, on their future political system or systems.

ANNEX

Letter to the UN Secretary-General

RE UN GOOD OFFICES IN SOMALIA

A broad spectrum of concerned Somali intellectuals have asked me to convey to you some observations on the Somali situation. Their main preoccupation is that the perspective of the world society or the international community may have been dimmed by the instability and multiplicity of the events surrounding Somali affairs. Hence the suggestion, particularly in view of the cruciality of the UN role, of my drawing the attention of the UN to the following.

Over two years have passed since the ending of the two decades of the dicatorship of Siyad Barre. Yet, there is still no sign anywhere of the anticipated post-Siyadism era of peace and plenty. Moreover, there is still no sustained return to the genuine democracy inherent in the Somali people's tradition of unceasing communal consultations.

Two interconnected factors are responsible for the prevailing lawlessness, which is so acute—for instance, in most of the central and southern parts of former Somalia—as to overwhelm our social norms and values, and thus inflict unimaginable horrors on the people.

1. The Remnants of the Culprit Regime

The first of such pernicious factors is the usurping of political power, in the territorial chunks of splintered Somalia, by the members of the overthrown regime. One would expect it to be self-evident that those who were members of the regime responsible for our present tragic predicament cannot head the determined communal enterprise needed to undo their own disastrous handiwork. Clearly their appertinance to the death-and-destruction regime, responsible for the material and moral disintegration of Somalia, permanently disqualifies them from all Somali political offices. They, however, seem to pretend, and with astounding success, that their waving a dubious tribal tag effaces all their past crimes. In fact, the remanents of the routed revolting regime have waved their counterfeit tribal banners all the way to the leadership of their vanquishers. The magical efficacy of their politicized tribal wands is due to the fact that each of the territorial entities into which Somalia got broken is founded on the same adulteration of our nomadic tribalism into its prevalent politicized souk version.

The extent to which our multifacted tribal structure, the efficacious mainstay of our nomadism, got adulterated in its politicized souk version is most tellingly illustrated by the case of General Mohammed Said Hersi "Morgan". General Morgan is, among other things, the devastator of Hargeisa and the author of the infamous Morgan Letter of 23/01/1987—prescribing and implementing the wholesale no-holds-barred persecution for the Issaaq clan, and the scortched earth policy for their land.

An excellent authenticated and annotated English translation of the Morgan Letter, dated 27/04/1987, is by former President of the Somali Supreme Court, Mohamoud Sheikh Ahmed—whose opposition to Siyad Barre's dictatorial bent led, within the first year of Siyad's rule, to his 1970 resignation from the then third highest post of the State. General Morgan's Letter and his other outrages were facilitated by the fact that Mohamoud Sheikh Ahmed remained the sole member of `the top echelons of the State personnel to so formally reject the supine acquiescence in Siyad Barre's increasingly blatant illegalities, and the creeping dictatorship in their tow.

The present emergence of General Morgan as a leading'"war lord" and one of the principal personalities of post-Siyadism shows how the Somali people's sanglant overthrow of Siyadism got diverted and then swallowed by neo-Siyadism. The way to General Morgan's effacing his blood-drenched past Siyadism and wallowing in the glory of post-Siyadism prominenece and leadership is that of the rest of the `war lords' leading the other parts of Somalia. He differs from most of the other neo-Siyadists, now controlling various parts of Somalia, in the way he differed from them under Siyadism—by being more prominent. All of Somalia's present variety of Siyadism-spawned leaders prop themselves on their respective tribal pillars. General Morgan has, however, metamorphosed into a veritable tribal hero.

The overwhelming sway of the tribal sentiment in our psyche is shown by the fact that General Morgan (whose identification with the worst excesses of Siyadism is second only to that of Siyad himself) is being now lionized as a tribal hero by the Majertein. True, the Majertein are General Morgan's tribe. But the Majertein are also: (a) the one tribe of the Darod clan to suffer Siyadism's wholesale collective persecution, and the first Somali tribal group to be subjected to its limitless savagery, and (b) the Somali tribal group whose present political leadership is collectively the best in Somalia, and whose top leader is (with the possible exception of Adan Abdualla Osman, Somalia first President) the Somali personality enjoying the widest pan-Somali prestige and sympathy—largely on account of the solidity and consistency of his uncompromising opposition to Siyadism.

What has to be remembered, in that connection, is that General Morgan and other neo-Siyadists now controlling the various parts of Somalia owe their localized supremacy to two weapons engendered by their membership of old regime, i.e. their Siyadism. The first is their prominence as public figures within their tribal constituencies; and the second is the financial muscle of each of them—invariably accumulated through corruption. The former dictator did not object to the communal prominence incidental to the public positions he assigned. That only enhanced the value of the patronage available to him. As to the corruption, he actually encouraged it in order to use it as a blackmailing means against the aides concerned.

2. The Problem: the Gun-Toting Proletariat

The man most directly responsible for the advent of the reign of armed **silic ku-nool** (which I translate as "proletariat") is (or was) certainly a distinguished Siyadist. He is Omer Arteh Ghaleb, who was so thankful to Siyad Barre for appointing him as his Prime Minister just a couple of weeks before his fleeing the Presidency under the improvised armed escort of General Morgan. Omer Arteh Ghaleb provides also the illustration of the lightning speed with which neo-Siyadism appropriated power from the non-leaderships of the victorious SNM/USC masses. Ali Mahdi Mohammed, whose rewarding links with Siyadsim included his wife being one of the legal advisors of Siyad Barre, was unilaterally declared, evidently by some members of the Mogadishu branch of the USC, as the provisional President of Somalia. The very next day, he appointed (or re-appointed) the same Omer Arteh Ghaleb, Siyad Barre's last Prime Minister, as the revolutionary Prime Minister for post-Siyadism Somalia.

Prime Minister Omer Arteh's first political step was certainly revolutionary in its effects. He announced over Radio Mogadishu a decree ordering all units of all the Somali armed forces (the army, police, custodial corps etc) to surrender immediately to the nearest SNM or USC guerilla units. As the depriving of a State of all its organized forces reduces it to complete inability to discharge its basic and crucial function of maintaining law and order, the Somali State immediately collapsed. The speedy effect of the inexistance of any Statal authority was the inevitable advent of the supremacy of the armed gangs and their era of devastating and often sanglant lawlessness.

3. The Solution: Returning to Consensus

The first step back to sanity is the disarming of all the present armed groups. Such initial total disarmament of all the armed factions and groups will lead: (a) to the end of the power of the war lords, and the myriad of independent or semi- independent freelance gangs and gunmen; and (b) to the restoration of the consensus-based authority of the traditional elders and the communal values they represent and uphold.

The second step is the formation of the biggest possible political entities. That is to say, the establishment throughout Somalia of governmental authorities which are based on the sponsorship of the customary communal leaders but whose import and jurisidiction are wider and more permanent. In other words, the formation, wherever they do not already exist, of governmental organs analogous to those of Somaliland and the North-East.

The third step is for the representatives of the governments of the various parts of Somalia to agree on the needed political system or systems. The new political framework for the whole of Somalia should be determined by consensus in conformity with our tradition for the settlement of important communal matters. Consequently, there should be no question of using any means of coercion against any of the participating governments.

APPENDIX 21

Memorandum by David Travers, Department of Politics and International Relations, Lancaster University

THE USE OF ARTICLE 99 OF THE CHARTER BY THE SECRETARY-GENERAL.

1. I have been asked to explore the use of Article 99 by the Secretary-General and suggest how this article might be used to greater effect in United Nations preventive diplomacy.

2. Article 99 states that the Secretary-General *may bring to the attention of the Security Council any matter which in his opinion may threaten maintenance of international peace and security*. And under Security Council rules of procedure if such a request is made the President must call a meeting.

3. The right to request a meeting of the Council under Article 99 has, however, only been formally used on three occasions: the Congo in 1960 (Hammarskjold); the United States' hostages in Iran 1979 (Waldheim) and the increased violence in Lebanon 1989 (Perez de Cuellar). But the Secretary-General has used this article in innovative ways to provide warnings and to pass information to the Security Council; to stimulate consultations among members and to provoke meetings of the Council; to engage in factfinding to establish whether particular disputes might threaten international peace; and in preventive diplomacy, often without any mandate from the political organs, to obviate any need for the formal use of the article.

4. The Secretary-General has made little formal use of Article 99 because he has believed that the necessary conditions for its successful use rarely appear to be present. First the public use of Article 99 is a dramatic act which will attract international publicity. The Secretary-General has taken an initiative on his own responsibility, that a threatening situation requires remedial action that can only be supplied by an urgent meeting of the Security Council. He need not do so. He could merely circulate his information to the members of the Security Council. He could consult with members of the Council and let them decide how to handle the problem. He could talk to the disputing parties and encourage one or both to make a formal request to the Council. And he could use one of the implied versions of Article 99 which are discussed below. Or he might decide that the threat to the peace might be better handled by quiet private diplomacy.[1]

5. Secondly it sets into motion a political process over which the Secretary-General may have very little control. The decision-making processes of the members of the Security Council—particularly the permanent who will play a major role in determining the outcome of the Secretary-General's initiative—are usually largely beyond his influence. The Council could make a determination under Chapter 7 that a threat to the peace exists, or could make a recommendation under Chapter 6 or it could fail to act. And if the Council was unresponsive this might induce widespread criticism of his judgment, diminish his prestige and perhaps reduce the chances of any useful role for either the Secretary-General or the political organs in attempting to avert the crisis.[2]

6. Thus the Secretary-General appears to take into account a range of factors when reaching a decision on whether or not to invoke formally Article 99.

(a) Does he possess the legal right in each particular instance to use Article 99?

(b) Is the use of Article 99 the most effective way of handling the issue?

(c) If it is, will he be sufficiently and reliably informed to present an independent, reasoned, impartial and persuasive case that international peace might be threatened and that the Security Council should act in a particular way?

(d) Would the Council meet quickly and would he have the necessary political support from Council members especially the permanent, and the non-permanent from the important regional groupings, to have the item inscribed on the formal agenda?

(The President places the request on the provisional agenda. The adoption of the agenda is normally regarded as procedural requiring 9 votes out of 15, and because the question is not substantive the veto does not apply. In the 11 member Council it would have required 7 votes out of 11)

---

[1] Leon Gordenker, The United Nations Secretary-General and the maintenance of Peace, Columbia University Press, New York and London 1967, p 140.

[2] Javier Perez De Cuellar, The Role of the Secretary-General in Adam Roberts and Benedict Kingsbury (eds) United Nations, Divided World: The United Nation's Roles in International Relations, Clarendon Press Oxford 1989, pp 65–66.

(e) Would the Council move immediately to a debate after hearing the Secretary-General's opening statement or would it consult and then adjourn thus casting doubts on the Secretary-General's judgment about the need for an urgent meeting?

(f) Would the parties be represented at the meetings of the Council?

(g) Would the ensuing debate be conciliatory and constructive or bruising and divisive?

(h) Would any substantive, useful resolution rapidly emerge with unanimous or a high degree of support or would the threat of a veto result in either a diluted recommendation, or a Presidential statement or no action?

(i) And finally what would be the effects of the debate and any resolution upon the attitudes of the parties and their allies and friends towards the particular issue that was threatening international peace and security? Would these be helpful or would the situation be made worse?

7. A further reason why the Secretary-General has been wary of formally using the Article is that on the three occasions that it has been invoked only once was there an entirely satisfactory outcome. In the case of the Congo the Secretary-General requested an urgent meeting of the Security Council in the morning of July 13 1960. He acted on information received from his representative Ralph Bunche and communications from the government of the Congo. With the breakdown of internal law and order, the military intervention of Belgium to protect its nationals and the secession of Katanga from the fledgling state he feared that other countries, particularly the United States and the Soviet Union, might be drawn in. He briefed members of the Security Council at length during lunch. He proposed that the United Nations provide assistance in security and administration, the despatch of United Nations troops and the provision of emergency food supplies. The Council met at 8.30 in the evening; and when it adourned at 3.30 the next morning the Council had approved a resolution which had been largely drafted by Mr Hammarskjold himself.[1]

8. In the case of the American diplomatic hostages in Iran the Secretary-General met a number of difficulties. The diplomats were seized on November 4 1979. The Secretary-General decided to use Article 99 on November 25 when it appeared that there was little chance of Iran and the United States reaching a negotiated settlement. Mr Waldheim hoped that the Security Council meetings and any resultant resolution would prevent the use of force by the United States which might not only disturb international peace but might prove fatal for the hostages; help to emphasise the importance of diplomatic immunity; provide an opportunity for a meeting between senior officials from Iran and the United States who had not met since the crisis started; and secure a call for the immediate release of the hostages and an international enquiry into Iran's allegations against the Shah.

9. The Council consulted on the 26. It met on the 27 and after hearing the Secretary-General's opening statement and an appeal by the President for the release of the hostages decided to adjourn until December 1. Mr Bani-Sadr the Iranian Foreign Minister could not leave until after the Holy Days. But the Iranians were willing to give a written guarantee that he would attend. In the meantime Iranian officials were able to offer reassurances that the hostages would not be harmed. The demonstrations outside the embassy would be suspended for the remainder of the religious holidays.

10. Mr Bani-Sadr, however, was dismissed by Mr Khomeini and the new Foreign Minister, Sadegh Ghotbzadeh, refused to attend the Council meetings. The Council therefore met in the absence of the Iranian delegation. A resolution which Mr Waldheim helped to draft was not passed until December 4. And when the Secretary-General went to Tehran on December 31 to see if he could establish a negotiating channel with the Iranian Government to seek the release of the hostages his trip was compromised by a United States' statement that if he was unsuccessful the Carter Administration would demand sanctions against Iran.[2]

11. And on the third occasion that Article 99 was formlly invoked Perez de Cuellar did not fully achieve his purposes. On the 15 August 1989, after an alarming escalation in the military confrontation in and around Beirut, and with the danger of even further involvement of outside powers the Secretary-General requested an urgent meeting of the Council. He wanted it to impress upon the parties to the conflict that there was an immediate need to halt all military activities and adhere to a ceasefire so that mediation efforts could continue.

[1] Brian Urquhart, A Life in Peace and War, Weidenfeld and Nicolson, London 1987, pp 146–147.
[2] Kurt Waldheim, in the Eye of the Storm, Weidenfeld and Nicolson, London 1985, pp 3–4. Urquhart, A Life in Peace and War, pp 322–323. Security Council Official Records S/13646, 25/11/1979. Letter dated 25 November 1979 from the Secretary-General to the President of the Security Council. Yearbook of the United Nations, 1979, Vol 33 (United Nations, New York, 1982) p 308. The Economist 1/12/79. p 35. New York Times November 26, 27, 1979.

12. The Council met the same day. But instead of passing a formal resolution, which Mr Perez de Cuellar was seeking, internal differences resulted in a Presidential statement which while meeting many of the Secretary-General's objectives did not have the same legal and political status.[1]

(There is a view that Mr Waldheim used Article 99 on July l6 1974 after Archbishop Makarious of Cyprus was overthrown by the Cypriot National Guard which was led by 650 Greek Officers. There are doubts about this. First he has never claimed then or later in his memoirs—he merely mentions that he alerted the Council—that he had formally invoked the Article. In the hostage crisis, however, he told a press conference before the Council convened that he had used the article and in his memoirs he states that he took advantage of this jealously husbanded article. Secondly he did not ask the President to convene an urgent meeting, nor did he claim that the incident was or might be a threat to the peace—perhaps because some Council members might have regarded a change of government, no matter how violent the method, as an issue of domestic jurisdiction and of no immediate interest to the Security Council. And thirdly Mr Rossides of the Republic of Cyprus on the same day requested an urgent meeting of the Council. I believe that the Secretary-General was, however, offering a prescient public warning to the Council through an implied use of the Article.)[2]

13. The Secretary-General faced therefore with what he believes to be potential or actual threats to the peace has used a variety of methods, *without formally invoking Article 99*, either to stimulate action from the Council or to express his concern.

l4. The first method is the confidential memorandum. This was used vainly by U Thant in July 1971 as an implied invoking of Article 99. He believed that international peace was threatened in the Indian subcontinent, yet neither the two parties India and Pakistan, nor the members of the Security Council wanted any action by the United Nations. Thant therefore wrote to the President of the Security Council on July 20. He stated that he was taking the unusual step of reporting on a question which had not been inscribed on the Council's agenda; that he was not in a position to suggest precise courses of action; that it was for members of the Council to decide whether consideration should take place formally or informally, in public or in private; that his purpose in writing was to provide a basis and an opportunity for such discussions to take place and to express his concern. In a press conference in September he stated that the situation in East Pakistan *vis-a-vis* the adjoining Indian states constituted a threat to international peace and security; that he had written to the President on July 20 and that he regretted that the Council had failed to act. The Council did not meet until December when war broke out but was unable to take action because of a veto.[3]

15. The second method is for the Secretary-General to hint that he intends to use Article 99 in the expectation that a member state will then call for a meeting of the Security Council.[4]

16. A variant is for the Secretary-General to inform the President of the Council of a threat to the peace, urge consultations the result of which is that a member requests a formal meeting. (Waldheim 26 September 1980: Iran-Iraq War)

17. Yet another variant is to draw to the attention of the Council a threatening situation, transmit documents and offer good offices. If this does not induce a meeting of the Council the Secretary-General has at least publically demonstrated his concern. (Waldheim: 30 March 1976 and 16 March 1978 Lebanon.)

18. A third method is to ask the President of the Council to call a meeting urgently but on his own responsibility. And then to state that Article 99 is not being used because the Secretary-General is reporting to the Council on an agenda item introduced by the President and because he is not in a position to make a judgment about the facts. (Hammarskjold 7 September 1959: Laos allegation of Vietnamese aggression and request for the Secretary-General to send an emergency peacekeeping force.)

19. A fourth method is to ask the President to convene a meeting so that the Secretary-General might report to the Council on information that he had received from his representative and from the United Nations Force Commander about an event that was serious in relation to international peace and security. (Waldheim l6 July 1974: Cyprus.)

[1] Report of the Secretary-General on the work of the Organisation. General Assembly Official Records 44th Session, Supplement No 1 (A/44/1) 12 September 1989 p 4. New York Times, August 8, 1989.
[2] Thomas M. Franck, Nation against Nation, Oxford University Press, Oxford and New York 1885 This view is at pp 125–126. Waldheim, In the Eye of the Storm, p 82. Urquhart, Life in Peace and War, p 255. Yearbook of the United Nations 1974, Vol 28, p 262. Security Council Official Records, S/11354 16 July 1974. Letter dated 16 July from the Secretary-General to the President of the Council S/11355, 16 July 1974. Letter dated 16 July from the Permanent Representative of the Republic of Cyprus to the President of the Security Council. New York Times, 17, 18 July 1974.
[3] Sydney D. Bailey, The Procedure of the Security Council, 2nd edition, Clarendon Press, Oxford 1988, p 76. U Thant, View from the United Nations, David and Charles, Newton Abbey, Devon, 1978, p 423. Urquhart, Life in Peace and War, p 222.
[4] There is evidence that all the Secretaries-General have used this tactic.

20. A fifth method is when the Council is discussing a threat to international peace the Secretary-General may draw new information to the attention of the Council and citing his responsibilities under Article 99 appeal to the Council to adopt a resolution that incorporates his suggestions. (Hammarskjold 22 July 1961: Bizerta question.)

21. And a final method to indicate his views about the gravity of a situation is to state publicly that if a member state had not called a meeting to discuss a threat to international peace and security the Secretary-General would have done so by using Article 99, (Hammarskjold: November 1956 Suez and Hungary questions.[1])

22. Article 99 has, however, played a central role in the development of the office of Secretary-General. If the Secretary-General is to be able to consider whether any matter might threaten international peace and security, if he is to provide early warning, he must be able to make an informed independent judgment. If the Secretary-General is not allowed to consult, to enquire, to investigate, to gather collate and assess information, is not allowed to maintain a rudimentary global watching brief, even in areas where the Council has failed to act because of a veto, then Article 99 would be erased from the Charter. Therefore the Secretary-General has gradually expanded the importance of the office by ceaseless consultations, conducting research, seeking opinions from the organisation's legal staff, touring capital cities, responding to requests for visits from troubled government leaders, appointing envoys and stationing staff in areas of tension with the permission of the host government, and sending expert factfinding teams to discover, for example, whether prohibited weapons have been used. Mr Boutros-Ghali, for example, in 1992 sent factfinding missions to Moldavo, Nagorno Karabakh and to Georgia. Another mission was despatched to Nagorno Karabakh in July 1992 to investigate but failed to substantiate Azerbaijani claims that Armenia had used chemical weapons.[2]

23. Article 99 has also contributed in part to the shaping of preventive diplomacy by the Secretary-General. Preventive diplomacy—consultations, appeals, factfinding, good offices, conciliation, mediation, peacekeeping, peacemaking and humanitarian operations—has usually initially been provided by the Secretary-General without a mandate from the political organs. The legal basis for this independent activity usually being the inherent powers of his office which draws upon combinations of Articles 1, 33, 97 and 99 of the Charter. The political organs, however, have endorsed settlements which have resulted from some of these independent activities.

24. The Security Council, the General Assembly, the Economic and Social Council and the Human Rights Commission have, additionally, used Article 98 to delegate good offices and other similar tasks to the Secretary-General. Sometimes where this has aroused controversy because of the antagonistic relationship between the addressee and the organisation the Secretary-General has detached himself from the resolution and executed the mandate on his own responsibility. And sometimes the Secretary-General has stimulated a good offices mandate from the Council.

25. The purposes of preventive diplomacy include:

(a) the provision of communications between states when diplomatic relations are strained, ruptured or non-existent;

(b) the interpretation of the behaviour of one state to another in an attempt to calm potentially dangerous situations;

(c) assisting in the removal of some of the sources of friction between states;

(d) helping states to negotiate with one another;

(e) providing supervising machinery to oversee negotiated settlements between states;

(f) to provide assistance for the victims of international and civil strife and of natural disasters.

26. From embryonic beginnings during Lie's tenure preventive diplomacy now makes ever increasing demands upon the Secretary-General and his office. There are four reasons for this.

27. First interested parties—who have included member and non-member states, liberation movements, insurance firms, ethnic groups and individuals—approached the Secretary-General for help to solve a variety of dilemmas which they believed fell within the ambit of the United Nations. *They considered that he had an obligation to assist them.* The range of requests covered not only the organisation's responsibilities in the peace and security field but also included the protection of individual and group human

[1] I have found extremely valuable for this section an unpublished paper by Walter Dorn: Keeping Watch for Peace. Factfinding by the United Nations Secretary-General. This is available in the Committee's files. Bailey, The Procedures of the Security Council, pp 74–78.

[2] Boutros Boutros-Ghali: Report on the Work of the Organisation from the 46th to the 47th Session of the General Assembly, September 1992. United Nations, New York, 1992. See Chapter IV Peace Endeavours and the Chart below.

rights; the safeguarding of diplomatic immunity; the supply of technical assistance for elections and referendums; the legitimisation of elections and other acts of free choice; the observation of peace negotiations; and the provision of humanitarian help for individuals and minorities, for victims of air hijacking, of hostage taking, of civil and international violence and of natural disasters.

28. Secondly they believed that the office of the Secretary-General appeared to be better equipped both politically and operationally than the political organs for providing a wide range of conciliatory and functional assistance. The Secretary-General and his executive staff had continuity of office. His central location within the political process of the United Nations allowed him to maintain a limited watching brief on international problems: to become the confidential adviser to governments and other entities providing that he continued to be regarded as neutral, independent, trustworthy and discreet. And any help that the Secretary-General might provide could be confidential, informal and unhampered by institutional procedures.

29. The Secretary-General could thus talk freely to all parties, including non-state entities and individuals, without having had to enquire into their political and diplomatic status. This informal assistance allowed parties to discuss their problems frankly, to make concessions with dignity and without public embarrassment and if they wished, to reach a settlement far more quickly than if every move was exposed to public scrutiny. This might have resulted in the hardening of positions, inflamed debate, the expending of diplomatic energy in justifying their policies and the possibility of political attack from a variety of sources.

30. Moreover, the Secretary-General could devote attention to problems or situations which might potentially be of long duration; he could normally respond with speed and despatch to urgent, unexpected and unusual problems; he could co-ordinate, if necessary and albeit with some difficulty, the resources of the United Nations family of specialised agencies and he had access to a pool of secretariat and governmental officials whose political, diplomatic and administrative skills could be deployed in a variety of situations at very short notice. And he could seek government help and support through the network of permanent representatives stationed at the Headquarters in New York.

31. The political organs, on the other hand, were less likely to be able to help governments and other interested parties to solve urgent, unexpected, delicate, emotional or complicated and deep-seated problems because of their institutional procedures which normally only allowed governments to appear before them; because there had to be sufficient interest in the problem for the political organs to vote the items onto their agendas; because of their political composition; because of the effects of a public debate on the problem which would provide opportunities for meddling; because of their normally slow and sometimes cumbersome decision making processes; and because of their inability, or, lack of creative imagination in devising new methods, to handle unusual problems.

32. Thirdly the Secretary-General has sought, despite firm opposition from most of the permanent members at some time, to play an active, independent political and diplomatic role. He has often helped to stimulate requests from the parties by reminding them of the facilities the organisation can offer. He has helped to negotiate agreements and allowed the parties to take the credit. He has legitimised agreements that the parties have reached in secret to protect them against criticism that they have made excessive concessions, and he has demonstrated that he is a skilled exponent of 'quiet diplomacy.'[1]

33. And fourthly he has offered his services privately and publicly when he believed that he needed to be on the record to express the symbolic concern of the United Nations in the peaceful settlement of disputes; when he considered that an appeal would compel the disputing parties publicly to commit themselves to a peaceful settlement; when he was convinced that he might be of practical assistance; when he had been approached by a large number of interested parties to offer his assistance to the disputants; when he considered that he could offer humanitarian help; and when he was deeply concerned that the political organs were prevented from acting by either diplomatic or legal or political considerations.

34. When the Secretary-General was thinking of offering assistance or received a request for his help, he had to make a careful judgment on how to proceed because his independent political, diplomatic and humanitarian roles rested on very fragile bases:

(a) Charter principles relating to peace and security, peaceful settlement of disputes, human rights etc,

(b) the legal powers of his office,

(c) the prestige of his office,

[1] Vratislav Pechota, The quiet Approach: A Study of the Good Offices exercised by the United Nation's Secretary-General in the Cause of Peace, A UNITAR Publication, New York, 1972. Diego Cordovey, Strengthening UN Diplomacy for Peace: The Role of the Secretary-General, in The United Nations and the maintenance of International Peace and Security, UNITAR, New York, 1987.

(d) the persuasive skills of the office holder and his staff,

(e) the Secretariat's innovative talents,

(f) the receptability of the disputing parties to his suggestions particularly the conditions upon which his help could be given and

(g) the willingness of the political organs, other states, organisations and individuals to provide assistance if asked.

35. The factors he appeared to take into account in his decision making were

(i) the political standing of the disputants or the requestee,

(ii) whether the nature of the tasks he was thinking of undertaking were compatible with his office, were conciliatory, practical and not likely to be counter productive,

(iii) would he be able to defend any potential action politically, diplomatically and legally and could he withdraw if changing circumstances exposed his office to criticism and attack, or if he believed he was likely to become a scapegoat,

(iv) could he anticipate what changes politically, economically and even strategically might result from his intervention,

(v) what impact could these changes have upon important states and political groupings,

(vi) to what extent might the parties attempt to influence his independent judgment, by, for example, leaking parts of conversations or negotiations to the press in order to develop public support for their position. If he wanted to maintain his role, if he wished to retain the confidence of the governments with whom he was negotiating the Secretary-General usually had to suffer with dignity the false accusations against him. If he were to attempt to set the record straight his usefulness to governments might disappear. If, however, he felt that the parties might renege on their commitments he might make a progress report either to one of the political organs or to the press.

(vii) would there be any important conflict of interest with

(a) *the permanent members of the Security Council* concerning his independent activities. If the parties were willing the Secretary-General usually informed the permanent members of his intentions and if necessary sought their advice and help. If the parties were not willing the Secretary-General decided when to inform the Security Council. If the Secretary-General's actions were criticised he would promptly reply that he *must* exercise his good offices in the settlement of disputes or differences when the states concerned requested it, even without any specific authorisation from the political organs. Thus the Secretary-General, where prudent, made every attempt to inform and gain the support of the permanent members but he was not willing to establish any precedents that he had to consult with, and receive a specific authorisation from the Security Council before he could act.

(b) *Other interested third parties*

(i) *Member States.* If the Secretary-General found that a member state was handling the problem he would either withdraw, or persuade the other state to allow him a free hand or try to work alongside that state.

(ii) *Regional Organisations*

Regional organisations have tended to claim that either they have exclusive initial jurisdiction or total jurisdiction over any problem within their geographical areas. The Secretary-General has tried to avoid conflicts of competence by suggesting to requestees that the regional approach be attempted first, which he sometimes re-enforced by public or private appeals to the disputing parties. He would only consider responding positively if his help was requested by both parties, or by the regional organisation; or if an extra regional state was involved, or if the regional organisation's efforts had been unsuccessful or if an important United Nation's principle was at stake which clearly exceeded regional considerations. And when he made a positive response he usually sought the support of the regional organisation.

(iii) *Functional N.G.O.s like the International Red Cross*

The Secretary-General normally worked in close co-operation with the Red Cross in the humanitarian field. Indeed in relief operations United Nations assistance was often channelled through Red Cross facilities.

36. The Secretary-General has, however, refused requests for his help for practical, legal and political reasons.

(a) When he had insufficient information about a situation or problem,

(b) if a request for assistance in helping to solve a problem involving two or more parties or governments was one sided,

(c) when he had been asked to perform functions which he did not believe were compatible with his good offices which were meant to provide conciliatory assistance:

(i) when he had been asked by a government to pass warnings or threats to another with which it was not in diplomatic contact.

(ii) when he was asked by one government to draw public attention to another government's alleged Charter violating behaviour, although this has been qualified to some extent where allegations of the use of illegal weapons are concerned.

(iii) when he was asked to negotiate on matters which he regarded as criminal.

(d) when he believed that there might be a more appropriate political organ, or international organisation or method other than good offices to deal with the difficulty.

(e) when asked to provide assistance to a state which had failed to accept the outcome of his previous help.

(f) when he had insufficient time to mount an operation.

(g) when he believed that acceding to a request might make a solution to dispute more difficult to achieve.

(h) when his assistance was likely to be extremely unpopular with the majority of the members and was likely to result in political attacks on his person and office.

37. It can be seen from the enclosed list of recent preventive diplomacy that the initiative for the Secretary-General's help can come from the parties, other interested states or entities, the incumbent himself and the political organs, and that the assistance is sought or offered at different stages in the various types of disputes. And that a variety of methods ranging from rudimentary diplomatic help to the mounting of large scale executive operations within the territory of a member state have been employed.[1]

38. The particular method will depend upon the interplay between the nature of the tasks, the conditions the Secretary-General attaches to his help, his desire to preserve the utility of his independent role, his ability to prevent conflicts of interest and his skill in obtaining co-operation from a variety of sources. And that the outcome varies from failure, partial success, the political organs mandating the Secretary-General to continue the activity and success.

39. *The British Government would like to see the Secretary-General make greater use of Article 99 in the sense of anticipating and trying to prevent conflict and the emergence of violence around the globe. How might this be achieved?*

40. First the permanent members will have to pay careful attention to the selection of a Secretary-General. If the full potential of preventive diplomacy is to be developed the organisation will need to avoid a person who either hoards or abuses the use of Article 99. It needs a Chief Officer who exploits opportunities adroitly in both the informal and formal use of the Article without long term damage to his relations with the members especially the permanent.

41. It has, however, been contended that in the past the Secretary-General has not formally invoked Article 99 when there were clear signs that international peace and security was threatened, but governments were unwilling for a variety of reasons to call a meeting of the Council, because he did not wish to offend the permanent members. They could prevent his re-election and could reduce the efficacy of his office by sustained political attack. Thus the deterrent value of Council meetings was lost. Potential wrong doers were not required to defend their policies in the full glare of international publicity. And the Council was not induced into either keeping the situation under constant review or taking defusing measures.

42. Therefore it is suggested that the Secretary-General should be elected for only one term which could be longer than the present five years. And that such an incumbent could draw upon his prestige with the other members of the United Nations and ignore the threats and the grumbles of the permanent members and call more emergency meetings. It is felt that even if the permanent members attended the Council meetings reluctantly they were not likely to attack a Secretary-General who could provide polit-

[1] This list is a sample of the activities of Secretary-General Boutros-Ghali, his staff and his representatives. It does not purport to be correct in every detail because of the difficulties in obtaining complete information, nor does it cover the entire range of his preventive diplomacy work because many of his most successful initiatives may never become public knowledge.

ical leadership to the Council and help the organisation to fulfil its responsibilities to maintain international peace.[1]

43. If, however, members felt that the Secretary-General should be allowed to seek re-election perhaps the dangers of his excessive dependence on the Permanent Members could be reduced if an agreement could be negotiated that if the secretariat after the most careful evaluation presented the Secretary-General with a warning about a possible crisis then the Security Council would meet either informally or formally to hear his assessment. Thus he would then only have to resort to the possible formal use of Article 99 if the agreement broke down or if he felt that his assessment had been heedlessly ignored.

44. Secondly the British Government might like to consider whether it should encourage the General Assembly to grant the Secretary-General the authority under Article 96 to seek an advisory opinion from the International Court of Justice. Mr Perez de Cuellar has pointed out that many international disputes are justiciable. If, for any reason, the parties fail to refer the matter to the Court, the process of achieving a fair and objectively commendable settlement and this defusing an international crisis would be facilitated by obtaining the Court's advisory opinion. Such authority would strengthen the role of the Secretary-General in preventive diplomacy and would also help in developing international law and norms as a basis for United Nations activity.[2]

45. Thirdly the British Government might like to explore with the Secretary-General and other interested states Dr Boutros-Ghali's suggestion of empowering the Secretary-General and *expert human rights bodies* to bring massive violations of human rights to the attention of the Security Council with recommendations for action. He believes that the United Nations has not been able to act effectively to bring to an end massive human rights violations and that the long-term credibility of the organisation will depend upon the success of the response to this .challenge.[3]

46. Fourthly the government should maintain a watching brief on the review that Under-Secretary General Marrick Goulding is conducting into the structure of his Department of Political Affairs and in particular whether the department has sufficient staff of the necessary calibre to support an expanded role for the Secretary-General in the field of preventive diplomacy.[4]

47. Fifthly the quality and the scope of information available to the Chief Executive needs to be improved. The Secretary-General has claimed that if he is to provide an early warning system he will need a reliable and independently acquired database. This might be done in four ways. First the Secretary-General might have his own diplomatic service. In the past representatives of the Secretary-General have reported temporarily from trouble spots. Perez De Cuellar, however, established political offices in Kabul, Islamabad, Tehran and Baghdad. And Dr Boutros-Ghali has created Interim Offices in six states of the former Soviet Union. If the number of these offices could be expanded the Secretary-General might then receive a flow of reliable information from his own staff stationed around the world. It has been pointed out, however, that members might object to the increased cost of United Nations diplomatic representation especially if the information they presented in debates and in consultations with the Secretary-General could be challenged by this independent reporting.[5]

48. A second suggestion is that the United Nations secretariat might explore the possibility of closer links with the secretariats of the regional organisations. And that there might be a mutual exchange of information about developments which might threaten peace and security and how these might be prevented.

49. A third suggestion is that the intelligence agencies of the permanent members might provide the Secretary-General and his senior staff with weekly briefings on questions affecting the maintenance of international peace and security. And that the Military Staff Committee might offer military intelligence and in particular supplementary information to that contained in the United Nations arms transfer register.[6]

50. There is a convention that the Secretary-General has to request information from, rather than having it pressed on him by, governments, if he is to remain impartial and independent. But a number of United Nations' bodies have already benefitted from national intelligence. The Chairman of the Special

[1] See Anthony Parsons, The United Nations and the National Interests of States, in Roberts and Kingsbury (eds), United Nations, Divided World, pp 57–59.
[2] Javier Perez De Cuellar, Report of the Secretary-General on the Work of the Organisation 1991. United Nations, New York, 1991, p 11.
[3] Boutros-Ghali, Report 1992, para 101, p 38.
[4] Memorandum by the Foreign and Commonwealth Office, The Role of the United Nations Secretariat in preventive Diplomacy, FCO/FAC/5/93, UN 153, para 6.
[5] Perez De Cuellar, Report 1991, p 9. Thomas Franck, The Good Offices Function of the United Nations Secretary-General, in Roberts and Kingsbury (eds), United Nations, Divided World, pp 92–93. Waldheim, In the Eye of the Storm, pp 215–216.
[6] Charles William Maynes, Containing Ethnic Violence, Foreign Policy, Number 90, Spring 1993, pp 15–16.

Commission on the disarming of Iraq has been provided with vital knowledge which he has filtered before passing it on to his staff. Similarly Hans Blix, the Director-General of the International Atomic Energy Agency, has been informed about possible violations of the nuclear non proliferation treaty and the international safeguards system. This information is held in a special cell within the Director-General's office to prevent premature disclosure, a practice which the Secretary-General could follow. And member states have provided the sanctions monitoring committees with intelligence information about alleged violations.

51. And finally the Secretary-General might have independent access to information from satellites He might be allowed to purchase time regularly on the French satellite surveillance service SPOT, which is now available commercially. Or the United Nations might acquire its own satellite to maintain a watching brief on world developments if members were willing to bear the expense. The organisation might also initially have to hire the expertise to be able to interpret this data. But a precedent has already been established. The United Nations Special Commission on the disarming of Iraq has already hired a U 2 plane from the United States to overfly Iraq regularly and the expertise to interpret the photographs.[1]

April 1993

---

[1] Maynes, Containing Ethnic Violence, p l6.

INDEX PREVENTATIVE DIPLOMACY

(i) Expression of Concern

(ii) Removal of Friction.

(iii) Political Appeals.

(iv) Diplomatic Immunity.

(v) Factfinding and Investigation.

(vi) Executing decisions of the Security Council.

(vii) Peacemaking.

(viii) Peacekeeping.

(ix) Post Conflict Peacebuilding.

(x) Electoral Assistance.

(xi) Humanitarian concerns—

(xii) Appeals.

(xiii) Humanitarian Emergencies—early warnings.

(i) Expression of Concern

Initiative	*Date*	*Action*
Secretary-General	March 1992	Expressed deep concern at the continued fighting in the region of Nagorno-Karabakh in Azerbijan. Situation particularly alarming because the two states had recently joined the United Nations, thereby assuming a solemn obligation under the UN Charter to resolve disputes by peaceful means.
Secretary-General	April 1992	The Secretary-General met on April 3 with the Israeli Permanent Representative to the UN and raised his concern at the situation in Gara.
Secretary-General	April 1992	The Secretary-General deplored the recent escalation of violence in the Middle East in which Israeli's, Palestinians and Lebanese had been killed.
Secretary-General	September 1992	Deeply deplored the loss of life which had occurred in Ciskei during a demonstration organised by the African National Congress.
Secretary-General	March 1993	Condemned the murders of Israeli civilians in Tel Aviv and Gaza and appealed for restraint by all sides in Israel and the occupied territories.
Secretary-General	March 1993	Conveyed to Prime Minister Rabin of Israel his serious concern about the situation in the occupied territories, stressed the importance of the implementation of Security Council resolution 681 (1990) on the protection of civilians in the occupied territories and that the unresolved issue of the Palestinian deportees might continue to be a stumbling block in the reintegration of the Palestinians in the peace process.
Secretary-General	April 1993	South Africa: deeply shocked and saddened by the tragic assassination on April 10 of Chris Hani; condemned the senseless act of violence which was aimed at disrupting the peace process in South Africa; appealed to all parties not to allow the incident to derail the multiparty constitutional negotiations.

(ii) Removal of Friction

Deportation of Palestinian Civilians

Initiative	*Date*	*Action*
Security Council Resolution 799(1992)	December 1992	The Council strongly condemned the recent mass deportation of Palestinian civilians from the occupied territories by Israel. And demanded that Israel ensure the safe and immediate return of those deported. Asked the Secretary-General to consider sending an envoy to the area to follow up on the serious situation there and to report to the Council. The Secretary General informed the Security Council that his special Envoy U.S.G. for Political Affairs James O.C. Jonah was unsuccessful in his mission to find a solution. He had therefore decided to send to Israel his special Political Adviser and Representative to the Multinational Peace Talks, Chinmaya Rajaninath Gharekhan of India. If this mission should prove unsuccessful, he would recommend that the Security Council consider taking further steps to ensure that its decision in resolution 799 (1992) was respected. The mission was unsuccessful.
	January 1993	Secretary-General, on 25th January 1993, recommended to the Security Council that it takes whatever measures "to ensure the safe and immediate return of the 400 Palestinians expelled by Israel in December." He warned that there was a growing perception throughout the international community that the Council by not pressing for Israel's compliance with resolution 799 (1992) and all other relevant resolutions did not attach equal to the implications of all its decisions.

(iii) Political Appeals

Initiative	*Date*	*Action*
Secretary-General's Envoy to the Former Yugoslavia	December 1992	Cyrus Vance attended extraordinary session of the Islamic Conference held in Jeddah, Saudi Arabia. He called upon the Organisation of the Islamic Conference to support the strategies adopted by the Security Council to end the conflict in Bosnia—Hercegovina and to consider how to support the constitutional ideas offered by the Co-Chairmen of the International Conference on Former Yugoslavia.

(iv) Diplomatic Immunity: Destruction of Venezuelan Embassy in Tripoli, Libya on 2 April.

Initiative	*Date*	*Action*
Security Council	April 2 1992	Strongly condemned the violent attacks on and the destruction of the premises of the Embassy of Venezuela in Tripoli that took place earlier that day and demanded that Libya pay the Venezuelan Government immediate and full compensation for the damage caused.
Secretary-General	April 2 1992	Secretary-General called in Libya's Permanent Representative to protest against the attacks on the Venezuelan Embassy; trusted that all measures would be taken by the Libyan Government to ensure the safety and security of foreign embassies and their personnel, of United Nations staff, currently serving in Libya and of all foreigners residing in that country.

	April 1992	Secretary-General's envoy (See Libya and compliance with resolution 731(1992)) reported that he had been assured by the Libyan authorities that there would be no more attacks on foreign embassies and that foreigners would not be prevented from leaving the country

(v) FACT FINDING:

Nagorno-Karabakh

Initiative	*Date*	*Action*
Secretary-General	16–21 March 1992	Secretary-General sent special envoy Cyrus Vance to gather information about the grave situation in the region.
Secretary-General	21-28 May 1992	Secretary-General sent a mission to study ways of assisting CSCE to bring about a peaceful settlement of the conflict there. Headed by Francesc Vendreli—Director of Department of Political Affairs. Mission took medicine and other humanitarian assistance.
Secretary-General	4-10 July 1992	3 recognised experts and two secretariat members investigated but failed to substantiate Azerbaijani claims that Armenia had used chemical weapons.
Secretary-General	November 1992	Secretary-General appointed Omar Halin his representative for Nagoma-Karabakh. He was sent to the region to examine what contribution the UN could make in support of the effort of the CSCE to bring peace.

Iraq

Security Council	April 5 1992	Requested United Nations Offices in Baghdad and Tehran to begin investigations into the air attack by the Iranian Airforce over Iraq on 5 April and to report, as soon as possible, to the Council to avoid any further escalation of the situation.

South Africa

Secretary-General/ Nelson Mandela	June 1992	Secretary-General informed the Security Council on 22/6/92 that he had received a telephone call from Nelson Mandela, President of the African National Congress, concerning the massacre in South Africa on 17 June; that he would meet Mr Mandela at the summit meeting of the OAU in Dakar 27/30 June; that he would discuss matter with South African Government; and would subsequently inform the Council of his assessment of the situation.
	June 1992	Secretary-General met with the Foreign Minister of South Africa in Lagos Nigeria on 29 June; discussed situation arising from Eoipatong massacre. South Africa presented its position: Secretary-General expressed his concern about the deteriorating situation resulting from the massacre and stressed the need for international co-operation regarding the situation in South Africa. He mentioned the constructive role the UN could play in reviving the Convention for a Democratic South Africa. The Secretary-General also held talks at various times with Mr Nelson Mandela(Dakar Summit) Chief Buthelezi, and Mr Makwetu. He urged all parties to

		resume negotiations and he reported on his discussions to the Security Council.
Security Council Resolution 765(1992)	August 1992 South Africa	Secretary-General appointed Cyrus Vance as his Special Representative—to recommend measures which would assist in bringing an end to the violence and increasing conditions for negotiations leading towards a peaceful transition to a democratic non-racial and united South Africa.

Liberia

Security Council Resolution 788(1992) November 1992	November 1992	Secretary-General appointed Trevor Livingston Gordon-Somers of Jamaica as his Special Representative for Liberia to evaluate the situation in Liberia.

Georgia

Initiative	*Date*	*Action*
Chairman of State Council of Georgia	Sept. 1992	Secretary-General promised to send mission of good will to Georgia. 12–20 September.
Security Council	January 1993	January 20 the Security Council decided to send a new mission to Georgia to assess the overall political situation in Abkhazia and to despatch a human rights factfinding mission to Abltaazia to look into allegations of human rights violations by both sides.

Moldova

Initiative	*Date*	*Action*
Secretary-General	June 1992	The Secretary-General expressed deep concern about the escalation of violence in Moldova, and sent a factfinding mission to Moldova. It was led by Gilberto Schlitter, Director, Department of Political Affairs.
Secretary-General President of Moldova	August 1992	Secretary-General's envoy to return to Moldova to supervise implementation of the agreement signed on 21 July by the President of Moldova and the President of the Russian Federation Boris Yeltsin. The agreement covers an urgent ceasefire and a political solution in accordance with the United Nations Charter and the Conference on Security and Cooperation in Europe. Mission visited Moldova 25–29 August. It reported that the situation has greatly improved. The escalation of violence had been reversed and the parties to the conflict had been co-operating in the implementation of most provisions of 21 July agreement. But conditions remained fragile and could rapidly deteriorate if negotiations towards an overall settlement did not progress quickly.

Tajikistan

Initiative	*Date*	*Action*
Secretary-General	September 1992	Secretary-General has sent a goodwill mission to Tajikistan and Central Asia, led by Raymond Sommereyns, a Director in the Department of Political Affairs. 13–23 September.

(v a) EARLY WARNING

Initiative	*Date*	*Action*
Secretary-General	June 1992	The UN is to open two interim offices in the capitals of Azerbijan and Armenia along with the United Nations Development Programme to observe the situation and study ways of providing humanitarian assistance to the refugees in the region.
		The offices were due to be operational in September, decision taken to open office in Georgia. Oct. UN opens interim office in Alma Ata in Kazakhstan.

(v b) HUMAN RIGHTS INVESTIGATION

East Timor

Initiative	*Date*	*Action*
Secretary-General	February 1992	Secretary-General sends Amos Wako, Attorney-General of Kenya and an international authority on human rights, to Indonesia on February 8, as his personal envoy to obtain clarification on the events that occurred in Dili East Timor on 12 November 1991. Will meet with Government officials, members of the Indonesian Commission of Inquiry and others concerned at the incident. He will then report back to the Secretary-General.
Secretary-General	March 1993	Further visit to Indonesia and East Timor.

Haiti

General Assembly Resolution 46/7	1991 Session	Secretary-General requested to support the OAS in restoring democracy in Haiti.
	August 1992	Secretary-General appointed a representative to be part of an OAS mission to Haiti.
Secretary-General's Representative OAS & parties concerned	Feb/March 1993	Agreement reached on an OAS/UN International Civil Mission in Haiti to monitor the human rights situation and initiate investigation of violations.
		UN component would be sent once a group of human rights experts and technical personnel had reported on conditions in the country. Deployment of observers began in March.

(v c) HUMAN RIGHTS

Initiative	*Date*	*Action*
Secretary-General Latvia	October 1992	Secretary-General reported that the information received and examined by the United Nations missions while visiting Latvia in October does not reveal gross and systematic violations of human rights in that country.

Secretary-General

Estonia

(vi) MANDATED TASKS: To persuade addressee to comply with Security Council resolution.

Initiative	*Date*	*Action*
Security Council Resolution 731(1992) 21/1/92	January 1992	Requested Secretary-General to persuade Libyan Arab Jamahiriya to comply with the resolutions to establish responsibility for the terrorist acts against flights Pan Am 103 and UTA 772 and contributing to the elimination of international terrorism.
Secretary-General	January 1992	Secretary-General appointed Vasiliy Safionchuk Envoy to Libya. Carried letter from Secretary-General. Met officials on 25–26 January and reported back to Secretary-General.
Secretary-General	January 30 1992	Meet with Permanent Representative of Libya Ali El-Houderi. Reiterated his request to Libyan authorities. The Ambassador said that he would go to Tripoli immediately to deliver the message in person.
Secretary-General	February 1992	Envoy went on two further visits on 24 and 27 February.
Secretary-General	March 1992	Met on 23 March with Permanent Representatives of Libya. The Ambassador informed the Secretary-General of his country's willingness to hand over two Libyans accused of involvement in the destruction of the two planes to the League of Arab States.
Secretary-General	April 1992	Appointed U.S.G. Vladimar Petrovsky as his special envoy. Visited Tripoli on 7 April.
Secretary-General	April 1992	Met in Geneva with Youssef Debri Special Adviser to Colonel Qaddafi.
Secretary-General	May 1992	Special Envoy met with Libyan leader Muammer-el-Qaddafi and Foreign Minister of Libya.
Secretary-General	August 1992	Further visit of Special Envoy to Tripoli.
Secretary-General	January 1993	In Cairo met with the Foreign Minister of Libya.
Secretary-General	April 1993	April 5, London. Met with President Hosni Mubarak of Egypt. Secretary-General of League of Arab States Estmat Abdel Meguid. Secretary-General received a message from seven Arab and African Ministers of Foreign Affairs regarding the Libyan question which he would convey to the President of the Security Council.

(vii) PEACEMAKING

(a) UN observers at peace conference

Initiative	*Date*	*Action*
South Africa/ Secretary-General	May 1992	United Nations delegation attended second session of the Convention for a Democratic South Africa in Johannesburg.
Mozambique	June 1992	Invited UN to participate as an observer in the Italian mediated talks between the Government and Resistenci Naccional Mocambieana.
Secretary-General	August 1992	Observers ready to attend CSCE negotiations on Nagorna-Karabakh. Preliminary peace talks held in Rome which were sponsored by CSCE were attended by a UN observer to look at arrangements for a ceasefire.
Latvia	September 1992	UN observers to participate in future negotiations between Latvia and Russian Federation on withdrawal of military forces from Latvia.
Secretary-General	November 1992	Appointed Chinmaya Gharekhan [Permanent Representative of India to the United Nations] as his Special Representative to the Multilateral Negotiations on the Middle East.
Secretary-General	November 1992	UN willing to be an observer at any meeting parties in Georgia hold at the request of the Security Council to resume the peace process.

(b) Diplomatic Assistance

Secretary-General	October 1992	Foreign Ministers of Indonesia and Portugal agreed to resume dialogue to search for a just solution to the question of East Timor under Secretary-General's auspicies. Dialogue would be a continuing process. Ministers would meet regularly.
	December 1992	Met with Secretary-General in New York. Agreed to continue efforts to solve question. Will meet again in Rome on 20/4/93.
Security Council	March 1993	Asked Secretary-General in consultation with the Economic Community of West African States to consider the possibility of convening a meeting of the President of the Interim Government of the National Unity in Liberia and the warring factions

(vii) PEACEMAKING—SOUTH AFRICA

Security Council Resolution 772(1992)	September 1992	Secretary-General appointed Former Under Secretary-General Virendra Dayal—special envoy to visit South Africa from 16–22 September to hold follow-up talks about the implementation of Security Council Resolution 772—to assist in the strengthening of the structures of peace set up under the National Peace Accord.
	November 1992	Secretary-General requested Tom Vraalsen, Assistant Secretary General of the Foreign Ministry of Norway and former Permanent Representative of Norway to the United Nations to undertake a mission to South Africa, starting November 23 to assess how the UN contribution to the peace process might be enhanced.

		Expected to report to the Secretary-General by 12/12/92.

(vii c) PEACEMAKING—MEDIATION

Initiative	*Date*	*Action*
		The Secretary-General's representatives are seeking to bring about a comprehensive political settlement in for example Cyprus, Afghanistan and Haiti.

(viii) PEACEKEEPING

Iraq

Initiative	*Date*	*Action*
Secretary-General	Continuing programme since April 1991	Under the terms of the Inter-Agency Humanitarian Programme for Iraq the United Nations Guards were to protect all programme staff, equipment and supplies. And Iraq agreed to take all required measures to facilitate the safe and rapid passage as well as delivery of humanitarian assistance commodities throughout Iraq.
Secretary-General	July 1992	Deplored attacks upon two Austrian members of UN Guards; attacks totally unacceptable; demanded that such incidents cease forthwith; expected full co-operation of Government authorities in ensuring the safety and well being of UN personnel.
Under Secreatry General for Humanitarian Assistance	October 1992	Announced that additional pledges of $10 million for UN Guards in Iraq. 108 deployed in Baghdad and Northern Iraq. Imminent increase now possible because of pledges.
Secretary-General	December 1992	After six trucks of the World Food Programme were timebombed outside the warehouses in Erbil, Northern Iraq, with 30 tonnes of flour destroyed, and after UN Guards safely defused another bomb on the 7th truck, the Secretary-General decided to assign UN Guards to strengthen the protection of the convoys.

South Africa

African National Congress—subsequent permission of Govt. of South Africa	August 1992	Secretary-General sent 10 observers to provide an independent observer presence at ANC demonstra tions which were held throughout South Africa on 10 and 11 August to call for a full transition to non-racial democracy.
Security Council on Recommendations of Secretary-General	August 1992	50 observers including 6 military were to serve in South Africa in' close association with the South African National Peace Secretariat in order to enhance the capacity of indigenous structures that can play a major role in the building of peace, both in the present and in the future. Angela King of Jamacia Head of Mission Headquarters Johannesburg. Full deployment expected by October.

Rwanda and Uganda

Rwanda & Uganda	March 1993	Secretary-General sent a mission to Uganda and Rwanda to explore with the two governments their request for a UN observer force to be stationed on both sides of the border.

Security Council Resolution 812(1993)	March 1993	Secretary-General invited to examine a request by Rwanda for the deployment of UN observers along the border between Uganda and Rwanda in consultation with the organisation of African Unity, and to consider the possible establishment of an international force under the aegis of the OAU and the United Nations entrusted with the protection of, and humanitarian assitance to, the civilian population.

(ix) Post Conflict Peacebuilding

Initiative Context	*Date*	*Action*
Security Council delegation for UNTAC Secretary-General Special Representative in Cambodia and the President of the Supreme National Council Prince Sihanouk	August 1992	Appeal to the international community for assistance demining activities in Cambodia. Although UNTAC involved in clearing landmines and providing training in mine clearing and marking a bigger operation was required which needed the assistance of the international community.

(x) Election Assistance

Initiative	*Date*	*Action*
Heads of State and Govt. of the Economic Community of West African States	July 1992	United Nations to facilitate the verification and monitoring of the electoral process in Liberia. Between May and July 1992, Secretary-General sent two consultants to Liberia to evaluate availability of population data and the situation of constituency maps. And to provide support to the Electoral Commission of Liberia. Secretary-General continuing to assist in the organisation and conduct of the planned election.
Secretary-General	1992	Provide Govt. of Ethiopia with assistance in the organisation of regional elections. Consultations about UN assistance for the conduct of the planned referendum in Eritrea. Technical team visited Eritrea in August 1992 to collect information for UN involvement in referendum. Assign two officers to Asmara to assist in initial preparations. Report to General Assembly in order to obtain a mandate for further action.
Secretary-General/ Mozambique	Sept. 1992	Secretary-General has made it clear that the UN stands ready to support the envisaged electoral process in Mozambique, including the provision of electoral specialists and other relevant assistance. At a Nonaligned Summit Conference in Jakarta on September 1 the Secretary-General, promised, at the request of the Foreign Minister of Mozambique to dispatch technical specialists to Mozambique immediately to see how they might assist in the electoral process. 4 Sept. Electoral team left for Mozambique. 6 Sept. Technical team left for Mozambique.
Secretary-General/ govts. concerned	June 1992	Told the OAU Summit meeting in Dakar Senegal that UN attached particular importance to technical co-operation activities which provided assistance to govts., at their request, with expert help in democratic

		elections, constitutional law and drafting national legislation affecting human rights. Currently involved in processing requests or carrying out verification missions in over 14 African countries.
Secretary-General	January 1993	Samir Sanbar of Department of Public Information appointed Secretary-General special representative for the United Nations mission to verify the Referendum in Eritrea (UNOVER) The referendum process in Eritrea will be completed in April 1993. Arrived in Asmara, Eritrea 15 February. 17 of 21 advance mission staff are in Asmara.

(xi) HUMANITARIAN CONCERNS

Initiative	*Date*	*Action*
Secretary-General	February 1992	Secretary-General's Personal Representative for Pakistan and Afghanistan Mr Seran received 9 prisoners of war released by the Afghan Government in response to an appeal by the Secretary-General. The prisoners were handed over to the International Committee of the Red Cross.
Secretary-General	March 1993	Appointed Benin Seran (now U.S.G. Department of Political Affairs) to deal with the questions of persons missing in action and prisoners from the Middle East area, including Israeli nationals.

(xii) APPEALS—FINANCIAL: HUMANITARIAN

Initiative	*Date*	*Action*
Secretary-General's Special Representative for Coordination of Cambodian Humanitarian Programmes —Shah A.M.S. Kibria	January 1992	Appeal for United Nations Border Relief Operations and programmes assisting some 350,000 displaced persons along the Thai-Cambodian border. Financial support needed for repatriation and mine clearance. International Committee of Red Cross claimed that Cambodia had the highest percentage of mine victims in the world.
Secretary-General	January 1992	Appeal for $621.6 million for Horn of Africa for next six months. Sum totally inadequate to meet all the relief requirements and covered only those groups in most urgent need.
Office of United Nations Disaster Relief Coordinator	January 1992	$145.2 million for continued humanitarian assistance to Iraq.
Secretary-General	January 1992	Appeal $50 million for Central Emergency Revolving Fund for disaster relief. "Tool which could be used quickly by Secretary-General to meet the most acute humanitarian needs around the globe." Target met in May.
Secretary-General	April 1992	Secretary-General appeal for food for Afghanistan. Danger situation might deteriorate further, causing widespread human suffering and malnutrition and resulting in new flow of refugees adding to the millions who had already sought refuge in neighbouring countries. Food distributed by UNHCR in Afghanistan.
Secretary-General	April 1992	Appeal to finance the reconstruction of Cambodia.

Secretary-General	May 1992	Revised appeal for humanitarian assistance in former Yugoslavia. Needed to prevent any more of the 1 million displaced persons from entering neighbouring countries.
Secretary-General	May 1992	Appeal for $854 million to assist drought stricken countries in Southern Afnca. June $526 pledged.
Secretary-General	June 1992	Appeal for $180 million to enable UN agencies to provide emergency humanitarian assistance for Afghanistan.
Secretary-General	July 1992	Updated consolidated Inter-Agency Appeal for $541 million for the Horn of Africa.
Secretary-General	Sept. 1992	Appeal for $434 for humanitarian assistance in the former Yugoslavia.
Department of Humanitarian Affairs	Oct. 1992	Appeal for Winter Plan for Northern Iraq.
Govt. of Egypt	Oct. 1992	United Nations to launch an appeal for international assistance for the victims of the earthquake in Cairo. (a) UN emergency cash grant of $550,000 for local purchase of relief items.
		(b) Sent two experts in search and rescue operations to Cairo.
		(c) Disaster Management Team, composed of representatives of international agencies in Cairo, set up two inter-agency committees for monitoring emergency and rehabitation needs.
Secretary-General	Dec. 1992	Deplored the poor response to his consolidated appeal in June for aid to Afghanistan.
		Assistance needed not just for refugees, but also for population as a whole for basic survival.
UN Department of Humanitarian Affairs	Dec. 1992	Immediate Emergency Appeal for Armenia and Azerbaijan.
UN Department of Humanitarian Affairs	Jan. 1993	Urgent appeal for $20.4 million in humanitarian assistance to Tajikistan, now in a state of civil war.
Afghanistan	Jan. 1993	Seeks UN emergency assistance for 90,000 Tajik refugees who have fled to Afghanistan due to recent developments in Tajikistan. Afghanistan was not even in a position to provide basic services to meet the needs of its own population.
Tajikistan	January 1993	Aid and assistance.
Secretary-General	January 1993	Consolidated appeal for $138.1 million in emergency humanitarian assistance to Afghanistan.
Secretary-General	February 1993	$762 million for humanitarian assistance to Eritrea, Ethiopia, Kenya and the Sudan.

(xiiia) HUMANITARIAN ASSISTANCE—EARLY WARNING

Initiative	*Date*	*Action*
World Food Programme/ USG for Humanitarian Affairs	April 1992	The World Food Programme issued an alert concerning the South Africa drought. Mr Eliasson warned on

		16 April that there would be massive starvation and a huge displacement of people without immediate food aid.

(xiiib) HUMANITARIAN EMERGENCIES

Initiative	*Date*	*Action*
General Assembly Secretary-General	December 1991 February 1992	Jan Eliasson appointed Emergency Relief Co-ordinator. He will be responsible for the co-ordination of emergency assistance and will work closely with, and have direct access to the Secretary-General in New York. He will assume responsibility for all emergency relief activities, including programmes currently underway in the Horn of Africa, South-East Asia, Iran, Afghanistan and Central America. He will manage the Central Emergency Revolving Fund established by the Secretary-General as a cash flow mechanism to ensure the rapid and co-ordinated response of the Specialized Agencies.
Secretary-General	February 1992	Secretary-General chaired a meeting in Geneva with Senior executives of NGO's concerned with emergency relief. He emphasised the importance of close co-operation in the humanitarian emergency sector with NGOs and regional organisations. It was agreed that: (i) UN should act as a trigger mechanism to alert international attention and serve as a catalyst to generate rapid response to the outbreak of emergencies (ii) political support by the UN was crucial in insuring the successful provision of relief (iii) timely early warning capacities were needed, and a greater exchange of information.

Humanitarian Emergencies

(a) Iraq

Initiative	*Date*	*Problem*
Security Council/ 688(1991) Secretary General	1992	Memorandum of Understanding between UN and Iraq had to be renewed every six months . Renewal due on June 30 1992. Between May and October both Mr Eliasson and the Secretary-General had to negotiate with the government of Iraq. Agreement, finally reached in October 1992—will remain in force until end of March 1993.

(b) Sudan

Secretary-General	April 1992	Secretary-General requested U.S.G. Eliasson to give special attention to the question of humanitarian assistance in Sudan, and in particular to persuade the Government of Sudan to allow the resumption of relief flights from Kenya. The Government of Sudan agreed on 21 April to allow UN relief flights from Kenya into 3 locations until the end of April. The UN relief flights had been suspended for 40 days.
		Problems Protection of Staff
Secretary-General	October 1992	Assistant Secretary-General Abdou Ciss and senior representatives from the Department of Humanitarian Affairs and the United Nations Children's Fund went

		to Nairobi to conduct a full investigation into the deaths of two UN staff members, a n.g.o. nurse and a freelance journalist in Southern Sudan on 26/9/92. The mission later reported that the Sudanese People's Liberation Army were responsible for the killings.
Secretary-General	January 1993	Two UN staff members were detained by the authorities of the Government of Sudan in Juba and their whereabouts were unknown. The Secretary-General expressed deep concern about the Security of United Nations and other humanitarian relief personnel waiting in the Sudan. The United Nations remained committed to providing humanitarian relief to all those in need throughout the Sudan, but its ability to do so was dependent upon the full cooperation of all authorities, in particular ensuring the security of the relief workers.

(c) Afghanistan

Under-Secretary General for	February 1993	4 UN relief workers were killed by unidentified armed men in mid-February in Afghanistan. Mr Eliasson requested that a full investigation be conducted by all national authorities and that additional measures of security be taken to ensure the safety of all relief workers in Afghanistan.

(d) Armenia and Azerbijan

Secretary-General	December 1992	The Secretary-General has authorized U.S.G. Eliasson to co-ordinate an urgent programme of assistance for Armenia and Azeebijan.

APPENDIX 22

Letter to the Clerk of the Committee from Irene Cross, UNTAC Electoral Unit, Kandal Province, Cambodia

This letter, written purely in my capacity as a private citizen, from one of your ex-freelance Hansard staff, comes to you from Cambodia, where the gechos are running about my feet as I type this in the candlelight on a battery driven laptop. The registration process has now started in our province. It is really a massive operation, and the local population seem eager to register (to collect the registration card seems more likely, according to our local staff). (I hope they are not going to be betrayed further down the line). I note that it has now been agreed to go ahead with the election in May.

I went in convoy the other day to deliver a Toyota 4-runner (where oh where is the best vehicle in the world—the land rover—another missed opportunity) to one of our remoter districts. We delivered four of them (it is rumoured that the Japanese Government has provided 50,000 of these vehicles as part of their effort), together with a lot of other stuff in five large UN lorries. The road was appalling; one metre deep potholes set in lesser depth potholes, the dust from the car ahead blocking your vision, the sun glaring down at you, no sides to the narrow wooden plank bridges barely wide enough to get the cars past, let alone the lorries, large potholes either side of the bridge, the planks rattling and groaning as you drive over them. Shall I wait until the car ahead has cleared the bridge? Shall I risk two cars on the bridge? The locals obligingly opening their gates and pulling down their fences so that you could drive through their gardens in order to avoid the deep pits filled with greasy, muddy water. The lorries were bumped about so much that the goods eventually danced off the back of the lorries; it took 20 minutes or so to reload. It took us 3 hours to drive 50 km, passing through deep countryside with small villages either side of the road among the palm and banana trees and rice paddies, many of which were flooded. I had two very polite armed guards with me who could speak only Bulgarian.

The purpose of this letter is to draw your attention to the really excellent work the UN Volunteers are doing in this whole business; I see them carrying the whole effort straight to the doors of every Cambodian villager; I see them working, working, working all hours under all sorts of disagreeable and difficult conditions (When we were told: don't forget to take your toilet things with you to Cambodia, they were not talking about soap. No one said that that meant a solid floor, a toilet, 6sq.m. of tiles, plumbing accessories, a plumber?) still smiling, still diplomatic, willing it all to succeed; (the UN said "There will be an election. Don't worry, it will be trucked, boated, helicoptered, motorbiked, walked to you and hey presto it is done—not without the UNVs though); they are adding a dimension that cannot be and could not have been put into any plan; they are the front rank UN diplomats—experienced, highly educated, mature men and women; professors, directors of ministerial departments, etc. in their own countries; soothing, reassuring, informing, charming, educating, convincing, training, managing, working, working, working—I feel the UN owes them something special. (Certainly none of them is being paid anywhere near as much as a UN typist here. (Most of the UN staff on location is purely administrative)). There may be from time to time some cosmetic congratulations to the UNVs, but something bigger is required. These UNVs are part of history, they are making history, they will go down in history.

When you are in the right place and at the right time, as and when appropriate etc., and I hope you will excuse my writing to you like this but I feel so strongly about it and I have seen so much here; a whisper in someone's ear, or a suggestion dropped elegantly over a luncheon table might work wonders. And so far the registration process, hard as it has been, will be nothing compared to the election process.

Moreover, look at it this way. There are so many border and other disputes here, a successful election means it's good for the UN's business.

Let me know if you would like any other information. Where oh where is British Telecom and the British Council (even the Australians)? The French are out here in force; I feel it would be a disservice to the Cambodian people to reinstitute the French language here when the French themselves are having to learn English, when Asia itself is learning English, because it is the language of computers, technology, business, commerce, tourism, etc. (What? Learn a third language?) The Cambodian people are anxious to learn English (certainly in Phnom Penh) and many Cambodians with even a modest knowledge of English are teaching it in their front gardens.

APPENDIX 23

Memorandum by the Foreign and Commonwealth Office

THE ROLE OF THE UN SECRETARIAT IN PREVENTIVE DIPLOMACY

INTRODUCTION

1. In his report "Agenda for Peace" published in June 1992, the Secretary-General defined Preventive Diplomacy as action to prevent disputes from arising between parties, to prevent existing disputes from escalating into conflicts and to limit the spread of the latter when they occur. In his view preventive diplomacy was integrally related to peacemaking (action to bring hostile parties to agreement essentially through peaceful means) and peacekeeping (deployment of a United Nations presence in the field.) These three strands were important parts of the concept of peace-building.

FORMS OF PREVENTIVE DIPLOMACY

2. In "Agenda for Peace" the emphasis was on various forms of preventive diplomacy, whose aim is the creation of confidence. The Secretary-General suggested there were actions that Governments could undertake such as exchange of military missions, formation of regional or sub-regional risk-reduction centres, or arrangements for the free flow of information between states, including the monitoring of regional arms registers. This was an area in which regional organisations had a contribution to make. For his part the Secretary-General said he would undertake periodic consultations on confidence-building measures with parties to disputes, and with regional organisations. He would make available advice from the UN Secretariat, where it was placed to give this. "Agenda for Peace" examined four specific areas in detail:

(a) Fact finding. The Secretary-General suggested that either he, the Security-Council or the General Assembly could initiate fact-finding missions. The nature and scope of missions would depend on the individual situation. The Secretary-General called upon Member States to provide him with detailed information on issues of concern, and undertook to supplement his own contacts by regularly sending senior officials on missions for consultations. The Secretary-General recognised that these activities did not preclude the Security-Council or the General Assembly from sending missions of their own, or inviting the Secretary-General to take the necessary action.

(b) Early warning. The Secretary-General recognised that a network of early warning systems already exists in fields such as environmental threats, risk of nuclear accident, natural disasters, mass movements of populations, famine and disease. But there was a need to look at this information in a political light to assess whether peace was threatened as a result, and, if so, what action the United Nations might take to alleviate the threat. He recommended studies by the Specialised Agencies of the United Nations, and undertook to make available to the Security Council the analyses of recommendations that emerged.

(c) Preventive deployment. The Secretary-General said that in times of a national crisis, a Government or the parties concerned might consider asking the UN to deploy personnel to help alleviate suffering through humanitarian assistance, or to limit and control violence. Lives could be saved and conditions of safety created in order to hold negotiations. Equally, in inter-state disputes, preventive deployment could take place on each side of the frontier to increase confidence, perhaps in cases where one nation feared a cross-border attack. The Secretary-General envisaged this kind of activity would be mandated by the Security Council where the Council assessed it was beneficial.

(d) De-militarised zones. The Secretary-General said that the concept of de-militarised zones was common at the conclusion of a conflict. However, de-militarised zones could also serve as a form of preventive diplomacy, as a means of separating potential belligerents, or at the request of one party, for the purpose of removing any pretext for attack.

ROLE OF THE SECRETARIAT

3. The Secretary-General has a key role in drawing to the attention of the Security Council any matter which in his opinion may threaten international peace and security under Article 99 of the UN Charter.

4. The Secretary-General monitors potential disputes through various types of visiting missions. In some cases he has used personal representatives. Greater use is now being made of fact-finding missions (for example in Tajikistan, Georgia, Moldova, Nagorno-Karabakh and the Israeli-occupied territories) and investigative missions (such as the one recently sent to Haiti). In addition, several "interim offices" have been established in places, such as Tbilisi and Dushanbe, where the UN is heavily engaged. The missions carry out a mixture of humanitarian and political functions, the emphasis of which changes depending on the circumstances. They report to the Secretary-General's office, the Department of Political Affairs, and, where relevant, to the Department of Peacekeeping Operations. The deployment of

an UNPROFOR contingent to the Former Yugoslav Republic of Macedonia was the first example of a preventive deployment.

5. There is no single Department in the UN specifically devoted to preventive diplomacy, though in practice the Department of Political Affairs takes the lead. Within UN Headquarters in New York, the Department of Humanitarian Affairs (DHA) and the Department of Peacekeeping Operations (DPKO) also have a role to play: DHA through its close monitoring of humanitarian emergencies and its relationship with humanitarian agencies in the UN system, and DPKO through its responsibility for operational deployments, whether for peacekeeping or for other missions. In addition, some programmes such as UNHCR and UNDP as well as the regional organisations can all have a role to play as part of a UN effort. As to other regional organisations, there are CSCE Missions, for example, in Vojvodina, Sandzak, the Kosovo and Macedonia in former Yugoslavia, as well as in Estonia and Georgia in the former Soviet Union.

6. At present, 26 desk officers for geographical areas in the Department of Political Affairs work on aspects of preventive diplomacy. A system of duty officers provides 24-hour coverage. Under Secretary-General Goulding (Political Affairs) is engaged in a review of his Department's structure, and this may lead to an increase in staff if it proves possible to re-deploy people from elsewhere in the Secretariat. The Department of Peacekeeping Operations is now establishing a situation room manned around the clock. The UK already seconds personnel at UN request to the Department of Peacekeeping Operations to augment the permanent staff. We have responded positively to the UN request to second personnel to serve in the situation room.

7. A number of Member States, including the UK, provide the Department of Political Affairs and the Department of Peacekeeping Operations with relevant political information on a regular basis. This is normally targeted with specific UN operations in mind. For its part, the UK is ready to respond to any request for specific information received from the Secretariat, as it has done in the past.

ISBN 0-10-021313-8
9 780100 213135

Printed in the United Kingdom for HMSO.
Dd.0508897, 7/93, C7, 3398/3B, 5673, 240988.